Red Queen

The Authorized Biography
of Barbara Castle

Red Queen

The Authorized Biography of Barbara Castle

ANNE PERKINS

MACMILLAN

First published 2003 by Macmillan
an imprint of Pan Macmillan Ltd
Pan Macmillan, 20 New Wharf Road, London N1 9RR
Basingstoke and Oxford
Associated companies throughout the world
www.panmacmillan.com

ISBN 0 333 90511 3

1 3 5 7 9 8 6 4 2

A CIP catalogue record for this book is available from
the British Library.

Typeset by SetSystems Ltd, Saffron Walden, Essex
Printed and bound in Great Britain by
Mackays of Chatham plc, Chatham, Kent

To Cecily and Isobel, the next generation

Contents

List of Illustrations ix

Acknowledgements xi

Prologue 1

1 Faith and Hope 5

2 A Woman Wot Speaks 19

3 Directing the Action 41

4 Ends and Beginnings 61

5 Jerusalem 82

6 Fresh Thinking 103

7 Bitter Lemons 135

8 Bombshell 165

9 A Keen and Dedicated Minister 186

10 Tiger 206

11 The Politics of Barbara Castle 230

12 The Whirlwind 257

13 The Eye of the Storm 275

14 The Battle of Downing Street 304

15 One of the Lasses 325

16 Yesterday's Woman 344

CONTENTS

17 Battling On 371

18 Defeat 393

19 The End of the Affair 419

20 Epilogue 447

Notes 457

Bibliography 480

Index 485

List of Illustrations

1 Barbara aged two, in party finery at a family wedding.
2 Frank Betts.
3 Annie Ferrand, the loyal and loving Muvvie.
4 Tristram and Marjorie, Barbara's older brother and sister.
5 Barbara aged eleven with T'ang, the first of many dogs she adored.
6 The Betts family, with Annie's parents and a truculent Barbara.
7 William Mellor in a *Daily Herald* photograph.
8 The essential Barbara: painstakingly stylish.
9 Barbara making the speech that led to her finding a seat and a husband: 'We want jam today!'
10 Mrs Ted Castle on her honeymoon, 1944.
11 Campaigning in Blackburn, 1945.
12 Utopian socialist. Barbara on the holiday she thought Robert Owen would have applauded for its spirit of common enterprise.
13 Barbara, ready to thrust herself between Nye Bevan and Clement Attlee if the exchanges got out of hand.
14 Hugh Dalton, Barbara and Ted on a Whitsun 'right to roam' walk.
15 Come dancing. Ted and Barbara live it up.
16 Barbara and Frank Cousins, allies against the Bomb.
17 The 1955 Equal Pay campaign, a rare instance of Barbara working in a cross-party alliance.
18 Party chairman at the start of the 1959 election campaign.
19 Attlee and Barbara on their way to save Aneurin Bevan from expulsion in 1955.
20 Housewife superstar.
21 Barbara had a reputation as a good cook, but she rarely had the time.
22 Heading for glory. Barbara at about the time of her appointment as Minister for Overseas Development in 1964.
23 Barbara and her dogs on the day of her appointment to the Cabinet.

24 Wilson's first Cabinet.

25 The informal Mrs Castle.

26 With Hastings Banda of Malawi, a comrade in the fight for freedom who became an oppressor himself.

27 On an early African tour as Overseas Development Minister.

28 At the height of her success as transport minister.

29 Promoting the seat belts campaign.

30 'B-day', 9 October 1967.

31 The most highly rated politician in Britain on holiday in Ireland.

32 'In Place of Strife.' In the end it was the trade unions who took Wilson and Barbara for a ride.

33 The pay-beds battle. Wrong time, wrong fight.

34 Battling Barbara.

35 1970 election.

36 Surrounded by Ted's roses at Hell Corner Farm where she lived from 1965 until her death in 2002.

37 Eightieth birthday celebrations in 1991.

38 Oldest friends: Barbara and Michael Foot.

39 Still as much socialite as socialist. Barbara in 1997, the year she set out to save the party from New Labour.

Acknowledgements

All pictures courtesy of the Castle Papers with the exception of the following: *Daily Mail*: 32, 33. *Guardian*: 34, 37. Popperfoto: 21. *Sunday Times*: 35.

Acknowledgements

Thanks are due to dozens of people who have given their time, experience, memories and encouragement and I am indebted to far too many to name. Specifically, I am grateful to Dr Tony Wright MP who originally told me that Barbara was looking for someone to write her 'life'. I owe thanks to many people at the *Guardian*, most of all to the editor Alan Rusbridger and the news editor Harriet Sherwood who first suggested a job-sharing arrangement which allowed me to work as a political correspondent and write a book as well as seeing my children, although not without two extended periods of leave. I also appreciate the kind support of friends and colleagues in room 15 and elsewhere in the Press Gallery, especially Primrose Skelton who kindly helped with research. Michael Crick has been a stimulating source of ideas and generous with his time beyond the call of friendship, as well as putting put me in touch with his agent Bill Hamilton to whom I am also grateful. Geoffrey Goodman has kindly and generously extended the benefit of his enormous range of knowledge and first-hand experience. Michael Foot sustained his friendship with Barbara even after her death, giving his time and encouragement. I am grateful to Macmillan for my unfailingly encouraging and usually patient editor George Morley and my bracing copy-editor Sue Phillpott. Much has been done to reduce factual errors and questionable judgements. What remain are, sadly, all mine.

Special dues are owed to the great legion of mothers, neighbours and friends on whose generosity and fellow-feeling I have leant all too often for unscheduled childcare, extra meals and the daily run of crisis management. In particular I am grateful to Alice Perkins and Magda Chorylek, and to my friend Vivia Robinson.

And of course, and more than anyone, to Cecily and Isobel and to Mark, for their unstinting encouragement and apparently unshakeable belief in this project.

Prologue

Barbara Castle was in her mid-seventies when I first encountered her some time around 1985. It was at a Labour Party conference fringe meeting, heavingly crowded, full of smoke and heat and bright white camera lights, a platform for another bout in the prolonged agony between left and right in the days when, like two people in an unhappy marriage, they could not stop picking another fight.

Barbara arrived a little late. She was not speaking; she had just dropped in with undiminished appetite for the political fight in which for so many years she had been a leading pugilist. Already, fifteen years or more before she finally conceded defeat, she looked not so much frail as fragile, like a piece of glass capable of carrying great weight but equally vulnerable to a careless gesture.

She was wearing her hair and her clothes with that peculiar kind of 1950s perfection (updated to a kind of low-key Joan Collins look for the 1980s) which on its own was enough to make her stand out in a crowd where dressing down had become a political statement. The atmosphere in the undersized function room was thick with sweat and bad temper and, everywhere, bodies – on the floor, leaning against walls, straining to see and to hear, to support or to jeer. There were TV cameras and microphones and notebooks and tape recorders.

Accompanying one of the cameras as a Channel Four News reporter, I had arrived early enough to have a seat almost at the front. Barbara made a small entrance – just enough for her presence to be registered – in the midst of the speeches, and came to rest standing beside me. Her hand gripped the back of my chair. Standing was obviously an effort. I gestured to her to take my seat.

With a rictus of a smile, she recoiled as if she had been threatened. She took her hand off my chair. If possible, her bearing became more resolute, her shoulders straighter and her concentration on the speakers more unswerving.

In that momentary stiffening of the spine, she delivered a salutory reprimand to the ill-discipline and self-indulgence which were wrecking Labour's electoral prospects, and my first taste of her extraordinary ability to project an image by the slightest gesture. This was Barbara on her way to becoming the iconic reminder of the virtue rather than the vice of passion in politics, the Red Queen of the traditional Labour movement.

Only ten years earlier, in the 1970s, she had been a different Red Queen, the Red Queen of *Alice in Wonderland* who would shout 'Off with their heads!' at the drop of the wrong-coloured rose petal or, in Barbara's case, a privately operated bedpan. The jibe came from right-wing newspapers, but there were plenty in the Labour Party who would recognize it from first-hand experience.

Politicians in the sunlit uplands of retirement tend to become pompous, chatty, avuncular, clubbable. They admit mistakes, embrace their enemies, chortle regretfully over defeats and develop an interest in their grandchildren. But Barbara didn't retire. In the great tradition of the evangelist, the true crusader, she merely allowed time to hone her convictions to a finer edge and carried on campaigning.

Years later, Barbara decided she needed her biography written. Partly, I think she was provoked, needlessly, by an unauthorized and unsolicited account of her life which was already in preparation. She did not like other people messing with her image. I suspect there was an element of ancient rivalry too. Patricia Hollis's brilliant biography of Barbara's old comrade (always a loaded term in Labour history) Jennie Lee had recently been published. Once again, the columns of newspapers were full of the beautiful, fiery Mrs Aneurin Bevan and her role in the history of the Labour movement.

I heard that Barbara was looking for someone to write her life, and leapt at the chance without considering her motives. It was a mistake Barbara herself would never have made. It was the first question to ask, she told me when we knew one another better. (We were discussing the then impending wedding between the Labour Chancellor Gordon Brown and Sarah Macaulay.)

So what were her motives? On one level, there was a straightforward commercial transaction. Always short of cash, she wanted to make some money out of giving me access to all her papers, which are destined for the Bodleian Library in Oxford. We agreed terms: it would be the 'authorized' biography. She would have the right to see the manuscript in draft and correct matters of fact. All judgement and opinions were to be mine.

Barbara has always understood about image, about the significance of personal style and the importance of symbolism. She was, after all, a journalist as well as a politician, married to a journalist, with a lifetime's experience of selling herself through an intermediary. Her most famous claim of her early years is that at the age of eight she wrote a manifesto for the first election of the peace in 1918: 'Citzuns! Vote for me and I will give you houses . . .' The tale, with its message of commitment and precocious awareness, first appeared in a newspaper profile in the early 1950s when she was a young MP in the Attlee era, and was rarely absent from them thereafter.

She was also, as a crusader, anxious to record her presence at the centre of the long, slow march towards socialism. She was an indefatigable diarist and observer of the Wilson governments in which, in her own subtly reworked account, she played a starring role, seducing the Prime Minister with her passion, cudgelling her enemies with her arguments. Her authorized biography was to be 'Barbara – the final cut', a summing up, not substantially different from what had gone before.

But she wanted more than that; she wanted some independent, or at least outside, confirmation that she had lived an important life, that she had made a difference, and had made it by force of will, not by some serendipitous chain of events. She wanted her life recognized and respected. She wanted, she told me often, a 'political' biography, not what she dismissed as 'kiss and tell' biography, a steamy saga of sex and scandal by the Thames.

There's the rub with an authorized biography. It gives you the key to your subject's papers, but not to her heart. Barbara, focused and ordered in the final phase of her life, had sorted her vast collection of letters, diary scraps and souvenirs, the scribbled notes on old cigarette packets, the cables and newspaper cuttings, all the dog-eared manky jetsam of passionate political argument. She had undoubtedly weeded out some parts of it; in old age, some events had almost certainly gone from her memory nearly as totally as they had been excised from her papers. What remained, she had collected into a library of her political life, occasionally illuminated by a glimpse of an earlier, more private existence.

The task I set myself was to rearrange these fragments so that Barbara's humanity was revealed beneath the driven, impassioned, sometimes doctrinaire, sometimes shrewish politician. Politics is a human activity, after all, driven by human emotions of ambition, sympathy and tribal identity. It was especially so for Barbara who was, despite a considerable intellect – and to quote Roy Jenkins whose à la carte approach to politics was so alien to Barbara – not an intellectual. She was interested only in one idea, the advancement of socialism. To this star she hitched her career, her standing, her self-respect.

Above all, Barbara declared that her love life was an entirely private matter except where she chose to write about it. She had been cajoled by the editor of her autobiography to divulge a little about sex in the Oxford of the late 1920s (she felt this made her a more truthful writer than Margaret Thatcher; did anyone suggest to her that her memoirs would sell better with a bit of sex?) and more about her long sexual and political affair with the socialist intellectual, William Mellor. Her husband, Ted Castle, was described affectionately, but she never pretended that he was anything more than an amiable second best.

Yet Barbara sought love. Like the actress she was, she wanted it and needed it. She liked men and she liked sex, and she knew, unless the image that comes through thousands of feet of grainy film and early videotape is all a lie, how to exploit herself. Unusually for a woman of her generation, she also had an informality of manner which added to the image of a woman in the habit of charming her way through life. She did believe she could make people love her and she saw it as an important and legitimate part of her political persona. I was merely the last of hundreds to be dazzled, at least a little, by her star quality, that unmistakable mix of style, courage, intellect and will power.

'Authorized' biography carries a certain stigma, a sense that the writer is under an obligation to the subject. Nothing so crude as approval, perhaps, but a subtle intimation of collusion, enough to taint independent judgement. Will every favourable opinion be taken as evidence of the subject's dominance over the writer? Or does the writer resort to undue criticism to avoid the charge of partiality? I have tried to be fair but not uncritical; impartial without being colourless. I have also tried to make sure my judgements are supported by the evidence. Consequently there is not, after all, much sex. There was an awful lot of gossip but no steaming letters of illicit passion, no death-bed revelations, no incontrovertible evidence that her account of her life was significantly less truthful than her enemies' description of it.

I am sorry not to be able to hear her verdict on my verdict. Contrary to those who believe she was motivated largely by vanity, there is copious evidence that she was prepared to listen to anyone who could back up their opinion with argument. She might have flinched, but I am confident she would have kept her word and left me to my own opinions.

1. Faith and Hope

Happy are they who live in the dream of their own existence, and see all things in the light of their own minds; who walk by faith and hope; to whom the guiding star of their youth still shines from afar, and into whom the spirit of the world has not entered. They have not been 'hurt by the archers' nor has the iron entered their souls. The world has no hand on them.

William Hazlitt, 1778–1830

Barbara Anne Betts, a romantic by nature, a radical by upbringing and a self-dramatist by instinct, was born on 6 October 1910. She was ambitious from birth, a daughter driven by the desire to impress her demanding father, Frank, a competitor determined to outshine her older brother and sister. In Barbara's memory of her childhood, there were only two people in the Betts household: there was herself, and there was Frank, a force of nature to be appeased, impressed and, if possible, manipulated. Frank, big, dark, hot-tempered, and Barbara, small, pretty, with Titian-red hair, were in colour; everyone else was in black and white.

In the Betts family, the political field was the only one worth fighting over. Frank was a radical activist. Barbara's mother Annie became a local councillor, her sister Marjorie a pioneer of the Inner London Education Authority and her brother Jimmie first a colonial civil servant in Nigeria and later an Oxfam field director. Frank Betts intended to found a political dynasty, and he was not easily thwarted.

The second great influence on Barbara was her own sense of herself as an outsider. Within her family she suffered what she imagined to be the permanent slight of being the youngest. Beyond it, she often saw herself as a misfit, struggling with serial personal injustices. At school and at university, she had less money than her contemporaries. Secretly, for in the Betts family it was an ignoble ambition, she longed to be rich. Yet if she felt being too poor marked her out in childhood, in her political career the reverse seemed to be true. Her background was too middle-class, she was too well-educated, too inexperienced in real hardship and financial insecurity. Seeking a socialist identity, she exaggerated and romanticized the economic difficulties of her childhood and encouraged the impression of a political commitment forged on the anvil of personal experience.

Frank Betts had been born in 1882 imbued with a Victorian confidence in the power of men to shape their destinies and a Marxist belief in the inevitability of the collapse of world capitalism. He made his living assessing taxes, but he devoted his formidable energy to trying to build a new world order of justice, equality and beauty. The offspring of Frank Betts were not so much children as the next generation, and his influence on Barbara was 'total'.[1] Frank was a member of the Independent Labour Party, the party that hovered over the gulf between revolutionary and parliamentary socialism. He was radical in his politics, generous in his support for the underdog, and determined that his two daughters should be educated to as high a standard as his son. 'Such things as scrapping hard, trying to help people, caring for my friends & regarding worldly success as dirt are ideas which always satisfied me completely,'[2] he once wrote to a friend.

Frank was the son of a solid and upright Coventry corn merchant, also Frank, a figure at the local Congregational chapel for forty years where he ran the Sunday school. The family lived near Coventry in the Berkswell area, in a smart villa called Villafranca, where Mrs Frank Betts was 'At Home' on the first and third Wednesdays of the month. The corn merchant saw his son's future in the new world of business and industry, and insisted that he study science. But Frank rejected what he saw as the sordid and risky business of money-making in favour of a safe career as a civil servant, a job which would give him the financial security to indulge in his real passions, politics, literature and drama.

Like his younger daughter, Frank indulged in a sense of injustice. He felt his father had cheated him of his true vocation as an Oxford don. He had a voracious intellectual appetite and learnt enough classical Greek, Icelandic, Spanish and Italian to read the literature in the original. Poetry, drama and fine art were equally important: he was an ardent, opinionated autodidact who began his lifelong friendship with Gilbert Murray, the Regius Professor of Greek at Oxford, by writing to ask his advice. 'I had often thought about Frank.' Murray wrote on hearing of his death many years later. 'He did a [sic] most remarkable work, both intellectual and political, and left his mark wherever he went. I like to think of his writing to me, so long ago, about the best way of learning Greek. So many many languages and literatures he tackled afterwards.'[3]

Frank published slim volumes of poetry, some at his own expense, but two were produced by Blackwell of Oxford. He had a taste for the epic, and a muscular belief in the inherent virtue of the fight which owed much to the socialist artist and writer William Morris, and suffered somewhat from what Morris's detractors called 'verbal wallpaper'. In the dark days towards the end of the First World War, Blackwell produced an edition of Frank's 'Ballad of King Richard'. It ends:

> Let him know this thing: it is his to strive
> E'en with a broken blade,
> And fail, one man against twenty men,
> Who rides on a Crusade.
>
> Tell him from me who have endured
> All toils he shall endure,
> One thing he shall hold for his reward
> Though all else be unsure:
>
> Not the City of Constantine
> The Paynim holds in his grip
> But with all high hearts, living or dead
> A crowned fellowship.

It could have become Barbara's battle hymn.

Barbara feared Frank's temper and dreaded his scorn. He demanded total silence, even at mealtimes if he was reading, and his study was a sacred place no child might penetrate. Barbara's friends found him alarming, and would tiptoe, stifling nervous giggles, past his study. He was very much the Victorian head of the family – 'a kindly man with a cutting tongue,' Barbara wrote later when she was adapting the story of her childhood for a 1960s audience. 'I was reared in irreverence: trained to challenge all the stale assumptions of a class-bound society. No hippie ever looked more unkempt than [my father] did with his badly cut hair straggling down under his battered felt hat, cigarette ash showering on his shabby overcoat, as he sat on the top of the tram on his way to work reading his beloved Greek.'[3] She carried his childhood strictures with her for the rest of her life, measuring her achievements against his expectations, never quite confident that she had done enough. By contrast, Frank saw himself as an astonishingly liberal and modern parent. 'It is a thing of yesterday the breaking up of the patriarchal

family, in which wife, child, servants, ox & ass only existed as limbs of the
family – & Father was the family. I am amazed when I consider the difference
between Barbara's childhood and my own.'[4]

Frank was big and dark, domineering and charming and, in later years,
rather shambolic, the kind of person who forgets to button his flies. He
spoke in a curious high-pitched voice. 'He was a tall man with black hair
that he allowed to grow rather longer than normal – that was because he
never had time to have a haircut, or didn't regard it as being important. He
would walk about with a hat just punched on his head anyhow, with a long
coat, rather a hawk-like look and a terrific grin from time to time when he
made a point.'[5] He loved dogs, hated the countryside, and called himself a
'Rabelaisian puritan'. After his death he turned out to be more Rabelaisian
than his family had realized: a long affair with a teacher called Nell emerged.
She was, apparently, a quiet and undemanding woman, but the discovery of
their father's duplicity towards them and their mother was a shattering
experience for a family brought up in awe of their father's exalted moral
standards. Barbara was unaware of the relationship when she began her own
long affair with a married man in the 1930s. Even when her father's adultery
had been revealed after his death, she clung to his old identity. In a *Daily
Herald* interview in 1961, she described him as a man of 'an absolutely
unqualified integrity and a high standard of personal conduct.'[6]

Barbara's mother, Annie Ferrand, small and fine-boned with a mass of
red-gold hair, met and fell in love with Frank just as the nineteenth century
and the Victorian era faded. Annie's family, like Frank's, had pretensions to
gentility. Her grandfather had been a bookseller in Stafford, but had died
young and the family had broken up. His son, Annie's father, had become
an insurance agent, while her mother had left school at twelve to work in
a factory making pens. Grandma Ferrand was a vivid figure in Barbara's
childhood memories, her link with the realities of working-class life, back-
to-back housing and a world where earning enough to live on was a more
urgent concern than discussing ideas and contemplating political action.

When she was seventeen, Barbara fictionalized a row between her older
sister Marjorie, who had just retreated from Oxford with a breakdown
brought on by overwork, and her 'dark, muddled, jealous' grandmother: 'Let
me tell you, my girl [learning] don't pay. And then you all sit round with
your fine talk and try and make them as haven't had your chances feel they
don't know anythink. Lot of trash, I call it. Tomfoolery, three parts of it.
And what about them as can't get schooling? Somebody's got to do the
work. Le'em wait on you, I suppose. I went to work at ten and that's all the
learnin' I got . . . you don't know you're born, some of you.'[7]

Frank's civil service career as a tax inspector – a 'surveyor of taxes' – enabled him to marry Annie when he was just twenty-three, she twenty-two. It was 1905 and he was earning the handsome sum of £200 a year. Barbara presented it later as an unequal marriage in which her father was entirely dominant, but a letter written in the year it took place conveys an atmosphere of shared enthusiasms. Music criticism was mixed equally with declarations of love. 'I hate dull people & books & places. Bad people have some interest even if they are ordinary, good none: cuss dullness. I love you 'cause you're sweet & beautiful & not a bit dull ever.' Annie was emotional, Frank domineering, and they clashed frequently. It was anything but a dull relationship.

Their first child, Marjorie, was born in 1906 and their second, Tristram (because his father, a character full of Wagnerian *Sturm und Drang* himself, liked the opera *Tristan and Isolde*), in 1908. They moved from Sheffield via Hull to Chesterfield, where Barbara was born in 1910. Two years later they travelled further north, to Pontefract. Barbara's earliest memories were of the old market town, which bridged the ancient traditions of rural Yorkshire and the nineteenth-century world of industrial labour. There was a ruined castle where Richard II had died, in which the children played, and the awesome sight of the miners, black with dust, on their way home from Pontefract colliery.

For Barbara, the youngest, it was an intensely competitive childhood. She was determined to keep up with her charming older brother and her clever, pretty sister. Her mother used to call her 'my beautiful little ugly' and regretted that she lacked Marjorie's regular features. In the struggle to shine in the eyes of her demanding father, Barbara insisted on starting school a year early. In 1914, as soon as she was four, she set off with Marjorie and Tris to walk from their semi-rural suburb to Love Lane Elementary. The buildings at Love Lane were basic and the plumbing rudimentary, but Frank believed in equality in education as the route to higher standards for everyone. 'If Nancy Astor had to send her children to Love Lane Elementary School, the lavatories would be flushed every day,' he declared.

The girls stayed at Love Lane until Marjorie was eleven and Barbara nearly eight, when they moved on to Pontefract and District Girls' High School. It had been open for less than ten years and was already overcrowded, although the head complained that now the council met the bulk of the fees, attendance was patchy. Its purpose was to prepare girls for womanhood: 'The great art of womanliness might best be summed up in the word "homemaker",' reported the chairman of the governors' founding prospectus. 'The young woman of today was the homemaker of tomorrow, and the sooner they got away from the fact that only 2½% of their secondary school girls went to Girton or Newnham and remembered only the 97½% who require the good, sound education necessary to make them true womanly women, the better.' But the climate was changing. In 1918 women over thirty were finally allowed the vote. Before Barbara left, the chairman of the governors was exhorting the girls to work for university scholarships and to train as doctors.

Her career at the High School was not distinguished. When she left, after three years, she was hovering around the middle of the class academically and underperforming in preparations for womanliness, coming seventeenth out of twenty in sewing. But both she and Marjorie won prizes, though Marjorie won more. Barbara showed an enthusiasm for public performance; was 'a dear little fairy' in Form II, and at prize-giving the following year she recited Walter de la Mare's 'Nod'. However, she failed to win the poetry-speaking contest, a disappointment she later attributed to the complications in rehearsal caused by an uncomfortable tussle over the correct style for recitation. Her teacher preferred the dramatic, her father the understated. Barbara, anxious to please them both, ricocheted between the two.

One of Frank's outlets for politics was drama: at the height of the miners' lockout, he produced John Galsworthy's *Strife* in the local hall (even though, he wrote later, 'Galsworthy was not a Socialist, and much of his work is thoroughly distasteful to a thorough-going Socialist mind: he is the laureate of the crushed worm, and we are Socialists precisely because we cannot at any price stand crushed worms'). Barbara had a part as a maid, which she muffed by tripping up on her entrance. Nonetheless, she found acting inspiring and identified powerfully with her audience of miners. These were to be enduring traits.

Frank rose through the ranks of the tax inspectorate and up the earnings scale so that by the early 1930s he was paid what was then the comfortable salary of about £1,000 a year. He treated the work with seriousness, emphasizing to Barbara the importance of accuracy and honesty in dealing with the state. The work brought with it the great advantage of security. In an ever more uncertain world, he could count on his job regardless of the vagaries of the economic cycle or industrial trends or consumer fashion. It also meant, when the First World War broke out, that he was in a reserved occupation: the Betts family, unlike most others, did not endure four years in the shadow of the telegram. There were, however, drawbacks of which the greatest was that as a public servant Frank could not openly engage in politics. So his political energies had to be contained in the theoretical and domestic arenas. And, because it was considered important that public servants concerned with the probity of their fellow citizens should not become too enmeshed in local life, the family was never entirely settled. At some point, they knew, they would be moved on.

It sometimes suited Barbara's account of herself to suggest that she grew up short of money. The Betts family was by no means rich, but they never experienced want. At a time when millions did, it would be more accurate to say that they never had enough money for all the things they wanted to do. No one went short in the Betts household. There was always a maid to help Annie with the three children, there were gardens and space enough inside for each to have a bedroom. There were sometimes seaside holidays and often excursions, wherever they were living, to whichever stretch of country or moorland was nearest. Throughout Barbara's childhood, the rich combination of compassion, charity and socialism meant the Betts home was a place for the desperate to turn. 'There was always someone sleeping on the sofa,'[8] Barbara once complained. During the 1920s, there was a lockout at the Pontefract colliery; Annie helped run a soup kitchen for the miners and their families, and children were occasionally fostered by the Bettses to make sure they had enough to eat.

Frank was the head of the family, the one who set the intellectual tone. For him Barbara wrote, at the age of eight, 'Dear citizuns, vote for me and I will give you houses.' Frank was said to have carried the scrap of paper around with him for years. And it was he who decided that the family should not sing 'Land of Hope and Glory' for the duration of the First World War, and later declared that the Boy Scouts and Girl Guides were organizations too militaristic for his children to join.[9] Instead they joined the Woodcraft Folk, the Co-op-backed youth organization set up by John Hargrave, another critic of the militarism of Baden Powell's movement.

For Annie, who made the family's emotional weather, Barbara wrote not political slogans but poems like 'Ma Mère', composed when she was about eight, which began:

> She is the sweetest thing on earth,
> The bestest ever born . . .'

Barbara loved her mother with a passion; she once (her mother remembered in old age) saved her pocket money for ten months to buy a bowl Annie had admired. High-spirited and unconventional, Annie was intensely loyal to her husband and children, all of whom loved her, exploited her and looked down on her. It was Annie who put up a maypole and got all the local children to dance around it, and who encouraged Barbara in a search for fairies at the bottom of the garden which lasted almost until her teens. Barbara sometimes found her mother cloying, but she shared her William Morris romanticism as well as a nostalgia for a make-believe world of medieval chivalry and clean, pure-minded young men, where heroines like Birdalone in her favourite novel, the painfully whimsical *Waters of the Wondrous Isles*, could combine physical perfection with a constant heart and unsullied courage with which to overcome all challenges both to her virtue and to her determination.

Years later, after the children had left home, it became clear that there was more to Annie than either her husband or her children had been prepared to recognize. In the 1930s, in the short gap between raising her children and nursing Frank in his final illness, she embarked on a brief career as a councillor: she lost her seat in 1937, in the local elections where Barbara was first elected, but the local newspaper felt that Annie had made an impact:

> Councillor Mrs Betts is the only Labour woman to have served on the Council, and her departure after a comparatively brief spell during which she has rendered splendid service, will be regretted. Having over 30 years' association with the Labour movement, she is particularly interested in such questions as housing, nursery schools, child welfare and kindred subjects, and has always held the opinion that the woman's point of view should be voiced in local authorities . . . In many spheres Cnclr Mrs Betts has given useful public service.

But all that lay far in the future.

In 1922, just before Barbara's twelfth birthday, the family moved to Bradford, the single most important event of her childhood. Bradford was the 'Rome of Socialism', the home of the radical left. It meant promotion for Frank, who became a senior inspector, and a larger, more comfortable house in Toller Lane in a suburb beyond the smell of the dye works and the sound of clogs on cobbles as the workers headed for the first shift, at 5 a.m., in the woollen mills on which the city depended. More importantly, it opened up the opportunity from which Frank would derive more pleasure than from almost anything else in his life: the chance to edit the city's socialist newspaper, the *Bradford Pioneer*. Pontefract had been a charming backwater, a kindergarten for socialist aspirations. Bradford was the hub, a place where things happened, a place that mattered even in distant London. It had a cultural life, a theatre and libraries and a concert hall – even a permanent symphony orchestra – and it had a political life.

In 1893, Bradford's political radicalism had given birth to the Independent Labour Party; Bradford produced some of the first Labour MPs, and it attracted social pioneers like Margaret Macmillan, who in the early years of the twentieth century brought nursery education and free school meals to the city. It was a testbed for municipal socialism, the London-based attempt to apply the principles of a welfare state to a single urban area by raising dole payments to the unemployed and investing in schools and public health. Bradford had a minority Labour council, one of the first in the country, which pioneered housing and educational reform. Barbara claimed later that it was the Bradford she saw then, the Bradford where socialism reached into every corner of people's lives in order to improve them and where 'property under threat fought back ruthlessly', that had shaped the whole of her political life.

Bradford's socialism came exclusively from the Independent Labour Party; all its Labour councillors were ILP and the party controlled a printing works and a cinema. The Temperance Hall was renamed the Jowett Hall after the Bradford reformer an ILP MP, Fred Jowett. Nationally, the ILP lived in a close symbiosis with the Labour Party, which it had helped to found in 1906 and to which it was affiliated, but it maintained its own conference, its own MPs and its own programme. Until Labour party constituency organizations were set up in 1918, individual members wishing to join did so through the ILP. Thereafter the two lived in uneasy and sometimes jealous partnership. The ILP's purpose, reaffirmed by its 1926 manifesto 'Socialism in Our Time', was to 'develop the Socialist objectives' of the Labour movement – defined as full employment and the nationalization of basic industries – a programme that was promptly disowned by the Labour Party leadership.

The 1920s, the years of unemployment and industrial disputes culminating in the General Strike, were the high tide of the ILP's popular success, during which its membership reached 50,000.[10] But its political centre of gravity was moving north from Bradford to Clydeside, drawn to the home of its leader Jimmy Maxton, where the extreme gradualism of Labour's national leadership was provoking extreme frustration in the men and women who lived among the idle cranes and dockyards. The ILP was always a sectarian, left-wing, working-class operation, in contrast to the trade unionist Labour Party, which at this point was surreptitiously shuffling towards the shoes of the dying Liberal Party and consciously seeking to be a party beyond class. In the febrile atmosphere of the early 1920s – when the Bolshevik revolution still looked as if it might be Russia's first successful export – the ILP was often a target for early witch-hunters scenting Communist plots.

In the 1922 general election William Leach, the editor of the *Bradford*

Pioneer, followed its founder Fred Jowett to Westminster as an ILP MP. Frank Betts, once he was home from tax-inspecting, now took over the newspaper. The *Pi* was the voice of the whole Bradford Labour movement, written, sold, bought and read by party and trade union activists. It prided itself on a tradition of distinguished writing. Before the First World War it had been the first to publish one of Bradford's most eminent sons, J. B. Priestley. Frank poured his energy and enthusiasms into the paper, but his editorship, which was plainly in conflict with his role as a public servant, had to be conducted discreetly. 'FB' wrote thousands of words for each weekly issue, art criticism, politics and cricket (his other great love) tucked in beside advice on hen-rearing and vegetable-growing sent in by other contributors. One issue of the period contains a review of Murray's translation of Euripides alongside an essay prompted by a Degas exhibition, which begins, not quite apologetically, 'It is a little tedious to discuss in these columns painters and carvers whose work is not accessible nearer than London . . . and yet the greatest artists, and Degas was one of the very greatest, are critics of life, intentionally or against their will . . . and their touch is as miraculous as great fiddlers'.'

The *Pioneer* set investigative journalism alongside art criticism; it exposed, for instance, the misdeeds of a Bradford alderman who had been making his own use of corporation property, for which he was sent to prison for seven years. Frank was an interventionist and a merciless editor. He had strong views about journaistic style; one young reporter, Vic Feather, later General Secretary of the TUC, noted, 'He used to say that the written word should be "clean as a bone, clear as a stream and hard as a stone", and that "two words are never as good as one". The first thing he ever taught me after I'd written my copy was to take out the first paragraph . . . and then take out all the adjectives.'[11] When, in late 1931, Frank was obliged by his employer the Tax Inspectorate to move on from Bradford, a shattering event for the whole family, he tried to replicate the experience by setting up a *New Pioneer*. He wrote to a friend: 'I'm crazy about the *Pi* – it's my job – what I was born to do.'

Bradford had two good schools: the Girls' and Boys' Grammar Schools. Barbara and Marjorie, despite failing the scholarship exam, were duly enrolled. The school fees – although between them no more than £15 a year – were, the girls were left in no doubt, a heavy burden. In truth Frank spent a significant amount of his income on trips to London for himself and, Barbara discovered much later, holidays abroad with his mistress. 'Paris is home and Toledo is heaven,' he wrote to a friend. Annie and the children, by contrast, spent their holidays in cold boarding-houses by the sea. Marjorie, nicknamed 'Dod' on an apparently anarchic whim of her father's, being the sensible and clever oldest child, was destined if at all possible for Oxford. Soon after they moved to Bradford, Professor Murray's advice was sought: 'Somerville too competitive,' Frank reported back in a letter from his parents' house in Berkswell. So Marjorie went instead to the less smart St Hugh's, from where she wrote to her younger sister offering embroidered petticoats and comfort for her adolescent anxieties. Tristram tried, and failed, to get into Oxford – something that was never afterwards discussed. Barbara suggested that, like his father, he had chosen to do the opposite of his family's expectations. But from Edinburgh, where he was studying agriculture, he wrote: 'They don't educate you, they fit you for a job. And that's why in missing Oxford, while it doesn't amount to a secret sorrow, I can still taste the gall.'

Barbara, left behind, fretted about growing up. She wanted her hair bobbed, to learn to dance properly and to know the facts of life. In all of these her father tried to thwart her. Often – in Barbara's eyes at least – intolerant, unimaginative and unsympathetic towards his younger daughter, he was scathing of her social ambitions: dancing was common, short hair, vulgar, and having a boy to tea was fast.

Barbara relied on her mother and on her one great schoolfriend, Evelyn Carter. Her mother was omnipresent, encouraging, loving and sympathetic. She made dens for the children in Toller Lane, she made Barbara pretty clothes and, above all, she reassured her that she was loved. Evelyn too had to rescue her from the anguish of self-doubt: 'You are loved,' she told her in one letter when they were both about fourteen, 'and you are *not* selfish'.[12]

Frank was pleading poverty again. He enjoyed living well and did not intend to be compromised by the expense of educating his children; he carried on with his trips to London, to the theatre, to exhibitions abroad, and justified them by writing about them. 'He had to have an audience,' Barbara reflected later. The children may not have been to blame for the financial constraints, but they were made to feel them. Tristram used to write anxious, self-justifying letters from Edinburgh detailing every penny spent (the cost of his laundry, his lodgings and every book he acquired). Barbara, surrounded by the relatively well-off daughters of Bradford's prosperous classes, began to nurture her sense of difference. Her reaction was to write school stories which suggest a child's longing to share the privileges of her classmates: 'The girls' parents were all rich, and the dainty frocks that the pupils wore did credit to [the school's] reputation of beauty and culture throughout. Miss Bradley was hard to please. Many applicants for a vacancy at this delightful place were rejected, for she would tolerate neither snobs, newly rich, nor black sheep.' In this story, the most popular girl in the school was a small redhead with an impish smile who saved the day.

Towards the end of the 1920s, financial constraints became real enough to force a move from Toller Lane to a shared house in St Paul's Road, off the Manningham Lane. It was a substantial Victorian house, and one still comfortably in the prosperous quarter of the city. Again, the children were blamed for the cash shortage. Supporting both Marjorie and Tristram at university was a heavy burden. However, there was enough money to send Barbara to France two years running, where she worked in a family teaching the children English and improving her accent before matriculation. From there she wrote letters of desperate homesickness to her mother. 'My bed is a double one and there is such snug room for you. I can picture you in your nightie, your pretty hair tousled, in bed beside me but I open my longing arms to empty air . . . goodnight sweetheart, you have built up for me a long thread of happy associations which are the very essence of my make-up. I am Mam's Baba and always will be.'

Through the *Pi* and his contacts with local MPs and councillors and the ILP Guild of Youth, Frank began to gather disciples, gifted young men and women already involved in the Labour movement. Two were to become important in Barbara's later life. Vic Feather, who at a key moment in her political career would become General Secretary of the TUC, was a grocery hand at Apperly Bridge Co-op when he first started writing for the *Pioneer*. He was two years older than Barbara, tall and handsome, the girls' heart-throb. Everyone was in love with him. They thought he looked like Rupert Brooke, dashing and vital, with his blond wavy hair. Feather felt a great debt to Frank, who among other memorable educational contributions first introduced him to the female nude in Bradford City Art Gallery. 'He asked me what I thought about a statue, a terracotta statue of a nude – and I was a little bit bashful, I suppose, because this wasn't the permissive society at the time . . . I remember him finishing by saying, "She's real, she's real, if you stuck a knife into her she'd bleed buckets of blood!" Buckets of blood!' And this was in a voice which carried all over the art gallery.'[13] He claimed later – possibly just to irritate Barbara, whom he never liked – to have had a crush on Marjorie, the 'clever, beautiful' sister. Feather thought Frank Betts 'a great man'. 'He was a man who really didn't *care* very much, it seemed to me, about the frivolities of life. I always regarded him as a great cavalier of a man rather than an austere character . . . a sort of King Charles rather than an Oliver Cromwell.'[14]

The second of Frank's protégées was a young woman called Mary Hepworth, who became and remained one of Barbara's few close friends. She was a cash-desk girl at the Co-op when, having been talent-spotted by Frank, she first met the dazzling teenage Barbara: '[Barbara] was absolutely lovely. She'd a yellow dress on and her hair was the colour of new pennies. You got such an impression of freshness, like spring.'[15] Barbara, she felt, was 'a little young', but she put that down to inexperience. Mary, only a year older, had already been at work for four years. To her, Frank was 'like my own private university tutor'.[16] She observed the tension between the two of them:

> [Barbara] had some sort of an intellectual battle with her father, who never felt that she did her brains justice. I think he expected too much from her at her age; he wanted her to be far more serious than she was . . . the scope of Frank's influence on Barbara was absolutely enormous. You're bound to take in an awful lot from a person like Frank just by being around. I think a lot was, in the nicest sense of the word, to *show* him that she could do it. Because she did rebel against being under his influence and I think that what she's absorbed from him, apart from her socialism, has been largely unconscious. And certainly, when she was younger, even unwilling.[17]

Through Mary, Barbara was able to gain a little freedom. Together they went off to the 1929 ILP conference in Derby, which Mary was to report for the *Pioneer*. Instead of coming home on the train they walked the sixty-odd miles back to Manchester, using the last of their cash to pay for meals en route. They slept rough, having warmed themselves up, where the opportunity presented itself, by climbing to the top of a hill, then in the morning would revive themselves by running down and, when they got to the bottom Barbara would plunge into a river.

Politics suffused daily life. There was an immediacy about the challenges of the 1920s that demanded a response: the need to avoid another war like the Great War, to tackle the terrible inequalities that still condemned families to the workhouse, men to Poor Law relief and children to malnourishment. Political commitment was not an optional extra, it was a state of mind that permeated every activity. In Bradford, the ILP Guild of Youth was only one of several social organizations sponsored by the party. Amateur dramatics were popular, also under the aegis of the ILP. Frank directed, Annie dressed and Barbara performed (in peripheral roles) a series of plays, often avant-garde, always political. They did Galsworthy's *Strife* again and Shaw, and the anti-Fascist Czech writer Carel Capek's *Insect Play*. Frank as a director was described as original in his ideas but merciless on his cast.[18] The family's pastimes derived from the ILP, and so did their friendships. The party was the backbone of their lives as it was for many others in dozens of towns and cities across the country. Amateur dramatics, rambling, camping, were typical of Labour-sponsored activities going on throughout Britain in the Depression years, the party – Labour or ILP – organizing events that attracted thousands. With a little trade union help and some fund-raising, day trips to the sea or plays or choral evenings came within reach even of the unemployed and their families.

From having been a diligent but indifferent scholar, in her last couple of years at Bradford Girls' Grammar School, Barbara's academic career took off. In her final year, the school organized a mock election to coincide with the 1929 general election; Barbara, of course, stood for Labour. She solicited from all Bradford's most famous sons, as well as its Labour candidates, posters and letters of endorsement. There was a hustings. Barbara, even to the younger girls, stood out. She could 'reach' an audience. 'She *made* you want to listen to her,' one contemporary remembered more than seventy years later. She became head girl, her school reports having brightened up notice-ably until in her last year she got straight As. To no one's surprise, except perhaps her own, she too was accepted, like Marjorie, by St Hugh's. For the first time, she experienced success and popular acclaim.

But to claim her place at Oxford, her father made it plain she had to find the money. She studied for months with a view to winning several awards, from the school and the county as well as an exhibiton from Oxford itself worth £30. But then, disaster: she was told her father earned too much for her to qualify for any but the Oxford scholarship. Frank said she could not go.

2. A Woman Wot Speaks

Ladies and gentlemen, we now have a unique phenomenon: a woman wot speaks.

Barbara Castle, Fighting All the Way[1]

There are two ways of wanting love. There is the way of sending out the whole force of one's vitality to a fair fight – perhaps to win, perhaps to lose, but certainly to fight. And there is the way of waiting outside as though love were a soup-kitchen and a marriage-certificate the soup-ticket, in the tremulous attitude of one cringing for charity.

Rebecca West, 'The Lamp of Hatred'[2]

Barbara was nearly persuaded that Oxford was not going to happen. She was not even certain that she wanted it to. She had romantic ideas about retiring to a remote and windswept farm where she could brush her hair and contemplate life, a kind of Lady of Shallott (Tennyson was another of her favourite writers). She had seen her clever sister Marjorie wear herself into a nervous breakdown and still fail to achieve the first-class degree that had been expected of her. She feared she too would fail.

Dons, like the mistresses at school, were not far-seeing, and exploited one's keenness. [Marjorie] had hated it all: the feverish competition to win a vacancy; the cram work for Higher Certificate and scholarships . . . sometimes [Barbara] felt she could not face the strain of hard work and narrow means for a culminating three years to come. She would break free and walk miles, work on a farm, and sit in a cool country bedroom brushing her hair in peace. But then – one wanted to learn, to know deeply and fully, to develop a scholarly mind and a clear brain, to quicken with appreciation before real beauty . . . even though the price was heavy, it was the only fine thing to do, to fight for it and get worn out and win.

It was Annie, her mother, who saved the day, marching into the town hall and taking the director of education through her household accounts. Bradford Council relented, and with a grant of £50 and another £50 loan repayable over five years – she would fall into arrears – and thanks to her mother's skill and diligence with a needle, Barbara had just enough for the journey south.

Barbara went up to Oxford, for the first time in charge of her own budget and seriously short of money. A contemporary, Nancy Burton,[3] had £50 a term compared with Barbara's £30 a year, and still found herself choosing between clothes and books. To make matters worse, St Hugh's did not even offer decent food; Barbara was reduced to relying on food parcels from home. But fuelled by her vitality and her nervous energy, she blasted her way into Oxford life. Her immediate reaction to the place was ecstatic: she wrote triumphantly to her grandparents from 'St Hugh's College Oxford!' that she had a 'dinky little room, at the end of a corridor – so it's got two windows'.

St Hugh's was in remote North Oxford, ten minutes' walk from the centre of town; the college was Victorian, forbidding, strongly Anglican: compline was said every evening in its chapel. It had been founded in 1886 by Elizabeth Wordsworth, great-niece of the poet and daughter of a bishop, and a champion of women's education. It was a prim and formal place, and its students were prim and formal too. Among these inconspicuous young women, Barbara, bobbed and pretty and full of life, immediately stood out. On the first night she met Olive Shapley, later an eminent broadcaster, who remained a close friend. 'Sitting around after supper, I was on a window seat with a sturdy, red-headed girl in a brown velvet dress with a lace collar, clearly made by her mother. We started to talk. She was a Yorkshire girl . . . she spent most of the evening telling me how infinitely superior the north was to the south, and what poor characters we southerners were . . .'[4]

Most of the other girls had come from boarding schools and were taking the next step on a narrow and well-worn path which would lead them into the Civil Service, or into teaching. In both, a marriage bar operated. Her fellow undergraduates lived, Barbara complained, dull, well-ordered lives and had dull, well-ordered minds. She was disappointed in them. Her poetry was not admired, and she failed to make the mark she had hoped in college drama. At first, though, she loved it all. The soft green country and the wide river, the golden stone of the ancient colleges, all appealed to the romantic in her.

Just before Christmas 1929, she wrote to Annie: 'This term has been dazzling – never has so short a time in my life been so crammed with "thrillin'" things . . . you will cuddle me when I come home, won't you Mam? And give me a lovely vac to console me for not being good at anything.'

Oxford gave Barbara the chance to develop her own ideas, away from the pressure of her father's demanding cross-examinations and her old school's narrow emphasis on qualifications. However, her politics remained strictly in the family tradition; it was her social life that blossomed. Soon after she arrived, Barbara switched from the French course for which she had been accepted to the newly introduced philosophy, politics and economics (PPE). It was not a success. 'Life seemed to be a succession of disjointed lectures and tutorials, linked to an excessively long list of set books, with no one to give it a central theme.' Her tutor was a plump woman without, Barbara claimed, any knowledge of politics or economics. So perhaps it was hardly surprising that Barbara found sex a more stimulating subject for study. Part of its appeal was no doubt the risk involved. The merest suspicion of any kind of sexual activity led to the culprit being sent down. The Oxford code of behaviour for women was constrained in the extreme. The places where they could go were controlled, and so were the people they could meet. Dancing in public rooms was banned 'under severe penalties', and undergraduates could learn to dance only with teachers licensed by the proctors (the university police). Women could go into men's rooms only with the express permission of the Principal and in the company of another woman 'similarly approved'. They could not travel in a car with a man unaccompanied by a second woman, or meet with a man anywhere.[5]

If the dons at St Hugh's were uncongenial – 'The staff . . . were . . . thin, pale, scholarly women, with dry, ironical humour, if any, and a delicate formality in dealing with the girls they taught,' wrote Nancy Burton – those at other colleges were worse. Barbara remembered one, lecturing on the Directoire period of the French Revolution, 'rais[ing] a snigger among the young men in his audience by remarking, "The name, I understand, has also been given to a certain type of women's knickers."'[6]

But there were compensations. Barbara fell in love – first with other women, for whom she wrote pages of romantic verse. To her Bradford friend Mary Hepworth who came to stay at Oxford several times she wrote:

> I am so all alone & young at heart
> I bring my humble adoration blind
> no longer, but a sweet necessity
> for older understanding on your part.

Later her affections were transferred to her fellow St Hugh's undergraduate,
Freda Houlston, 'a dark, strikingly attractive girl'.[7] Barbara often referred to
her 'difficult' path to sexual maturity; perhaps lesbian experiments lay along
it? They were not uncommon. But far more common, in the kind of girls'
boarding school atmosphere engendered at St Hugh's, were romantic but
entirely spiritual 'pashes' between girls.

   In her second year, however, men prevailed and there were no more
poems to girlfriends. Barbara, Olive Shapley thought, was very attractive.
'She was small and pretty, and I think she disliked being pretty. She had
these beautiful fine features, lovely little nose and beautiful skin and hair, and
I think she would rather have been more dramatic looking.'[8] She enjoyed
having a comet-like tail of men in pursuit, a reaffirmation of her prettiness
and a boost to her fragile self-confidence. She claimed later that she had been
'racked with inferiority complexes'; it was not the impression she gave
contemporaries as she powered her way through a social life that left her
exhausted and reliant on Virol and other energy-enhancing patent remedies.
One admirer, a student at the trade-unionists' Ruskin College, proposed
marriage. Theirs, he felt, could be a partnership to rival Beatrice and Sidney
Webb's. 'I think you are as sincerely socialistic as myself,' he wrote earnestly,
promising to kiss every strand of her spun-gold hair when they met the
following Sunday, regardless of her 'tantrums and selfishness'. But Barbara
was determined not to marry, not even someone who had been miserably
unemployed for two years and whose love letters included long quotations
from 'The Red Flag':

>   No saviour from on high delivers
>   No trust have we in prince or peer
>   . . . Each at his forge must do his duty
>   And strike the iron whilst it's hot.

   Barbara was strong, opinionated, self-absorbed and inclined to see herself
as under-appreciated. Occasionally, however, she was ambushed by her
inferiority complex. She would awake in the small hours overwhelmed, as
she wrote in another poem to Mary, by 'self-hatred and despair and jealousy'.
A photograph of her, soberly posed with her grandparents at about the time
she first went up to Oxford, shows her hiding behind a heavy fringe and
looking off-camera. Her brother and sister, by contrast, are open-faced and
look coolly straight into the lens. The evidence from contemporaries suggests
that the confident Barbara who climbed out of windows and over locked
gates under the nose of the porter, who careered about Oxford in an

acquaintance's open-topped car and once smashed into a milk-float, predominated, while the other Barbara emerged largely retrospectively, when the shock of a poor degree undermined the social triumphs and made them appear nugatory, as her father had always warned her they were. She feared, all her life, that her temper and her selfishness made her unlovable. Although she lived at the centre of a constant whirl of activity and admirers, letters from friends and lovers show that she often demanded reassurance.

Tristram – who had renamed himself Jimmie at a girlfriend's suggestion – went to Oxford to do a postgraduate diploma before joining the forestry service in Nigeria. They were the most devoted brother and sister Olive Shapley had ever met. They 'admired each other, liked each other, did a great many things together'. As he prepared to leave for Africa, Barbara wrote a typically emotional letter home: 'We *must* have the cottage[9] for a week before Jimmie goes, mustn't we? Last memories – unbearably brief! I'm sorry to be so sentimental, but Jim has pretty well taught me how to get the best time when young, & even when he comes back on leave there will be no repeating it.' She was almost as emotional about her shortage of cash, although she had a little more than the 2s 6d (12.5p) a term she claimed in her autobiography. 'Thanks for the 5/- [25p] . . . money slips away. I spend 2/6 every Friday on the Labour club dinners. But they are well worth it – I wouldn't dream of missing them. Last week we had Maurice Dobb address us on The New Russian Revolution – he was very good & a charming man.' She told her mother that she feared becoming a sponge on her richer friends, and then told her how dear Freda had given her £2 to buy a new dress, since her old one had been worn three times. She wrote in desperate terms about laundry she had sent home if it was not returned immediately.

There was little political content in her affectionate, demanding letters home. She was absorbed in the petty logistics of college life and the fun and excitement of being a social success.

Men [Nancy Burton said] were our hidden agenda: Oxford was a great marriage market. In a way this was recognised by the elaborate rules to penalise us for staying out late at night, bringing men into College, going away without permission, even for the day, going unchaperoned to a man's rooms. Of course all these rules were broken, but the punishments for being found out were severe . . . one felt that the dons simply did not accept sexuality as a factor in the life of scholarship, and that they treated their students as potential scholars, postulants in an order, rather uneasily open to the world. One don said to us . . . 'Women have no rights, only duties.' A tremendous undercurrent of innocent sexuality pervaded Oxford: so many men, so few girls. An endless debate: should one go to bed with the current boy, shouldn't one? Sexual radicalism was in the air, its gurus came to Oxford to address the undergraduate societies. But birth control, as it was then called, presented a severe problem. The clinics would only provide for married women, and only a few, mostly women doctors, in London could be relied upon to help.[10]

Barbara, who had still not managed to find out as much about the facts of life as she felt she needed to know, despite sending off for a sex manual on which she then tested her St Hugh's friends, was responsible for bringing one of the gurus to Oxford.

The gynaecologist and sexologist Norman Haire had recently published *The Comparative Value of Current Contraceptive Methods* in which he encouraged a frank and scientific approach to sex – in startling contrast to the experience of most of the undergratuates – arguing that women must reach orgasm for their physical well-being. Unsurprisingly, his talk to the Labour Club, followed by personal interviews with all those who wanted advice, was a sell-out. (Jimmie reported back to their parents that Barbara had been making enquiries about the meaning of 'masturbation'.[11] His disapproval of his sister's interest in sex, however, did not deter him from seducing her friend Olive a few months later.[12])

By her own account, Barbara had more or less abandoned academic work after her first term, a rebellion against the long, diligent hours spent studying when she was at school in Bradford. Olive, however, remembers Barbara working as well on playing: 'The outstanding thing about her was her dedication to her aims. We all thought it would be nice to get a First and nice to be beautiful, but she was the only one who did anything about it. I remember her creaming her face and hands at night and wearing gloves, drinking fruit juice, eating rusks and reading some obscure economics handbook at the same time. She was determined to be balanced. I was quite scared of her at times.' According to Olive, Barbara worked considerably harder than most of her friends, and unlike them, with a very clear objective: to get into politics. She took the same attitude to the highly fraught task of losing her virginity. It was something she thought she needed to find out about (and later, in a spirit of competition, to write about in her autobiography, 'because I knew Margaret Thatcher wouldn't say when she lost her virginity'[13]). She claimed it was an unsatisfactory experience. The poetry she continued to write suggests it did not put her off.

Already, the political arena was the one in which she was most confident and assured. Not clever enough to shine in the academic premier league, nor remotely rich enough to compete among the diamond-bright Brideshead generation, politics offered her a purpose great enough to overcome her self-doubt, and at the Labour Club she was a figure of some consequence. Her friends were people who shared her politics. At the Oxford Union, women were not allowed even to speak; there was no overt sex discrimination at the Labour Club. In her second year Barbara became an officer, although even that organization could not quite see its way to electing a woman as its chairman.[14] In the summer of that year she and some friends campaigned across Oxfordshire, proselytizing for the League of Nations. They called themselves the 'Caravan Girls (from Oxford)', leafleting the villages and addressing people in such martial tones that even retired colonels were prepared to come and support them:

> Someone said the League was not good as it had not published a Fixture Card. – But IT HAS stopped four wars and prevented at least three others . . . settled half a hundred Disputes . . . fought typhus in Poland . . . settled nearly a million Greek refugees on the land . . . IT IS Stamping out Slavery, Suppressing the White Slave Traffic . . . Organizing Peace so as to abolish War. IT CAN do ever so much more, if Public Opinion (that is YOU) will back it . . . Speakers: The Caravan Girls (from Oxford).[15]

In August 1931, around the mid-point of Barbara's second Oxford summer vacation, the second Labour government collapsed. The events of that long, sad summer, the sense of working people betrayed and hope vanquished, captured and shaped her political imagination. She was not alone. Both left and right of what remained of the party found their prejudices confirmed. The left – the ILPers and their sympathizers among party activists, like Barbara – blamed MacDonald's lack of radical fervour for his weakness in the face of the bankers and international capital. The right – trade union leaders and councillors – was equally confident that a failure to make the needs of workers pre-eminent had led to the betrayal of the party.

Barbara, debating at the Labour Club in term time and writing for the *Bradford Pioneer* in the vacations, had had a good vantage point from which to observe, as Ramsay MacDonald steadily abandoned Labour principles and finally agreed to lead a National Government, predominantly Conservative, committed to maintaining the value of the pound regardless of the damage inflicted on jobs and the economy. The last crisis came when, pressed by international bankers, MacDonald and his Chancellor Philip Snowden demanded more public-spending cuts, including 10 per cent off the dole on which three million families relied. The decision was endorsed by the first woman cabinet minister, the Minister of Labour, Margaret Bondfield.

At the end of the summer, Barbara delayed returning to Oxford for a few days so she could report for the *Pioneer* from Scarborough on Labour's first post-crisis conference. One incidental result of this trip was to make a lifelong enemy of Vic Feather, who had thought the job was his. Feather, influenced by Frank, had become heavily involved in practical politics, working among the desperate poverty of Bradford's unemployed. He was one of a small gang which went on occasional forays to steal pigs from the local landlord to supplement their diet. He cannot have been amused to discover he had been dropped in favour of the editor's undergraduate daughter. Elbowing him out of the way so she could report the Scarborough conference was a decision for which Barbara may have paid a heavy price when, nearly forty years later, he was General Secretary of the TUC and she, Employment Secretary.[16]

The Scarborough conference ran from 5 to 8 October; Barbara celebrated her twenty-first birthday on 6 October. But Scarborough was memorable for more than her finally achieving what was then voting age. It was at this wind-blasted Yorkshire seaside resort that the trade unions took control of the party and set in train the events which were to lead to the disaffiliation of the Independent Labour Party. The long tension between Fabian gradualism, the steady process of constitutional and economic reform, and the ILP's demand for swift and radical transformation was to be resolved by the new brutalism of the trade-union block vote on the conference floor.

In the public mind, MacDonald was the saviour of the nation, but there was no shadow of doubt within the party that his desertion was an act of base treachery. The new generation of leaders had a terrible inheritance from which to refashion the political arm of the Labour movement. Foremost among them was Ernest Bevin, creator and leader of the Transport and General Workers' union, the dominant personality on the TUC, and among many other achievements, the builder of Transport House. A short walk from Westminster, Transport House became the home not just of the union, but of the Labour Party National Executive and the TUC. It became Labour's central command, the point from which all attacks by the left were anticipated and rebuffed, the embodiment of opposition to Barbara's wing of the party.

It was at Transport House that the course of the Scarborough party conference, and so the course the party itself would take for the next five years, was mapped. With a general election expected shortly, internal support for the party was shored up by expelling MacDonald. There was no doubt where party members' duties now lay. Arthur Henderson, MacDonald's Foreign Secretary, became the caretaker leader. The message was to be continuity and discipline. MacDonald's betrayal was to be blamed on the bankers, not the party structures. Those who argued otherwise could not expect to remain in the party. The ILP, which a year earlier had decided that its thirty-seven MPs should observe their own, ILP, discipline wherever it conflicted with the Labour Party's, was to be instructed to toe the line. Candidates at the imminent election who refused to sign up risked having official Labour candidates run against them.

At Scarborough, Arthur Henderson made all this plain in his opening speech. He attacked the ILP as the 'organised conscience' of the Labour movement. It was the word 'organised' that spelt trouble as far as the party was concerned. Barbara – 'BB' in the columns of the *Pioneer* – disagreed.

> Henderson . . . had failed to explain away why ILP members should be considered rebels when merely advocating the measures demanded and defined by previous Labour conferences. Henderson did not seem to believe in too much control by the Conferences . . . details of policy were the business of Cabinet, and the parliamentary party must obey these details, rather than the Conference decisions . . . The Party was still clinging to the idea that Socialism was two or three generations removed and was still discussing what to do in the crisis after next. The left wing policy all through the conference has been to press home the urgency of the problem . . . and to urge the party to grasp the fact that is is a new situation which can only be dealt with in a revolutionary manner.[17]

In her report of the second half of the conference, which appeared the following week, Barbara recorded that Ernest Bevin had dismissed the ILP's favourite remedy for alleviating poverty: swingeing taxation. 'Socialism by taxation has proved impossible,' he had told delegates. Barbara disagreed. In a personal commentary, she declared that the great source of Labour's strength 'lies in its determination to stand by the unemployed, whatever financial calamity may threaten, for in this crisis those who stand by the unemployed must stand for revolutionary Socialism'. She echoed the call of the ILP leader Jimmy Maxton: 'The people are not going to respond to academic resolutions, but to the demand for working-class power, power, *power!*' In the general election less than three weeks later, the National Executive Committee not only refused to endorse ILP candidates unless they took a loyalty oath: some even had official Labour candidates standing against them. Both parties paid the price for discord. The ILP now had just four MPs, while Labour lost all but 46 of the 287 seats it had won in 1929. It seemed possible that instead of destroying capitalism, Labour was to be destroyed by it.

For the Labour left, no further evidence of the right's perfidious instincts was ever again needed. But for many ordinary non-sectarian party members, the electoral disaster was confirmation of the need to keep the movement together, against boat-rockers of either faction. It also distorted the Labour Party's understanding of economic alternatives. MacDonald and his Chancellor Philip Snowden believed that the British Empire's survival depended on sticking to the gold standard regardless of the impact on their supporters. Yet when, within weeks, the National Government was forced to devalue, disaster did not follow. In fact, it marked the beginning of the recovery. Bankers were not after all omniscient. Orthodox economics took a severe blow to its credibility, but Barbara saw in the episode a more political message. 'The lesson I learned,' Barbara summarized a lifetime later, 'was that Labour governments cannot survive by adopting the economic policies of their political enemies.'[18]

Finally, relations between Labour Cabinets and the party became an issue. The left was always frustrated by the innate conservatism of its leaders. The demand that the party have some control over Cabinets increased. Moreover, even before Prime Minister MacDonald committed the final betrayal of splitting the party when he led a handful of Labour ministers into his new National Government, he had already allowed unemployment to double; nearly three million people were out of work by September 1931. Mistrust of the leadership became established as the hallmark of the Labour left. In the immediate aftermath of the formation of the National Government, however, it was the trade union movement that emerged, through its strength on the National Executive, as the controlling influence on the party. At the same time many individuals, like Barbara's friend Olive Shapley, looked further left. The October Club, a Communist-front organization which later took over the Oxford University Labour Club, was founded. Olive joined. Barbara did not. In the early 1930s, 'Communists were very sectarian, got drunk, wore beards and did not worry about their examinations,' according to Denis Healey, who was recruited himself at Oxford a few years later. It is not clear which of these characteristics alienated Barbara, but she eschewed Communism. 'I sympathised with the Bolshevik revolution as much as [Olive] did, but always retained a cautious streak.'[19] In a grand gesture, she led the move by the Oxford University Labour Club to depose its honorary president, Ramsay MacDonald. G. D. H Cole, the man who wrote Labour's 1918 constitution, was elevated in his place.

Back at Oxford for her final year, with Jimmie gone, Barbara was sobering up, or so she reassured her parents. 'I have got beyond the desire for ordinary flirtations now & can discriminate. The result is that I have a much clearer mind for work . . . For the first time, my heart is in my work & it is not merely a nuisance to be hurried out of the way. It is a comfort to find I am basically intellectual after all & not merely sensual. I had my doubts at one point.'[20] If she was taking work more seriously, part of the reason was a new tutor. Agnes Headlam Morley was the daughter of a diplomat, herself a Conservative candidate in the 1931 general election and a transforming influence on many young women she encountered. But there was simply too much work to make up. Barbara could not abandon her heady experimenting with life. She sat her finals, but then instead of studying for her viva (the final, oral part of her degree), she absented herself with some friends and nearly missed her viva altogether. To her utter and unmitigated despair, she graduated with a third.

It might have been worse. It was still possible to get a fourth. But her shaky self-belief was shattered: she had, after all, done all the things her father detested. She had behaved in what he would call a common and vulgar way, and this was the result.

Failure was a severe blow in Barbara's personal battle to measure up to her father's expectations. Frank, however, seems to have been less disappointed than Barbara feared. Nor was he surprised. Mary Hepworth was still his protégée as well as Barbara's good friend. From London, where she was trying to succeed as a novelist, she had reported back to Frank on her weekends with Barbara. In a letter of February 1932, Barbara's final year, Frank told Mary: 'Promiscuity is certainly uncongenial for most people – it does not satisfy normal needs. It is tiring and palls – & it cannot be fitted into the structure of a purposeful life – it tends to divide instead of harmonizing the personality.'[21] Much prouder of his children than they could see, Frank decided Oxford had failed Barbara rather than the other way round. His enthusiasm for the ancient universities was fading and he even warned Mary against trying to get a place at Ruskin, the trade union college from which many students without formal qualifications won diplomas and places at the university proper. The mood on the left generally was becoming hostile to intellectuals and their institutions. Frank, writing to Mary again after Barbara's results, thought Oxford had done her no good at all: 'I feel a long way off Babs, because she has just now the most undergraduate mind ever, I feel. Full of the brightest and most unreal ideas. When I think of my own ideas – like certain books I have, battered with 30 years' use & repeated rereading, & Babs' readiness to take any view she fancies & defend it, I simply feel I want to wait till she has some sense.'

It was not only Barbara who was making Frank dyspeptic. The special dispensation he had gained from the Tax Inspectorate to stay in Bradford until Barbara finished school had long ago expired and in 1931, after nine years, he could delay the Inspectorate's demands no longer and was moved to Hyde, on the edge of Greater Manchester. Frank loathed Hyde, later blighted as the home of the Moors Murderers, Ian Brady and Myra Hindley, and later still of the serial killer, Dr Harold Shipman. 'I individually and personally hate every dirty brick between home & office,' he told Mary; describing another office he had been visiting, he went on: 'The effect is of a Dickens novel dropped in the mud & the mud over all the pages; and what sights, what twisted faces; & several deaf or shamming deaf, & that kind of stupidity which is a positive quality . . . It's all to me part of the image of the neighbourhood – like scraping some of the scurf off the dirty ground that stretches for miles & miles.' Olive Shapley remembered going to stay with Barbara in Hyde in 1932, the year Barbara graduated. 'It had rows of small grey houses, steep cobbled streets, sad little shops, clanging trams and a grim park on a hillside . . . at that time Barbara longed with [a fierce] intensity to get away from Hyde.'[22]

It was not all bad. There was a little more money now that Marjorie and Jimmie had left home and Barbara herself was about to start earning. The house was larger, with a pretty garden, and Hyde was a gateway to the Peak District. In September, Glyn Jones, a boyfriend who became a successful colonial official, wrote from Northern Rhodesia: 'Your letter this week tells me that in spite of the disappointment of your people, you have managed to get your charming head in fit condition for maintaining its bloody and unbowed appearance.'[23] Frank was soon reporting to Mary that Barbara was recovering from the shock of not doing well in her finals. 'Babs is much less unhappy than I expected. She is just dropping Oxford and its damnable inheritance & except for occasional outings with anyone available, concentrates on hard reading, shorthand & Labour politics. We don't say very much to each other but are in pretty close touch.'

Barbara, together with three million others, was unemployed. She had been offered a job by the 'impressionable' editor of one of Hyde's local papers, but it had folded before she could start. She was determined not to become a secretary or a teacher, but there was little prospect of other work. Consequently, she had a lot of time for politics. The left, still in confusion after the devastating 1931 election results, was struggling to contain the tension between reform and radicalism. If the party split, could it ever win power again – and would it deserve to, if it was prepared to compromise on its objectives? The ILP was the outspoken tribune of radical – even revolutionary – ideas. Labour, now led by the sympathetic George Lansbury, a pacifist and a man who had been imprisoned rather than levy what he thought was an unjust tax on the people of Poplar, where he was mayor, was nonetheless firmly under the control of the trade unions who disliked the ILP's politics and were deeply hostile to its refusal to respect party discipline.

Barbara was always instinctively on the side of the romantic. But Frank believed in the solidarity of the Labour movement. Behind closed doors he was one of the leading voices in the Hyde ILP to argue against disaffiliation.[24] At a special conference in Bradford in July 1932, Hyde was one of a significant minority of constituency parties – about a third – that opposed it, but the ILP majority voted for disaffiliation. It turned out to be a disastrous decision. Purity meant obscurity: by 1935, ILP membership would be down by three-quarters. If its leaders' calculation had been that a defeated Labour Party could be overtaken from the radical left, it could not have been more wrong.

The ILP had been teetering on the brink of divorce with the Labour Party for so long that plans to replace the ILP as the voice of the activist and the source of radical ideas were well advanced when the break finally came. While MacDonald was still trying to square the Labour Party and the international bankers in the summer of 1931, G. D. H. Cole, whose lectures Barbara had attended at Oxford, had established the Society for Socialist Inquiry and Propaganda as an 'intellectual ginger group' to strengthen the Labour left. It proposed 'not a series of isolated and uncoordinated forays into capitalism but concerted action designed to transform the basis of the economic system "at a blow"'.[25]

The Coles, Douglas and his wife Margaret, were a Fabian phenomenon, for fifty years providing much of the intellectual drive and organizational energy which shaped the early Labour Party. For this latest project, they had recruited many of the most eminent names on the Labour left. They included Frank Horrabin, the lover of 'Red' Ellen Wilkinson, the Jarrow MP who was to lead the hunger marchers, and a younger man, William Mellor. Mellor was a journalist and socialist propagandist who had co-written a book with G. D. H. Cole. But Cole's greatest coup had been to persuade Ernest Bevin that the SSIP offered a real opportunity to bring together the trade union and intellectual wings of the party. Bevin agreed to chair the new body.

After the ILP had voted to disaffiliate in July 1932, the large minority

who disapproved of the decision – including Frank and Barbara – joined
Labour. They were led by another Frank, Frank Wise, 'the man from the
City', a civil servant turned businessman and, from 1929 to 1931 an MP and
the lover of the young and beautiful Jennie Lee. Working-class Lee stayed
with the disaffiliated ILP. Wise led the ILPers who wanted to heal the breach
with Labour. He made contact with the SSIP and after some months of
negotiation the Socialist League was formed, a union between the intellectual
drive of the SSIP and the manpower of the old ILP – several thousand
strong, organized in branches around the country.

It began inauspiciously. Bevin failed to get the chairmanship of the new
body against the objections of the ILPers, and refused to serve on the
executive. The numerical predominance of former ILP members – which
alarmed Cole too – meant, Bevin was sure, that sooner or later the old
sectarian tendencies would resurface. But for people like Barbara, the League
seemed to legitimize the decision to stay with the Labour party instead of
deserting with the real working-class radicals under the leadership of the
Clydesider Jimmie Maxton in the breakaway ILP.

Barbara had encountered the SSIP first when she had attended a meeting
in the basement of a shop in Manchester. 'I remember how depressing I
found not only the bleak meeting place, but the remoteness of the "intellectuals". They did not seem to me to be in touch with the real tough world
I knew in places like Hyde.'[26] There was little evidence that the Socialist
League would be any different: not only had Bevin refused to serve, but
the executive of the new body was dominated by Oxbridge graduates. The
League began to prepare the ground for a new Labour government by
identifying the sources of resistance to socialism and planning how to
overcome them. It was to hear William Mellor on the role for which
socialists in north-west England must prepare that Barbara and her mother
went to a Saturday meeting in Hyde.

Mellor, immaculately turned out in an expensive suit, with a silk
handkerchief in his breast pocket and carrying kid gloves, made no concessions to the poor and the unemployed that he addressed as he toured the
country appealing for their support and educating them for the work ahead.
Mellor believed the first phase in politicizing the workers was to make them
aware of their condition. 'I have just spent as much on my lunch as you earn
in a week,' he told his audience. 'How much longer are you going to put
up with it?'[27] Barbara was entranced by this novel way of accommodating
the radicalism of the prosperous classes with the muscle of the working class.
(Mellor was not alone. Tom Driberg, a future left-wing colleague of Barbara's
at Westminster, was chronicling the doings of the 'bright young things' as

the *Daily Express*'s first William Hickey. He, too, excused himself with the defence that he was 'politicizing' the workers.) Barbara's mother was also bowled over. Mellor was invited back for tea. Within months, he and Barbara were lovers. Mellor was already forty-four, only six years younger than her father and exactly twice Barbara's age. He was glamorous, confident and married, with a baby son. He became her mentor, her alternative father, a man who loved her totally and compellingly. Unself-aware as she was, she saw the parallel: 'Mellor was in many ways much like my father. They were of that same bigness. He was about my father's generation, a bit younger than my father but considerably older than I was. And just as my father could not tolerate trash, whether it was self-seeking, pecuniary ambition or a vulgar Sunday newspaper in the house, or whatever it was . . . nor could Bill Mellor . . . He did for me what Dad did for Mary Hepworth.'[28]

Frank had been disdainful of Barbara's love life. In one letter to Mary, he wrote: 'What distresses me is the vulgarity of Babs' attitude with a long tail of men, mostly second rate, dragging at her heels. The only possible comparisons would burn holes in the pages of an asbestos edition of *Lady Chatterly's Lovers* [sic]. But fox terriers figure in the simile.'[29] Jimmie, briefly visiting from Africa, was even more critical of Barbara's relationships. One was with a man called Styles. Styles, too, seems to have been married, and Barbara always insisted their relationship was entirely platonic and based on a mutual love of dancing. It ended badly, judging from allusions to it in Frank's letters to Mary. 'Babs tells me you have been told of last summer's episode. At the time I was not to tell you. I tried to behave calmly at the time but the result is I cannot bear the sight of Styles.'

In the autumn of 1932, at about the time of the formation of the Socialist League, Barbara had finally found a job, demonstrating in shops and stores in the area the products – ranging from sweets to crystallized fruits – of a wholesale importer, Samuel Hanson's. For the first time, she was brought into close and regular contact with people who had no safety net between their job and the dole. She tried to persuade her fellow workers to join her as a member of the Shop Assistants' Union and stand up for their rights. They pointed out that they would lose their jobs if they did.

The demonstration work was often cold and always dreary. Once Barbara had to dress as Little Nell and sell humbugs. But it gave her some financial independence. Moreover, although she continued to live at home, her confidence was returning. Her father, still resenting living in Hyde, wrote more approvingly of his youngest daughter to Mary. 'Babs is good in that she seizes on to every possibility of life this place offers & is only horrid when all doors to activity seem shut.' Frank had told Barbara, 'the only way

to learn public speaking is to speak in public', and she followed his advice
exhaustively. She was propaganda secretary to the local Hyde party. She had
to organize meetings and was always first reserve if a guest failed to turn up.
She began to read widely about politics and economics, and to prepare her
speeches with exhaustive and detailed research, a habit that persisted all her
life. Her political skills were improving all the time, Frank told Mary.

> She would be Labour candidate if she had another 6 months before the
> adoption to make headway. As it is, her chance is poor. The local women
> hate her because she is pretty & clever. Quite a successful meeting Tuesday
> – Susan Lawrence[30] [chairman of the Labour Party in 1930] & a crowded
> hall. Babs spoke – clearly & *well*. SL [Susan Lawrence] came in half way
> through her speech – got excited – paid Babs a handsome public compli-
> ment & seized her after to find out all about her. But Babs will not be
> backed by the Hyde end of the division & the other end are only just
> getting aware of her possibilities.

Politics was once again providing her with both her social life and her
raison d'être. About this time Mellor became a regular visitor, taking her out
to smart little restaurants in Manchester and occasionally for drives in a hired
car. Mellor did not drive: 'I belong to the car-hiring classes,' he declared,
sitting back behind the chauffeur, his kid-gloved hands folded on his lap.[31]
He was the son and brother of Unitarian ministers – the most radical of the
Nonconformist Churches – and he had been intended for the ministry
himself. In preparation, he had been sent to Manchester College,[32] Oxford,
where he rebelled. He left Oxford for London and in 1913 found a job on
the *Daily Herald*, the trade union paper, which at that time was kept afloat
by collections raised at political meetings. Like many on the left he bitterly
opposed the First World War.[33] He was imprisoned for a while as a
conscientious objector, but was taken back by the *Herald* immediately the
war ended, as its industrial correspondent. In 1920 he published *Direct Action*,
an extended essay on the need for workers to use their muscle for radical
reform. It is a classic of Marxist orthodoxy. 'The war that began in August
1914,' he wrote, 'resulted not from a threat to freedom and democracy, but
from a threat to the interests of the Allied Capitalists from the Capitalists of
Central Europe. The "State" that was in danger was "the Executive Committee of the Capitalist class." Fortunately five years of war [have] resulted in
bringing that State into even more imminent jeopardy.'[34]
    The book was dedicated to his wife of barely a year, Edna. Barbara
always portrayed Edna as a weak creature who relied on William for

emotional support. Her son Ronald paints a different picture, of a politically aware and active woman who, having lost a brother in the first war, campaigned for the League of Nations and the Peace Pledge Union. As importantly, she was financially independent, with money of her own from her family's successful brass foundry in Rotherham.

When Barbara and William met, the *Herald*, of which he had become editor, had just been taken over by the publishers Odhams. The TUC – in effect, Bevin – still controlled the editorial line. As a result William had been elevated to the Odhams board, and after twelve years of marriage had just become a father. The family lived comfortably in a flat in Battersea in south-west London, overlooking the park; Mellor was well off, careless with money and plainly enjoyed impressing Barbara, whose previous social outings, she claimed, had been restricted by poverty to a cup of tea in the local tripe shop. According to Barbara, the attraction was instant and mutual: 'Physically, he was my kind of man: tall, black-haired, erect, with a commanding presence and strong, handsome features.'

There was a certain inevitability to the seduction. For Barbara, a relationship with a glamorous senior intellectual was an attractive idea in itself. An affair – especially a semi-public one, as this became – demonstrated an independence from convention and, with such a man as William Mellor, a seriousness of purpose. It also provided her with an entrée into the highest reaches of left-wing politics. So it was hardly surprising that she, young and still unsure of herself, fell in love with him. 'For good or evil,' Beatrice Webb wrote in her diary in 1931 after a conversation with another leading figure of the left Ellen Wilkinson, 'the political emancipation of women and their entry into public life has swept away the old requirement of chastity in unmarried women.'[35]

For Mellor, it must have been a more complicated business. He was married, and a father, and he wanted to get into parliament – three good reasons for not becoming entangled with a woman half his age, however attractive. And he saw himself as a man of high moral principle. Revealing the affair in her autobiography, Barbara said that she had 'led him to bed'. His justification, in the end, for their relationship echoed his justification for parading his affluence before an audience of workers. Early in February 1934, he told her: 'In the end I am a socialist and an agitator because I want a free world in which human relationships shall be free from the constrictions and restraints imposed by, . . . and taboos that spring from, religious . . . fears. I'm a politician only because this world as it is kills individuality, destroys feedom and fetters human beings . . . We may have to go through hell to get there but even that wouldn't be too big a price to pay.'[36] A few days later, he wrote again: 'You've let the real me come out of its hiding place, you've loved (I know) that real me, you've made it possible for self-imposed repressions and surface coverings to disappear, and you've talked to me in a myriad ways that were beautiful.'

In March he wrote suggesting they spend Easter together. It would be a major step in their relationship.

> You will, I know, believe me, when I say that I have thought until it's hard to think any longer about all that might be said by the world about our doing this. But when all my thinking is over I come back to this: both of us are strong enough to know what we can bear & what we cannot; both of us are honest enough to face before we start the 'dangers' (the word is ill-chosen but you will understand); both of us care for each other so that we should guard one another against hurt. I believe we can be together in happiness & contentment of mind & spirit. Limitations of expression there may be, but companionship and love will be there . . . So far as any 'moral' question arises I have tried in what I have just written to give my answer. If it be fact that the world would frown on us for being to each other what we are and for letting something of what we desire find fulfilment in such a way – then the world is foolish and unwise.

The early days of their affair were, like the early days of most love affairs, a switchback ride of drama and misunderstanding. Barbara was now getting cold feet. The Easter weekend was a disappointment. On the Monday, William wrote from the Midland Hotel, Manchester: 'Sweetheart, tonight I seem to have lost you just when we were so close to each other. And I can't bear to lose you . . . When I tell you I love you, then comes your reply, "Sorry, William, I'm in control." In control of what? God knows you're in control of me.' Barbara was not so in love that she did not realize the risk inherent in an affair with a married man who had shown no intention of leaving his wife. William responded to her concern. A couple of days later, he wrote again: 'Another step on the honesty road has been taken. Last night I told my wife. Not to have done so would have been to smirch the love you and I have for each other; not to have done so would have been unfair to you and to her; not to have done so would have made what is, and now will continue to be, beautiful, clean and holy into something furtive or stolen.'[37] It was, however, only to be a half-loaf. He would not leave Edna immediately; she was to be 'led gently' to the idea of divorce. Nonetheless, Barbara's parents were let into the secret. William was relieved: 'My dear, I'm incredibly at peace and incredibly happy. We've set our faces towards the light and we've done it honestly and openly in the eyes of those who matter.' Frank said to Barbara, 'I never expected a man to come to me and tell me that his intentions towards my daughter were strictly dishonourable.'[38]

The eyes of those who mattered did not, however, include anyone outside either immediate family. For the next eight years, Barbara lived partly in the shadows of Mellor's life. Again and again, he promised he would leave Edna at the right moment. The right moment never arrived.

Love and politics were far more exciting than Barbara's physically demanding but unsatisfying work touting dried fruit around the North-West. Mellor's second-hand accounts of high politics in London, sent almost daily, did little to lift her spirits, and neither did the occasional weekend with him. She wrote apologetically in April 1934: 'Until I have settled this question of my job, I can't find complete, full happiness in our love . . . while I stand low in my own estimation, while I move and work in an atmosphere which jars and frets, I can't take delight in offering myself to you.' However, she found in herself a spirit for direct action that was a tonic for her bruised self-esteem. 'Tonight I am to speak at the Stockport League of Youth inaugural meeting. I shall speak well because you have given me conviction and infused my politics with a sense of reality. When I really believe in anything I can make others believe in it too. Never before have I thought my speeches could have any importance or my political work any real value. Now I see myself as the medium of a message which has a power of itself, independently of the medium.'

The same sense of a wider purpose made her more confident, she told William happily, in argument too. She reported one successful encounter with the husband of a 'progressive female soul', who had invited her to speak at a meeting. 'He was a fascinating man . . . clever & provocative . . . He and I launched into a first class argument while the females applauded and rejoiced – "at last we have found someone who can stand up to him" . . . afterwards he said seriously to me: "You've argued well. Don't overtire that brain of yours – it's too dynamic – like an avalanche."'

Barbara liked to think of herself as a slightly raffish, unconventional character:

The place [the family home in Hyde] is full of cheerful domestic activity – rooms upside down with spring cleaning & meals taken picnic-fashion anywhere. I've put on my nice old overall & am pottering round washing stockings, writing to you, sipping coffee, smoking & playing records. In a few minutes I shall retire to my room & read about Frauenbewegungen

[Germany's women's movement]. There's something elemental & satisfying about the busy-ness of a home like mine. I'm ruined irretrievably for respectability & also the conventionalities that take up so much time.

Barbara already saw herself as bolder and cleverer than most women but she was anxious that men were not taking her seriously, that her prettiness was all they saw. Having grown up in an environment where – apart from a tendency to patronize her mother – women were treated with some seriousness, she was shocked to discover that it was not the same everywhere. Even Oxford, where the restrictions on women had been so manifestly petty, had not prepared her for the way women were simply dismissed in the real world. She took to her bed in moral outrage after watching a fashion show at a grocery exhibition: 'Came out feeling sick – I'll have some remarks to make on Wednesday about the attitude to women in *this* country! . . . You wonder why I have a profound mistrust of men when the man-made system of this country *stinks.*' She complained often to William that she did not trust men, and that even he was more interested in her body than her brain. Barbara's attitude to her semi-public affair with Mellor must have owed something to the prevailing view on the left that true sexual freedom would be one of many benefits of a socialist state. William and Barbara were merely sampling its delights a little ahead of most others. But Barbara showed little interest in the feminist arguments of the day, which to most young women had begun to appear faded and irrelevant to world economic crisis and the rise of Fascism.

In the 1920s and early 1930s, many socialist women had argued that all women, regardless of class, were as much the victims of the capitalist system as their proletarian brothers. But, it was claimed, middle-class women lacked the will to fight for the kind of radical social and economic change which would benefit working men and women. Furthermore, gender issues – equal pay, birth control and the right of married women to work – were controversial and it was convenient to dismiss them as middle class.

In the 1918 debates on the party constitution, some women had warned that demanding separate women's sections of the party would lead to women being excluded from the rest of the party's activities. By the early 1930s, that was palpably true. Not only did the women's sections fail to get the main party to discuss issues important to them, but nor could their perspective be heard in debate on 'men's' issues. In 1929, women's representation at the party's main annual conference was dramatically reduced by the declaration that instead of five hundred women members, constituencies must have 2,500 to win the right to send a second delegate to conference. The demand for the right of the women's conference to put three resolutions a year to the main conference was rejected in both 1929 and 1931. Soon even the campaign for constitutional reform became dormant. When constitutional changes were discussed at the annual conference in 1936, the campaign for women's representation on the National Executive went by default. By then, Barbara appeared to be avoiding all gender issues, preferring, like many of her women contemporaries, to be 'less aggressively feminist than independently feminine', as one of the new women's magazines described it. Later, quoting Rosa Luxemburg, she too would declare 'my sex is irrelevant'.[39]

But there was horror in Britain at the fate of the Frauenbewegungen at the hands of the Nazis, who had effectively closed down all but their own Deutsches Frauenwerk. The Nazi organization had reversed hard-won equal-pay legislation, and promoted the myth of the ideal woman bound to hearth, home and the perpetuation of the Aryan race. For sympathizers in Britain, women's rights not only remained surbordinate to the achievement of socialism, but became bound up in the fight against Fascism.

'I'm afraid of men's greed and ruthlessness,' Barbara wrote, 'I'm afraid of the crushing of beauty and life. I've been brought up among the perils of debt and I shall never lose the sense of the danger. I feel kinship with those who always live on the borderline. Oh William, if the workers would only dare to fight.' Barbara and William, unable to do much together, wrote almost daily to describe their political campaigning: speeches to hostile audiences, street-corner meetings in howling gales, May Day parades. In 1934 Barbara was in Stockport, William in Leeds. 'As I walked, I thought of my lover,' Barbara wrote, 'walking too in some other procession, feeling no doubt like me – slightly ridiculous but defiant of ridicule and underneath inspired by the thought of solidarity and power.' William was indeed marching too: 'I walked about two and a half miles at the head of a procession passed [sic] streets that made one's heart sick. They weren't "officially" slums – just back to back houses in dead ends . . . I did a stream of hot and angry vituperation which "got" what was left of the crowd.' The Herald duly reported his speech: 'Mr Mellor expressed disgust at the conditions in which many of the people of Leeds were living. "I have seen Leeds today," he said, "it doesn't want a Socialist Council. It wants dynamite . . . you cannot do that without destroying the capitalist system."'

The few surviving letters between Barbara and her parents suggest they were less sanguine about the relationship than Barbara later chose to remember. The affair with William marked a turning point in the balance of power at home. Barbara had struck out on her own, establishing her potential tin the eyes of the leaders of the Labour movement. From being the dominant influence in her life, Frank faded quite abruptly from daily consideration. In contrast, their glowing, determined and able daughter became the focus of her parents' lives, a source of pride to whom they were now the willing slaves. They had no option but to accept William on whatever terms Barbara was prepared to tolerate.

'Mother has accepted my references to our Buxton rendez-vous without a quiver! Her only complaint was "now I shall be left alone to entertain grandpa". Envy and frustration are at the bottom of most moral judgements – which sounds thoroughly catty but which is actually a profound & sympathetic analytical judgement. Nothing my dear can give me a sense of sin in my love for you! And I do love you. Barbara.' But the lack of certainty was straining Barbara's nerves. Towards the end of May, William tried to reassure her. 'Last night, when I got back, Edna & I had another talk. It was not too easy for either of us but it marked, I believe, another stage towards happiness for her and for you & me . . . you're not to worry or trouble about this. I tell you because you have a right to know & because were I not to tell you our love would be hurt . . . I and you alike must know what each of us is thinking and saying & doing for without that there would be a failure to make our love, what it is, big and fine and clear.'

'You see this double life can be rather difficult,' Barbara responded. It was about to get more complicated still.

3. Directing the Action

Here and there will be found groups of workers who consciously strive to awaken their comrades to the full meaning of the Class War.[1]

William Mellor, *Direct Action*

Barbara was making the best of Hyde. She planned to run for the council, and she wanted to learn to drive. But she was also desperate to get away. For eighteen months she had been working in the department stores of the North-West trying to sell the products of her employers, Samuel Hanson & Sons of Eastcheap. It was two years since she had graduated from Oxford: it was time to move up or move out. In April 1934, she wrote to her London boss, a Mr Dunning, to remind him that he had promised that her work as a demonstrator was only a pilot scheme. He responded by inviting her to London, where he offered her a new and better job. Ecstatic, she wrote to her parents:

> Ever since Oxford I have been battling with great self-distrust, the misery of which has made me restless and irritable. Gradually I'm winning back my self-respect – intellectually and in every other way. If I can establish myself securely in this job then I shall be able to hold up my head again . . . I haven't come to London in any careerist, worldly sense. I have come both with a sinking heart and with rising hopes. I *will* show my worth and my power to earn a worth-while livelihood! . . . Every scrap of careerism in me has drained away – I'm not the lass I was at Oxford now. You know that, don't you? But I've still got that craving to 'make good' . . . to show my abilities and my powers in my contact with my fellow men.

Barbara's political character was formed in the grey and threatening climate of sectarian political struggle which overshadowed the left in the

years from 1933 until the outbreak of war in 1939. Radicals and gradualists
floundered in the face of the rise of Fascism, while fear and loathing of
militarism was constrained by suspicion and hostility towards the new power
of Soviet Communism. The party mood swung wildly over the issue of
rearmament, and it was echoed in contradictory conference decisions. Only
reluctantly did the leadership come to accept, from 1937, that war might be
unavoidable. Even then, the left clung to the hope that political and
economic rather than military measures might prevail.

Barbara wanted to be part of the struggle. More than that, she wanted to
succeed, and to be seen to succeed. She was also determined to be with her
lover, William Mellor. With him, she could move to the heart of political
life, bypassing the traditional Labour woman's route to Westminster of a
slow and uncertain rise through her trade union or local government.
Through Mellor, she would be taken directly to the top of the left of the
Labour movement. For the next five years, the political and the personal
were intimately interwoven in an exhausting and ultimately futile pattern:
Mellor's struggle to persuade the Labour Party to form a united front with
all the parties of the left against Fascism became entangled with her own
fruitless attempts to persuade Mellor to leave Edna and their son Ronald.

She had reason to be optimistic. The economy was steadily improving.
Nationally, unemployment was dipping below two million; Ramsay Mac-
Donald's largely Conservative National Government was claiming that more
people were in work than ever before in British history (a statistic which
next resurfaced in the prolonged recession of the 1980s). In the South,
depression had only ever been a second-hand experience brought home by
the hunger marchers from the silent shipyards and pits of the North and the
coalfields of South Wales. Heady with excitement, Barbara found a cheap,
furnished flat near the British Museum and threw herself into her job as a
sales supervisor, responsible for organizing demonstrations of Hanson's goods
around the country. Soon, she felt her immediate boss was blocking her. She
decided to repeat the move which had worked so well a few months earlier:
she wrote again to Mr Dunning. This time, the effect was disastrous. In the
early spring of 1935, she was sacked. Now she had no option but to pursue
her ambition to be a journalist and a politician.

On the strength of her two years' working for private industry, Barbara
maintained a lifelong belief in its inefficiency and what she was later to call
its 'hierarchical rigidities'.[2] A similar impact was made on her approach to
politics by her close involvement in the Socialist League as it embarked on
confrontation with a pragmatic, trade-union-dominated Labour leadership.

The Socialist League gave Barbara an outlet and a justification for her instinctive activism. She arrived in London just as its brief life was coming to a climax. After a year, 1932–3, of earnest propagandizing on behalf of the Labour Party, the League was starting to become a threat to it. Just as G. D. H. Cole had feared and Ernest Bevin had warned, the new organization was becoming frustrated with the limitations of propaganda. The urge to develop a programme and set itself in internal opposition to the Labour Party was growing, and Mellor was among its leaders and a powerful influence on the man who paid its bills.

In mid-1933 Frank Wise, who had snatched the leadership of the League from Ernest Bevin's unifying grasp, had suddenly died. In his place had been elected the extraordinary figure of Sir Stafford Cripps. Tall, rich and increasingly ascetic, Cripps was married to Isobel, granddaughter of Mr J. C. Eno, the fabulously wealthy founder of Eno's fruit salts. Cripps's aunt was Beatrice Webb, celebrated student of the working man's life and midwife to the Labour Party. His father was Lord Parmoor, who had begun his political career as a Conservative but ended it as a Labour cabinet minister. Stafford himself grew up in luxury in London and at Parmoor, an enormous house and estate in the Chilterns, and subsequently acquired a smaller estate in Gloucestershire which, after his brilliant career as a barrister gave way to an equally spectacular but less conventional career in politics, earned him the sobriquet of the Red Squire. Always generous to friends and political sympathizers, he personally lived a frugal existence. Stricken with a stomach disorder while working in an armaments factory during the First World War, now reduced to vegetarianism and frequent cures in foreign spas, Cripps had swerved from mild progressivism in the 1920s to a headstrong radicalism in the 1930s. The man who had been invited by Ramsay MacDonald to become Solicitor General in his 1929 administration (bringing with it a knighthood), became in the 1930s a close associate of the Communist leader Harry Pollitt.

The Socialist League's first concern was with preparing for a return to government. To that, the growing menace of Fascism in Italy, Germany and then Spain was added. The League's position on both domestic and foreign affairs was further complicated by attitudes to the Communist Party and the Labour leadership's fear of fellow travellers, those Communist sympathizers who, at the least, risked undermining Labour's appeal to cautious voters and, at the worst, might try to subvert Labour itself. The Communist Party of Great Britain had repeatedly tried to affiliate with Labour in the 1920s only to meet with rebuffs. In the early 1930s, it chose a different route: to work alongside Labour and draw the infinitely larger Labour movement into its sphere of influence.

Mellor, dark and driven, with all the evangelical fervour of a son of the manse, was one of the League's leading figures, a member of its National Council throughout its four years in being. He wrote passionately to Barbara about the poverty he saw on his campaigns around the country, and with loathing of the leadership he believed impeded the kind of radical transformation of power which alone could rebuild society. Foremost among his targets was Ernest Bevin, who not only controlled 10 per cent of the conference vote as general secretary of the transport workers' union, but was also chairman of the National Council, linking the Labour Party's National Executive, the parliamentary leadership and the trade unions. It was not uncommon for members of the audience at political rallies to faint from hunger, while the streets of Britain's biggest cities were disfigured by 'unspeakable poverty, narrow and dingy streets, houses filthy outside and God knows what inside . . . children in rags'.[3] Yet the party leadership was still failing to respond with any sense of urgency, let alone with radicalism. Bevin, Mellor railed, 'is not a socialist, he's a regulator of capitalism with the [trade unions] as junior partners and himself as their king'.

The League was specifically committed to planning for the return of a Labour government: wherever its strength was adequate, it set up groups to study what needed to be done by an incoming government, how it should be done, and what the obstacles were likely to be. It gave its members a sense of purposeful work, a 'will to action'. Its concern was that, having achieved a Labour majority, the government would then backtrack on its commitments, as the last one had. The battle was to convince the party of the need for desperate measures. In 1932, radicalized by the events of the previous year, conference had accepted the need for the immediate nationalization of the joint stock banks. By 1933, the pragmatists, led by Hugh Dalton, were regaining control.

Dalton came from an even grander – if less rich – background than Cripps. His father was tutor to two of Queen Victoria's grandsons, one of them the future George V. He described Cripps's increasingly apocalyptic visions of the threats facing the next socialist government as an 'adolescent Marxist miasma'.[4] He and Bevin were, together, a powerful force for moderation in Labour's policy development. The less the leadership responded, the more apocalyptic the League's predictions became. In January 1934, Cripps provoked outrage when he warned that the House of Lords and Buckingham Palace too could be expected to oppose a socialist government. The following month, William wrote a letter of angry frustration to Barbara:

I sat this morning listening to and arguing with eight of 'our leaders'. To them there is no need for urgency or for challenge. They are blind to realities. They think in terms of aeons of gradualism, of nice methods, of taxation, of 'being fair' to the capitalists, of anything but of a capitalism that knows neither/nor [sic] competition. I came away near to hopeless, and even as I write to you the sense of defeat, of the crushing of all that I care for in life comes over me in great and nigh uncontrollable waves. They don't believe in socialism. It's only a word they use; they look upon society today as a kind of mistake, not as the result of inexorable forces . . . They're afraid of what they appear to preach because now they've got to practise. Perhaps we all are. Here am I with a job, with a bank balance, with ties and responsibilities, with a 'nice wife'. What am I prepared to risk? Everything, I pray in my heart.'[5]

William, who often suffered from what would now be called stress, took himself off to a comfortable hotel in Eastbourne to recover his spirits. From there he sent Barbara a shortlist of the candidates who might lead a 're-inspired' Labour movement. Cripps he dismissed for not being a stayer. His favourite was a young MP from the Welsh valleys. Aneurin Bevan, still in his thirties and Ebbw Vale's MP since 1929, was not a Leaguer, because he saw its separatist instincts, 'It's the Labour Party or nothing,' he told Jennie Lee that year. Mellor saw his talents and his flaws. 'Background, A1. Brain first-class. Power to move people. But has he patience? Has he a simple and ruthless enough mind? Does he like caviar too much?' Bevan, he wrote to Barbara approvingly, wanted a transformation of the party structure to circumvent the dead weight of the trade union bosses:

In his view the existing machine has got to be smashed by a deliberate effort to reorganise the political movement on the basis of individual membership and constituency parties, with the local Trade Unionists members, but not through their organisation. Then, and here he's definitely right, the whole purpose of the industrial movement has got to change; it has to become revolutionary and cease to be part of the system . . . The League, expanded and recharged, might become the spearhead. We're neglecting the whole problem of the organisation of revolt in the hope – which seems to me incredibly slender – that the present machine and the present leadership will somehow soon see the light.

There was a new alternative for those who longed to 'organize revolt'. With the rise of Hitler, the British Communist Party, following instructions from Moscow, reversed its opposition to social democracy and once again renewed its application for affiliation to the Labour Party. It envisaged a united front of those with common policy objectives, among them the Socialist League. Mellor told Barbara in a letter in February 1934 that the outlook was not yet gloomy enough to take such a schismatic decision.

> I feel that we are reaching a point when people like myself will be forced to match our strength and skills with the machine and within the machine by a direct challenge to it as unrepresentative. But for the time being we must not give up the fight to change. To go out now means simply isolation. If we go out we must take with us not merely a coterie but a considerable section of the constituency parties in the Labour Party. Then and under those conditions I'll be ready to talk 'United Front.'[6]

But, within the next year, Mellor, who shared the general dislike of the Communists (he said they had undermined the revolutionary fervour of the working classes 'by shouting at them'), became convinced a united front was the only route for the left. 'I wish I had more faith in the Labour Party – or alternatively, more faith in the Communist Party . . . one can't be a party to oneself.' Barbara took him to task for a lack of coherence. 'First you say United Front means "patient endeavour to undermine from within" and then later that we may be driven outside the machine if we can take a sufficient following with us and that "under those conditions I'll be ready to talk United Front". May it not be that the [Communist Party] has merely realized the necessity for getting outside the machine sooner than we have?'

Already overtures had been made. On 24 April 1934 William reported that the League had been invited to meet two of the leaders of the breakaway ILP: Fenner Brockway, who came to regard the disaffiliation as the worst mistake of his life, and the ILP leader Jimmy Maxton himself, to 'talk over the question of ways and means of securing working-class unity . . . I doubt whether anything will come of it, but it seemed to me utterly impossible to refuse Brockway's invitation.'

The rump of the ILP was haemorrhaging members. Within two years of disaffiliation, a mere four thousand remained, less than a quarter of the membership at the time the vote on disaffiliation had been taken in 1934. It was no longer an organization with the power to rock the Labour Party, and it no longer had the ear of the media. Within a united front – the argument went – the left, including the Communist Party, would once again find a voice. That the Labour Party would gain nothing and risk much by the association was a weakness never openly addressed by Mellor or Barbara. But long years of dealing with attempts by the Communists to affiliate or infiltrate had hardened the Labour leadership's collective heart against anything which could be construed as an association with Communism.

Mellor was playing high-stakes politics: he was nursing the constituency of Enfield where he had been selected as an official Labour candidate. A by-election was due. He had just published a pamphlet calling on the Co-operative movement to make way for real socialism, which had even frightened fellow Leaguers, and there was no evidence that his abrasive style of campaigning was winning voters. Asked at a youth conference, 'Are you going to win Enfield?' he replied, 'I haven't the slightest idea. I'm trying to make the workers of Enfield, Socialists.'[7]

At the League's conference at Whitsun 1934, it made its challenge to the Labour hierarchy explicit. Contrary to its original undertaking, it endorsed a radical alternative programme, 'Forward to Socialism', based on the assumption that Britain was on the brink of a Fascist takeover. A newspaper was founded, the *Socialist Leaguer*, edited by Frank Horrabin, which provided Barbara with a new journalistic outlet. After the conference, Mellor went to Cornwall and spent a month away from both his family and his mistress, happily dividing his time between sea trips with the local fishermen and long-distance politics by post. The focal point now was Labour's conference in October, where its own programme 'For Socialism and Peace' – regarded as the most radical ever put forward by Labour – was to be debated. Unimpressed, the League tabled seventy-five amendments: wanting to spread the confrontation with the Labour leadership among the constituency parties, Cripps encouraged them to move some of these amendments, but Mellor was determined that the League should fight under its own banner.

Back in London, William discussed tactics with Barbara: 'I hope you'll approve of the way I've carried out your suggestion on Reference Back,'[8] William wrote. 'You'll see I've put in the guts of Forward to Socialism with the idea of forcing a straight decision. Whether Cripps or Brailsford[9] will agree with our tactics this afternoon will show, but since the declaration of aims is partly Cripps' probably they will ... Inwardly I'm elated at the prospect of facing the Labour party Executive with a clear challenge – it's been a dream of mine for years.' In the *Socialist Leaguer* he wrote that the League 'should no longer be a "mere umbrella" for "loyal grousers" but an instrument for co-ordinating what I would call Marxist opinions and action within the wider Labour Movement'.

When the utopians of the League finally did battle with the pragmatists of Labour at Southport in October, the League was resoundingly defeated. William personally moved most of the amendments which embodied the League's programme. These included a condemnation of the League of

Nations (for which Barbara had been campaigning only a couple of years earlier) which called for its substitution by an alliance of workers in every country. A general strike should be called if a British government declared war. Barbara, for the first time, was made to understand the rage the left's wilder ambitions could provoke among the rest of the party. 'I was shaken by [Arthur Hendersons[10]] fury, but William battled on unperturbed, and won reluctant admiration for his courage and oratorical stamina. The votes in favour of our amendments were derisory.' In fact, in 'For Socialism and Peace', Labour had drawn up an extensive and radical plan, paving the way for a 1935 manifesto committing the party to extensive nationalization, large programmes of regional aid and the development of health and welfare services.

The League's response was to embark on a journey that would end in open confrontation with Labour. At a special conference in November 1934, it resolved to become a mass-membership organization in its own right, built on preparations for opposing international Fascism.[11] William called for the creation of 'A Will to Power' – a development of the theories he had first advocated in 'Direct Action', recognizing the need for constant agitation to fulfil the left's desire for movement, for a sense of involvement in battle.

Barbara was present at both the conferences, but she was there in Mellor's shadow, not in her own right. Later she bitterly resented her isolation from the main political arguments, handicapped, at least in hind-sight, by her relationship with a man who was plainly no closer to leaving his wife.

At the end of August, William had promised that he was ready to leave Edna, although this was not the only possible solution, as he saw it:

> There are three courses that can be taken by us. We can continue as we are with all that is involved on the credit & the debit side alike; we can break with all that means; we can follow the road that will unite us as man and wife, with all that may spring from that following. I would repeat quite calmly that I am ready to follow this latter road, for journeying along it we shall find the beauties and joys that we have already known become fixed and permanent comrades of our lives.
>
> Not a single possible outcome of this declaration has been slurred over in the making of it. I know all that is involved personally and politically for both of us. I know, too, that were I not to make it I should be false to myself . . . You know my mind now. There are the three paths. Not one is easy, but one must be trodden. I want to know your mind.'

Barbara's side of the correspondence has not survived. From William's daily letters to her it seems she was uncertain about making a commitment, and even more of his readiness to free himself. On 24 August he had explained that saying she, not he, had to decide their future did not indicate a lack of commitment from him. It was a sign of his respect for her right to make her own choice: 'If your decision be my decision I have no fears . . . that our life would be beautiful and that for both of us inner peace and harmony will flood in permanence through us. But though *I* have no fears, what matters is *you*. . . . and you know that in me there is understanding of your fears lest the "seagull part of you" should be smothered, lest your inner need for freedom and independence should be hurt, lest your "wild joy" should find itself denied of outlet.'

Two days later, he wrote again. 'Barbara dear, I love you and the hardest thing in the world is not to be able to express that love in all its fullness. But there, what is that but trying to influence? It isn't really but lest it become so I'll write no more.' In December, Edna told him divorce was unacceptable to her. 'I propose in a few weeks to leave my wife either with her agreement or without it,' he told Frank and Annie. Barbara wrote to her parents a day or two later. 'Don't worry about the latest news. I'm not. I don't think Edna has yet faced up to the situation and I've not given up hope that she will. William & I have agreed that when he leaves her he will move into a bachelor flat of his own and we will keep outwardly as we are for the next few months until we have exhausted all possibility of an agreement. Then we will re-consider the situation. I don't want any more dislocation than is necessary.' The correspondence is inconclusive. But William did not leave Edna.

Somehow, Barbara was surviving in London. Their political friends knew of the affair. William was a glamorous and attractive figure, and Barbara partied with the socialites of the left, people like Dick Mitchison, an old Etonian left-winger, who became a Labour MP in 1945, and his writer wife Naomi. Barbara met other writers like Storm Jameson, as well as Nye Bevan and Jennie Lee. Barbara was not entirely comfortable with the smart socialist set, though.

No Mam, London isn't 'getting' me – or the London crowd [she wrote at about this time]. 'You should have seen me at Naomi's party – a little aloof, refusing to smoke, drinking very little, listening to the intelligentsia, watching the freaks (Margaret Cole for instance!), liking some people (Pritt & Gollancz & Madame Maisky[12]) & gladder than anything to see Jennie & Aneurin arrive – jolly & sociable & natural . . . Taken in the mass, I *hate* the intelligentsia ... Naomi Mitchison's a queer woman – quite mad in some ways & far too emotional for my liking. PS could you make it Sanatogen instead of Pink Pills?

Jennie Lee and Nye Bevan had married in October 1934; Jennie on the rebound from Frank Wise's death eighteen months earlier. Their marriage had the effect of underlining Barbara's own uncertain status. She told her mother she had felt too ill to go to their wedding party. She and Jennie, despite their superficial friendliness, neither quite liked nor quite trusted each other. Jennie had a beauty that Barbara, attractive as she was, could not begin to match, and an assurance Barbara had yet to acquire. William and Bevan conflicted politically, despite Mellor's admiration for him. Mellor did not trust Bevan – who had a notoriously wandering eye – with Barbara. Barbara admitted Bevan made a pass at her one morning when she had gone round to their flat. Her response to the incident was telling: 'I disentangled myself with some embarrassment and crept out, feeling like a small-town puritan.'[13] Barbara's social self-confidence would never match her confidence in her political skills.

It was a black time for Barbara and for William: William's by-election campaign in Enfield had ended in failure despite, as William told her mother, Barbara's 'working like a Trojan and speaking like an angel'. Barbara tried to present it as a kind of victory: they had added five thousand to the Labour vote, on 'a 100% left-wing programme'.[14] Instead, it was a portent: in the general election in November of 1935, Labour's representation would only creep up to 154, and although the party's share of the vote was back up to 1929 levels the result was a profound disappointment.

The left, inside and outside the Labour Party, was fragmented and disheartened. Mystifyingly, neither continuing recession at home nor the rise of Fascism abroad was rallying support for their position. The Socialist League had interpreted the failure of Labour's election manifesto as a vote of confidence in their more radical one, but a recruiting drive on this basis was a failure. Only the Communist Party seemed, in its own small way, to thrive.

The Communists were receiving instructions from Moscow encouraging some kind of united front; such cross-party alliances had won the election in France and were opposing Fascism in Spain. At the same time, the League was on the brink of a new and fundamental disagreement with the Labour leadership. In line with its criticism of the League of Nations as an instrument of capitalism, the Socialist League opposed League of Nations demands for sanctions to be imposed on Italy after its invasion of Abyssinia in 1935. The only response to a capitalist war, the League argued, was a general strike.

The row over the correct response to the rise of Fascism and the instability in continental Europe that spanned party conferences from 1934 to 1936 constituted another wedge driven between the Socialist League and the party. (It was also the cause of a disagreement between Barbara and William: Barbara was berated by her brother Jimmie, home on leave from Africa, for failing to understand how desperate the Abyssinians were for help. Barbara admitted to unease, but no more. She felt vindicated subsequently, however, by the ineffectiveness of the League of Nations' efforts.)

Cripps and Mellor decided it was time for the final break: a united front must be established, regardless of the response of the Labour Party. At home, the South Wales miners had elected a Communist president, Arthur Horner. The hunger marches, the success of the Communist-led National Unemployed Workers' Movement, and the popularity of Victor Gollancz's Left Book Club, contributed to a mood of optimism. By the middle of 1936, civil war had broken out in Spain. Hitler was backing Franco's Fascist forces. Mellor had never lost contact with the ILP disaffiliationists. Now, Cripps put him in charge of negotiations with Harry Pollitt, the secretary of the British Communist party. While Mellor and Pollitt talked, Barbara, who had moved again and now lived in a flat in Coram Street in Bloomsbury, fed Pollitt sausage and mash and was charmed, just as Cripps was, by his self-effacing manner and his relish for her cooking. She, like Cripps but unlike Mellor who was always more sceptical, either overlooked the Communists' motivation for seeking a united front, or believed that opposition to Fascism was more important than the Communist desire to capture the Labour Party.

Mellor's involvement in the Front, his outspoken campaign in Enfield and his criticism of the Labour leadership brought him into further and even more serious conflict with his employers. Although the *Herald* was now run commercially, the unions still had control of editorial policy, and they did not like Mellor's stand. '[He] offered to resign from the Socialist League, but apparently that's not enough . . . they want him to cease all writing, speaking or standing for Parliament,' Barbara wrote home, despairing. 'I'm a bit low tonight, haven't even got my husband[15] near me for comfort & not much prospect of having him in the future now. But I *won't* have him stifled! . . . saw Maurice [her former boss] the other day. William told him we were going to get married.' In March 1936, William was sacked.

He rescued himself from unemployment by borrowing £500 to set up a journal for Labour supporters in local government. The *Town and County Councillor* provided both him and Barbara with jobs. Barbara was to earn £4 a week. Another letter to her mother echoes the trials of Birdalone, the heroine of her favourite childhood novel, the *Waters of the Wondrous Isles*: 'I hope I can win through to my husband without too much upset and pain. It isn't an easy choice, Mam, to choose a man with so many penalties attached to the having of him. In many ways it would be easier to go back. But we love each other genuinely – it isn't infatuation – and that means we are "home" to each other, absolutely part of each other . . . "courage" and "love" has always been our motto to each other.' There are hints that even if Barbara was prepared to be patient, her parents were getting restive. 'I want you to learn to love my William & accept him as part of the family – completely. I know it will take time & cannot happen in a moment . . . he's developed a worldly crust which so far I only have been allowed to penetrate . . . this holiday [in Cornwall in June] has shown both of us that we can't be apart much longer and William says Edna realises it too, though she hasn't said anything. We have to be patient and let realisation come to her slowly.' Still nothing changed. The truth was that William almost certainly could not afford to leave Edna. In December 1936, he wrote to Barbara on *Town and County Councillor* headed paper:

> I have spoken to Edna this morning. I have told her that you have for months been working with me on the *T&CC*. I have told her that we still want to marry. I have told her that the strain is at times overpowering. I have told her that we are at a crisis. I have told her of your suggestion that you should meet her and of my doubts as to whether it would help. I have told her that what we are trying to do is to win economic independence. I have told her that the consequences of the crises, arising from tearings apart, are utterly incalculable. Finally I told her that I might be with you tonight. Please let me know whether the 'might' is to be 'shall'.

William remained her lover and her mentor. After the 1935 general election, however, Mellor acquired a second disciple and Barbara a close and enduring friend. Michael Foot had deserted his family's Liberal tradition – his father and one of his brothers were Liberal MPs – for Labour. After contesting Monmouth in the general election at the precocious age of twenty-two, he had come to London to work as a journalist. Cripps, whom Foot had met at Oxford where he had been a friend of his oldest son John, sent him to see Mellor, with a view to getting work on the *Town and County Councillor*. Barbara's friendship with Foot was uncomplicated and stimulating; their backgrounds were similar, and so were their outlooks – radical, passionate, romantic. Three years younger, Foot had gone up to Oxford in the same year that Barbara came down. He was quick and funny and clever, and a much needed companion, someone to ease the enforced loneliness of the mistress of the married man. Sixty years later he denied there was any more to it. He claimed that he knew about the affair and, if nothing else, loyalty to Mellor would have made it unthinkable for him to take his relationship with Barbara any further. Barbara always claimed she was not beautiful enough for Michael, Foot that he was too ugly for her (he was still suffering from chronic and disfiguring eczema). They read together, sometimes for fun, often in pursuit of political knowledge – Marx, Beatrice Webb, Dickens – a reading course prescribed by Mellor.

Some weekends Barbara took Michael home with her, taking advantage of his car, although she was careful not to visit if Marjorie, now married and with small children, was likely to be there. She did not, she wrote brutally, want to be there if Marj's 'brats' would be 'yowling at my bedhead'.[16] Foot tried to teach her to drive, a project previously postponed because of a shortage of both money and opportunity. Barbara managed one return trip to Nottingham, where her parents had moved from Hyde, before Foot gave up his car. Many years later, he claimed she had written his car off on the way home. 'It put a strain on our relationship,' he said.

Through Foot, Barbara also got to know Cripps more informally. Cripps, who existed modestly in London, at weekends lived up to his image as the Red Squire. At Filkins, his estate in Gloucestershire, the millionaire, teetotal and vegetarian lord of the manor entertained generously. Barbara, who could never quite contain her competitive streak even when it might have been in her interest to do so, was delighted to beat him at tennis and to argue with him relentlessly. His wife Isobel was to become a kind friend.

She also started looking for a seat. In June 1936 she was interviewed at Hertford. 'It's a hopeless constituency,' she wrote home, 'but what is worse is [that] it is vast and largely agricultural. However, everything turned out ideally: they fell for me, applauded my speech vigorously, damn nearly selected me & only just decided in favour of a middle-aged, stolid gentleman with a detailed experience of agricultural matters. I was informed I was a very close runner-up.'

Meanwhile, progress towards achieving the United Front was being made in the tight, complex circles and spirals that define left-wing alliances. The Socialist League was acting as broker between the Communists and the rump ILP, who wanted to settle grudges originating on the battlefields of Spain, Late in 1936 the Front's objectives were agreed. It was to achieve 'the unity of all sections of the working-class movement within the framework of the Labour party and Trade Unions in common struggle against Fascism, Reaction and War, and for the immediate demands of the workers, in order to develop the strength and unity of the working class for the defeat of the National Government.'[17] The agreement marked a high tide of Communist influence.

In tandem with the 'Unity Campaign' for a united front, Cripps decided to launch a newspaper, a vehicle to 'advocate a vigorous socialism and demand active resistance to Fascism at home and abroad.' It was to be called the *Tribune*, and was scheduled to be launched in January 1937 to coincide with the launch of a mass campaign for the United Front itself. William would edit it; Barbara and Foot together would write a column on trade union affairs called 'Judex', after the column William had written twenty-five years earlier for the infant *Herald*. Barbara and Foot were also in charge of getting the copy of their star columnist, Aneurin Bevan to the paper on time which came to be a notoriously difficult task. Mellor, Barbara and Foot worked closely together. William, dangerously casual with his and other people's money, would stand them expensive lunches at Simpson's-in-the-Strand whenever things went particularly well; the problem was that the money was *Tribune*'s, not his.

Mellor was now chairing the League, and Barbara, aged twenty-six, had been elected to its executive, the youngest member. But the appetite for alliance with the Communists was faltering. At the Labour party conference in Edinburgh in autumn 1936, it had seemed that the Communists would at last win affiliation. In the event, the motion was defeated by about three votes to one, and the call for a united front by an even greater margin. News of the first Soviet show trials, and the conduct of the Communist factions in Spain contributed to the abrupt decline in confidence. Equally, the forceful responses from the Labour National Executive fatally undermined the campaign.

It was plain that any united front would not include the main body of the Labour movement. The declaration Cripps and Mellor had drawn up with the Communists and the ILP was put to the full Socialist League at a tea room, incongruously, in the West End of London, in the wake of a carefully timed warning from the Labour National Executive that disaffiliation would follow its acceptance. Many Leauge members did not want to force the issue to disaffiliation, and anyway had not been consulted about the Front. (The negotiations had been conducted in secrecy – ironically, since Cripps had just lent the League's support to a new movement of the constituencies that was trying to bring openness and democracy to the Labour party.) As a result, the declaration was approved only by a narrow majority, and with twenty-three abstentions, on a minority vote.

On 1 January 1937, the *Tribune* was launched in a mood of optimism.

Cripps, much impressed by the success of Victor Gollancz's Left Book Club, the one organization on the left that seemed to be prospering, believed the *Tribune* could, in a matter of weeks, reach a circulation of 50,000, at 2d (less than 1p) an issue. Cripps wrote encouragingly after the first issue. 'I have read the *Tribune*, every line of it (including the advertisements!) as objectively as I can and I must congratulate you upon a very first-rate production.'[18] To critics, Mellor, Barbara and Foot seemed wholy owned subsidiaries of the Cripps's empire. *Tribune* became known as 'Cripps Chronicle' while Dalton dismissed the League as 'a rich man's toy'.

The United Front and the *Tribune* were supposed to feed off each other and on the mood of anxiety and impotence created by the spread of Fascism. At first, the Front appeared bouyant. At its inaugural rally, a week after *Tribune*'s launch, more than 3,700 pledge cards were signed. An average of 1,500 supporters came to the next half-dozen meetings.

But as it had warned, the National Executive had disaffiliated the Socialist League within days of the launch of the United Front campaign. In March 1937, it was decided that individual participation in the campaign, which of course entailed appearing on platforms with Communists, was also incompatible with Labour Party membership. Mellor and Cripps had to choose between the United Front campaign and the League. The National Executive would not take the final step and proscribe the League – preventing Labour Party members joining it – as long as it abandoned its campaign for a united front. Mellor believed it was a price worth paying; the League had vital work to do through Labour Party members. Cripps refused to abandon the United Front. Barbara backed Cripps. At the special conference convened at Leicester on 17 May 1937, she told delegates that dissolution did not mean defeat:

> The Socialist League stands unrepentant before the Labour movement for its action in entering into agreement with the ILP and CPGB to conduct a campaign for unity of the working class against the National Government. It stands unrepentant because it believes the workers of Great Britain cannot at this crucial moment afford the luxuries of apathy, drift and division . . . Driven into a corner by the weakness of its own arguments the National Executive has resurrected as its one objection the finances of the Unity Campaign. The cry of 'Moscow Gold' is heard again.'

Dissolution 'was not a funeral, but a conscious political tactic'.[19] Cripps sent her a warm note of congratulation on her 'statesman-like' speech.

★

Barbara's career as a journalist – her only source of income – was still
dependent on her work in the *Town and County Councillor*, which she had
largely taken over from Mellor. *Tribune*, which continued despite the collapse
of the United Front, offered more interesting possibilities. In the autumn of
1937 Cripps dispatched her to the Soviet Union to report on the condition
of women and children there. It was her first big opportunity. In the style
of breathless enthusiasm which was typical of *Tribune* features, she wrote a
series of seven one-thousand-word articles that appeared in October and
November.

> Many a short-sighted visitor to Russia has been shocked by external evidence
> of poverty. 'But,' they exclaim, '*our* workers enjoy better transport, better
> houses, better paved streets, smarter shops, better clothes than these people!'
> But the Russians don't get alarmed. The coming of the luxurious they know
> is 'all a matter of time'. And in the meanwhile they enjoy what capitalism
> can't offer its workers: security today, hope of abundance tomorrow . . .
> here is no shadow of slump and unemployment – only an insatiable demand
> for more and yet more workers. It explains the Stakhanov movement
> [rewarding exceptional productivity]; throws light on the Trotskyist trials; is
> the key to the anti-abortion law and the role of women.[20]

It was a dishonest piece of reporting. In a postcard home she described the
poverty as 'repellent, particularly housing, clothes, transport; then they go
and intoxicate you with lavish provision for children, mothers & general
education'. The articles provoked controversy. Her assertion that although
abortion had been outlawed in 1934, birth control advice was freely available
was questioned. She denied that it signalled a return to bourgeois values.
'The steady increase in Soviet Russia's population is proof in my opinion
that Soviet women are bearing children because they are happy and secure'.[21]

There was a storm of protest from *Tribune* (the 'the' had been dropped)
readers. 'How deeply the left craved to give the benefit of all the doubts to
Moscow!' Michael Foot would write in an apologia marking the twenty-first
anniversary of *Tribune*. 'No one who did not live through that period can
quite appreciate how overwhelming that craving was.'

Cripps had not sent Barbara to the Soviet Union to bring back tales of
the Stalinist terror or to undermine Soviet social policy, although some
Tribune readers clearly thought he should have. In the final piece of the series
she explained defensively: 'When the *Tribune* decided to send me to Russia,
it was in order that I might study the present position, economic and cultural,
of the Soviet women and children. Just before I left the editor warned me
that I was not being sent in order to engage in the Trotsky v Stalin

controversy, or to become yet another authority on the inner meaning of Soviet internal and foreign policy.'

Whatever Cripps wanted of her, Barbara herself was entirely committed to the now defunct Socialist League policy of achieving socialism even at the temporary cost of democracy. As she and William Mellor often told each other, it might be hell getting there, but it would be worth it in the end. In common with the Webbs and other pilgrims to Moscow, she was expected to approve of what she saw, and so she said she did. Victor Gollancz, Moscow's leading apologist, refused to publish Orwell's *Homage to Catalonia* even before it was written, because he knew it would attack the Communists in the Spanish Civil War, while John Strachey, a member of the distinguished literary family who had left the Labour Party in protest at its gradualism but refused to join the Communist Party, said that after reading transcripts of the show trials he had been entirely convinced of the 'authenticity of the confessions'.

Barbara was stubborn when challenged, a characteristic that made her formidable in argument but also blind to the weaknesses of her position. A more imaginative or a more confident and independent-minded journalist might have written more of what she saw; but Barbara, who was still only twenty-six, could be unexpectedly naive. Coming back by train from Moscow with a bust of Lenin and a copy of the Soviet constitution in her luggage, she was searched by the Nazi in Berlin. They did not find either item of contraband; instead they were overwhelmed by her collection of shoes. Barbara saw herself as the embodiment of a new spirit, simultaneously capable of frivolity and of high-mindedness. For a magazine called *Everyman's* she wrote in 1936 a thinly disguised piece about her own faith:

> The fact that the modern girl goes walking on the downs on a Sunday, or cycles round the countryside, plays golf, or rushes about in a sports car, does not necessarily prove that she has no depth of character or lacks a serious side to her nature. It may prove just the reverse. In many cases it is because she has formed her own conception of religion and the meaning of worship. Above all she passionately opposes ugliness and will have nothing to do with a faith which presents goodness as drab, meek and unlovely. Her sense of higher things becomes translated into a search for the Good Life – beautiful, gay and courageous with its own code and its own commandments . . . young women go out into the world today with a deep sense of their duty to society and to humanity . . . only those forms of religion which are in touch with modern realities and modern moods have any hold over the young today.

★

By the end of 1937, matters were coming to a head between William Mellor and Sir Stafford Cripps. *Tribune* was struggling. Cripps and his co-backer, George Strauss (another wealthy Tory renegade, later a long-serving Labour MP) had invested the phenomenal sum of £20,000 to keep it afloat. Then, Cripps, who suffered chronic ill-health, had disappeared and reappeared on the political scene, set on the very policy he had formerly opposed: the aim was no longer a united front of the working class, but a popular front which would include anti-Fascist forces of all classes. *Tribune* was also to move closer to the successful Left Book Club, whose founder, the ubiquitous Victor Gollancz, was to help fund its debts. When Mellor refused to change the paper's editorial line, Cripps dismissed him – and invited Foot to take his place. Foot, in a typical gesture of loyalty, flatly refused. When Foot suggested the sacking of Mellor merited further discussion, Cripps declared this impossible. He was about to leave for the West Indies. The triumvirate of William, Barbara and Michael were left feeling, as Dalton had jibed, like 'a rich man's playthings'. Mellor, devastated and unwell, took off on a banana boat to South America. Barbara and Michael, who had been planning a holiday, went to France together, where Barbara lectured Michael relentlessly about world politics. It was decidedly unconventional for a couple who were not lovers to holiday alone together, but both insisted that apart from Barbara rushing with concern into Michael's adjoining bedroom when she heard him having an asthma attack it was an entirely innocent sojourn. They arrived back just as Chamberlain returned from Munich declaring 'Peace in our time'. Foot, typically, said that a week with Barbara gave a whole new meaning to the expression.

Mellor was thrown back on the *Town and County Councillor*. But soon that journal was in trouble as well. Isobel Cripps generously bailed it out. There were wounding rumours about Mellor's temper and some innuendo about his bookkeeping skills; he and Barbara suspected Victor Gollancz as the source – they had distrusted him since he had gone into partnership with Cripps on *Tribune* and converted it to the Popular Front. Barbara, who always had a keen sense of injustice, wrote angrily to her mother that 'flat lies' were being told about William. 'Gollancz, we have every reason to believe, is spreading fairy stories about the matter [of William's dismissal from *Tribune*] all over the country, and we are helpless.' Cripps inadvertently contributed to the bitterness when he wrote to William's partner on the *Town and County Councillor*, a Mr Wallis.

> Wallis got a most peculiar letter from Stafford yesterday [Barbara wrote to her parents], saying he felt he had been treated 'unfairly' over the accounts

in the past, but that he knew it wasn't Wallis's fault; and that when he returned he would discuss . . . the possibility of saving the 'remnants' of the paper! It is a letter insensitive to the point of insult . . . It is the kind of letter that hurts William . . . He is convinced Stafford is trying to get him out of the *T&CC*, as he did out of the *Tribune*. Well, we knew it would collapse without him . . . I've written a normal chatting letter to Isobel.

Isobel Cripps responded with calm and tact.

I am glad you wrote as you felt. Your saying that William is now considered a blackguard and Mr Wallis a minor thief, is the very first I have ever heard it suggested. Yes – I know you to be full of pluck, and my only answer to you at present is, to beg you to think quietly and patiently during these next few weeks, & to do all you can to persuade William to do the same.

There are times when certain things are inevitable, & if one has cared very much for them, it is hard, desperately hard, not to let things at the moment seem completely one sided & unjust. So – I do beg of you once again to do all you can to look at things squarely & not arrogantly, with as constructive an attitude as possible under the circumstances . . . Isobel.

William Mellor had a notoriously short temper as well as a casual attitude to money. Cripps was equally capable of arrogance and thoughtlessness, as well as some erratic reasoning. They were not a combination likely to last. With Barbara however – despite her loyalty to William – Cripps remained on kind terms, as emerged after 1945.

Once again, Barbara threw herself into practical politics. In 1937, she had been elected to St Pancras Borough Council in London, an area of political life where women were beginning to advance. Central government was just starting to ask local councils to make preparations for war. Barbara, whose parents had given shelter to Spanish refugees, had heard terrifying accounts of aerial bombardment in Spain. On her way back from Russia she had been caught up in an air raid practice in Berlin, which had finally convinced her that war with Germany was imminent. Still backing a united front, she nonetheless decided, rather than rely on the likelihood of a general strike, to take practical steps to mitigate the effects of bombing. She took up the issue of air raid shelters with vehemence, doing copious research on appropriate protection, harrying government ministers about their inadequate proposals for shallow 'Anderson' shelters, which only offered protection from bomb blast when all human instinct was to go underground. She worked assiduously, as she told her mother in a typical lament about her shortage of time and money: 'Next Friday I have to make a speech, next Sunday I have a committee meeting; the weekend after that I have an important council group meeting; the weekend after that a conference. Also, if I am to pay 30/- or so for spring cleaning, I just haven't got 18/- or even 10/- for fares. (I made up my budget yesterday & I find that allowing nothing for clothes, holidays or dentist, I am still 5/- a week overspent!)'

As usual, Annie was invited to fill the breach. Perhaps she could come and do the spring cleaning for her, Barbara suggested, adding kindly: 'If it would upset your plans, why you must tell me & I must postpone spring cleaning, that's all.'

Barbara was not given to introspection. But if she had taken stock as war broke out in September 1939, she might have given a disheartening account of herself. She was nearly twenty-nine, locked into an affair, now in its seventh year, with a married man who seemed unwilling or unable to leave his wife. She wrote to her mother, in a sad attempt to be positive: 'What if William doesn't care enough to come & take me away? Why should I be so bitter. Do I love him merely for what he brings me, or for what he is?'

She cast about for ways of earning a living compatible with a career in politics; she thought of doing another degree; she tried to get a job as secretary to the Fabian Society. Marjorie, running a home, three children and already a councillor tipped for greater things, advised war work of some kind. Meanwhile, Barbara's erratic and inadequate income came from a regular commitment on a failing journal – the *Town and County Councillor* was technically bankrupt by 1939 – and trade and weekly magazines like the *Grocer*. In the Labour movement at large she had acquired a damaging reputation as a left-winger prepared to associate with Communists. Her only powerbase was St Pancras council.

4. Ends and Beginnings

War opens minds that were sealed, stimulates dormant intelligences,
and recruits into political controversy thousands who otherwise
would remain in the political hinterland. It is with these new,
eager, virgin minds that Labour must concern itself if it is to breast
the tides of war and emerge from it holding the leadership of the
nation.

Aneurin Bevan, 1940[1]

War suspended normal politics: by 1940, less than ten years after the great
betrayal of 1931, Labour ministers once again sat beside Conservatives in a
coalition government, by-elections went uncontested, the war burden was
shared. The internal party battles that had dominated the 1930s became
irrelevant. This state of suspended political animation gave Barbara the
opportunity to metamorphose over the course of the next five years from a
struggling freelance journalist, the mistress of an ageing and controversial left-
winger, into the youngest woman MP in the House of Commons, a political
figure in her own right.

In the year between the Munich Agreement and the outbreak of war in
September 1939, the left struggled to find a way of defeating Fascism without
sustaining capitalism. It was Aneurin Bevan who began to articulate the view
that if the Labour leadership had the courage, war could be made into the
death rites of capitalism. If Labour insisted, it could be a people's war and
the people would be the winners. Labour's leadership was more prosaic. It
saw only that war was coming. Hitler had to be opposed, even at the risk of
delaying the advance of socialism. In this spirit, after three years of confused
and anxious debate, the party had formally abandoned its opposition to
rearmament at its 1938 conference.

If William Mellor continued to scorn the idea that Fascism could be opposed on anything other than a class basis, Barbara was beginning to hesitate. Bevan had always preferred a cross-party popular front to a class-driven united front because he could see that while Westminster was the seat of power, nothing would happen unless Chamberlain was overthrown. This could not be done by the left alone while Labour was in a minority in parliament. After the Munich crisis in 1938, Cripps too had considered a parliamentary move against Chamberlain; but he was also pursuing with an enthusiasm which seemed to increase in direct proportion to the hostility he met from the Labout leadership, the notion of an extra-parliamentary popular front of all parties opposed to Fascism. He had dropped his united front demands for socialist objectives in the hope that his campaign would thus attract Liberals and even progressive Conservatives like Harold Macmillan and Robert Boothby. Bevan became one of his most prominent supporters. 'From Parliament itself nothing can be expected. It is jaded, tired and cynical. It can be stirred from outside, but only from outside,' he told an 'Arms for Spain' meeting in January 1939.[2]

The voters were sending conflicting signals. In October 1938, at a famous by-election in Oxford, the Labour candidate Patrick Gordon Walker (a man who never prospered in by-elections)[3] was forbidden by the party leadership to stand down to give a popular front candidate a clear run against the Conservative. In the event, Quintin Hogg[4] won the seat for Chamberlain and appeasement. But only weeks later a popular front candidate, the journalist Vernon Bartlett,[5] did succeed against both Labour and Conservative opposition when he won a by-election at Bridgwater in Somerset after a campaign marked by attempts by supporters of the Left Book Club to persuade the Labour Party locally to back his candidacy.

Early in 1939, Cripps finally overreached himself with the Labour Party leadership. Even his old friend Clement Attlee, elected 'temporary' leader after Lansbury's resignation in 1935, realized he could no longer protect him, despite his personal sympathy. Cripps presented to the National Executive, which had been convened specially to consider it, a memorandum calling for a mass appeal to all anti-Fascist forces. The NEC rejected it overwhelmingly. Cripps immediately launched a direct appeal for support to the local parties and to every other organization he considered progressive. It was a 'prepared and organised campaign to change Party direction and leadership' and as such it was intolerable to the leadership, who throughout the 1930s had been deeply suspicious of any possible link with Communism. Cripps must be expelled. Bevan offered his immediate support for a campaign 'to unite the forces of democracy and freedom'. '[Cripps's] crime is my crime,' he declared. Cripps continued to organize his mass petition, calling 'upon the parties of progress to act together and at once for the sake of peace and civilisation' by forming an international 'peace alliance'. The campaign caught on in the constituencies, and the National Executive responded to it with extreme toughness. The threat of expulsion was extended from Cripps alone to any who supported him, and at the end of March it was enforced on Cripps, Bevan and dozens of other activists. Meanwhile at Westminster, leading right-wingers like Hugh Dalton went unpunished by the Labour Party despite publicly backing the campaign for rearmament at whose head stood Churchill – the man, the left liked to point out, who had ordered the troops in against the South Wales miners in 1910. Attlee feared that to move against Chamberlain without the backing of the Churchillians risked making his opposition look sectarian. The Churchill faction claimed it did not want to replace Chamberlain. This impasse continued until after the fall of Norway in May 1940 – and the abortive British expedition to try to prevent it – and even then Chamberlain was not technically defeated in the vote forced by Labour. But the revolt of over a hundred of his backbenchers was enough, together with Labour's refusal to join his government, to force Chamberlain, finally out of No. 10 (although he continued in Churchill's Cabinet).

Far harder for the left to comprehend, on 23 August 1939, Soviet Russia and Nazi Germany signed a non-aggression pact. The left took it as a shocking and incomprehensible betrayal, a bizarre and inexplicable alliance between good and evil. Many who had turned to Communism as the only effective defence against Fascism now retreated in horror. Only a handful were ready to argue that Britain and France had been prepared to see Hitler attack Soviet Russia; that Britain's failure to respond to Russia's overtures for a defensive alliance left Stalin with no option but the non-aggression pact with Germany. Initially, Barbara was among the shocked. Later, however, she wrote, 'I learn that Aneurin Bevan thinks the pact a brilliant move.'[6] Mellor, who had continued to argue for a united front of the left including the Communists, and to suspect that whoever won a capitalist war would turn on the workers, was entirely undermined.

Once war was declared, a kind of peace – or at least an absence of war – descended on the Labour Party. Although the National Executive tried to impose loyalty pledges before it would allow the expelled members back, Bevan, strongly supported by his South Wales Miners' Federation, was allowed to return the following year without a commitment to orthodoxy. Cripps, however, did not rejoin the party until 1945.

Mellor, who had been blacklisted as a parliamentary candidate in 1937 after the United Front debacle, had now been selected for the safe seat of Stockport. In normal times, there would have been a general election in 1940 at the latest. For Mellor this held out the prospect of a return to the centre of the political stage, but for Barbara it complicated the chances of a divorce. What was a private difficulty would, once he became a public figure, become a scandal. With the onset of war and the suspension of elections, on the other hand, the problem might be resolved. Yet the prospect of marriage seemed as distant as it had for the past six years. Mellor was fifty-one and, effectively, unemployed. Barbara thought he was too mentally depleted to be pushed again on the question of divorce. She was terrified of war, her nightmares fed by the vivid accounts of aerial bombardment from the Spanish refugees living with her parents, and she was ready to pack her bags and leave London and Mellor for the safety of provincial Nottingham. 'It would be hell here in the war. I should have no money, no light, no cinemas and no boyfriends!' she wrote to her parents. But the next day she changed her mind. Her nerve, she said, steadied. Perhaps she could not face separation from Mellor, but more probably she was busy with her council work, with what turned out to be the premature evacuation of thousands of local children, and with her new role as an air raid protection warden. She had also been seconded to the Metropolitan Water Board by Minister of Supply Herbert Morrison, who 'loved to appoint women to positions which they had never held before'.[7]

Barbara was busy, but she was also lonely. War – and especially the Blitz, when it started in June 1940 – made life too disorganized to keep up with friends easily. Ironically, the companionship of her best friend Michael Foot (whose mother was encouraging him to marry Barbara, although the two women had never met)[8] had been lost because of his loyalty to Mellor. After Cripps had sacked Mellor as editor of *Tribune*, Bevan had taken Foot home and telephoned one of his good friends, Lord Beaverbrook. As he dialled the number, he said to Jennie Lee: 'I've got a young bloody knight errant here. They sacked his boss so he resigned. Have a look at him.'[9] Beaverbrook launched Foot on to another plane – one of country houses and beautiful women and well paid jobs, first on the *Express* and then on the *Evening Standard*. Barbara was left behind, writing for the *Grocer*. Their paths now rarely crossed.

Nonetheless, Barbara stuck doggedly to her self-imposed objectives. She was desperate for a regular income but, appalled at the idea of returning to an all-women environment like St Hugh's ('sleeping with women!'), not at the expense of joining up, and she now began work on an idea for a book about the Blitz for Gollancz. But early in 1941 she found another journalist,

Ritchie Calder, later Lord Ritchie-Calder, was doing the same thing, so she went to work for him instead: he paid. When the book was finished, Calder invited her to join a special unit working on psychological warfare. The location of the unit was so secret, even he claimed not to know where it was. Barbara, fearing such a commitment would impinge on her political career and perhaps not wanting to leave Mellor behind in London, turned the job down. Instead, when conscription for women was introduced in 1941, she became a temporary civil servant, an administrative officer in the fish division of the Ministry of Food. She spent the rest of the war finding ways of rationing kippers and making palatable a fish called snoek.

During the Blitz, Barbara's gas main had been blasted, leaving her Coram Street flat with no usable cooker and no hot water. It was the excuse she needed to move in with Mellor. Edna's money had a few years earlier provided a large, modern house on the edge of Hampstead but she and their son Ronald had gone to Cornwall to escape the air raids. It was not the love nest of Barbara's dreams: Mellor's niece, a young doctor (who was told by him that Barbara had been bombed out), lived there too for some of the time. Mellor was on night shifts, having found a job at last – the *Herald* had taken him back. It was commonplace for people who still had a sound roof over their heads to offer accommodation to friends and neighbours forced out of their own homes. When the family returned, Barbara stayed close by, moving into the top half of a maisonette in a nearby street.

By the third year of the war Barbara and Mellor were nearly ten years into their affair. The London Blitz had ended; Barbara had almost for the first time a regular job and a regular income. She was beginning to tire of waiting. She and William considered giving up on the notion of a divorce and openly living together. It would have been a controversial, but not unheard of arrangement. William Beveridge of the eponymous report lived for three years with his future wife, Janet Mair, in the master's lodgings at University College, Oxford, until her first husband died and they were able to marry.

In a letter written on 6 March 1942, William assured Barbara that he had raised the whole question with Edna.

When I got back last night – over an hour late – Edna was waiting. Quietly and I hope in a way you would have approved I told her of our decision. *For the present* [Mellor's emphasis], I said, we had decided to propose a modus vivendi based on our right to be with each other . . . and our desire to do all that was *possible* to help Edna and the boy. Two or three times I stressed that this proposal was *for the present* and added that if Edna agreed you and I would talk together about its working out.

When she asked me whether you had considered your own position I told her very firmly that you were a serious minded woman, alive to and conscious of all that was involved in the fact of our love. Beyond that I did not go because I felt – and believe you do too – that the nature and content of your anxieties is something that no one but you and I have any right to know. I did, however, say that I was certain in my own mind that I could live in happiness with you – this in answer to a question as to whether 'for the present' meant that I was liable to swing back again.

Mellor was back at the *Herald* in a subordinate capacity, and he was struggling to get his career back into shape. He wrote to Barbara again a couple of days later, but with none of the ebullience of his early letters, to warn her that he could not take a Sunday off because it was his chance to be 'virtually in charge'. There was no decline in his reckless generosity, though. A few days later he reported that he was 'still shaking from the blow' of picking up the tab for lunch with Percy Cudlipp, the *Herald*'s editor, but 'it was all very friendly and pleasant'. It was almost his last letter to her. In early summer 1942 his doctor told him he had a stomach ulcer. He must take six months' rest, or have an operation. His job was plainly too insecure to contemplate a prolonged break, so he opted for the operation. At first it seemed to go well, but then complications set in. On 8 June, two weeks after the operation, he died.

A couple of months earlier, on fire watch one night, William had written Barbara a love letter that came close to being an apology. 'I have loved you since the first day I saw you. And after ten years – it's nearly that, sweet – rich with lovely memories and black with the recollection of my own cowardice in not following the course love set, I know now that my love is deeper, more compelling, more understanding and finer, I hope, than at any time.' Mellor, who had never squared his horror at the idea of deserting his family with his desire to be with Barbara, in the end betrayed them both.

Supported by Michael Foot, Barbara went to the funeral. Fortunately, according to her son, Edna stayed at home and the two women never met. Barbara fled London the next day to stay with her sister Marjorie, from where she wrote to her mother in Nottingham. Annie was nursing Frank, who had retired early, sick with Parkinson's disease.

Mam darling, It really doesn't matter whom one talks to about one's loss – or whom one 'turns to' in words. Words are useless things. The thing that matters is to know in one's heart that one is loved, that one's sorrow is shared, that there is a corner to creep to when one is desperate. This whole business has brought home to me inexorably that the only real human contact is of the spirit. When Mellor died on Monday, I hadn't seen or spoken to him for 5 days. That wasn't a point of any relevance to me. When I saw him the previous Wednesday – suddenly struck low – weak & bewildered & powerless while his life's energy ebbed away – I knew I was helpless to do anything for him. All I could do was not to add to his worries by the physical presence of my anxiety. So I told him myself, 'I'm not coming to see you again until you're stronger. That's not because I don't want to. It is because I love you'. He smiled & nodded & we were near to one another. As near as anything on earth could make us, all those 5 days through. I never spoke to him again. I went to the funeral to pay tribute to Mellor like any other comrade of his in the Movement. I was glad I did, although at one point I thought I'd never get through it with the control I'd sworn to myself I would not break. Michael and Ritchie [Calder] stood round me like a bodyguard, sheltering me with understanding, & Krishna [Menon, a fellow St Pancras councillor and later Indian High Commissioner] took me home. It was a genuine goodbye from genuine mourners, with real comradeship.

After Marjorie, Barbara fell back on the kindness of Jennie Lee, who less than ten years earlier had not been with her lover Frank Wise when he died suddenly, and knew the devastating loss both of bereavement and of grief compounded by exclusion from the recognized ranks of the intimate mourners. It was Jennie who took Barbara in until she was able to go back to work.

Mellor, with his 'raw puritan cantankerousness'[10] and vile temper so like Frank's, had shaped Barbara's politics; she never left his influence entirely behind. He was the 'granite conscience'[11] of the left, a mantle Barbara later aspired to for herself. She did not carry his Marxism with her, but she agreed with the credo he spelt out in the first issue of *Tribune*: 'It is capitalism that has caused the world depression. It is capitalism that has created the vast army of the unemployed. It is capitalism that has created the distressed areas . . . It is capitalism that divides our people into the two nations of rich and poor. Either we must defeat capitalism or we shall be destroyed by it.'[12]

Other threads of Mellor's beliefs ran through her thinking. From his guild socialism she absorbed a faith in worker participation. Nationalization, which kept the old power structure in place, would not achieve all of its ends. She shared his belief in the power and importance of demonstrations and agitation in building and sustaining support for socialism, and a predisposition towards the Soviet Union as its home, however flawed. She echoed his hatred of wars between capitalist powers. And she learnt about being in a minority, about being on the losing side. Above all, she believed that politics was a crusade, fervent, immediate and all-embracing, which demanded near-total commitment. Atheistic almost as an article of faith, nonetheless she, like the former Labour leader George Lansbury, believed: 'If we cannot within the framework of our party get together a body of men and women, especially young men, who will see the cause of Socialism as a religion, to be served as St Francis, Savonarola and Tolstoy served their faiths, all our work is hopeless.'[13]

Mellor became a central part of Barbara's later image, an idol to garland with tributes. Occasionally, privately, and many years later, she might admit that he had been weak and that she had been a fool to let him take her youth. But in the aftermath of his death she felt herself 'haunted by his unfulfilled spirit, like Hamlet's father it bids me see that the fruits of his suffering are gathered for his rightful heirs'.[14] He gave her, she said at the pinnacle of her career, a 'philosophic mould': 'Something to hold on to, so you don't get shoddy and you don't get mean, you don't get ambitious and climbing and pecuniary, you've got something to hang on to all the way . . . this was the quality of his Socialism . . . for him, politics was a quality of living. This is what *my* socialism is about.'[15] It was a romantic ideal, a long way from the realities of practical politics. But it was the essence of her enduring appeal.

William was dead. Cripps was abroad as ambassador to Moscow, from where he returned in glory after the entry of Russia into the war on the side of the Allies and joined the government. Domestic politics was beginning to revive. The left needed a new leader, Barbara a new mentor. Aneurin Bevan became both.

In 1941 Bevan had taken over the editorship of *Tribune*. He had had his column; now he had the whole paper as a platform, and he could take his demand for a war for all the people out of the House of Commons, where he was risking the outraged disapproval of his own leadership by attacking Churchill's premiership, to a wider audience. If the British press was substituting treacle for ink, as he claimed, he was using vitriol. Labour, by refusing to join the National Government under Chamberlain, had ensured that in the end he would have to go. When Churchill formed his first coalition government in May 1940 there were fifteen Labour ministers, five of them in the War Cabinet, with Attlee as Deputy Prime Minister and Bevin as Minister of Labour. Bevan, who to no one's surprise was not among the fifteen, thought Labour had underplayed its hand in negotiations for the coalition and had failed to make it clear that on the home front the policies had to be Labour's. Labour support should have been traded, for example, for improved benefits, instead of allowing the Conservatives to 'remodel the social services in accordance with Tory principles'.[16] It was a scandal, he believed, that Chamberlain and other leading appeasers had been allowed to remain in government after their defeat, but it proved that the Tory Party had not changed. In Bevan's opinion, under the rhetoric they were all Fascists.

Virtually single-handed, Bevan fought in the Commons and in *Tribune* a brilliant, coherent and deeply unpopular campaign against the national hero Churchill, whom he described as the embodiment of the kind of society the war must end. 'Mr Churchill is the spokesman of his order and of his class, and that class and that order [are] dying,'[17] he wrote confidently as the Battle of Britain raged. (Churchill once told Cripps, weeping, 'I *am* England.')[18] Bevan professed outrage that Churchill, the leader of a National Government, should have taken the leadership of the Conservative Party from the now dying Chamberlain, accusing him of 'draping' the Tory Party in the national flag. When – after a prolonged onslaught from Bevan about his conduct of the war – Churchill was finally able to celebrate victory at El Alamein in November 1942, Bevan renewed his demands for Labour to turn its attentions to the 'new, eager, virgin minds' opened by the war and capture them for its cause.

Minds were indeed being opened by the war. It had brought an unprecedented degree of social mobility; the impact of the depradations of ten and more years of terrible poverty on millions of families was suddenly thrust into the faces – and homes – of their more prosperous fellow Britons. Recruiting sergeants complained about sickly and weedy conscripts. In small provincial towns and rural villages, evacuee children with anaemia, sores, eye inflamations – all the diseases of poverty – were exposing the middle classes to the realities of life for the families of unemployed or low-paid factory workers. It was a hard, practical lesson on the existence of the two nations Mellor had written about in the first issue of *Tribune*. The paper had often turned its attention to the state of the poor. In March 1937 Storm Jameson, provoked by a new survey of malnutrition, had contributed an epic diatribe:

> Any middle-class mother spends in a week more *on milk alone* for one child than the total amount the wife of an unskilled worker or an unemployed man has left to spend on providing all the food for two children. Just think quietly about what this means – to the two underfed children. Widespread malnutrition is a fact which no chatter about minimum standards can conceal, except from the wilfully blind, and from the spokesman of a government which applies means tests to babies and hands their profits to armaments manufacturers on a plate.[19]

A few weeks after El Alamein – the battle Churchill called the 'end of the beginning' – the Beveridge report was published. The drily titled official publication, *Social Insurance and Allied Services*, would transform the domestic political agenda. 'From now on, Beveridge is not the name of a man; it is the name of a way of life, and not only for Britain but for the whole of the civilised world,' Sir William Beveridge immodestly told his young assistant, Harold Wilson. And for years it seemed a reasonable claim. In the words of one historian, he delivered 'the prince's kiss'[20] to assorted ideas for long-overdue reform of social welfare. He also awoke a nation dulled by three years of coalition government. A statistician by training who had in 1938 told Beatrice Webb that 'he was not personally concerned with the welfare of the common people', Beveridge famously wept tears of disappointment when asked to inquire into welfare because he had hoped to be asked to run the wartime manpower effort. But he had had a lifetime's experience of welfare. He had introduced the first labour exchanges (in 1908) and set up the first insurance scheme against unemployment, introduced by Lloyd George in 1911.

Now in his sixties, Beveridge was a man looking for a place in history. It took him only eighteen months to devise a system to tackle the 'five giant evils' – want, ignorance, disease, squalor and idleness – a scheme which in all its fundamentals endures still. To the Treasury's alarm, however, it rested on the assumption that there would first be put in place three essential under-pinnings – a national health service, universal children's allowances and a commitment by the state to full employment. Social security would be based on insurance jointly paid for by the individual, the employer and the state. An insurance-based scheme meant, most importantly, that benefits would be an individual entitlement that could not be eroded by the harsh and hated means test.

It was not, however, a socialist scheme. Beveridge's sentiments were Liberal – he was to be, briefly, a Liberal MP. His early experience of welfare schemes had been for a Liberal government. So his own was a hybrid of old Liberal ideas of self-reliance, in that it was contributory, and Lloyd George Liberal views about the role of the state, in that it was compulsory and state-organized.[21] Bevan, who would have preferred a redistributive, tax-based scheme, immediately saw its potential. 'Sir William has described the conditions in which the tears might be taken out of capitalism. We should not be surprised therefore, if all unconsciously by so doing he threatens capitalism itself.' It is odd that he did not see that the scheme might equally be the saviour of capitalism. Bevan, however, believed that giving primacy to welfare in the state's priorities might sound the death knell of pre-war society. 'To keep [the people's] bodies healthy, to ease their minds, to release their souls – these are the first claims on the State. The claim of property must come second.'

The Conservative Chancellor, Sir Kingsley Wood, tipped off by his officials about the likely budgetary implications of the Beveridge proposals, had contemplated suppressing the report. Failing that, the government was prepared to disown it. The officials who had worked on it with Beveridge were instructed to withdraw their names. It was to be Beveridge's own work. Reports of the unease in government reached the outside world. On the eve of publication there were queues at the government stationers, HMSO. Sixty thousand copies went almost immediately; in the end, an astonishing 600,000 were sold. Beveridge himself became a hero of wartime Britain, 'the people's William',[22] and having by his judicious leaks built up a head of steam for his report's publication, he now led the way in creating a demand for its implementation, addressing meetings around the country. The National Government, in a sign of its growing distance from the sentiments of the country, attempted to head him off. It played for time, hoping the clamour might die down. Then in the new year Bevan used his *Tribune* editorial to declare – in a theme that would recur throughout the rest of his career – that the report was the route to moral rearmament: 'If Britain shows that she has the courage, imagination and resilience to embark on a social experiment of such a magnitude in the midst of war, then she may once more assert a moral leadership which will have consequences in every sphere of her activies.'

More than two months after its publication, in February 1943, Labour finally forced a debate on the report in the Commons. (Ernest Bevin, who had an old quarrel with Beveridge, had declared parts of the report 'unacceptable to the unions'.[23]) It was a difficult moment for the Labour ministers. Herbert Morrison had to defend the government's refusal to authorize implementation, and fifty-seven Labour MPs voted against the government. In March that year, Jennie Lee stood in a by-election in Bristol on a platform for its immediate implementation.

At Labour's party conference held at Central Hall, Westminster, in May, the leadership knew it would come under pressure on the Beveridge report. Barbara, attending for the first time as a delegate, was well prepared. If there was a single issue on which she could talk and be guaranteed an impact, it was on Beveridge. 'No delegate has ever arrived at a Labour Party conference more determined to get to the rostrum or more terrified at the thought of standing up before that large, stolid and critical audience,'[24] she wrote. Word had gone out from Labour headquarters at Transport House to start candidate selection for the next election.[25]

The speech Barbara made was to change the rest of her life. From it flowed her marriage and her parliamentary career. With it she proclaimed on the national stage an enduring concern for social welfare and a scepticism about the political role of trade unions. To the speech itself she brought fifteen years of political campaigning and a natural flair for the dramatic. She cheeked the chairman who, she complained, had taken too long to call her – 'I began to think there was no equality of women in the Labour movement' – and told the union bosses on the platform: 'We of the rank and file of the constituency parties say to the trade union movement that the Beveridge issue is as axiomatic to us as the Trades Dispute Act is to them.' Finally, she turned to the delegates themselves to deliver her peroration: 'Jam tomorrow but never jam today – that is what the government is trying to say to the people, but we want jam today!'

Barbara became an instant heroine of the rank and file. If her success had stopped there, it would have been a useful asset in her search for a seat. However, it was picked up by the *Daily Mirror*'s man at the conference Garry Allighan, who went back to Fleet Street and suggested to the night editor Ted Castle that he make a feature of it. The paper had already been campaigning for Beveridge. The following morning, Barbara was on the front page. Her career as Labour's pin-up girl was launched. The *Mirror*'s picture showed her with clenched fist thumping down on the lectern, in the other fist copious notes. She wore round, thick-rimmed spectacles (it was a long time before she was photographed again in spectacles of any kind), her hair was pin-curled, and she wore a smart tailored jacket.

Bevan was impressed. He 'began to take notice of me, politically', and arranged for them to speak together at a fringe meeting about democratizing the union vote at conference. Bevan was campaigning for an end to coalition government and a resumption of normal political life, but had been defeated at both 1942 and 1943 conferences by the power of the trade union block vote. 'The trade unions are no longer paying affiliation fees to the Labour Party. They are paying its burial expenses,' he complained angrily. Barbara later claimed he stole her ideas. 'I was surprised when he grew increasingly restive during my speech, refused questions and quickly closed the meeting down. I was even more surprised a few days later to read an article in *Tribune* by Nye himself advocating exactly the same line. I had a lot to learn about politics.'[26]

Ted Castle was interested enough to go himself to Westminster to meet the woman he had put on the front of the newspaper. They spent the afternoon talking politics together. He was impressed by her feel for politics, and even more impressed that she treated Aneurin Bevan as an equal. Most of all, he was struck by her looks. He arranged to take her to the theatre. Ted was just thirty-five, nearly four years older than Barbara. He had been married and had a daughter, and was in the process of divorcing. He was a bit of a lad, quick rather than clever, gregarious, successful with women, at ease with himself in a way that Barbara was not. Years later when Barbara was in Cabinet, Ted, betraying a certain predictability in his outlook, told a journalist:

This was the first redhead I'd ever gone out with, the first one I'd known in fact, and they'd always been represented to me as fiery, quick-tempered, and, to some extent, illogical. In the first few days I was trying to find out whether there was any truth in this. I soon saw the quickness of reaction, the fact that injustice or distortion or any irritation can make her blow up into a real storm very quickly . . . any unpredictable thing could set her off into a very eloquent denunciation at top speed and with great vigour.[27]

Ted wanted to be an MP too. He and Barbara spent their courtship proselytizing for Beveridge, hoping to impress constituencies looking for a candidate. They became something of a star turn,[28] touring the constituencies they could reach from London, sometimes together and sometimes separately. Shared experiences in different places – it was like the early days of her affair with Mellor. But little else was. Barbara feared that Ted was shallow. He looked a bit too much like the screen actor David Niven, he was dapper, he had a 'neat moustache'. He could not have been less like either the saturnine Mellor or her real prototype husband, dark, shaggy Frank Betts. About nine months after they met, she wrote to Ted: 'I'm dearly fond of you and a little afraid of you, because I still don't really know you yet. And this strange hankering to get at the bottom of you is something you can't understand & don't really approve of. Then, too, I believe that living is essentially a very serious business in which the spirit is much more important than the flesh.'

Barbara had a seriousness and an intenseness about her that was belied by her startling good looks. She trod, not always successfully, the narrow line between exploiting her appearance and being taken seriously. Achieving objectives through charm and flirtation became as integral a part of her style as her toughness and her temper. During the Blitz it had become of talismanic importance to her not to rush for shelter with an unmade-up face. Her passion for clothes was unabated; she was continually bullying Annie to make or alter something for her. When her parents moved house, she wrote desperately of a skirt: 'If it gets lost the mainstay of my winter wardrobe will have gone.' She asked for clothes for Christmas and birthday presents, and when clothes rationing came in – restricting her, she moaned, to the wardrobe she had for years been too poor to replenish – it seemed, on a personal level, almost as bad as the Blitz. Her appearance was her carapace, her defence against a world in which she did not feel quite comfortable. She never mastered the light-hearted, inconsequential small-talk of London parties. She sometimes covered her uncertainty with flirtatiousness, which some contemporaries claimed was not misleading. In the lament of many attractive, independent women, she felt that men were only interested in sex: 'I only know that with every instinct in my body I treasure physical fastidiousness as spontaneously as I delight to dance and express my high spirits in friendly sociability. The men I like to dance with here . . . leave me utterly cold sexually. The two things just don't seem to me to have any connection. I know now why William used to beg me to curb my high spirits and frank sociability in the company of the average male.'[29] Equally, men, especially misogynistic trade union leaders, suspected her of being fast. Nice girls did not love dancing quite as much as Barbara did, nor did they stand up for themselves in political argument quite so vehemently.

Ted and Barbara were opposites. Barbara had a tendency to the solitary; she was quick-tempered but careful and thorough, strictly self-disciplined, always living on her nerves or something stronger. Ted was laid-back, casual and instinctive. In common they had socialist politics, a love of the country-side and a passion for walking. Ted also had working-class parents, whom Barbara instantly adored, 'simple, gentle and devout people without a touch of worldliness'.[30] Her own father was slowly dying, her mother absorbed in caring for him. Her sister Marjorie, although hundreds of miles away in Wigan working as a personnel officer, had shown her the pleasures of normal domesticity, of a kind they had never enjoyed with their domineering father. Her nieces and nephew were beyond babyhood and proving amusing companions. Her brother Jimmie was in Africa, also married, although his wife had had a serious stroke and they were not going to be able to have children.

Before she met Ted, Barbara was alone, lonely and broody, and she was thirty-one. They married just over a year after their first encounter, on 28 July 1944. It was almost exactly two years since William had died. The left's aristocracy, Nye Bevan and Jennie Lee – who in the aftermath of Frank Wise's death had married Nye with some misgiving – stood in for Barbara's friends and family, kept at bay by Hitler's new V-bombs. The night before the wedding, Ted had resigned from the *Mirror* because the man who brought them together, Garry Allighan,[31] had been sacked – unfairly, Ted thought. Ted got a job on *Picture Post* within twenty-four hours, and after a decent interval Barbara took over Allighan's column in the *Mirror*. It was journalistically undemanding, dealing with problems from the Forces ('Barbara Betts, the Forces' Friend') but it gave her a familiarity with, and the opportunity to air her views on, housing, demobilization and jobs.

The marriage was to be almost as tempestuous as her parents'. There were dramatic accusations of infidelity on both sides. There was a time when Ted found Barbara's success difficult to live with and drank slightly harder than was good even for a hard drinker. They survived.

After nearly ten years without an election, there would be a transformation at Westminster, whoever won. Many MPs were retiring, and with so many likely applicants at war it looked like easy pickings for those at home. Barbara had already put out feelers for a constituency for the election. Despite her determination to stay in London to pursue her political career, she had had a quiet war until she burst on the scene at the 1943 conference – in contrast to the men elected with her in 1945. Harold Wilson, at that time a temporary civil servant of a rather more elevated kind than Barbara – economist at the Board of Trade rather than an administrative officer (albeit senior) in the fish division of the Ministry of Food – had, in his political life, been seconded to the board of the Fabian Society, while Barbara had merely written a chapter on pensions for a Fabian pamphlet. Hugh Gaitskell, a temporary civil servant in the Board of Trade, had captured Maynard Keynes for the right through the XYZ Club of economists and politicians while Barbara had travelled the country in some discomfort, arguing for Beveridge and a better world.

The barriers facing a woman who wanted to be an MP were no less high for being unremarked; for the men, finding a winnable seat was straightforward. Wilson landed Ormskirk after only one other interview; James Callaghan had been selected for Cardiff at the first attempt. Denis Healey was selected in absentia (although not for a winnable seat) while he carried on fighting through Italy. Roy Jenkins went to just two interviews before being selected, also for an unwinnable seat. Barbara went to half a dozen interviews and applied for many more.

But her party conference gambit had borne fruit: within a month, Oldham invited her to apply for selection. Crewe, Exeter, Stockton and Macclesfield all followed suit over the next few months. Sometimes she got interviews. Often she did not. Blackburn, a Lancashire mill town, approached her towards the middle of 1944. The women's section had insisted that unless there was a woman on the shortlist of six they would strike. The men told them to find a candidate, so they had approached the north-west regional women's organizer. Barbara's years of campaigning in the region paid off: her name went forward – but not as a 'woman candidate'. She had an equivocal relationship with the question of the role of women in the Labour Party: feminists or class warriors? Both cared about the same issues, but from different perspectives. Feminists – dismissed as middle-class by many women in industrial constituencies – thought equal pay had to be fought for as a matter of justice; class warriors wanted it to prevent women taking men's jobs at lower rates of pay. Birth control, for feminists, was a matter of giving women independence; socialists saw it in terms of economic survival. In theory, a woman's route to power within the party had been established through the local women's sections. Women also had separate representation on the National Executive, to try to counter the overwhelmingly male dominance of the trade unions. There was an annual women's conference, but it had no power to make policy and could only hope to influence it at the periphery. What women's issues gained by having an identity, they lost by being marginalized, and it has always been easy for male-dominated Cabinets to hold back reforms that might redress the balance. Women, collectively, could be and were corralled behind a veil, segregated to perform useful but minor tasks; breaking through to power called for a high degree of courage and determination. Of more than 1,600 candidates in the 1945 election, just eighty-seven were women, and only twenty-four were elected. Many of the women who succeeded in 1945, like Bessie Braddock, Alice Bacon and Edith Summerskill, as well as Barbara herself, stood out for their exceptional personalities.

Barbara never doubted that socialism was more important than feminism. Yet, though her priorities were socialist, her priorities within socialism were strongly influenced by being a woman.[32] The empowering experience of war, which had made the demand for women's votes irresistible in 1918, was in 1944 encouraging women in constituency parties to find their voices. Blackburn, like other mill towns, was in the vanguard. Women in textiles earned the rate for the job, just like the men. In 1929 Blackburn had elected a woman MP: Mary Agnes Hamilton, novelist and biographer of both the Webbs and Arthur Henderson, 'an extraordinarily able woman who created a profound impression among people in Blackburn about her ability'.[33] She had been one of only fourteen women in the Commons, nine of whom were Labour. (All nine lost their seats in 1931.)

Blackburn was unusual in the North-West for lacking a Nonconformist tradition and a Liberal political past. Although there was a significant minority of Roman Catholics, it was an Anglican town, and usually a Conservative one too. Without a Liberal base, the Labour cause took root early. Its first socialist MP had been Philip Snowden, MacDonald's Chancellor of the Exchequer, who won the seat in 1906 when there were only thirty successful Labour candidates altogether. Snowden's opposition to the war had cost him the Blackburn nomination in 1918 but in 1929, the year Labour first became the biggest single party, the town sent two Labour MPs to Westminster, only to lose them again in 1931. It was still Conservative-held in 1945; one seat was considered winnable. Winning both was only an outside chance.

In the spring of 1944 Barbara had been ill. Her health was never robust, and she had succumbed first to shingles and then appendicitis. Nonetheless, she ignored doctor's orders and made the long train journey north. There were two reasons for her determination. The Blackburn Labour agent, George Eddie, had been drumming up support for her. Jim Mason, later the chairman of her constituency party, was a bomber pilot in the RAF, and was one of several party members to be summoned back to Blackburn for the selection conference with specific instructions from Eddie to vote for Barbara Betts. Eddie, a remarkable figure, had been a conscientious objector in the First World War and (like Mellor) briefly imprisoned in Dartmoor. In the 1920s, he had been agent in Jimmy Maxton's Glasgow Bridgeton seat, but he had come south in the late 1920s. He was to be a vital ally for Barbara. Eddie wanted as many rank-and-file members as possible to obstruct a group of trade unionists who would prefer a trade union activist to a London-based journalist. Jim Mason duly applied for leave, which for political purposes was an automatic entitlement. Eddie must have been confident that he had fixed it for Barbara. Ted had arranged for *Picture Post* to do a photo-spread on the final selection process.

Blackburn had been built on cotton, and cotton was already an industry in decline. Barbara described 'cobbled streets, dim street lighting, dilapidated schools . . . I could not find anywhere to eat unless a comrade gave me hospitality out of the family's rations.'[34] The town was smoky and grimy, its fabric still recovering from the long years of depression when nearly half the town had been out of work. The housing was bad, the population falling. Like many Labour seats, it was the kind of place where party workers collected the weekly subs on a Friday night before the money went. But over the previous twenty years, Eddie, who was about to become leader of the council as well as party agent, had built a thriving Labour Party ripe for some evangelical socialism.

Barbara, up against five men, gave it to them. She was also determined to have the last word. 'Barbara wanted to go on last and so make the best impression but I think she was due to be first or second. So she beat it back to her hotel for handkerchiefs or something and came back and actually spoke last. She put up a damn good show. A tiny girl, with a trim figure and that shock of red hair. And when she spoke it really made an impression.'[35] 'I want you to forget two things,' she told the packed and smoke-filled hall, with only a few women here and there in the crowd. 'The first is that I am just out of hospital. The second is that I am a woman. I'm no feminist. Just judge me as a socialist.'[36]

The effect of her looks and the passion with which she spoke left the outcome beyond doubt. The final factor in her favour was that Blackburn was a two-member borough constituency – two candidates were being selected to stand on the Labour ticket. The trade unionists got their man, John Edwards, backed by the Post Office Engineers, and Eddie got his left-winger. The two were comfortably ahead of the rest of the field.[37] Eddie immediately took Barbara firmly in hand. The party did not agree with married women using their maiden names. It was still six weeks before her marriage but she became, for all political purposes and soon even for journalistic ones, Mrs Barbara Castle. They might have chosen a woman, but there was a limit to what the party could take.

Within a matter of weeks, Barbara had acquired both a promising parliamentary constituency and a husband. In Europe, the Allies had started to advance through France. The war was in its closing stages. Barbara's future, which only a couple of years ago had looked so bleak, had been transformed.

At Westminster, Aneurin Bevan was simultaneously escalating his campaign to dissolve the coalition before the end of the war in Europe and renewing his attack on trade union influence in the party. He foresaw the Tories being swept to power on the back of military victory, while the impetus for radical reform drained away in the neutered politics of coalition. He now called for a Labour-dominated 'coalition of the Left', to embrace the parties which, unlike Labour, had been contesting and winning by-elections during the war. Barbara took up the call. She and Bevan also continued to raise the question of democratizing the voting system within the party. Barbara had worked out a scheme that would split the trade union block vote: half of it would be exercised nationally, but the rest would have to be used through individual trade union affiliations to constituency parties. She had sent a memorandum explaining her proposal to the NEC.[38] There had been no reply.

Her complaint was that Labour was so dominated by the unions that the individual party member could have no influence. Individual membership had fallen by nearly half in the war years, from 409,000 to 219,000, while trade union membership was rising. Yet it was the individual members whose hard work won elections. With another Labour candidate, William Warbey,[39] she warned that the appearance of control by the trade unions and the interests of the manual workers was tending to alienate potential support among black-coated workers and what she described as the 'new middle classes'. It was time to abandon trade union-style bargain and compromise, they argued, in exchange for confrontation with the capitalist enemy. Having won the argument in 1937 to increase the number of constituency party seats on the Executive from five to seven, they hoped, ambitiously, to redress the balance against trade union influence. 'There is nothing anti-union in a campaign to strengthen the electoral units of the Party which in their preparations for the winning of power would be only too glad to bring the local unions into partnership,' their proposal concluded optimistically.

Another Labour intellectual, Harold Laski, was also attacking the dominance of the unions. Together, they provoked an angry response from the top. Ernest Bevin, seeing the old divide opening up between individual and trade union members, accused them of bringing discredit on the party.[40] In retaliation Laski warned that the day of the corporate state was approaching, when the workers would be excluded from cosy deals stitched up by government, employers and union bosses. He and Bevan stressed the importance of allowing the rank and file to think and speak for themselves. They denied they were attempting to divide the movement: 'Strength from the unions and social purpose for the Party; those are still the twin merits which justify the trade union basis of the British Labour Party,' Bevan wrote in May 1945.[41]

On 7 May Germany surrendered. Attlee, as Deputy Prime Minister, refused to sustain the coalition until Japan was defeated, which was expected to take another year. Churchill formed a Conservative government and an election was called for 5 July, with a further three weeks to allow servicemen to vote. Barbara's election message was ready. She was endorsed by Herbert Morrison, the man 'who put her on the Metropolitan Water Board' and who came to Blackburn to launch her campaign: 'She will add lustre to Parliament. Send her there!' Cripps and Bevan came too. It was at best a marginal seat, and the chances of returning two Labour members seemed remote. However, barely one candidate in twenty was a woman, and

Barbara, pretty and controversial, was easily the best copy. Looking neat and unalarming, and without her glasses, throughout the campaign she figured prominently in the pages of the local papers. Her image, she decided, should be womanly. She used a picture of herself 'curled up in an armchair darning one of her husband's socks'. Asked if she would come and live in the constituency, she retorted that she was old-fashioned and would live with her husband. But, she added, she'd put Blackburn on the map. Ted was coming to terms with being the candidate's husband, an 'election bachelor', complaining that he had had to come to Blackburn to get a button sewn on. Marjorie came to help, and brought her older daughter Sonya, then aged nine, to reassure the voters that Barbara really was a housewifely type. (No one corrected the mistaken assumption that she was Barbara's daughter.) Barbara was exhausted; behind the scenes she frequently lost her temper, and her party workers wondered how she would manage in parliament.[42]

In public she assured the voters of Blackburn of her competence and range of experience, and reached out to servicemen overseas: 'You have had to bear an unfair share of the war's burdens'. Her priorities, extracted from Labour's programme 'Let us Face the Future', naturally put ending the war at the top and the 'socialization' of fuel, power, transport and iron and steel at the bottom, with the economy and welfare reform in the middle. She was left-wing, but in the reasonable tones that would not keep wavering Tories awake at night. She was, it was said in her election literature, 'rebelling against the idea that poverty and ugliness are necessary evils. So she set out to get the training in economics, in political science, in industrial organization to equip her for the fight against them.'

People remembered the 1945 election for the rest of their lives. They said the campaign itself felt different. It was the first general election for ten years, and it came at the end of nearly six years of war. In the election of 1935, Labour had still been tainted with economic failure and internal division, but as members of the coalition government, Labour ministers had looked safe and reliable (despite Churchill alleging during the campaign that a Labour government would be a 'kind of Gestapo'). A country emerging battered from a war which had for the first time conscripted the whole nation, was attracted to the idea of winning the peace through the same spirit of common endeavour. People who remembered the Depression, including the middle classes, who had now seen for themselves the impact it had had on children and families, wanted a fresh start. There was a demand for change, for improvement. The Beveridge report was still selling well. Bevan's polemic *Why Not Trust the Tories?* reminding people what had happened before the war, sold fewer copies but a still phenomenal eighty thousand.

There was, Barbara's agent later recalled, 'an evangelical air' about it all. On the final evening of the campaign, what would nowadays be the extraordinary number of twelve thousand people gathered in the centre of Blackburn and spontaneously sang 'Jerusalem'.[43]

Still Barbara feared they could not win. But when the results were declared on 26 July, Blackburn's Labour candidates had swept the board. Disproving the theory that women don't vote for women, there was only the narrowest difference in votes for the two successful candidates, who between them took 52 per cent of the total. (A Liberal candidate from the 'Women for Westminster' movement scored a respectable 6,096.) At Westminster there were 392 Labour MPs, 21 of them women, of whom Barbara was the youngest. From the steps of the town hall she told her supporters. 'There is overwhelming support in Blackburn for a bold advance.'[44] She devoted the next thirty-five years to its pursuit.

5. Jerusalem

President Truman: 'You've had a revolution.'
King George VI: 'Oh no! We don't have those here.'[1]

1 August 1945 felt so like a revolution that Labour MPs, gathered for the first time at Westminster to hear a King's Speech from a majority Labour government, burst into a chorus of 'The Red Flag', a richly ironic gesture since the bombing of the House of Commons meant that MPs now sat in the House of Lords. From this bomb site[2] the new Jerusalem for the dawn of which Barbara's constituents had sung so lustily a month earlier was now to arise. The government of 1945 changed the political future of Britain, and the generation of young MPs which now entered parliament for the first time would trail its glory across Labour politics for more than thirty years. Four Labour leaders[3] – including two future prime ministers – entered parliament for the first time on that first day. Many friendships and alliances that were to shape the party's future were made over the next five years. For Barbara, the triumph was marred by personal tragedy. Just before the election, her father had died. He had been ill with Parkinson's disease for more than three years and his death was not a shock, but it deprived her of his final blessing and of the pleasure of showing him how triumphantly she had fulfilled his dreams.

Labour's victory, beyond the euphoria, was also less of a revolution than it at first appeared. The shift of power in the economy, itself a natural progression from wartime controls, was not matched by any shift of power within the Labour Party. The political barons behind whom the young MPs found themselves forming up almost from the start of the parliament had first been active in the 1930s. The manifesto owed much to Dalton's work ten years earlier, while divisions that were to emerge by the end of the first five years had been sketched out in the angry pre-war battles. Attlee, Bevin,

Morrison and Dalton, who had held the party in their unbending grip throughout the earlier strife, still made up the high command. The only new blood was Cripps, readmitted to the party in time to stand as a Labour candidate. This was not the Cripps who had so vehemently demanded a popular front, however. He was still rich, eccentric, vegetarian and ascetic but 'the practice of statesmanship'[4] had smothered the Marxist prophet and left a strangely neutered politician, one who came not by political passion but by personality alone to dominate the government, an able and ambitious individual who was to be the 'planner of the new order of social democracy'.[5]

The old guard was still in charge, and many of the same rebels were still challenging them. Chief among them was Bevan. During the war he had scandalized the British public, including Barbara,[6] by insisting that Churchill was fallible. He had repeatedly demanded an end to the coalition and an alliance of all left-of-centre parties to take on the Conservatives. At the 1944 Labour Party conference, delayed by D-Day until December, Bevan was elected to the NEC for the first time. At the same conference, a new rebel emerged: Ian Mikardo, the candidate for Reading – where he had once been so impressed by Ted and Barbara's double act in praise of Beveridge – called for the manifesto to include an explicit commitment to expand nationalization 'to the land, large-scale building, heavy industry and all forms of banking'. To the horror of Herbert Morrison, the custodian of a carefully inoffensive programme, the Mikardo resolution was carried overwhelmingly. The commitment was later watered down significantly, but the manifesto still pledged the government to nationalize coal, gas, electricity, steel, the railways, road haulage and the Bank of England.

Bevan thought the success of the Mikardo proposal 'a victory of cardinal importance'. Without state control, there could be no true socialism because there could be no planning. 'In practice it is impossible for the modern State to maintain an independent control over the decisions of big business. When the State extends its control over big business, big business moves in to control the State. The political decisions of the State become so important a part of the business transactions of the combines that it is a law of their survival that those decisions should suit the needs of profit-making. The State ceases to be the umpire. *It becomes the prize.*'[7] Bevan, who had argued that the war must be fought for the right reasons, now sought to impose on a nervous party leadership the will to ensure that it had been. During the war, Bevan had used *Tribune* to shape the left's expectations. He personified the determination to transform Britain, to see 1945 as a revolutionary moment, the moment when the 'ordinary man' could finally claim his dues and make democracy fulfil its potential. His pamphlet *Why Not Trust the Tories?*[8]

defined the role of the politician in educating the voter to exercise his power: 'He either steps back into the shadows of history once more or into the light of full social maturity. Property now rules with his permission. At any moment he can withhold it. But he must be brought to realise that he must either make the threat good or withdraw it altogether . . . The people must be brought to see that social affairs are in a bad state, because the people themselves have not clothed the bones of political democracy with the flesh of economic power.'

Bevan had replaced Mellor as Barbara's mentor. She regarded him as a 'poet' of politics, his socialism the embodiment of her own conviction that it must touch all of life, even its most mundane aspects. But the admiration was distant. On a personal level Bevan left her feeling small, provincial, under-educated. He was widely read in what he would call 'liberal literature'; he had a prodigious memory, a genius for phrase-making and a capacity for argument that equalled even Barbara's. She in her turn was all the things he was not: disciplined, studious, diligent and acutely tactical. It was said that Bevan 'couldn't stand' her. He and Jennie had been the only friends at her wedding, but it was not an intimate friendship.

Bevan's claim on a cabinet post was irresistible. Attlee made him Minister for Health and Housing. From that position, he could comment on the progress of the government as a whole only indirectly, through *Tribune*. Both Jennie Lee and Michael Foot (his closest political confidant and from 1948 *Tribune*'s editor) now sat on its editorial board. Never had the newspaper been read so carefully by so wide an audience. The conflict between the elderly, gradualist leadership and the young radicals only needed igniting.

Sir Stafford Cripps had become President of the Board of Trade, a vast department with over a hundred divisions, responsible for the global task of boosting Britain's overseas trade. During the war it had also acquired responsibility for administering the thousands of controls on imports, the direction of raw materials, and the production and output of every industry in the country. The task of the Board of Trade had been to ensure that all sectors involved in the war effort got as much as possible of what was needed, and to distribute the remainder fairly among consumers. In effect, the Board's regulations gave the state a say in every nook and cranny of daily life from dictating whether rubber should go to engineering or the manufac-ture of corsets, to deciding if machinery to make nylons or machine tools could be imported.

Sir Stafford invited Barbara to be his Parliamentary Private Secretary, a toehold on the lowest rung of the power ladder. She abandoned her resentment at his treatment of Mellor; to work for the man seen as the 'leading figure in the country'[9] as well as the senior left-winger in Cabinet was an offer she could scarcely refuse. It was an important but distant relationship. Cripps's workload was Stakhanovite. He told Barbara that she could see him at any time but that if she wanted to submit a paper to him it must be no longer than half a side (a rule also imposed by Attlee). He showed her what a good minister could do, if he was determined and confident. In a review of a biography of her old boss in *Tribune* in 1957, she wrote:

> Stafford Cripps was a moralist who purged his sense of guilt in politics . . . one of his weaknesses was that he tended to see himself as a messianic figure who, by a lightning tour of a continent or a factory, could personally solve problems that had grown stubborn with years. Humility was not his strong point. Cripps's great contribution was that he was unafraid . . . he was one of those rare ministers who dominate their departments and win civil servants over to novel policies . . . claiming the right to form his own judgements, he was prepared on principle to support the right of other people to form theirs and to campaign vigorously in support of them.

He may, in the public eye, have become a statesman, but he never became a disciplinarian, nor entirely lost his sense of fun. Once, on an official visit, he made Barbara eat a bowl of raw carrot provided by their hosts for their distinguished vegetarian guest – 'We mustn't hurt their feelings. Eat it up.' He left her, in hindsight, admiring: 'He could not be panicked out of his principles . . . he was a man of great political courage which found its highest fruition in party terms.'[10]

Barbara did her best with the job. Cripps was prepared to encourage her to contribute to office discussions and to let her see the workings of a department. He even invited her to contribute to policy formulation, until the departmental officials revolted. Barbara's admiration of Cripps was shared by another of the new intake, the youngest member of the government and one of Cripps's two junior ministers. Harold Wilson was six years younger than Barbara but an ambitious move by Cripps provided her with an early insight into his potential.

Cripps brought to politics a lack of guile bordering on the unworldly. After a desperate year for the government, on 9 September 1947 he sought an interview with the Prime Minister, where he informed Attlee that he should step down in favour of his Foreign Secretary, Ernest Bevin. He suggested that Bevin should also control a Ministry of Economic Affairs to coordinate the government's fraught efforts to plan and rebuild the post-war economy.

Attlee's response to this frontal assault was typically restrained. He merely suggested that it was Cripps, not himself, who should have a new job, and if he thought strong planning was necessary, then he must become Minister for Economic Affairs. Wilson would replace him as President of the Board of Trade, which would become one of the departments of Cripps's new economics empire. Before the change could be formally effected, Dalton was forced to resign as Chancellor after inadvertently disclosing some trivial budget information to John Carvel, political correspondent of the *London Evening Star*, before his budget speech. The information appeared in the newspaper before Dalton got to his feet in the Commons. Cripps became Chancellor of the Exchequer. He chose not to take Barbara with him – he told her he was sure she would not be interested – to his new posting, but assured her that Wilson would want her.

Barbara rebelled; she had already suffered the disappointment of seeing her fellow Blackburn MP, the smooth, handsome John Edwards,[11] promoted from being her co-PPS to junior minister in his own right. She went to tell Wilson she was resigning. Almost Wilson's first act as the new President and the youngest member of the Cabinet for 130 years was to soothe her and persuade her to stay on as his Parliamentary Private Secretary. It was the start of the most important political relationship in Barbara's career.

Barbara and Harold got on, developing a deeper bond than their shared Yorkshire, grammar school and Oxford background. Each recognized the other in themselves. Barbara described Harold as 'a mixture of dogged ambition and a lack of self-confidence'.[12] They were both driven, determined, competitive and ultimately a little insecure. Their alliance owed something to their sense of the snobbery of the public-school-educated Gaitskellites – and their successors, the Jenkinsites – against whom they would fight for the next fifteen years. 'We had no time for the products of softly-cushioned privilege,' scoffed Barbara. Both Barbara and Harold were clever, but they liked facts rather than intellectual argument, theatre rather than opera and not too much of either. Their Oxford had been circumscribed by academic effort and a shortage of cash. After his father lost his job, Harold had won a scholarship, which enabled his father to move to look for work. Both the Wilsons and the Castles lived modestly, and enjoyed modest, unpretentious pastimes. Gaitskell, who did not often trouble to notice Barbara, wrote of Wilson: 'You don't feel that really you could ever be close friends with him, or in fact that he would ever have any close friends . . . How different he is from John Strachey [a Communist-sympathizing cabinet minister], with whom one may often disagree but who is a real person with interests and feelings rising above politics, and with whom one can have that emotional and intellectual intercourse which is really the stuff of friendship.'[13]

The grandness and overt superiority of the public-school gang of Gaitskellites did not intimidate Wilson or Barbara; it infuriated them, it made them hostile and unreceptive to their ideas.

Harold and Barbara were not close socially. In fact Harold, with young children and a wife who hated politics, saw few parliamentary colleagues away from Westminster. Nor was it an equal partnership. Harold was always the stronger, the more successful, usually the better performer in the Commons. He was the cleverer of the two, the man with the best Oxford first of his year in PPE – a lifelong source of solace, even if it did not quite make up for failing to become a Fellow of All Souls. Barbara still preferred to forget her academic performance at Oxford. Harold was cool where Barbara was passionate; he was unemotional where Barbara was a romantic. Harold could remember reams of statistics; Barbara could quote pages of Shakespeare and Tennyson. Above all, Harold was 'political' as well as a left-winger. He would duck and weave, strike deals and make concessions. Barbara became his conscience, possessor of the bedrock of beliefs against which all policy was judged. It could make her appear judgemental and hectoring. Harold learnt to be relaxed and sometimes even witty. Barbara could administer a blistering put-down, but she never mastered relaxation.

Barbara complained that she always had to do the dreary business of sitting behind Harold in the Commons, while his other PPS, a Dundee MP called Tom Cook, went on interesting and, in post-war England, scarce foreign trips. As she had two prolonged stays in New York during this time, her complaints were less well-founded than it might seem. But in 1949 she finally persuaded Harold to take her on a long export promotion journey around Canada. His officials told her that it was the wrong trip for her to go on, that the Canadians' approach to women was highly conservative, but she insisted. As they had predicted, she spent the entire voyage by train and plane across Canada segregated from the business end of affairs, eating bad food, surrounded by dull women and trying to find British goods for sale in the shops (which was hard).[14] The excited reception the newspapers gave her may have been some compensation. She was variously described as 'vivacious', 'Titian-haired' and 'blue-eyed, neat and pleasant'. She confided to journalists that she was a 'little' older than Harold – thirty-seven, she said, when she was in fact thirty-eight, a birth date slippage which, as forty approached, tended to recur.

The trip also gave rise to much speculation, which lasted for the rest of their lives, about her relationship with Harold. Pictured on the trip, they look like Mr and Mrs Average from the New Britain. Harold is already a little plump, with a small, neat moustache (which went when he decided he looked old enough not to need it). His hair appears to be receding. Barbara is wearing an unusually unbecoming hat and a coy smile. Even close associates became convinced that there had been an affair, which Barbara went to great lengths to deny. She said Harold reminded her of Ted. He liked women, but he was 'not a philanderer'. (If she really believed that of Ted, she was alone in her opinion.) 'Certainly Harold never tried to seduce me. In the nearly forty years I worked with him all I can remember is one rather fumbling kiss. He liked a little flirtation but it was verbal rather than physical.' Barbara was a flirt too, and perhaps it was their style when together that misled her friends. On the other hand, the gossip could possibly have been true.

There is some circumstantial evidence. Preparing to write her autobiography in the late 1980s, Barbara taped an interview with William 'Billy' Hughes, an MP from 1945 until 1950 and thereafter Principal of Ruskin College. Discussing the affair between 'Red' Ellen Wilkinson and Herbert Morrison and Wilkinson's support for him in his abortive plot to challenge Attlee for the leadership in 1945, Barbara commented that having an affair with someone makes you likely to support them in leadership challenges. 'You should know, Barbara,' joked Hughes. 'Yes, I should, shouldn't I?' she responded, laughing. Barbara was to be one of Wilson's most prominent backers in his two bids for the leadership. In later life she was occasionally heard advocating to other women the merits of sleeping their way to the top.[15] She thought that how you got there mattered less than what you did once you had arrived.

Attlee had made the most of his landslide: the government was fulfilling its manifesto commitments with breathless haste. Coal and rail were nationalized; gas and electricity followed soon afterwards. Bevan, Minister for Housing and Health, had overcome the doctors' and the Tories' opposition, and the National Health Service Act was on the statute book. It was the economy that caught the government unawares.

On 6 August 1945, only five days after the new parliament met for the first time, the United States dropped the atomic bomb on Hiroshima; on the 9th, a second bomb was dropped on Nagasaki. On 14 August, Japan surrendered. A fortnight later, Attlee announced to the Commons that the Americans had taken the underpinning out from the British economy. Lend-Lease, the arrangement by which American raw materials and food were supplied for the Allied war effort, was ended. From that moment, the UK would have to pay dollars for all American goods, even those already shipped and in transit; and, after nearly six years of war, the UK was already facing a dollar famine. This should not have come as a surprise, for American law stated that the agreement ended the moment hostilities ceased. But no one had expected the war to end as quickly as it had. The Treasury had done no contingency planning. Between September and December 1945 a $4.6 billion loan was negotiated, but with an American administration deeply out of sympathy with the socialist economic policies of the Labour government, Britain had little bargaining power. Dalton, Chancellor of the Exchequer, feared 'an economic Dunkirk', but the terms of the loan could not be improved. Although it would provide dollars in the short term, this was at the cost of Britain being hurried into a fixed exchange rate with the dollar. There would be insufficient time and too few dollars for industry to invest and start producing again for the export market. Repayments would start in a year. There was a real danger that the economy would go into meltdown, as it had in the crisis of 1929–31 after the bankers had insisted that the pound could not be devalued. And it was all because of a foreign and defence policy many in the party opposed.

'The American Loan is primarily required to meet the political and military expenditure overseas,' wrote Sir Richard (Otto) Clarke, a Treasury official, noting a conversation with Maynard Keynes, who had negotiated it. 'If it were not for that, we could scrape through without excessive interruption of our domestic programme, if necessary by drawing largely on our reserves . . . the main consequences of the failure of the loan must, therefore, be a large-scale withdrawal on our part from international responsibilities.'[16] In a style typical of the whole Cabinet's casual approach to spending levels, Dalton made some efforts to secure defence cuts, and managed to get a 5 per cent reduction. Attlee called for a hastening of demobilization. Efforts were made to ease the manpower shortage, which in turn was slowing production. In the midst of the negotiations, Barbara made her maiden speech in the Commons, demanding that demobilization be speeded up. 'My own constituency of Blackburn has a big housing programme on which it wants to embark. It has educational reforms it wants to undertake. It has a cotton industry which needs textile workers.'[17] It was a competent maiden speech, dealing with a local issue with national implications, as the convention demanded. But it also indicated frustration at the slow pace of domestic economic expansion – the very thing now jeopardized by the outcome of the negotiations for the American loan.

There seemed little doubt that the stringent terms were motivated by

American hostility to Labour's nationalization programme. It was not the only aspect of British policy in which the Americans would indirectly intervene. The USA was determined that Britain should not retreat from its old imperial obligations, especially in Asia, and that it should share the burden of containing the Soviet Union there and in Europe. The left questioned the American analysis of Soviet Russia's expansionist aims, particularly once this was used as a justification for increasing British military spending at the expense of domestic programmes. At the heart of the argument, which was beginning to undermine the government, lay Britain's willingness to follow America's lead and to direct foreign policy, across the globe, towards containing Communism.

Barbara was strongly opposed to the loan. She believed that continuing wartime controls would allow the economy to survive without it and its crippling terms. She discussed her fears, briefly, with Cripps, who as one of the Cabinet 'Big Five' of Attlee, Bevin, Dalton, Morrison and Cripps himself, had been closely involved in the crisis that had preceded it. She told him her conscience would not let her support the loan. 'Your conscience is wrong,' he said. Nonetheless, Barbara went into the No lobby that night with about twenty other Labour colleagues. The left's anti-Americanism, which became such a destructive force in the 1960s and 1970s, was founded on the suspicion that there were American interests that wanted to destroy British socialism. 'It is clear,' the *New Statesman* declared, 'that on the matters that most affect Britain today, the United States is nearly as hostile to the aspirations of Socialist Britain as to the Soviet Union.'

Barbara, who had a tendency to believe herself unfairly treated, extended at will this sense of injustice to her cause. She always believed that the split that developed in Labour after 1946 need not have happened. It was 'their' fault – the fault at first of Attlee and especially of Bevin and his visceral anti-Communism, and later the fault of the Gaitskellites and especially Hugh Gaitskell's stubbornness and the determination of his clique to see him take the party leadership.

The centrality of foreign policy to the issue was exposed by the second significant political friend Barbara made among the 1945 intake: Richard Crossman. If Wilson was her obvious soulmate, Crossman could not have been less so. He was a product of just the privileged background that she disdained: the son of a High Court judge, and educated at Winchester, having taken a scholarship to Oxford he became a philosophy don – a post to which he had just acceded when Barbara came up herself. Unsurprisingly, the New College don with a particular interest in Plato and the impoverished St Hugh's undergraduate engrossed in practical politics had not encountered each other. Nor was their 1945 alliance immediate. Barbara observed grimly that Crossman regarded her as a 'junior' member of their group, and complained that his conversations were always tutorials. By the early 1950s, though, he was noting in his diary with approval that she was 'shrewd' and 'always had something interesting to say on any subject'.

Crossman was large and self-assured and very clever. He was also unreliable – 'double-Crossman', a man who was 'disliked and distrusted or liked and distrusted'. His socialism was, he said, prompted by a 'bump of irreverence'. He did not share Barbara's emotional commitment to the cause, nor did he ever understand the importance she attached to being loved by the party. He confessed to his wife Zita his surprise when he discovered that his amendment to the King's Speech in November 1946, which was to precipitate the divisions within the party, had aroused more than intellectual interest at the meeting at which it was discussed: 'I have been thinking about this for so long with my head that I had forgotten that other people have hearts and feel passionately.'[18] The very fact that he and Barbara were such opposites may have contributed to their friendship. Just as Barbara valued Ted's working-class parents, Crossman enjoyed the Castles' modesty of life. They were the acceptable face of a different class from his own, people whose instincts were different, but in whose company he could relax on equal terms.

Crossman, unlike Barbara, travelled light ideologically; it enabled him to see more. In November 1946 he had been in the United States, from where he reported in the column he wrote for the *Sunday Pictorial*: 'America may not be politically isolationist today, but she is economically isolationist. We in Britain should be foolish to count on any understanding or co-operation from this post-war America in facing our own difficulties. America believes in a free-for-all internally and externally.'

In fact, the Marshall Plan with its huge investment in Western Europe and Britain – and its stimulus to Europe to work in concert – was only months away. But it was the frame of mind that mattered. America was not going to do Britain any good turns; why, then, should British foreign policy be dictated by America, especially an America whose hysterical anti-Communism was exposing the British left to suspicion and vitriol? That same month, Crossman, with a small group of other left-wingers from which Barbara, as a PPS, was excluded, decided to table an amendment to the King's Speech spelling out an alternative foreign policy. It was the first breach of the general edict not to make trouble that had gone out from the leadership at the start of the parliament. The amendment called for the government to 'review and recast its conduct of international affairs so as to

afford the utmost encouragement to collaboration with all Nations and
Groups striving to provide a democratic and constructive alternative to an
otherwise inevitable conflict between American capitalism and Soviet communism'. Appearing to equate America and the Soviet Union was a clumsy
mistake, and Crossman himself was trounced by Attlee in the debate. Nonetheless, a hundred Labour backbenchers failed to vote for the government.

The excess of emotionalism over intellect demonstrated by this embarrassment inspired Crossman, together with Michael Foot and Ian Mikardo,
to retreat over the Easter of 1947 to the Crossman cottage in the Chilterns
to put together a coherent body of left-wing ideas. The result was *Keep Left*,
an energetic forty-seven-page pamphlet which exhorted the leadership to
'tell the people!'. 'Don't be afraid of party controversy. This is a socialist
revolution, not a National Savings Week.' The pamphlet was full of practical
suggestions, some of which were rapidly taken up. Cripps's idea for a
Minister of Economic Affairs, bringing together the Treasury and Board of
Trade had been one of *Keep Left*'s recommendations. (Equal pay and more
nurseries to help women back into the workforce would take about fifty
years longer.) The pamphlet warned against future loans, called for cuts in
luxury consumption and controls on raw materials and – in a passage
attributed to Crossman – a foreign policy built around Europe as a third
force. Europe, it was proposed, could be the solution to the real problem
between East and West. If Europe was used to contain Germany so that it
was in neither the Soviet nor the American sphere of influence, then
European security could be achieved, bringing with it all the economic
benefits of scaling down military obligations. Barbara, not invited to contribute to the pamphlet, was in total agreement with its views. *Keep Left* was the
spur for a small and disparate group of backbenchers to start to meet to
discuss the policies of the next Labour government. Barbara was among the
regular attenders.

The economic situation did not improve. Dalton, whose policy of cheap
money allied with controls Barbara thought adventurously socialist, had to
change tack. His colleagues, whom he dismissed as 'easy-going and muddle-
headed', failed to realize that the dollar well was capable of drying up. The
winter of 1946–7 was the worst in the century. British industry, which had
never lost output through fuel shortages during the war, now went on to
short time. The vital export boost was delayed. Still, spending continued to
rise. In July, convertibility with the dollar was introduced according to the
terms of the American loan; in August, it had to be suspended indefinitely.
In November, Cripps took over at the Treasury and Wilson took sole charge
of the Board of Trade. Then, suddenly, the pressure eased. 1948 was a boom

year, and with Marshall Aid in the pipeline, spirits lifted. So too did consumer pressure. Wartime controls, which had once been accepted in a mood of grim resignation, were becoming bitterly resented. There was a sordid case of bribery involving a minister in the Board of Trade itself, which served to illustrate the dangers of imposing a system on a public that no longer gave its consent.

Throughout the year, Wilson slowly eased the pressure: children's shoes, then all shoes, then furnishings were freed from controls. On 5 November, in a laborious piece of Wilsonian PR, over two hundred thousand further licences and permits were abolished in what Wilson claimed was a 'bonfire of controls'. Early the following year, clothes rationing, which had caused Barbara such grief when it came in, was finally ended.

Churlishly, Barbara was unimpressed. However she felt personally, she had come to realize the importance of controls in a socialist economy. The Keep Left group had been earnestly debating the issue. Their economic mentor, the Hungarian-born Tommy Balogh[19] – a constant in the shifting fortunes of the left – had convinced them that controls would always be necessary to influence the balance of trade, as an alternative to deflation and as a way of containing inflation. In defiance of her ministerial master Barbara wrote a pamphlet *Are Controls Necessary?* arguing that the only alternative to controls was to allow prices to rise and thereby undermine wage stability. Inflation would endanger the commitment to full employment. Controls *were* socialism. It was a popular view on the left, which looked askance at Wilson's enthusiasm for dismantling the regime.[20]

The left had reason to be anxious about Wilson's 'bonfire of controls', but its consequences were not those the left had predicted. In the boom of 1948, consumer demand had taken off. After ten years of restrictions on every aspect of domestic life, there was a hunger to spend. Industry could not keep up, and exports fell. At the same time, an American recession reduced demand in Britain's most important market. Meanwhile, public spending controls were almost non-existent: Cripps's exhortations to rein in were, like Dalton's, ignored, through either ignorance or incompetence. The British economy was heading for crisis, the first of a series which for the next half-century would come at shorter and shorter intervals. In July 1949 the decision was taken, in the greatest secrecy, to devalue the pound by 30 per cent. Devaluation would not take effect until mid-September.

Devaluation in itself was a political disaster for the government. It marked the end of what for the next two generations of Labour politicians were always the miracle years, the years that shaped post-war Britain. It was also a great blow to national prestige, with profound effects around the

world: a third of all the world's transactions were still conducted in sterling.
But the serious damage was done at home.

It is unlikely that the argument between the gradualists and the radicals
in the party could ever have been resolved peacefully. In just three years,
the bones of a programme which had been Labour's objective for the
previous ten had been made flesh. There would always have been vehement
debate about where to go next. It was devaluation, however, that set the
party's most powerful personalities against each other. It pulled the pin
from the grenade. The machinations between Harold Wilson and the two
other young economics ministers, Douglas Jay[21] and Hugh Gaitskell, in
the days before the final decision to devalue laid the groundwork for
much of the internal warfare which followed. These three young men had
been responsible for the economy, despite having just nine years in parliament between them, while the ailing Cripps took a cure in Zurich. First
Jay and then Gaitskell were converted to the need to devalue. Wilson,
however, was held to have trimmed and dithered over the decision, saying
different things to different people before finally accepting that it had to be
done. To inflame the personal tensions, it was clear that Cripps was too ill
to last much longer as Chancellor. Wilson was accused of allowing his
desire to be Cripps's successor to influence his judgement on a matter of
the greatest national importance. Whitehall turned against him. When
Cripps did finally retire, a year later, it was Gaitskell who succeeded to the
chancellorship.

After devaluation, deflation. The Treasury demanded cuts. Social security
spending was examined. Bevan, opposing his old ally Cripps, fought to
protect the NHS. He escaped the imposition of cuts in spending on health,
but was forced to abandon the principle of free prescriptions. The scene was
set for a much graver confrontation.

Only the first whisper of the need for cuts had reached Barbara. In early
September 1949, Barbara had set off to see for herself the isolationist,
materialistic, ideological enemy which, by contradiction, was home to the
embryonic new world government – the United Nations. She had been sent
as a delegate to the UN General Assembly. The delegates travelled across the
Atlantic in luxury on the *Queen Mary*, where Barbara fell in with a Texan
millionaire who invited her back to his ranch. New York fulfilled all her
expectations and confirmed her prejudices: it was a city without historical
charm, or even a river embankment. Worse, for Barbara, who was in mid-
Atlantic when devaluation was announced, nylons cost ten shillings a pair. 'I

don't like New York. It's garish, it has no roots; its geometric regularity
strikes a chill; it has only one, rather scruffy Central Park – there is nothing
to *do*,' she wrote to Ted. But the letter was swiftly followed by a postcard
requesting her jodhpurs (Ted had insisted she learn to ride on their honeymoon) so that she could ride in the park. To her dismay, she had been put
on the Assembly's Social Committee and her brief was world prostitution –
women's issues, she snorted. At first, the work struck her as 'detailed,
technical, exacting – and futile', but she soon realized its potential. For the
first time she had expert back-up – a team of young diplomats – to help
prepare a speech, and she loved it.

The General Assembly was a pressure valve for all the tensions building
between the Communist world and the West in the early days of the Cold
War. Barbara found herself in confrontation with the Soviet delegate, who
accused Britain of 'forcefully recruiting' Soviet citizens from German displaced persons camps and imprisoning them in Britain in Nazi-style work
camps instead of allowing them to fulfil their wish to return to the
motherland. The Associated Press agency picked up the story: 'Britain
accused the Soviet Union of using genocide, forced emigration and slave
labor as a matter of state policy,' its report read. 'The charges were hurled at
Russia in a vitriolic speech by British delegate Barbara Castle in the United
Nations Social Committee. Her speech was interrupted by Chairman Carlos
Stolk of Venezuela' – in his opinion she had overstepped the mark – 'just
after the youthful member of parliament had indignantly charged the Russian
rulers with having "a genocide habit of mind" which enabled them to wipe
out whole nations for the unproved crime of a few individuals.'

The assault – in marked contrast to her pre-war praise for Soviet
women's policies – assured her of the enthusiastic attentions of the press.
'Mrs Castle, a slim, pretty red-head in her early thirties [actually thirty-
seven], became flushed and excited as she piled up example after example to
back up the charges,' AP reported. The newspapers were just as excited. She
was sparkling 'with so much vitality you feel you'll get an electric charge if
you argue at closer range than [ten feet],' one reporter said, while the *Houston
Post* described her admiringly as 'more like a socialite than a socialist'.

Her energetic social life in New York left a lasting impression on the
diplomats who encountered her. There was salacious gossip about her
behaviour. She was taken to a film premiere by Britain's Permanent Representative to the UN, Sir Alexander Cadogan, and told Ted that she was
fighting off the attentions of admirers: 'May I whisper that some of [my
nights] are *voluntarily* lonely.' Hardly comforting for Ted sitting at home in
post-war austerity, waiting for the food parcel she had sent him ('The big

tins will feed *us*, small tins you,' she pointed out in case he should mis-
understand).

Ted and Barbara had been married for five years. They were hoping for
children, but children did not arrive. Barbara had been anxious after only a
couple of years; after four, she was sufficiently desperate to be prepared to
experiment with the pioneering fertility treatment then available. It was
intrusive, uncomfortable and demoralizing, so – she wrote later – they soon
abandoned the task and left it to nature. Some of Barbara's friends assumed
that she was suffering the after-effects of an abortion, but it was not uncommon
for married women in public life to be childless. Barbara, however made no
secret of her disappointment, and for a time it put a severe strain on her
marriage.

    But there were compensations. It is hard to envisage her unrelenting
devotion to politics or their hectic social life surviving motherhood. Ted,
who had no contact with his daughter from his first marriage, was an
enthusiastic host. He introduced Barbara to mass entertaining, specializing in
Christmas parties. In the days before Labour's family rows got too painful,
their guests were drawn from across the 1945 intake; James Callaghan (an
occasional visitor to the Keep Left fold) and the Prime Minister's right-wing
PPS Geoffrey de Freitas as well as the noisy, opinionated Keep Left group
were all invited. Michael Foot brought Jill Craigie, the film-maker he
married in 1949, who would berate another guest, Harold Wilson, for his
inadequate investment in the British film industry until Foot told her to stop.
The only person missing, usually, was Crossman, who disliked partying with
his colleagues.

    Barbara was far richer than she had ever been before. Ted had a good
job as assistant editor of *Picture Post*; she was earning £1,000 a year as an
MP, and topping it up with freelance journalism. They could afford to rent
a comfortable flat in North London and later a cottage in the Chilterns for
Ted's parents. One bank holiday weekend, she and Ted responded to a rail
strike by cycling from London to Stockbridge in Hampshire, a distance of
about seventy miles. Her other great passion was walking. They spent
holidays walking across southern England, and later, in the 1950s, travelling
to Yugoslavia. In 1946, Dalton had set up the National Land Fund with
£50 million to enable the state to accept land in lieu of death duties. He
saw land thus acquired for the National Trust or the Youth Hostel Association as a kind of national war memorial. In 1948 Tom Stephenson, the
secretary of the Ramblers' Association, invited Dalton and Barbara and a

small group of other MPs to walk part of what was to become the Pennine Way – three days and forty-five miles. Accompanied by a flattering number of reporters and photographers, Barbara in box-pleated tweeds leapt across the bog on the arm of Hugh Dalton. Ted was some way behind, the out-of-focus figure at the edge of the picture. Barbara wrote ecstatically in the *Spectator* afterwards:

> ' Is it worth it all? Why does one do this sort of thing? Here at last is the cairn and the answer – the cairn crowning the summit of 2,900 feet (the photographers dropped away a thousand feet ago), and the answer in the encircling view: the silver ribbon of the Solway, the Lakeland landmarks, Ullswater, Helvellyn and Langdale Pikes, the line of foothills passed on the way up two hours ago, and to the North, the Cheviot itself. Who would not walk with death and morning on the silver horns?[22]

The well-reported walks became annual events. Opening up the country to ramblers was, Barbara believed, part of the socialist mission to improve life in the round. The National Parks contributed with town and country planning as much as the health service in providing a decent quality of life for everyone. It was 'socialism in action'.

Barbara also took Ted off on camping holidays. They were her idea of utopian socialism made real, as she wrote of one holiday: 'How to have a holiday for 46/- a week per head: Robert Owen[23] would have approved of this holiday for, if it is to succeed, everyone must contribute his share to the little community. And everyone does, because the work is part of the fun. From the moment the morning sun winkles the sleepers out of their tents there are volunteers in abundance. While father lights the primus to make tea, someone fetches the milk; another couple carry water . . .'

The Enid Blyton tone sits improbably with Barbara the class warrior, who was beginning to emerge at Westminster as having a particularly savage dislike for Tories in general and Churchill in particular. One Tory newspaper found her so abrasive that it described her as 'something between La Vengeance and La Pompadour of the Barricades'.

Barbara was struggling to find a style in parliament. She could not escape playing to the novelty value of being a woman, and nor did she want to, however determined she was to avoid being corralled by 'women's issues'. Newspaper features clucked over her style and talked salaciously about her sex appeal. Later, one panting writer in the London *Evening Standard* would describe her as ranking with Marilyn Monroe and Zsa Zsa Gabor: 'It is a combination of animal magnetism, provocation and a challenging twinkle in the eye.' The press attention was hardly unsolicited. She dressed with provocative chic, and took infinite pains over her appearance. She wore hats into the Commons which caused such excitement, proceedings were interrupted. She was, after all, a journalist herself; she knew the cast of mind. Through Ted's link with *Picture Post*, she was commissioned to interview the Prime Minister for a lavish photo-spread, the kind of opportunity not often offered to backbenchers. It was as anodyne an exchange as one would expect from a new backbencher facing her own Prime Minister. There was just a sniff of a story in her suggestion that the government's foreign policy was less than socialist, a suggestion Attlee denied in his customary monosyllables.

Hugh Dalton, a hate figure for Barbara in the 1930s, was proving an amiable colleague in parliament – occasionally a little too amiable. Despite his reputation for being homosexual, she found his instincts 'normal enough'. Dalton also had a reputation for encouraging young talent, and Barbara was among those he thought worthy of encouraging.

But her apparent success did not endear her to all her colleagues, whether male or female. Nor did her single-minded pursuit of her interests. Barbara remembered doing the can-can with her friend, the Liberal MP Megan Lloyd George. People who knew her less well regarded her tongue with fear and her success in the media with hostility. 'In the early days of the 1945 parliament she did not have an easy time,' recalled the motherly Leah Manning, a veteran of the 1929–31 parliament. 'Her very success as a young member aroused jealousy . . . more than once, I found the girl . . . vulnerable and in tears in the Lady Members' room.'[24] There were sneers at the amount of time and effort she put into her appearance, and suggestions that the ladies' lavatory should be renamed 'Barbara's Castle'. Being a woman at Westminster was still largely uncharted territory. The difficulties went far beyond the inadequate facilities available. The place was full of men. Not only were there more than six hundred male MPs to twenty-four women, but almost all the staff were men too. When she was appointed Cripps's PPS, there was some astonishment in the press. How, people asked, could she do her job of finding out what backbenchers thought, when she could not go into the smoking room and talk to the chaps? Technically, of course, she could go into the smoking room, but she admitted it was not a comfortable atmosphere; few women ventured in.

Speaking in the Commons was the most difficult challenge, and one Barbara felt she never quite conquered. Public speaking was one thing; trying to keep the attention of several hundred men who wolf-whistled and jeered and heckled was quite another. Unsurprisingly, the woman who had survived as one of a tiny minority was unsympathetic to the complaints in 1997 of those women who came in with a hundred others.

One description in the *Herald* gives an indication of the struggle: 'A woman in a white frock stood undaunted for 20 minutes in the House of Commons last night against the concerted attempt of 200 Tory men MPs to shout and laugh her down.' Barbara's response to the trials of speaking in the Commons was to fight back, but it was impossible to fight without shouting. Shouting destroyed any attempt to sound reasonable, and she was accused of being coarse, shrill and vitriolic. One man, later one of her most senior officials, once saw her bump into Churchill in a corridor outside the chamber, which caused her to drop all her papers. The old man, applying his legendary charm, stooped to pick the papers up for her. 'Winston was due to go away to some international gathering, and in the most graceful way she wished him well . . . and I thought that was not at all in keeping with her behaviour in the Commons.'[25]

In 1950 the *Yorkshire Post*'s correspondent found her to be one of the best backbenchers in the Chamber. Commenting on her attempt to introduce a bill to extend the protection of common law to prostitutes (a result of her learning about the subject for her UN appearances), the *Post* declared she 'contrives successfully the difficult task of being a vocal woman MP without losing femininity – no easy task . . . but the House likes her best when she gets a bit waspish with Dr Edith Summerskill.[26] And this surely is a worthy achievement for a woman Member.'

Away from the Commons, Barbara presented herself as the committed housewife, cooking and cleaning and sewing on buttons, at the same time defending the right of women to go out to work. 'What is the attraction to women of work outside the home? It brings into their lives greater variety, more self-reliance, a sense of status, above all, economic independence,' she wrote in *John O'London's* weekly in 1952. 'If a woman is always given the menial jobs of life, is it to be wondered that her mind becomes a rubbish heap full of bits and pieces?' She could never quite disguise her view that women who stayed at home had rubbish heaps for minds. It did not endear her to the wives of colleagues, although most men would probably have agreed. However, she went out of her way to encourage all the women who worked with her to pursue their own careers. In the 1950s, the future Speaker of the House of Commons, Betty Boothroyd, was her secretary, while another future MP, Jo Richardson, ran the Keep Left group. There were many others.

Surviving in such a male-dominated environment only increased Barbara's desire to be judged as a success in that world. In the Commons, however, she found herself increasingly arguing for women's causes, not least because women's groups approached her to represent them. She was put on the committee scrutinizing the detail of the National Insurance Bill. With a left-wing colleague, she tabled dozens of amendments most of which she also moved. It was an area she already knew, and it required a diligent study of the detail, which she enjoyed. She fought for a lower pensionable age for spinsters on the ground that they had lost their potential husbands in the first world war. She also tried, and failed, to prevent married women being allowed to opt out of contributions to the National Insurance Scheme, fearing correctly that it would lead to millions of widows being left dependent on an inadequate pension if they outlived their husbands.

The Keep Left MPs were anxious about the post-devaluation cuts and the drift in government policy. An election was pending, a manifesto was being drafted. Barbara, Michael Foot and Richard Crossman wrote a follow-up to *Keep Left*, which was published in January 1950. Entitled *Keeping Left*, it is a statement of faith, its quasi-religious tone intensified by the evocation of one of the heroes of the English Civil War, Colonel Thomas Rains-borough: 'Really I think that the poorest he that is in England hath a life to live as the greatest he.'

Rainsborough's belief in equality was reflected in *Keeping Left*'s analysis of how to make democracy produce an egalitarian society. It is an owner's manual for those who have recently purchased democracy and now, imbued with a confident faith in the willingness of all the moving parts to cooperate, want to transform it from a form of government into a form of society. Read in the knowledge of what was to come, it is remarkable for its inoffensive and mainstream approach. It dealt in ringing phrases – 'Unemployment,' it declared uncompromisingly, 'is the industrial equivalent of capital punish-ment.' But it recognized that full employment also presented a challenge: '[Full employment] not only emancipates the worker; it lays upon him responsibilities which were previously the monopoly of the ruling class. Now it is the worker not the employer who has the whip hand in negotiations.' Consequently, there must be a 'recasting of economic and social relations' and 'socialised incentives to replace bankruptcy and unemployment'. It also recognized that economic realities had moved on since 1945. Nationalization was now less important than full employment and 'fair shares' as an aim – 'The last 4 years have taught us to distinguish aims from means.' Oxford economist Tommy Balogh had submitted a paper arguing that nationalization was not a panacea and was already tending to lead to inefficiency and bureaucracy. Its conclusions – a restatement of those of *Keep Left* – are less interesting than the light they shed on the way the left was working. The right of the party might dismiss the left's conclusions as utopianism, but they were ideas around which the party could unite. What was damaging was that on the eve of an election, the left chose to address the party rather than the country.

Barbara was a careful constituency MP. Her majority was narrow, and the electoral boundaries were being redrawn by the Boundary Commission. Until 1945, the link between constituencies and their MPs, especially Conservatives, was tenuous. In the first post-war government Labour had pioneered the idea of the constituency 'surgery', where the member was available once or twice a month to listen to their voters' problems. It was the kind of practical politics Barbara was good at and she enjoyed the social-work aspect of her job. But there was little she could do about her voters' biggest problem: the steady decline of the cotton industry and the consequent unemployment and low pay. Where there had, in 1920, been 145 mills employing 70 per cent of the workforce, by the 1960s fewer than 10 per cent of those with jobs worked in textiles. The population was falling, the housing stock was bad, social problems like drunkenness rife. In the late summer of 1946, Barbara had spent a week at Manchester College of Technology learning about the science of weaving, and another week alongside the women in one of the mills in her constituency. In 1949, she co-wrote a pamphlet setting out a regime of controls and investment to reinvigorate the industry. But cotton was dying, undermined by cheaper labour and higher investment in the Third World.

The Labour Party in Blackburn was under the control of two remarkable men: George Eddie, later Alderman Sir George Eddie, and Tom, later Lord, Taylor. Eddie was party agent for forty years, and for half of that time was also the leader of Blackburn Borough Council. He ran the party, which was a joint venture between the local unions – represented by the Trades Council, which was dominated by the Weavers' Union – and the ward parties. It became a highly efficient vote-winning machine, keeping Black-burn Borough Council uninterruptedly controlled by Labour for twenty-three years. In a trend newly popularized by the left, Barbara would report back to the Trades Council every month at a meeting attended by several hundred. The party was relatively well off, able in the days before MPs received travelling allowances to underwrite Barbara's election expenses and her train fares as well as retain an agent and an assistant. Its income came mainly from the Saturday night dances at St George's Hall in the huge civic centre that contained several different-sized halls and in which the police station was incorporated, which had the merit of making problems with

drunkenness rare. Labour and Conservatives were allowed the income from
the dances on twelve Saturdays each, the Liberals on two. Each weekend, up
to a thousand people queued all afternoon to get in at 2s 6d a head. Politics
in Blackburn was the beneficiary. Barbara was not required to get involved
in any of the detail of local organization, only to do what she was told by
her agent. It was not always an easy relationship. Roy Martin became the
assistant agent in 1948 and later succeeded Eddie as agent until, in 1968,
funds ran out as membership fell and the Saturday night dances gave in to
the challenge of the newly opened bingo hall. Martin remembered Barbara
completely losing her temper on one occasion and throwing herself on to
the floor, drumming her heels like a toddler in a tantrum. He also remembered Ted's response: 'Get up, you silly –.'

As his successor on the Council, Eddie chose Tom Taylor, a young man
whom he met through the local Congregational church. Taylor, who had an
even more uneasy relationship with Barbara than Roy Martin, not only
became leader of the Council but also chaired its education committee.
Controversially, he introduced special centres for recent immigrants – of
whom Blackburn's mills attracted thousands during the 1950s and 1960s –
where children studied until they knew enough English to be able to cope at
school. He also put a ceiling of 7 per cent on the number of immigrant
children in any one school, and bussed them around the town. He became
a major figure on the national education scene, and was later given a life
peerage by Callaghan, which did nothing to endear him to Barbara. Between
them, Eddie, Taylor and Martin controlled the town for nearly fifty years.

At the 1950 general election, the last remaining two-member constituencies like Blackburn were abolished; Blackburn was split into two. Blackburn Labour Party had to choose which of its MPs would be selected for the
safer of the two new seats. Barbara won. The other Blackburn MP, John
Edwards, once her fellow PPS and promoted over her, deserted for a safer
constituency. Nationally, in the general election in February, despite polling
a million and a half more votes than the Conservatives, Labour only scraped
back: its Commons majority was down to eight. It was an inauspicious
relaunch for a government from which the key players were disappearing,
defeated by age and long service: Bevin and Cripps were both very ill;
Dalton, although still in the government, was marginalized. The economy
was struggling, and worse lay ahead. The 1950 election was was one of those
Labour might have done better to have lost.

6. Fresh Thinking

This movement did not start yesterday. It is a very old one in its thinking. We do not need to go into conference to find out why we are here at all. You would have thought some of these people had only just arrived in the socialist movement. You would have thought that the history of the socialist movement began when they came into it. The history of the socialist movement looks as though it is beginning to end when they came into it.

Aneurin Bevan, Tribune rally, Manchester 1955

The relations within the parliamentary party and on the NEC now degenerated into a bitterness the party had never known before . . . looking back, I now accept that the Bevanite row helped to keep the party out of office for 13 years.

Barbara Castle, *Fighting All the Way*[1]

Two antagonistic personalities came close to destroying the Labour Party in the 1950s. For most of the ten years after the 1950 election, the visceral dislike of Bevan for Gaitskell ('He's nothing, nothing, nothing') and of Gaitskell for Bevan ('Bevanism is and only is a conspiracy to seize the leadership for Aneurin Bevan'[2]) divided the party into armed camps between which no civil exchange was possible. Ambition was a major factor in the struggle, but not the only one. Certainly, each thought he should be party leader, and was determined the other should not. But they were also the personification of the dilemma that still divides Labour: their conflict was a battle for the meaning and direction of the Labour Party, a fight to save it for government on the one hand and for socialism on the other. In the

1950s, Attlee's dogged determination to hang on to the job he had held since stepping in as a caretaker in 1935 prolonged and exacerbated the divisions.

The world in 1950 was already very different from the world at the end of the war. There were jobs to spare and a growing sense of economic security. The conditions that had appeared to make socialism inevitable now seemed to be dissolving. The Tories were coming to terms with the post-war settlement while Labour struggled with the problem of how to respond to an opposition that was no longer a bogey for ordinary working people, and to an electorate with only a fleeting interest in the politics of revolution. A slew of essays and books by the party's intellectual tendency reflected the struggle to come to terms with the fulfilment of a programme which had been ten years in preparation. These ideas became the new missiles in Labour's internal warfare.

Superficially, the Bevan–Gaitskell contest seemed just another round in the continual left–right tension that had marked the 1930s and 1940s. For Bevan, it was partly about their class and their experience – the two factors that made him a socialist leader and Gaitskell a careerist. His most scathing dismissal of Gaitskell, repeated in various forms but always fundamentally the same, was 'He's an intellectual. I'm a miner.' Gaitskell, a man with no roots in the movement, no experience of the working class, was incapable, Bevan believed, of being the same kind of socialist as he was. 'A young miner in a South Wales colliery, my concern was with the one practical question, where does power lie in this particular State of Great Britain and how can it be attained by the workers? ... It will be seen at once that the question formulated itself in a different fashion for us than it would have done in a new, pioneering society or in the mind of someone equipped by a long formal education. In such cases the question shapes itself in some such fashion as, "How can I get on?" '[3]

Gaitskell, in turn, believed profoundly that the Bevanite approach rendered the party unelectable and that Bevan could never be Prime Minister. 'I said in the middle of one of the discussions to Hugh Dalton, "It is really a fight for the soul of the Labour Party." More people understand that this was so now. But who will win it? No one can say as yet. I am afraid that if Bevan does we shall be out of power for years and years.'[4] He was convinced that in a two-party system elections had to be won on the middle ground. In later years, he had one eye on the Liberals as potential support. It was also his refusal to take refuge in woolly statements, his determination to say what he meant and mean what he said, that contributed to the depth and duration of the split. As Crossman remarked before the 1952 party conference, after he had taken advantage of their old acquaintanceship to parley privately with him, Gaitskell was stubborn to a degree. 'I could feel an obstinacy which I don't think was there two years ago, whenever an idea was broached which contradicted his idea of Labour policy.'[5]

The Bevanite struggles could not have happened had there not been a genuine, if exaggerated, conflict of views deeply held by significant minorities on both sides. It was the need to respond to the accommodation with capitalism, which Labour itself had engineered in government, that enabled the parliamentary party to draw itself up into factions behind their champions and to carry on the campaign as bitterly as their leaders. They were, as Roy Jenkins later observed with rueful elegance, cut off from one another: 'Bevan was petulant and vain but he was on the frontier of being a great man, and he was certainly a great talker and a great wit. To shut oneself off from any concourse with him was like forgoing the opportunity to talk to Fox or Disraeli.' Both Bevan and Gaitskell insisted that policy rather than personality was at issue but it soon became impossible to distinguish between the two. Every party election became a trial of strength. Every election had a candidate or a slate of candidates from each side. And every issue had a Bevanite approach or a Gaitskellite one. There were major casualties along the way. It became impossible to conduct rational debate about policy development. Much of the argument was carried on in the press. Editorially, the newspapers were all Gaitskellite, but the Bevanites had *Tribune* and the *New Statesman* as well as columnists in several of the mass-circulation papers. Journalists learnt to present every difference of emphasis within the party as a split. Free speech in the party suffered, and voters grew cynical. The currency of politics was devalued, and the tensions were never fully resolved. Like a forest fire not quite extinguished, they could revive at the drop of an insult.

Motivated by her admiration for Bevan and her sympathy for his policies, and almost equally by her personal dislike of Gaitskell, Barbara was at the epicentre of the Bevanite camp. It was the kind of politics in which she had grown up, watching her father plotting against a Conservative–Liberal pact in Bradford, arguing against the right in the Socialist League. For a romantic like Barbara, being a Bevanite was partly about being on a crusade, setting out to recapture the Jerusalem of the parliamentary leadership from the Gaitskellite infidel. By contrast, the Gaitskellites felt cornered, beleaguered, outnumbered. 'The very existence of the Bevanites and their popularity,' Crossman recorded Jenkins telling him late one night, 'was the major factor in making [Jenkins] loyal to Gaitskell. In the sort of hopeless fight Gaitskell was waging one had to stand by him . . . We on the right feel every force of demagogy and every emotion is against us.'[6]

The antagonism between Gaitskell and Bevan had been apparent before the election. When they were in Cabinet together again, it developed from anatagonism to hostility and finally to a bitter and irremediable breach. Attlee appeared to set out to offend Bevan, Gaitskell to confront him. Bevan would finally lose his nerve and his temper and behave unforgivably.

Back in office in 1950 with a tiny majority, a new election likely within a couple of years, the Attlee government limped on. 'We have office without authority or power,' Dalton sadly observed. And, he might have added, without any big ideas, or any majority with which to enact them. Instead, as tends to happen to governments without clear ambitions, this one was nearly overwhelmed by events. Ministers began badly disposed towards each other. The right – Attlee did nothing to discourage it – was inclined to blame Bevan for the small majority. During the campaign he had intemperately remarked that he hated the Tories, who in his mind were – in a phrase that became notorious – 'lower than vermin'. Attlee let it be known that he thought this indiscretion had cost them a million votes. Herbert Morrison claimed up to fifty seats had been lost. On a less personal note, Gaitskell thought the manifesto – which contained little beyond a renewal of the still unfulfilled commitment to nationalize steel – had been too radical. Bevan was equally convinced it had not been nearly radical enough. Attlee now proceeded to behave in such a way towards Bevan that a far less sensitive man than Bevan would have suspected conspiracy.

Bevan expected promotion. He had had five successful years as Minister for Health and Housing, he was now one of the most senior ministers still fit and well, and he had a huge following in the party. In particular, he would have liked to become Colonial Secretary. But all Attlee proposed – acting on Bevan's own recommendation – was splitting off his responsibilities for housing. Bevan would keep his role as Health Minister, but in charge of a smaller department. It looked like a calculated insult to Bevan. To the Keep Left group, not yet anything more than a huddle of supporters on the touchline, it was a sign that this new government was drifting away from socialism.

In March, within weeks of the election, the North Koreans invaded South Korea. American troops, under General Douglas MacArthur and with a UN mandate and British military support, launched a counterattack. MacArthur threatened to take the fight all the way into China in a further assault on Communism, a prospect that appalled the British left. The Americans now demanded a huge increase in military spending by Britain. The defence budget would have to rise by £100 million.

Any Treasury official casting a searching eye over the Whitehall spending departments would have picked out Bevan's health ministry. The hospital service of his new NHS was costing considerably more than predicted. There had had to be a series of supplementary estimates. Cripps, meanwhile, was still ill and Gaitskell was deputizing as Chancellor. Gaitskell, in common with most of the right, thought Bevan's NHS had been too ambitious and had no principled objection to the introduction of charges. He and Bevan had already been over the terrain once, after devaluation. Now he persuaded Cripps that, given the upward pressure on the health budget, charges were an appropriate way of saving money. Bevan made it plain it was a resignation matter for him. For the time being, the Treasury backed off. When Cripps's ill-health forced him to resign in October, there was little doubt that Gaitskell would succeed him. Wilson was disappointed to be eclipsed, but Bevan was furious that his own title to the job had been overlooked. He wrote to Attlee to warn him it was a betrayal of the party. 'I think the appointment of Gaitskell to be a great mistake. I should have thought it was essential to find out whether the holder of this great office would commend himself to the main elements and currents of opinion in the Party. After all, the policies which he will have to propound and carry out are bound to have the most profound and important repercussions throughout the movement.'[7] According-ing to Wilson's biographer Ben Pimlott, it was the senior civil servants who dictated the succession. Bevan, neither an economist nor an economics minister, would have been an unlikely candidate; a man who had fought to the point of resignation on budget cuts was an impossible one.

Instead of one of the three great offices of state, the home office, the treasury and the foreign office, Bevan was offered the Ministry of Labour. It was a sideways move to a department that would have thrown him into constant contact with his lifelong opponents in the trade union movement. For months he refused to move, only conceding defeat in January 1951. There is evidence that Gaitskell was anxious to have him replaced as Health Minister to ease the path of his budget plans. '[Bevan's move] might make a lot of difference to my financial policy. It is too early to speak but it may be the removal of the obstacle in the way of general economy in public expenditure.'[8]

The Americans were now pressing for another, even greater increase in the British defence budget. Gaitskell told Cabinet that another £1.1 billion – a 30 per cent increase – would have to be found. From the start, Bevan made it clear that he was uncomfortable with the proposal: he did not believe the defence industry could absorb so much investment all at once, and he thought it was the wrong thing to spend scarce resources on. However, his new role as Minister of Labour gave him responsibility for National Service. In a speech in February, he wound up for the goverment, defending an unpopular decision to extend National Service to two years. The debate ended with a substantial left-wing revolt against him. In the bitter arguments that followed, this speech was taken to be an endorsement of the rearmament programme.

The Korean War was not the only cataclysmic event to strike the Labour government that March. Terminal ill-health finally forced out the second of the government's Big Five, Ernest Bevin. Attlee needed a new Foreign Secretary. A braver Prime Minister – perhaps, it is said, the Attlee of 1945 – would have risked Bevan in the job, as many people later (much later) believed he should have. Instead, he gave it to Bevan's bitterest rival, Herbert Morrison. To see a lesser man take the job that he wanted and for which he believed himself well fitted was a shattering blow to Bevan. It was not the only one. That same month, Gaitskell told a cabinet subcommittee what further cuts he had in mind to meet the cost of rearmament. His budget would include dental and opticians' charges and prescription charges. Bevan, backed by Wilson at the Board of Trade, said again that protecting the principle of a free health service was a resigning matter. Gaitskell retorted that if he was not allowed the charges, then *he* would resign. In negotiation with a dying Bevin, standing in for Attlee who was in hospital, Gaitskell conceded prescription charges, while disarming further criticism by balancing the £23 million raised from what came to be known as 'teeth'n'specs' charges with an increase in old age pensions.

For days, Bevan teetered on the brink of resignation. He interpreted, probably correctly, Gaitskell's decision as a personal attack. 'Am I not worth £23 million?' he demanded angrily. Some of his closest friends tried to persuade him to stay. John Freeman, a junior minister and later a leading Bevanite until he resigned to go to the *New Statesman* in 1955, told him to wait for a bigger issue. Attlee, still in hospital, sent a message telling him to 'think of the Movement'.[9] Significantly, James Callaghan led a deputation of junior ministers to warn him against being seen as the man who divided the party: 'We know the Party's interests will only be served if we *all* go into a general election together.'[10] Jennie Lee, however, and Michael Foot both thought he should go. Their counsel was decisive. On 22 April 1951, twelve days after the budget introducing the charges had been unveiled, Bevan finally resigned. Harold Wilson and John Freeman resigned with him.

It was immediately and damagingly apparent that Bevan had resigned on an issue about which the parliamentary party was not greatly exercised. Gaitskell's budget, in which the charges were announced, was generally regarded as a brilliant success, and its author 'an acknowledged star' and 'a new force in politics'.[11] Bevan was rattled. In an inchoate personal statement to the House, he turned his intemperate invective against Gaitskell. Barbara later wrote glumly: 'The Keep Left group had acquired a leader who would put us on the political map but at a heavy price.'[12] Once Bevan had resigned, his cheerleaders in the Keep Left group would become a Bevanite group, his private army. Gaitskell, history strongly suggests, deliberately forced Bevan out of government. But at that stage there were no Gaitskellites, and it was Bevan and the Bevanites who were seen by the press and by the parliamentary party as the wreckers, and it was a perception that never changed.

For the next few days Bevan did nothing to help himself. At his first PLP meeting after his resignation, under some provocation from Gaitskell who repeatedly and wrongly claimed that Bevan had not objected in Cabinet to increased arms spending, he lost his temper. A young and impressionable Tony Benn, at that point rather taken with Gaitskell, recorded the meeting: 'When Nye rose he shook with rage and screamed, shaking and pointing and pivoting his body back and forth on his feet. His hair came down, his eyes blazed and I thought at times that he would either hit someone or collapse with a fit. The spectacle absorbed us completely. He accused Gaitskell of a reckless frivolity of argument. He screamed, "I have been martyred by the platform", a tragic insight into his persecution-ridden mind that shocked us all.'[13]

Meanwhile, Harold Wilson's personal statement was a carefully constructed explanation of the reasons behind his decision to resign. Barbara was struck: 'As I listened to him I realised once again that this backrooom boy had developed into a skilled strategist. This man, I told myself, is hell-bent on the leadership ... Nye never trusted Harold again.'[14] Wilson – less charitably described by Roy Jenkins as 'a bureaucrat turned opportunist'[15] and by Hugh Dalton as 'Nye's little dog' (sometimes just 'dog') – was, at least in Barbara's hindsight, already beginning to eclipse Bevan as a man of action. At the time, however, Barbara regarded Wilson, despite their former relationship as minister and PPS which ended only with Wilson's resignation, as a rival. It was mutual. While Harold had been travelling the world largely invisible except to readers of the financial press, Barbara had been establishing her reputation in the party; frustrated, like other able left-wingers such as Richard Crossman, by Attlee's refusal to promote her, she and others on the left set about establishing themselves in the highest echelons of the party.

Barbara had been trying to get on to the National Executive Committee for almost as long as she had been an MP. The NEC was a relatively unimportant body when Labour was in government. In opposition, however, it played the central role. In effect, it was the party's board of directors, controlling policy development, publicity and organization. Elected annually at the party conference, membership was almost entirely in the gift of the block votes of trade unions, which were counted in millions. Individual party members could elect their nominees to just seven of the twenty-nine places. In 1946, Barbara had overcome her distaste for the separation of women from the mainstream of party activity and run for the women's section. It was clear from her result – 800,000 votes below the lowest vote of the four elected – that there was no point in running again without a union alliance behind her. In 1949 she made a well received speech to conference about the need for financial controls, at which the Durham miners' leader Sam Watson (one of the few trade union leaders of whom Bevan approved) offered her his support if she would stand the following year. In 1950 she was duly elected – in absentia, since she was on her second visit to the UN – to the women's section.

Barbara did not allow the fact she had union backing to inhibit her views. In particular, the pamphlet *Keeping Left* had contained a violent attack on the way trade unions were run, including a passage referring to 'the mutual back-scratching jobbery of the type that decides the election of the women members of the Party's National Executive'.[16] She was clearly not going to get union backing again. Moreover, by the run-up to the 1951 conference, the Bevanites were preparing their own slate for the constituency section of the party. If she was to establish herself as a senior member of the team, Barbara would have to be on that slate. Wilson argued that he would have a better chance, and she should stand down for him. Barbara would not, she said. She discussed it with Dalton as they walked together on the fourth of their hikes to promote access to the countryside. Dalton, who had no love for Wilson, 'encouraged her to refuse'. In the event, they both stood.

The 1951 party conference was the making of the Bevanites. Before it, they were a loose grouping, open to such disparate pamphleteering talents as Roy Jenkins and Jim Callaghan. After the conference they became a threat, a destabilizing force, feared and distrusted. The hegemony of the trade unions and the parliamentary party was rudely challenged by the ordinary party members, irresponsibly led – in the eyes of the right – by a self-promoting bunch of 'frustrated journalists'. The result of the elections to the National Executive came as a thunderbolt, and not only to the right. The fact that Bevan was elected top in the constituency section was not the startling development – it was that Barbara had come second. This was an astonishing personal triumph. She was the first – and for sixteen years (she was elected every year until 1979) the only – woman to succeed in the constituency section. It was her first attempt, a confirmation of her judgement as well as her appeal. It catapulted her from the inside pages of *Tribune* to the front rank of the left and the front pages of the national newspapers – 'Bevan's new lieutenant', pictured smiling confidently at Bevan, who has one hand gingerly on her shoulder. Two other Bevanites, Ian Mikardo and Tom Driberg, the eccentric, rampantly homosexual former 'William Hickey', were also elected. Only Herbert Morrison, Hugh Dalton and Jim Griffiths remained from the old leadership. An admirer sent her a limerick:

> There was a young redhead named Barbara
> Who charmed all the conference at Scarborough
> Her poll was so high
> She came second to Nye
> Now Dalton will no longer 'harbour her'.

Had it not been for the imminence of the general election, the struggle might have begun immediately.

Labour fought the 1951 general election, which came immediately after the party conference, from a position of weakness and uncertainty. The voters, still subject to many wartime controls six years into the peace, were restive; Labour won more votes than it has ever done before or since, but the Conservatives were returned, with a majority of just seventeen. It seemed possible that the Tories might not be able to last a full term, and in the battle that now broke out there were often faint cries of warning of the alienating effect of division, on the voters, emanating from those whose gaze was not focused on the enemy on their own benches.

The Bevanites were yet to become the coherent group that their detractors were already denouncing. Crossman and Freeman considered ending 'the pre-election controversy' then and there, and would have liked Bevan to go into the shadow cabinet (then called the parliamentary committee). Bevan, however, had decided that he wanted to be free to speak. The matter was not discussed further. The episode defines the nature of the relationship between Bevan and the Bevanites. Each needed the other, but they rarely worked in partnership. Occasionally it would be Bevan who would move in their direction. More often, he would unexpectedly make a stand on an issue and the Bevanites would rush to line up behind him. Over the next few years the rush slowed and the numbers diminished until Bevan found himself almost alone. But for the year from the election defeat in October 1951 until the group was compelled to disband in late 1952, the two were more in harmony than at any other time. Barbara was personally closer to Bevan's approach to politics than other, more intellectual Bevanites. She was drawn to his romanticism and his passion; but she shared their frustration with Bevan's apparent desire to achieve ends without willing the means.

Internal party tolerance was a commodity highly valued yet repeatedly challenged by the left. The right came to see it as a disaster. It was a matter of pride that the party's standing orders had been suspended in 1946, allowing backbenchers to vote against the government without serious fear of reprimand throughout the parliament, an arrangement which had allowed Barbara to survive as a PPS despite taking part in revolts which in more regulated days would have forced her to resign. Such tolerance was intended as a recognition that there were no longer organized factions. Arguably, to some extent it delayed their formation. However, Bevan – who had, of course, been expelled once already, in 1938–9 – and Barbara in particular had reason to remember that the Socialist League had been disbanded in order to avoid expulsion for being 'a party within a party'. At some point, it was likely that the Bevanites were going to hit the same buffers.

In December 1951 around twenty Bevanites, including Barbara, arrived at Buscot Park in Oxfordshire, home of their most wealthy supporter, Gavin, Lord Faringdon, for the first of what became frequent if irregular policy weekends. Buscot Park had before the war been the lavish seat of a railway baron, with liveried footmen and a fleet of 'pea-green Rolls-Royces',[17] but by this time was somewhat reduced in grandeur. Only one of the Rolls-Royces remained. The 'conference', as described by Crossman, illustrates both the relationship between Bevan and the group and the attraction Bevan had for Barbara.

Nye has a tendency to regard as defeatist anyone who states [difficult] facts. Yet under the pressure of discussion he reacts extremely well and suddenly, on Saturday evening after trying at dinner to get out of having an evening discussion, he got interested when we forced one on him. He began to consider seriously the practical ways of facing these long-term problems [the defence budget and the economy]. Even here, however, he slipped into believing that a powerful debating point is a solution to a problem . . . The Group indeed was a bit scared of facing facts for fear of finding the problems insoluble. Of course, it may well be that the problems *are* insoluble – this is a type of philosophic fatalism which I find acceptable enough but which Nye, as a sensible politician, instinctively rejects, as does Barbara Castle. A certain amount of utopianism is really essential. The question is whether you can control it, and keep it within reasonable bounds.[18]

The Buscot weekends were a mix of earnest debate on world events and future domestic policy, and boozy games of snooker; they were almost as social as political. The regular Bevanite meetings were, in the eyes of the party managers at Westminster, more compromising. They took place every Tuesday lunchtime in the comfortable surroundings of Crossman's house in Vincent Square, a ten-minute walk from the House of Commons. In the Keep Left days, these were intimate, relaxed events that focused on future policy. During 1952 they became increasingly preoccupied with the conduct of their political campaign, deciding positions to be taken on forthcoming debates and how the group should vote. Barbara was a regular, with a seat beside the fire that she regarded as her own. Bevan, who hated policy discussion, was decidedly irregular. He, alone of the Bevanites, had been in parliament in the 1930s. He had a better feel for what was acceptable to the leadership, and he was aware of the damage already done to his prospects by appearing schismatic.

It was in foreign and defence policy that Bevanism came closest to being an original and coherent doctrine, owing more to Bevan than to the efforts of his disciples. This was only partly because its impact, in the form of rocketing defence expenditure, was so burdensome on the domestic agenda. Bevan was convinced that the reaction of the West to the Russian Revolution of 1917 had forced Russia in on itself and corrupted its ambitions. He feared the West was having the same effect on China, after *its* revolution in 1948. He also doubted the American conviction that China was inescapably a Soviet sphere of influence, and – economic determinist that he was – he gravely and reasonably questioned the Soviet Union's capacity to fight the kind of war in the West for which America was insisting on British preparedness. Moreover Bevan and the Bevanites, who so often argued about detail and even basic analysis, shared the conviction that confrontation would merely provoke more confrontation. In short, the Bevanites refused to accept the whole substructure of British foreign policy. In their view, a mistaken interpretation of the world situation was forcing Britain economically and militarily into the arms of an America that had already proved itself threateningly hostile to British socialist objectives.

One of the debates at Buscot had been on the defence budget. In March 1952, parliament held the annual vote on the defence estimates. This triggered events demonstrating either malicious intent by the leadership or, more charitably, a wilful misunderstanding of Bevanite sensibilities and of what strength, on this issue at least, Bevan could command.

Churchill, now back in No. 10, had announced that the rearmament programme would have to be spread over four years, rather than three. He confirmed (pointedly and with delight) Bevan's thesis that Gaitskell's rate of spending was unsustainable. The Labour leadership, apparently genuinely believing it was making a conciliatory gesture to the Bevanites, proposed an amendment accepting the Tory programme (which was, after all, its own) but doubting the government's ability to achieve it. The party line was to abstain on the government's motion and, of course, to vote for the party amendment. In effect, it was asking Bevan, Wilson and Freeman to support the policy over which they had resigned. The Bevanites were affronted, and rebelled. They abstained on the party amendment, and voted against the government. In total, fifty-seven Labour backbenchers recorded their support for Bevan's position. After the vote, they marched back into the Commons together, a direct challenge to the leadership that could not be allowed to pass. Crossman – in a letter which was mysteriously treated as an ultimatum – had tried to persuade Attlee to modify the party line on the grounds that both international and economic circumstances had changed. He had feared 'the press would hardly notice' their stand. Instead, it was splashed across all the front pages and there was excited talk of expulsions. Bevan, veering dramatically away from his former caution about schism, exacerbated attitudes by announcing that he would not be bound over to toe the party line, and privately he and Foot talked rather wildly about setting up an alternative socialist party.[19]

Whatever Bevan and Foot felt, the Bevanites did not want to be expelled. Barbara was appalled. She and Wilson both counselled caution. Crossman resolved to give no one an excuse to expel him.[20] Attlee – assumed to be in hock to the trade union leadership and the shadow cabinet – felt he had to assert his authority, even at the risk of expulsions. Some of Bevan's closest supporters suspected the intention was to drive out the hard core: 'To expel fifty-seven would disrupt the Party; to expel five or six might be its salvation.'[21] At the PLP meeting the following Tuesday, there was vehement confrontation as Attlee proposed the reimposition of standing orders and a pledge from every member to abide by majority decisions. To Attlee's chagrin, the mood of the party was for peace rather than revenge. A conciliatory motion calling only for the introduction of a redrafted set of standing orders was overwhelmingly supported. The Bevanites had a few more months of freedom.

In April, compounding the suspicions about his ambitions for the leadership, Bevan published a political testament. The expulsion threat had been ideal advance publicity; a publishing sensation was predicted. In the event, *In Place of Fear* was badly reviewed and contributed little to the future debate about the direction of the Labour Party. Bevan had written it in a hurry, during the months since his resignation (although he had first started working on it towards the end of the war), and he had shown it to neither Crossman nor even Michael Foot, both brilliant polemicists and loyal supporters. The book sold well – 36,000 copies – but not nearly as well as *One Way Only*, the third of the Keep Left pamphlets, which appeared soon after the resignations of Bevan, Wilson and Freeman, with a foreword by Bevan, and sold 100,000 copies. It is an indication of her emotional, utopian approach to theoretical politics that Barbara – diamond-hard in her analysis of practical problems, rigorous in argument – found in *In Place of Fear* the apotheosis of her socialist faith. It became her holy writ, a source of inspiration for the rest of her life. It also provided her, fifteen years later, with the inspiration for the title of her own most ambitious project – to reform trade union law – which she called *In Place of Strife*.

Bevan may have hoped *In Place of Fear* would silence the sneers of the intellectuals. It is a sweeping, emotive, blurred canvas with some sharply penetrating insights, especially into the developing world and the impact of the appropriation of resources by the West, an issue he brought into public debate. 'Soon, if we are not more prudent, millions of people will be watching each other starve to death through expensive television sets.'[22] The critics accused Bevan of ignoring his own warning about becoming a prisoner of the past. 'We seek to imprison reality in our description of it. Soon . . . we become the prisoners of the description . . . our ideas degenerate into a kind of folk-lore . . . As we fumble with outworn categories our political vitality is sucked away and we stumble from one situation to another.' Critics searched in vain for tangible ideas about how socialism, its origins now described, might develop. Loyalists described the book as setting a mood, as the utopian socialist William Morris had in 1890 set a mood in his novel *News from Nowhere*. Bevan had once chosen as his epitaph a Morris verse:[23]

> Rest, comrade, rest.
> Cull we sad flowers to lay on your sad breast:
> There till the world awakes to love, we leave you:
> Rest, comrade, rest.

Barbara, who had read Morris both at home and under the tutelage of William Mellor, shared Bevan's love of Morris's nostalgic romanticism. Heavily underlined in her own edition of *In Place of Fear* (signed, but without a message, by the author) is Bevan's description of the character of democratic socialism:

The philosophy of democratic socialism is essentially cool in temper. It sees society in its context with nature and is conscious of the limitations imposed by physical conditions. It sees the individual in his context with society and is therefore compassionate and tolerant. Because it knows that all political action must be a choice between a number of possible alternatives it eschews all absolute prescriptions and final decisions. Consequently it is not able to offer the thrill of the complete abandonment of private judgement, which is the allure of modern Soviet Communism and of Fascism, its running mate.[24]

Bathos? Or 'the most apt and memorable' hymn to democratic socialism ever written? Foot believed the latter. Bevan's more recent and less partisan biographer John Campbell disagrees. He describes it as 'a sad confession of political bankruptcy. On this evidence Bevanism, if it was dependent on Bevan himself for inspiration, was a road that led nowhere. Socialism was still the shining city on a hill; the emerging compromise of welfare capitalism was a sell-out; but Bevan could offer no route forward from one to the other, only an appeal to faith.'[25]

The summer session of parliament in 1952 was dominated, it was generally recognized, by the Bevanites. Barbara took little part in the big set-piece attacks on government policy. She was respected as a tough debater, but she never felt comfortable in the kind of broad, sweeping attack that Bevan in particular, but also Crossman and increasingly Wilson, could pull off. The right of the party viewed their success with hostility; but it was not their legitimate activity in the Commons that alarmed them as much as the triumph of an experiment in grass-roots education out in the provinces.

At the 1950 conference in Margate, Ian Mikardo and a handful of other left-wingers had organized a Tribunite brains trust – a panel of four speakers who answered questions from the floor. It was a straight copy of a successful radio programme. The idea immediately took off, and panels were dispatched to constituencies around the country, sometimes at the rate of three or four a week. This was Barbara's forte, and provides one explanation of her unpredicted triumph in the constituency section of the 1951 conference. Each week she appeared in front of up to a thousand party activists, the same kind of audience of enthusiastic party workers that she had already learnt to handle so brilliantly at the party conference:

The 'star' turn was, as one would expect from a successful television performer, auburn-haired Mrs Barbara Castle. Mrs Castle is a master – or should it be mistress – of emotional appeal. As an effort in demagogy [her definition of socialism] had its merits. It was almost a breath-taking piece of rhetoric, brimful of sentimentality, yet strident in its denunciating passages of those who do not conform to the Socialist conception of life and the way of living. It got the longest and loudest applause of the night.[26]

The panel toured the country either in the red van that *Tribune* acquired specially for the purpose, or occasionally in Gavin Faringdon's remaining pea-green Rolls-Royce. Mikardo organized the panels and often chaired them. He divided the participants into categories: there were 'natural teachers' like Wilson and Crossman, advocates like the MPs Geoffrey Bing and Julius Silverman, and six others 'who had the gift of words not merely to educate and convince but also to inspire'.[27] Barbara was one of those. Even on the 'Costa Geriatrica' in Worthing, a crowd of of nine hundred turned up. 'They queued and paid,' said Mikardo, 'because they believed what we believed and they got from us the evidence to confirm and reinforce that belief.'

In August 1952, for the first time the Bevanites were written up by a journalist as a 'party within a party'. The brains trusts with their money-making activities constituted one part of the charge. The second was 'their' newspaper, *Tribune*. *Tribune*, which had been edited by Michael Foot since 1948 and now had both Bevan and Jennie Lee on the editorial board, was (in the narrow terms of a party newspaper) going from strength to strength. In 1951 it had been a paper to which Roy Jenkins contributed fairly frequently. Now it carried the Bevanite line, often vehemently stated, into hundreds of constituencies; at its height, it had a circulation of 18,000. It was an energetic critic of the party leadership, freely discussing events on the National Executive as well as promoting the brains trusts; perhaps most dangerously, it carried model resolutions on current issues for local parties to table for debate at conference.

By the end of September, when the party gathered in Morecambe for the annual conference, both leadership and rank and file were in a state of heightened tension, fed by headlines in the Sunday papers such as 'End the Bevan Myth'.[28] The leadership knew it was in for a difficult week, and already suspected the left of underhand organization. Herbert Morrison, who had been approached by Ted Castle for help in finding a seat, wrote back telling him he would do what he could – but only if Ted stopped 'stirring up' trouble by running an NEC slate. On the Monday, the first full day, there were unprecedented scenes when ballot papers for the NEC election were issued. 'Practically the whole hall was emptied and a football scrum poured into the room outside . . . normally at Conference the Executive has to appeal every hour during the afternoon to delegates to take up their voting papers. This year there was no need. They all knew what they had come for.'[29]

The results were announced the next day. The Bevanites had nearly swept the board in the constituency section, taking six of the seven seats: Barbara was second to Bevan again, and Wilson and Crossman were both elected too. Dalton and Morrison were off. (Several months later, Ted, trying to impress Dalton, admitted that constituencies had been told to vote for the four Bevanites and no one else. He offered to get Dalton back on the NEC at the next elections.) The exile of the two old-timers was greeted with cheers and catcalls. The conference, even Foot admitted, was 'rowdy, convulsive, vulgar, splenetic; threatening at times to collapse into an irretrievable brawl'.[30] Dalton, understandably, was even less charmed by it: 'This was the worst Labour Party Conference, for bad temper and general hatred, since 1926, the year of the General Strike.' The NEC elections were not the end of the matter. Conference proceeded to accept several Bevanite resolutions, including a big increase in the nationalization programme.

This was not, the right felt – and probably some of the left agreed – any way to run a party. The following weekend Gaitskell, who had been third runner-up, sharply escalated the conflict in a speech at Stalybridge near Manchester which amounted to a declaration of war. He alleged infiltration and attacked *Tribune* for creating a climate in which it was possible. As many as a sixth of the delegates at conference were 'Communist or Communist-controlled', he said. Then, anticipating what was to become a familiar theme as he endured repeated rebuffs by conference: 'Let no one say that in exercising the right of reply to Bevanites we are endangering the unity of the Party. For there will be no unity on the terms dictated by *Tribune*. Indeed its very existence so long as its pages are devoted to so much vitriolic abuse of the Party Leaders is an invitation to disloyalty and disunity. It is time to end the attempt at mob rule by a group of frustrated journalists and restore the authority and leadership of the solid and sensible majority of the Movement.'

As soon as MPs returned to Westminster, Attlee joined the attack. 'Drop it. Stop this sectionalism. Work with the team. Turn your guns on the enemy not your friends.'[31] A resolution was tabled, calling for the 'immediate abandonment of all group organisations within the Party other than those officially recognised'.[32] Bevan immediately, and without consulting any of his so-called party, announced the dissolution of his group in the columns of *Tribune*. 'To continue the Group now is to perpetuate schism,' he told Crossman. 'If you were to continue the Group in these conditions and I were the Leader, I would have you expelled. The Group is intolerable.'[33]

But others argued that it would be a betrayal of all the activists who had supported them at conference. A compromise was agreed: to throw the Bevanite meetings open. At the key party meeting on the resolution, to take place on 23 October, Barbara, together with John Freeman, sought to try to get consideration of the resolution delayed until after the shadow cabinet elections, when its new members could consider it.[34] Attlee forestalled them, and the vote to disband the Bevanites was carried by 188 to 51.

Bevan chose to underline his new determination to be loyal by standing for the deputy leadership against Morrison and was defeated by 194 to 82. He was, however, elected to the shadow cabinet – but only just. He was bottom of the twelve, the only Bevanite, sentenced – as Michael Foot saw it – to 'incarceration by his own hand'.[35] On the face of it, the battle was over. The party leadership had reasserted its authority, the party conference had been overruled. The *status quo ante bellum* was safely restored.

Barbara's role had been peripheral in the arguments over tactics. Her instinct, as it had been fifteen years earlier in the dispute over the Socialist League, was to play for caution. In the aftermath of the defence revolt, she had advised against forcing the issue; after Morecambe, she again recommended delay and further discussion. Her behaviour contrasted with her growing public reputation for impetuosity and rabble-rousing. 'How can you be taken seriously when the alternative Labour leadership consists of Tom Driberg and Barbara Castle?' Crossman was asked.[36] In a fragment of diary, Barbara recorded: 'I am in trouble for a reply at last weekend's brains trust at Lowestoft.' It was the day of the Queen's coronation, 2 June.

> I said I didn't see what all the fuss was about as the Queen had been exercising her powers perfectly satisfactorily for the last 18 months. I said I hoped this would be the last Coronation of its kind we should see, it was so unrepresentative of ordinary people . . . I think there is no doubt this is a minority view, even among the working class . . . as I write this the Queen's correct & piping girlish voice is enunciating the formulae of dedication; Winston has just introduced her on the radio, exploiting the romantic mood of the moment to its fruitiest uttermost.

No doubt it was what she thought, but it looked even to her friends on the left like another example of the avid garnering of personal publicity with which she had come to be associated. She wore attention-seeking hats. She presented herself as Mrs Castle, Ted's cook and housekeeper, the housewife next door, when they had in fact employed a housekeeper since they married. In part, it was an attempt to meet the prejudices of the press, which regarded as peculiar in a woman her capacity to handle complex issues with authority. In May 1953, for the first time, she was invited to speak at the Durham Miners' Gala, a high accolade of throbbing emotion. Until the death of the coal industry, the Gala was an annual event of almost unparalleled importance in the Labour calendar. 'Up early to watch the incredible procession [of miners and their banners] from the balcony: it lasted over 3 hrs & I saw 2 hrs of it, struck by the naïve mixture of religious sentiment & simple militancy which is the miner.'

She had a charisma that generated attention even without easy one-liners at brains trust sessions. She had become the prima donna of the Labour movement, a vivid contrast to the women of the right and the hatchet-faced and solidly built hammers of the left like Alice Bacon and Bessie Braddock. She was a quick-witted television performer and a terrier-like opponent of the Tories in the Commons. When an elderly member of the House of Lords declared that he found women in politics inappropriate, she snapped back that she found peers in politics inappropriate. The danger for her was that she was all too frothy, too lightweight, ultimately too feminine. The things for which she was famous were undermining the fame she wanted to achieve, as a major player in the premier league. She lacked gravitas, depth, authority. She had still to establish herself as a serious politician who might one day be considered a potential leader. The press loved Barbara, but could not quite place her. Westminster was rife with lurid and salacious gossip about her, some of which was still circulating forty years later. The right had long memories. A woman as flirtatious and attractive was plainly available. The only question was to whom? Men's affairs were accepted and ignored. Barbara was the subject of fevered rumours, especially since Ted's reputation for marital fidelity was even more dubious. To fuel the speculation Ted and Barbara argued, publicly and furiously. It was a high-octane relationship. Hugh Dalton, who knew them both from their walking campaigns, reported: 'Ted is terribly difficult about everything. Barbara is taking too much benzedrine or is very strained.'[37]

In June 1953 Ted was at last selected for a by-election, at Abingdon. There was a Conservative majority of five thousand to overturn, and it was a virtually hopeless seat, full of racehorse yards whose head lads repeatedly complained that Ted's loudspeaker van upset the bloodstock. He was competing with the coronation (and his wife's controversial remarks about it), and midsummer apathy had struck. But with a general election once again considered imminent and the party anxious to show unity, he had a steady flow of high-level supporters. Gaitskell and Callaghan as well as Crossman all spoke at the eve-of-poll rally, but on the day the Tory – Airey

Neave, who would become Margaret Thatcher's close adviser and who twenty-five years later was murdered by the IRA – won with a slightly increased majority.

It was another blow to Ted, who had also been dropped after only a year as editor of *Picture Post*. Later that year, he found some consolation in another political role when he became the unofficial Bevanite constituency organizer dubbed the 'national agent' in the press. He and a 'second eleven' of non-parliamentary Bevanites – mainly the staff of *Tribune* – identified sympathetic candidates and constituencies with vacancies and mobilized the vote for the Bevanites at conference. They also tried to win converts in the trade unions. 'Most of the second eleven's activities were secret,' Ted said later, 'but I think our antagonists guessed its existence . . . always Aneurin had a real fear of causing a split in the party.'[38] The logical reaction to defeat by the parliamentary party was to continue campaigning in the constituencies, with the avowed – if unstated – intent of encouraging them to select Bevanite candidates. It was a pretty distant prospect, and in the lingering mood of vitriolic division in the Commons, demonstrated by the weight of votes cast against Bevan, there was no chance at all of winning over enough MPs for a Bevan leadership victory.

Politics may have been the cement that kept Barbara and Ted together. If Barbara was thought in some circles to be a little too keen on self-advancement for total ideological purity, Ted was seen as her personal ginger group, constantly revving her up. There was little they did that did not have some political content. If they went on holiday it was with fellow politicians, and sometimes with a political purpose. In 1951 the Castles and the Crossmans – Dick with his second wife Zita, who died tragically and unexpectedly the following year – went to Yugoslavia and met Tito, whom Bevan had taken up. Yugoslavia, Bevan thought (and Barbara agreed), with its attempt to steer a path between East and West, was a model for the development of international relations.

Bevanism at Westminster was in a cul-de-sac; its old members kept their heads down. But in Vincent Square, the ban on Bevanism was being quietly defied by a small group. Barbara and the other five Bevanite NEC members, together with Jennie Lee, Michael Foot and John Freeman,[39] continued to meet discreetly at Tuesday lunchtimes. Bevan was rarely there, spending much of 1953 abroad. In May, Barbara observed that he could not make up his mind how to respond to the confused proposals for the new Labour programme, 'Challenge to Britain'. 'Nye seems uncertain whether he wants a fight, or unity on as big a policy victory as possible . . . with a flash of vivid sincerity, he admitted that an agreed document is likely to be much less evocative than a controversial one: "If we balance this document, we shall also bleach it." This dilemma seems to symbolise Nye's own contradictions. [The] office produces a final draft so drawn [up] that we are not quite clear [as] to what [the] next Lab Govt. [will be] committed in way of financial controls, taxation & investment.'[40]

A heavy lethargy seemed to settle over internal party politics. Barbara, Wilson and Crossman were all getting increasingly frustrated by what they considered Bevan's almost dilettante approach to his responsibilities as their leader. Barbara and Bevan still irritated one another on a personal level; Dalton and Crossman both observed at about this time, without enlarging on it, that *he* did not like *her*. Despite their shared intuitive and emotional political instincts, they were otherwise very different. Bevan was capable of great political originality, as Crossman often noted, but was almost impossible to tie down to methods or consequences. Barbara was the opposite. She rarely generated orginal ideas. In that sense she was not a creative politician. But she was sharp about tactics, shrewd about consequences and prepared to be honest about likely difficulties. The wilder fringes of conference – moving resolutions on general strikes to bring down the government, voting through impossible programmes – she regarded as absurd, and she was ready to tell the group so. 'The Party, freed from the restraints of government, has regained all its old reformist fervour but without any idea of how it is going to pay for reformist advance. As I put it at meetings: "How do we think we are going to be able to afford these costly advances in 1954/5 when we couldn't afford them in 1951 at the peak of post-war productivity?" '

Meanwhile, Barbara's informal alliance with Wilson was strengthening. They both lived in North London, and Wilson would stop at her flat at Cholmondley Court in Highgate to pick her up on their way to NEC meetings at party headquarters in Transport House, giving them time to agree a line.[41] At the party conference in Margate in 1953, Barbara – in a remark as revealing of her attitude to conference as his – complained: 'Nye as usual anxious for none of us Bevanites to speak but himself . . . Harold, who had been allocated finance, *very* anxious to speak.' She then devised a way of allowing Wilson to get his way. 'He spoke well when his time came & is obviously strengthening his position all the time.' However, she and Crossman both found Wilson's willingness to use 'not too scrupulous methods' distasteful. Crossman had observed that Wilson, who had persuaded the Bevanites to accept Bevan's decision to disband without letting them know that Bevan had already sent to the printers an article announcing it, had unblushingly 'diddled' forty of his colleagues.

At Margate, Bevan and Barbara came first and second again in the constituency section. Eyebrows were raised at the result. 'The NEC vote showed no change but some surprises none the less: Nye & me both over the million & both polling more votes than there are members of the LP! Harold up to 3rd place . . . we are still solidly getting the backing of the CLPs [constituency Labour parties] despite the most determined efforts of the right wing to oust us. People say there is a passionate desire for unity: well, they've got it all right.' Jennie Lee, with whom Barbara was not on cordial terms, told her there was a 'great serenity' about the conference. Barbara, for all her caution about splits, was anxious to see the Bevanite group revived. Back at Westminster, Bevan told her to wait until the shadow cabinet elections.[42] But they were as disappointing as the previous year's: he was still twelfth – in, but only just. Wilson was the first loser. Bevan ran for the deputy leadership as he had in 1952, and did worse. Still, Barbara wrote, he was unwilling to take action: 'He continues to oppose the revival of an organised group & is very spasmodic in attending lunches at [Dick Crossman's]. It is very difficult to see what his tactic is at present; despite the Parliamentary Committee rebuff, he still seems to cling to the idea of unity in the face of the imminent election & of getting back on the inside of the next Labour Government.'[43] Crossman echoed the feeling. 'Nye is deeply disturbed by his lack of success in the election to the deputy leadership and feels that he is in a dead end. Should he go on leading a Group which seems to repel everybody else from supporting him? But if the Group is disbanded doesn't he lose his position on the Left and would he be a prisoner once again, as he was in the Cabinet? All this makes him needful of self-confidence and so very self-assertive and volatile.'

The left had not entirely abandoned the field. *Tribune* continued to publish pamphlets. In April 1954, Barbara and the other five Bevanite NEC members had published one on the latest policy preoccupation, German rearmament. The question of whether Germany should rearm so that it could contribute to the defence of Europe against the Soviet threat, uniquely for this era of raw left–right division in the party, cut across factional lines. The left found themselves for once in harmony with Hugh 'No guns for the Huns' Dalton, until the pressures of the factions drew them back into their respective camps. But the bones of the argument were essentially those that had persuaded Bevan, Wilson and Freeman to resign three years earlier. The Americans were demanding a greater European contribution towards containing an enemy the threat from which the Bevanites – although they did not dispute Soviet military intentions – believed was exaggerated; and they were resorting to confrontation, when the left believed more could be achieved through negotiation. The pamphlet *It Need Not Happen* dwelt on the alleged revival of German Nazism and dismissed the proposal to rearm Germany as part of a new European defence community as 'not an alternative to a German national army but merely the first step to its creation'.[44] Drawing the front line down the middle of Germany made 'World War III inevitable'. Germany should be united, neutral and democratic, an unfrightening buffer zone. The Bevanites' willingness to find a middle way for the Soviet Union contrasted unfavourably with an offensive cartoon in *Tribune*, showing the Labour leadership arm in arm with jackbooted Nazis, dancing round a maypole.

It was an article of faith for the Bevanites that America, in the grip of its McCarthyite anti-Communist witch-hunts, was a malign influence on world affairs. Since 1951 Bevan had been making a powerful case for confronting the threat of Communism in Asia and Africa by ending the conditions that made it attractive – colonialism and poverty – rather than by military containment. He helped launch a new awareness of the problems and needs of what is now called the Third World, a campaign picked up by Wilson, who in 1953 wrote *The War on World Poverty*, a book which in its turn inspired the aid charity War on Want. Barbara, like most others on the left, took up the cause of the anti-colonial movement. Soon, post-imperial Asia became another battleground in the Bevanite–Gaitskellite war.

In May 1954, Barbara went off by herself to stay with her old friends Dick and Naomi Mitchison at their house in Scotland. The trip aroused more gossip, especially after she was rushed to hospital with a wisdom tooth problem but because of a bed shortage was put in the maternity wing. If some great crisis in her marriage had been reached, however, as some speculated, it did not prevent Ted from writing to her full of the latest development in the long Bevanite saga:[45] Bevan had resigned from the shadow cabinet.

This time his grounds for concern were American actions in Indo-China, where France had already been fighting the Communist leader Ho Chi Minh for seven years. The American Secretary of State, John Foster Dulles, wanted 'united action' against the Communist threat. On Tuesday 13 April at the Bevanite lunch, with Bevan himself there for once, the question was the main topic of conversation. That afternoon, unexpectedly, the Conservative

Foreign Secretary Anthony Eden announced that some kind of 'NATO for Asia' was under discussion: a policy of military containment – polarization between Communist and capitalist – to parallel that in Europe was being proposed. Attlee gave cautious support for the idea, and Eden's statement was almost over when Nye barged down to the front bench, red-faced and angry, took his place and denounced the plan. This was obviously intolerable behaviour. The following day he walked out of the shadow cabinet and at the PLP meeting that night, he was left with no option but to resign. It was a reaction to the impotence he felt at being outvoted in the shadow cabinet and on the National Executive, the kind of emotional spasm he was later to condemn so offensively in others at a party conference.

Of all the implications of Bevan's behaviour, the most immediate was a vacancy in the shadow cabinet, which would go automatically to the first runner-up in the shadow cabinet election – Wilson; but it was at first assumed that he could not possibly take it. That, however, was to misjudge Wilson's ambition and the discontent of some of the Bevanites – particularly, or maybe only, Crossman – at being asked to support Bevan in a decision taken impetuously and without consultation. Wilson took Bevan's seat. Barbara, up in Scotland, thought he was wrong. 'I assumed that HW would refuse to fill the place & was amazed to read a few days later that he'd accepted . . . My mental comment was: "If it were anyone but H I'd say it was the decision of a very brave man."' Back in London, she was told by Ted that Crossman had encouraged Wilson to think of accepting the seat, even though the other Bevanites were against it. On 3 May she wrote:

> In the House today I ran straight into Dick who clutched at me like a drowning man. It was obvious that he was very unhappy, feeling guilty about the role he had played. ([John Freeman] described it as being tricked once again by intellectual arguments into personal disloyalty: this time to his own rebel colleague, Nye.) Dick launched into a detailed justification of himself & Harold: 'If you'd been here you would have been terrified about the mood into which Nye was drifting: a position which was leading him logically out of the Party. His behaviour to Harold was utterly high-handed: not only did he not say a word to him beforehand, but he hardly spoke to him after. If he will not accept any of the obligations of comradeship, what right has he to demand blind loyalty?

Barbara, at Crossman's suggestion, went to see Nye, who was at home in Cliveden Place. 'I rang Nye who was cordial & went to have tea with him in his little top study. I found him friendly but very very bitter . . . It

had never occurred to him that it was a snub to Attlee . . . he was furious
with Harold & Dick: "Never once did Harold come & see me: he was too
busy conspiring with DC. They had already told me I had better resign
myself to becoming the prophet of the Left, leaving the practical leadership
to others. It is a role which I do not fancy for myself."' Barbara argued that
he must take some positive action. Bevan rejected the idea of formally
reviving the group, and attacked Crossman bitterly. As for Wilson: 'The
trouble with H,' he told Barbara, 'is that he wants the best of both worlds
& you can't have it.' Barbara went on: 'Then [John Freeman] arrived &
between us we got him into a better humour, agreeing to come at least to
the next lunch.'[46] It is evidence of her rising status that Crossman thought
that had Barbara been there on the day of the resignation, she (and Michael
Foot, also away) might have persuaded Bevan that it was right for Wilson to
join the shadow cabinet; or it may be further evidence, as John Freeman
said, of Crossman's notorious inability to comprehend normal standards of
loyalty.

Bevan, already angry and pessimistic, now took a further decision that
the Bevanites found almost inexplicable. He had been particularly angry at
the impasse in which he found himself – the constituency parties' favourite,
but stymied at every turn by the unions. He believed that outside the
'irresponsible group of trade union bureaucrats'[47] he had support among their
membership, and he decided he would challenge Gaitskell in the contest for
a new party treasurer to replace Arthur Greenwood, who had just died.
Treasurer was one of the key roles in the party machine, the link between
the unions and the party, carrying an automatic seat on the NEC. Gaitskell
had been defeated for the constituency section of the NEC every time he
had stood. But with the backing of the most right-wing of the union leaders,
Arthur Deakin of the Transport and General Workers, the treasurership
looked his for the taking. That, Bevan argued, would be a betrayal of the
will of the party. Challenging for the position would be the logical outcome
of the campaign that he, Bevan, had been fighting against union domination
of the party since the 1930s. Having thrown up the shadow cabinet (and
then failed to attend the debate on the very issue on which he resigned), he
was proposing that he abandon his other power base on the National
Executive. It was a particularly Quixotic decision, for if he had been able to
win union backing, he would hardly have needed to become treasurer in
order to convert the unions to Bevanism. Bevan insisted that it was a way of
exposing the 'ruthless and cynical' exercise of power by the Transport and
General Workers' Union and the General and Municipal Workers' Union.
However, in order to contest the position, which he knew before he began

he could not win, he would have to resign from the constituency section, and deprive himself of his one position of power in the party – and the Bevanites of his leadership.

The mood in the party was once again as bitter as it had been in the heyday of parliamentary Bevanism, before the group was formally disbanded. The right of the party was further inflamed when *Tribune* and the *New Statesman* returned to the forefront of the Bevanites' defence. Herbert Morrison wrote an intemperate piece for the right-wing journal, *Socialist Commentary*. Then, a month after Bevan's resignation, Bevan, Barbara and the other Bevanites on the NEC, in a discussion on German rearmament, were bitterly attacked for 'disrupting the basis of this movement'. Edith Summerskill, dedicated opponent of the Bevanites, claimed opaquely that 'Dick and Barbara were victims of their own temperaments'. It was Mikardo, the organizer (and regular visitor to Eastern bloc countries), who was the real villain, she believed. Attlee, beyond monosyllabic put-down for once, accused them directly: ' "I don't see that it is primarily a matter of policy [Barbara's diary note quoted him as saying]. Things are brought in from time to time like German Rearmament. It is a fine emotional cry but there is no fundamental difference. Nor over South East Asia. To my mind our so-called left-wingers are often unconsciously the catspaw of more designing elements." ' Bevan, for once, did not lose his temper when he felt he was being unfairly attacked.

> Nye at this weighed in moderately but firmly to lift the whole horrid squabble on to the political plane . . . there was a cleavage of opinion on policy that could not be disguised. Members of the Executive were saying he was the 'catspaw' of fellow travellers & communists. There was this much truth in it: that the activities of the 'Bevanites' kept in the Labour Party many people who would drift into the [Communist Party] otherwise; he warned Herbert [Morrison][48] 'You can proscribe us, silence us, disaffili-ate us tomorrow & you will then find the CP in this country double its membership because so many people, seeing the [Labour Party] deprived of all militant leadership, will join the CP.[49]

The Executive, predictably in the Bevanites' view, was unimpressed. Dis-agreement in public with NEC decisions was thenceforth banned, except on the subject of German rearmament, which from respect for the party's long tradition of pacifism was regarded as a conscience issue. Bevan railed against Morrison's vision of an 'emaciated' party, ready to be carried into a centrist coalition. Then, he told Barbara, ' "The Trade Unions will realise it is not in

their interests." "Who will they choose then?" I asked, "Alf Robens?"[50]
"No," said Nye complacently. "Me."'

The charge of Communist subversion, with its McCarthyite overtones, was one levelled repeatedly at the Bevanites. As Barbara implied in her comment on the 1953 NEC results when she and Bevan managed to get more votes than there were party members, conference appeared to be less than watertight. In the parliamentary party, there had been a handful of expulsions for Communist membership, and loyalty oaths had been demanded of twenty or so MPs who had telegrammed congratulations to Pietro Nenni after the pro-Soviet leader of the Italian socialists, who were in an electoral pact with the Communists, had come to power. Certainly the Bevanites were aware of fellow travellers who sometimes supported them in the lobbies. Thomas Braddock had been a member of a front organization called Socialist Outlook and joined the CP in 1952. John Platts Mills, Lester Hutchison, L. J. Solley and Konni Zilliacus were also expelled, although the latter was readmitted and even came back as an MP. Equally, the Bevanites were very much less hysterical about Communists and Communism than many on the right of the party and in the country generally. Crossman wrote sometimes for a Communist-front journal called *Labour Monthly*, maintained a cheerfully friendly relationship with the Soviet ambassador and was aware of but relaxed about other colleagues' links with the CP. Bevan regarded another MP, Sydney Silverman, as 'more than 50 per cent' Communist. If the state of play at Westminster was reflected in the country, it appears that, rather than the Bevanite group being a front organization, Bevan had some justification in claiming that their militancy kept some Labour Party members within the fold while arguing a coherent, democratic, non-Communist alternative to the leadership.[51]

In July 1954 Barbara and Wilson, depressed by what they considered Bevan's 'running from responsibility', tried to engineer some kind of exit from the dead end into which he had driven himself. She suggested to Bevan, who would have no official status in the debate on German rearmament, since he had resigned from the National Executive, that he join it from the conference floor.

But when I put this to Nye in the smoke room, his lip curled. 'Me speaking against the red light? No thank you. I have better platforms than that!' This chilled me almost more than anything he has said & reinforces Harold's view that Nye has got himself into a completely non-cooperative frame of mind. It is increasingly difficult to see what his plan for power is & I am beginning to think we were wrong to let him run for the [Treasurership].

It looks as though he is relying on a crisis to catapult him into power à la Churchill . . . it is difficult to see a crisis which will leave Bevan the obvious leader.[52]

By the end of 1954, the Bevanites finally appeared routed. At the party conference in Scarborough that autumn Bevan was beaten two to one by Gaitskell for the treasurership; most gallingly, it seemed the constituency vote – at least according to Crossman's calculations – had split equally between the two candidates. The leadership had narrowly won the argument on German rearmament, after the small Woodworkers' Union had been leant on to change its vote. Finally, Bevan, infuriated that Wilson had taken his place at the top of the constituency section as well as in the shadow cabinet, made a splenetic and incoherent speech remembered for ever after for one phrase: 'I know that the right kind of leader for the Labour Party is a desiccated calculating machine who must not in any way permit himself to be swayed by indignation. If he sees suffering or privation or injustice he must not allow it to move him, for that would be evidence of the lack of proper education or of absence of self-control. He must speak in calm and objective accents and talk about a dying child in the same way as he would about the pieces inside an internal combustion engine.' This was intended as a response to Attlee's recent attack on emotionalism. Everyone took it as a sneer at Gaitskell. Barbara was in despair. She sat next to him on the platform on the last day of his membership of the NEC. 'I have made a perturbing discovery about him. His favourite doodle is writing his own name.'

The division between Bevan and Wilson was opening up fast. *Tribune*, trying to promote Bevan's attack on the trade unions, blasted at Arthur Deakin of the Transport Workers. On the NEC Wilson refused to defend *Tribune*'s behaviour. He was leaving Barbara behind, too. For the first time he had beaten her in the NEC vote. Discussing who should run for the shadow cabinet in the autumn, Wilson had vetoed her idea of extending the slate (presumably to include her). 'Obviously he sees the future in terms of a left monopoly for HW,'[53] she wrote angrily. But it was a fait accompli. Wilson, Crossman also noted, was going to be the new leader of the left. His preferment in government by Attlee in 1945 had given him a start which neither Barbara nor Crossman (who probably did not want to, anyway) could make up. But there was more to it than that. Wilson had a broader reach than Barbara, a cooler approach to political discourse. He was also a less divisive figure, careful to keep his fences well mended and sensitive to the susceptibilities of others. Crossman, like Barbara, had seen his talent early on: 'His complacency must be unique, but he has a good mind, is an excellent member of a group and is likeable into the bargain.'[54]

As for Barbara, she still repelled more people than she attracted by the vehemence with which she expressed herself. She was not interested in cooperation, which might lead to compromise, but in proving that she and her point of view were right. Friends who she thought betrayed Bevan or the Bevanites received stinging rebukes. When one MP, Desmond Donnelly (who regularly told Hugh Dalton everything that happened at Bevanite meetings), attacked Bevan – and then, later, wrote to congratulate her on her NEC election result – she responded in outrage: 'I can respect political decisions reached with care & heart-searching. I cannot respect decisions based on personal spite & personal frustration. Your speech was not an effort in search of truth, but in search of the headlines. Well, you have them. But take care. You have started on a path that will lead you far away not only from your comrades but from your self-respect.'[55]

Bevan once again retreated into caution: he vetoed Mikardo's plans to relaunch the brains trust, and failed to attend the Commons debate on the foundation of the South East Asia Treaty Organization, over the inception of which he had resigned. On a vote on the issue of German rearmament, which of all the Bevanite fights had been the most controversial and the best supported, the Bevanites decided to abstain.

Bevan, as Crossman had observed, was always more volatile when he was in a weak position. One issue, which came to dominate Labour politics for a generation, had been slowly gathering momentum over the past four years: the question of whether Britain should have an atomic bomb, and if it did, in what circumstances it could be used. In March 1954 America had exploded the first hydrogen bomb in the Pacific, launching a new, more devastating weapon with which to assert its world hegemony. The government announced that Britain was to manufacture its own thermonuclear bomb. Barbara, in common with many women, Church leaders and some left-wingers, saw this new generation of weapon as a moral question. It was morally wrong even to have in the national armoury a weapon capable of causing such terrible and widespread destruction, and there could be no question of first use. However, she never carried the moral argument to its logical conclusion. If it was morally wrong to use such a weapon and by implication to gain from its use, Britain would be obliged to leave NATO, which sheltered under the American nuclear umbrella. She made a compromise between principle and expediency which left her exposed to the jeers of more rigorous critics.

The position that all Bevanites could support was to pursue talks, to disarm through negotiation. There should be talks between the four nuclear powers, the USA, Russia, Britain and France, in effect to achieve disarmament before there could be more nuclear armament. The party leadership, however, implicitly endorsed the government's decision to build and if necessary use the new weapon. In the Commons defence debate in March 1955, Bevan – who had already breached standing orders by canvassing support for the motion calling for talks after it had been officially rejected by the PLP – demanded to know whether a Labour government was prepared to use the British bomb in the face of an overwhelming conventional threat, or whether it was a deterrent to be used only in response to a nuclear attack. His assault on Attlee was if anything stronger than his assault on the government, and his line of attack was clearly a breach of the official party position. In the vote sixty-two MPs rebelled with him against the party line. They included Barbara, although she disapproved of his style, but not Crossman or Wilson and some other Bevanites. The particular absurdity of the situation, as Barbara knew, was that Bevan did not share her reservations about the bomb itself. He made it quite plain in the debate that he saw no moral or legal distinction between 'the hydrogen bomb, the atom bomb or even saturation bombing'.[56] To the suspicious onlooker, it appeared that Bevan was cynically jumping on to a party bandwagon to restore his standing in the party. As his biographer John Campbell put it, 'What Bevan had succeeded in doing was to put himself at the head of the unilateralist faction with whom he did not fundamentally agree, while appearing to signal once and for all that he was not interested in working constructively for unity.'[57]

A majority in the shadow cabinet and on the NEC (led by Deakin again) demanded first the withdrawal of the whip from Bevan and then his expulsion. But the party rank and file were equally determined that he should stay. Legalistically, although he was guilty of a breach of discipline, it was hard to argue that he had breached standing orders; in practice, his demand for clarity on policy was a blatant attack on Attlee. To compound the difficulties, Bevan's proposal that the party's official policy should be to demand arms talks had been accepted. Once again, it was Barbara on whom Crossman called to woo Bevan back into the party. Together they went to Bevan's new pride and joy, his farm, Asheridge, in the Chilterns, where he had taken to his bed with a tactical outbreak of flu. All Barbara's reservations about Bevan's character were reinforced. She had told Crossman that she had been embarrassed to find Bevan voting with her, knowing they disagreed. (Crossman, who interpreted Barbara's stand on the bomb as a 'fanatical' search for a conference issue,[58] attributed her embarrassment to rage: 'I later learnt that she was intensely resentful of Nye's climbing on her and Tony

Greenwood's bandwagon and taking it over!') Bevan wanted the Bevanites to resign from the NEC if he was threatened with expulsion. Barbara told him he had to apologize to Attlee. 'Nye shouted like a petulant child, "I won't! I won't."' However, along with their efforts to avoid his expulsion they talked him into cooperating. At the critical party meeting, Bevan assured Attlee that he would never again exploit the H-bomb emotionally in a campaign and would never try to launch a third party. But a motion calling for the withdrawal of the whip was carried by 141 to 112. It now all rested on the NEC, which had to ratify the PLP's decision.

Crossman used his old-school-tie network to meet the enemy. Gaitskell came to Vincent Square for a drink and revealed how obsessively he regarded the Bevanites: 'Bevanism is and only is a conspiracy to seize the leadership for Aneurin Bevan. It is a conspiracy because it has three essentials of conspiracy, a leader in Bevan, an organisation run by Mikardo and a newspaper run by Foot.'[59] He knew there was a Bevanite network in the constituencies, and he was determined to 'clean it up'. Crossman pointed out that the Bevanites were no longer a homogenous group. A centre-left group was emerging, at least in his imagination. At the NEC the sense of retaliatory persecution persisted, and it was only Attlee who persuaded them to allow Bevan to make a statement to a special NEC subcommittee before any decision was taken. Barbara was the only Bevanite on the committee. She took Bevan in hand to make sure the statement was appropriately apologetic, and then bounced the NEC by inadvertently telling Bevan to come an hour before he was due. Bevan apologized to 'Mr Attlee for any pain I may have caused him'.[60] At the full NEC he escaped serious retribution, although he came in for some tough, Gaitskellite-inspired strictures on his future behaviour. The party narrowly managed to close down the issue just as Churchill resigned and handed his party to Sir Anthony Eden, who immediately called an election.

It was not quite the Bevanites' last hurrah. As few doubted it would be, the election was comfortably won by the Tories, who got the credit for ending rationing and engineering an economic boom which, for the first time in many people's experience, was bringing material prosperity. The Tories won an overall majority of fifty-eight.

Barbara came closer to losing her seat than she ever did before or after. She spent a tense forty-five minutes at her count after her agent had warned her that on his figures, which had always been reliable in the past, she was out.

For three quarters of an hour the word spread like wildfire round the King George's Hall at which were present some four or five hundred people, spectators and counters, that Barbara Castle was out. And Barbara knew she was out. And Barbara's reaction to this was just a drop of the face – it was just perceptible – and a little artificial smile and then she became natural . . . and she told me afterwards that during that time she'd been deciding what she would do in life now – journalism. She'd go back to journalism.[61]

She was in, but the threat of defeat and Labour's poor performance had forced Barbara to review her own contribution. She had been in parliament for ten years. She was an established national figure, familiar from television discussion programmes and newspaper front pages. But the years of deep and painful division, she had to acknowledge, had damaged the party. It was plain that Bevan could not win the leadership, and it was hard to see that anyone but Gaitskell could. Five more years of opposition lay ahead. If it was not to be five more after that, the schism had to be healed. In one sense, Barbara came back to Westminster after the 1955 election no longer a Bevanite. Yet emotionally, Bevan himself remained for ever her flawed but brilliant hero.

After the election, Barbara insisted on standing for the shadow cabinet, a gesture of intent towards unity. She trailed in among the losers, behind Crossman but ahead of Mikardo. Of those elected, Bevan came seventh and Wilson fifth. It seemed that Wilson was already the left's new leader – if he was still of the left. Barbara was not ready to abandon Bevan, even though both Wilson and Crossman had made it clear that when Attlee finally went – and it was now rumoured that he would retire in October – they would back Gaitskell. Crossman told Bevan he had no one to blame but himself: 'You've got to understand that many of us know all the drawbacks of Gaitskell but accept him as inevitable because you've ruled yourself out.' Barbara, still angling for a way of giving Bevan a chance, went to see Attlee to try to persuade him to stay on for a little longer, which she hoped would give Bevan some desperately needed time to recommend himself to the party again. At that autumn's party conference she attacked the right, accusing them of trying to force Attlee out, prompting an ironic Low cartoon of Barbara as Joan of Arc holding a protective shield over the Labour leader. In December he announced his resignation.

Barbara, who had always found Bevan's incorruptibility one of his most endearing features, returned from a trip to Kenya to discover to her horror that he had shown himself prepared to act as cynically as any right-winger. He had offered a deal to Gaitskell, suggesting they both stood down to give

Morrison, his oldest and most sustained critic in the party, the leadership. Bevan, like Barbara, believed his only hope of achieving what he wanted was to gain time. The tactic did nothing for his chances. Gaitskell understandably rejected his overtures and trounced Bevan, 157 to 70, with Morrison, the last of the pre-war leadership, polling just 40.

It was time for a new beginning.

7. Bitter Lemons

The sight of an Englishman had become an obscenity on that clear
honey-gold spring air.

Lawrence Durrell, *Bitter Lemons*[1]

With Gaitskell as leader, Barbara and the Bevanite rump felt as if the party
was under enemy occupation. Barbara had been frustrated by Bevan's erratic
behaviour, but she had been much further from being reconciled to a
Gaitskell candidacy than either Crossman or Wilson. Gaitskell was a mystery
to her, someone with whom she had nothing in common beyond membership of a party – a party even on whose purpose they could not agree. In
Barbara's view, his predominant and least attractive political trait was his fear
of alienating the floating voter, while his abrasive style and his passion for
'provocative clarity' were bound sooner or later to find out the party's
conflicting cultures. The bomb, and later the purpose of the party itself
as expressed in the pledge to public ownership made in Clause 4 of its
constitution, were to provide an object lesson for Gaitskell's successor on the
importance of unity, and the need for balance and compromise if it was to
be attained.

After Gaitskell's victory, politics at home was clearly going to be an
uncongenial battlefield. Gaitskell was unshakeably in the ascendancy, even
if he had never won the backing of the party's constituency activists at the
annual conference. Bevan and Wilson were soon in the shadow cabinet,
Wilson as shadow chancellor, Bevan as shadow colonial secretary. Crossman
was sent off to draw up a scheme to give people 'half-pay pensions'. Wilson
swore a private oath of fealty to Gaitskell.[2] Bevan did not need to – he had
nowhere else to go. However, although his supporters thought the job
demeaning to his status in the party, Bevan was happy to shadow colonial

affairs. He had been writing and talking about the future of the colonies, where seventy million people still lived in varying relationships to the mother country, since 1950 – nearly a decade ahead of Harold Macmillan's 'Wind of Change' speech. It was an area the left hoped to establish as a cornerstone of a new world order, where free, democratic and independent countries could group together, perhaps under the umbrella of the Commonwealth, as an alternative power bloc to the United States and Soviet Russia.

Bevan argued that it was up to Labour to act on behalf of the inhabitants of Britain's colonial territories, without their own representation in Westminster, and to raise the grievances of people whose struggles for independence were, the left argued, blocked by a right that was both capitalist and racist and prepared to use excessive force to perpetuate white regimes. Africa in particular offered the left what was literally a black-and-white issue, a straight fight between right and wrong in which they were uncomplicatedly in the right, and the Conservatives, with their eager defence of the white settlers' rights over the Africans', equally emphatically wrong. Africa gave the party a cause over which there was no need to squabble. Here was a green-field site, where it could start again to build a new, fairer and above all a better-planned world. Concern for correct behaviour was a natural extension of the left's instincts about morality and justice in politics, of its Nonconformist tradition and its view of the wider role of socialism as 'a way of making a reality of Christian principles in everyday life',[3] a benign influence on the lives of ordinary people everywhere. It was a view in which more difficult questions about independence, questions of process and method, and the conflict between self-interest and a new world order could be subordinated to a higher moral purpose.

Barbara's own interest was encouraged by her brother Jimmie, who had been working as a forester, mainly in Nigeria, since the early 1930s. He introduced her to some of the few Africans who managed to get to Britain to study, and he wrote often from Nigeria about the nastiness of the climate, the loneliness of his work and occasionally about contacts with black political movements. Barbara, with her conventional instincts, had been slow on the uptake. 'I found it hard to grasp at first that the African natives with whom [Jimmie] went into the bush to preserve and plant trees had minds and traditions of their own and were getting restive under white rule.' Jimmie came back from Africa in 1955 and went to work first for the Fabians and then for the Oxford Campaign for Famine Relief, which in the early 1960s was to become Oxfam.

Unlike India, where a Labour government had overseen independence in 1948, most of Africa was considered, even by progressive opinion, to be at least a generation away from majority rule. In 1950, the Labour Colonial

Secretary Patrick Gordon Walker had exiled the future president of Botswana, Seretse Khama, from what was then the British Protectorate of Bechuanaland, for 'disrupting the life of his tribe'. He had married Ruth Williams, a white Englishwoman, while studying law in London. The same Labour government that had pushed through independence for the subcontinent had, before losing office in 1951, countenanced developments in Africa calculated to delay it. Among these developments was the Central African Federation, which originated with white-dominated Southern Rhodesia's desire for a broader economic base than agriculture. Northern Rhodesia's copper deposits and burgeoning industrial base had seemed a logical partner, and the British establishment had been persuaded that federation offered the opportunity for stable and prosperous development. The official principally identified with the development was a young man called Andrew Cohen, who was to become Barbara's first Permanent Secretary. The proposed federation would link not only Northern Rhodesia (which became Zambia) but also Nyasaland (later Malawi) with Southern Rhodesia. In the process, the Africans of Northern Rhodesia and especially of Nyasaland – where there were few white settlers – who had benefited from a far less racist approach by businesses interested in exploiting the local mineral wealth, would lose all protection and come within the ambit of Southern Rhodesia's Europeans and their whites-only constitution.

The 1950 Labour administration had been prepared to accept the plan, but before they came to appreciate the depth of African hostility to it they had lost office. With a Tory Colonial Secretary, Oliver Lyttelton, who was enthusiastic about the potential for copper, the Federation was established in 1953. The Movement for Colonial Freedom sprang from opposition to its foundation. Africa was becoming a fashionable cause, espoused by figures beyond those dismissed by Roy Welensky, Prime Minister of Northern Rhodesia, as the 'short-haired women and long-haired men'[4] of the Fabian Society. It was an abiding interest of Harold Wilson who, as one of Attlee's ministers, had been involved in setting up the UN's Food and Agriculture Organization.

The 1950s in Kenya were scarred by the Mau Mau's campaign of terror against white rule. The response – to some savage murders of women and children – was brutally, and apparently arbitrarily, repressive. As well as the terrorists, hundreds of entirely innocent Africans were rounded up and subjected to inhuman treatment. By 1954, there were rumours and reports of torture and maltreatment of prisoners, and a group of left-wingers including Barbara, Crossman and Tom Driberg had repeatedly raised the issue in parliament. But the Colonial Secretary from 1954 to 1959, Alan

Lennox-Boyd, would reveal nothing. In particular he would not publish the resignation report of one Colonel Young, a City of London police officer sent on secondment to reform the Kenyan police. Lennox-Boyd, 'a guardsman type', Barbara thought, 'imbued with the conviction that the British ruling class, both at home and overseas, could do no wrong',[5] argued in the official record that Young had made no complaint of abuses by the Kenyan police until his resignation, and had described their alleged obstructionism in detail only after his resignation had been accepted. The tone of Lennox-Boyd's minute suggests, in the style of quasi-sympathetic character assassination familiar in public life, that Young must have succumbed to an outburst of emotionalism, a comforting charge the authorities later made of his deputy when he too complained of abuses by the Kenyan police.[6]

Young's report was an uncompromising condemnation of the workings of the Kenyan police force, in particular the Kikuyu Home Guard, the more damning for coming from a serving British police officer. The summary, in the studied official language of the Colonial Office, said:

> [Colonel Young] cited malpractices committed against Mau Mau suspects, alleged that these malpractices were condoned by Officers of the Provincial Administration in the troubled areas who had hindered the police in investigating such alleged offences, and further alleged that the Governor of Kenya had attempted to interfere with the police investigation into one such incident . . . In Col. Young's view, unless the police were given a greater measure of independence in the performance of their functions than they at present possess in the emergency areas, no progress could be made towards regarding the Kenya Police as impartial custodians of the law commanding the trust and confidence of the people.[7]

Refusing to reveal any of this, the government stuck to the terms of the agreed letter of resignation, which were explosive enough. In it, Young declared that the activities of the Kenyan police – the Home Guard – 'seriously jeopardised' public respect for its political independence, and he condemned its lack of discipline that led to abuses of power. In the face of stonewalling from the government, little progress could be made. A few weeks later, however, Barbara noticed another mysterious death in custody in Kenya reported briefly in the press. She got hold of the details of the disciplinary case that followed. The resident magistrate had strongly criticized the two white police officers charged with beating to death an African, Kamau Kichina, after an alleged theft. The details of his torture were set out: 'He was flogged, kicked, handcuffed with his arms between his legs and fastened behind his neck, made to eat earth, pushed into a river, denied food for a period', before the magistrate concluded: 'He was never brought before a magistrate in the proper manner and he received no trial whatever, the right of all British subjects. Thus he must be deemed legally innocent of the offence.'

But the charge of murder had been dropped and most of those involved had escaped any kind of sentence. Barbara got the NEC to condemn the murder, and made her attack in *Tribune*: 'In the heart of the British Empire there is a police state where the rule of law has broken down, where the murder and torture of Africans by Europeans goes unpunished and where the authorities pledged to enforce justice regularly connive at its violation.'[8] Lennox-Boyd once again refused to provide details and condemn events. So Barbara approached Colonel Young directly. He confirmed that he had resigned because he had been unable to consider the security forces as separate from the state. He promised to help Barbara uncover the true story of Kamau Kichina. Finally, in a move that both covered her costs and promised her publicity for her findings, Barbara got the *Daily Mirror* to pay for her to go out to Kenya to establish the facts. In Nairobi she looked at the court records, which showed the doctor who conducted the post mortem had been leant upon to change his findings from death by beating to 'unexplained' death. The records also showed that a colonial officer had incited the beating and had faced no punishment at all. It was harder to find other cases; one attempt to interview detainees ended with a farcical conversation with a District Officer which, after she had asked to be allowed into a camp, went as follows:

DO: 'I cannot allow that. These men are dangerous. A woman must not be
    with them alone.'
Barbara: 'I am not a woman, I am a Member of Parliament.'
DO: 'Madam, I can only go by appearances.'[9]

Nonetheless, she managed to find another case of wrongful detention and beating, and on the morning of her departure examined the weals on the backs of more Africans who, wrongly accused of being Mau Mau terrorists, had been beaten up when they demanded the return of their confiscated property. The incident was witnessed by an acquaintance of Barbara's brother who wrote approvingly to Jimmie of what local Europeans regarded as her 'scandalous' behaviour: a white woman publicly examining the naked backs of black men. 'I call her tops.'

Back in London, Barbara wrote a series of articles for the *Mirror* under the headline, 'What Price Justice? – Kenya, Land of Fear'. She was a hero, not least because of the vilification heaped upon her in the Commons by the Tories. 'Is my Rt Hon. friend aware with what contempt responsible public opinion in Kenya will regard the conduct of Mrs Castle?'[10] one Tory backbencher demanded. Lennox-Boyd himself said she had 'gone out to support conclusions at which she had already arrived . . . that I believe is bound to rob a great deal of what she said of its value'.'[11] The charge was fundamentally true, but so was the fact that she found what she was looking for. Nonetheless, defending the rights of the untried against the Fleet Street lynch mob, who were determined that all black Kenyans were implicated in the indiscriminate brutality of the Mau Mau, was a course guaranteeing fame and abuse in almost equal measure.

There is now evidence to show that Lennox-Boyd was aware of a policy of violence by prison officers in the detention camps. If a Mau Mau detainee sounded the tribal 'howl', it was taken as an assertion of symbolic defiance. According to a report from the colonial Attorney General, Eric Griffiths-Jones (who had been a prisoner of war of the Japanese himself), 'It was essential to prevent the infection of this [howl] spreading throughout the camp, and the "resistor" who started it was put on the ground, a foot placed on his throat and mud stuffed in his mouth. In the last resort, a man whose resistance could not be broken down was knocked unconscious.'[12]

Over the next ten years, Barbara established an extraordinary reputation in English-speaking black Africa. Her ability to bring to public attention the politics of colonial decline, her unflinching stand in the Commons and in her journalism for the right of Africans to choose for themselves how they were governed, made hers a revered name in some African circles. White Britons working in Africa, where the Churches fought a courageous campaign supporting and encouraging the development of liberal black politics, regarded Barbara with more qualified enthusiasm. Colin Morris, the 'fighting parson', who as a Methodist minister met her in Northern Rhodesia, found himself warning her not to be too simplistic.[13] An African-based journalist, Frank Barton,[14] was appalled at her ignorance even of the fundamentals of African politics. On the other hand, she was valued as someone who could bring the attention of the British media to their problems. Morris, who was sometimes in danger of his life and often in danger of being deported, regarded her as his ultimate guarantor. If anything happened to him, she would make sure it did not go unnoticed.

In 1958, when for a year Barbara had her own weekly newspaper column in the *Sunday Pictorial*, she went to observe the first treason trial in South Africa. A young Nelson Mandela was among the 156 defendants.

The Drill Hall was a ramshackle building with a corrugated-iron roof, an almost comically informal setting for an important trial, with the accused lined up in rows in front of the magistrate's chair, so near to the press table that I could almost touch them and could certainly chat to them . . .[15]

They were acquitted. It was an irony, she observed, that the magistrates in South Africa, unlike those in Britain's colonies, were drawn not from the administration but from the independent ranks of the bar.

She caused a storm of outrage when she entertained an African in Meikles, the unofficially whites-only hotel in Salisbury, Southern Rhodesia, and took up the campaign against the Central African Federation in Northern Rhodesia, earning the bitter hostility of the white regime. Morris, who had shared a platform with her in Blackburn, wrote to her on his return to Northern Rhodesia: 'I am still living down the Blackburn meeting. One can get away with sodomy, blasphemy and adultery, but to speak on the same platform as Barbara Castle puts one completely beyond the pale as far as the white Raj is concerned.'[16] In 1961, as president of the newly formed Anti-Apartheid Movement, she organized a silent vigil outside the Commonwealth Heads of Government Conference in London against South Africa's continued membership.

Africa and the rights of Africans were a cause, a campaign, a platform from which Barbara could argue for socialist values. In part it was Bevanism by other means, a deliberate attempt, now the group was disbanded, to continue the fight for socialism by organizing sympathizers to campaign on specific issues.[17] Yet colonial policy seemed a second-league affair, beneath the notice of the main players on the political stage, a staging-post in Bevan's acceptance by the Gaitskellites; within a year, after backing Gaitskell's brave and principled opposition to the Suez invasion, Bevan was promoted to shadow foreign secretary. Barbara's colleagues in the Movement for Colonial Freedom were the committed but eccentric – people like Fenner Brockway, and Tony Benn in his politically experimental stage, while the MCF's lay supporters came from the vegetarian fringes of radical politics, 'bearded anarchists and . . . bicycling Christians'.[18] Barbara's determined championing of the MCF marked her out in the press, and no doubt in the minds of the right in the Labour Party itself, as a particular kind of woman socialist: obsessive, shrill and doctrinaire.

Barbara's journalistic career flourished in a mutually beneficial relationship with her campaigning voyages around the fading empire. The *Sunday Pictorial* column enabled her to push her claim to be taken seriously as a politician. Dick Crossman had arranged for her to succeed him after he

decided to write a twice-weekly column for the *Mirror*. Crossman, like
Michael Foot, was a brilliant polemicist, risk-taking, insightful and capable of
lethal outbursts of frankness. It took a kamikaze Labour politician to write,
as he did in 1957, that only four of the trade union-sponsored MPs in the
Commons were competent enough for junior ministerial office, while his
comments on the leadership of the party frequently infuriated loyalists, not
least for their accuracy. Barbara turned out to have little to say that people
had not heard before. Her style tended to the weighty and her sentiments to
the predictable. Haranguing the party's timorous leadership was a favourite,
and her descriptions of what would now be called her human rights
campaigns conveyed the passion she felt, but lacked the readability that might
have made more converts. Her extraordinary ability to capture an audience
in a speech never quite transferred to the page. In June 1958, after just a
year, the editor Hugh Cudlipp tactfully terminated the contract.

Barbara's most regular outlet was the *New Statesman*, and apart from the
legendary Kingsley Martin who edited the weekly from 1930 until 1960, her
best contact on it was John Freeman, the dashing MP who had arrived in
uniform on the first day of the 1945 parliament, resigned as Minister of
Supply along with Bevan and Wilson in 1951 and then left parliament to
take up the assistant editorship of the paper in 1955. Every Friday, Barbara
would turn up at the paper's office at Great Turnstile Street for the weekly
conference where, with a floating cast from the intellectual left which almost
invariably included Crossman and sometimes Wilson and the economist
Tommy Balogh, they debated – or in Barbara's case argued passionately –
about the editorial line. Freeman influenced her writing and disciplined her
thinking. He always took what became known as her 'annual conference
article' each September, where she could expound a vote-winning theory on
the eve of the NEC elections. She, in turn, valued his criticism and his
compliments.

Barbara's journalism brought in much-needed cash, and allowed her to
travel. Ted's career was in decline. He had been promoted to editor of the
weekly *Picture Post* just as its politics were realigned. In 1951, the paper lost
its left-wing slant and he was sacked. For a time, his only income was from
editing a newsletter for the Yugoslav embassy. Later he returned to the *Mirror*
as night editor on the picture desk. 'I'd have to take a loaded shotgun down
to the print room to get them to change anything,' he told friends.

Africa was only one of Barbara's destinations in the 1950s. In the main,
she travelled to developing countries, but she was also a regular at the annual
Anglo-German conference of social democratic parties at Königswinter, and
she went to Paris to study economic planning for a series in the *New*

Statesman. At the end of 1954 she went to China on a delegation of parliamentarians and distinguished artists (including Stanley Spencer, who was in the midst of his 'Christ at Cookham' series, and the watercolourist Dennis Matthews). It was an unparalleled but controversial opportunity to see the country for the first time since the Communist revolution. China was at the epicentre of the American struggle to contain Communism. The Korean War had ended only a year earlier, and the US saw China as the major source of instability in Asia. There was also criticism of human rights abuses within China. Bevan, who had gone there in an earlier delegation, disputed the American description of internal repression as aggression and therefore incompatible with UN membership. Labour's policy, as it had been with the Soviet Union, was to woo the embryonic superpower through trade and cultural contact.

With the prospect of unprecedented access, Barbara kept a regular diary of her travels, which began with a vodka session in Moscow, where she stopped off en route, on her forty-fourth birthday. It was just a year after Stalin's death; the tourists were eager to find evidence of a lifting of the atmosphere of repression and scope for rapprochement, as well as evidence of the success of the new form of command economics that Communist countries were pioneering. Barbara began with a rare excursion into art criticism:

> The most interesting thing about the new Russia is its failure to produce a modern idiom in architecture, painting or furnishing. Dennis Matthews agrees with me that the paintings are hideous and the new buildings just imitation American sky-scrapers. The new University of 6,000 students looks like a battleship riding the night with red lights swinging from mast to poop. Inside it is hideous in its brash grandeur . . . The backcloth of the stage is a grim representation of Soviet youth marching through hammers and sickles to their glorious destiny. Everything is thick and unshapely like Soviet women's legs.

However, she found Soviet factories and laboratories better equipped than their British equivalents, and the evident poverty of Moscow's citizens aroused no suspicions:

> The thing which astonishes all the time in this country is the contrast between the splendour and cleanliness of the surroundings (University, Exhibition Hall, Metro, Bolshoi Theatre) and the scruffy, drab, even unkempt appearance of the crowds that throng through them. It is not merely that they are drably clothed; they look every inch proletarians, sons

of toil, manual labourers, peasants, who have no pretensions to taste in clothing, furniture or personal belongings yet who obviously enjoy the luxury of their surroundings.

Barbara was eager to learn the secrets of the planned economy, and her diary is mainly a dry catalogue of Russian marketing techniques and food distribution practices.

In China, she found more evidence of the powerful impact of planning in bringing industrialization and employment to backward regions, despite the West's reluctance to export machinery which could strengthen the backward economy. Her account resembles that of a Board of Trade official with a knowledge of textiles and a determination to get to grips with the dynastic succession. She saw the Kwang Tung reservoir being built almost entirely with manual labour, 'tiny blue-clothed figures swarming everywhere . . . men were digging tunnels with shovels and carrying the stone away in baskets slung on poles and carried on the shoulders of two men. There seemed more baskets than trucks and little donkeys plodded by weighed down with loads of brushwood . . . a male voice gave us a song expressing his passionate desire to go and fight in Korea.' In a market, Barbara bought an embroidered panel in which 'two cranes have a good time in pairs'. She was still the earnest tourist who, twenty years earlier, had reported on the liberating impact of Communism on Soviet women. Stanley Spencer told her about his soul – 'If my soul feels it, the paint's all right' – and the delegation argued about whether the Chinese were right to build an enormous conference hotel in the midst of a shanty town. Barbara defended the Chinese:

> I argued that in every society there must be some luxury to satisfy the cravings of the most high-minded of us. In Labour Britain, we had never attacked the capitalist ideology, we had provided the security of the welfare state but left people with the desire, and the opportunity, to contract out of it (capital gains, football pools, legacies, etc.). In these backward areas the government must concentrate all its energies on getting people to contract in; luxury therefore must not be private but communal. Ellis [a fellow Labour MP] and I were heartened on our drive to the factory to see how many buildings of direct value to the workers are going up: flats, sports stadium, gymnasium, hospital, trolley bus station, road widening. So long as bureaucracy does not corner the luxury, a few palaces won't hurt.

Uncritical of Communist China, she risked a serious breach with Bevan and Jennie Lee by appearing to support the Tito regime against the imprisoned dissident Milovan Djilas. Apart from Ted's work for the embassy, Yugoslavia was a favourite left-wing holiday destination, and Barbara met Tito on at least two occasions and other Yugoslav politicians much more often. In the *New Statesman*, she wrote approvingly of the Yugoslav experience of worker participation and sympathetically of the need to stop the great experiment being derailed by dissent. After a long informal conversation in Belgrade with a senior Titoist, who told her that Djilas was jeopardizing progress because of his opposition to workers' control, she concluded: 'If [progress] is real on the economic front then one is only justified in demanding this freedom of political organisation on western lines if one is prepared to see emerging in Yugoslavia a party committed to the destruction of the whole concept of workers' councils, and I frankly don't think that Yugoslavia can stand the strain of that political battle at the moment.'[19]

In 1956 she was on Khrushchev's side at the notorious dinner given in London by the NEC for the new Russian leader, at which George Brown[20] questioned the Soviet Union's commitment to world peace and provoked a tirade from Khrushchev about Britain's perfidious betrayal in 1939 which had forced the Russians into the arms of Nazi Germany. She was on friendly terms with Eastern bloc ambassadors. The left believed conciliation was more effective than confrontation, and Barbara looked for no evidence to undermine her belief. Equally, the left no longer believed in the inevitable collapse of capitalism, but Barbara shared with Wilson, Bevan and Balogh an earnest faith in Communist command economies as the pathfinders to a more just society. She also possessed, perhaps to a greater extent than the others, a blind spot where repression and restriction, the reverse side of the coin of planning and control, were concerned. Her attitude was shaped by a reaction against the right's constant identification of Communism as the source of instability and its paranoid fear of importing revolution. But it was also strongly influenced by a moral conviction that material prosperity was not the only, nor even the most desirable, objective. Justice, equality and participation all seemed at least equally valid, and this view made her less critical of those regimes which appeared to share her values than was justified by a dispassionate appraisal of the facts.

The overwhelming moral issue for the left in the mid-1950s was the nuclear bomb. It had also become, because of Bevan's truculence shortly before the 1955 election, his issue, the last vehicle for Bevanism. The conjunction of moral high-mindedness and political opportunity was to prove explosive. It provided unmistakable evidence after two years of quiescence under Gaitskell that for a significant section of the party it was only on sufferance that he remained its leader. Once Britain started testing its own H-bomb, Barbara quickly saw its likely political impact, while Crossman at first saw it entirely as a defence matter and regarded its acquisition as an unpleasant but unavoidable kind of weapons upgrade. One night in 1955, he and Barbara had argued for three hours:

> It was an extremely good discussion, but the longer she talked, the clearer it became that her only real argument was that we must appeal to morality 'by refusing to enter the thermo-nuclear race'. She repeated this eight or nine times in the course of our talk but she was reluctant to admit that we'd been in the race for nine years and even more unwilling to explain how, by simply not manufacturing the bomb while remaining in NATO, protected by the American strategic air force, we should cut a very moral or edifying figure.[21]

Labour's nuclear policy became the focus of all the grievances and tensions of a party engaged in a complex but more muted struggle to redefine its purpose in the new age of affluence. The bomb issue and the call for unilateral disarmament were appealingly simple, morally satisfying and damagingly divisive, surrogates for the real battle for the party's future. In the three years from 1957, there were to be two set-piece battles on unilateralism. The first, which reached a tormented climax at the party conference that autumn, seemed to be Bevan's final betrayal of Bevanism. The second, three years later, nearly destroyed Gaitskell.

The trigger for renewed concern was the 1957 defence White Paper which revealed that Britain was building its whole defence policy around its nuclear capacity, working on a new generation of thermonuclear weapons and proposing drastic reductions in conventional forces; by implication, nuclear weapons were to become the ultimate labour-saving device. Barbara and her fellow unilateralists demanded that Labour policy should be for tests of the British bomb to be abandoned. In effect, that would mean stopping the building programme and raising again the question of the whole structure of Britain's defence policy, including membership of a nuclear-armed NATO. Gaitskell, also seeking clarity but on a different premise, was well aware of the implications and resolutely refused to accommodate the unilateralists. Barbara accused him of intransigence in his defence of a shadow cabinet proposal for a negotiated cessation of testing. 'It seemed to me as if he wanted to railroad the parliamentary committee's resolution through the meeting against the wishes of an enormous minority or perhaps even a majority.' But Gaitskell did concede that tests should be 'postponed for a limited period'. She observed happily, 'The most interesting thing about the whole business is that this latest "revolt" has taken place during Nye's absence in India, so nobody can blame it on *him* . . . Dick [Crossman] has spent all his time muttering that we evaded the real issue, but I told him he was merely over-compensating as usual for his own intellectual uneasiness. There is no doubt that this has been a tremendous victory for the rank and file.'[22]

Barbara devoted the spring of 1957 to the bomb question. UN disarmament talks were under way and she used her contacts at the Soviet embassy to try to find out what their position was. Russia was proposing cuts in conventional forces and a ban on the use of nuclear weapons; the United States, fearing they could be overwhelmed by Soviet conventional forces, refused to abandon nuclear weapons. She tried to understand the science of bomb-making and likely future developments, and she read everything she could find on the impact of a nuclear explosion. She undoubtedly saw political advantage in the campaign; and once she had focused on an objective, she could not avert her eyes.

That Easter, 5,000 people gathered in Trafalgar Square, including Barbara, Mikardo and Tony Greenwood. They called it the H-bomb campaign; it subsequently became the Campaign for Nuclear Disarmament. One objective was to build a head of steam for conference, encouraging constituencies to send in resolutions. But it would be a mistake to believe, as Crossman suspected, that Barbara was exploiting the issue only to emerge later as the conference darling. She believed profoundly that it was immoral to build a weapon apparently capable of rendering large parts of the world uninhabitable. Once Britain had the bomb, she argued, preparation to use it would begin, and conventional warfare would become impossible. She told friends at dinner in the summer of 1957: 'Preparing for all-out nuclear war is the inevitable logic of our having the bomb. We can't afford both the nuclear arms race and conventional arms. I therefore urged we should see the possession of the bomb as a bargaining counter by being ready to give it up before we tested it.'

Bevan, shadow foreign secretary, had appeared to support the unilateralist cause, without spelling out his position in detail. He wrote a piece in *Tribune* in May headlined 'Destroy the Bombs before They Destroy Us!' and he spoke often of the scope for moral leadership on the issue. But for most of the summer he was out of the country. Fresh from a meeting in the Crimea with Khrushchev, with whom he had discussed the whole issue, he returned in time for the NEC meetings which would decide the line to take at conference. Khrushchev had persuaded him, Bevan said, that if Britain gave up testing it would set a benign circle in motion, leading first to Russia and then the USA also stopping nuclear tests. Under pressure from Barbara he agreed that would mean a wholesale revision of defence policy, but it would have to be faced. 'Nye said he had thought about this issue more than any other political problem in his whole life and had come to the conclusion that this *was* what he meant.'[23]

There seemed a real danger that Gaitskell, who was thought to be underperforming against the Conservative Prime Minister Harold Macmillan and a Tory Party miraculously restored after the Suez fiasco, might be defeated on two fronts at the impending conference. If the first was on defence, the second – and in terms of the internal balance of power, the vital one – was on Gaitskell's first attempt to modernize the party's attitude to nationalization. In 1956 Anthony Crosland, with whom Gaitskell had a very close relationship, had published his book *The Future of Socialism*. Like Bevan's *In Place of Fear* four years earlier, it set out to explain what socialism was for. Unlike *In Place of Fear*, it was responding to the new mood of affluence, seeking to answer the question in the context of full employment, a National Health Service and the welfare state. And, unlike *In Place of Fear*, Crosland's book was dispassionate, temperate, classless, forward-looking – and would be enormously influential. In one of the key passages, Crosland expressly destroys the case for old-style nationalized monopolies on the very social grounds that for Barbara always justified it:

> Socialism, whether viewed in social or ethical or economic terms, will not be brought much nearer by nationalising the aircraft industry. A higher working-class standard of living, more effective joint consultation, better labour relations, a proper use of economic resources, a wider diffusion of power, a greater degree of co-operation, or more social and economic equality – none of these now primarily require a large-scale change in ownership for their fulfilment; still less is such a change a *sufficient* condition of their fulfilment.[24]

Under Crosland's influence, Gaitskell instituted a policy review intended to lead the party away from nationalization as an objective towards other goals of equality and personal freedom. The NEC subcommittee set up to consider the subject carefully included Bevan as well as Wilson. The left was to be tied in to the committee's findings. Once their deliberations were completed,

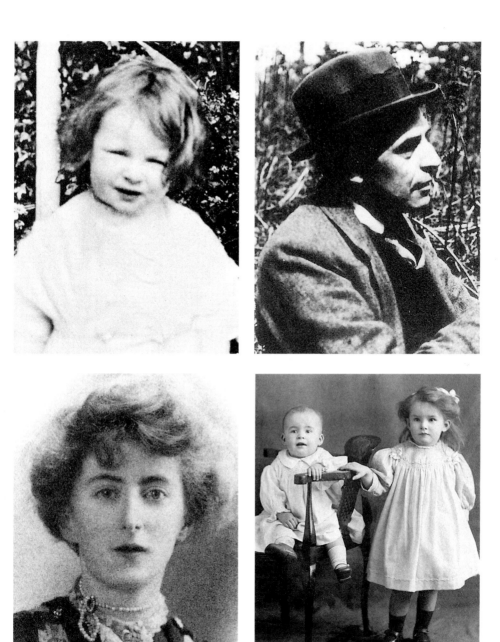

TOP LEFT: Barbara aged two, in party finery at a family wedding. TOP RIGHT: Frank Betts. 'He would walk about with a hat just punched on his head anyhow, with a long coat, rather a hawk-like look and a terrific grin from time to time when he made a point.' ABOVE LEFT: Annie Ferrand, the loyal and loving Muvvie. ABOVE RIGHT: Tristram and Marjorie, Barbara's older brother and sister, aged one and three.

TOP LEFT: Barbara aged eleven with the long hair she hated and T'ang, the first of many dogs she adored. TOP RIGHT: William Mellor in a *Daily Herald* photograph. ABOVE: The Betts family, with Annie's parents and a truculent Barbara, her hair newly bobbed. RIGHT: The essential Barbara: painstakingly stylish.

ABOVE LEFT: Barbara making the speech that led to her finding a seat and a husband: 'We want jam today!'

FAR LEFT: Mrs Ted Castle on her honeymoon, 1944.

ABOVE: Campaigning in Blackburn, 1945.

LEFT: Utopian socialist. Barbara on the holiday she thought Robert Owen would have applauded for its spirit of common enterprise.

FAR LEFT: Barbara, ready to thrust herself between Nye Bevan and Clement Attlee if the exchanges got out of hand. Note Harold Wilson observing from a careful distance.

OPPOSITE BELOW LEFT: Hugh Dalton, Barbara and Ted on a Whitsun 'right to roam' walk. Barbara admired her old enemy Dalton's performance as Chancellor. He made a pass at her.

OPPOSITE BELOW RIGHT: Come dancing. Ted and Barbara live it up.

LEFT: Barbara and Frank Cousins (back to camera), allies against the Bomb.

BELOW: The 1955 Equal Pay campaign, a rare instance of Barbara working in a cross-party alliance.

WOMEN DEMAND EQUAL PAY

TOP: Party chairman at the start of the 1959 election campaign, Hugh Gaitskell awkwardly gripping Barbara's fist, perhaps in a pre-emptive strike. ABOVE LEFT: Attlee and Barbara in fleeting partnership on their way to save Aneurin Bevan from expulsion in 1955. Tom Driberg getting in the picture from behind Attlee's shoulder. ABOVE RIGHT: Housewife superstar. 'I have the normal womanly instincts,' Barbara told interviewers.

the review returned – in May 1957 – first to the home policy committee, on which Barbara sat, before finally being approved by the full NEC.

Barbara, predictably, disliked *Industry and Society*, the paper that emerged from the policy review. On the home policy committee in May she described it as 'negative and uninspiring', and recorded that Bevan had 'tried to get the whole thing abandoned on the grounds that we had too many documents for the Conference'. 'I expressed the view that I thought the document would do more harm than good, partly because it was so complacent in tone about such things as consumer consultation, public accountability and workers' control, and partly because when it did make suggestions they were not only trivial but clarified to the point of sterility.'[25] Nonetheless, it was passed by the National Executive and so became part of official policy, subject to conference's approval. In July, on the eve of its publication, she condemned it again in discussion with the *New Statesman*'s editorial board, and soon her disapproval was widely known. There was a rumble of criticism and the charge of disloyalty was levelled at her, culminating in a bitter piece by Crossman in the *Mirror* – 'If it is a betrayal of principle, then the betrayal has been committed unanimously by the whole of the National Executive.'[26] One view held that she was only attacking the document to buy off critics on the left, and Bevan, who had nominally been a member of the drafting committee, came in for even harsher criticism. The main thrust came from *Tribune*, where Jennie Lee famously called it 'too pink, too blue, too yellow', attacking on the symbolic absence from the document of any 'shopping list' of companies to be nationalized, and a proposal instead that government shareholding could be an alternative. The authors of *Keep Left* had rejected the shopping-list approach, which, Bevan reminded Barbara, was 'a false statement of priorities'. All the same, it became the litmus test of true socialist thinking.[27]

That summer, Bevan made several speeches apparently in favour of unilateralism. Crossman suspected he had been provoked by the criticisms of his role in *Industry and Society*. Barbara, who addressed another Trafalgar Square 'Ban the Bomb' rally a fortnight before conference, was meanwhile trying to ease the party line to the left, arguing for a unilateral renunciation of testing and a commitment to no first use; but she was also prepared to accept a fudge. At the first discussion about how to handle conference, on 19 September, she raised her fear that Bevan – at that stage still in the Crimea with Khrushchev – was going to be put in an impossible position at the party's annual conference in Brighton, forced to defend a position with which he was personally at odds. She accused Crossman of pushing too hard for clarity: 'He has to have the Party's sufferings spelt out in all their inescapable detail. I sometimes think that Dick's love of intellectual flagellation makes him quite unfit for politics.'[28] The row between them over the *Industry and Society* document had sunk relations between the two to such a low point that there was even speculation that Barbara was trying to head the poll in the NEC elections by getting Dick thrown off. It might explain why, a week later, at the second NEC discussion about the line to take at conference, Crossman accused her of needling Bevan (newly returned) into saying that unless he could rule out manufacture as well as testing, he would be unable to speak for the Executive. It would be a major shift in policy which had not been considered. Crossman pointed out that the first consequence would be to reverse the popular decision to end National Service. The alternative was to leave the question of manufacture open. Discussion was then suspended until the eve of conference, by which time the motions for debate would have been selected. The hope was that some middle way might emerge. Instead, the NEC was forced to reach a decision on what was to become the legendary 'Norwood resolution', arguing for a complete renunciation of all manufacture and testing. The Norwood constituency was reputed to be in the hands of the Trotskyites, and its support for the unilateralists' position was at the least an embarrassment, and in Barbara's view risked alienating conference altogether.

Bevan had had a night's heavy drinking and arguing with Sam Watson, the Durham miners' leader. Watson, one of the few union leaders Bevan respected, had convinced him that his future was as Foreign Secretary, and that it was a job incompatible with unilateralism. Bevan had argued his way round his position with close friends like Michael Foot and the journalist Geoffrey Goodman. Barbara reported that Bevan had told the NEC in a rehearsal of the speech that was to devastate conference a couple of days later, '"The question, was how could Britain exert the greatest possible leverage on world affairs in order to avoid a world war. [Unilateralism] effectively destroyed every international undertaking in which we were engaged and was a denouncement of our alliances with the US. It must mean that we must deny to them any facilities for the use of the bomb anywhere in the world where we have influence or control . . . We had nothing to put in its place."'[29] Yet Bevan was also still determined to argue that nuclear weapons were so terrible that they were worse than the danger against which they were being used.

After the NEC meeting Barbara and Ted bumped into Wilson. 'We met Harold on the sea front and his comment was "It is now quite clear to see the lines on which Nye is thinking. He's not merely planning to be the next Labour Foreign Minister but a world statesman, and I believe he will achieve it." I added, "Another Nehru". "Exactly" said Harold. But whether Nye will get away with it on Thursday depends purely on whether his eloquence is up to standard.'[30]

He did not get away with it. Bevan's speech, splenetic and incoherent, caused hurt and outrage – less for what he said (although his disavowal of unilateralism came as a shock to those who had not read the small print), more for the brutality with which he said it. Bevan under pressure was always unstable. That Thursday, his description of unilateralism as an 'emotional spasm' and his refusal to go 'naked into the conference chamber' were delivered, delegates believed, with an angry vehemence that could only come from a man betraying his conscience. The 'unilateralist' resolution was defeated, and worse for the left, Gaitskell was immeasurably strengthened. And for the next two years, almost until the very end of his life, Bevan was seen as the captive of the right. The left, whom he had not led for years, could now hardly even worship his memory. The motion was thrown out by more than five to one. To complete the rout of the left, *Industry and Society* was approved by a margin only slightly narrower. Crossman observed that the party extremists had been curbed. 'The two most important emotions of the Labour Party are a doctrinaire faith in nationalization, without knowing what it means, and a doctrinaire faith in unilateralism, without facing its consequences.'[31]

The old Bevanites suffered from Gaitskell's new confidence. When parliament reconvened the following month, Dick Crossman was not put on the front bench to defend his pension policy against the Tory attack, despite a huge personal success at conference when he launched the pension policy. 'Fortunately for me,' he wrote afterwards, 'I saw right in the middle Frank Cousins, who is the ideal [Workers' Educational Association] three-year tutorial class member – a long, not very intelligent face, which nods when it's got it at last.'[32] Barbara found Bevan truculent and disengaged and was still not reconciled with Dick.

> I think Dick's ambition is overwhelming him and he has got himself into a vicious circle . . . normal conversation and discussion with him is impossible and I am not the only one who avoids talking to him. It is a great pity because there is obviously now complete disagreement on the Left. It is impossible to know where Nye stands. Jennie approached me in the corridor today . . . under great pledges of secrecy she told me that he was going to tell the Parliamentary Committee that they were driving him

[Bevan] too far and that there were limits to his patience . . . she went rambling on about how hurt Nye had been at the aspersions cast by some people on his honour, and how he was suffering for the cause of unity.'[33]

Another colonial movement had meanwhile caught Barbara's eye. After years of trying to shed responsibility for the Mediterranean island of Cyprus, a British territory since the Treaty of Berlin in 1878, it had become the front line in the Cold War. So vital was it considered to British interests that in 1954 a Conservative minister had declared that independence would 'never' be possible.

Barbara and the Movement for Colonial Freedom were arguing for a new party statement on the island's future. At conference she had caused a squall by setting a timetable on independence for the colony, a unilateral shift of National Executive policy. She had declared: 'We are not like the Tories, talking of a vague and misty future when we talk about self determination . . . we shall endeavour to complete this freedom operation for the people of Cyprus during the lifetime of the next Labour government.' Back at Westminster, she found the foreign affairs team of Callaghan and Bevan going back on her commitment. Meanwhile, in Cyprus itself, a terrorist campaign led by Greek Cypriots was claiming an alarming number of lives among British troops, while the minority Turkish Cypriot population attacked Greek Cypriots and opposed any agreement short of the partition they believed was essential to protect their safety. Drafting the NEC policy, Bevan refused to allow a timetable to be inserted. 'Do you want progress, or merely agreement with the Greeks?'[34] he demanded of Barbara. 'Nye is becoming so statesman-like, that it is clear some profound metamorphosis has taken place,' she complained in her diary.

The following year, Cyprus offered Barbara her own chance to meta-morphose from the boat-rocking self-publicist of the tabloid headlines into someone who might be taken seriously in a future Labour government. In May 1958, the Conservatives, in collusion with Callaghan and Bevan, delayed a debate on new government proposals for the independence of Cyprus pending their consideration by the Greek and Turkish governments. Afterwards, Bevan told a protesting Barbara, '"If we were to give self-determination immediately there would be riots in Istanbul . . . it's no good doing this at the price of bloodshed." To this I said mildly, "Anyone who feels sick at the sight of blood ought not to be Foreign Secretary these days," which Nye didn't like very much. "If these proposals fail we shall have another Palestine."' It emerged that the governor of Cyprus, Sir Hugh

Foot,[35] had briefed Bevan and Callaghan. Barbara commented in her diary: 'Once again the worrying thing about all this is that Nye, who has spent his political life denouncing the 'empiricism' of the right wing leaders of the Labour Party, is being driven more and more as he faces office towards empirical solutions and is temperamentally constrained to turn them into high moral attitudes.'[36] On 11 June, she was told by Callaghan that the one chance of persuading Cypriots to accept the new proposals was for Labour to support them. On the 19th, Macmillan finally revealed his non-negotiable plan which, to the dismay of Barbara and colleagues who wanted self-determination for all Cypriots, took the future of the island out of the hands of its people and placed it firmly in the grip of Athens and Ankara.

Macmillan's document 'Ambition for Partnership' was a counsel of despair. It abandoned the effort to get agreement between the two Cypriot communities and proposed instead separate development for each, under a joint legislative council controlled by the Governor which was widely felt to be too weak to hold the island together. It was, said Bevan, 'spiritual partition'. Greece and Turkey alike were invited to send a representative to oversee the arrangements – a sop to the concern among NATO bureaucrats that tension between two of its members was threatening the effort against the Communist menace in which the Cyprus bases were key. Their fear was not without reason: Greece had just suspended cooperation with Turkey. Perhaps the most important feature of the plan was that it was – as the Conservatives admitted – 'designed to put the future of the island out of discussion for seven years'.[37] It was to come into force, without further negotiation, in October. According to one Athens-based diplomat, Macmillan had been round the Mediterranean capitals 'slapping his proposals on the table.'

In September 1958, through Labour's international officer John Hatch, who had been working on his own plan for an independent Cyprus, Barbara was invited to Athens by Archbishop Makarios, the Greek Cypriot leader. Barbara was a person of standing in the party: she was vice-chairman,[38] and shortly to become chairman, an office awarded on the basis of length of service on the NEC. Makarios, meanwhile, had been exiled as part of the British response to the escalating violence in 1955 and was widely regarded as the main inspiration for the terror campaign, while his commitment to union with Greece, *enosis*, was the main obstacle on the Greek side to a settlement. Barbara decided to make a tour of the region, funded partly by the Greek government,[39] not an unusual move by a backbench MP but one requiring some caution and a careful assessment of the motives of the sponsor. The Greeks were looking for a way to derail the Macmillan plan.

Delay through diplomacy was one arm of the strategy; the second was to smear the name of the colonial power.

Barbara's reputation as a champion of the rights of the nationalists against the colonial security forces was now well established. It seems likely that she went not only to talk to Makarios, but as a guest of a Greek government that hoped she might undermine the British position by investigating allegations of brutality made against British troops.[40] The use of excessive force in Cyprus had been a cause célèbre on the left for most of the previous two years,[41] and the Greek government and Makarios had made much of it. Thirty-five thousand British soldiers were trying to handle a highly organized terror campaign being run from the hills with devastating efficiency by a retired right-wing Greek officer called Colonel George Grivas. One or two British soldiers, and sometimes more, were being picked off in ambushes and street shootings every week. It would be impossible to accuse the British military of excessive measures without appearing to be siding with the Cypriot terrorist movement, Eoka. It was, as Barbara had been repeatedly told, a highly sensitive moment to make the trip.

She did not blunder in immediately, however. She found Makarios full of charm but suspected that he was trying to encourage Labour to promote its own plan for the independence of Cyprus in order to jeopardize the Conservative government's. She made it clear to him that the only chance of formal support for independence would be if he anounced his own similar plan first. To her surprise, he indicated that he was indeed prepared to abandon *enosis* and embrace a guaranteed independence for the island. The British ambassador Sir Roger Allen, to whom Barbara recounted this concession, reported back, unimpressed: 'It is clear that this offer is designed partly to frustrate the execution of our plan and in particular the appointment of the Turkish Representative and partly to enlist support for the Greek case.'[42] The Greek government on the other hand, whose Prime Minister Barbara saw next, welcomed Makarios's proposal and, again to Barbara's surprise, indicated an enthusiasm for abandoning enosis, a strategy Prime Minister Karamanlis made clear they espoused only because of pressure from the Greek Cypriots.

But Barbara found the Turks deeply sceptical about any Greek move. And when she finally arrived in Cyprus to meet Governor Sir Hugh Foot, she was told firmly there was to be no alternative to the Macmillan plan. Barbara, believing that with Makarios's offer she had a diplomatic coup on her hands of the kind that would establish her as a heavyweight, and had even tried to persuade Sir Hugh that she would claim no credit for it.

Her focus then switched to the treatment of Cypriot villagers by the security forces. On her first night in Cyprus, there were four terrorist shootings including that of the newly arrived American consul. 'It was not the purpose of my visit to enquire into the conduct of the security forces in this emergency,' she wrote disingenuously in her autobiography thirty years later. She spent two of the three days she had in Cyprus investigating claims of brutality, and there was plenty to investigate. In her version of events, Barbara always insisted that her interest in the brutal treatment of the local population by British troops was triggered by a remark volunteered by the Governor, who had already set up a special investigation group to deal with complaints. She said he warned her that some villagers would tell her of bad treatment, and he went on to remark: 'I do not mind so much if the soldiers get a bit rough when they are engaged in hot pursuit. What would worry me is if they started to do it in cold blood.' There is no note of this remark in her diary, which is entirely focused on her diplomacy.

Barbara's key contact in Cyprus apart from the Governor himself was Charles Foley, the editor of the *Times of Cyprus*, an English-language paper he had founded three years earlier. It was his paper that had first highlighted the accusations of brutality. At dinner with him she met Michael Triandefyl-lides, a member of the Cypriot Human Rights Commission, whom she fell for. He was, she noted, 'a most intelligent & attractive lawyer . . . [he] told me that hundreds of atrocities had been carried out by Security Forces, as well as general rough treatment. He himself had raised many of these cases in vain. He suggested I go to Paphos, where a soldier with the Argyll and Sutherland Highlanders had been shot dead about ten days earlier.'[43] Foot had sent in a special investigation team after allegations of maltreatment of Cypriots, which found no one had been detained in hospital though there had been some minor injuries. Somehow Barbara persuaded Sir Hugh to allow the lawyer to be her escort on a trip to the detention camp at Pernomi. There the detainees made claims of maltreatment which Barbara herself regarded as extravagant.

She was on her way back to Athens for a final meeting with Makarios when a *Daily Herald* reporter asked her to comment on the allegations of brutality. She recalled, in 2002, that she told him what she remembered Sir Hugh telling her – that 'the troops were permitted and even encouraged to use unnecessarily rough measures after a shooting incident on the grounds that they were engaged in hot pursuit'. There is a subtle but important change of emphasis between her first note of his remark and the way she repeated it, which suggests she was remembering her interpretation of his remark and not the remark itself. When the reporter queried the word 'encouraged', she remembered that she withdrew it. There is no record of this conversation in her contemporaneous diary. But the *Herald* reporter sent back the quote. It was front-page news.

But there is in the diary, a glowing description of Makarios, whom she met again on her way back through Athens to draft his statement of renunciation of *enosis*. 'He manages to appear as though he is smiling straight at you, while really curious shutters are going up and down over his eyes. None the less, I like him. His gentleness, coupled with a steeliness of purpose, is very impressive. I don't think "wily" is the right word for him . . . There is a very real sincerity, and if he uses his wits, who can blame him?' In her diary she also wrote: 'He talked very precisely, very quietly, always through an interpreter. He didn't make it clear at first that his idea was to launch the plan through me. I think at the back of his mind he thought the Labour Party would come out with it first and he would then associate with it.' She added, 'I had not the slightest doubt in the sincerity of Makarios.'

She was impressed with his understanding of Labour's own problems: he told her he understood why her party could not openly support an independent Cyprus. 'They would seem to be stabbing their own soldiers in the back,' he told her. He convinced Barbara that he too was making a sacrifice. She wrote: 'My heart went out to Makarios. It will be a dreadful blow to his people to give up *enosis*, and it must be a dreadful humiliation to him to have to advise them to do so. He is pinning all his hopes now on the LP backing him up. I pray heaven I can persuade them to do so.' Barbara was stunned with her success. She tried to identify a motive. 'I still cannot believe all this international manoeuvring has been channelled through me. How did it happen? Why was I chosen?' Nonetheless, she couldn't resist the image of herself as 'a diplomatic Mata Hari envoy'.

Barbara flew home anticipating a hero's appearance at party conference as the woman who had saved Cyprus – and, incidentally, British soldiers – from further fratricidal conflict by persuading Makarios to abandon *enosis*.[44] To her dismay, the charge of brutality beat her back to London; even more damagingly, the reaction of a right-winger on the NEC, Jim Matthews, also preceded her arrival home. Barbara had dismissed Matthews, privately, months earlier as an 'exhibitionist loudmouth'.[45] He was an old soldier and a recent bitter critic of Barbara's conduct in the dispute over *Industry and Society*. By the time she arrived back in London on 22 September, Matthews's attack on her 'deplorable' remarks about the behaviour of the British troops, was headline news. Instead of the hero returning with olive branches with which to garland the left, she found herself a political pariah. However much of a cause célèbre the ill-treatment of Cypriots was among the left, the largely right-wing press were in no doubt that it was disloyalty verging on treachery to criticize troops who went in daily fear for their lives and lived cooped up in camps, effectively under curfew. The day after her return she was called in for a very public carpeting by Gaitskell, Bevan and Callaghan. Bevan nodded as Gaitskell bitterly attacked her for criticizing British troops while she was abroad. He also questioned her suitability for the party chairmanship. She was guilty, as far as they were concerned, of naively jeopardizing the election and condemning the party to years more in opposition. She would retain the chairmanship, but she was barred from speaking about Cyprus at conference. The diplomatic breakthrough she thought she had achieved was dismissed. Later, one of Gaitskell's team briefed a journalist that the party leader thought she had simply been used as 'Makarios's messenger girl'. Barbara left the dressing-down session after an hour, 'pale and agitated', according to gleeful political journalists.

The headlines were savage: 'Babs Boobs', 'We Disown Barbara', 'Mrs Castle Carpeted'. The right-wing *Daily Sketch*'s columnist Candidus, who led the attack, referred to 'the most disgraceful episode in Barbara Castle's political career . . . coming at a time when Cyprus has never been more trigger-happy, or a just solution so delicately in the balance, it is political dynamite'. She was accused of giving comfort to the Eoka terrorists and her suitability as next party chairman was again questioned. Barbara tried to put her side of the argument. She told the *Daily Mail* and the *Daily Telegraph*: 'In one village, villagers showed me their injuries, hospital dockets and receipts for the cost of treatment, thus showing the government's investigations were inadequate.'[46] But no one wanted to know. Nor did many want to hear about her meetings with Makarios. When she spoke at a conference fringe meeting of the Movement for Colonial Freedom, she was shouted down by Empire Loyalists who chanted 'Traitor, traitor' until Ted leapt at them and had to be restrained.

Tony Benn, still close to Gaitskell but sharing Barbara's interest in Cyprus, was appalled.

Barbara Castle's statement about roughness by British troops in Cyprus is headline news. But Barbara's main contribution has been to bring back from Athens news that Makarios is willing to ban [*sic*] Enosis. This is staggering news that transforms the whole situation. Only the Vice Chairman of the Party and a firm supporter of Cypriot freedom like Barbara could have got this interview and helped to shape this new policy. But today she went to see Gaitskell . . . he saw fit to issue a statement afterwards in effect repudiating her. Without paying tribute to her diplomatic achievement with Makarios he concentrated on the object of the press hunt . . . and thus encouraged it. I was so sick that the Leader should have repudiated a colleague who was in difficulty. It was such a poor demonstration of the Gallup poll mentality defeating ordinary instincts of personal loyalty and leadership.[47]

More damagingly, at the party conference a sustained attempt was made by the right to use the row to unseat Barbara from the chairmanship. It came to nothing but it was followed by a steady flow of articles and profiles asking whether she had what it took, despite her undoubted ability, to handle life at the top. 'Responsibility and respectability – even the shreds of it that come from being a PPS – did not sit easily on her pretty shoulders,' wrote the *Daily Mail*.

Makarios was right about the difficulty of selling his new position. Colonel Grivas was not impressed with the news, sent immediately by the Archbishop: 'I yesterday made a statement to Mrs Barbara Castle, the MP, by which I virtually created a new situation . . . Although this new line could possibly be described as a retreat, it is what the situation, coldly appraised, requires.'[48] The response from Grivas – whose Eoka never gave up the dream of enosis – was to step up his campaign of violence. The day the party conference ended, a sergeant's wife, Katie Cutliffe, was callously murdered in the street in Famagusta while out shopping with her teenage daughter and a friend.

Barbara was ambushed by journalists with this latest news, and the story began all over again. She had been widely criticized for not spending time with the troops. Newspapers made good the omission. Less widely reported in the British press was the news that two Cypriots had died, crushed to death in the ensuing round-up, while a young girl had suffered a fatal heart attack. More than a hundred Cypriots were injured in what a subsequent inquiry found had been an attempt to force people into a truck so violently that those in front were trampled underfoot by those behind them. The coroner said the security forces had used 'a degree of force that would appear to be entirely unjustified'. The families of the dead were awarded compensation and Macmillan's papers suggest that, had he been pressed, he would have conceded in parliament that excessive force had been used.[49]

In due course, a moral victory for Barbara took shape. First Bevan and then Gaitskell cautiously took up the Makarios approach. Within six months, Cyprus became an independent state. Half a generation later it was partitioned. But the episode further damaged Barbara's image. Confirming the prejudices of the party leadership, the press was happy to embellish their caricature of her as a politician who need not be taken seriously. Afterwards, Gaitskell told confidants that he would never give Barbara a serious job in government.

Even her friends, like the *Times of Cyprus*, wrote that she had to make a choice: was she going to accept the discipline of being Labour Party chairman or waste her talents and risk becoming that stock figure of the party, the recalcitrant left-winger? The attempt to use the episode to oust her from the party chairmanship was another illustration of her vulnerability to those on the unscrupulous right who regarded her as a dangerous, divisive troublemaker.

There was, unsurprisingly, no succour from the Tories. The Colonial Secretary, her old bête noire Alan Lennox-Boyd, refused to meet her immediately and in the end she did not get a chance to brief him until mid-October. But from the official record, it seems that he was unwillingly impressed with her grasp of the situation. Although there was criticism of her failure to see that *enosis* might still happen under guaranteed independence – it would only take a plebiscite, after all – her observations of the Turks' determination to achieve partition and the alarm in the Greek Cypriot camp were taken seriously. However, in a Commons debate at the end of the month, Macmillan dismissed her as a patsy, commenting: 'To reinforce the diplomatic efforts of the Greek Government at the North Atlantic Council, Archbishop Makarios, at the beginning of the last week of September, launched a new propaganda campaign.'

There was one last sting in the tail. During the 1959 election a Tory candidate and later MP, Christopher Chataway, attacked Barbara for accusing British troops of 'torturing' suspects. Barbara, never able to let an issue drop where she felt wronged, sued. After briefing a Labour MP QC with no experience of libel who had volunteered to represent her case for nothing, Barbara lost. She and Ted faced having to sell their newly acquired country cottage to pay her £8,000 costs, until Morgan Philips, the party's general secretary and an old opponent, generously organized a fund for her.[50] Reviewing a book on the Cyprus Emergency by Charles Foley in the *New Statesman* in June 1962, Barbara reflected on the whole experience:

[The book] does not spare the Governors who failed, including Sir Hugh Foot, perhaps the most wretched failure of all. Nor does it spare the Labour politicians, including myself, who drew back dismayed when they realised how successfully the government had embroiled the army's emotions in its colonial war. No political leader in Britain dared denounce the ill-treatment of Cypriots in the Famagusta round-up following the murder of Mrs Cutliffe . . . The lesson of this book is that once a colonial war breaks out we all become its prisoners.

★

In March 1959, Barbara once again challenged the British colonial authorities in Kenya. She had begun to hear rumours of a massacre in a camp called Hola, and enquiries confirmed that eleven detainees had been beaten to death in a new campaign intended to destroy their adherence to the Mau Mau cause. The victims had been so malnourished in the camp that they suffered from scurvy, a condition which made them peculiarly vulnerable to the kind of injuries caused by being beaten. The prison governor had claimed they died of poisoning from contaminated water. This time Barbara scored a direct hit. Her enquiries revealed that the governor had expressed concern to his superior about his instructions to make 'eighty-five desperate hard-core Mau Mau detainees work against their will', which had led to the beatings. Yet no one but the prison governor was to be censured, and even he was to be retired on full pay. Barbara rose to the occasion: 'Can Hon. Members let these proceedings go through without censuring a man like that for sheer downright incompetence? I am not accusing anybody here tonight of sadism. I am accusing them of incompetence so overwhelming as to amount to criminal negligence that goes all the way up the line.' She spoke for nearly three-quarters of an hour in a long and careful indictment of all those involved, culminating in Lennox-Boyd. 'When this terrible shame comes upon the Colonial Secretary, whether he willed it or not, and he does not act, he shows he does not deserve to hold office.'[51] What she did not know was that Lennox-Boyd had offered his resignation and it had been refused by Macmillan, who wrote in his memoirs that if Labour had forced a vote on the issue, at least ten Tories would have voted against their government.

The campaign absorbed much of her time and effort. She was inundated with letters from Kenya from men alleging more abuse. When she raised the issue with Lennox-Boyd he told her they were time-wasters, or worse. 'If the honourable lady is receiving a large number of letters from detainees, it is all part of a campaign to smear the security forces and the administration in Kenya,'[52] he told her. She was sneered at in the lobbies and criticized in the press, even when her questions uncovered brutality. She was accused of publicity-seeking, not least by Lennox-Boyd himself. Sometimes she claimed defiantly that 'the beastlier people are to me the more sure I am of my own rightness', but on other occasions she admitted that she worried whether she was doing the right thing for the wrong reason.

As the 1959 election campaign began, a journalist on the *Evening Standard* once again asked whether Barbara was made of the right stuff. 'Is she to be an electoral asset in the vital days ahead, or is she to be her old, uncompromising self, a liability to the party and a pain in the neck to the unions? It is for her to decide.'[53] Labour went into the campaign with its organization overhauled by Harold Wilson and a confidence belied by the polls, which showed a significant Tory recovery. It was to be a foretaste of the 1987 campaign: glossy manifesto, poster sites, photo-calls – and at the end of it, a one-hundred-seat Tory majority. Labour Party unity was symbolized by a campaign poster of Barbara, looking like a Butlin's redcoat, standing between Gaitskell and Bevan. A cynic might have thought she was keeping them apart. But it was not Barbara who was about to stumble, but Gaitskell. Cautious, persuasive, moderate, in the final days he took only one risk. It was the wrong risk: he promised tax cuts, forgetting that no one votes Labour for lower taxes. In the view of colleagues and commentators alike, he had reminded the voters of what Crossman called Labour's 'financial insincerity'. The day after the results – showing the party with its lowest share of the vote since 1935 – Gaitskell, shattered, informally invited some of his 'intelligent young men' along to talk about what to do next. Their analysis, according to Roy Jenkins,[54] blamed the party's third defeat in a row on a range of issues from the unpopularity of nationalization, via the unpopularity of Labour councils and trade unions, to a general sense that the party was old-fashioned. As Bevan observed, it was unpopular because it was Labour. A series of articles, most notoriously by Gaitskell's close associate Douglas Jay, called for radical reform, including a redefinition of Clause 4 of the party's constitution which at that time made public ownership the party's main objective. Gaitskell, on a brief visit to Crossman, told him that constitutional reform was overdue and he wanted the party to be entirely restructured on a federal basis, giving MPs the same rights to elect representatives as the constituencies and the trade unions.[55]

The defeat had reopened the unresolved tensions within the party. Both Bevan and Wilson – the latter not invited to the Gaitskell election postmortem and now, according to the whispers, under threat of demotion from the role of shadow chancellor which he had held for the last two years – scented an opportunity, which Gaitskell's ambitious and unsettling proposals for constitutional reform could only enhance. Meanwhile, the proposals engendered an unprecedented (and unacknowledged) common agenda between Barbara and the Labour leader. Gaitskell seemed to be offering the reduction in trade union control of the party for which she had campaigned for years. The unions, however, were not going to tolerate Gaitskell's reforms, as Walter Padley, general secretary of the Union of Shop, Distributive and Allied Workers, and an MP, made clear at the first post-election

NEC meeting. Barbara was alarmed that Gaitskell's dramatic proposals might provoke such a backlash that it would be impossible to consider any change at all. It was Gaitskell himself who saved the day: '"Surely you are not suggesting that there is no case for any reconsideration of the constitution at all?" . . . It would be quite wrong for us to assume that there was nothing in the party that needed to be studied and changed. For all his faults [she concluded in a rare moment of enthusiasm], that man has courage.'[56] Bevan ridiculed the idea of in-depth surveys to discover why people had voted as they had. Barbara summed up his argument: 'People never voted for the reasons that they said – or even thought – they did. No one was going to admit, for instance, even to himself, that he was indifferent to the well-being of old-age pensioners. He therefore found an excuse to rationalise his self-interest.' Bevan warned the trade unions that their lack of zeal had contributed to the party's defeat. 'It is no satisfaction to us if we are going to the cemetery to know that the trade unions are paying the funeral expenses . . . the individual trade unionist votes at the ballot box against the chaos caused by his own wildcat strikes.'

Bevan, now sixty-two, was back at the peak of his form. The party was split again, and this time no one could doubt that Gaitskell was to blame. It was trade unionists against intellectuals, offering new alliances in the old battle of right against left. Away from Westminster, the opposition to Gaitskell's plans to redefine the party's objectives rapidly mounted. Barbara, as party chairman, opened the conference, abbreviated because of the election, in Blackpool in November 1959 with a tumultuously received fundamentalist defence of socialism and a reminder of its ethical base which, she implied, the Gaitskellites had forgotten:

> We have spent 50 years of political life proving to the people of this country that economic and social morality go hand in hand . . . The morality of a society is not created in a vacuum. It springs from the way it organises its economic life and distributes its rewards. Today we live in a society in which the bonds of common interest have been deliberately loosened by Government policy. The highest virtue lies in looking after number one, and the greatest merit is being strong enough to do it . . . economic might has become social right and the Devil has taken communal interest.

If people rejected socialism, the answer was not less socialism, but more education. At the last election, voters had been 'suckered' by the Tories.

The only way to attack inequality is at the source. Radicalism without socialism is an also-ran . . . either we must convince the people of this country that they – and not a few private interests – should control their economic lives, or we shall shrink into an impotent appendage of the windfall state. And this is the real case for public ownership. We don't want to take over industries merely in order to make them more efficient, but to make them responsible to us all.[57]

Look at the triumphs of state enterprise and nationalized industries, she went on – the sputnik now circling the moon, the hovercraft developed by the National Research Development Corporation, Nimrod, the giant atom-smasher at Harwell.

Do we believe that our moral aims can only be achieved by economic means? Are we prepared to affirm therefore that what Nye has called 'the commanding heights of the economy' must be publicly financed and under public control . . . once we have agreed about ends we can be as flexible as we need about the means of achieving them.[58]

Gaitskell, sitting beside Barbara on the platform, now backtracked on the original prospectus.

We have no intention of abandoning public ownership and accepting for all time the present frontiers of the public sector. Secondly, we regard public ownership not as an end in itself but as a means – and not necessarily the only or most important one to certain ends . . . we do not aim to nationalise every private firm or to create an endless series of state monopolies. While we shall certainly wish to extend social ownership in particular directions, as circumstances warrant, our goal is not 100% State ownership.

And, since nationalization was no longer the goal, it was more sensible to say so, instead of having the party's objective defined as the achievement of nationalization, when that was a means, not an end. As one delegate, the Bevanite MP Benn Levy, pointed out, 'If there is any person in this hall who thought those two voices were speaking the same language, then he is very deaf indeed. One might even be forgiven for thinking that one of them at least was addressing a different party conference!'

It was, by common consent, Bevan who saved the day. In what was to be his last conference speech, he played for the unity of the trinity of chairman, leader and deputy. 'What does that make me?' Barbara remembered him saying. 'The Holy Ghost?'[59] 'I agree with Barbara, I agree with

Hugh and I agree with myself, that the chief argument for us is not how we can change our policy so as to make it attractive to the electorate. That is not the purpose of this Conference. The purpose is to try, having decided what our policy should be, to put it as attractively as possible to the population.' On their way back from Blackpool, in one of their last conversations, Bevan – 'more charming to me than he ever has been' – told Barbara that hers was 'the best chairman's speech I ever heard'. Gaitskell is now a prisoner, he said. 'The real question,' Barbara concluded, 'is whether he is now prepared to work to a sustained and thorough strategy to switch the party on to a socialist track. Certainly the moment has never been more propitious in view of the attitude of the trade unions.'[60] Bevan arrived at the conference, one cartoonist observed, on the back of the leadership tandem and left it on the front. He was in charge. But by January 1960 he was seriously ill in hospital with cancer, and although he rallied a little, by July he was dead.

When the news of his death finally came, there was universal dismay. Barbara said she was 'sick with shock'. 'His presence is with us all as vividly as it was before his illness began. A sense of loss pervades everyone. What will Parliament – and Party conference – be like without him?' She had already written his obituary for the *New Statesman*. 'I have been frequently dealt with by him in scathing terms. I have been politically abandoned by him, too, more than once. And yet, there it is: I am overwhelmed with despair – and with love.' She did not eulogize. He did not ask you to agree with him, she wrote, but if you did you strung along. 'It is an astonishing tribute to the power of the man that, though loyalty was for him so often a one-sided obligation, so many thousands did string along, with a personal devotion that no other political leader of any party, except Winston Churchill, has been able to command in my day . . . He made socialism . . . appear like common sense patriotism, and patriotism in its turn the ally, rather than the enemy, of a wider humanity.'[61] Bevan, despite his flaws, remained in her view the greatest exponent of socialism of her lifetime, a poet of politics. After his death, Barbara and Jennie Lee stalked with suppressed hostility around one another, each believing herself the better champion of his legacy. At heart, Barbara was always a Bevanite.

8. Bombshell

Ah! When shall all men's good
Be each man's rule, and universal Peace
Lie like a shaft of light across the land?

Alfred Lord Tennyson, 'The Golden Year'

At the end of 1959, Barbara's friend Richard Crossman voted her his woman of the year: 'In the House of Commons, she is the only opponent whom ex-colonial secretary Alan Lennox-Boyd[1] really fears. Then at our Labour party conference at Blackpool where she was chairman she simply stole the show from Bevan and Gaitskell by making what is usually a purely formal introduction the most powerful speech of the conference. I should add that she is equal to men on their own ground without ever once unfairly exploiting her very considerable feminine charm.'[2] Barbara's tenure as chairman had established her as a significant figure within the party. There had been no more embarrassing storms, and the courage and correctness of her stand on the Hola massacre in Kenya in the summer of 1959 had added retrospective justification to her earlier criticisms of the conduct of colonial officials. In the new parliament, she had been disappointed not to be elected to the shadow cabinet, but Gaitskell overcame his reservations about her and gave her a middle-ranking front-bench job as shadow minister of works, a job, which, according to his biographer Francis Wheen, Tom Driberg believed he had been promised. Gaitskell allegedly thought 'mucking about with curtains for embassies' would be the perfect occupation for his ageing gay friend. Barbara had an entirely different idea about what the job involved. The brief covered the Palace of Westminster. Soon the newspapers were full of reports of the absurd conditions under which MPs were supposed to work: the scandalous shortage of desks, offices and telephones which Barbara

had been complaining about ever since she had come into parliament fifteen
years earlier.

Barbara Castle was in her fiftieth year, but few meeting her for the first
time would realize it. She had anyway been taking a year off her age since
she was thirty-eight, although (to her later regret) she never went as far as
disguising her age in *Who's Who*. She told one interviewer that she saw
herself as thirty-five and she always would. She was still strikingly good-
looking, as slim and stylish as she had been ten years earlier. She was also still
the object of much lubricious speculation. The outside world might, slowly,
be changing, but Westminster was as much a male society as it had ever
been. On one level, she had to handle a mix of ostentatious gallantry and
blatant lasciviousness; on another, a constant belittling by men who regarded
a woman as even worse than a left-winger. 'Men are so terribly sex-
conscious,' she said. 'If a man disagrees with you in public life, he's also
probably resenting you sexually. Sex resentment colours a great deal of
masculine opinion.'[3] There were not nearly enough other women to offer
protective cover. After the 1959 election, only thirteen Labour MPs were
women, and across the parties there were only twenty-five altogether. Most
responded to the resentment Barbara identified by dressing inconspicuously
and conducting themselves earnestly; no one doubted Barbara's seriousness,
but inconspicuousness was an alien quality. After fifteen years in the House,
she was no longer the youngest woman MP, but set against the cast of elderly
trade unionists and over-promoted councillors, she dazzled.

At Oxford and immediately afterwards Barbara had made no secret of
her sexual independence. Ted made little attempt to hide his, even after he
was married. She had written, early on, a poem to him which suggested
strong disapproval of casual sexual encounters:

> You talk of love in bawd, but never Keats;
> Cultivate music halls in dubious streets;
> And frankly glory in chastity.
> Woman is fleeting game, to be brought low
> And being won, to be despised so.[4]

Yet, in the closed and libidinous atmosphere of Westminster, it was generally
assumed that she was more than just a flirt. There was gossip about her, and
about Ted. One friend of them both said: 'Ted was a bed-hopper. He was
not faithful, always patting bottoms, a bit cocksure', while Barbara was
regarded as 'very close' to John Freeman. Colleagues on the *New Statesman*
observed an affectionate informality between them.[5] But Freeman was not

the only person with whom she was linked. There were also tales of threatened divorce and salacious talk about how many of the Parliamentary Labour Party might be cited in court. 'There are actual accusations against one's morals,' Barbara complained bitterly to one interviewer.[6] In the deeply personal and intense left–right battles, sexual innuendo was just one more area over which to fight, and those most avid for gossip were often Barbara's political rivals. Maybe the gossip was correct; it hardly marked her out. Hugh Gaitskell was absorbed in an affair with Ann Fleming, the wife of James Bond creator Ian, while Wilson's private secretary Marcia Williams was involved in a long affair with, and ultimately had two children by, a married political journalist, Walter Terry.

There was also talk about her erratic behaviour. Crossman recorded furiously how she got up in the middle of a small and important dinner party insisting that she had to go and look something up in the library. 'Nothing would restrain her, so she popped off without saying good-bye. If she wants to know why she's unpopular, I could tell her.'[7] Similar stories emerged from her 1954 sojourn with the Mitchisons at Carradale in Scotland, where gossip had it that she had gone with her marriage on the brink of total breakdown.

But however fraught their marriage may sometimes have been, Barbara and Ted stuck together. In 1958 they had bought a small cottage in the Chilterns, the Beacons, at Cadmore End. Ted's father had been a professional gardener. Ted, with time on his hands, took it up. Barbara, who had grown up with dogs and always wanted one, gave Ted a puppy for his birthday – called Aldie, short for Aldermaston, at first the destination and later the starting point of the CND marches of the late 1950s, 'because he loved marching'. The creature became a child substitute, loved by them both, and its death in 1969 caused days of anguish and even inspired Barbara to write poetry for the first time in twenty-five years. Ted, an only child, was close to his parents, who played an important role in both their lives as a source of quiet, undemanding, undramatic normality in contrast with the residual rivalry and other challenges of Barbara's own family. Mrs Castle, Barbara's mother-in-law, had a particularly soothing phrase that she brought out whenever Barbara complained (as she often did) of some injustice or slight. 'It isn't *meant*, dear,' she said, a remark Barbara typed out on a piece of paper and kept beside her. The Castle parents still lived in Hampshire, and until Barbara and Ted bought the cottage their house was often a base for walking holidays, an idyll about which Barbara could romance. 'To the candidate fresh – or jaded – from the General Election, to stay in our New Forest hamlet is a refresher course. It is the perfect corrective to high level campaigning, not because one escapes from politics to a world of ragged robin, cow parsley and star of Bethlehem, but because one is brought back firmly to first principles, like a University graduate reawakened to the meaning of the alphabet.'[8]

Ted, in the words of a friend, was still 'trailing himself humiliatingly round the selection conferences', the choice restricted by his known Bevanite allegiances. But after 1959, he abandoned the quest. He was a local councillor in Islington and became in 1964 an alderman of the Greater London Council. Westminster politics, however, were experienced, or endured, at second hand. 'Barbara would return from the Commons,' said a councillor colleague, 'her eyes glittering with rage, having not had the opportunity to make a speech she had been sitting all day to make. "Make it to us," we said, and she did, marching up and down between Ted and his friends.' At times Barbara's success must have been galling. Towards the end of the decade, if not before, their relationship changed. She was starting to value Ted for his emotional support. The Cyprus experience had been shattering for the bile released against her, in person as well as in the press. The tougher the going, the more she needed him in the background, encouraging and reassuring her. She became more careful with the image of her marriage, simultaneously promoting Ted's forbearance and her own ordinariness. Sometimes the two conflicted. In August 1962, she complained in the *People*: 'It makes me mad to see how otherwise decent and well-behaved husbands expect their wives to be cook, cleaner, valet and general run-about. One husband I know [leaves] his clothes in a heap on the floor every day . . . who taught him to behave like that? His doting mother."[9]

In real life, Barbara had little patience with women who were mere housewives; chat about clothes she could always find time for, but women who had no occupation outside the home she dismissed with something like contempt. Yet she saw the value of being considered a mere unthreatening housewife herself. She rarely mentioned that she also had a housekeeper. 'I have the normal womanly instincts,' she insisted, and she and Ted were pictured washing up. She was a pioneer of the housewife-superstar role picked up by Margaret Thatcher and parodied so brilliantly a few years later by Dame Edna Everage – just an ordinary woman who applied the valuable skills of housewifery to politics and economics. She was photographed buying saucepans and cooking as well as looking like a film star with her long cigarette holder and painted nails. 'I've never seen life as a choice between a career and a family. I married a Socialist I met at a Labour Party conference. We share the same political enthusiasms. I have no children but that is not my choice. I see no reason why a woman should not be in parliament and bring up a family too.'[10] To another interviewer she said, 'I am particularly lucky in being married to a man whose instinctive reactions to so many things are exactly the same as mine. We have a harmony and companionship ... I am a very happy woman.'[11] Yet politics still mattered more than anything else. The compliment she most treasured, she said, was when she was described as ' "the only woman who met the men on their own terms". Now I wouldn't feel the same pleasure if my husband or anyone else paid me a compliment about a new hat or suddenly said that I looked pretty.'[12]

Much of the attention Barbara attracted in the media was provoked by her contradictions. She produced a noise disproportionate to her size and her sex and completely at odds with her appearance. For, if it was considered unusual for a woman to be so openly ambitious, it was considered almost improper for her to be so unmistakably feminine, to like showy hats like the astrakhan number she bought in a Moscow department store. She ignored conventions about the muted colours redheads were supposed to wear, and she always wore jewellery, usually large and ostentatious. Her secretaries would be sent around London to collect clothes from the dressmaker or the cleaners, while she would struggle for an hour to iron a blouse meticulously even if she was going to wear a jacket over the top. She was a perfectionist to the point of self-indulgence. But it was all part of her femininity; and being feminine, she said, was about being true to oneself. 'In the end a woman in public life will be accepted for her ability to do what she is setting out to do.'[13] The idea that she somehow had a man's brain in a woman's body she dismissed as a piece of male arrogance, 'which assumes that anything that works at all efficiently must be of the male gender'.

She used interviews to present a kinder, gentler Barbara, almost apologizing for the tiger-like image engendered by her performances in the Commons and on television. She suffered terribly from nerves before she spoke, she explained, and it was the attempt to compensate that produced the hard-as-diamonds, battling Barbara. 'I see a much gentler person than others see ... I'm constantly astonished at the impression I give people of being an aggressive, tough person. One is much more warm-hearted, I think, more hesitant.' But what she was most scared of was fear itself, the fear that would lead her to push to the front to escape from danger, or to back off from an argument. Not having enough courage to stand up for what she believed, she regarded as a fatal weakness. 'There are great temptations to play safe,' she admitted. 'And then I think a slow moral corruption sets in ... the higher you go the more you've got to lose. It becomes easier to argue with yourself. And it can be a very tricky thing indeed, this. You need timing and you need judgement and you need courage.'[14]

Her courage was not doubted, but her judgement was. 'You always know when she's there,' wrote one sketch writer, praising her contribution to the debate on the Hola massacre. 'Pale and vivid and watchful ... in attack she provides one of the most awesome sights the House of Commons has to offer. She crouches forward, her glowing head lowered, gathering herself for the assault ... sometimes she makes a kill; sometimes she misses her spring and suffers for it.' But hers was not an easy personality, and she knew it. 'I suppose that I have a domineering manner. At times it makes me look as if I am a bully. People think that I am bitter and aggressive ... I am very self-absorbed.' There is a suggestion in her comments that the quiet and the self-effacing were somehow lesser people. She asked rhetorically, 'What *can* it have been like for those Victorian women? – fancy having to pretend all the time you were a fool.'[15]

There was always a sense of drama, observers noted, around Barbara. She was an actress. 'The third-floor flat on Highgate Hill has the appearance of a stage set. Pale sun streams through bay windows. The walls are white and lemon. There is an off-white carpet ... The telephone rings. All that is needed to complete the theatrical illusion is for a handsome redhead in pink mules and a long cigarette holder to rush in and answer it breathlessly. Enter the chairman of the Labour Party, at the rush. She is a redhead. She wears pink mules.'[16] Her friends sometimes groaned at the way she saw life and politics as a performance art, but more often admired her for it. Crossman spent more and more time with her. 'Anne [his wife[17]] and I spent Sunday morning walking on the beach with Barbara and Ted which gave the gossip columnists a great deal to write about Barbara's paddling. What a girl she is! This conference publicity is like blood to a ghost. She throve on it, though sometimes she had slight indigestion.'[18]

While Bevan lay dying in the spring of 1960, the Labour movement prepared for another paroxysm of dissent. Out of respect for the sick Bevan, the debate on Gaitskell's constitutional reforms had been delayed until March, but in the interim, the sequel to the party's 1957 nuclear-weapons crisis was rapidly unfolding. It was to become hopelessly conflated with Gaitskell's desire to reform the way the party worked. Barbara was at the forefront, determined to take the opportunity, if it came, to unseat Gaitskell, although without a very clear idea of who should replace him. Gaitskell and Barbara rarely encountered each other except in battle. Once they had to travel together to Hull and back – he was 'an arid companion', she said afterwards. Barbara found small-talk difficult, and they clearly could not discuss politics without fighting. Their approach was culturally and emotionally different – the visceral against the intellectual, the passionate against the rational – but, as Ben Pimlott observed in his study of Wilson, it was the style that contrasted more than the substance. The points of agreement were there, but neither was constitutionally able to look for them. According to Anthony Howard, political correspondent of the *New Statesman* from 1961 to 1964, who saw them both and was particularly close to Gaitskell,

> Gaitskell really loathed her, in a way he didn't loathe Dick . . . He told me after the Cyprus row, 'I could strangle her with my own hands'. He had absolutely no respect for her; he didn't rate Barbara intellectually. Dick was cleverer than him, Harold was an Oxford don – but Barbara got a third class degree and he was a tremendous intellectual snob. 'Third class mind' he would say. He didn't expect Alice Bacon or Bessie Braddock to be tremendous intellectuals, but if you had been to Oxford and muffed it, then you didn't count.[19]

Gaitskell was set on establishing control over the party by using his strength in the PLP to dominate Barbara and the left in party conference. It was an intentionally confrontational strategy, forfeiting the confidence even of the trade union wing of the movement. Without Bevan, the left was fragmenting. Barbara was not even among Gaitskell's most extreme opponents. They were led by Michael Foot in the offices of *Tribune* and Ian Mikardo in the Commons; Barbara was gravitating towards Wilson and the centre-left.

In January 1960, as the gravity of Bevan's illness became apparent, she and Crossman had met Wilson and discussed whether he would challenge for the deputy leadership. Barbara was more enthusiastic than Crossman, who thought the party should not have 'two Oxford dons' at the top. In Barbara's mind, Wilson was less than perfect, but probably the only possible challenger. First, however, Gaitskell's grip on power had to be loosened. The party was internally divided again on defence; the old German rearmament issue had been reopened by the proposal to arm West Germany with nuclear weapons. Then, far more cataclysmically, it emerged that the development of Blue Streak, the system intended to deliver Britain's H-bomb, had been abandoned. Once again, the whole structure of Britain's defence policy had to be re-examined. The question to be answered, Barbara said, was how to stop the spread of nuclear weapons. The options for Britain, she wrote in a long article in the *New Statesman* in May 1960, were fourfold: to buy American weapons, to make her own, to internationalize control, or to abandon 'all ideas of nuclear weapons that are in any sense our own'. The latter was her preference. But again she left unanswered the question of whether Britain could shelter under NATO's nuclear umbrella, or indeed whether opposition to nuclear weapons should be carried to the point of destroying NATO itself.

In March, trade union opposition had forced Gaitskell to concede defeat in his attempt to redraft Clause 4. The party would continue to aspire to common ownership of the means of production. Barbara and Crossman between them secured the victory by insisting that Gaitskell's redefinition was merely a 'restatement and amplification' of the orginal Clause 4. Jennie Lee, of whom Barbara was never more dismissive – 'Jennie, as the widow-elect of the great man, intervened with dignity (and was listened to in respectful silence)'[20] – successfully proposed a further compromise incorporating the key Bevanite reference to 'the commanding heights of the economy':

> [The Party] is convinced that [the] social and economic objectives can be achieved only on the basis of a substantial measure of common ownership in varying forms, including state-owned industries and firms, producer and consumer cooperation, municipal ownership, and public participation in private concerns. Recognising that both public and private enterprise have a proper place in the economy, it believes that further extension of common ownership should be decided from time to time in the light of those objectives by an extension of common ownership substantial enough to give the community power over the commanding heights of the economy.[21]

Gaitskell said at the end, 'I have given up a good deal this afternoon.[22] He was forced to look for other ways of taking control of the party, as the campaign against the bomb returned to challenge his authority.

By mid-1960, it was clear the tide had turned among the trade unions on the issue of nuclear weapons. In the Commons in March, a month after the cancellation of Blue Streak, Barbara and Crossman led a rebellion of a hundred on an official Labour defence motion. At Easter, the first CND march from the Aldermaston nuclear research centre to London ended triumphantly when one hundred thousand people gathered for the biggest demonstration ever seen in Trafalgar Square. Barbara was a member of CND, but never made the whole pilgrimage. She, Ted, Aldie the dog and at least once her nephew, Marjorie's son Hugh McIntosh, would set off with Michael Foot and the photographers, but by nightfall they would be tucked up at home in bed. CND was like feminism for Barbara, a distraction from the main aim and a magnet for a worryingly varied bunch of supporters. Nuclear weapons might be immoral and a good cause around which to build support for the party, but the main focus of political activity had to be on winning the world for socialism. In 1960, it looked for a few heady months as if the two aims could be combined. Trade union conferences began passing unilateralist motions that would bind their delegates at the Labour Party conference in the autumn to vote against the bomb. On the right, as defeat loomed, there was serious discussion about whether it was time to split the party and lose the troublesome vote-losing left.[23] Barbara seemed determined to provoke the right-wingers. Late in April, she used the tail-end of an NEC meeting – after Crossman and Wilson had left and so were unable to restrain her from a course they thought mistaken – to bounce the party into committing itself to review its defence policy in consultation with the TUC. For the right, the spectre now loomed of two arms of the Labour movement – the unions and the rank and file through the NEC – agreeing a defence policy which the third arm, the PLP, could not accept. The need for reform of the constitution, to give the greatest weight to the PLP, suddenly became pressing. Anthony Crosland wrote a Fabian pamphlet arguing that while conference represented a mere fifty thousand activists, the PLP represented twelve million voters. A significant number of trade unions that had already decided to support a unilateralist line, for the first time lined up against the right to prevent constitutional change undercutting their policy objectives.

At the forefront of the demand for unilateralism was Frank Cousins, now leader of one of the biggest unions, the Transport and General Workers', a member of the NEC and author of a unilateralist resolution to conference.[24] In June, he came out against the draft NEC policy that had been drawn up by the defence review committee, because – Barbara was told by George Brown, the right-wing ex-trade unionist – Gaitskell had deliberately set out to provoke him. 'Brown is firmly of the opinion that Hugh was determined not to accept any draft which Cousins supported, because of the interpretation that would be put on it.'[25] She went to see Cousins to try to persuade him to accept the draft so that Gaitskell, not he, would be isolated. She warned Gaitskell to his face that the party would not tolerate the 'arbitrary personal rule' that his refusal to accept majority decisions would mean. However, when the outside left, Victory For Socialism, an organization backed by Michael Foot and Ian Mikardo whose mission was to revive the Bevanite left in the constituencies, called for Gaitskell to go, triggering a vote of no confidence among Labour MPs, she backed the leader. Gaitskell won by 179 votes to 7. To her rage she was reported as abstaining or even voting against. 'Do you really think I could go on serving on the front bench under a man in whom I had refused to express confidence?' she demanded with dramatic outrage, when she was directly challenged. At the first party meeting she restated her position. 'I very much enjoyed getting up and saying sweetly, "I want to point out that I did not abstain on the motion of no confidence yesterday – I voted for – and I think that those of my colleagues who leaked to the press the statement that I did [abstain] might have had the courtesy to confirm the fact with me first." A lot of people looked uncomfortable.'[26]

In July 1960, constitutional reform was shelved and the leader resolved to make the bomb issue into one about who ran the party. Crossman believed he had found a compromise between the party and Frank Cousins's Transport and General resolution, but Gaitskell refused to accept it or even to talk to Cousins. The TGWU's resolution called for an end to the testing, manufacture and use of nuclear weapons, and opposed missile bases in the UK. Unsurprisingly, Gaitskell regarded this as a unilateralist move (although Cousins insisted that, by leaving open the issue of NATO and Britain's existing arsenal, it was not). Unilateralism was widely portrayed as a Communist-inspired doctrine, even though the official Soviet position continued to be multilateralist. Yet such was the tide of opposition that when in September, Barbara, Crossman, Wilson and Tony Greenwood met, the unspoken question was whether Gaitskell could survive: 'We all agreed it was a good tactic to show that Hugh was unwilling to talk with Frank Cousins under any circumstances even to avoid a split at Conference and a possible defeat for the platform.'[27]

By the time the party gathered at Scarborough at the end of the month, neither side was arguing about the bomb at all, but about who was boss; and Gaitskell's speech left his audience in no doubt that, having lost the first round of his battle – to reform relationships within the party – he was launching round two. He challenged the unilateralists to show that they were not also neutralists who could not in all conscience stay under NATO's nuclear umbrella, and he accused some of using the motion to try to unseat him from the leadership. That, he insisted, was a job for the parliamentary party, and it would be unforgivable to do it by exploiting 'a policy in which you did not believe'. But his real message was saved for the end. He ridiculed the idea of the sovereignty of the party conference, by which he and other multilateralists were supposed suddenly to reverse their beliefs and fall into line 'like well-behaved sheep'. Gaitskell was not prepared to be bound by conference decisions. We may lose the vote, he warned, 'but I think there are many of us who will not accept this blow need be mortal, who will not believe that such an end is inevitable. There are some of us, Mr Chairman, who will fight and fight and fight again to save the Party we love.'

Gaitskell had made one of the best speeches of his life. Yet this was his third significant defeat in almost as many months. First, he had lost in his attempt to replace Clause 4; second, on the eve of conference the National Executive had insisted that conference decisions were sacrosanct; finally, at conference itself he had suffered four separate defeats on resolutions relating to the bomb. Yet with one phrase his leadership was saved. Any other outcome, it was considered even by Labour-supporting papers like the *Daily Mirror*, would have been disaster. 'The Party is still wide open over the H-bomb. Still faced by grave perils. Still looks like a sitting duck if the Tories should spring a snap General Election. But the ardour and brilliance of yesterday's H-bomb debate has undoubtedly inspired the Labour Movement throughout the country. It has made politics exciting. And Labour can succeed only when politics are exciting . . . Anyone who opposes [Gaitskell] seems likely to get a derisory vote from Labour MPs.'[28]

Most commentators thought Labour had been left 'helpless', 'vulnerable', possibly even – some on the right speculated – unable to survive. Barbara believed it was no moment to stop kicking, even if she knew victory for the left was virtually impossible and the damage caused by pursuing it possibly irremediable. Back in London, she invited the left-wingers on the NEC to discuss the next steps. Wilson, looking unhappy, was told he must challenge Gaitskell. 'We brought some pretty tough pressure to bear on him [she wrote in her diary], telling him in effect that if he did not challenge Hugh now, he would be finished as far as the left was concerned, and become a prisoner to the Right Wing. However, he was obviously very unwilling to stand and sat looking more and more miserable.' Crossman recalled 'this little spherical thing twirling round in dismay'. Tony Greenwood surprised everyone by saying that he would stand, and was going to resign from the shadow cabinet. Barbara surprised everyone even more by offering to stand herself. 'But the group agreed it would be better to have a former member of the Shadow Cabinet do so provided he was making it clear that he was not doing it on unilateralist grounds.'[29] Crossman remembers the evening differently: 'But oh dear, dear, dear. Suddenly it became clear that Barbara's one ambition was to immolate herself and thereby to establish that women can be Leaders and Prime Ministers. She was nearly in tears insisting that she had the right, and later I went out into the kitchen and found Tony Greenwood with the uncomfortable job of deterring a termagant from suicide. If she had been the candidate, it would have been a farce.'[30] It was a brutal assessment, but undoubtedly correct as far as the likely vote was concerned. Barbara was also right. To have a woman standing would have forcibly transformed attitudes to women in parliament. It was another fifteen years before it was tried.

Greenwood's determination to stand forced the hand of a reluctant Wilson. He phoned Barbara in Blackburn to tell her of his decision. 'My mind works more slowly than the rest of you,' he claimed. He did not want to challenge. He had not, he knew, the smallest chance of success. At best he would look opportunistic, at worst he might sacrifice the support of the centre which he had been carefully trying to consolidate, and end up, instead of a prisoner of the right, a prisoner of the left. In the event he ran his campaign on a unity ticket, unity being defined as Gaitskell backing down on all his objectives of constitutional reform, and on a new defence policy reflecting the Scarborough vote. On 3 November 1960 Gaitskell was returned as party leader by 166 votes to 81. 'We thought this was pretty good under the circumstances,' Barbara wrote, and the inner core of the Wilson group retreated to Tony Greenwood's house to discuss whether Wilson – who had promised Greenwood he would not – should run for the shadow cabinet. Barbara told him he must: 'The situation at present was that we were not fighting clear cut actions but an amorphous atmosphere of sabotage but . . . we had to play this on the simple theme of "who wants unity?" We had run Harold on the unity ticket and it seemed to me it would do violence to that if we now asked him to come out and lead a split.'[31] Harold, she said, was 'lyrically grateful' for her 'brilliant analysis'. He was duly re-elected to the shadow cabinet.

Barbara, having exposed the exact scale of the division in the PLP, now sought to unite the party again while keeping Gaitskell isolated. She was determined to find an accommodation between Cousins and the party's defence statement. Crossman, party chairman from 1960 to 1961, wanted to evade direct confrontation by going back to first principles and drawing up a whole new foreign and defence policy. Barbara thought Gaitskell would spend the intervening period 'stumping the country and putting interpretations on the Cousins line which widened the breach in the party'. 'After about a half-hour shouting match on these lines we agreed to refer the matter to Harold for his views and I went away exhausted and fed up.'[32] To her dismay, Gaitskell and the right had a firmer grasp on the NEC than the left had appreciated. The centrists, faced with an apparent choice between the man they knew and Wilson, Crossman or Castle, stuck with Gaitskell. From the high point of the 1960 Labour conference, the cause of the left rapidly slumped in popularity. The following year at Brighton the Scarborough defence decisions were overturned by huge majorities. Gaitskell had not got the reforms he wanted, but his grip on the leadership was more secure than ever. 'The policy and the leadership issue are settled,' Crossman told conference in 1961. Gaitskell felt strong enough to demote Wilson from shadow chancellor to shadow foreign secretary. There was to be no reconciliation. Neither Barbara, who had resigned with the others from the front bench to back Wilson's challenge for the leadership, nor other leading left-wingers like Crossman, were to be forgiven.

Early in 1963, Barbara went on a *New Statesman*-funded trip to examine the independence movements in the Middle East. She was in the bazaar in Cairo when she heard the news that was to transform her political future. After a sudden and mysterious viral infection, on 17 January Gaitskell had died. The runaway bus, the subject of such frequent speculation in political columns, had finally cut down a leader widely thought to be at the height of his powers. Labour had been ahead in the polls for more than a year. Gaitskell's critics were muted by their own failure, and perhaps by the prospect of power. Whoever won the the leadership could reasonably expect to be the next Prime Minister. There was little doubt who the candidates were for the succession: George Brown, the working-class right-winger with a drink problem, was the party's deputy leader. Only the previous autumn he had defeated a challenge for his job from Wilson by 133 votes to 103. But that was when MPs were choosing someone who could work with Gaitskell. By the time Barbara was back in London, it was becoming clear that the contest for the leadership would be much closer. However, she had no part to play in managing Wilson's leadership bid. She was excluded from the campaign, which was largely run by a 'patronizing' Crossman and the conspiratorial figure of George Wigg, a former soldier and self-appointed expert on defence and security. She was on the sidelines when, on St Valentine's Day 1963, Harold Wilson, aged only forty-six, was elected by 144 votes to George Brown's 103. James Callaghan, who had stood as the sober, hard-working candidate of the right, retired after the first ballot having divided the establishment vote, and left Wilson the clear front-runner.

'My political life is beginning again,' Crossman wrote a fortnight after Gaitskell's death. Barbara was not so sure. Once before, when she took a front-bench appointment from Gaitskell, she had chosen to put the party (and her own frustration with opposition) ahead of her convictions, only to throw up responsibility for the battle – Wilson's abortive leadership challenge – a few months later. She knew that Wilson's election was no sign of a major realignment of the party: 'My heart was in my mouth when Harold took over the chair . . . As the winner for whom many people had voted as a *faute de mieux*, he had a . . . difficult task and picked his way carefully. His very difficulties added conviction to his statement that election to such a position created first and foremost a sense of inadequacy.'

Wilson's election marked the start of an armistice between the parties' warring factions. Barbara wanted him to launch in with a 'clarification' of the position on Clause 4. He wisely ignored such sectarian advice and awarded Gaitskellites the jewels in the front-bench crown. Of his defeated rivals, Brown reluctantly took the home affairs portfolio, while Callaghan was shadow chancellor.

Barbara, complained that he was showing no loyalty to his friends, even those who had, like her, given up front-bench jobs in 1960 to campaign for his first challenge against Gaitskell. 'He then asked me to be patient with him if he could not immediately make all the changes he wanted to.' He told her he had made Patrick Gordon Walker shadow foreign secretary because 'he was a man of straw and he wanted to be his own For. Sec.'[33] A couple of days later, she wrote: 'Harold has now announced Dick [Cross-man's] appointment [shadow science minister] which contains a rebuff for me in that he has balanced it by appointing Charlie Pannell[34] minister of works. Ironically, this was the job Hugh gave me and which I gave up when I backed Harold against Hugh.' She went to see Wilson to complain. 'I said that I had, in fact, felt that as this new subject ['works' included new house-building] was so important I had almost volunteered in the light of the reconciliation with Hugh Gaitskell after the Brighton conference [in 1962] to come back on the front bench to deal with it. HW assured me he had tried to get both Dick and me back on the front bench before HG died but G would not hear of it retorting: "Why should I annoy Alice Bacon[35] for the sake of Barbara?"'

As usual, she felt the injustice deeply. Wilson shored up his left flank at private dinners, reassuring his old friends that nothing had really changed. He claimed that sitting in shadow cabinet among the Gaitskellites 'was like Khrushchev trying to govern through a Czarist Cabinet'. On another occasion there was a debate about the appropriate style for Wilson to adopt on television. 'Ted chipped in with: "The only thing you ought to do, Harold, is to be yourself." Grinning impishly Harold said, almost *sotto voce*, to me: 'If I had been myself, I should never have become the leader of the Labour Party.'[36]

The truth was that it was easier for Wilson to overlook Barbara than risk promoting her. She remained a highly controversial figure. Within the party she was known for arguing with an occasionally intolerant vehemence that frightened the less robust; outside the party she was a symbol of the dangerous left-wing, a constant threat to the more moderate leadership. Crossman, probably her closest friend, doubted her judgement.

For her part, she was still inclined to believe that to make concessions in circumstances other than abject defeat was cowardice. 'Harold thinks that a phrase will always settle anything because words can always be made to mean what you like,' she remarked. But she was not one of the irreconcilables like the Victory for Socialism stalwart Judith Hart, who had won Jennie Lee's old seat in Lanarkshire. Barbara had struck out on an independent path, pursuing, in particular, her disarmament and colonial interests. She worked with the Movement for Colonial Freedom and the Anti-Apartheid Movement, and with Crossman on the bomb – although their positions were significantly different. She had tried to bridge the unilateralists and the party mainstream, even if that meant trying to move the party's centre of gravity towards unilateralism.

After three consecutive election victories, the Tories were running into trouble. By-elections were going against them, and a brutal cabinet reshuffle by Macmillan had failed to restore his fortunes. The Profumo affair, relatively insignificant in itself, delivered the final blow. Macmillan's handling of it suggested that the post-war generation of Conservative political leaders had had its day and, as sleaze contributed to the end of the long Tory reign in the 1990s, so Profumo did in the 1960s. Barbara played only a small part in the affair, but it revealed both her terrier-like determination and the dismissive attitude to her of Labour's new leadership.

George Wigg had, or imagined he had, good security service contacts. From them he learnt that the Conservative War Minister John Profumo was having an affair with a young woman called Christine Keeler, and so too was a Soviet attaché, Eugene Ivanov. Wigg claimed that there were security implications because – as he told Barbara later – 'a Soviet official does not do anything by accident.'[37] The first she heard of it was at a dinner in her flat, where she was entertaining the new party leader. 'In the course of the evening [Wilson] had a mysterious conversation with George Wigg about [John] Profumo and his carryings on with the call girl Christine Keeler. Wigg was very excited about it all.'[38] Salacious gossip at Westminster was commonplace but Wigg insisted that there was a serious point at stake about the conduct of the War Minister. Keeler's name was in the news because another boyfriend was on trial for trying to shoot her, but she had disappeared and was thought to be in hiding somewhere.

Ten days after the dinner, on 21 March, there was a debate in the Commons about the imprisonment of two journalists who had refused to reveal their sources in a completely separate spy saga involving a navy clerk

called John Vassall, who had just been convicted and sent to prison for
eighteen years. 'Barbara came in saying she was going to blow the gaff on
Profumo, under the protection of parliamentary privilege,'[39] Crossman
recorded, plainly doubting her ability to do so without making a mess of it.
'George Wigg and I thought we had better get in first, using fairly careful
language.' Barbara, egged on by Ted looking down from the strangers'
gallery, in a speech purporting to be about where the public interest ended
and press sensationalism began, hinted that Profumo might be involved in
Keeler's disappearance. 'If accusations are made that there are people in high
places who do know [where Keeler is] and who are not informing the police,
is it not a matter of public interest?'[40] Crossman told her afterwards that what
she had suggested would be actionable outside the House, and there was a
general feeling that she – as well as Crossman and Wigg – had been wrong
to use innuendo against a minister who was on the whole rather popular and
who, in conducting a discreet affair, was doing no more than many of his
colleagues. The next day, Profumo's private secretary rang Barbara to tell her
that Profumo was to make a personal statement. 'I did not even dress! I
dashed down to the House without even washing and arrived just on time
. . . Dick and George told me that every Tory MP was expecting Profumo
to announce his resignation. Instead he braved it out with Macmillan by his
side looking grim . . . nobody believes we have heard the end of the
matter.'[41]

Profumo told MPs, in what three months later he had to admit was an
outright lie, that he had met Keeler only a few times, at the house of a
society osteopath called Stephen Ward. Crossman was worried that their
intervention had been tawdry, and was aware of muted distaste even within
the Labour Party. Barbara made no note of such feelings, and *The Times*
wrote a leader supporting the critics. After the weekend, the excitable Tory
MP for Arundel, Captain Henry Kerby, who had spent the war involved in
cloak-and-dagger skulduggery, approached Barbara to encourage her to keep
pressing. 'Almost bursting with indignation he told me: "Every Tory in this
place is sickened by the whole thing. We cannot do anything because we
have been showered with dire threats of instant excommunication if we press
the matter . . ."'[42] Whipped along by media innuendo, over the next few
weeks, the affair escalated to the point of hysteria. Barbara, to the alarm of
more fastidious colleagues, urged another, oblique attack. 'It is very difficult
to make security points stick [as Wigg wanted] but it would be enough to
establish that Ward was engaged in disreputable activities[,] living off young
girls[,] to get official action taken against him on these grounds to show the
Government's behaviour in its true light.' Ward, who later committed

suicide, wrote to Barbara, protesting that he had not been a pimp; a woman wrote anonymously claiming she had been recruited by him. Dozens more letters flooded in, advancing conspiracy theories and claiming to know killer facts. On 21 May, Ted sent Barbara in great excitement a copy of a statement Ward had just made to the *Herald*, saying that he had 'placed before the Home Secretary certain facts about the relationship between Christine Keeler and John Profumo'.[43] On 5 June, Profumo returned from a late spring break in Italy with his wife to apologize to a packed House of Commons for 'misleading' MPs. He resigned, abandoning politics altogether. Barbara, 'safely away in Italy', according to Crossman, and unaware that a general ban had been placed on all Labour MPs appearing on television for fear of appearing to gloat over one man's misfortune, jotted down some notes for an article about establishment cover-ups and 'the closed circuit of loyalty to those who speak in the right accent and wear the right tie'. By the time she was home again, the moment had passed.

The Profumo affair was a disaster for the Tory government. The party did not have time to recover before the general election. For once it was faced by a united Labour Party, with a leader who, despite the misgivings of the party, seemed to be capturing the mood of a country suddenly shedding the habit of deference. The Profumo episode contributed to the mood. So did the decline of empire and the discovery that British civil servants abroad were capable of compromising the standards of integrity and discipline on which every schoolchild was still raised. At the same time, the general rise in prosperity made people more independent, more interested in looking around them, more questioning. Barbara had been wrong in her 1959 conference speech to blame Labour's third election defeat on the selfishness of affluence. Watching on his family's first television set as Barbara talked in Blackpool of how the Tories had 'suckered' the voters with their promise of wealth, the seventeen-year-old Neil Kinnock in Nye Bevan's Ebbw Vale constituency later remembered. 'I looked at our centrally heated prefab with its bathroom and fridge and fitted carpet, and I thought affluence was a bloody good idea.'[44] It was secure people, not frightened ones, Kinnock believed, who voted for radical ideas. As the general election approached, it seemed he was right.

In October 1960, Barbara had quietly passed her fiftieth birthday. Her life had developed a pattern. She and Ted were based at their flat in Highgate. At the weekends, the cottage became the centre of their lives. Barbara's mother, Annie – 'Muvvie' – often came with them. After Frank's death in

1945, she had moved south to Golders Green, to be closer not only to Barbara, but to her elder daughter Marjorie who had also moved to London after the war. Marjorie, with her husband Alistair McIntosh, who had become principal of the City of London College of Commercial Education, and their three children, Sonya, Philippa and Hugh, lived in Putney. Jimmie was now a field worker for Oxfam, based in southern Africa. So glamorous in the 1930s, Jimmie was still a magnetic, dangerous character for his nephews and nieces, who called him 'Uncle Devil'. To his sisters, especially his younger one, he was simply dangerous. He had retired a widower from his career as a forester in Nigeria and was to marry, unsuccessfully, twice more. He was also on his way to developing a drink problem. Oxfam colleagues remember him staggering into ornamental ponds after dinner and packing nothing but bottles of Scotch for trips away. He had a cruel taste in practical jokes and was rude and domineering, even – according to one colleague who was with him when he tried to drive without stopping through a guerrilla roadblock – when faced by wild-eyed men with guns. Forty years later, one of those present remembered that, 'We were allowed to sit in the shade by the side of the road while they decided what to do with us. Jimmie was made to lie face down in the road in the full sun, for hours. Even after they decided to let us go on, he was rude to them.' Equally, they remember a man who knew his job brilliantly, understood and loved Africa, and had the serious drinker's ability never to betray in working hours the smallest sign of incompetence.

For his friends and family at home, his drinking was a menace. He would descend on Ted and Barbara in the country and 'capture' all the pubs where they liked to drink. When he and Barbara were together they would argue, just as they had argued with their father as children – stoking each other up, shouting passionately, furiously and sometimes cruelly.

Marjorie, her children felt, was never at home. She was a sociology lecturer at Bedford College, part of London University, and was as steeped in politics as Barbara. She was a Battersea councillor, a member of the London County Council and, since 1961, had chaired the LCC Education Committee where she had been intimately involved in plans for the new Inner London Education Authority, which was to centralize the London boroughs' education policy and management. Her politics were gentler and more compromising than her sister's. She was unenthusiastic about her children's commitment to CND and, to his rage, had sent her son Hugh to the public school Bryanston. Marjorie was Barbara's best friend. Barbara was too busy with politics and too engrossed in her own life to cultivate women friends.

Bevan's death had merely made relations with Jennie Lee more difficult. In 1957, for example, she wrote: '[Jennie] gave us a vague panorama of [her and Bevan's] Moscow and Poland tour – leaving us, as she always does, with a sense that they have been in some private stratosphere from which they have graciously descended for a moment to discourse with ordinary mortals. She has an irritating habit of implying that they have the ear of the almighty in a way denied to rank-and-filers like us.'[45] After Bevan's death there was no improvement: 'Jennie . . . tartly rebuked me for calling Nye a "magician". Her self-appointed role as guardian of the tomb becomes a little cloying at times and I think we are going to have trouble with her attempt to pose as the voice of the philosopher beyond the grave. Any obective reference by anyone to Nye sets her hackles rising. He must be worshipped whole or she will want to know the reason why.'[46]

Barbara's secretary during the 1960s, Elaine Strachan, gave one journalist an unflattering and vivid account (which she later bitterly regretted) of working for Barbara. Strachan arrived in Barbara's office at the height of the campaign she had initiated to end the system of making women pay to go through a turnstile to use public lavatories. This was the Barbara Castle the public knew best – the woman prepared to work tirelessly and argue vehemently in pursuit of a useful but hardly glamorous objective. The campaign attracted hundreds of letters of support.

> Once she got her teeth into something she didn't let go till she won. It was something to admire. I never met *anybody* like her, let alone a woman. She was a hard task-master, she didn't suffer fools gladly . . . She's got a tremendous memory for detail and she never forgot anything and she never seemed to make any mistakes. She likes to be able to tell you something and not explain herself. She used to frighten me. In fact she used to terrify me.

Once, Elaine Strachan realized too late that she had made a mistake booking Barbara's sleeper to Blackburn. Judith Hart, for whom she also worked, had to take her down to the bar and 'fill her with gin' to give her the courage to face Barbara on her return. Barbara was not a woman, Strachan observed, with whom one could relax, let alone get close to. Even at the hairdresser, there would be letters to dictate. 'I don't think she likes women very much. She prefers men,' Strachan concluded.

But for Barbara, Marjorie, whose habit of indulging her demanding younger sister had never faded, was different. Each September, after Marjorie's children were back at school, the two left their families for a week of what they called 'pootling', walking or cycling around the countryside. Marjorie perhaps needed the break as much as Barbara. Both women were obsessively, exhaustingly hard-working, but Marjorie also suffered from debilitatingly severe headaches. In the autumn of 1963, they set off with the objective of finding a new house for Barbara and Ted, on whom the cottage-dwellers' nightmare had dawned: the route for the new M40 from north-west London to Oxford was going to come within a few hundred yards of the Castle back door in Cadmore End.

Only a few miles away, Barbara and Marjorie found a village called Ibstone. It was a pub, a school, a straggle of pretty cottages, an expanse of village green with a cricket pitch and the house where the feminist and writer Rebecca West had lived since the war. Down a track which led only to a couple of farms, they came across a small farmhouse with a converted barn attached: perfect, they thought, for Marjorie's family and for Ted and Barbara; half each. The only hurdle was the cost.

Christmas 1963 was spent, as usual, with the two families together. Even though the children were now grown up, Ted was Father Christmas. There were outings and parties. 1964 promised to be a climax to the two sisters' years of effort, the fulfilment of the dreams on which their father had nurtured them as children. The general election had to come some time in the year. Labour was still favourite to win, and Marjorie was also running to be a member of the new Greater London Council, which was to replace the London County Council. But there might be even greater rewards to come. Wilson had finally felt secure enough to invite Barbara to join his front-bench team. Since October, she had been the party spokesman on overseas aid. Marjorie, meanwhile, had been approached about taking a seat in the House of Lords. It seemed that she as well as Barbara might be ministers in a Labour government.

In May 1964 Marjorie was elected to the GLC as one of the four members for Hammersmith, the borough with the biggest Labour majority in the capital. On 4 May, the same day her first grandson, Mark, was born, she suffered a catastrophic brain haemorrhage and within twenty-four hours she was dead. Barbara was devastated. The woman whose public emotions were normally reserved entirely for politics wept uncontrollably in front of her secretary in her office, in front of colleagues in the Westminster canteens, and on the shoulder of her old friend Richard Crossman, whose wife Zita had died in tragically similar circumstances. Marjorie was, said one obituary, 'renowned for thinking and speaking about complex controversies with clarity, common sense and imagination'. A Labour colleague, Barbara Wootton, wrote: 'Marjorie McIntosh had a greater zest for life than almost anybody that I have known. I have often seen her furious at the frustrations of academic or public life, but never disheartened or even visibly tired. Good fortune and her own splendid vitality combined to give her a full share of what any woman would most desire – a rich and happy family life, a successful career of her own, and abounding opportunities of service to the community.'[47] The Tory Education Minister Sir Edward Boyle, who was involved with her in planning London's education service, had been a good friend. She was, he wrote, 'an excellent and most stimulating conversationalist, formidable in controversy . . . and possessed of a personality which was a most attractive combination of vivacity and moral seriousness'.[48]

9. A Keen and Dedicated Minister

We should have a full-dress Ministry of Overseas Development under a keen and dedicated minister of cabinet rank.

Harold Wilson[1]

Harold Wilson transformed Labour into a party for the young, the creative and the compassionate. After Profumo, the Conservatives were branded in the public imagination as defenders of an outdated establishment and of the privileges of birth. Macmillan's decision to retire in the autumn of 1963, and his replacement by Sir Alec Douglas Home, a man who (like Tony Benn) had renounced his title so that he could lead the party, not only reinforced in No. 10 the whiff of the grouse moor left by Macmillan but, just as the economy took a dive, brought the arithmetic of the school room[2] to Cabinet. In contrast, the Nonconformist grammar school boy with the brilliant Oxford degree in economics looked innovative and exciting, an echo of President Kennedy across the Atlantic, and Wilson demonstrated a sure-footed ability to exploit his advantage. In his first conference speech as leader in the autumn of 1963 he promised to bring science into the heart of government: 'The Britain that is going to be forged in the white heat of this revolution will be no place for restrictive practices or for outdated methods on either side of industry,' he said. But at the heart of his message there was also a promise to the Third World. 'A Labour government would initiate a State-sponsored chemical engineering consortium to meet the needs not only of Eastern Europe, but far more important, of developing Commonwealth countries. We would train and we would mobilise chemical engineers to design the plants that the world needs.'[3] Compassion abroad was to be as much a part of the promise of the next Labour government as modernization at home.

The polls were in Labour's favour, but as the election came closer, the gap narrowed. On 15 October 1964, Labour crept rather than swept back into power. The majority was only five. Yet Wilson and the media between them had brought the expectation of revolution to such a crescendo that anything less than sustained radicalism was going to be a disappointment. The left had been swept as enthusiastically along as the mainstream. Michael Foot had even written a laudatory biography of Wilson (which he later disowned). After thirteen years, half a political lifetime, of 'Tory misrule', the battle for socialism which had been forced to a halt with devaluation in 1949 could be resumed.

Barbara, who had never moved on the establishment's inside track, remained a little sceptical. She was a shrewd judge of the prospects for the left. She knew her Wilson; she knew he was a pragmatist, like the later Bevan whom Barbara used privately to criticize for ruling by empiricism rather than ideals. She knew his cabinet appointments would indicate the extent of his determination to break with the cautious Gaitskellite past, and she had no confidence that he would be brave enough to take her on. She understood that she presented Wilson with a challenge; bringing her to the top table would be a significant gesture. Her *New Statesman* colleague Anthony Howard had written a piece for a Sunday paper speculating on Wilson's first Cabinet which, although praising her as the first woman to 'smash the sex barrier', suggested there was no certainty she would be in Cabinet. However, when she had seen Wilson at an election eve rally, he had raised her hopes by asking her when she would be back in London. But by Friday afternoon, the day after the election, she had heard nothing. Defiantly, she retreated to the cottage at Cadmore End and slept late. At 9 a.m. on the Saturday the phone rang and Wilson's private secretary told her the Prime Minister wanted to see her; to the official's sceptical astonishment she said, 'Does he? Why?'[4]

Barbara saw Wilson that lunchtime. She had spent an anguished morning deciding what to wear and she had lost her voice, but when she emerged on the steps of No. 10 in Marjorie's 'old brown straw hat'[5] the triumphant smile and confident wave showed a battle won. She was Minister for Overseas Development, and she had a seat in Cabinet. Barbara knew how deeply she was in Wilson's debt. 'Aid was clearly a minority preoccupation. So when I swept into that sunny ministerial room on Monday October 19th I was borne up – not for the first or last time – by Harold's personal interest.'[6]

Wilson's decision to put Barbara – doyenne of the the Anti-Apartheid Movement and the Movement for Colonial Freedom, defender of the rights of Africans and exposer of the wrongs of colonial officers – into the Cabinet was more than a reward for her loyalty. It was an insurance policy. She would be the public keeper of his conscience, guarantor of his principles, the outward symbol of his government's embrace of the left wing of Labour's broad church. She knew the real Harold. She would make sure Harold never forgot.

She would also be an ally, his own woman, the cabinet minister whose career was entirely at his disposal. She had no support in the parliamentary party, as the annual elections to the shadow cabinet showed. Her best result had been in 1959, after her year as party chairman, when she was fourth of the losers. In the year of the 1964 election she had been equal twenty-second in a contest in which only the first twelve were elected. Nor had she support in the trade union movement. Her only independent power base was on the National Executive. Wilson singled her out from the rest of the left, ignoring the most sectarian – Michael Foot, Ian Mikardo and Tom Driberg[7] (who wrote Barbara a sad note of congratulation). As the gloss wore thin on Wilson's administrations, these three were to provide damaging commentaries on his record. Nonetheless, in its first post-election issue, *Tribune* was able to welcome the Cabinet in enthusiastic terms: '*Tribune* takes over from Eton in the Cabinet,' it shouted, over pictures of half a dozen of its regular contributors in their new roles as members of Her Majesty's Government.[8]

Wilson had also made peace with the talent on the right. Barbara thought he had overdone conciliation, but liked the promise of the new departments that he created. George Brown was in charge of a new Department of Economic Affairs that was to draw up a national plan; James Callaghan was Chancellor of the Exchequer and Patrick Gordon Walker was Foreign Secretary. Another right-winger, Frank Soskice, was Home Secretary. Of the left there was only Dick Crossman at the Ministry of Housing, Tony Greenwood at the Colonial Office, Frank Cousins at the Ministry of Technology and Barbara herself. Her detractors put it about that she owed her place only to some special hold on Wilson (by transparent implication, sex). Some said she was his 'alternative Marcia', his socialist conscience in the parliamentary party and in Cabinet as Marcia Williams was in his private office.[9] Although Marcia was a private figure and Barbara always a public one, there were parallels in their behaviour, tempestuous – sometimes temperamental – and intimate. They brought an energy and a fierceness to their politics in contrast to the cool, calculating, buttoned-up Wilson.

Barbara was the only woman in Wilson's Cabinet, and only the fourth to have reached the top in British politics.[10] Her old friend John Freeman wrote in the *News of the World*: 'The women who have ever served in the British Cabinet can be counted on the fingers of one hand. But even in this honoured group, Barbara Castle stands out like Miss World at a meeting of the Women's Institute. Let nobody, however, be deceived by her spectacular charms. This is one of the toughest and ablest of our politicians . . . even her bitterest political enemies – and she has a few – would agree that she has the capacity to rise further.' He sent her a personal note from the *New Statesman*: 'Dearest Barbara, We all (& I above all) send you our fondest love & best wishes. I am so proud of you & so happy for you. Love as always – John.'

In his first year as party leader, Wilson had been at pains to stress his continuing interest in overseas development. A policy that would make a start at delivering the transfer of resources from rich world to poor, which he had first advocated in 1953, was an integral part of the party's programme, and one to which left and right subscribed. Barbara had placed it at the heart of her own manifesto at the 1959 conference when she had appealed to the party to offer a 'noble lead'. 'Let us denounce the hideous colour bar; let us declare frankly that we are out to liquidate the last remnants of colonialism; let us make a big feature of our pledge to help those in backward countries struggling with the burden of brutish poverty our own workers carried only fifty years ago. In other words do not let us forget, in the scramble for votes, that the biggest thing which distinguishes us from the Tories is our belief: "I am my brother's keeper – and his friend." '[11]

In the final year of opposition, Barbara had launched an ambitious campaign for a world development agency to replace the self-interested, ad hoc and overlapping aid efforts of the developed world. She accused the Tories, who had responded to some of the problems of which she spoke by establishing a Department of Technical Cooperation, of using aid as a form of neo-colonialism. She visited North Africa and Uganda to see for herself the confusion and waste on the ground caused by the failure to coordinate different programmes which had anyway been started without reference to local needs.

> Every country is giving its dollops of help for motives which have nothing to do with the prime purpose of securing the economic development of the recipient countries of the world [she told the Commons in February 1964]. They are giving help for reasons of national prestige, or for political motives to sustain certain regimes as against others, or for reasons of rivalry in the cold war, or for reasons of their own internal economic self-interest. Because the motives are wrong, the help bears no relationship to the results in terms of maximum economic development.[12]

In October 1963, as part of his 'White Heat' speech to conference, Wilson had specifically promised a separate Overseas Development Minister

and in a newspaper article set out his ideas. He had been influenced by the
newly founded American Peace Corps.

> The Ministry will be central in Labour's work for peace. It will mobilise
> technicians and teachers, doctors and farm specialists for service abroad. It
> will be a 'ministry of munitions' calling forth from British industry not the
> weapons of destruction but the munitions of peace . . . The ministry will
> place research contracts . . . to devise new ways of increasing food produc-
> tion We shall be engaged not on a tip-and-run raid on world poverty but
> on all-out WAR. We shall mobilise the energies and abilities not of the
> few but the many.[13]

Barbara would later retort to an interviewer who suggested she had
schemed for the job: 'As it happened the man I believed in is now Prime
Minister. No one's more surprised than myself that here I am without
making any concessions.'[14] As usual, it was a little less than the truth. One
of her attributes as a politician was to take nothing for granted. 'Plums don't
fall in plain girls' laps,' she would incant, and neither did the Ministry of
Overseas Development.

Wilson's conference speech had prompted the Fabian Society to start
work on a blueprint to turn the new ministry from a political slogan into
reality. Each month from early 1964, the Fabian working party sent Barbara
a paper setting out their progress. Each paper suggested the department would
need a minister 'of Cabinet rank'; each paper was returned with 'of Cabinet
rank' crossed out, and 'a minister in the Cabinet' written over the top.[15]
There was not even any clearly stated opinion that a separate department was
the best solution; it risked creating rivalry and confusion, and it could be
isolated and weakened by other pressures. 'Separate,' warned the May 1964
working paper grimly, 'does not necessarily mean independent', and independence was the quality most needed. 'Decisions on where [aid] is spent and on
what are . . . important. A new organisation therefore should be strong
enough to resist pressures from other Government Departments and from
politicians to arrange its programme according to non-development criteria.'[16]

The ministry was to signal an entirely new approach to aid: it should not
be about aid at all, but about development, and development had to be
established as a notion independent of foreign policy, of trade or of the
economy. The recipients must believe 'that the Labour government is
entering into a partnership with developing countries and not dispensing
charity'.[17] Improving coordination by separating aid out from the different
departments which currently administered it was going to be a big political

challenge. While the new Department for Technical Cooperation, which was an adjunct of the Foreign Office, could be the heart of the new ministry, it would also need to take over most of the work of the Colonial Office, which would be 'reduced to a Ministry for Islands',[18] while some of the work of the Foreign Office and the Board of Trade would also be taken over. Ultimately it was the Treasury that would have to be squared, for the biggest obstacle to a whole new department was that it might not have a big enough budget to justify its existence. The Fabian group had pointed out that if it had only 2 per cent of government spending – 0.65 per cent of GNP – a separate department would not justify the staff needed to run it. And the biggest challenge of all would be to sell the idea of aid to a public which firmly believed that charity began at home. 'For the first time in history it is now technically possible to do away with poverty, disease and ignorance . . . it is probable also that the financial resources are available to apply this knowledge . . . certainly current and apparently effortless expenditure on armaments suggests they are.'[19]

Barbara's putative Permanent Secretary was Sir Andrew Cohen, currently running the Department of Technical Cooperation. Persuaded that the Civil Service would not be willing to implement socialist policies, Barbara was doubly suspicious because she knew him as the architect of the now defunct Central African Federation, against which she had campaigned so vehemently ten years earlier. Later, his wife Helen confided to Barbara that he had said he would never work for a woman; possibly, he just meant Barbara. In a startling lapse of protocol, Cohen was not even in London when her appointment was announced. Barbara was furious. Later, she called his absence 'shameful'.[20] However, in the argument over aid, he was on her side. A year earlier, at a lecture in New York, he had called for professionals to integrate a period of work in a developing country into their career, and set out his own commitment to the developing world. 'Relations between countries, even world peace itself, will be threatened unless, as between the more southerly and more northerly countries of the world, standards of living, levels of education, scales of national wealth can come together instead of growing apart.'[21]

Barbara, avoiding any reference to his earlier role in central African affairs, merely observed that he seemed paralysed with shyness. He was 'a huge, crumpled intellectual',[22] so much larger than Barbara that they came to be nicknamed Elephant and Castle. He had been Governor of Uganda and one of Britain's Permanent Representatives at the UN. Barbara invited him and his wife to tea in Buckinghamshire. 'I found that I took to the Minister–Permanent Secretary relationship quite naturally. I was completely at ease,'[23] she wrote later.

She was not at first, however, completely happy with Sir Andrew. Although he was regarded as 'a flamboyant left-winger'[24] in aid circles, she thought he was a bad judge of people, and she complained to friends about the lack of support her officials were giving her as she struggled to extract powers and personnel from the other ministries concerned with aid. She said she lost count of the number of times Cohen came to her in a day saying, 'Minister, while of course the decision is entirely yours I would be failing in my duty not to tell you how unhappy it makes me . . .' Slowly, though, they developed a mutual respect for one another. She found him creative and sympathetic to Britain's continuing obligations to the old colonies. Within a few months she was defending him against what she considered an unjust attack in an extreme-left African publication. On 17 January 1965 in the *Sunday Times* the two were described thus:

> They are a natural pair, Socialists both, with drive and imagination in their contrasting ways – she with her impetuous, idealistic mind, he with a vigour trained by scholarship and several years' experience in the field as Governor of Uganda and Britain's Representative on the UN's Trusteeship council. They work late like young pioneers, and Sir Andrew has been heard to remark with relief that she is his first Minister since Alan Lennox-Boyd inclined to produce a bottle of whisky when the rest have gone home.

However, much of the rest of her new department was staffed with stiff ex-colonial civil servants repatriated from Africa and Asia, often still convinced of the infallible superiority of Britain and the feebleness of the governments of the newly independent countries. Unlike Cohen, she complained, they were never on her side.

Before Barbara had even met her new Permanent Secretary, a decision had been taken at the heart of government which decided the fortunes of Wilson's first two administrations. Wilson, together with his new Chancellor and the Secretary of State for Economic Affairs, were told that the predicted budget deficit was £800 million and that there were only two options: devaluation or some form of import controls. Before Labour had come to power, there had been no forewarning that economic circumstances would be so bad, and no planning had gone into considering a response to them. Wilson knew about controls, and about the political cost of devaluation, from when he was last in government. Deflation would be inevitable. Yet he had resigned because of spending cuts. He chose the import surcharge, determined to avoid the deflation that would spell the end of all the party's plans, based as they were on continuing growth. In fact, although sterling recovered, the recovery was short-lived. Every sterling crisis thereafter provoked a bout of deflation and spending cuts. It was an unpromising background against which to educate British taxpayers about their moral obligation to share their wealth with the developing world.

Barbara's new office was outside the geographical boundaries of the Whitehall village, in Stag Place, in a modern office block overlooking the gardens of Buckingham Palace. She set about realizing her dream of taking politics out of aid with an energy that reflected the urgency Wilson himself had promised when he had talked of his 'first hundred days of dynamic action' in a broadcast the summer before the election. She would tell a civil servants' conference in the early 1970s:

> Put yourself in my place. Twenty-two years as a backbench MP – a good one as a matter of fact – party activist, constituency Member, the whole of whose political life up to then had been given meaning by representing, quite deliberately, a certain section of society, and expressing its aspirations. Coming out of that Cabinet room very excited, I was charged with a responsibility, the Ministry for Overseas Development . . . [The Permanent Secretary] is there on tap, filling the horizon. One goes into the office, the first thing in the morning. 'Oh Minister, we had prepared for the fact that there might be a Ministry of Overseas Development. Here is the whole thing worked out.' . . . There it is, waiting for you to take on board. Civil servants have been working away at it while you have been battling for your political life.[25]

Barbara was determined to bring in outside expertise; it was part of Labour mythology that officials would obstruct a socialist government. She believed officials should be there to deliver her priorities. But to establish what those priorities were, she wanted political people around her who could give her the evidence she needed to make a political case. A dispatch rider was sent to collect copies of the Fabian document on the structure of the department, for the instruction of the officials. Barbara herself turned to the Labour-supporting chairman of the food giant Booker McConnell, Sir (later Lord) Jock Campbell, an old friend. They lunched. The next day several closely argued pages of advice arrived. Most of them re-emerged nearly a year later in a government White Paper. 'Yours is a colossal operation – establishing a new Ministry, creating a new Government policy to meet perhaps the greatest challenge of the age . . . I suppose the main strategic objectives are the social and economic development of the underdeveloped countries, and the raising of all the living standards of their peoples, in order to further the progress and peace of mankind as a whole.' Treat it as a military operation, Campbell told her. He divided the task into different fronts: technical, financial, projects, investment and trade policy. He recommended an analysis of the available resources and of the requirements and priorities of the individual developing countries and the other sources of aid available to them. 'This leads to planning, and I am sure we must be careful not to say or imply arrogantly: this is what we in Britain can and mean to do – take it or leave it. I think a very early move of your Ministry must be for small missions to visit individual areas and countries, and to sit down with representatives of their Governments to take a hard, practical look at their own plans, problems and priorities . . . this process of examination will disclose the lamentable lack of effective plans.'

Economic planning was to be Barbara's god, as it was the whole government's. She had studied it, written about it, visited France to see it in action. And planning's first tool was information: Barbara sought out economists and development experts. One of the two most important was Tommy Balogh, old friend and Keep Left supporter. Balogh had convinced Wilson[26] – and Barbara – that the Russian rather than the US model of economic growth was the pattern for the future. 'The central control of her economy is a powerful help . . . all in all it is likely that Russian output per head will surpass that of Britain in the early 1960s and that of the US in the mid-1970s unless our progress is speeded up.' This was the doctrine Barbara believed could profitably be applied to the developing world. Her second expert was Dudley Seers, brought back to England from Addis Ababa where he was working for the UN, to become Director General of Barbara's economic planning staff. By the time she published her White Paper the following summer, she had assembled a team of more than a hundred experts to advise the department and lend their expertise to developing countries. Less than two weeks after taking office, Barbara set out the remit of her new ministry. The detail was a little sketchy, but the ambition was plain: 'to contribute its utmost to the solution of one of the dominant problems of the world, the social and economic inequality between the highly industrialised countries and the rest of the world'.[27]

The most ambitious objective of the new department was to establish the moral imperative of aid, an obligation quite separate from Britain's foreign or economic interests and one that must be preserved from the predations of the Treasury regardless of economic conditions at home. It was the twentieth-century equivalent of the white man's burden, a duty of fair shares imposed by the values of ethical socialism. Wilson, who came from the Nonconformist background that was providing Africa with 'fighting parsons' like Colin Morris, wrote in the Fabian Society's overseas development magazine *Venture* that aid could not be restricted to ex-colonies. 'I do not see the aid policies implicit in the plans I have described as being rigidly confined to the Commonwealth. In Africa, particularly, the borders of the new independent Commonwealth nations are a legacy of colonialism, arbitrarily carved out of the African continent by past imperialism.'[28] Aid was not a surrogate for empire, but a morally based attempt by the rich world to promote the social and economic development of the poor. A dedicated ministry would spotlight the gulf between those two worlds. 'We recognise that it is in the nature of aid that we should accept an economic sacrifice when giving it,' Barbara wrote in her White Paper. 'This does not mean that the present economic sacrifices cannot yield benefits to us in the future. It means that these benefits should not be the main motivation for giving aid and they must not conflict with development.'[29] The ultimate objective was a World Development Agency to administer aid as a form of redistributive global welfare. A British Ministry of Overseas Development would be one of its cornerstones.

Yet when it came, in the autumn of 1965, it was clear that the White Paper was a well-disguised admission of defeat. Barbara was forced to accept that the Whitehall reorganization implicit in the plan for a separate ministry had been an overambitious target for a tiny department that still existed more in her mind than on paper. The Foreign Office, the Treasury and the Colonial Office all proved effective defenders of their territory, and at this stage she lacked the political punch to shift the ministers at the top. 'The central purpose of the new Ministry is to formulate and carry out British policies to help the economic development of the poorer countries,' the White Paper stated, on the question of the ministry's role. But,

> in relation to dependent territories the Colonial Office remains responsible, in consultation with the Ministry, for budgetary aid, while the Ministry in discharging its responsibility for development aid, acts in agreement with the Colonial Office. The Treasury continues to bear the main responsibility for relations with the International Bank for Reconstruction and Development, in co-operation with the Ministry. The Ministry is not responsible for military aid, which remains under the Foreign Office, Commonwealth Relations Office and Colonial Office.[30]

★

The White Paper did not describe the reality of Whitehall power relations in all its complexity. 'Military aid' was a term capable of wide interpretation, and neither the Ministry of Defence nor the Foreign Office was prepared to surrender influence. There turned out to be more 'highly sensitive political questions' than Barbara had anticipated. Relations with other ministers were fraught with arguments: notably over Malta, still – before the retreat from east of Suez – strategically significant, and east Africa, where there were fears that the Communist Chinese were ruthlessly exploiting the demand for major structural investment.

The Maltese problem was a stark example of what Barbara had so often denounced. The right-wing, pro-British government of Borg Olivier was in debt. Olivier had applied for aid so that he could avoid raising taxes, a move that might cost him the impending election. In such an event, the victor would be Dom Mintoff, who was suspected of Soviet leanings and who might deny Britain the use of the strategically important dockyards. Barbara was furious that £1.2 million of her bilateral aid – nearly a quarter of the total – was being used for such low purposes. 'I could hardly believe my ears . . . I nearly burst a blood vessel arguing. Harold could see clearly that this was nothing but a political bribe. However he did not like the prospect, which the Defence boys hinted at, that, if Mintoff were returned, he might offer the base to Russia in order to twist our arm. Personally, I believe that is so much gobbledy-gook, but I was overruled.'[31]

East Africa was a simpler problem: Tanzania and Zambia were keen to develop their own transport systems which would free them from dependence on the southern African route. In particular, they wanted a railway to link their mineral industries. It was a long-held ambition, but repeated surveys suggested it would be prohibitively expensive to build and there would be inadequate demand to generate the necessary return. These were, however, Commonwealth countries with whom relations were already tense because they felt Britain was failing to make a stand on Rhodesia and South Africa. More alarming still, the Chinese had promised to build the railway – although with Chinese labour, which was currently a stumbling-block in any deal. Barbara was unwilling to offend a country whose leader Julius Nyerere was a fellow socialist whom she knew well. She was uncomfortable with his frequent accusations that Britain used aid only as a form of neo-colonialism. But – backed on this occasion by Cabinet – she was not prepared to bend her own rules on aid on grounds of political expediency alone. Like Wilson, faced with a crisis that could not be resolved without damage, she hit for the long grass. Her ministry would prepare a new survey on the route and economic viability of the railway.

In opposition, Barbara had highlighted the absurdity of countries borrowing only to pay off interest charges. One-third of foreign aid in some countries, she said, was simply recycled straight back to the banks. Departmental research argued that given the absence of the infrastructure in developing countries to collect taxes, with export markets hard to penetrate and above all with the need for these countries to invest every penny they could raise, the practice of demanding interest payments severely reduced the effectiveness of the loans themselves. In June 1965, she announced that interest-free loans would be available to certain – not exclusively Commonwealth – countries. India, for example, which was spending a third of its foreign aid on debt, would be eligible, but so would some Latin American countries where two-thirds of the aid went straight back to Western bankers. The announcement, made with great fanfare and received with enthusiasm – 'the most imaginative step yet taken towards a genuine aid policy', said the *Economist* – was less radical than it seemed. Most aid loans were already interest-free in the early years, although end-loaded to compensate; and there were already doubts about the ability of the poorest countries to repay even interest-free loans. The proposal also brought out the latent hostility to aid. The *Daily Telegraph* complained: 'It is surely one of the curiosities of British politics that, when the nation is in debt up to its eyebrows and the Government judges it right to bring in a new corporation tax which heavily discriminates against private overseas investment, the aid programme rests sacrosanct, beyond the reach of vulgar economy.'

One of Barbara's most important objectives was to win over *Daily Telegraph* readers to an appreciation of the value of aid. Publicity and promotion were essential, and she recruited Chris Hall, an abrasive but effective *Sun* journalist (whose wife worked for Dick Crossman), to manage her press relations. Hall had been a journalistic colleague of Ted's, and shared the Castle passion for walking.[32] He had first met Barbara more than ten years earlier when he had helped campaign for Ted at the Abingdon by-election. One winter's day they had walked from the Castles' cottage at Cadmore End to Ewelme, about ten miles distant, discussing how to educate the public in what aid could do.

The idea of aid, as Barbara often pointed out, was popular with the public at large. The new charities like Oxfam and War on Want, as well as Voluntary Service Overseas, were well supported. But only the state could deliver consistent, carefully targeted aid, and she was determined to win wider public acceptance of state involvement and the disbursement of large sums of taxpayers' money. In its manifesto, the government had promised to increase spending on aid to 1 per cent of GDP, almost double the 0.65 per cent currently spent. But in the mood of crisis which had already enveloped the government, she was struggling to keep her current budget. She and Hall decided to use her own experience of visiting Africa to educate and inform. The public would see what she had seen of the problems and absurdities of aid which built steel plants where there was no market, and refused to fund a new college because aid given specifically to buy British goods had not been spent. India and Pakistan were first on her itinerary, but the most spectacular of her trips in terms of the coverage generated back in Britain was that to east Africa in the summer of 1965, where Hall found a pretty baby for her to cuddle in what would be widely seen back home as an arresting image of Lady Barbara the Great Mother[33] nursing the infant states of post-colonial Africa. (The baby had first been taken down to a stream for a bath. 'The child,' Hall remembered, 'was encrusted with dirt.'[34]) The press loved the pictures from Africa but one little black baby was not enough to slacken the grip of the Treasury and the Department of Economic Affairs on the cash. The idea of aid might be popular, but the actual needs of the developing world had not captured the hearts and minds of the great British public, at least not as refracted through the press. Nor, it seemed, had it captured the hearts and minds of the ministers on the public expenditure committee, gathered on a Sunday afternoon in July 1965 to pore over Barbara's bid for her share of next year's spending programme.

Barbara had prepared for the Sunday session by calling her officials to Cadmore End the day before to scrutinize the arguments one last time. She believed – or claimed to believe – that her request was modest, at least more modest than she would have liked. But her old enemies Jim Callaghan and George Brown, backed by Frank Cousins, demanded further cuts. 'One of the bleakest days of my political life,' Barbara mourned in her diary, ignoring the wider financial crisis facing the government.

> My careful preparation of an opening submission went for nothing: Jim didn't want to hear it. Instead they jumped into hostile cross-examination . . . when I pointed out that if we did not get the additional sum for which we asked . . . it would mean either no general purpose aid for India or the abandonment of [the steel plant at] Durgapur, Frank said viciously 'India never wanted Durgapur till we put it into their heads'. And when I pointed out if Durgapur was abandoned the UK steel plant-making industry would be in the soup, George Brown said savagely, 'Perhaps they would go out then and look for some real exports.' They obviously couldn't care less about the Party's commitment to 1% of GNP. They dismissed aid as irrelevant.[35]

Aid for the coming year was one victim of the sterling crisis that was now leading to negotiations for a loan from America. The publication of Barbara's White Paper, with its specific spending implications, was another. In negotiation, her officials had been forced to concede point after point. Now she was told it could not be published at all, for fear of frightening the bankers. Only in extreme circumstances could arguments be taken from committee to full Cabinet, but for Barbara the fight was just beginning. 'How my colleagues must hate Harold for putting ODM [the Minister for Overseas Development] in cabinet,' she acknowledged. She told George Brown when they chanced upon each other at a Buckingham Palace garden party (which she felt constrained, as a minister, to attend): 'I was created. You may not have liked the fact but I exist and you have got to come to terms with me.' Wilson told her to cool it. Leave it to the following week, he advised, so the foreign bankers bailing Britain out weren't left with the impression that they were lending the UK millions 'just to spend on soup kitchens for Africans'.[36]

The following week, the extent of the economic crisis became apparent: £90 million of reserves had gone in the past few days – a tenth of the total. So Barbara was surprised that when the issue finally came up in Cabinet a week later, Callaghan offered a compromise, allowing her £225 million rather than the £216 million he had originally proposed. It was still substantially short of the £250 million she insisted she needed to fulfil her commitments, as she pointed out crossly (sending Callaghan a note of gratitude at the same time). And there was a trap: her budget was not to be inflation-proof. It took another day's battle to get the budget basis restored to constant prices (and under her successor, the decision would be reversed again). So she had more or less won on the budget, and shortly afterwards she was able, by sharp political manoevering, to reverse the decision about publishing the White Paper. Immigration controls were currently being proposed in the light of the mounting pressure from Asians facing persecution in East Africa. Wilson had expressly ruled out such controls two years earlier. Barbara saw her chance. She suggested that if her aid White Paper came out at the same time, it might 'take the bad taste . . . out of our people's mouths'.[37]

Newspapers observed the White Paper's ingenious stretching of resources and allowed themselves to be distracted from the minimal increase in spending. Barbara's determination to improve the quality of aid through technical support was well received. New academic posts were to be created and other academics were recruited to advise overseas, creating a kind of Peace Corps of around four hundred agricultural and economics experts.

Only the left noticed with dismay the disappearance of the one per cent pledge; this became another grievance, joining unease about Wilson's pro-US stance on the Vietnam war and the government's failure to make real cuts in defence spending, while the document's simultaneous appearance with the immigration White Paper merely added to a sense of government cynicism.

Five years later Dudley Seers, the economist Barbara had brought in to run her economic planning staff, would describe her as a minister of 'outstanding determination and energy'.[38] However, he was less impressed by the government's record on aid. The responsibilities of power, he said, had merely made Labour nationalistic. By 1970, the amount of cash for aid had effectively fallen below the levels the Conservatives had been committed to spend. George Brown's 'National Plan' which, only a month after Barbara's White Paper had projected a growth in personal consumption of 21 per cent over five years, had called aid an 'economic burden' which would have to be 'scrutinised with particular care'. 'The August White Paper and the September National Plan express the two souls of Labour,' Seers wrote,[39] 'one, generous and far sighted, conscious of international responsibilities and opportunities – the other, narrow, nationalistic, materialistic . . . the long-hairs against the skinheads.'

After its enthusiastic welcome for the new government, the left had developed a hangover. Economic stringency was only one of the betrayals. Steel nationalization, which was supposed to be justified by its importance in national planning, had been deferred after two backbenchers threatened to rebel. Defence cuts had been delayed. Worse was happening overseas, where Wilson's intimacy with Kennedy's successor President Johnson, and his refusal to condemn increasing American involvement in Vietnam, had lit a slow-burning fuse. The early decision to honour a contract to supply arms to South Africa was another grievance. One African delegate at a Commonwealth conference reported that when he had complained to Barbara about the sale of Buccaneer aircraft to the apartheid regime of South Africa, she had lectured him on the need for exports to pay for pensions.

In fact, Barbara found herself frustratingly party to decisions she felt she could not influence. In Cabinet, her status as the minister for the smallest and newest department meant she was at the far end of the table on the Prime Minister's extreme left, often almost out of earshot of the debate between the key players – the Chancellor, the Foreign Secretary and the Defence Secretary – who sat in a cluster at the centre. 'It is extraordinarily difficult to make any impact in Cabinet,' she wrote in her diary after a year of trying. 'So many important things are mumbled over in a throwaway tone between the PM and the nearest ministers that it is almost like shouting in church to strike a positive note or express one's anxieties. But from the far end of the table I try to hack my way through the deadening atmosphere, and challenge some of the placid assumptions.' In 1973 she returned to the theme. 'In my innocence when I went into Cabinet government in October 1964 I still believed . . . that Cabinets were groups of politicians who met together and said, these are the policies we are elected on, now what will be our political priorities?'[40]

By later standards, Wilson's Cabinet met and argued exhaustively. Often, however, its ministers were merely approving decisions already argued out in the much smaller cabinet subcommittees where many of the most important issues were debated and finalized. At Cabinet, as Barbara frequently lamented, it was too late to start unpicking conclusions reached earlier. However, her position as head of the new department did give her a frequent (though not automatic) seat on the defence and overseas policy committee, or OPD, the key committee linking Britain's shrinking defence capabilities with the search for an alternative source of stability in the newly independent countries of Asia and Africa. It took her into the heart of the issue which, after the economy, became for the left one of the most controversial of the administration: Rhodesia.

The story of the government's response to the Rhodesian crisis is a study in the power of official inertia to overwhelm and disarm political action. As the *Sunday Times* observed later, 'The real dynamic of the campaign was not the attempt to win a battle. Rather it was the desire to conceal, for a sufficient time, the fact that battle had been refused – so that the denouement would appear eventually as a form of victory.'

'We are on a collision course with Southern Rhodesia,' Arthur Bottomley, the Commonwealth Secretary, told the OPD at its first meeting after the 1964 election. It was not unexpected news. The crisis in white Rhodesia where Ian Smith, the smooth-talking ex-Battle of Britain pilot, was Prime Minister, had been building since the Central African Federation had started to unravel in 1960. Britain's objective was to impose on Rhodesia an independence constitution that would pave the way for (black) majority rule. Britain's handicap was that she had no obvious way of stopping Rhodesia assuming independence on a constitution that would guarantee white ascendancy. It was unthinkable to endorse white supremacist rule, but it was hard to see how it could be averted. Duncan Sandys, the Conservative Colonial Secretary in the previous government, had told the Commons in 1963, 'We have long ago accepted the principle that Parliament at Westminster does not legislate for Southern Rhodesia except at its request.' However, to concede defeat on the issue would alienate black Africa and world opinion and be completely unacceptable to the left and many others. Black Africa wanted Britain to lead the open and outright opposition of the entire Commonwealth. Establishment opinion in Britain argued that to do so would precipitate a unilateral declaration of independence which, once done, could not be undone without the use of force. But force, as the Defence Secretary, Denis Healey,[41] repeatedly emphasized to Barbara, was not only logistically difficult – 'Our nearest base was Aden, as near to Salisbury [Harare] as London is to Cairo' – it was emotionally fraught. White Rhodesians were literally Britain's kith and kin, often settlers who had arrived from the UK only after the Second World War, in which they had fought. Crossman observed that even the language, the use of 'unilateral declaration of independence' (UDI) rather than 'rebellion' or 'revolt', indicated a pacific response.[42] Wilson was repeatedly advised that the correct action, indeed the only action open to Britain, was to play it long: to delay, to negotiate and ultimately, Barbara feared, to compromise by recognizing Rhodesian independence without properly safeguarding the future of the African population, which massively outnumbered the whites.[43]

If the threat of force was ruled out, the other option was economic sanctions. However, there was a widespread fear that they would do more harm to Britain than to Rhodesia because Rhodesian coal fuelled copper-mining in Zambia, which supplied nearly half Britain's copper needs. Any interruption would severely damage British engineering as it was feared that UK sanctions against Rhodesia could trigger retaliatory action on coal exports to Zambia. Replacing Rhodesia as a source of coal would send the price of copper soaring. Sanctions against Rhodesia's tobacco industry would force Britain to use scarce dollars buying American tobacco. Attempts to stop oil getting into Rhodesia, according to the official advice, were unworkable and anyway unlikely to make a big impact on what was still a largely agricultural economy. Rhodesia also had highly permeable borders, and in Mozambique – still Portuguese-controlled – and South Africa, two neighbours that were fervent supporters of white rule. (Many of these drawbacks were uncomfortably true, but when sanctions were finally imposed, Wilson insisted, disastrously, that they would bring an end to UDI in 'weeks not months'.) One by one the options put forward for the 'war book' that Wilson had assured Barbara was under preparation for use in the event of UDI, were knocked down in cabinet committee.

Meanwhile diplomacy secured nothing. Official visitors to Salisbury returned impressed rather than horrified by Ian Smith, persuaded of his good intent and convinced that all that stood between him and an agreement with Britain was his Cabinet. But his cabinet, dominated by people sympathetic to Apartheid, was to prove immovable.

In October 1965, as Labour reached the end of its first year in power and the tension over Rhodesia rose to new heights, Smith made a final visit to London, seemingly still flexible. Wilson, talking tough, planning to try to get round the 'kith and kin' dilemma with a UN force operating out of Zambia, rather than sending British soldiers to suppress UDI, and discussing blockading the Mozambique port of Beira through which Rhodesia's oil was transhipped, made a return visit to Salisbury. There he discovered Smith had after all not been flexible at all.

At last Wilson started to address possible political reactions to UDI. There was talk of undermining any breakaway regime by instructing civil servants, who had taken an oath of loyalty to the Queen, not to support it. The idea of direct rule from London was examined. Barbara tried to identify a group of moderates who could form an interim government while progress was being made towards majority rule. How should Britain respond if the African members of the Commonwealth recognized a black government in exile? Worse, how could Britain avoid backing Smith if violence broke out? Barbara knew Wilson was desperate for a deal, and on 30 October watched in horror as he made a disastrous tactical blunder. In a radio broadcast, he explicitly ruled out the use of force. Barbara thought that each of Wilson's moves was no more than an attempt to delay UDI, little better than an act of appeasement. If he cracked further, made more concessions, she decided she was ready to resign.

In early November it was tacitly acknowledged that UDI was unavoidable. One last diversion was being feverishly debated: Smith had accepted a Royal Commission to consider a new Rhodesian constitution, but there was nothing to stop him vetoing its findings. A last Cabinet on 2 November, only nine days before Smith's dramatic declaration, argued bitterly over the options. The majority wanted to continue to play for time, allow the Rhodesians to back off. Barbara noted sourly, 'If the white Rhodesians are going to get away with UDI why should their morale crack?' Her colleagues fumed with patronizing impatience as Barbara fought on, against more talks. She lost, but still felt the fight had been worthwhile. 'I was overruled of course but I left feeling that my opposition had produced a more tolerable attitude.'[44]

Crossman, increasingly impressed with Barbara as a minister, agreed. She had, he wrote, a hold on Wilson's conscience. She was the left-winger closest to him. 'True, she has been overruled in Cabinet – each new stalling device was proposed by Harold, opposed by her and accepted by the rest of us. But he has paid her enormous deference . . . she was allowed to speak and be listened to at length. On the last day Harold Wilson said that he hadn't slept well the night before because he had been worrying about it. That is most unlike him . . . She got under his skin in a quite extraordinary way.'[45] Barbara exploited her influence. She inspired a Commons motion backing the position she had taken, arguing for a stiffer British position on the threatened UDI. Although she had a long and, she admitted, indiscreet conversation with its author, David Ennals, a newly elected MP with an interest in Africa, she nevertheless claimed she had not intended him to table the motion. Wilson, however, saw it as a deliberate breech of collective responsibility. Crossman agreed. He thought she had 'got away with gross misbehaviour',[46] but Wilson had his revenge. She was not invited to the emergency OPD meeting that followed Smith's rejection of the British terms on 7 November. Out in the cold, she had to wait until the full Cabinet, which met on three consecutive days culminating in Smith's declaration of independence being brought to the cabinet table at 11.15 a.m. on 11 November.

Having failed to avert UDI, the government now had to decide how to respond to it. To the mounting irritation of some of her colleagues, Barbara fought on through OPD and Cabinet, stubbornly and at length. She demanded military intervention to prevent Rhodesia blocking electricity supplies to Zambia, and despite a public outcry she refused to cut aid to those countries that had broken relations with the UK over its failure to respond more aggressively. She was well aware of how intensely her intransigence irritated her colleagues. On one occasion, she turned on William Ross, the Scottish Secretary who, behind the scenes, was egging her on, and told him to do some of the fighting himself: 'Cabinet is tired of hearing me on Rhodesia.' Perhaps she might have won more sympathy if she had had fewer, clearer objectives, instead of firing across every front that opened on the Rhodesia issue. To the jaundiced observers in Cabinet, it seemed she was merely posturing, exploiting her exceptional access to Wilson and his peculiar patience with her to argue her doctrinaire – the pragmatist's rebuke of choice – approach to a crisis which only realpolitik could resolve. Even Crossman, who shared her doubts about Wilson's firmness of purpose, could no longer tolerate her hectoring advocacy. Wilson himself, tolerantly, reported to her that another minister had said: 'Look at her. She only has to waggle that bottom of hers and she gets it all her own way.' In December, even Wilson lost patience. He may have been worried that Barbara might resign, thereby damaging his credibility with an important part of the party, but he was in need of reshuffle elsewhere, so a reshuffle taking Barbara out of overseas affairs it was to be.

Wilson regarded reshuffles as a kind of political chess. Against the misery of making people unhappy could be set the satisfaction of striking a balance between containing ambition, promoting talent, pleasing the party and delivering policy. It was high art, and after a year in power working with a team imposed on him by the party's practice of electing a shadow Cabinet in opposition, he could legitimately clear out the dead wood. In a Cabinet that contained the political talents of Denis Healey, Roy Jenkins, Dick Crossman and Tony Crosland as well as Barbara Castle, there were two overwhelming inadequacies: the Home Office, under the ageing and ailing Frank Soskice, and Transport, in the bumbling hands of a Scottish ex-miner called Tom Fraser. There was speculation that Barbara was earmarked for the Home Office, one of the three great offices of state. One evening just before Christmas, Wilson called her into his office in the Commons to tell her that she was the central figure in his first reshuffle. On her all else depended. He proceeded to address her, according to the account in her diary, with a mixture of sympathy and flattery. Overseas Aid was a frustrating business, he suggested, with spending so tight – and it was so divorced from domestic affairs. And he needed her elsewhere. It was not, however, contrary to all rumour, the Home Office he wanted her for. It was Transport.

10. Tiger

Put a Tiger in your Tank

1960s petrol advertisement

To be offered the Ministry of Transport was a crushing disappointment but Barbara turned it into a platform for her talents. Within the year, even some right-wingers were prepared to consider her a potential leadership contender. Some of the gloss had been rubbed off Wilson; Barbara, by contrast, seemed sure-footed, glamorous and brave, 'the party's greatest electoral asset, after Mr Heath'.[1] The most controversial woman in British politics had metamorphosed into the most successful.

In Whitehall terms, Transport was only a small shift up the food chain from Overseas Development. It meant leaving the ministry that had given her a constructive role in an area of politics she had made her own, without any real rise in cabinet status to compensate. Transport had always been politically uncontentious, a backwater – even, according to Crossman, a reputation graveyard – and she would be taking over from a minister who had been, in her view, little more than a cipher. Wilson was tolerant of her hesitation. It was not uncommon for his cabinet-making aspirations to be thwarted by the ambitions of his ministers (Denis Healey later refused to move from Defence and Roy Jenkins rejected Education). He assured her she would benefit from wider experience of domestic affairs, and emphasized the importance of delivering the integrated transport policy to which the party was committed. 'I can't hold the party otherwise. And the party is the key to everything.' Sleep on it, he said. 'I must have a tiger in my transport policy, and you are the only tiger we've got.'[2] The next day, she said yes.

Crossman was confident of the reason for the move: 'I am sure Barbara has paid the price for her pertinacity in taking the black African point of view and in being the one member of the Cabinet prepared to prevent a settlement in Rhodesia. She was moved because he didn't want her formidable, old-fashioned, left-wing conscience there preventing him [from achieving] some kind of settlement with the Smith regime'[3] A few months later, Barbara herself noted crossly: 'I have been watching the Rhodesian developments on TV without having the slightest idea of what the Government is planning or doing because I am not a member of the special committee on Rhodesia. No doubt when we face a major crisis on this I shall be consulted – but by then it may be too late to influence events.'[4]

As 1965 ended, she bade her farewells at her first department. Her senior officials – and the economists she had recruited – were almost universally sorry to see her go. 'It was as though someone had switched off the current . . . it was like a morgue here,' one Ministry for Overseas Development official said. Cohen sent her a warm note[5] on her departure. She had been lucky to have him, she came to realize. He 'showed her how Whitehall worked', according to one commentator briefed by Barbara's press officer for an article praising her record. 'Tapping economic expertise and enthusiasm from the universities, she managed to weld the regular civil servants and outsiders into creative partnership, and though since she has left credits have been slashed and her successor is no longer in the Cabinet, the competent and up-to-date administration she created is likely to survive.'[6] It was thirty years before the Ministry of Overseas Development regained its status. It became a job for placemen, or for people being shuffled politely out of government. Over the next three years it had three different ministers. Not until Clare Short was made minister in 1997 did it return to Cabinet rank.

If Transport was not quite the leap into the political centre-field she had envisaged, it would still move her into the heart of domestic politics. It was a dangerous ministry because, like the Home Office, it covered thousands of public-sector jobs, millions of people's daily lives and major issues of safety. It was a place where bucks stopped unpredictably. It was also a department where a politician could, literally, make his name, as the Liberal MP Leslie Hore-Belisha had before the war when he had introduced flashing beacons at pedestrian crossings. Callaghan used to joke that he would be remembered only for pioneering the introduction of catseyes in 1948. Wilson saw the advantage of someone who could stamp their personality on the department. Nor had Wilson been exaggerating when he told Barbara that the party had expectations. Under ex-miner Tom Fraser, the department's underperformance had been so serious that a cabinet subcommittee had been set up to bolster him and shame his civil servants into action. In his

memoirs, Wilson blandly observed, 'I had entirely miscalculated the glare of
publicity which beats down on the ministry – mainly because so many
newspaper readers are motorists. [Tom Fraser] had been treated pretty
cruelly.'

Barbara could not even drive, the first transport minister in a generation
who had never learnt. Wilson assured her that her non-driving status would
be an advantage. Publicly, she blamed Ted's unwillingness to share a car, but
in truth she had been defeated by it.[7] Michael Foot, who thirty years earlier
had tried to teach her, wrote to congratulate: 'My dear Barbara, How much
will you pay me to suppress the full scandalous details of what really happened
when I taught you to drive? Consider your financial affairs carefully before
replying. It will need to be substantial to suppress a story as good as this.'[8]

It was more than an advantage. The idea of a Transport Minister who
was not only a woman in the boiler-suited world of engines and footplates
and trade unions and railways, but a woman who had never even taken a
driving test, was greeted with glee by news-hungry journalists as the quiet
Christmas break ended. Barbara captured the moment with a spectacular
demonstration of her flair for self-promotion. On her first day at her new
department in Southwark, she was pursued up the stairs by photographers
and it took an hour for them all to photograph her. Barbara could not
suppress her delight. 'Papers full of pictures of me. My appointment was the
sensation. The fact that I couldn't drive had almost, as Harold predicted
when I tried to use this as an argument against appointing me, turned out to
be an asset.'[9] She called the press in to hear her spell out her preliminary
ideas. In an atmosphere more film premiere than new ministerial appointment (an event not usually marked at all), Barbara – in scarlet, with heavy
gold costume jewellery and the years falling away so dramatically it was
rumoured for long afterwards that she had had a facelift – talked policy; they
wanted to hear about driving. Was she going to take it up? Definitely not,
she said – 'No, for the sake of marital harmony.' Laughter. 'One family, one
car, means one husband, one car,' she declared, seducing a dozen reporters
with a quote. The *Guardian*'s (male) correspondent wrote: 'Splendid stroke
in the sex war. But on whose side?'[10]

That morning, Barbara ditched her old image as vituperative and
dangerous and reinvented herself as an attractive woman who was going to
talk sense about issues that concerned ordinary people. At the age of fifty-
five (although she only admitted to fifty-four), when most of her female
contemporaries were settling into grannyhood and knitting-patterns, Barbara
was flirting her way across the front pages. 'The Taming of A Toughie' was
the headline to one of many flattering profiles.

'The secret really in public life,' she told the *Sun* a few days after her appointment, 'is to be a *person*. Winston Churchill, for instance. People felt he was a person. For some reason – some of it through their cramping themselves with self-restraint – women often emerge as admirable administrators but not as *people*. You've got to be yourself. You've almost got to defy the public: "*That's me. Take me or leave me.*"'[11]

Her adulatory reception marked the start of the long process of changing the way women politicians were perceived. '"She may be pretty and have red hair, but she *can't* be both tough and feminine"' was the popular view quoted in the same *Sun* profile by Susan Barnes, later the wife of Barbara's cabinet colleague Anthony Crosland. 'Can't she? Tigresses can fight tooth and nail, but no one ever suggested they weren't profoundly female creatures . . . men are considerably less dismayed by aggressive women when they are clearly and unmistakably women – and decorative as well. Mrs Castle is.'

Mrs Castle used her decorativeness in the service of political aggression. On a trip to Birmingham at the height of her popular success – and in the midst of a confrontation with lorry drivers and their employers – she and her press officer Chris Hall, who had followed her from ODM, pulled off a shameless stunt.

> At one viaduct which I was due to inspect, a demonstration of road hauliers and drivers was waiting for me, banners aloft, with the slogan, 'Hands off Road Transport'. I, of course, was whisked on to the road works by the officials accompanying me, but Chris and John Gunn [Principle Private Secretary] got together, arranged for a site office to be made available for me and invited the demonstrators to depute ten men to talk to me . . . men, banners, photographers, reporters and I crowded into the small shed. One of the hauliers offered me a cigarette, another hoisted me on to the table where I sat showing my knees. They crowded eagerly round me to pose for a photograph, and with that instinct of mine I whisked one arm round the neck of the chief road haulier employer and the other round the neck of a lorry driver. The employer leaned his cheek against mine and cooed happily, 'My wife will divorce me when she sees this.' . . . If the press use all this, it really should be a scoop.[12]

Over the next two years she rode this dangerously double-edged persona with a sureness of touch – 'that instinct of mine' – that continually exploited its benign potential without quite toppling into the grotesque. In an era that had just discovered teenagers she was almost geriatric, yet she guaranteed publicity for whatever event she attended. No new stretch of motorway was opened, no bypass unveiled, without Barbara in the foreground looking chic (despite her frequent moans to women journalists about the lack of time she had for shopping). But it sometimes exacted a heavy cost: outdoor visits were punctuated by frequent trips to makeshift ladies' rooms. (Overheard on one such trip: 'Marples [her Tory predecessor] used to sleep on these visits. This woman spends all her time in the lavatory.') When the Queen opened the new Severn Bridge, for which Barbara found time to get a 'daring' new hat, the next day's papers, she complained, were almost all about the hat, and where they weren't, they were about her refusal to curtsey. She was unabashed when Prince Philip challenged her name on the bridge's commemorative plaque. 'That's pretty cool. It was practically finished before you came along,'[13] he said. 'I intend to be in on the act,' she retorted.

To media relations she brought a level of manipulation that New Labour's Peter Mandelson later took years to recreate. Her press people were always consulted during the policy debates in her office: at the end of the political argument, she would turn to them and ask how the idea would play in the media. She was punctilious about the timing of stories; good news must be spread across the week. Angry memos were sent out when timing went wrong. Wherever she went, her press entourage was there, antennae twitching. They found her reliable, a professional, an actress always ready to play her part. There was to be a stunt a week, self-promotion disguised as political propaganda. But she would not do gimmicks. An attempt by Chris Hall to persuade her to travel occasionally by public transport – something bound to be picked up, she was so widely recognized – was dismissed as a non-starter however much it might impress the London newspapers.[14]

The twice-a-week visits to the hairdresser were a fixture in her diary. If there were dangers in her emphasis on her femininity, they only became clear later, when the media shifted from admiring references to her hats to derogatory descriptions of her red-hot temper and an alleged tendency to tears when thwarted. And there were warnings that, for a serious politician, she was playing a dangerous game. Even admiring profiles could not resist defining her by her style: there were descriptions, in serious newspapers, of 'small fists banging on the table', and there were often sexual undertones of a kind more appropriate to a Ginger Rogers in cabaret than to a serious politician in Cabinet. Colleagues who wanted to undermine her, needed only to hint at her sex appeal to confirm suspicions that her success had some not unrelated explanation.

★

Addressing star-struck transport reporters at her first press conference, Barbara had promised 'brave new thinking'. Transport was a perfect test bed for the next generation of post-war socialism, a chance to make good the mistakes of the first.

The process had been initiated before she had even signed in for the first time at her new department. At a post-Christmas brainstorming session of her new team, Tommy Balogh, at this stage her mentor at every turn, had introduced his protégé Christopher Foster.[15] Foster was a young left-of-centre Oxford economics don who had co-written a *Socialist Commentary*[16] paper on a future Labour government's transport policy in the early 1960s, and a sharp critique of British Railways management published in 1964. With them was left-winger Stephen Swingler, the junior minister at the department and an old friend of both Barbara's and Wilson's. From amid the gossip two distinct policy strands emerged: the need for a proper description of what was meant by transport integration as a starting point for doing something about it; and the need to get rid of the Permanent Secretary Sir Thomas Padmore before doing anything else. Padmore, once apparently destined for a dazzling career at the Treasury, had been sidelined by Churchill from the Cabinet Office years earlier and in 1962 had come to rest as a force for inertia at the Ministry of Transport.

Swingler regaled the others with tales of Padmore's incompetence, his lack of interest in the area and his apparent belief that all Labour's ideas for transport were unnecessary. The civil service view was that once the massive 1950's motorway programme was complete, there would be little more for the department to do. Swingler's description of Padmore at work confirmed Barbara and especially Balogh in their deep suspicions of officials exposed to long periods of Tory rule. Padmore was already established in Labour Party mythology as the reason for the apparent cancellation of the integrated transport policy for which it had been waiting so long. He was seen as a classic example of the newly identified phenomenon of mandarin power, which had become a fashionable topic for discussion in newspaper columns. One former senior civil servant had just published a book condemning the Civil Service as 'an archaic non-profession . . . which has not even the saving grace of being efficient'.[17] Harold Wilson, a wartime civil servant with an instinctive respect for his former colleagues, had set up the Fulton Commission, the first major inquiry into the Civil Service since the Northcote–Trevelyan inquiry a hundred years earlier.

Unfortunately, Foster had lunch with an old journalist friend, Peter Jenkins of the *Guardian*, soon after the post-Christmas meeting. Barbara's determination to move Padmore was his juiciest bit of gossip. Naively, he was mortified to find, on his first day at the department, that the *Guardian* had splashed the tale across its front page.

Arriving to start work at the department, Barbara was prepared to find signs of hostility. She was not disappointed. Morale in her new ministry, now described with open contempt in government circles as a failure, was low to subterranean. She found her welcome 'chilly', her private office staff 'devoted to her predecessor' and the atmosphere peculiarly masculine. She wanted action quickly, lest such a climate 'solidify around her'. One of her ministers, John Morris, said the politicians were treated 'like an army of occupation', met not with sabotage but with resentment, especially in the private office. (Foster, an outsider, with the kind of donnish, high-table background that most senior officials recognized, had a different perception.)

Barbara wanted to move Padmore to give the party a victory over the Whitehall machine. It would enhance her standing both in the party and in the ministry. She regarded working with good and sympathetic officials as essential to effective policy-making, and there was no chance of victory if every skirmish was conducted in the public eye. Foster's leak united Whitehall against her. Where before it might just have been possible to move a senior civil servant discreetly at a politician's behest, in the full gaze of the Westminster village it was now virtually impossible. The nominal impartiality of officials was too important a doctrine to flout openly. Roy Jenkins – who had got the job of Home Secretary for which Barbara had been so confidently tipped – set about tackling his entire private office structure. But by aiming off the Permanent Under-Secretary Sir Charles Cunningham, who had been in the job for ten years, he achieved Cunningham's early retirement with barely a ripple.

Barbara was furious with Foster; but the damage was done, and Padmore dug in. Mistakenly, she did not abandon the mission. There was a tense scene between Permanent Secretary and Minister. She would not be able to oppose the 'wilder ideas of the [PLP] transport group' she warned him, because if she did they would think she was doing his bidding. He responded suavely, 'Surely no one would think that of you. Everyone knows you are a very determined woman.' The following day, in a second confrontation, tempers frayed further. 'Once again I had to repeat that I had discussed his move with the PM but it was still open. He told me flatly that he would fight: he wasn't going to take the can back for a weak Minister [Tom Fraser].'[18]

Barbara tried a direct appeal to the head of the Civil Service, Sir Lawrence Helsby, and was told politely but firmly that it was unprecedented for permanent secretaries to change on appointment of a new minister. Her repeated appeals to Wilson to honour the commitment to allow her to choose her own Permanent Secretary, made when he appointed, her went unanswered. 'He seems to be running a private war with the civil service, despite the outward correctness of his relationship with it, and I feel he doesn't always come out on top,' she said in May as she began to realize that Padmore would never go. Marcia Williams, from even closer at hand, would agree later: 'When [Wilson] went into Downing Street he regarded the civil servants as colleagues and friends . . . they didn't control him, but they managed to handle him and they certainly had the measure of him and his personality.'[19]

Barbara now tried a more indirect tactic, cooking up a conspiracy with George Brown at the Department of Economic Affairs. Brown was anxious for reasons of industrial development to see transport policy overhauled. But an attempt to move his smart young Under-Secretary Douglas Allen (Permanent Secretary at the Treasury from 1968 to 1974) from the DEA was repeatedly foiled after farcical scenes which included the new Home Secretary Roy Jenkins and Barbara sitting in the Home Office wondering how to get hold of George Brown by telephone without alerting officials to their plan. Thereafter, every time Barbara spotted a job opening suitable to Padmore's status, it was mysteriously taken by someone else. Padmore was saved by the loyalty of colleagues both to himself as an individual and to the doctrine of neutrality. In the end he outlasted Barbara, who was reduced to admitting defeat and to bringing in her own man, J. D. Jones, to work alongside Padmore while Foster, who was not a civil servant at all, took the lead on policy development. The frigidity of the relationship at the top is illustrated by Barbara's notes to Padmore and in his correspondence with her. 'The Secretary may care to see this,' she scribbled on an outline of a major policy speech she was about to make, to which Padmore replied: '[The proposals] . . . although they might well be useful, seem likely to strike most people as pretty trivial.' Only after Barbara left the department did Padmore admit to her successor that he realized he had been stale for several years. He left almost immediately after Barbara and joined a civil engineering group in the private sector. Later, the failed operation to move him would be cited as an example of Barbara's intemperate empire-building. In the meantime she was left in a state of mutual mistrust with her most senior official, grumbling at the injustice of being held responsible for everything that happened in her department but without the power to hire and fire the people who worked for her.

Transport was a department where politics and principle collided. Barbara's first major decision was about politics. In January 1966, there was a by-election in Hull North. It was a Labour-held seat. Wilson was anxious to hold a general election to try to secure a working majority and victory in the by-election would be a good launch pad. The people of Hull, one of the more inaccessible corners of Britain, wanted a bridge over the Humber estuary which, it was argued, would open up the whole east coast of England. Approval was said to depend on a satisfactory regional development plan. Barbara ignored this, and at a by-election meeting in Hull gave the bridge the go-ahead. 'I pledge to Humberside that when the development plans of this region have been agreed between the planning authorities and this government, then you will have your Humber bridge,' she promised the voters. 'It was the most flamboyantly political decision she took,' economics adviser Foster said.[20] When it opened in 1981, five years behind schedule and more than four times over budget – the cost had risen from £19 million to £90 million – she was declared the project's godmother. 'Leave Harold Wilson out of it,' she told critics at an event celebrating its opening. 'He didn't know I was going to make that announcement [on the bridge]. The Conservatives only ever built north–south roads, there was no money for regional development. I believed in it. I meant it, and you got it!'[21] The Humber Bridge was always referred to by Conservatives as 'Mrs Castle's pork barrel'. For nearly twenty years it was the longest single-span bridge in the world, and it remains an object of great beauty and little economic merit, continually struggling with the debt incurred by overambitious projections for its use.

However, the Hull by-election was won on a 5 per cent swing to Labour, and within weeks Wilson had called a general election in which he secured a majority of ninety-seven. It was the first substantial majority Labour had achieved since 1945, yet it had been a flat campaign ('the most boring I have ever experienced' Barbara wrote) which Wilson had kept deliberately low-key. Labour's share of the vote rose from 44.2 to 47.9 per cent, and for the first time since 1951 the party won more than thirteen million votes. The Humber Bridge set a pattern for decision-making in transport that made the bypass map of Britain by the end of the 1980s look as if it had been designed by the marginal seats campaign unit at Conservative Central Office.

Action was Barbara's ministerial trademark. From the luckless Tom Fraser, Barbara inherited a massive road safety bill. Nearly eight thousand people a year were dying on the roads, and hundreds of thousands were injured. It was a field in which an energetic and determined minister could make a name tackling the vested interests of the vast and influential motoring lobby, who regarded as inalienable the motorist's rights to drive while drunk, to drive dangerously fast and not to wear a seat belt. To curtail these freedoms, the lobbyists argued, would be the action of a domineering, bureaucratic nanny state – a sentiment shared across the political parties. Roy Jenkins, for example, was unhappy with speed limits and seat belts – even though the number of road deaths was rising so fast it was projected to reach five hundred thousand by the turn of the century.[22] Road safety was ultimately a matter for the individual, not for government intervention, and laws that did not command popular respect would only bring the law itself into disrepute, Jenkins held.

The motoring lobby could with justification argue that the rate of increase of road casualties lagged far behind the rise in car ownership. However, the evidence of the striking impact of some road safety measures had converted the policy-makers in the department. Only the political will to sell them to parliament and to the public was lacking. The Road Safety Bill introduced the breathalyser, extended the 70 mph speed limit trial and required new cars to be fitted with seat belts. The breathalyser was an American invention which superseded the 'drunkometer', a 1930s device for measuring the amount of alcohol in a driver's bloodstream. British police still relied on the traditional method of asking a suspect driver to walk down the white line in the road, but the arguments in favour of the breathalyser – it was portable, reliable and almost instant – and its potential to cut road deaths and serious injuries were overwhelming. Resistance was also intense – sustained by popular heroes like Britain's Formula One 'Racing Driver of the Year', Stirling Moss, who poured invective on 'socialist hypocrisy'. The bill had not completed its passage through the Commons by the time of the 1966 election, however, and it was lost.

As soon as parliament resumed, decisions had to be made on the legislative programme for the new session. Barbara, already identified with the Road Safety Bill's fortunes, struggled to restore it. Consumer protection measures and leasehold reform (a long-held party ambition) were shunted aside to make room for 'her' bill. In fact its content had been largely decided by her predecessor, although she appeased the motoring lobby and the police by dropping plans for random breath testing (a concession she later regretted). Justifying this change, she said that the risk of the police alienating the public, together with the possibility of women on their own being stopped by potential impostors, had persuaded her that a tighter drawing-up of the bill was more appropriate. On the other hand, she increased the penalty for driving while drunk from a fine to automatic disqualification.

What Barbara brought to the bill was her unremitting determination to get it on the statute book. It provoked a media storm. A year earlier, Barbara had been photographed being kissed by Hastings Banda, the new President of Malawi, which resulted in an extraordinary storm of racist hate mail. Now her postbag was bulging with angry letters from aggrieved men; but there were also touching letters of gratitude from wives 'allowed to go to the pub for the first time' if only so that they could drive their menfolk home. And there was even a death threat, which Scotland Yard took seriously enough to provide Barbara with a bodyguard for a fortnight. He was she exploited to the full for the benefit of the media. The detective assigned to the job bought the Castles drinks at her local pub, and they all walked home for the cameras. The impact of the breathalyser was even more startling than predicted. The official forecast of lives likely to be saved was two hundred a year. At the end of the first five months, eight hundred people were alive who statistically would have died without the breathalyser. Serious injuries were down by 15 per cent. Over the first Christmas, in 1967, deaths fell from 158 in 1966 to 98.

Backed by an unprecedented advertising budget of over £1 million, Barbara managed to turn public opinion so that it was at least facing in the right direction to see the transformation the new device had brought. On 11 October 1967 she noted in her diary: 'I find that I have forgotten to mention B for Breathalyser day! [two days earlier] This is an indication as to how coolly I have taken the introduction of the social revolution . . . for which I am responsible. The fact is that, having gone into all the arguments myself very thoroughly, and all the medical evidence, I have just assumed that the new law was the most natural thing in the world. Yet far from coming a cropper over it, I seem to be sailing through.' She could in justice claim to have launched a social revolution – although persuading the British driver to abandon drinking and driving turned out to be more of a process than an event.

Barbara's promotion, as Wilson had anticipated, had not only offered a placebo to the left, but distracted Barbara herself with an issue that played to her political strengths – decisiveness, a capacity for administration and a flair for personalizing policy. Transport presented a serious challenge to a left-wing minister who wanted to reconcile contemporary change with socialist aspiration. Public transport of all kinds was in decline. In the Attlee era, the party had created a nationalized railway and road haulage system out of the legacy of wartime controls. But now the landscape had altered dramatically. The Conservatives had partially denationalized road freight, while the number of cars in private ownership had exploded from 1.5 million to 9.5

million. The party's policy-making machinery had not yet absorbed this profoundly unsocialist development. Its response to the anticommunal, individualistic vice of car ownership, which was undermining collective enterprise – bus services as well as railways – was to revert to the post-war plans for nationalization of road services as well as rail. When, in 1960, a Labour transport spokesman had said 'The ownership of a car ... is beginning to replace the ownership of a house as the expression of a man's sense of independence and self-respect'[23] he was not indicating a change in policy to reflect it. Only slowly were the party's policy-makers coming to terms with the social impact of private travel, and asking questions about how to ensure fairer access to it.

Car ownership was traditionally associated with the prosperous – to such an extent that the laws restricting the use of cars by candidates in election campaigns (for example, for taking voters to the polling station) had only been liberalized in 1958. The establishment to a man were motorists, instinctive defenders of the freedom of the road as a fundamental liberty not to be curtailed without heavy political cost. The AA and the RAC between them boasted more members than all the political parties put together. Although Barbara brought to the ministry long experience of public transport, she was not entirely opposed to private cars. She and Ted owned one, while her ministerial car and its driver were a vital extension of her office. Nonetheless, at least once a month for more than twenty years she had travelled by overnight sleeper from London to Blackburn via Manchester. She had years of first-hand knowledge of railway stations with no regular linking bus services, erratic local connections and the practical implications for the traveller of under-investment in rolling stock and track improvements. The fate of British Railways was a matter of personal familiarity as well as political concern. Furthermore, thousands of jobs as well as thousands of miles of track were threatened by the radical cuts proposed by the former British Railways chairman, Dr Beeching.[24] But as well as railways, the political left now increasingly wanted cars, and open roads to drive them on, and protection for the growing number of jobs in the car industry. And, not least because of the work of Barbara's in-house economist Christopher Foster, they wanted a coherent, planned system to reconcile the two ambitions.

In the previous ten years, the proportion of freight traffic travelling by road had risen from 44 to 61 per cent, although less than a third was carried by the private sector; while four-fifths of all passenger miles were now travelled by road, more than half by private cars and motorcycles. The age of mass private travel had dawned, and it was predicted to expand exponentially, causing congestion, delay (already estimated to cost £2 billion a year) and environmental damage while simultaneously provoking crisis in public transport. Loss-making bus and train services which had once been cross-subsidized from profitable ones were now being closed down altogether. Where the Attlee government had had to adjudicate between two rival forms of public transport, the problem now was how to keep any public transport going at all. Party policy called for a national transport plan to coordinate urban, industrial and regional development needs; and, 'given the lamentable performance of the Ministry of Transport',[25] for a powerful transport board to be set up to do the work. But it was clear that a Labour Transport Minister could no longer afford to focus only on the interests of the trade unions in the nationalized transport industries. Although car ownership was a measure of affluence that mirrored regional prosperity – in 1966, there were four people per car in Surrey, while in parts of Glasgow there were eleven[26] – policy had to reflect the need for both the car and the train. Barbara declared: 'In such a situation it was no use trying to turn back the clock. I refused to be a King Canute' – a charge levelled against her by the AA – 'trying to force people onto railways which could not take them where they wanted to go. If the private car had brought the boon of mobility to millions of people, which it clearly had, then that boon should be available to everyone. We then must collectively face the consequences and deal with them through new arrangements which reflected the new facts.'[27]

The party wanted to make road users pay the real costs of their journey. Unlike rail charges, which included the cost of track construction and maintenance, signalling and operations, the costs of driving a truck or a car failed to reflect the amount of money needed for construction and mainten-ance and the development of road systems. To make journeys reflect those costs implied a steep increase in charges on private road users. To offset this, it was proposed that the real cost of rail track and station closures in terms of the cost of alternative journeys and the impact those journeys would make on congestion should be included in the calculation of the 'unviability' of any given route or station. Foster had pioneered the concept of 'social cost' in his analysis of the benefits of the proposed new Victoria tube line in London.

From his prompt box in the Cabinet Office, Tommy Balogh exhorted Barbara, as she wrestled with conflicting objectives, at least to 'give expression to the general principles which would animate your Ministry. This is one thing which your predecessor never got round to doing.' Within two months she had the bones of her policy worked out. She showed them to Padmore, who reported them to the Treasury, who tried to stop her announcing them in case they had spending implications. But she ignored the instruction. Labour, she told a party local government conference in February 1966, recognized the right of everyone to own a car. (She even promised to 'democratize' car ownership, although no scheme was developed despite an attempt by Tony Benn to interest her in a national leasing arrangement.) There would be a rail network to meet the country's social and economic needs and an expanded road programme accompanied by restraints on car use in urban areas. There would be a new national freight authority to coordinate freight movement and ensure the competitiveness of rail freight and there would be planning at national, regional and town level. And there was the issue of road safety. All these ideas appeared a couple of months later in a White Paper on the ministry's work.

Barbara had found a new passion: policy development. Her underlying seriousness as a politician was always the counterbalance to her flamboyant press image. The kind of starry-eyed enthusiasm that once filled letters home now poured into her work at the ministry. Diary entries grew sparse under the pressure.

> Hard at work on National Freight Authority and White Paper policy. I've really got the boys thinking! It is amusing to see them trying to reverse the instinctive reactions which they imposed on Tom Fraser. What fascinates me about a Minister's job is the difficulty of knowing when to stand out against official advice. Some of it (e.g. on technical problems) is invaluable, and civil servants are also the reservoir of knowledge about parliamentary battles, the reaction of interested organizations, etc. Yet there are limits to the purely technical, and even these types of judgement overflow into, or are influenced by, political and economic attitudes.[28]

Many of her officials, and both of her ministers, John Morris and Stephen Swingler, found her an open but challenging boss. One official regarded life with Barbara as 'a ball'. She spoke as she found, she argued vigorously and rationally, she was clever and hard-working. Above all she had the ear of the Prime Minister, and she usually got what she wanted. But she risked trying to do too much, too quickly. Even Wilson warned her against thinking only of the next day's headlines. Her first White Paper, her departmental mission statement, was heavily amended in Cabinet and panned in the press for failing to carry enough detail.

Encouraged by Crossman at the housing department, Barbara applied planning to transport in a way that had never been attempted before. Transport could become big politics, she believed, reflecting and influencing a whole range of decisions about where people lived and worked. Urban traffic schemes could be designed to provide fast, seamless travel by a variety of means, while preserving the town centres that traffic was threatening to destroy. She had, Crossman noted, moved the centre of gravity of planning from his department (where he was thirsting for a move) to her own. The transport crisis had triggered shelves of investigations and inquiries. The most celebrated of the early 1960s came from an urban planner, Professor Colin Buchanan. In a report for the transport ministry, he had recommended separating the car and the pedestrian without compromising the car, envisaging science-fiction cities elevated over motorways and roundabouts and car parks. The sense of siege endured by those inside such a structure was not anticipated, but fortunately, in most areas the extensive redesigning of urban traffic flows was found to be prohibitively expensive.

Barbara, only slightly more modestly, proposed devolving power to specially created urban passenger transport authorities, which would have extensive powers to control bus services – newly renationalized – and to coordinate them with suburban rail services, which they would also control. Grants would be available for infrastructure developments such as new connections between different forms of transport. The private motorist had to be made more aware of the real cost of his choice of transport: passenger transport authorities could introduce road-pricing and extend parking charges, the proceeds from which could be redirected to other transport objectives. Devolving decision-making on transport was practical. It was also political, since the burden of unpopular decisions would fall on local authorities. (Ted was the vice-chairman of the GLC's traffic committee.) The idea of road-pricing caused horror on the left: rationing by purse, journalists suggested. Barbara denied it would discriminate against the poor; if it was properly structured. 'What it would do,' she told one critic,[29] 'is to penalise the anti-social motorist against the social motorist.'

Her biggest headache in her attempt to shore up public transport was the railways. Although they played a vital role in moving people around, their main income came from carrying freight. Under the previous Tory government, British Railways had been substantially reorganized and devolved in preparation for the long-awaited return to profitability (reversing a ten-year deficit). This was the motive behind Dr Beeching's draconian pruning of the infrastructure and the proposed closure of more than two thousand stations and eight thousand miles of track, one-third of the total length.

Barbara had been persuaded by Foster that neither BR nor the road haulage industry, represented by Sir Reginald Wilson, chairman of the

Transport Holding Company, all that was left of the Atlee government's attempts to integrate transport, could effectively integrate road and rail – indeed, they undermined it by trying to protect their own interests. The proposed national freight authority would impose integration on road and rail, directing freight perhaps by a licensing system to whichever mode was most economically efficient. But if the national freight authority was to be a genuinely integrating force, Barbara was warned, it would have to be guided by economics and not by a desire to protect the railways. The railways in their turn would have to take a huge stride into the modern age, and introduce the kind of accounting practices that would allow their services to be accurately and transparently costed. Unless the freight authority was seen to act in the best interests of business, there would be a counterproductive explosion in lorry fleets owned directly by companies which were not covered by regulation. Barbara rejected the argument on political grounds: the country 'has willed the continuance of an extensive railway system'[30] and one way of making it viable was to use it as much as possible. It had been agreed, she continued, that short-haul freight should travel by road: it was only justice that long-haul freight should be directed on to rail. She told the TUC, which wanted to renationalize all road haulage, as it had been under Labour's 1948 Act, under a British transport commission: '*I* am going to be the BTC.' In other words, integration would be imposed from the top. She devised a complex system of quantity licensing to restrict the amount of freight that covered long distances by road, to be introduced once a new container-freight service was nationally available. The licensing system was never used.

At the heart of the problem was the parlous state of British Railways management. But the management of nationalized industries was part of the dialogue of conflict between left and right. Anthony Crosland had used it to argue against further nationalization in his book *The Future of Socialism* ten years earlier. The left had always opposed 'Morrisonian' boards that replicated the private sector's approach to management. Barbara still believed in the importance of worker control, although in the argument to come it was hard to detect any lingering influence of William Mellor. She accepted that some nationalized industries were badly managed, but she was discovering that ministers lacked the levers to do much about this problem. The only real scope for movement was through her power of patronage: she appointed the chairman and board of BR. When Labour came to power in 1964, Dr Beeching was replaced by Stanley Raymond. Raymond was an industry man, an edgy character, a Barnardo boy who had worked his way to the top first in the army and then in public transport. During a brief period in the trade union movement he had made powerful friends now in the Labour Cabinet; both Jim Callaghan and Ray Gunter at the Ministry of Labour were old allies.

Raymond had been in the job a little over a year, presiding over BR's worsening fortunes, when Barbara arrived at the ministry. Their relations began badly: it was reported that he, like Padmore, was to be sacked. Raymond, notoriously thin-skinned, was outraged. But their relationship – at least as far as she was concerned – seemed to recover. In February 1966, she persuaded him to submit to a management review so as 'to give BR realistic financial targets' and identify the 'social cost' element of the operation. They worked together to reassess Beeching and agree a track length longer than Beeching's but in theory short enough, at eleven thousand miles, to be viable under a new subsidy regime. (The network they decided on survives virtually unscathed today.) Meanwhile, the review was revealing the chaos of BR management already described by Foster in his own 1964 survey. In July 1967, Barbara was told by the independent experts in the joint steering group overseeing the review that Raymond would not be able to deliver the change in management culture and practice that was the industry's only hope.

> The main outcome of the review was that the loss-making social services should be subsidised explicitly but that even if the Government subsidised all the so-called social services, the railways would still make a loss. [BR] was less efficient in its use of people and assets than other railways. Its administrative overheads were exceptionally high. It was a mammoth management task to turn it round ... The inquiry had shown up the painful inadequacy and lack of management skill and initiative of most of the BR top team.[31]

Raymond had to go. 'I must force him to resign,' Barbara accepted coolly. 'I suggested we must draw the attention of eminent journalists to the fact that the report is a scathing indictment of BR management ... I hope the comments in the press will bring a reaction from Raymond that will give me my chance.'[32]

She now threw herself into the job of finding a successor for the biggest job at her disposal. Almost immediately, the glamorous figure of the young Peter Parker was suggested by her old friend (Lord) Jock Campbell. Parker, recommended as a socialist, had been on the Booker board while Campbell was chairman. Barbara fell for him, for his charismatic charm and leadership potential. He was keen to come. But the first round of discussions faltered after her department united to argue that, charismatic as he mi̱, lacked both practical and theoretical experience of running a huge ε like British Railways. He had not been chosen to succeed Campbell top of Booker the previous year, and he would need the underpinni̱ ̤r a strategist (a job Foster would have liked) and a financial director – Parker's expertise was leadership. Under departmental pressure, she agreed to consider other candidates. None, in her view, matched Parker.

Inevitably, rumours of her intentions spread and seeped into the newspapers. Suddenly anxious to avoid humiliating the sensitive Raymond despite her earlier decision to undermine him in the press, she decided on a sideways move. 'Having thought a great deal about this I have come to the conclusion it would be altogether too cruel – as well as too risky – just to sack him outright. In any case I have no power to do so: I would have to blackmail him into resigning.'[33] She would offer him the chairmanship of another area of her empire, the as yet non-existent freight integration council. The offer was made in an interview hastily arranged to pre-empt more speculation (Raymond had to be called out of a critical meeting with the unions). He was deeply wounded, and understandably furious. He 'stalked out, cold with anger', Barbara wrote, and 'almost spat at me'. Foster recalled: 'It had been an appalling experience for her. She was white and shaking. His rage had been volcanic. All his pent-up insecurity as a Barnardo boy had poured out.'[34] But the plan worked. When his departure was finally confirmed, the *Financial Times* wrote: 'The steering group had the advice of several consultants some of whom are said to have been astonished by the techniques and methods used by the railways.' *The Times* was more cynical: 'Since he became chairman, the fortunes of the railways . . . have gone sharply into reverse and a near-record deficit of £150m is expected this year. There is some evidence that he is being made the scapegoat.'

Now Barbara had lost her BR chairman before finding a replacement. Various other names were suggested: John Morris, her railways minister, went all the way to Canada for a long interview with Douglas Macmillan, the man who had saved the railways there. But, after a few days' contemplation, Macmillan decided he didn't want the job. Harold Wilson wanted her to consider Alf Robens, the former minister and coal board chief, but Barbara was determined to have someone as like Parker as she could find. Finally, she went back to the man himself. However, in the protracted interval between first and second approaches, a new, and this time irrecoverable, sterling crisis had erupted; devaluation ensued. Parker was still enthusiastic, but only on condition that he and his board of management were paid the rate for the job. In effect, that would mean a 50 per cent increase in BR's most senior salaries. Alternatively, Parker would have to take a 12.5 per cent cut. In the aftermath of devaluation, pay rises at the top were out of the question.

Barbara regretted her clumsiness, thinking that if she had insisted at the start, she would have got the pay increases through. The ICI chairman Lord Melchett had only recently been recruited to run the steel industry for £16,000 a year (nearly twice a cabinet minister's £8,500 salary), well above the going rate for nationalized industry chairmen of £12,500. Parker, however (whose credentials were only partly enhanced by an Oxford romance with a rising star in the Labour Party, Shirley Williams), was perceived in the press – rapidly informed of all developments – as greedy, a view possibly encouraged by his white Rolls-Royce and personalized number-plates. 'I can't get rid of the [rail] deficit for you if you don't give me the tools,' she complained to Callaghan at the Treasury after a steamy interview, followed by a Cabinet where the plans for her proposed national freight consortium were finally approved – 'But what use is that?' she asked herself disconsolately.

Do the railways have the right management? asked the Nuffield transport economist Denys Munby. 'The importance of organisational change can be exaggerated. But the importance of good people can hardly be over-emphasised. The railways have not had enough of them.' Parker himself – who did finally become chairman of BR, but ten years later – was anxious not to burn bridges. He sent Barbara a personal note: 'You know that my heart is in all that you are trying to do. I am very sorry not to have been able to make out the case for urgent action on the salary structure for senior management. Despite all the difficulties of the post-devaluation period, I remain convinced that what I have recommended would be the lesser risk of many that must be faced – and indeed would be soon seen as straightforward, firm and fair.' Barbara was furious with herself. 'It is the only time since I have been a Minister that I have wobbled like this, and I am paying for it.' Others believe she was victim of a conspiracy to preserve the job for a railman, not a whizz-kid businessman from the private sector (even one who was a serving board member of British Steel). For Raymond's friends in government, unable to prevent his dismissal, could at least stop Barbara getting the successor of her choice.

Management reform had been central to the plan to revive BR and to give it a fighting chance against road transport. In the end, Barbara was forced to promote Raymond's deputy, Bill Johnson. When she saw him on 7 December 1967, she made no attempt to sign him up to reform, just as there had been no attempt to see whether Raymond himself would implement the kind of changes the joint steering group believed were essential. Barbara introduced no mechanism for holding Johnson to account, or of requiring him to work in a new way. Barbara had allowed her grip to slip on the only lever she had inside British Railways. Her fury with herself was overwhelming: 'Oh, Barbara, you ought to be ashamed,' she wrote; she had dithered when she should have decided. But she also blamed Foster, who had told her that Parker could not do the job on his own, for being critical of her candidate. Jock Campbell told her that it was because he wanted the job himself, something Foster still vehemently denies and on which Barbara never directly challenged him. Foster himself believes that her failure in this episode – partly caused by her obstinate refusal to drop Parker as a candidate – confirmed BR's decay. Within months, BR was rejecting the department's demands for cost accounting, thereby denying the outside world (and itself) the figures that would have allowed it to take informed decisions on the basis of accurate information.[35]

There was a symmetry to the situation: while Barbara was haggling with colleagues over several thousand pounds a year for a new chairman and board members, the existing BR board was refusing to pay train guards a productivity bonus that management said had not been earned. A strike was on the cards. The damaging cycle of uninspired management and bad industrial relations – and lousy train services – continued unbroken. Barbara's mishandling of the replacement of Raymond – she was accused of 'hawking the job round', unable to find a successor, for months – meant it was impossible to have a discussion about the real problem of under-resourcing and poor management, as Raymond himself pointed out in an article in January 1967 in the *Sunday Times* in which his anger was barely concealed. 'We have got to establish some reasonable means of dealing with appointments to these exposed positions on the boards of nationalised industries . . . nationalised industries have to compete with other employers for scarce manpower.' But it was plain he saw his sacking as an act of personal vengeance. 'We ought by now to be able to take these appointments out of politics or at least say which are political appointments and which are career appointments.' He had never understood women, he said – a sentiment which aroused less sympathy than he had perhaps anticipated. 'Spare Rib Blues', a poem by Peter Dickinson, appeared in *Punch* soon after his dismissal.

> When God created women, Stan,
> He gave 'em feeble little wits.
> Unlike that noble creature, Man,
> Whose mighty brain conceives a plan

Of solemn and prodigious span;
And when (hard cheese!) it falls to bits
He blames a woman if he can.

But God made girls to please the view
Of you and me and other chaps,
To cook, and bear a child or two,
And in the intervals to coo
Admiringly at me and you,
And when (bad luck!) our plans collapse
To scuttle off and fetch the glue.

No wonder we and all our peers,
Sir Stan, are sadly baffled by
A woman who, amid the jeers
Of Men beset by Manly fears,
Astounds our brains, affronts our ears
By talking better sense than I
Or you have talked for years and years.

As the crisis over BR management reached its climax, Barbara was also in the final stages of preparation for her Transport Bill. Based on five White Papers published over the previous eighteen months, and the longest piece of non-financial legislation introduced since the war, it was published on 6 December 1967. It was a prodigious piece of work and a hugely ambitious programme: as well as setting up the National Freight Authority and giving it extensive powers, and reforming the BR board, it allowed for the renationalization of bus transport and enabled the establishment of the first passenger transport authorities, hiving off powers from myriad local government functionaries and giving them considerable additional ones, to allow the imposition of coordinated services.

There was more to come on road safety. Scientific principles were to be applied: to find out why accidents were happening and how to stop them, she introduced accident analysis and road safety units across the country. In addition, she made the fitting of seat belts compulsory in all new cars, introduced a driving-instructor register, confirmed the 70 mph speed limit – despite drunken assurances from George Brown that driving at 100 mph down the motorway was perfectly safe – and, in the age of the hit song 'Terry' ('He rode into the night/On his motorbike/I cried out to him in fright/Don't do it, don't do it . . .'), raised the minimum age for riding bigger motorbikes, mopeds or scooters from sixteen to seventeen. She also reprieved hundreds of miles of Britain's ageing canal network, a move which won her the undying admiration of a small but dedicated group of enthusiasts. Finally, she planned to nationalize the largely ailing docks so that their development could be better planned.

Although she rejected the complete renationalization of road haulage, Barbara introduced ways of improving pay and conditions for lorry drivers. She suggested giving them the ten-hour day they sought, and using the tachograph, the 'spy in the cab', as its guarantor. (This was less popular when drivers realized it would monitor every moment spent at the wheel.) Frank Cousins, now out of government and back as general secretary of the Transport and General Workers' Union, was unpersuaded by her arguments. 'Frank Cousins' socialism,' Barbara remarked bitterly of her former cabinet colleague on several occasions, 'stops at the door of the cab.' Michael Foot hailed the bill as the government's first real socialist measure. No one else on the left could see much socialism in it, but thought none the worse of it for that. Alan Watkins, soon to become a devastating critic, wrote in the *New Statesman*: 'Mrs Castle opposed both the unions and the Labour Party's traditional wisdom . . . Mrs Castle is a good minister.' Norah Beloff, Wilson's bête noire on the *Observer*, suggested she had bamboozled her detractors with policies quite at odds with the rhetoric which described them. 'There was a shudder of alarm that she might be irrelevantly doctrinaire. She encouraged this herself by always insisting she was carrying out a 'socialist' transport policy (by which she meant one with a social conscience).' The experts were enthusiastic. Denys Munby in the *Journal of Transport Economics and Politics* wrote: 'Mrs Castle's dirigisme throws over both the traditional Socialist dogmas of "coordination by nationalisation" and the naive belief that competition in the transport industries will solve every problem without any coordinated control of the market as a whole.' The *Financial Times* praised her innovatory approach to state control, introducing holding companies rather than old-fashioned nationalization: 'This seems to be the best way yet devised of giving public industries a taste of the disciplines of private enterprise.' The Croslandite *Socialist Commentary* observed, 'Nothing Mrs Castle does is ever short of controversy. But . . . most people who have been wrestling with the problems of transport policy over the last few years would say that at last, and dangerously late in the day, a coherent strategy has now been found.'

The opposition, on the other hand, chose to believe Barbara's rhetoric and declared the legislation the wild act of a left-wing extremist. Even though the *Economist* found it 'better than Beeching'[36] and praised its approach to BR's management problems, a young, rich and ambitious future Tory minister, Peter Walker, was reported to be paying £10,000 out of his own pocket to mount a campaign against it, backed by the Road Hauliers' Association and the right-wing Aims of Industry group. They invented a character called 'Transport Bill', with a bowler hat, striped trousers and a spanner in hand, captioned: 'It's your money he's after.' Alarming costs were imputed from the legislation, on flimsy evidence.

The bill dominated the 1967–8 session of parliament. It had 169 clauses and 15 schedules. Even its admirers described it as a pantechnicon, while the Tories' declared intention was to fight it line by line. Behind the scenes, however, Crossman – now Leader of the House and responsible for the day-to-day work of the Commons – and his shadow, the emollient Willie Whitelaw, soon struck a deal which involved shedding some parts of the bill. Barbara crossly refused. 'I certainly have no intention of dropping anything.' The suggestion was repeated on various occasions thereafter. Auberon Waugh, who devoted many column inches in the *Spectator* to Barbara-baiting, reported one approach in February: 'Apparently she fell into a rage, and the two men retired with their tails between their legs.'

But support for the bill was wavering. Peter Walker's road industry campaign was emphasizing the new costs that would fall on industry, just as devaluation was making it more competitive. The bill was attacked for protecting uncompetitive and overmanned rail at the expense of efficient and flexible road transport. It was beginning to bring in too many bad headlines. Early in 1968 Wilson put Barbara, after more than two years in the job, on the transfer list. The bill was destined to fall short of being the memorial she had intended and Wilson's decision to dismember the bill team was an act verging on political vandalism. He argued that the job was done. It is not clear whether he reckoned with or without Padmore's desire for revenge or the aim of Richard Marsh, the man chosen as Barbara's successor, to pursue a less controversial course.

Marsh took over in April, and immediately dismantled the more collect-ivist provisions of the legislation and diluted Barbara's plans for dock nationalization, so that once again public ownership became only a support for a less successful industry instead of a means of coordinating investment and development. Fuming, Barbara condemned him as a man with a 'slovenly mind' and no socialist feeling. Foster – left behind at Transport, his relation-ship with Barbara at an end because of her private suspicions about his role in the Parker affair – went to see her to complain about the misery of working for the new man. 'Dick Marsh was not only lazy, but completely cynical. He had no ideas of his own on transport and spent his time saying how little he thought of mine,' Barbara reported. 'His only theme was efficiency, but he had no clear idea how to achieve it.'

In his autobiography Marsh described his method of getting the mammoth Transport Bill through standing committee with a casual disregard for the niceties of debate: 'I made a habit of purchasing a couple of bottles of Scotch which I kept in a committee room nearby and encouraged the more vociferous members of the standing committee to go and have a drink at my expense . . . To celebrate the end of the Transport Bill, we held a party and I calculated that I had spent £48 on free whisky to stop government supporters talking in the course of the committee.'

Barbara had been in the job for two years; Marsh was there for six months. Then the department – like the Ministry for Overseas Development – was dropped from the Cabinet.

11. The Politics of Barbara Castle

Is this really the rebel whose elevation to the Ministry left a hole
in the left ventricle of Labour that no one has filled?

Norah Beloff, *Observer*, July 1967

1967 was Barbara Castle's *annus mirabilis*. She was constantly in the public
eye, and the public eye could rarely fault her. She had all the attributes of a
successful cabinet minister with further yet to climb and she was identified
with distinctive policies for which she had been seen to tackle a variety of
vested interests in defence of the ordinary traveller. Those policies had won
her wide public support and, partly in consequence, a growing fan club
within the party. Moreover, as one observer noted: 'She has the distinction
of being the minister of whom the Treasury is most afraid. Her old terms of
friendship with the Prime Minister and his principal economic adviser, Dr
Thomas Balogh, mean that she can sometimes by-pass the Chancellor's
veto.'[1] After three years in government, the waters of the establishment
seemed to have closed over Barbara's head. She was 'bustling Barbara' now,
a woman in a hurry to bring to people's lives not radical change but order, a
clever pragmatist admired by the *Economist* and the *Financial Times*. Her
political appeal carried to new corners of the public and the party. Her
resolute advocacy of policies distinctly her own was contrasted favourably
with Wilson's shiftiness and the trimmers elsewhere in Cabinet.

Barbara's triumphs shone the more against the background of a government which within weeks of its 1966 election victory had become enmired
in grave economic chaos. She had achieved a kind of political respectability
that she would have scorned a few years earlier. Exposed to the realities of
government, forced to accept Bevan's 'language of priorities', she grew
irritated by the hostility of the left, which refused to acknowledge the

financial dangers threatening the government. 'I am appalled by the purely destructive mood into which the Left has got itself – not least Michael [Foot]. The Government is on the edge of complete disintegration of a kind from which Labour would not recover for twenty years, and I cannot see that it would benefit anyone to push it over the edge,' she complained in the midst of one of the periodic financial crises.

Her own ideas about policy became more subtle as she became absorbed in the detail of making abstract ideas work in practice. There was less space in her life for theorizing or for the comfort of ideological rectitude, and more for the pragmatic search for solutions. In March 1968 she wrote, 'One can't carry out economic changes except through the natural instruments. The latter can be adapted, but not to the extent of cutting across the natural grain . . . [My philosophy] is that self-interest is the most powerful force in the world – not least among our working class supporters – and that the secret of success must be to mobilize that self-interest for progressive ends. In other words we shall only achieve Socialism (in the sense of disinterestedness) by stealth.' In the *Sunday Mirror* in October, Anthony Shrimsley observed the change: 'She has, despite her femininity, the not easily acquired reputation in Whitehall of being a Minister who is very much boss in her own department. Intellectually she is flexible. It is difficult to live in a Labour cabinet if you are not. Administratively she is something of a toughie. "I don't think you ought to be a minister unless you are willing to do two things," she says. "One is to listen . . . the second thing is to judge." '

This was a different side of the Barbara Castle who used to frighten voters with the vehemence of her opinions; who had once, a Labour parliamentary colleague confided to the *Sunday Times*'s profile writer, appeared coarse, threatening, a virago. 'Most reasonable people felt uneasy with her, the way she leant across a table, chin jutting, *spitting* out her answers.'[2] The media, faithfully reflecting her popularity in the country, learnt to love the new Barbara. For month after month she topped a regular Opinion Research poll on the most popular minister, with a positive rating throughout the summer of 1967 of 18 (12 points ahead of her nearest rival, James Callaghan) which soared to 26 in November, the month after the breathalyser was introduced. It was a summer of headily flattering profiles, tipping her for promotion in a pre-conference reshuffle and culminating in a picture in the *Mirror* for which Barbara had semi-posed in mid-holiday, pony-trekking in Ireland. In saucy seaside-postcard style, in pedal-pushers astride a pony, she was the sexiest thing he had seen for years, Wilson told her later. He had stuck the picture on his shaving mirror, he said. (The predicted promotion, however, did not come.)

She was, one writer exclaimed, Labour's Lady Astor, more phenomenon than personality. Even the Labour right had discovered a heroine, someone, they thought, on whom they could agree with the left. Brian Walden, one of the bright young men elected for the first time in 1964, told his local paper the *Birmingham Post* in November 1967:

> When Labour was in opposition, Barbara had a legendary ability to persuade the Speaker that she was a frail, friendless woman who simply had to be called to speak in the debate to make up for the cruel blows of an unheeding world. In reality, she has more guts and vision than any six ordinary men put together. She is a ruthless in-fighter who knows exactly what she wants, and has a carefully thought out plan for getting it . . . If the Prime Minister appointed her Chancellor of the Exchequer tomorrow (and plenty of people wish he would) she would still have been a Minister of Transport whom nobody is ever likely to forget.

At the party conference that autumn, she got the nearest thing to a standing ovation she had ever had, and people came away muttering that she was the best politician in Cabinet. However, after three years in government, the left was less impressed. They were not sure that this seemingly more calculating, less passionate, Barbara was still one of them. After two years topping the constituency Labour Party section of the NEC, she slipped to third, behind two prominent left-wing critics, Tom Driberg and Ian Mikardo. Those political writers who knew their Labour Party spotted the problem coming. In July, Norah Beloff tried to explain the apparent conflict between Barbara's traditional and current positions:

> It might be deduced she must be either wretchedly frustrated or insufferably hypocritical. In fact, she is neither: as a doer, rather than a thinker, she is now willing to compromise on doctrine as long as she can genuinely feel that she is making a tangible contribution to the well-being of the public and the credit of her party . . . to most left wing MPs . . . she remains a shining beacon. Whatever they think of Government, most of them, most of the time, feel reassured to know she is in there, rooting for their causes.

What Barbara could not ignore, however, was that she was a member of a Cabinet doing just what the party had promised not to do in opposition. Deflation and cuts instead of expansion and growth had become the hallmark of an economically beleaguered government. How could she justify supporting such a government? The general election victory in March 1966, treated with indifference by most, had been greeted by the left with soaring expectations. Their subsequent disappointment was all the greater. With a ninety-seven-seat majority, the left had a much freer hand to operate inside its self-imposed constraint of not endangering the government's survival.

As early as August 1965 a *Tribune* correspondent had written: 'What of the Left leaders in Parliament? Tell them off on your fingers, comrades, and think of their words and deeds in recent months while the Labour movement has been sold down the river.' Crossman, with his troublemaker's instinct, saw it early. Within months of the 1964 victory, he had invited Michael Foot and Barbara to dine with Frank Cousins and himself for a 'little left-wing conspiracy'. He found Barbara devotedly loyal to Wilson. 'She really does have certain left-wing views and she has done a fine job in her Ministry . . . But heavens alive! She has become difficult in the process. She spent the evening lecturing us on our responsibilities. Before the evening was out it was perfectly clear that there was no question of a left-wing alliance between us.'

She also lectured journalists on the burdens of office: 'Before the election of 1964, when I was making Left-wing speeches I always defined a Left-wing government as one that would seek fundamental changes and not just ride the easy tide. Fundamental change isn't created overnight. Meantime you've got to live with reality. You have to live with your overseas relationships and with your balance of trade. If the bailiffs are at the door you may have to give them the grand piano when you want to go on with your music lessons,' she said to Anthony Shrimsley in the *Sunday Mirror*. She thought the critics were naive and damaging in their refusal to acknowledge the problems the government faced. In July 1967, she wrote angrily after more criticism of the decision to cut demand at home rather than defence commitments abroad: 'Can't they realise there has been a revolution in our defence policy and that East of Suez is dead? This is of epoch-making importance to Britain . . . it is a tragedy they can never give this government credit for anything.' This was a new Barbara, a Barbara gone native in the very 'cosy embrace' of Whitehall which she had claimed to be determined to resist. She was seduced by the opportunities of power. Challenged at a *New Statesman* party, she lectured her friends: 'I was immensely stimulated by the difficulties of government. I just couldn't get away from the fact that there is more morality in responsibility (and therefore inevitably some com-promise) than in agitation.'

If she was growing impatient with the criticism of her old friends on the left, they were furious with her. On Ian Mikardo she made little impact with her explanations and justifications. Michael Foot, having been ignored in 1964, had refused an offer of a job in 1966 when Wilson approached him to become Minister of Technology. Barbara was sufficiently alarmed by Foot's anger – focused that day on Wilson's refusal to condemn American action in Vietnam – to discuss with him the question of whether she should resign. According to notes that did not appear in her published diary, he told her not to. 'Very diff for you,' her note of his reassurance goes. 'You yourself are doing a first class job. I think you should stay.'

Her explanations mattered even less to the next generation, the young left-wingers who had been elected in 1964, people whose faces Barbara scarcely recognized. This new left were not middle-class intellectuals like Barbara herself and her old allies Crossman and Wilson – and Foot – who had just spent thirteen years out of power; they were a generation more working-class than hers, men who had fought in the war and been trade unionists in peace, who had learnt their trade on the front line of industrial politics and whose power base was the new, radical trade union movement. To this new left, she was a collaborator in a government increasingly hostile to trade unionists and ordinary Labour voters at home, immoral in its support for America in Vietnam and discreditable in its failure to act decisively on Rhodesia. Michael Foot and Ian Mikardo led the revival of the old Bevanite group in parliament. About forty strong, it met at first secretly and then openly as the Tribune group (named after the newspaper), always careful to avoid breaching the rules. The Tribune group's objective was the traditional one of keeping the government up to its commitments. Its methods were equally traditional: opposition in parliament up to and including rebellion in the division lobbies, but stopping short of bringing the government down.

If Barbara was fierce with her old comrades on the left, she was gentler with the young MPs like Norman Atkinson and Eric Heffer, leading lights in the new left. She acknowledged their right to criticize. Their job, she told them, was to 'keep banging away at principles . . . to force us to change [details] back into principles from time to time in order to see how far we've strayed', and she was a vociferous defender in Cabinet of the right to dissent in the PLP. When Wilson shattered the three-year relaxation in parliamentary discipline and warned rebel MPs that although every dog was allowed one bite, they might 'lose their licences' if they did it repeatedly, she reminded him forcefully that she had voted against the government four times as a PPS and Cripps had tolerated it.

More than any other minister, she felt reliant on her standing in the constituency parties for a sense of security in government. She had no traditional power base in the parliamentary tribes of left or right, no sustaining regional alliance. In opposition, she had never succeeded in being elected to the shadow cabinet, and she knew there was a danger of being tainted by her association with the decisions of a right-wing Cabinet. Even in 1965, when the great majority of the party still accepted that the government's tiny majority and the likelihood of a new general election required cautious handling of policy issues, she had worried that a lack of radicalism would jeopardize her performance in the annual NEC elections. Crossman (still feeling jaundiced towards her after her lecture on his responsibilities) recorded her neurosis: 'Throughout the weekend Barbara Castle was continually saying, "Oh dear, Dick, what shall we do? I believe we are going to be knocked off the executive this time. It's the young ones who are going to win." I told her . . . the ministers would get all the votes . . . I am unlike Barbara in this respect: the elections for the National Executive don't dominate my life; in her case it is a chronic disease.' That year Barbara topped the constituency section.

The following year, she began to wonder whether she could sustain the conflicting roles of cabinet minister and representative of the constituency activists on the National Executive. She agonized over the rival demands of loyalty to collective responsibility in Cabinet, and loyalty to the party represented by the NEC. In 1966 she had toyed with the idea of not standing at all. She discussed it with Tony Benn, whose diary entry suggests some cynicism about her motives. 'I think in the back of her mind is the fear that she might be defeated and that she is losing her role as the leader of the Left. I doubt if she would be defeated. But I told her frankly I would rather be defeated than give up my place . . . Anyway I spoke frankly to her and I would be surprised now if she decided to give up.' Benn dismissed Barbara's idea that they should consult Wilson. But Barbara went ahead. Wilson, who valued Barbara not least as a messenger trusted on both sides, soothed her out of it: 'You [Barbara, Benn and Crossman] are the people the rank and file want . . . Jim Callaghan is the one who might get beaten.' Only Crossman decided to stand down and even he backtracked after Frank Cousins's resignation from government, because Barbara warned him that Cousins might 'stir up the left'. The following year, 1967, however, he did stand down, to be replaced by Tony Crosland. Barbara had by then completely changed her mind. 'If they want my seat they'll have to fight for it.'

'It's no Morecambe,' she said in 1967 as she herself slipped two places down the rankings while the ratings of the left soared. But if it was not a repeat of 1951, the year she had led the Bevanites to victory for the first time, still the left had turned. The long summer of party unity, begun in 1961 and reinforced by Wilson's accession to the leadership, was over. There was a lengthening charge sheet against the government. In his book *The Politics of Harold Wilson*, published in 1968, Paul Foot, nephew of Michael, self-confessed and incorrigible sectarian, had claimed a lump in his throat when he looked back to the promise of Labour's election victory only two years earlier. 'The quarrels, the arguments, the strikes and lock-outs, the bitter theoretical wrangles of the last thirteen years, had been smoothed over and bypassed with the injunction, "Get the Tories Out". In the past seventeen months of minuscule majorities the injunction had been reiterated even more earnestly . . . No wonder in the hour of victory that *Tribune* bellowed: SOCIALISM IS RIGHT BACK ON THE AGENDA.'[3]

Foot's polemic was more than a devastating rant. It identified a deeper problem with Labour, a development the old left had failed to notice. Wilson had sold out to corporatism. Politics was dying, stifled by the embrace of big business which had finally captured Labour and was subverting its radical energies to create, not a climate for reform, but a contented consensual consumerist electorate. A similar charge was made in the 1968 *May Day Manifesto* by a group of prominent left academics, artists and playwrights including Raymond Williams, R. D. Laing and Arnold Wesker. They too saw a Labour seduced by big business (which had adapted itself from laissez-faire capitalism to monolithic corporatism) into softening its rhetoric and abandoning its historic mission to end poverty and unemployment through a transformation of the state. Labour as a vehicle for radical reform was bankrupt, now interested only in building consensus in order to stay in power.

The grounds for argument were plentiful. On the back benches, Barbara would have opposed many of the decisions that the government of which she was a member was now making. The Common Market, Vietnam, Rhodesia and industrial policy all provoked major rebellions of one kind or another in the six years from 1964 to 1970. In Cabinet, she often argued the left case, giving her a value to Wilson beyond her personal loyalty. She was the government's sounding board, the authentic voice of the party, a minister whose instinctive response to a proposal was likely to be reflected by the awkward squad in parliament. Callaghan and Jenkins, even Crosland, sought her out to discuss the general direction of government. In return, she defended the principle of collective responsibility with the gradualist's refrain:

> You shouldn't go into a Cabinet unless you are prepared to be part of a collective view . . . it can't survive if the members claim the individual right to go off at a tangent on this or that . . . I have to ask my colleagues to support my policies. I need their strength. The moment you try to fragment the collective attitude you make strong and effective government imposs-

ible. So long as I remain, I must accept completely what it involves. And
when I do not want to accept what it involves, I should leave it.

But the frustration inherent in trying to influence government decisions
was a recurring theme. While Barbara believed passionately in cabinet
government, at least as far as it gave her the scope to intervene in other
people's decisions, she found it harder to accept their interventions in hers.
She was furious when Cabinet rejected her appeal for a higher salary to
secure the services of Peter Parker at British Railways. But unknown to her,
the decision to devalue – a decision of incalculable consequence – had
already been taken in secret by the Prime Minister and the Chancellor. It
was another forty-eight hours before it was reported to Cabinet, and then
only so that its members could start to consider the deflationary cuts that
would have to accompany it.

Despite hours and hours of cabinet sessions during which Wilson listened
solemnly and then summed up manipulatively, few major decisions were
actually taken round the famous coffin-shaped table. The long argument
about retreating from east of Suez, which was intimately linked with
American support for sterling and with Wilson's refusal to condemn US
bombing in Vietnam, was conducted almost entirely in a subcommittee, the
defence and overseas policy committee (OPD). So were the major decisions
on Rhodesia and on applying to join the European Economic Community.
Cabinet government, outside critics believed, was more a way of establishing
collective guilt, a mutual mingling of blood, than a democratic process. Most
ministers accepted that collective responsibility was a myth, and some nodded
through even the biggest decisions unless they had a departmental interest.
But Barbara was a fundamentalist, always on the case – although occasionally,
if she regarded the opinions as predictable, she would draft speeches and
draw up shopping lists in Cabinet. (Once, to her great satisfaction, Wilson
ticked her off for breaking the Cabinet rules and taking notes – which she
did whenever there was a debate important enough to feature in her diary –
as she scribbled 'buy lavatory seat' on her weekend to-do list.)

She was less critical of the constraints of collective responsibility than she
was, for example, of the doctrine that made her responsible for every activity
affecting her department without giving her the right to choose her team of
officials. She railed against the more junior cabinet ministers' lack of
influence, not least because of their physical distance from the action at the
centre of the cabinet table. She described one meeting, in the midst of the
July 1966 sterling crisis: 'As [Wilson] droned on no one would have guessed

that a major political drama was being played out – one never does at Cabinet. I don't know whether it is is a deliberate tactic on Harold's part or just that casual, low key manner of his, but I always feel in Cabinet as if I were in a cocoon, cut off from the vulgar realities of political conflict.' She sympathized with the young Peter Shore,[4] sitting silently in one of his first cabinet meetings: 'This is the creeping disease of Cabinet government and Dick himself once suffered from it. There is only one cure for it (as long experience on the NEC taught me). You must just speak your mind and ignore the sneers.' The courage to intervene, however, also needs an equal and balancing skill: judgement, to know when to fight and when to stay silent. The flaw in Barbara's cabinet career was that she talked too much, too often. Ministers who knew her outside Cabinet before seeing her at work inside it were stunned. She even queried the grammar in a Rhodesia White Paper. 'If I can't have any principles, I do like a little punctuation.' It was a trait that cost her allies and even friends, and ultimately undermined her career. No other prime minister, she acknowledged in a rare reflective moment, would put up with her.

Wilson kept a tight grip on the nature of debate in Cabinet. When Barbara tried to argue that steel nationalization had run into trouble because of a lack of political will, she was swiftly silenced. 'We must conduct this discussion on the basis that everyone round this table is as much a Socialist as anyone else,' he said firmly. Disagreement was to be strictly impersonal. All the same, people on the outside usually heard of her speeches to Cabinet, and journalists were always well briefed on her various successes. Profile writers observed the distance she discreetly placed between herself and Wilson, not only on issues like Europe where she made no secret of her dissent, but also on Vietnam and other unpopular policies such as abandoning plans to raise the school-leaving age. Without risking the charge of disloyalty, she beamed out rays of disenchantment through discreet lunches and visits to the tea room in the Commons and through chance encounters at parties, or events like an anti-apartheid fund raiser in the middle of the night at a West End theatre.

Occasionally, Wilson used Barbara covertly as his link with the left. In December 1967 – a fortnight after the devastating experience of devaluation – Wilson felt he was being bounced by George Brown and Denis Healey into lifting the arms embargo on South Africa to allow naval equipment to be exported. They argued that the deal, worth £100 million, would protect thousands of jobs; Wilson knew the party would not forgive him if he reneged on his pledge, made while still in opposition, to end all arms sales to the apartheid regime. He also suspected a Healey-inspired operation to avert the worst of the post-devaluation cuts in defence spending. He devised a plan to activate the PLP against his cabinet colleagues, a device not made any more attractive by his opponents' extensive use of similar means. Barbara – 'little Barbara' she was, that afternoon when she was called into his office – was solicited to find likely candidates on the back benches to table a motion condemning any change in the status of the embargo. To force Cabinet's hand, another stooge was to be found to ask him a question on the subject in the Commons the next day. Wilson then used his answer to indicate to the Commons that policy was unchanged, although of course not necessarily unchangeable (a sop to George Brown, who had been away and could not be consulted). By the time Brown was back, it looked as if the mood in the party, as expressed in the Commons motion, was so unanimously opposed to any policy change that none would be possible.

It was Crossman who saw the huge peril of this blatant attempt by the Prime Minister to bounce cabinet colleagues by provoking parliament against them. Wilson offered a compromise, proposing a way of lifting the South African embargo without affronting the pledge to keep it. He saved the day for Healey and Brown, now strongly backed by other ministers like Jim Callaghan, who had already told young backbench MPs at a private dinner that the embargo might have to go, and Ray Gunter, who commented: 'There are other Socialist principles and one is full employment; it is alright for us to be lofty when we shan't pay for it; the British worker will feel differently when he loses his job.' All this spilt out into the weekend press in a sordid display of party in-fighting and in particular a series of vitriolic attacks on Wilson's cabinet management. White with fear or anger – Barbara could not decide which – he called a special Cabinet and demanded collective repudiation of the accounts circulating in the press, or his position was untenable. 'The credibility of the government is dependent on *his* credibility, and Cabinet must be ready to restore it,' she noted. Cabinet accepted Wilson's argument: arms sales to South Africa were taken off the agenda. It was a Wilson victory, but at a heavy cost. He could argue that others conspired against him. But to have the Prime Minister himself manipulating party opinion was to grant a licence to disloyalty of which his rivals were to take full advantage. It did Barbara no credit either; it left an impression of her not just as a loyal, but as an unprincipled friend of an unprincipled Prime Minister.

Barbara, while loud in her public defence of the Prime Minister, privately blamed Wilson for keeping his friends at too great a distance and surrounding himself with the enemy. Why were there no left-wingers at the top of the hierarchy? she moaned to a colleague. Why did he always promote the right?

At the end of that month, Benn, reviewing 1967, also noted in his diary: 'I was beginning to be aware of the grave dissatisfaction of the Party with the leadership.'

High on the charge sheet of the left against the government stood immigration. From outright condemnation by Gaitskell of the first Immigration Act introduced by the Tories in 1961, by late 1963 Wilson had moved the party's position into acceptance of the need for some immigration controls. When Callaghan took over the Home Office, just as Kenyatta was seeking to make life unbearable for Kenyan Asians who had kept their British passports after independence, he introduced very tight restrictions on the number who could enter the UK. Barbara, after an all-night session on her Transport Bill, slept through the vital discussion in Cabinet, and any attempts on her part to modify policy details later were futile. For all her attempts to be involved in the decisions for which she would in the end have to take responsibility, Barbara found that she had no time to survey the broader sweep of government business; nor, absorbed in the fascinating detail of making and shaping a policy, did she always want to. She gloated over Crossman's enforced idleness as Leader of the House, a cabinet minister with no department to run, in contrast to her own importance on what she referred to in passing as her departmental throne: 'I am so intellectually and emotionally absorbed with the evolution of my own Socialist policy in my own field that I haven't time to worry about my morale.'

There was one issue, however, for which she was never too busy. As she watched Wilson play for time on Rhodesia, insisting that Smith was still someone he could do business with, she genuinely feared that she might be forced to abandon her career. It was a prospect which, like defeat in the elections to the party's National Executive, haunted her. Would there come a time when, after a life devoted to politics, she would have no moral alternative but to bow out? How would she handle the conflict between a deep and fundamental conviction and an act of the government to which she belonged and which for all its failings was still better than a Conservative one?

In late 1966, according to her diary, she gave serious consideration to resigning. She feared that Wilson – increasingly anxious to secure a deal to end UDI before the imposition of mandatory sanctions, which it was feared would severely damage the UK economy – was ready to sell out. Emissaries were sent to Salisbury and Cabinet discussed terms for reopening negotiations, in breach of the commitment not to make any deals with an illegal regime. Barbara, who had always thought the UK's negotiating position verged on appeasement, was determined that any promise from Smith to move to majority rule had to be backed up by a UK military presence in Salisbury, to serve as a constant reminder that the UK was witness to the Smith regime's fulfilment of its obligations. When Wilson himself went to meet Smith aboard HMS *Tiger*, off Gibraltar, Barbara told herself she was resolved if necessary to risk everything. It would have been an enormous sacrifice. At the end of 1965, on the strength of her huge leap in salary as she went from the back benches to Cabinet – an extraordinary rise from her MP's salary of a little over £1,000 to more than £8,000, she and Ted had bought the house that she and Marjorie had found on their last holiday together – Hell Corner Farm in Ibstone. She would also lose the 'sheer intoxication of administrative responsibility'. Unrecorded for posterity was the thought that in its place would come – perhaps – the leadership of the left on the back benches, a role to which she had aspired so often in the past. After walking in an unusually reflective mood along the Embankment, she wrote:

I would [resign] tomorrow rather than have a wretched conscience over Rhodesia which would poison all my enjoyments . . . I even began to enjoy the thought of release from that endless flood of paper which comes between one and so many sensual experiences. The truth is I am not ambitious as a man is ambitious. Creative work of some kind is vital to me – even power of a kind – but not 'success' in terms of office. I can always write; influence things. Does this make me different from a man? And, if so, does it give me a special kind of strength?

Her resolve was never put to the test. Smith rejected Wilson's approaches. It is hard to judge whether, after such a long struggle to reach the top, she would actually have gone. On the whole she was dismissive of resignation as a political weapon, and her change of heart on resignation from the NEC shows how hard a move it would have been for her, even without the financial complications it would have entailed. Less than three years later, when her whole industrial relations policy was abandoned in ruinous defeat, she once again backed away from a course she had considered almost daily for weeks. She knew – as Michael Foot was just concluding – that if she wanted real influence, the cabinet table was the only place to be.

Rhodesia was the issue of conscience for the left that was always simmering but never quite came to the boil. The story of the economy was different. Criticism of Wilson's economic management was now widespread on both wings of the party. His decision to opt for deflation not devaluation,

and his ultimately futile attempts to contain wage inflation, would scar
Labour's self-confidence for more than a generation.

Influenced by the powerful memory of devaluation in 1949, Wilson held out
against such a move until he was left with no other option in the autumn of
1967. By then, trying to avoid it had already done as much damage as might
have been caused by a realignment in 1964. In 1965, Barbara's aid programme was among the smallest – if not the least – of the casualties. In the
July measures of 1966, there was another round of cuts. Wilson had promised
to reinvigorate the economy; in the event, deflation further undermined the
economy's productive capacity, Labour's welfare programme was curtailed –
even the first pensions increase had to be delayed – and tensions within
Cabinet were sharpened. The underlying cause of economic instability was
sterling's role as a reserve currency, required by international agreement to
be maintained at a set value. It was also a trading currency, with reserves
held around the world over which Britain had no control. Perceived as
overvalued (although some expert opinion now argues that it was not) and
with the UK lacking large reserves of its own, sterling was a favourite target
of speculators. It was also the national virility symbol. For the pound to come
under pressure was a national humiliation, as newspapers reminded their
readers almost every day. Callaghan himself, it was said, would anxiously stop
colleagues to update them on its health, as if it was a favourite aunt.
    The pound's weakness was a result of the trade gap. Britain was not
making enough from its exports to cover the cost of its imports. Every
economic boom sucked in imports and drained Britain's reserves, until the
trade deficit provoked a run on sterling and the Treasury was forced to
introduce a new round of deflationary cuts in government spending and
personal consumption. Opinion about the cause of Britain's failure to export
competitively, like opinion on the appropriate value of the pound, was
mixed. Tommy Balogh, Wilson's economic adviser and Barbara's personal
economics tutor, argued influentially that if industry was more competitive,
the balance of payments problem would be eased. But attempts to invest in
modernization were defeated by the need for deflationary policies prompted
by the very problem – under-investment – that the moves were intended to
solve. To break the downward spiral the state must intervene, through fiscal
measures and subsidy, to encourage modernization, promote investment and
play a key role, through indicative planning, in encouraging and reviving the
'right' kind of industry. To avoid, or at least minimize, inflation, a prices and
incomes policy of a undefined nature would be needed.

In practice, deflation had caused growth to stall and only prices and incomes policy remained of the plan. Over the years that followed, trade unions and collective pay bargaining backed by industrial muscle were increasingly identified as the principal causes of the country's economic ills. Barbara, on whom Balogh was hugely influential, was forced to accept that some deflation was unavoidable. But she argued throughout the Wilson years for alternatives to cuts in public spending and for the use of controls on imports and later on capital movements to protect the pound in a way which would not, she believed, damage the domestic economy.

Even in oppostion, Wilson had indicated that pay restraint would be necessary. A new euphemism, acceptable to the unions, made its appearance: 'the planned growth of incomes'. In the context of sustained economic growth, it seemed some constraint on free collective bargaining might be tolerated by the TUC in a new 'partnership'. But even before the election, Frank Cousins, the Transport and General Workers' leader, had sharply reminded politicians why trade unions existed: 'If we do not fulfil the purposes for which members join unions, to protect and raise their real standard of living, then the unions will wither and finally die,' he had told his union in 1963. Another, later, trade union leader described unfettered collective bargaining in less poetic terms. It was, said Sid Weighell of the National Union of Railwaymen, 'the philosophy of the pig trough, where those with the biggest snouts get the most'.[5]

A Labour government had controlled prices and incomes before in partnership with the TUC. Between 1945 and 1951, the Attlee–Bevin axis had restrained incomes without quite violating the principle of free collective bargaining. Part of the explanation had been the creation of the welfare state: pay restraint in return for free hospitals and schools and proper pensions. Perhaps as importantly, the trade unions – like the rest of society – still tended to the deferential, while mass unemployment was for many an experience rather than a folk memory. By 1964, circumstances were less favourable. After a generation of full employment, the public had downgraded trade unions from their post-war national-hero status into the 'I'm alright, Jack' villains of the piece. The trade union link was once again a problem for the party's image-makers, and the unions recognized this. Considerable efforts were made during the 1964 election to keep strikes down; negotiations on wage claims in both the docks and the steel industry were extended. However, there was a widening gap between union leaders, the intimates of prime ministers who served in cabinets, and the membership, who saw tax and inflation eating away at their real wages at the same time as new technology theatened jobs and new working practices challenged old habits.

Government thinking, owing much to the success story of the Attlee government, had not kept pace with changes within the trade unions. The Ministry of Labour was a backwater devoted to conciliation whose top officials had – like Wilson himself – cut their teeth in the ministry during the war.[6] The first cautious moves to disrupt this approach came from George Brown, whose new Department of Economic Affairs bridging Labour and the Treasury was to fall victim to conflicting aspirations. Brown, like the TUC General Secretary George Woodcock, thought the DEA could be the realization of the dream of giving the unions a permanent voice in the shaping of economic policy. 'Our people aim higher than the mere satisfaction of their basic fodder requirement. Our people want to play a bigger role in society, and take more decisions as citizens, and to live in a society of which they can feel proud,'[7] Brown announced early in the new government. More prosaically, the Prime Minister wanted the DEA to circumvent Treasury orthodoxy; and the most cynical regarded the new department as a plaything for Brown, the sometimes troublesome deputy party leader. The DEA had responsibility for the prices and incomes policy as part of an overall brief to develop a national plan, but not for fiscal or monetary affairs, which stayed with the Treasury.

Brown won support from both sides of industry for the idea of some unspecified voluntary cooperation with government machinery to monitor prices and incomes, which evolved into the National Board for Prices and Incomes. Its outline joint statement of intent was announced, in a ceremony at Lancaster House, with the kind of fanfare customarily reserved for the signing of international treaties, a deliberate signal of how significant a part the control of prices and incomes was intended to play. The trade unions accepted, in March 1965, a policy setting out a formula for establishing a pay 'norm', linked with the national economic growth rate. The norm could only be breached if the pay of one sector of the workforce was 'seriously out of line', or if a group was found to be earning less than was needed for a 'reasonable standard of living'. Both definitions were so vague that they spawned a hundred acrimonious disputes.

Given the conditions, so optimistically envisaged, of an expanding economy and rising living standards, the voluntary plan might conceivably have slowed the rise in wages. But within weeks of the election, sterling was facing a crisis. The leeway for pay rises shrank; within three months, there were worried discussions about a pay freeze. The 'partnership' deal was headed for disaster before it had gone to the printers.

By August 1965, the government – still less than a year old – decided it had to introduce statutory powers to impose a requirement to give advance warning of pay and price rises and to strengthen the National Board for Prices and Incomes. The TUC objected. The government twisted arms – the 1966 election was imminent. The TUC agreed to operate a voluntary wage-vetting system. The plan only squeaked through their annual conference, an early warning of the loosening of the control of the traditional leaders over the traditionally led within the union movement. Already the prices and incomes policy, the essential weapon in the government's plans for defence against inflation and sterling crises – lacking any other which anyone believed would work – was taking the government directly into confrontation with its bedrock support.

The first evidence of the slowly brewing conflict was the resignation of Frank Cousins, the TGWU leader, from the Ministry of Technology, carefully timed to coincide with the day the legislation was introduced, 3 July 1966. Cousins always insisted Wilson had promised that despite the White Paper laying out the plans, no statutory policy would ever be introduced. The legislation, Chancellor Callaghan believed – entirely wrongly, as it turned out – would trigger 'massive foreign support' for sterling and it was further cursed when Wilson, fed up with George Brown's drunken bad manners and offensive demeanour (he once said trade union leaders only responded to 'frequent kicks in the shins'), shifted the detailed implementation of prices and incomes policy to the Ministry of Labour, run by the right-wing trade unionist Ray Gunter.

Meanwhile, the National Union of Seamen had gone on strike and, in May 1966 – only weeks after the election victory – the limitations of the government's pay policy were not so much written as splashed across the wall. The seamen wanted a package which was predicted to add 25 per cent to their wages bill, clearly steering a tanker through the pay norm. Attempts at conciliation failed. There was wide sympathy for their case on the left, who pointed to the pay-norm-busting settlements recently authorized for judges and senior army officers. The government, seeking a way that looked tough on pay but which might lead to a settlement, set up an inquiry under the business magnate Lord Pearson, which recommended improvements in the employers' offer. The TUC recommended acceptance, but the union negotiators broke with the TUC .

Wilson was in no position to back down. He believed confidence in the pound depended on holding down pay. With nowhere else to turn, he made the two interventions that were to linger sourly in the memories of his critics and would define the dispute as a watershed in his government's relations with the broad Labour movement. With the first he alienated the trade unions and their supporters in parliament, and with the second he affronted the left. He declared that the strike – bound, by seizing up the docks, to have a devastating effect on trade and consequently on sterling – was 'a strike against the State – against the community'. Here was a Labour prime minister suggesting the unpalatable truth that a part of the Labour movement was undermining the good of the wider community, that what was good for one union might not be good for them all. It foreshadowed the breach between unions and government that was to climax with Barbara's attempt to bring trade unions within the law. Furthermore, the Prime Minister asserted that the strike was led by Communists, a 'tightly knit group of politically motivated men', a remark that startled everyone, including Barbara, as well as members of the emergency strike committee like John Prescott, who had been an official Labour candidate at the 1966 election. On a wider front, it alienated all those on the left who regarded attacks on Communism as low trade fit only for the right – a 'surrogate for thought', Tom Nairn once called them in the *New Left Review*. '*I'm* politically motivated. *Harold Wilson*'s politically motivated,' Ian Mikardo pointed out.

Finally, at the beginning of July, the strike was settled, and on terms that the government might have accepted weeks earlier. There were lessons to be learnt. First, a statutory prices and incomes policy risked making every pay claim one against the government as well as the employer. Second, even if the TUC was still prepared to stand by the government, it could not be relied upon to deliver. Third, there were going to be problems in the party – both on the left and among trade-union-sponsored MPs (not coterminous groups), who had been appalled at Wilson's attack on the seamen. Denis Barnes, Under-Secretary at the Ministry of Labour, later called it 'the most damaging national strike since 1926'.

Barbara loyally supported Wilson. She was convinced of the role that prices and incomes controls could play in achieving both the productivity boost the economy needed and a measure of the redistribution that socialism demanded. She argued her case in Cabinet at the height of the NUS strike in June 1966, shortly before Cousins resigned. Crossman was impressed: 'Barbara Castle fired off and really made a very good speech on a socialist prices and incomes policy. She behaved as I should really behave, she was a Cabinet minister playing that role.' Her recipe was a cap on higher salaries and a special dispensation to raise the pay of the worse off, and – most radical – a national minimum wage, a move which could have been used to remind trade unions of the potential for benign government intervention in their affairs.

★

To the public Barbara was one of the government's few success stories. She was becoming more and more important to a Prime Minister beginning now to scent conspiracy all around as he repeatedly forced his Cabinet to accept deflation. He suspected Callaghan and Brown of operating a pincer movement against him to force devaluation. The reaction to his interventions in the NUS strike illustrated his vulnerability. He was becoming increasingly frustrated with the trade unions, whom he suspected of backing Jim Callaghan (who was seeking their support to take over as party treasurer) against him. The old left was rediscovering the trade unions' instinctive preference for free enterprise over socialism whenever their own interests were at stake. Barbara and Wilson, old Bevanites both, were frustrated if not surprised that the union movement, which had willed the party into being, was capable of undermining it in office. They could not see the reverse of their argument: that a Labour government's job was to create the conditions in which trade unions prospered. The old argument about the balance of power in government between unions and the Labour Party, seemingly laid to rest by the harmonious Attlee era, was back.

The NUS strike and Frank Cousins's resignation were among the factors that triggered the worst of the episodic crises of international confidence in sterling experienced so far. Once again devaluation was ruled out, despite the objections both of the right, who saw Britain's future in Europe, and of the left (Shore, Benn and Crossman, as well as Barbara), who wanted Britain independent of both Europe and America. Callaghan declared that to devalue 'out of failure' would be catastrophic. Barbara was convinced it was an imperative, out of failure or not; when Wilson accused her of 'being taken for a ride' by the Europeans, who were demanding devaluation as the price of entry into the EEC, she retorted that on the contrary she wanted Britain to be free of the international obligations imposed by sterling's position as a reserve currency and able to choose its own role in the world. She may not have appreciated the deflation that would ensue.

On 12 July 1966 Cabinet was warned that another £500 million of deflation was unavoidable. Wilson promised it would not come from public spending cuts. All effort was focused on pay policy. The results of a year and a half of 'voluntary' pay restraint were unimpressive. The TUC wage-vetting committee examined six hundred cases in its first five months. But it had 'no real effect on any',[8] and was said to be making no attempt to compare them with the 3.5 per cent norm. According to one industrial relations expert, Denis Barnes, increases were running at double that. Among other measures, the prices and incomes legislation now going through parliament would be made even tougher. Extra powers would be introduced, allowing the government to impose a freeze on all wages and – if a way could be found – on price rises, for six months, with a 'period of severe restraint' for a further six months. The government would have the power to reverse increases that breached the code. In the last resort, sanctions would be imposed. Ultimately, that could have meant imprisoning trade unionists for non-payment of fines (although the DEA thought they had got round that by extending the right to deduct any fine from the defaulter's pay packet). Michael Stewart, the inoffensive MP for Fulham and former Foreign Secretary, who had swapped jobs with George Brown and was now running a reduced DEA, promised that the new powers were 'strictly limited, of temporary duration and specifically designed to support and encourage the voluntary principle'. TUC Congress reluctantly approved the plans by the narrow margin of 344,000. In the House, fifty backbenchers rebelled, but the legislation went through. In Cabinet, Barbara had also expressed concern about the sanctions: 'A Labour government couldn't survive giving itself statutory strike-breaking powers,' she said. Callaghan, the movement's Vicar of Bray on pay policy, declared: 'Prices and incomes policy is part of the educational processes of the consequences of full employment in a democracy.'

In an attempt to make incomes policy at least bear down less hard on the poorest, Cabinet began again to give serious consideration to the question of a minimum wage, which Barbara believed was an imperative. A committee was set up to consider it, but the Labour Minister Ray Gunter was unenthusiastic. Reflecting the trade unions' hostility, he warned that it would be inflammatory in an era of tight restraint and would pre-empt all wage increases for the year. He recomended family endowment (a form of tax credit) as a better way of dealing with the problem of the low-paid.

The government had promised that the powers over pay and prices would be renewed annually; consequently, the arguments were revisited with unsettling frequency. In February 1967 unease surfaced again. On the National Executive, the union members rebelled against renewing the powers. The talk was of disaffiliation, of breaking the historic link. Why, they demanded, had the government gone anti-union? It was a question that was to haunt Barbara for the next three years. However, she was prepared to consider it dispassionately. 'Free collective bargaining and full employment are incompatible. What are the implications of all this? Possibly that an effective Labour movement will be driven to find another basis than the unions. And yet that would be a pity because one of Labour's jobs is to make the unions political. Left to fulfil a purely industrial function, they will become merely an arm of capitalism, as in America . . . I don't know whether we are just educating the unions or breaking with them.'

The TUC decided to undermine government policy by operating unilaterally: it would draw up its own economic analysis and its own pay norm recommendation annually, and devise a way of strengthening its pay-vetting committee. In this proposal, with its emphasis on the need for self-regulation rather than statutory control, Barnes later saw a continuous thread stretching from the original 1964 'partnership' to the 'social contract' of ten years later. Faced with the adamantine independence of the TUC, Wilson conceded a return to a degree of voluntarism. In April 1967 Callaghan declared that 'an incomes policy in a free society won't work'. But privately, faced with more backbench unease, Wilson talked angrily of the 'primitive worship of free collective bargaining' among trade union MPs. There were whispers of another 1931, another breach in the broad church of the Labour movement provoked, again, by resistance to deflation. The 1967 Prices and Incomes Act, the government's second, gave the TUC a new role administering voluntary controls on incomes, while statutory powers remained to deal with prices and dividends and labour organizations not affiliated to the TUC. But Barbara's doubts about the utility of the unions as a channel for government intervention, and the correspondingly reduced role for individual responsibility, were growing.

At a high-summer meeting at Chequers of Wilson's old friends on the left, Barbara argued in favour of floating the pound and putting the responsibility for maintaining its value on the workers themselves. 'Now you are on your own,' she wanted to say. 'The defence of the value of your money can only be conducted on the factory floor.'

In August, Wilson radically reduced the scale of the DEA's responsibilities and put the young Peter Shore in charge of day-to-day affairs while taking personal overall command himself, thereby dashing Barbara's ambition to have the job. She continued to criticize the lack of coherence in a government that could introduce selective employment tax to encourage the growth of jobs in manufacturing, and then use it as an instrument of deflation by allowing prices to rise to cover the cost of its introduction rather than holding them down and depressing profitability.

In September 1967 she warned Ray Gunter against letting an NUR guards' pay claim through, on the grounds that it would only trigger a catch-up round. 'This isn't social justice, it's anarchy. Of course Tribune is backing the guards on the principle that true Socialism consists of supporting any industrial claim, regardless of its effects on other workers. But to me this is nonsense. The religion of Socialism is the language of priorities and that means daring to choose between one claim and the next, to work out proper relationships between the different members of society. Left-wingism that consists of burying one's head in the sand and avoiding all awkward choices just makes me sick.' Later (26 September) she argued in her diary: 'But I still feel we are attempting too much, taking too much on the Government, letting everyone else ride away on their individual irresponsibilities. Interventionism won't succeed if it merely reinforces the worker's or manufacturer's personal dynamic.'

Meanwhile, the distance between the TUC leadership and union delegates was uncompromisingly displayed at the autumn Congress. The policy of support for the government's pay policy was rejected and a motion condemning its intervention in free collective bargaining overwhelmingly passed. For different reasons, there were strikes and work-to-rules in the docks, on the railways, on London construction sites and at northern engineering works. The CBI declared the country was 'bleeding to death'.

In November, at last, Wilson and Callaghan were forced to give up the long defence of the pound. Devaluation was formally announced on the 18th, but only after Callaghan had failed to lie convincingly about his intentions in the Commons, and £100 million from the reserves had been lost (Barbara later recorded with savage pleasure) in the few hours before the foreign exchanges closed. Barbara, still arguing for a floating pound, doubted that a devaluation of 14.3 per cent was enough. But the decision was taken well away from cabinet influence. Another £500-million cuts package was to follow: more deflation, more pressure on pay policy.

Such a catastrophic – although hardly unpredicted – event brought political turmoil in its wake. A barely disguised blame game was now carried on in the corridors of Westminster and in the newspaper columns. Callaghan, in a sombre speech openly confessing to the total failure of government economic policy over the past three years, somehow gained in stature. Wilson, the cheeky chappie declaring the pound in your pocket was still worth the same, a phrase intended to reassure Labour voters who it was feared might believe they would only get 19/6 instead of £1 in their pay packet the next week, saw his stock slide still further. Peter Jay, economic editor of *The Times*, wrote: 'The prime minister has been the prime mover behind the maintenance of the old exchange-parity of sterling. Not only that, he has also been the chief architect of the policies that in the end made that position untenable.' The author was the Chancellor's son-in-law. It was hardly surprising that Barbara as well as Wilson scented conspiracy.

In the aftermath came the battle over post-devaluation policy. Barbara, like other colleagues outside the innermost ring of decision-makers, was increasingly frustrated at the apparent absence of any strategy. Early in the new year of 1968, she was in bed with pneumonia – a casualty of her own work addiction – but nearly every day for a fortnight she got up to go to Cabinet to argue over where the cuts would fall. Jim Callaghan had resigned from the Treasury and been replaced by Roy Jenkins, who called the spending negotiations which followed devaluation, 'Cabinet government by exhaustion'. Barbara, enraged at the piecemeal approach, demanded a better system: 'We should never get people to accept the cuts unless we made people feel we had a better strategy this time. The whole purpose of the exercise was to reduce demand . . . my fear was that we were merely going to depress growth again . . . finally on P and I policy, it would be impossible for us to sell restraint to the unions – to deny the busmen their £1, for instance – unless we made some sacrifices ourselves. I was therefore in favour of a 10 per cent cut in Ministers' salaries.'

But the Treasury set out on a deliberate policy of deflating the broad economy, and consumer demand in particular. Real wages (except cabinet ministers' – Barbara's appeal fell on stony ground) were not to stand still; they were to fall. In February, as the now annual consideration of prices and incomes policy began, Jenkins demanded a squeeze. Devaluation had produced a shift of power in Cabinet: those who opposed intervention in free collective bargaining – especially the influential Callaghan, now Home Secretary and party treasurer, and Crossman – were outside the immediate area of economic policy decision-making. At the much reduced Department of Economic Affairs, the young Peter Shore was an ardent supporter of Treasury policy. Roy Jenkins believed there was no alternative.

Barbara, who had talked her way on to the Cabinet's industrial committee, argued for her vision of a socialist incomes policy. Either, she said, you have wage control to make capitalism work, or a 'planned growth of wages as part of Socialist planning'. She wanted a prices and dividends freeze to match that on wages, and a wealth tax. 'If this is another gambit to restore the confidence of capitalists we shall finally destroy the confidence of our own movement. This is our last chance and we are in mortal danger.'

Outside Whitehall, the opposing forces were gathering. In the past year, the two biggest trade unions, the Transport and General and the Amalgamated Engineers, had elected left-wing general secretaries: Jack Jones and Hugh Scanlon were loudly opposed to any impediment to free collective bargaining. Their influence would almost certainly be decisive in the councils of the TUC. In March, less than six months after devaluation, there was another international financial crisis as the post-war world economic system creaked towards obsolescence. In London there were two repercussions: more deflationary pressure, and the resignation of Foreign Secretary George Brown, who would storm out of government for the last time.

This came close to being Wilson's darkest hour: a failed economic policy, industrial relations in chaos, the parliamentary party in uproar and by-election swings delivering safe Labour seats into the hands of the opposition. Under such pressure, the man whom Callaghan once described as 'a fighter who never lacked courage when his back was to the wall'[9] turned once more to the two friends in Cabinet on whom he knew he could rely: Crossman and Castle. Crossman was always, personally if not politically, on the edge of the inner circle, offering advice, hanging out with the kitchen cabinet, fulfilling his self-appointed role as philosopher prince to the Prime Minister. But Wilson rarely consulted Barbara, old intimates though they were. The times when he sought her out – by phone or in person – for a general discussion could be counted on one hand, and nearly always coincided with a desperate need for friends. Barbara was Harold's creation, ultimately loyal despite her frequent criticism of him to his face and to their mutual friends, and prepared to acknowledge – for example, when there was a frisson of excitement about the chances of her replacing George Brown as deputy leader – that Harold had given her the break she would not have had from any other leader. 'I don't personally think I shall climb any higher because I only got where I am by a fluke. If Harold hadn't manoeuvred his way to power I would probably be still on the back benches, or a very minor Parliamentary Secretary in a right-wing Labour government. I know how lucky I have been. If I were drafted I would take on any job, but I am not going to elbow, scratch or scramble.'

Barbara did not really think so little of herself, and she showed herself perfectly willing to scratch and scramble later on (as well as having a blazing row with Wilson when he threw his magnanimity towards her in her face). But, as when she was young – though now only occasionally – she could be the victim of gut-wrenching moments of self-doubt. Ted was her emotional prop, a constant source of reassurance, although friends thought he was almost more ambitious for her than she was for herself. In these weeks, with even her Permanent Secretary Sir Thomas Padmore telling Ted she was bound to be promoted, the newspapers tipping her, backbenchers and her ministers whispering encouraging thoughts in her ear, she seemed truly the most powerful woman in Britain.

But Barbara's standing was less certain than it seemed. The erosion of the left's support had continued. Her friends and admirers – like Shirley Williams,[10] George Thomas (later to be Speaker of the House) – pressed her to be more accessible, to spend more time in the tea room. So did her advisers. But although she did make occasional efforts, it was not her style. She operated at the centre of attention, as a leader, not a consensus-builder.

She was impatient of the opinions of people who did not come from her wing of the party, unwilling to acknowledge a shared objective, suspicious of right-wing plots and conspiracy which her own growing distance from the party merely encouraged. She was uncomfortable in the male clubbiness of Westminster, not because it was male – she loved male environments – but because it was clubby. In the long hours of late sittings spent by most MPs in the bars, the tea room and the smoking room, politicians stopped being sectarian, and united in a shared feeling of being a misunderstood elite, appreciating that whatever their views, they had more in common with each other than with the voters outside. Barbara, however, was always a politician of the left; while her colleagues drank and smoked and occasionally seduced one another, Barbara sat in her room off the ministerial corridor behind the Speaker's chair and worked.

This isolation from her old allies, together with her growing reputation as a determined and practical minister, was drawing a significantly different group of admirers. In her department John Morris, a right-winger who had gone to work for her in a spirit of adventure rather than optimism, was a fan. Outside it, individuals from across the Labour Party were coming to accept her as an important figure in the party. She had become respectable.

George Brown's resignation, on 14 March 1968, came as the pound wobbled perilously close to a second devaluation. His complaint was that he had not been included in the party that had rushed to Buckingham Palace to see the Queen to arrange a bank holiday, in order to effect the closure of the financial markets and an international currency realignment. There was a suggestion that little attempt had been made to find him. Later that evening, he had come and sat next to Barbara on the front bench as her Transport Bill was being debated, and had talked loudly but unspecifically about the difficulties of his job. 'And then he went on to say that anyway, we had better face it, we were getting old. He and I were getting pretty bloody well near to sixty, though it took some realising. "You don't look it and I don't feel it" . . . I hadn't been too worried when he had skipped through the division lobby with me at ten o'clock, unbuttoning the back of my blouse.' However, rumours of his intention to resign trickled into the long night sitting, picked up by Barbara as she dashed out for a cigarette or brought into the Chamber by whips and backbenchers fresh from the bars.

Next day, Brown failed to show up for Cabinet; by nightfall, he had finally resigned as Foreign Secretary. The successful accomplishment of a repeated threat raised an unexpected difficulty. Could he stay as the party's deputy leader? The immediate conclusion was that he could not; the speculation was that the contenders in the poll to find a replacement would be Jim Callaghan, Roy Jenkins – and Barbara. For the first time in her political career she was being seen as someone capable of appealing to more than a narrow faction of the party, the crowning political achievement of her three and a half years in office. Barbara professed disdain. When the news that she was being tipped was brought to her by John Morris, she observed:

> Frankly I haven't a chance, except in a situation in which the Right wing take over and want me there as a left-wing prisoner . . . it is strange how uninterested I am in such intrigues. I have never tried to chat up Members in the tea-room. I could never go through the calculating climb to power that Harold did. Frankly I am not interested in that sort of activity. Usually I bury myself behind a newspaper trying to catch up with the day's over-crowded reading.

A few days later she was told by Norman Atkinson, one of the 'new' left, that 'the party wouldn't wear a woman!' But neither the party's misogyny, nor Barbara's sincerity, was ever tested. The party was so alarmed at the prospect of a contested election that George Brown was encouraged to stay on as deputy leader, preventing any damaging jostling for power and keeping him tied to the government – and muzzled in the press.

Barbara had set a blistering pace at the Ministry of Transport, helped by the team of experts and politicians she created and led. She and her two ministers – Stephen Swingler, the public-school-educated polemicist, and John Morris, young enough to survive to become the only member of Tony Blair's 1997 Cabinet with previous experience – were described in the *Daily Telegraph* as 'Transport's Triumphant Triumvirate'. 'All three are articulate – none more so than the leading lady – all three seem to know their homework and together . . . form a tricycle through the wheels of which spokes are hard to put.' After Barbara was moved, Swingler went to the Department of Health and Social Security and in February 1969 died of pneumonia aged only fifty-four – killed, Richard Marsh unkindly observed, by the Transport Bill (others thought his early death more likely to have been hastened by his lifestyle). John Morris went to the Ministry of Defence, and was sent away for a rest by the MOD's senior doctor. Even Barbara's health – not for the last time – gave out under strain: at the end of 1967, the first breathalyser Christmas, she was in bed with flu, too ill even to appear on television to celebrate the triumphant vindication of her policy.

Barbara's two years at the Ministry of Transport established her ministerial character. She was energetic, enthusiastic and determined to get it right. In the run-up to making any decision, her officials and advisers would find her open, free-thinking and interested in listening to everyone's point of view. She never pulled rank. 'She was enormously open to argument. She didn't have ideas of her own, but she knew what would run.'[11] But once her mind was made up, people recognized that it was almost impossible to persuade her to change it. Officials and advisers learnt to get their arguments in early. Although she blamed herself for dithering over the appointment of Peter Parker, others thought her mistake was to continue to hanker after the chairman she could not have at the cost of considering how to get the best out of the one she could. Christopher Foster thought she was 'good at rational meetings, less good at irrational ones, where people did not want to be persuaded'.[12] She had, she would brag, 'the killer instinct', a view Stanley Raymond would have endorsed. After one bruising encounter with a critical journalist, her railways minister John Morris told her, 'I wouldn't be married to you for any money but you will be Prime Minister one day if your health holds out.'[13] Morris had never spoken to her before she was appointed, and had thought of her only as a 'red-haired left-winger'. He was amazed to find that she was entirely undoctrinaire in ministerial meetings, consensual, looking for agreement – a lion lying down with the lambs, he thought. He would see her two or three times a day (when he became one of Denis Healey's ministers, they met once a month), and he said that she taught him everything he knew about being a minister. 'She always did her homework. Every morning, her briefs would be marked and underlined with points she wanted to follow up.'

The geographical arrangement of the ministerial floor of her department illustrated her priorities. As well as space for her Permanent Secretary and her ministers, room had to be found for her special adviser. Her press officers were also at hand; and there had to be a ladies' lavatory and somewhere for her to change. This was usually the hardest to achieve. Policy and her personal press relations dominated her departmental life. Some suggested that she was sexually predatory, that she had used flirtation as a way of attracting attention and smoothing her path for so long it had become instinctive. And in the department, where she ruled as of right, it could be overpowering. Visitors reported that she 'devoured' her junior officials, and her manner with some trade union leaders appeared to verge on the intimate. Her style alarmed the buttoned-up civil servants hovering beside her, and they in turn felt it embarrassed the subjects of her attentions. Others were simply dazzled by her informality and direct manner. She once told a delegation of motor-cyclists who had accused her of being biased against them, 'Too bloody right I am. I'd get rid of the lot of you if I could.'[14] Morris, who often travelled with her, agreed she used 'feminine wiles', but unconsciously. He never saw her cry, although she was not above asking her private secretary to go and buy her some cigarettes or a new lipstick, if she wanted some privacy. 'She was an intimate person. She went out of her way to meet people, to make them feel comfortable. She was a very big public figure.'[15]

At her first Miners' Gala in 1955, the Durham miners' leader Sam Watson had told Barbara, after her impassioned attack on the Conservatives, that she ought to represent the miners in negotations because 'you really believe the cost of living is going up'. 'It is!' she retorted hotly. To have believed otherwise but to have argued it anyway would have been cynical. She regarded cynicism as the enemy of political integrity, and the conviction never deserted her,[16] although it sometimes took a high level of self-deception to maintain. The NUR leader Sid Greene once took her out to lunch in the midst of a difficult negotiation. 'It'll be war,' she said, if there was no agreement. '"No more of these nice lunches with you." "Oh, I don't know," drawled Sid. "You don't have to take these things too seriously." But I repeated grimly, "It will be war." '[17]

She always meant what she said – at least at the time she said it. She usually believed she was right, too. She was not interested, once her mind was made up, in hearing the other side of the argument. She was not interested in putting herself in the other person's place; she wanted them to agree with her. Unlike her hero Bevan, who would argue one position at night and the opposite the following morning, often in the very words of his opponent, she would not allow an argument to move her at all. She might be overruled, but never persuaded. She viewed people with flexible opinions with grave suspicion. In Cabinet, where the trait was most openly paraded, she was generally admired for her strengths as a departmental minister; but her determination to fight her corner regardless of wider concerns, to go to the Prime Minister and get decisions reversed, and her relentless and solipsistic pursuit of her objectives, dismayed and irritated others. 'She never knew when to keep her mouth shut' was a widespread opinion. The Parker affair prompted one revealing diary entry. 'How can one plan or execute a policy effectively when one is stymied at every move by one's colleagues' quirks?' she moaned. 'As I told some of them, the fact that the Government's policy is in a mess is all the more reason why one Departmental part of it should score a success. But with the *Evening Standard* reporting me Top of the Political Pops again, they aren't likely to be in any mood to help me to another triumph. Home to bed, utterly exhausted.'[18]

12. The Whirlwind

I have at last moved from the periphery of the whirlwind into its
very heart.

Barbara Castle, *The Casle Diaries 1964–1970*[1]

For they have sown the wind, and they shall reap the whirlwind.

Hosea 8:7

By 1968 Harold Wilson's hold on power looked as shaky as the soon-to-be-
abolished Lord Chamberlain's hold on censorship. There were demands for
a National Government, a ministry of all the talents. Lord Mountbatten, the
Queen's cousin, together with the newspaper magnate Cecil King, got as far
as drawing up a list of ministers. The calls were a reflection of a more general
unease. Students in London and Paris and on American university campuses
protested angrily about war, imperialism and capitalism, and their radicalism
seeped into the British trade union movement. It was the beginning of the
end of the post-war era, the start of the terminal decline of the optimistic
certainties that Keynes and a generation of economic growth had brought.
Most members of Harold Wilson's government were nearly old enough to
be the grandparents of the rioting students; their best idea had been to lower
the voting age from twenty-one to eighteen. There were no new weapons
with which to fight the combination of inflation and rising unemployment,
nor the old enemy of a dodgy balance of payments and a weak pound.

George Brown's resignation, in the midst of a world economic crisis,
further imperilled the British economy. A second devaluation threatened; the
Treasury once again prepared to deflate. Four days after Brown's resignation,
Roy Jenkins had warned the country when presenting his first budget that
there was 'two years' hard slog' ahead. But the left was in revolt, deeply

hostile to government policies on Rhodesia, Vietnam and immigration as well as the economy. On 28 March, Labour was badly defeated in three by-elections, making six in a row, advance warning of catastrophe in the local elections.[2] Wilson was now under siege – from a hostile press which had long since abandoned its honeymoon with the Prime Minister, from his party at Westminster and, he often believed, from within his Cabinet. The South African arms incident had seen an assault on his authority by Healey, Brown and Callaghan. Jenkins, supported by a Gaitskellite band in government and on the back benches, was equally mistrusted. It was time to contain his enemies and promote his friends. Of the latter, the one whom he could most trust was was Barbara, rescued from back bench obscurity by his patronage, transformed through his support in Cabinet into a political superstar.

It was, however, Crossman who recommended to Wilson a 'Mark 2' Cabinet, a wholesale restructuring. The Prime Minister was enthusiastic, and not only because the idea would divert the 'Wilson must go' faction in the press. It would be a timely reminder to his cabinet critics that it was he who had the power to hire and fire. Crossman himself, Wilson proposed, would be the principal beneficiary. He would command a united Department of Health and Social Security in the first of a series of appointments to create departmental overlords. There was talk of an inner cabinet, not of the kitchen cabinet cronies, but of the major departmental ministers, charged with looking beyond their immediate responsibilities at the overall direction of the government. Barbara would be one of them. But which?

Six months earlier the speculation had been that she would move to the DEA; instead, Wilson had effectively wound it up. Now the speculation that she was in line for a major promotion revived. On the Whitehall net, the views of the top officials were, and are, a major factor. Padmore, still clinging tenaciously to his job as Barbara's Permanent Secretary, told Ted that the Cabinet Secretary Burke Trend rated her highly. A few days later, there was confirmation: Crossman took Barbara out to lunch to repeat to her what Wilson had just told him: 'Barbara is to be the new inspiration; she'll spark the new model. Tell her that today when you see her at lunch but don't tell her any more. She's to make the whole difference by taking over relations with the trade unions.'[3] She was to become the economics overlord. Barbara reacted with horrified excitement. 'My prime task is to take over the trade unions. The thought terrifies me . . . it was simple at Transport because I inherited a policy vacuum . . . But to take over at this stage a mess of policies which other people have created would be a very different kettle of fish. Anyway someone has got to do it so I might as well have a shot.'[4]

Wilson apparently hoped that Barbara, having silenced party grousing over the lack of a transport policy, might somehow pull off the same coup with the prices and incomes policy; after four years of abrasive tension between the DEA and the Treasury, it must be taken as a sign of his desperation to contain the ambitions of his Chancellor that the Prime Minister was prepared to contemplate reviving the near-moribund DEA. If he had been braver, or the pound stronger, perhaps he might have risked Barbara in the Treasury itself.

Crossman, as usual, had said more than he ought. Barbara, disguising how much she knew, went to see Wilson in order to suggest he do what Crossman had already told her he was planning. However, he had changed his mind, not about the cabinet of overlords, but about her role in it. He wanted her to be Leader of the House. It emerged that Chancellor Jenkins had vetoed her appointment to a beefed-up DEA. Barbara, furious, insisted that her skill at handling the trade unions and the party rank and file would make her invaluable in an economic department. She would be the embodiment of the party's commitment to the working class. Wilson was unpersuaded. Late that night, just as she and Ted were getting into bed, Downing Street summoned her back. There followed an hour of high drama: Wilson – perhaps because he still wanted her to become Leader of the House – was now offering her Ray Gunter's job at the Ministry of Labour. This was a sideways move, not a promotion, and if Transport had been a risk for her, Labour spelt certain oblivion. 'I could see my whole hopes of at last getting into the inner Cabinet fading away simply because the Minister of Labour would not have rank high enough in the hierarchy.'

Ted, who had driven Barbara back to No. 10, was called in to see if he could persuade her to take the Leader of the House job. Ted thought she should. Barbara dismissed him as a romantic. Wilson suggested the Ministry of Labour could be extended to include prices and incomes. 'Harold outlined his new idea while I sat moaning with my head between my knees.' They discussed renaming the department, to break its link with Labour's first woman cabinet minister Margaret Bondfield, who had cut the dole in the midst of the Depression and then resigned in ignominy. Barbara suggested it should be called the department of labour and productivity. Wilson pointed out that with a woman minister, this could lead to ribaldry. With nothing decided, the Castles returned to Islington.

While Barbara had been drinking with Wilson, Crossman in his self-appointed role as oiler of wheels was dining with Roy Jenkins. The following morning, the Chancellor invited Barbara in to explain, in the most flattering terms, why he thought two strong ministers at the two economic depart-

ments was a mistake. He thought she should go to the Home Office, he
suggested smoothly, and be Leader of the House at the same time (two jobs
that would keep her very busy and well off his economics pitch). Later that
day, she saw Wilson again. Jenkins, he told her angrily, had had the temerity
to ask him to settle nothing while he, Jenkins, was in Washington. To
Wilson (ignorant of the fact that Barbara had suggested the approach in the
first place), Jenkins's intervention appeared just the kind of high-handedness
his reshuffle was supposed to end. 'He has tried to tell me how to run my
own Cabinet. I told him he had better remember who was Prime Minister.'[5]
Wilson was now convinced that what was indeed to be called the Department of Employment and Productivity – that is, the Ministry of Labour,
with the main remaining duties of the Department of Economic Affairs
tacked on – was the right place for Barbara to go. Although leaving Jenkins
with the upper hand, it would force him into harness with Barbara: she
would be Wilson's spy in the Treasury cab. Still Barbara stalled: she could
not, she believed, do the job that needed doing without much greater status
in Cabinet. It was Crossman who found the solution. The following day, in
a rare instance of a politician acting against his own interests, he persuaded
Wilson to offer Barbara the title of First Secretary, a rank revived for George
Brown in 1964 to give his role at the Department of Economic Affairs parity
with the Chancellor's. Crossman himself had just been promised the rank
but he regarded it as unnecessary (he had, after all, the ear of the Chancellor
and the Prime Minister and an unusually detached attitude to his political
career: he was already planning to become editor of the *New Statesman* in
1970). Wilson asked him if Barbara really cared so much about status. 'No,'
Crossman replied, 'but she cares about power, and she's right.'

Barbara meanwhile had gone off with Ted to be the guest of the Queen
at Windsor Castle for the night. Wilson had thoughtfully warned her to be
careful what she put in her suitcase, as she would have it unpacked for her.
When his sister had been invited, to her mortification her corn plasters had
fallen out. Barbara reported a 'disappointing' dinner with the Queen ('Poor
woman! I don't know which of us is more under the spotlight!')[6] eaten off
silver plate with Prince Charles beside her – they got on famously and she
invited him to visit her department – and she had slept the night in the
splendid Minister's Room. At seven the next morning, she was on the phone
to Crossman for a progress report. He broke the news about her enhanced
rank: Barbara now felt she had both the status that would allow her to make
something of the job and a place at the table where the major economic
decisions affecting the future of the government were taken. She leapt at the
offer, which was capped when that evening – in a call made from the station

master's office at Euston minutes before she left for Blackburn on the sleeper
– Harold Wilson told her he would like her to be, not a minister, but a
Secretary of State as well as First Secretary. Double promotion, confirmation
of her status as the 'hottest ministerial property outside Downing Street'[7] –
the 'most powerful woman politician in British history', according to one
excited newspaper account.

After days of negotiations, Barbara was finally confirmed in her new role
on 5 April. Happily, she wrote in her diary: 'Well I am in the thick of it
now, for better or for worse – probably worse.'

The appointment shot Barbara up the cabinet rankings. She was, at last, on
all the most important cabinet committees, in particular the economic
strategy committee and the defence and overseas policy committee (OPD).
Her new prominence was reflected in the cabinet seating plan: from being
out at one end, often unable to hear debate, she moved to the centre
opposite the Prime Minister. She was in a position to influence him in
Cabinet; she and Dick Crossman planned to do more through the new inner
cabinet or 'parliamentary committee' that Wilson had also set up, which they
wanted to be devoted to focusing government effort. It turned out to be less
powerful than they had hoped, because Wilson decided it was safer to gather
his rivals around him rather than exclude them.

As far as other colleagues were concerned, his promotion of Barbara
rankled, and not only because some cabinet members preferred to consider it
a return for old favours rather than an acknowledgement of her success, or
even the kind of normal patronage indulged in by every Prime Minister.
Ray Gunter was furious that a woman and a left-winger – to whom he had
always referred as 'leather knickers' – had displaced him. More widely,
Barbara was thought to have got her own way unfairly, even against the will
of Cabinet. Callaghan accused her of repeatedly undermining his attempts as
Chancellor to control public spending by going to Wilson behind his back.
She did nothing to lessen the criticism, continuing to operate in Cabinet as
she had always done, with a mix of flirtation, charm and passionate, overlong
interventions. She saw herself as the Cabinet's ideological canary, unafraid of
warning them when they were losing sight of what she thought were proper
socialist objectives – making her, by irritating implication, the only real
socialist among them. She was prepared to bore her audience into submission,
overriding their sighs and sneers ('she went on and on like a mechanical drill'
according to one colleague[8]). Her chair had to have a cover put on it after
she complained that her stockings were repeatedly laddered, and her male

colleagues accused her of leaving early to go to the hairdresser's (in fact, her hairdresser's appointments were always first thing in the morning).

Out of Cabinet, her relations with Wilson were relaxed to the point of intimacy. She found him charming and admired his brain – though she suspected that, like most politicians (in her opinion), he did not match up to her intellectual rigour. But she forgave him. 'I am in the sort of relaxed relationship with him that enables me to chip in, tapping him on the knee firmly to stop him in mid-course and say doggedly, "Harold, listen to me." At which he grins and listens till he interrupts again. I think he knows I have considerable affection for him, even while I despair sometimes over his ideological limitations and am ready to resign, if necessary, if his tactical subtleties ever betray my beliefs. He knows, too, that I will always be honest with him.'

Crossman described the pleasure she and Wilson had 'niggling over details of negotiations' together. They drafted amendments and raged about possible plots brewing against him. Some people saw Wilson as a Boy Scout who never grew up. Crossman thought Barbara a Girl Guide: he, like Jenkins and Healey, could never quite resist a sense of superiority at the unpretentious lifestyle and middlebrow interests of the Wilsons and the Castles. Crossman once caused deep offence to Mary Wilson by refusing to drink Nescafé.

To outsiders, it was Barbara and Crossman who were the closest pair in government. They were 'the terrible twins', always in each other's company, enjoying a relationship of mutual support characterized by rages and rows that survived bitter political disagreement to become even closer. In April 1968, Crossman eulogized Barbara's talents:

> She is probably the biggest personality in the Government today. Already she's a natural number two and if she weren't a woman she would be a natural number one: she could quite conceivably be the first lady Prime Minister. Of course she's appallingly highly-strung and she's older than she should be for the leadership. Moreover, she overstrains herself. Nevertheless, success freshens her vitality in an amazing way. She has the personality to control any Ministry not only by sheer willpower but also by intellectual domination. What distinguishes her from Harold as well as from Roy is that she's still a real socialist as well as a woman of immense gusto and courage in negotiations.

Crossman was a demanding ally: he would telephone at all hours, experimenting with ideas, insisting on a response. But Barbara adored being with him. She described one afternoon at Crossman's big old farm house in

Oxfordshire, where he lived, she said, like a kulak, enjoying his new heated swimming pool: 'We swam solemnly up and down for a good half an hour. What I love about Dick is the way he always enjoys everything that happens to or belongs to him. It shows a capacity for enjoying life which keeps him perilously and entertainingly human.'[9]

Over the next few months, a third pattern in the cabinet kaleidoscope was perceptible. Roy Jenkins and Barbara Castle were forced into each other's company by their shared concern for the level of pay settlements and the development of a strategy to deal with them, and they both found it a less distasteful experience than they had expected. Crossman (who, Barbara reassured an anxious Wilson, just had one of his pashes on Jenkins) often provided the table around which they gathered to try to defuse some new pay crisis or moan about the latest Callaghan perfidy. Jenkins flattered and charmed, respectful of her ideas and seeking her advice. Barbara relaxed her suspicions a little, and genuinely admired the ambition of his first budget: 'It certainly was an impressive performance, but more important still it depended for its effect entirely on its intellectual content and marshalling. Its brilliance is proved by the fact that the most swingeing Budget in history left our people positively exultant.'[10] She continued to regard him as a dilettante, the kind of politician who wanted to give it all up after a couple of hard nights, and thought he was essentially cold at heart, but she respected his political judgement and admired his liberal instincts. 'I have the feeling that it would not really break his heart if the Government fell,' she wrote, 'provided he could write its history.'

Barbara's appeal to Wilson rested on three factors: that she had a rapport with the unions, a rapport with the left in parliament and a rapport with journalists. The first two assumptions were mistaken, and without them the third was a mirage. Once she became the instrument of pay policy, no amount of rapport would preserve her relationship with the trade unions, while her relationship with the left at Westminster was already under strain and, with the new intake, largely undeveloped. As for her fans in the media, they were always fair-weather friends.

Wilson, two years earlier, had watched Barbara steer the NUR away from a challenge to the embryonic prices and incomes policy with a passionate twenty-minute speech delivered late at night at his first beer and sandwiches session at No. 10. It was such a memorable speech, delivered at such a critical moment, that Wilson recalled it four years later when writing the memoir of his first two administrations. 'Here Barbara Castle . . . was most helpful. With little encouragement she spoke for twenty minutes, weaving a web of hope: higher productivity and higher wages in the not very distant tomorrow.' While close observers of the industrial relations scene saw the deal as a warning that a statutory prices and incomes policy would lead both to even worse industrial relations and to direct confrontation with the government, in Wilson's view – and her own – it was proof of Barbara's ability to talk to trade unionists in their own language. So successful was she deemed to be at handling the unions that Cecil King, the megalomaniac newspaper proprietor who hated Wilson (and Barbara), nonetheless thought that in his fantasy National Government she would have to have a role 'because she was so popular with the trade unionists'. Now she was to become the nation's head of human resources.

Barbara's experience of tough negotiating with the unions at the Department of Transport was a misleading guide. There she had been a quasi-employer, with something to give in return for concessions or compromises – enhanced job prospects or better conditions in return for a more relaxed attitude to demarcation, as in the dispute over the new container trains which she had solved in early 1966. At her new department she would be the policeman, with nothing but sanctions in her armoury, the role played by her Ministry of Labour predecessor Ray Gunter.

Barbara's relations with Gunter were a truer reflection of the attitude of the old union right. She had been at loggerheads with Gunter since her Bevanite days, and after her sacking of his friend Stanley Raymond he was more hostile than ever. Losing his job to Barbara was the final blow. He reluctantly accepted the job of Minister for Power, then in June resigned, protesting, like Brown, at the way government was being conducted. Gunter was typical of the old school of trade union leaders in other respects. His nickname for Barbara, with its overtones both of toughness and sexuality, suggests a dislike for women in power that was echoed in the upper reaches of the trade union hierarchy, which were virtually a woman-free zone. Business was conducted from the basic principle that might was right and solidarity was for men. This attitude to women was equally prevalent in the Labour Party at Westminster, where fewer women MPs had been elected in 1966 than in 1964 despite the surge in Labour members, and where about a third of backbenchers as well as some cabinet ministers had close trade union links. The Transport and General Workers' Union alone sponsored twenty-six MPs. Wilson had watched Barbara triumphantly exploit her gender in the men-only world of Transport; he expected her to capture another citadel of male chauvinism at Employment.

Her new department had been transformed by its extra responsibility for prices and incomes. During the war, the Ministry of Labour had nurtured industrial relations more or less regardless of cost. Even in the 1950s,

Churchill regarded it as the department for 'keeping the home front quiet'.[11] Little had changed by 1968, according to Bernard Ingham, who had recently been recruited to its press office from the industrial staff of the *Guardian* via the Prices and Incomes Board. It was a Whitehall cul-de-sac. 'The department moved at . . . a gentle tempo . . . [it] sought to promote industrial health and safety and the interests of the disabled who wanted to work . . . it studied trends in manpower requirements. It looked after the unemployed and tried to find them work . . . it was a noble department of State, and anyone with an ounce of social conscience could be proud to serve it.'[12] Its role was conciliation. Adding to its brief the entirely different tasks of imposing government-set pay norms and controlling the machinery of prices and incomes policy – the weapons of deflation – changed it from being a department for peace and prosperity into the front line of the war to save the pound. It became the conduit for union hostility to government policy, and its minister the focal point. Just perceptible in the media excitement of Barbara's appointment was a zephyr of doubt about whether she was the right person for the job. Was a politician whose main political characteristic was conflict the right person to soothe the angry world of industrial relations? And could a minister who believed in leadership rather than persuasion build support for prices and incomes? Or was Wilson, in appointing her, signalling a willingness to do battle on both?

Industrial relations were in chaos. Where 2.7 million days had been lost through disputes in 1967, in 1968 the final total was to be 4.6 million.[13] It was widely observed that national wage agreements were a sham: increasingly, pay deals were struck at individual factory level. The government's incomes policy was busted almost daily by ad hoc deals with local workforces, and there was little union leaderships could do about it – let alone the TUC, a federal organization that functioned only to the orders of its strongest members. In the late 1960s those were the Amalgamated Engineering Union – soon to be led by Hugh Scanlon, which had an active Communist clique at work in the executive – and the Transport and General Workers' Union, where Jack Jones was effectively taking over from Frank Cousins. Jones was a new kind of trade unionist; he had a socialist agenda and believed his union should be in the vanguard of the fight for socialism. Unlike Barbara, unfortunately, he did not regard a prices and incomes policy as a weapon to achieve it.

Nonetheless, as she remarked in a series of self-congratulatory passages in her diary, Barbara was confident she could find a way of working with the grain. She had reason to feel that the General Secretary of the TUC was a potential ally. George Woodcock, a Lancashire cotton-weaver who had subsequently taken a first-class degree in PPE at Oxford, was a thoughtful but unfortunately not forceful leader of the trade union movement. (Tony Benn thought he was a 'terrible old bore'.)[14] In the early 1960s he had warned his leading members that 'the free-for-all cannot continue unabated; it will bring regulation by unemployment or legislation'.[15] He believed that a *voluntary* incomes policy was a necessary part of the bargain between trade unions and the state, a quid pro quo for the government's commitment to full employment and part of the trade union movement's responsibilities, in return for which it was entitled to a say in the way the economy was run. The National Economic Development Council, which brought together employers, unions and government – ironically, established by the Tories – was, he believed, a pattern for the future. Unfortunately for Barbara, who was to take his reassurances at face value, he was regarded with suspicion by the union barons, who assumed his attempts to raise their sights above the next wage round were merely a bid to accrue more power for himself and the TUC. To some extent they were right: he envisaged the TUC as the collective voice of all working people, and it was on that basis that it should have a seat at the top table of power. But if it was to be more powerful in the formulation of national policy, it would need more power over its members. The viability of that equation was to become central to Barbara's plans over the next two years.

Meanwhile, the parliamentary left was lining up to argue against a prices and incomes policy. A group of Tribune MPs were among the first to set foot in Barbara's new office in elegant St James's Square, fifteen minutes walk across St James's Park from Westminster. These were the authors of the pamphlet, 'New Economic Strategy', who condemned 'the government's acceptance of classical Tory deflationary measures as a method of solving our economic problems', who believed that the government was heading 'all the panicky way back to Philip Snowden and the disastrous Ramsay MacDonald government of 1929'.[16] They came to tell her that the new prices and incomes legislation – which she had challenged herself in Cabinet – must at the very least be delayed so as to give the TUC's voluntary policy one last chance. The TUC had proposed returning to their voluntary system, with a 6 per cent ceiling. Barbara said it would turn out to be 10 per cent; it was unacceptable. The choice, she believed, was between a backbench rebellion, accompanied perhaps by a rift with the unions, and another devaluation, 'which would put social democracy out of office in Britain for the next 20 years'.[17] If the alternative to losing power was sending trade unionists to prison for breaching the pay norm, then she would do it. (And I would go with them, she added obscurely, but dramatically.) Ian Mikardo, the driving force behind the Tribunites, a dour sectarian with an unexpected penchant for flowery language, told her: 'You are a marvellous woman and we love you dearly, but even you can't make us think a cesspool smells like roses.'

Defence of the statutory prices and incomes policy was her first priority. Where Wilson was uninterested in its transforming potential, Barbara had long convinced herself of its ability to achieve significant change and could marshal fluent and persuasive arguments to back her case up. Nearly two years earlier, in the summer of 1966, as Frank Cousins teetered on the brink of resignation, she tore into him over his refusal to accept statutory controls and set out what a proper, socialist, policy might achieve. 'Let's go ahead with the bill, but seize the opportunity to set an entirely new climate. The majority . . . welcomed the policy, not merely as an alternative to deflation, but as a redistributive measure. I therefore suggested that we should announce we were going to introduce minimum wage legislation; say there would be a norm of nought for twelve months, only to be exceeded against absolutely watertight productivity agreements.'

In late 1967, she had made an even more determined case that pay policy could be an instrument of a new, modern socialism. This, she argued, would be a socialism for a technocratic age, where the minimum wage, productivity awards and the 'social wage' − state-funded health care, schools, training and public transport − should all combine to achieve a fairer distribution of the national income and a more equal society.[18] It was hardly an extreme position. Until the late 1960s, the public difference between the two main parties on state intervention was one of degree, not principle, and within Labour only the least ideological on the right were beginning to wonder whether the damage done by the unintended consequences of government economic micro-management might actually undermine their socialist objective.

Having argued so often that an incomes policy could be a weapon in the socialist armoury, Barbara immediately set about trying to prove it. Her new Permanent Secretary Denis Barnes was summoned, like her permanent secretaries at her earlier departments, to tea in the country, now at Hell Corner Farm, and told that 'incomes policy was socialism'[19] (a claim treated with astonishment when relayed back to other officials).[20] The challenge, she and Barnes agreed, was to improve productivity so that pay rises could be justified. There was to be a new unit dedicated to achieving this, within her department. She was warned that the unions were less enthusiastic: rising productivity threatened jobs.

Before any of the long-term problems had really been addressed, the government's third round of prices and incomes legislation for 1968–9, giving even tougher powers to the government to delay and to restrict pay and price increases to 3.5 per cent, had somehow to be guided through parliament against committed left-wing opposition. Barbara was still not familiar enough with the material to speak confidently on the subject in the Commons. On the second reading, thirty-five left-wingers abstained. She was exhausted by the demands she had imposed on herself in her first few weeks at the job – launching into wage negotiations, attracting once again a blaze of publicity – so exhausted, in fact, that she could hardly get her words out at her first party meeting. She had left behind all her close advisers. Chris Hall, her press spokesman, had stayed at Transport, one eye on a future career with the Ramblers' Association. He had been one of her most important allies at the department, a Labour man who knew both the party and the press, as well as being a personal friend whom she trusted completely. Her expert adviser, Christopher Foster, had been rejected for the alleged breach of trust of opposing Peter Parker's appointment; and although she had recruited another strong adviser at the Department of Emloyment and Productivity in Derek Robinson, a labour economist on secondment from Oxford, he lacked the smooth social skills that had enabled Foster to parley with officials in their own terms.

Barbara was at their mercy in a way she had never been before, dealing with a highly complex, fast-moving subject that was almost as central to the government's survival as Roy Jenkins's work at the Treasury. A dangerously heady sense of impending martyrdom started to colour her diary entries. The new job, she wrote with one eye on posterity, was a move to 'the very focal point of unpopularity. And yet,' she went on, 'I know I couldn't do anything else. If I go down in disaster as well I may, at least I shall have been an adult before I die.'[21] Her friends noticed a new uncertainty in both her public performances and her private persona as she struggled to find her feet. Her health was on a perilous edge; she suffered frequent stomach trouble and throat infections, and as she drove herself harder and harder, exhaustion was never far away.

Political help within the department was equivocal too. Barbara's new junior minister was a young Birmingham MP called Roy Hattersley. He was a keen Jenkinsite, so keen (a veritable snake, claimed Tommy Balogh) that Barbara had been advised to replace him with someone more sympathetic. She refused. It was one of her strengths that she saw no need to surround herself with yes-men. Hattersley made no secret of his opinions, not least on the pay policy. He thought this round of legislation had to be the last, and he warned Barbara against sounding too hawkish on it. Jenkins was equally uncertain about its merits, but convinced it was indispensable to calm the bankers. Callaghan, who with the departure of both Brown and Gunter was about to become the only trade unionist in Cabinet, had cooled rapidly since he had left the Treasury. In May 1968, he too made it clear, in a speech to the firemen's union, that this legislation had to be the last. 'Three and a half years is long enough.'[22] There was a row in Cabinet about his apparent criticism of government policy, but Crossman too thought it would be impossible to renew the legislation. The point was effectively conceded when the backbench rebels were promised that if the government wanted to bring in more legislation at the end of 1969, it would not attempt to renew existing legislation but go back to first principles. In the face of opposition from MPs and trade unionists, Barbara was almost alone in arguing the merits of the policy, rather than its necessity.

While the bill ground through parliament, attracting record numbers of rebels, Barbara herself underwent an intensive course in the realities of running a pay policy. Every major dispute stopped at her desk; it was on her say that the department – and often Barbara herself – intervened. Her officials, watching her slip cash to one woman trade unionist[23] (to help the strikers' families) after a long negotiating session, wondered what they had been landed with. She was regularly letting through pay settlements exceeding the government norm on a variety of pretexts[24] (which rarely included the truth: that the claim was coming from a sector of the workforce that the government could not afford to alienate without dire economic consequences). Between April 1968 and April 1969, wage rates increased at around 5 per cent and actual earnings by 7 per cent against the government-set norm of 0–3.5 per cent. Barbara claimed that her policy was aimed first and foremost at holding down prices. Tackling price increases meant running a policy at odds with the Chancellor's: the Treasury was out to deflate, to hold down wages and let prices rise. Treasury officials briefed influential sectors of the press against her. The *Economist* predicted disaster if she failed to hold down wages and took instead 'the easier but disastrous role of temporarily delaying price increases . . . she has got to be stopped'.

Furthermore, Barbara was not confident she had Wilson's support. 'Will you back me?' she asked anxiously on the question of fighting the Treasury's determination to allow prices to rise. 'I put you there, didn't I?' was all he would say in response.[25] However, later he sent her a copy of a minute he had written to Jenkins instructing him to agree a line on prices. 'Perhaps the three of us should meet to agree on instructions to be given to the economic advisers who could . . . provide a basis for an agreed policy – and an agreed line in dealing with the press.'[26] It was a mess, and Barbara knew it: 'I have to go on justifying a policy which three quarters of the Cabinet no longer believe in, and pending its winding up I am being publicly bullied into enforcing it on the weaker brethren . . .'[27] Christopher Foster, still hoping to get back on her staff, wrote to warn her of the appearance of confusion. He wanted her to present the prices and incomes policy as a positive and deliberate strategy linking output, prices and competitiveness – an ambitious instruction which would have taken all Barbara's self-belief and powers of persuasion. And, as Foster himself acknowledged, innovation at a time of crisis was a dangerous path to follow.[28]

Barbara, the nation's industrial troubleshooter, was hunting with the hounds but at first her instincts remained entirely on the side of the hare. Increasingly close encounters with trade unionists who seemed either unwilling or unable to stop strikes, and the discovery that employers were more amiable than she had expected (she was on good terms with both John Davies, the Director General of the Confederation of British Industry, and the former Tory minister Aubrey Jones who ran the Prices and Incomes Board), together with some careful management by Jenkins (who went out of his way to bring her into his confidence on the vulnerability of sterling), slowly shifted her internal balance. The turbulent state of industrial relations and the emphasis Wilson was placing on pay policy as the way to save the pound completed the process of turning the trade unions into a public enemy. If only strikes could be stopped, the message went, then there would be an economic transformation. In vain did labour economists point out the real impact of lost production on the economy – only 0.1 per cent of working days were lost to strikes. Increasingly, public opinion demanded not an accommodation with the unions and their representative body the TUC, but something like a victory over them. As early as the end of June 1968, after only three months in the job, Barbara was talking of introducing some kind of sanction against trade unions that failed to exhaust negotiating procedures before coming out on strike.

The national appetite was for some radical action that could magic away the dyspeptic headlines: the Tories, in a policy paper called *A Fair Deal at Work*, had already committed themselves to making contracts between unions and employers legally binding, a deceptively simple and therefore popular solution which would make strikers who breached a contract liable to damages and, potentially, imprisonment. So far, Labour had avoided committing itself by referring the matter to a Royal Commission, a move intended to 'take the politics out of industrial relations'. Since 1965, the former Labour MP turned High Court judge Lord Donovan, and eminent academics, journalists and trade unionists, had been pondering the issue. Ray Gunter, as Minister of Labour, had picked the members of the Commission; his choice suggested that the report would shy away from the iconoclastic.

By the spring of 1968, after three laborious years of inquiry and millions of words of evidence – Wilson had originally resisted the idea of a Royal Commission because, as he jocularly complained, it would take minutes and spend years – Donovan was ready to report. Already the newspaper leader writers were predicting it would be a damp squib. Some observers read Barbara's appointment as Secretary of State for Employment and Productivity as proof that Wilson intended to meet the challenge. Gunter had had to go because he was at heart a 'voluntarist', an old-school trade unionist who firmly believed in the tradition of keeping the government out of industrial relations. Certainly, most of the old Ministry of Labour shared his opinion. But the Permanent Secretary Denis Barnes and especially his deputy Conrad Heron belonged to the radical tendency. They thought the unions needed saving from themselves, and had started to recruit freethinkers from outside the department. Among them was John Burgh, a young civil servant from the Secretary of State's private office at the Department of Economic Affairs – the front line of the battle against wage inflation – whose new job was to head the team preparing to respond to the Donovan Commission.

A fortnight before the report was published, anticipating intense pressure and always enthusiastic for action, Barbara warned cabinet colleagues she would probably want to bring in a short bill in the next session of parliament. Officials had already seen most of the Commission's draft, and it confirmed expectations: it was a thorough, indeed exhaustive, analysis of the way industrial relations worked at national level, and of the way they did not work. But – it was widely felt – it entirely failed to reflect the urgency of the need for a solution. It blamed breakdowns on out-of-touch union officials and employers, on the excessive number of trade unions represented in negotiations – far more than in the United States or what was then West Germany – and in particular on ill-defined negotiating procedures. However, far from responding to the national appetite for intervention, it reaffirmed the principle of voluntarism central to traditional trade unionism and recommended a slow programme of grass-roots reform.

The Commission's caution was yet another obstacle to a radical approach to industrial relations. Not only was it offering no springboard for legislation, it would give all the defenders of the status quo an argument for inaction. Barbara's immediate public response on the publication of its report on 13

June 1968 hardly suggested anything different. She promised to consult. A
month later, when the Commons debated it, she actually noted the need to
disguise the department's 'non-existent' line on it.

But by the autumn of that year, Barbara's own experiences – her
increasingly desperate attempt to stem the flow of wage demands which were
ever more widely perceived as the cause of sterling's weakness, as well as the
political pressure for some assertion of authority against unofficial strikes –
had convinced her that some kind of government action was essential. It was
obvious she was unlikely to get another round of prices and incomes policy
through the PLP; she was dogged by industrial disputes which should have
been resolved without strike action, such as the 'recognition' row at the
newly nationalized British Steel, where the skilled workers' unions vied for
power with the manual unions in a dispute which threatened shortages for
every steel user in the country. When the TUC intervened to settle the
dispute under the terms of the Bridlington Agreement on poaching – coming
out in favour of the manual unions – it seemed to prove it was unable to
judge impartially between the rival claims of its members. By contrast,
Barbara found a willingness among employers to do business. Talks she had
set up in an effort to improve the damagingly bad industrial relations in the
motor industry indicated common ground between employers and unions.
The employers had offered increased recognition for the unions, including
'check-off' (allowing union subscriptions to be deducted from the pay packet,
with members opting out rather than in), in return for an honouring of
agreements.

The political pressures were even more overwhelming than the industrial.
The CBI, as the main representative of the employers, was demanding legally
enforceable contracts and a rationalization of the plethora of unions fighting
for their lives in a changing industrial world by every means at their disposal.
The press was full of reports of unofficial 'wildcat' strikes in which the
actions of a handful of workers were allegedly jeopardizing thousands of jobs.
In the bitter atmosphere provoked by the passage of the new prices and
incomes legislation there was no enthusiasm for constructive conversation or
a cool public debate on the issue that underlay both the report and the whole
question of industrial relations: the role of trade unions in a social democratic
society.

The theory of the 1960s corporate state assumed that trade unions, like
employers, were partners in power with the duly elected government. Trade
union leaders shared knighthoods and peerages with the bosses of the CBI.
As General Secretary of the TUC, George Woodcock had virtually open
access to No. 10. He himself was a proponent of reform, at least in as far as

it meant strengthening the TUC. Barbara's own officials were anxious to present themselves not as union-bashers, but as genuine seekers after a way of strengthening them so that they could play their part more effectively. However, as the government came to rely more and more on the TUC, the TUC became less and less able to deliver the consent of its members, represented by individual trade union leaders, who in turn had become less and less able to deliver their rank and file. When Barbara later declared that power had passed to the shop-floor, there was an outcry at the implications – but no questioning of the truth of the assertion.

Ten days after the Donovan Report was published, Barbara used an interview with Stephen Fay in the *Sunday Times* to set out her position on the trade union movement: 'It is constantly torn between the collective political commitment and the sectional view,' she observed – optimistically, in view of all the evidence that trade unions were wedded to the sectional view – 'particularly when a Labour government is in office.' She went on boldly to assert that a prices and incomes policy was implicit recognition of the trade unions' role in policy-making. 'The trade unionist at the point of production should be treated as an adult contributor to the whole problem of prices and productivity and therefore of management . . . they are very important people in our society . . . *they must behave like important people* [author's emphasis]'. Over the next year, the plea to unions to accept the responsibilities that went with the power given to them by a government determined to maintain full employment was made with mounting urgency and equal futility.

Meanwhile, Barbara had to continue to defend the government's policy on prices and incomes. She was bitterly aware that despite her interventions she was having little success in making the policy an instrument of social justice. She railed bitterly in Cabinet against the Chancellor for giving in to the demands of the groups with the greatest industrial power. Why, she fumed in her diary, should the tally clerks in the docks get their full pay award just because they could bring exports to a halt, when she could not approve increases for lower-paid and industrially weaker groups unless they were fully backed by productivity agreements? In July, she accomplished the first of her tasks at the department: the new legislation extending the government's powers for another eighteen months was passed. Her old friend Ian Mikardo, whose refusal to acknowledge either the potential of the policy or her efforts to make it work during the passage of the bill had infuriated Barbara, drove the message home when he wrote with laborious irony to decline an invitation to mark the bill's successful enactment. 'I've nothing suitable to wear. My best sackcloth and ashes which I last wore at a party to celebrate the successful reimposition of prescription charges is showing signs of wear. Moreover my taste for hemlock is somewhat less zestful than it used to be . . . Please publish a list of those who come to your party. It will make interesting reading in the Constituency Labour Parties and the Trade Unions.'

In the autumn of 1968, first the TUC and then Labour's conference overwhelmingly rejected statutory pay policy. At their conference in Blackpool, the trade unions ensured pay policy was rejected by five to one. Barbara's lectures on the need for a reviled policy, which in the previous year could only be shown to have held down earnings by 1 per cent, made no impact. 'If you do nothing about incomes,' she declared in an interview in the September issue of Labour's *Economic Brief*, 'sustained economic growth, rising earnings and permanent full employment cannot be achieved. That is why we need an incomes policy which compliments other measures to help our balance of payments by acting directly on costs instead of indirectly through restraining demand.' She angrily denounced the 'hypocritical protestations of socialism'. But already she knew some other way would have to be found to lift productivity and improve industrial relations. Her attention focused on the opportunities provided by the Donovan Report.

13. The Eye of the Storm

As a socialist, Barbara Castle was convinced that it was impossible to plan the economy if pay was left unplanned. By the same token it would be impossible to make progress towards socialism if the industrial scene was disfigured by indiscipline.

Edmund Dell, *A Strange Eventful History:*
Democractic Socialism in Britain[1]

The decision to legislate on industrial relations destroyed Barbara's career. Taken in a matter of weeks in the late autumn of 1968, it was a bold attempt to deliver up to her patron Wilson the Holy Grail of industrial peace and the simultaneous political humiliation of the Tories. She had set out to produce a policy that would be more eye-catching than the Conservatives', to prove that in 1968, 'the year of the strike', the government still governed. Yet, where she intended to restore the government's standing, she succeeded only in bringing it still lower; and where she sought a personal triumph, she ended by being vilified throughout Labour circles. The circumstances that made legislation desirable also made it almost impossible to achieve.

Barbara wanted a political triumph; but she wanted it on her terms. It was also, it went without saying, to be a socialist triumph. She wanted finally to assert the primacy of the political over the industrial wing of the Labour movement, just at the moment when the industrial wing, fearful for jobs, goaded by insensitive management and threatened by technological advance, had become more radical and militant than it had been at any time since the General Strike forty years earlier. Barbara did not look to see if the troops were gathered behind ready to follow; she believed that good leadership brought its own support. A rational assessment of the conditions would have shown her that although she had the Prime Minister with her, she had few other friends in Cabinet, and the admiration of the PLP was rooted only in her success; while the trade unions were increasingly hostile to the government and in particular – after nearly a year in office – to Barbara, the instrument of a policy of holding down wages and allowing unemployment to rise.

As events unravelled, people began to ask why Barbara, of all people – a left-winger, a party animal – had tried to storm Labour's citadel. 'Energy and idealism collided,' one respected observer remarked,[2] 'and energy won.' Of all the interpretations of her actions, this is the most misleading. She had no ideological difficulty with legislation; she did not come from the wing of the Labour movement which regarded the party's first task as promoting the interests of the trade union movement. If she had, she would not have threatened it with the law. For Barbara, Labour was the instrument of socialism, and the purpose of the link with trade unionism was to educate the working class in its benefits. She believed the state had both a legal and an economic role as arbitrator between the interests of the producer and of the consumer. A more pragmatic minister – like her deputy Roy Hattersley – would have looked at the wider political scene, at the deepening hostility to government intervention, and decided discretion was decidedly a better bet than valour. Barbara believed she was acting in pursuit of socialism. Discretion was no part of her make-up, while valour was her stock-in-trade.

However, there was no immediate sign that she intended to bow to public pressure and use the Donovan Report as a springboard for legislation. Almost nothing seemed to happen in the department between its publication in June and the brainstorming session that would take place in her office at the department in November. The employer's agenda was well known: to achieve the power to make legally binding contracts with trade unions, and for the plethora of small unions to be replaced by fewer but much larger ones. The TUC wanted nothing done by government at all. Barbara was unimpressed. 'I can't see any revolutionary changes being carried through unless the Government is prepared to impose them on an unwilling TUC,' she wrote after a meeting with the TUC's George Woodcock and her childhood aquaintance Vic Feather who was his deputy. Woodcock himself acknowledged that by fighting the pay policy, the TUC had ruled itself out of the kind of role in government of which he had dreamed.[3] There was a desperate need for action of some kind, but little evidence from Barbara's diaries and papers that the Donovan Report would be any more successful than most other Royal Commission reports in providing a blueprint.

During the autumn of 1968, the pace of events began to quicken. After the government defeat on the floor of the party conference on pay policy, it was plain that the party would not survive another round of statutory controls. Meanwhile, an unofficial strike by twenty-two machine-setters at Girling Brakes in Merseyside caused five thousand others in the motor industry to be laid off. Barbara had suggested to the motor industry employers that they should keep larger stocks of such components; they had retorted that it was the most uneconomic way of running a business. The internal problem of continuing the prices and incomes policy, and the external problem of anarchic industrial relations, were driven home. At the Conservative Party conference the week after Labour's, the Tories made much of their new trade union policy, 'A Fair Deal at Work': it was a comprehensive plan intended to turn trade unions into bodies governed by statutory law. In order to preserve their immunity from action for damages, unions would have to register with a new industrial relations authority; agreements they made with employers would be legally enforceable. Sympathy strikes, inter-union disputes and the closed shop would be illegal. There would be a compulsory cooling-off period, and secret strike ballots. A new industrial court would adjudicate.

The Tory policy had a double effect: it increased the pressure on Barbara to act, and, politically, it eliminated some courses of action. A few days later, Barbara discussed the Donovan Report with officials: 'I held forth about the need for us to have our own discussions about whether we accept the Donovan analysis and above all our own philosophy of the role of the trade union movement in the present day.' She demanded a weekend of brainstorming. It was fixed for the following month, the weekend of 15 November.

Barbara was a believer in 'big' politics, the single, all-embracing solution. She wanted drama and action, not the long, slow haul of gradualism. The Transport Act had been an attempt to introduce at a stroke an integrated transport policy. The aim of the Sunningdale[4] brainstorming weekend was to devise a policy which in one bill would simultaneously make further attempts at pay policy redundant, settle all current unofficial strikes, render further unofficial action near-impossible, reform the processes of industrial relations in line with Donovan's recommendations, and leave the Tories high and dry. As one correspondent later observed, she had 'to steal Mr Heath's thunder and to save Mr Wilson's bacon, all in the same tumultuous breath, in time for the next election'.[5]

Unsurprisingly, the Sunningdale conference was attended with some scepticism, at least by Barbara's ministerial team of Roy Hattersley and Harold Walker.[6] The newspapers were full of the Girling dispute, the damning statistics of unofficial strikes, and criticism of Barbara's inequitable approach to pay policy, which had led her to refer a tiny increase in construction workers' pay – 'the builders' penny' – to the Prices and Incomes Board. Almost all strikes, press reports pointed out, were unofficial, and even though strikers constituted usually only a small number of workers, they accounted for 75 per cent of working days lost. The right-wing weeklies were sounding the death knell of the government's policy. The *Economist*, demanding, as usual, further deflation, was the most chillingly authoritative: 'Incomes policy has broken down and to the most alarming extent. That extent is shown by the way in which employers, convinced that inflation is inevitable, are falling over themselves . . . to grant large wage increases; and to proclaim their confidence about bogus productivity deals in which no cool efficiency expert could believe.' Denis Barnes, the department's Permanent Secretary, told his new recruit Bernard Ingham that unemployment would double every decade until 'we got on top of the trade union problem'. The prediction turned out to be an underestimate.

The advice from the left was no more palatable. Tommy Balogh had just sent Barbara his analysis of the current economic outlook. Writing with the next budget, now under preparation, in mind, he warned her that productivity and therefore competitiveness were still lagging disastrously behind Britain's rivals. The prices and incomes policy had to continue, he insisted. The trade unions had to be brought on side to make it work, but with social, not financial, incentives. The same message came from columnists: in the *Spectator*, Auberon Waugh asked if Labour was actually trying to lose the next election. He painted Barbara as a socialist from an Ealing comedy, being maliciously indulged by the Chancellor: 'In her simple warm-hearted bossy way [Mrs Castle] sees it as an essential part of socialism that there should be a planned increase in wages . . . alias a freeze. The workers may not like it at first, but in their heart of hearts they know that teacher knows best'; while Roy Jenkins, he speculated, egged her on only in order to demonstrate that socialism was 'politically unviable and economically irrelevant'.

At the party conference in Blackpool, the National Executive had called for a wide public debate on pay and incomes policy. But no public debate was to emerge from the Sunningdale weekend's deliberations; the participants were all sworn to silence. Barbara was planning a complete reversal of post-war industrial relations policy by ambush.

In another self-deception of the kind to which ministers appear to fall prey after some years in office, she also wanted, at least retrospectively, to divorce industrial relations reform from the failure of the prices and incomes policy and the need to find an alternative. The attempt only made her critics more suspicious. The link between the two was uppermost in the minds of many of the participants at Sunningdale, and had always been explicit among the members of the Donovan Commission. As the Commission had pointed out: 'Actual earnings have risen far above rates laid down by industry-wide agreements, and disputes procedures laid down by industry-wide agreements have been greatly strained by the transfer of authority to the workplace [where] bargaining . . . is fragmented and chaotic and largely uncontrolled by employers' associations and trade unions.' Peter Shore, minister at the Department of Economic Affairs, was determined that industrial relations reform must focus on bringing trade unionists into line. 'On the left it was absolutely clear to anyone who thought about it, that if you wanted full employment you had to have an incomes policy. No problem if you don't want full employment, then you can use unemployment to regulate the market. We had to drive this into the heads of a lot of blockheaded trade unionists.'

Most participants at the Sunningdale weekend arrived believing that maintaining full employment demanded a way of overriding the market and holding down the cost of labour. That meant curbing the trade unions' right to drive up their members' pay to the highest level the market could stand. However tactfully it was presented, industrial reform was going to mean weakening the trade union movement from which the Labour Party had grown and on which, for finance at least, it still depended.

'She wasn't an intellectual,' Bernard Ingham wrote later, 'but she liked to get the philosophy right.' Barbara was cautious in her approach to major decisions, and her preparations for Sunningdale were meticulous. She read and annotated a series of papers prepared by officials like John Burgh and expert advisers like Bill McCarthy, the labour lawyer and academic. Industrial relations were a sphere (like transport) in which most of those involved traditionally regarded untrammelled independence of action as an inalienable right. As government intervention had almost invariably been aimed at curtailing trade union strength it was an understandable position, although illogical in the new era, when the Wilson government was starting to intervene to help trade unionists – for example, to protect employment rights and introduce redundancy pay. Among politicians and commentators, and trade unionists like George Woodcock, there was also a lively sense of the damage done to the community by some strikes. However, the doctrine of non-intervention was not one to be breached lightly. Donovan had examined the idea of making pay deals legally enforceable, and rejected it on the grounds that procedures for reaching agreements were so archaic that they were the main cause of disputes – logically they should be the starting place for reform. If Barbara was to advocate 'systematic and positive' intervention, it would require a clear set of objectives which intervention should be able to achieve. She pondered trading the commitment to full employment and the enhancement of the social wage, in return for allowing the government to constrain the unions' freedom of action. To a limited extent, that had been the formula which had produced relative industrial calm in the Attlee years. Some trade unionists, though, might reject any help from government as compromising their independence. In the end, she scribbled on a piece of departmental notepaper, 'Do governments know best, or does not the free play of other power forces engender some remedies a government might not initiate or could never impose?'

The policy which emerged was Barbara's, but the officials had long since decided intervention was necessary. The old Ministry of Labour had said as much in its evidence to the Donovan Commission. Burgh now repeated it.

> The doctrine of non-intervention . . . no longer corresponds with the facts . . . There can be no assurance that the unguided process of voluntary collective bargaining will produce the best possible result for the community generally. Put bluntly, the country's elected government is better placed than either side of industry or any other private interests, to assess the common good. When it judges the common good to be threatened by either side or both sides of industry, the government should have the power to take the necessary remedial action.

Typical of the gestation of Barbara's programmes, the atmosphere at Sunningdale was more cerebral than political, one of diligent effort. (According to Sir John Burgh, 'It was an interesting collection of individuals and there was a sense of a genuine search for the way forward.'[7]) The highly controversial decision to overturn Donovan's main recommendation, against legislation, appears to have been taken almost without a murmur of protest. 'The real question is not whether there should be legislation on industrial relations, but what sort of legislation it should be,'[8] Burgh's discussion paper pronounced uncompromisingly. The old principle that government, and the law, stayed out of relations between employers and unions must go; the tension between the right of the employer to use his capital as he saw fit and the right of workers to combine as a counterweight, which had exercised the minds of lawyers and legislators for a hundred years, should be permanently resolved. In an economy in which a small dispute in one sector could seriously damage many other businesses, as the Girling dispute was doing even as they deliberated, the government was responsible for securing the good of the whole community. Peter Shore laid out the case with particular force. 'Whole effect of strikes changed,' Barbara noted him saying as she gathered her thoughts at the end of the first day, 'they affect community rather than employer. E.g. dock strike is a blockade of the nation. State has right to intervene where national interest threatened, regardless of merits of dispute.'

Shore's was a personal spin on what was now becoming a widely held position. Barbara's PPS John Fraser, who was also at the seminar, recalled the mood: 'We had to do something. The trade unions behaved like the Vatican State, as if they were an independent power. Yet they had been given everything. We had public ownership, but the miners and the railmen had no compunction about going on strike. They had inherited the earth and still they wanted more.'[9] Donovan's reservations about legislation were dismissed; the report's weakness, Barbara felt, was that it had looked at industrial relations in the abstract, without considering the impact on the national economy of any breakdown. While it had done much good work on the causes of industrial anarchy, its focus had been too narrow. The report had come up with a cumbersome proposal, giving powers to the new Commission for Industrial Relations (whose establishment was the one recommendation on which Barbara had immediately acted) to register unions and, as a condition of registration, impose standards on their negotiating procedures. Without registration, unions would forfeit their legal immunity for breach of contract. But this, the Donovan Report acknowledged, would take years to have any real impact and, as critics immediately remarked, even unions and employers with model negotiating procedures had trouble with unofficial strikes.

Having accepted the justification for government intervention, the conference considered what form it should take. Peter Shore and John Fraser believed contracts should be legally enforcible but, with the Tories already committed to the idea, it was politically unacceptable – and premature, pre-empting necessary reforms in negotiating procedure. Aubrey Jones, the chairman of the Prices and Incomes Board, wanted the state to force a reduction in the number of unions in the same way that it was making companies merge in the interests of a more modern economy. He called for a new, powerful judicial body that would register not only unions but the agreements they made, and then police them. It was an idea that went further even than the Tories' plan for an industrial court, Barbara noted. The labour economist (and subsequent Labour peer) Bill McCarthy proposed a govern-ment-imposed framework of 'desirable objectives', with sanctions that would be 'specific, immediate and observable'. Barbara disagreed, and stirred the argument. McCarthy was dazzled by her style. 'She never let anyone know what she thought, she just probed and probed, challenged and challenged.'

That night she sat up alone, summarizing and developing her ideas. State intervention, she considered, need not mean using the law against trade unions, or sanctions. It could be directed towards a range of positive ends, including 'effective and acceptable agreements at appropriate levels', preventing disputes and implementing a prices and incomes policy, and it could also be used for developing management and extending worker participation. But 'the chief problem was how to prevent workers themselves acting against the longer-term interests of the economy. *It was essential to find a means of reconciling the interests of the producer and the consumer.*'[10] Barbara's strategy was to remind the unions that they had a wider role than serving their members' interests. It was a strategy that owed nothing to her experience of implementing the prices and incomes policy and much to her romantic aspirations for what collective action could achieve.

By the Sunday morning, she had mapped out the headings of a White Paper. She swept down the staircase at Sunningdale with what amounted to the skeleton of her industrial relations strategy in her hand. Sitting curled up in informal intimacy in an armchair in the main conference room, she set out her proposals. She was prepared to legislate for state intervention in certain circumstances. The key question was not whether sanctions were justified, but whether they would be effective in securing improvements. She wanted government to have the power to impose a cooling-off period in 'unconstitutional' strikes – that is, where dispute-resolution procedures had not been exhausted before the decision to strike was taken – and the power to compel employers to return to the status quo until negotiations were complete. She also wanted to impose secret ballots where strikes would jeopardize the national interest, and powers for the new Commission for Industrial Relations enabling it to impose settlements on recognition disputes, backed by financial sanctions. Unions should register with the CIR, which would be able to scrutinize their procedures to ensure they had been modernized. The CIR's inquiries would be directed by the Secretary of State; decisions on when a cooling-off period or conciliation pause should be imposed would be taken by the Secretary of State; secret ballots would also be at the behest of the Secretary of State. Barbara, who as Transport Minister had declared that she would be the driving force behind the integration of the various sectors, was now proposing to become the arbitrator of the nation's racked industrial relations.

Almost as a footnote, she rejected the idea of trying to involve the TUC in the role of policeman; the individual unions would not accept the loss of sovereignty involved. But they would be offered a broad programme of workers' rights that would strengthen the trade union movement. The Tory agenda of legally enforcible collective agreements, a ban on sympathy strikes and the closed shop was rejected.

Her officials were impressed. For Bill McCarthy it was a revelation. 'In the morning, all [the experts] went home and the only people left were the civil servants, and Barbara. She came down, this tiny little person, and sat in this great chair, with a piece of paper covered in her handwriting and it was marvellous, it was what we were going to do, how we were going to thread our way through all these difficulties . . . and she asked me to write it.' John Burgh thought well of her too: 'It was a very impressive performance. She had obviously done a great deal of work, and she was completely in command.' Other enthusiasts included Peter Shore. 'I wanted to find ways of limiting, or indeed stopping, the power of the strike weapon being used against our incomes policy, and frankly to stoke up inflation. I was delighted with what I thought were Barbara's very strong proposals.'

Barbara was exhilarated, triumphant. 'A fabulously successful weekend,' she exulted in her diary. 'We agreed that we would never get anything positive out of the TUC and the government would have to risk giving a lead.' At last, 'the woman who introduced the breathalyser' had a real project in hand. Yet the history of the next six months of the Labour government is a story of retreat and defeat, a political catastrophe that saw Barbara's ideas unpicked stitch by stitch and her support ebb away, until finally only she and Harold Wilson were left. Her political career would never fully regain the heights it reached that weekend at Sunningdale.

The seeds of disaster were germinating already. Roy Hattersley, who had left Sunningdale on the Saturday night, was horrified at the direction she had taken. 'I have no philosophical objection to the imposition of more rigorous laws to control the conduct of trade unions and their members,' he wrote in a detailed minute the following week. But, he argued, employers did not use the powers they already had to enforce contracts because they soured relations, so why should the government risk it? 'If they were applied, the sanctions would dislocate the union/government relationship. If they were not applied, the government would appear ridiculous . . . sanctions could not stand any practical test. They would unite the whole union movement against the government.' He thought the government should stay out of direct involvement, and the clamour for action should be met by removing what obstacles there were preventing employers and unions from making enforcible agreements. Industry should be its own policeman. Barbara, who never quite knew what to make of Hattersley but suspected him of being in the enemy camp, was unconvinced. Hattersley had yet to learn – perhaps was not interested in learning – that to influence Barbara it was necessary to get in before the decision was taken.

Meanwhile, she was testing out her ideas. She tried the conciliation pause in the Girling dispute, by setting up a court of inquiry (a device common at the time for beleaguered employment ministers trying to find fig leaves behind which official pay policy could be decently breached) and demanding that the strikers return to work pending its findings. They refused. A helpful backbencher was primed to ask her a question in the Commons 'so I can drive home to our own people how outrageous it is that these unofficial strikers should refuse to go back to work pending the findings of my court of inquiry. In this way I hope to prepare the way for the legislation I have in mind.'[11] In parliamentary terms, there was little time left to act. Already the 1968–9 session was well advanced. There would almost certainly be only one more session – and that not a full one – before a 1970 general election. Legislation had to be on the statute book before then. Within a fortnight of the Sunningdale weekend, Harold Wilson had a draft copy of Barbara's White Paper on his desk.

Early December 1968 was another low point in the fortunes of Wilson's administration: the Tories were repeatedly challenging him to show he was not scared of the trade unions by legislating to contain them; Jenkins had had to introduce a mini-budget at the end of November, and there was no confidence that it had done enough. Another devaluation was rumoured, and on one day there was a run on sterling that wiped out £100 million of the reserves.

In this context, Wilson was probably as relieved as he was delighted to be presented with Barbara's draft White Paper and a positive course of action. 'As I said to Marcia, Barbara has not so much out-Heathed Heath as outflanked him.'[12] The White Paper was called, inoffensively, 'Partners in Progress', and it opened, 'There are necessarily conflicts of interest in industry.' All the ideas for intervention that Barbara had sketched out at Sunningdale were there, with a sweetener of extended trade union rights. Workers were to have the statutory right to belong to a trade union, legal protection against unfair dismissal, protection in relation to sympathetic strikes and the closed shop. Workers dismissed for refusing on the grounds of conscience to join a union would be entitled to compensation. She hoped, and certainly came to believe, that it was a 'charter of trade union rights', a genuine and considered attempt to strengthen trade unions so that they would be in a position to play their proper role as responsible members of the corporate state. It was an ambition astonishingly at odds with the interpretation trade unionists were likely to put on it, as Barbara herself knew.

Wilson agreed that they should take the high ground by storm. There were to be no leaks. A special committee would be set up; the cabinet gossips were to remain in ignorance. The great Wilson–Castle gamble with the future of the government was to depend on secrecy. Early in the new year, their plan would be unleashed, they believed, to startled approbation. A handful of cabinet ministers would have to be let in on the secret: Roy Jenkins, as Chancellor, was of course among them, while the law officers were beavering away trying to find a way of introducing sanctions that would not end up with trade unionists being sent to prison. But the third main player in Cabinet, Jim Callaghan, was deliberately kept in the dark – and not simply because of his tendency to gossip. Indeed, suspicion of him and his motives was so great that Barbara would not even allow her officials to consult his at the Home Office in discussions about appropriate and acceptable sanctions.

But the Wilson governments, with their constant personal and political tensions, was the leakiest in living memory. And this plan was no exception. The Chancellor's PPS, Tom Bradley, was a staunch trade unionist. Jenkins showed him Barbara's White Paper. Bradley told his mate on the *Guardian*, Ian Aitken. Aitken, one of the shrewdest of political observers as well as an old campaigner on the left of the Labour Party, immediately saw the flaws. If the Commission for Industrial Relations was to have the power to impose fines on unions that failed to observe its rulings, there would have to be sanctions for non-payment. Non-payment of fines in England and Wales, as Barbara herself was uncomfortably aware, meant imprisonment.

The gaffe was blown. The *Guardian* splashed the story on its front page on 12 December. It was followed up by every other paper, all of them adding their own snippets of information. Not only was the element of surprise now compromised, but the people whose support, or at least neutrality, was most needed were being conditioned to oppose the proposals. A damage-limitation exercise now began. On 15 December, after a meeting at Chequers, a small group of trade union general secretaries, including Frank Cousins, were briefed informally on cooling-off periods and strike ballots. These ideas were not well received. On the 19th, on the spur of the moment, Barbara decided to outline her proposals to George Woodcock, now in his final year as General Secretary of the TUC. After six years of effort, Woodcock had despaired of persuading the unions of the role the TUC might play in government if only they would cede sovereignty to the umbrella body. Barbara had taken his defeat as a green light for government action; most others would have taken it as at least a warning signal, if not a veto. Barbara was reassured by Woodcock's reaction to her proposals: 'He listened to my full résumé in silence and then, to my surprise, said that he didn't think there was anything there that need alarm the trade union movement. I could hardly believe my ears!'[13]

Barbara's cabinet colleagues, alerted by the leaks, were furious that a major departure from government policy was being planned without their knowledge. Dick Marsh, Barbara's successor at Transport and a trade unionist, rang the Cabinet Office, enraged. 'There'll be hell to pay in Cabinet,' he warned the official who took and minuted his call. On 16 December the ad hoc committee agreed that the draft White Paper should go to full Cabinet on 3 January for approval, with a view to publishing it the following week.

Barbara now lost her nerve. With the papers buzzing with guesses and partial leaks, which she felt were giving a misleading impression of her White Paper, she decided to take Woodcock's advice. She would personally brief the TUC – and, in the interests of even-handedness, the CBI – before telling Cabinet. The decision backfired disastrously. Three of the government's bitterest critics – the ex-cabinet minister Frank Cousins, his anointed successor as general secretary of the TGWU Jack Jones, and Hugh Scanlon of the Amalgamated Engineering Union – were already fired up to oppose the White Paper. Ignoring Barbara's request for secrecy, they left the meeting to brief the press on their total hostility to any government action on industrial relations. In the news lull between Christmas and the new year, a nation replete with turkey and plum pudding had plenty of time to digest the thousands of angry words. By the time Cabinet was recalled three days into 1969 to be given the first official sight of the plans, the opposition was already drawn up, banners flying. And it had a direct line into Cabinet.

Barbara's relations with Jim Callaghan had been marked by mutual dislike for most of the last twenty years. Where Barbara was an Oxford-educated ex-journalist with a middle-class background, Callaghan was a working-class ex-trade union official who had never had the opportunity to go to university. To some extent their mutual dislike was a reflection of the relationship between the intellectual and the working-class arms of the movement. But there was more to it than that. Callaghan did not rate Barbara and – as he told the *Guardian* commentator Peter Jenkins – he could not understand why she had been promoted from her position as 'a nobody, dishing out Treasury money to faraway countries, while he [Callaghan] was Chancellor . . . what is more she has no understanding of the trade unions or the nature of the Labour Party'. (There was also a fundamental difference in style; years later, Callaghan told her, 'You know, I was never really interested in politics.') He thought Barbara a neurotic conspiracy theorist; Barbara thought that wherever Callaghan was involved, her suspicions were entirely justified. After all, he had been Wilson's most threatening opponent in the leadership elections in 1963; Wilson's failings in government, it was generally assumed, could only redound to Callaghan's credit, even if devaluation had been a severe personal blow to the ex-Chancellor. By the start of 1969, Callaghan's ambitions to succeed Wilson were an open secret. Barbara and Crossman regarded themselves as Wilson's personal bodyguards, or at least the protectors of the Labour left, which they feared would be ruthlessly suppressed under a Callaghan administration. Callaghan, in a move widely seen as advancing his ambitions, had just become the party treasurer, a job which entailed close and frequent contacts with the party's main financial sponsors, the trade unions. And he had been, as an official of the Inland Revenue Staff Federation, a protégé of Douglas Houghton who in his turn was now chairman of the Parliamentary Labour Party and the main independent conduit of party mood to the Prime Minister. Houghton maintained exceptional links with the unions: he had been a member of the TUC General Council from 1952 until 1960. Callaghan and Houghton were a formidable alliance.

Barbara tried to tackle Callaghan head on. The night before the first full cabinet meeting, she met him to discuss the White Paper privately. The next day she reported, in a breakfast-time phone call to the Prime Minister recorded in the official papers, that Callaghan had warned her that he 'would oppose and argue for Donovan, in accord with moderate trade union opinion'. She suspected he had already been sounding out that opinion, and was going to take his line straight from them. According to Callaghan, 'From the moment I set eyes on it I knew that such a proposal, which ran counter to the whole history of the trade union movement and to the ethos of the Donovan Report, could not succeed. Barbara galloped ahead with all the reckless gallantry of the Light Brigade at Balaclava.' If Barbara was the Light Brigade, he was commanding the Russian guns pounding from the safety of the hills.

But that first day in Cabinet, it was not Callaghan but Dick Crossman who led the assault against the White Paper. Barbara had finally taken him into her confidence two days earlier and found him furious that he had not been part of the ministerial group in on the secret. Barbara wrote off his criticisms as pique at being excluded. In fact, whatever his motives, his attack exposed both drafting weaknesses and flaws in the White Paper's practical application. Although Barbara felt her exposition had gone well, Crossman

recorded: 'Barbara made her first mistake by speaking for forty-five minutes
. . . and as it got on towards midday it became clearer and clearer that she
wasn't all that conversant with the details of her scheme. She is able and
driving but like all the rest of us she is an amateur, quite new to trade union
law and legislation, a tremendously complex subject.'

Opposition had been anticipated: that was the justification for trying to
ambush public opinion. But there was support coming in too. A poll of
trade union backbenchers in *The Times*, ahead of the publication of the
White Paper, reported that a majority were 'unworried' by it. A wider poll
of trade unionists in the *Sunday Times* also found support for intervention
among rank-and-file union members, while letters of support from private
individuals flooded in. Christina Foyle, notoriously hostile to union membership for her own employees at her eponymous bookshop in Charing
Cross Road in London, wrote Barbara a fan letter: 'You always carry on
courageously and manage to remain beautiful into the bargain.' The *Economist*, often the government's sternest critic but at the same time no friend
of the unions, put Barbara on the cover and declared that her ideas (still
not published) were 'some steps towards the right policy'. Encouragingly, it
came to the very conclusion Wilson most wanted to read. 'The fact that
[the government] has proffered them [industrial relations legislation] is a
heartening sign for the New Year that this bruised, battered, bulldozed
Labour ministry still has the courage to try to do some innovating work in
the national interest.'

Praise from such quarters if anything exacerbated the anxiety of Barbara's
cabinet colleagues. In the new cabinet committee that she had been forced
to accept to look at the detail of the White Paper, she was fighting line for
line with Crossman and now also with another close political friend, Judith
Hart, the Paymaster General; while from around the corner at the Labour
Party headquarters in Transport House, worrying rumours were heard of
threatened resignations, with Callaghan at the centre of it all. But it was
Crossman's opposition that was most public and, since he was Barbara's
closest ally in Cabinet, the most wounding. He had too many good friends
in the press and was too fond of gossip ever to have been an entirely reliable
confidant, and when he had a grievance it inevitably found its way into the
public eye. Soon the *Guardian* was reporting his hostility to the White Paper
and his success in checking Barbara's 'indecent haste', while the *New
Statesman* ran a long attack on Wilson for abandoning cabinet government
and taking major decisions in small cliques – unmistakably the result of a
session with Crossman.

It is not uncommon for a government to use the hostility of its natural supporters as a kind of virility symbol, proof that it is operating in the national rather than the sectional interest. Wilson was gambling on a massive popular response which would leave the union leadership isolated and biddable. But Barbara wanted to play a slightly different game. She was convinced that her proposals could be sold over the heads of their leaders to the ordinary trade union members. If Barbara captured their support, their leaders would be forced into line by the power of democracy. Debate on the draft White Paper became a battle over who best understood the man and woman on the shop-floor 'the keeper of the cloth cap', in Peter Jenkins's memorable phrase. On 15 January 1969, after a week spent in bitter wrangling with some of her closest political friends over the value of her proposals – even in the final full Cabinet there was a row over whether any recent 'unconstitutional' dispute would have been affected by the planned conciliation pause (it concluded that it would not) – the draft was finally approved for publication. That night, in an uncharacteristically bitter entry, Barbara wrote in her diary that she was sure she would succeed. 'I hope so! I do want to make Dick and Judith eat dirt. Their assumption of superior concern for rank and file feeling has been almost more than I could bear. I have a hunch that I can carry people with me on this and I only hope that proves true.'[14]

It was in that frame of mind that the title for the White Paper was finally approved. Barbara, more aware than ever of the importance of image, had been wrestling with ideas for weeks. It was only at the final drafting meeting with officials in her office, on the eve of publication, that the clinching phone call came. It was from Ted, languishing in hospital after undergoing tests on his heart. Barbara went back to her desk to take the call. 'Yes!' her officials heard her shout. 'Ted's done it!' she cried as she returned to her seat. 'In Place of Strife!' The echo of Aneurin Bevan's testament *In Place of Fear* was exactly what she wanted, a way to keep the banner of her left-wing convictions flying over a document which, even though one civil servant warned that it 'read like a WEA lecture',[15] she now feared would alienate all her oldest political friends.[16]

Any calm assessment would have confirmed her doubts. Even Barbara, described by Crossman as 'very cross' after a *Guardian* leak about the effectiveness of his opposition to her proposals, and exhausted by the constant drafting and redrafting which filled her evenings and weekends, had her moments of anguish. 'Of course I am swept with doubt from time to time as to whether I have entirely misjudged reactions. If I have I shall have mortally damaged my political career.' Her Permanent Secretary tried to reassure her: ' "You've made history," Denis Barnes said to me. "It would be I who first shackled the unions," I replied gloomily. "You know that isn't true, Barbara," he replied. "Three years ago I decided we could either sit back and let the trade union movement disintegrate or we could take it in hand. I am absolutely sure our proposals are right." '[17]

Wilson was also being given urgent warnings by his own officials. The Cabinet Secretary himself, Burke Trend, anticipating the demand to speed up the timetable for legislation, minuted his advice against rushing a bill through (pointing to the difficult experience of Barbara's last bill, on transport). Wilson's junior economic adviser, Andrew Graham, another Oxford economist, set down his anxiety about the role the industrial relations policy was intended to fulfil, warning that it could not be taken as a substitute for an incomes policy. Using an argument that came to haunt the public debate, he questioned the impact of strikes on output. Of five billion days worked each year, no more than five million were lost through strikes. Even if that was trebled to account for knock-on damage, the impact on productivity was tiny – and the White Paper was neither expected nor intended to stop many strikes. Yet legislating on it would make legislating again on prices and incomes politically impossible.

But most damagingly, in order to persuade the Crossman–Hart alliance to accept the inclusion of the conciliation pause (which they thought meaningless and likely to be interpreted as a back-door pay freeze) it had been agreed that a lifeline should be thrown to the TUC. A form of words was to be inserted that would open the prospect of negotiation, if the unions could come up with a satisfactory alternative. The original strategy of blitzkrieg was dead. The prospect was no longer of a swift bounce, but of a prolonged dialogue with a virtually implacable foe. Moreover, Barbara herself accelerated the retirement of the intellectual, ineffective George Woodcock from the leadership of the TUC so that he could head her Commission on Industrial Relations – clearing the way for the TUC to be led by a man who disliked her intensely.

Vic Feather, the Rupert Brooke lookalike of her youth, had risen through the back rooms of the TUC. He had been Woodcock's deputy for nine years, responsible for negotiations with the 'Ministry of Labour'. Some dismissed him as a bureaucrat, but as an eighteen-year-old he had been on the front line in the General Strike in Bradford. It was an open secret among industrial correspondents[18] and even Barbara's own officials[19] that he hated her with a vehemence that went far beyond the irritation she regularly caused. To Bernard Ingham over lunch one day he dismissed her thus: 'I knew that girl when she had dirty knickers.' Feather became acting TUC General Secretary in March 1969; in succeeding George Woodcock he was determined to impose his own identity on the organization for which he had worked for more than thirty years. He was ready to fix, but he was unlikely to make major concessions. This was the figure with whom Barbara now had to find some kind of compromise.

On 17 January, the White Paper was published. The initial enthusiasm in the press – notorious for its own lamentable industrial relations – now cooled. The *Guardian* was always opposed, while even the *Daily Mirror* thought that with the scope she had built in for ministerial intervention Barbara was taking too much power when she should have left it to employers and workers to make contracts that stuck. From the *Mirror* to the *Financial Times* the view was that she should have kept politics out of it. The *Guardian* accused her of paternalism when '[w]hat British labour relations need, above all, is more muscle and courage among trade union leaders and employers'. Barbara herself now came under the strongest personal attack that she had endured in her entire cabinet career. Alan Watkins, often critical in his *New Statesman* column, told her over a lunch which she had hoped would improve their relationship that he didn't like her, 'because you are a button pusher. Button pushers are dangerous people.' Elsewhere, she was accused of 'staging a performance of Elizabethan power and rage. She pleads, cajoles, flatters and swears roundly; at the finale hot tears explode from her like fireworks'.[20] She was also accused of exploiting her closeness to the Prime Minister,[21] described sneeringly as 'one of her more effective devices', and of overweening self-confidence: 'Her belief in her own powers of persuasion is almost unlimited.'[22] One of the briefers was her own Permanent Secretary, who would walk his friends in the press corps round the gardens of St James's Square, hidden by the plane trees from the windows of the department at No. 8. Not surprisingly, the stories rattled her, and she couldn't hide her discomfiture from everyone. After her first, thinly attended, meeting with trade union MPs on 'In Place of Strife', Charles Pannell, an old colleague, wrote reassuringly to her: 'Your performance was impeccable and afterwards you said to me that you wanted someone to love you. Many do.'

Maybe they did. But that did not stop opposition crystallizing against the proposals as the PLP got together again at the end of January. The combination of the Tribunite left, the trade union right and the trade-union-sponsored MPs added up to a majority against her proposals. Trade union sponsorship was a powerful factor, having often secured the member's constituency for him or, occasionally, her through the system of gathering nominations, it also paid for most or all of their constituency expenses and sometimes ran to office support at Westminster. Meanwhile it was reported

that Callaghan, as party treasurer, had suggested to the unions that he might
be able to get the White Paper toned down if they would raise from a
shilling to 1s 6d the fee they paid for each member affiliated to the Labour
Party. (The number of members decided the union's voting strength in
Labour Party affairs.)

Other tentacles of political reality were gaining a hold on the White
Paper. With the connection between industrial relations and the prices and
incomes policy never clearly analysed, the two were becoming entangled
despite Barbara's efforts to pretend they were only distantly related. As
predicted by the Prime Minister's office, further legislation prolonging the
statutory controls on prices and incomes was now considered impossible. But
the Chancellor, receiving regular visits from an International Monetary Fund
anxious to see where its latest loan was going, needed a gesture of serious
intent towards the containment of wage inflation. In February 1969, the
threat of economic meltdown seemed sufficiently real for the inner cabinet
to discuss 'Hecuba', a plan to float the pound and introduce more draconian
deflation than any so far seen. As Crossman had predicted, Jenkins was
pushing hard for a quick 'interim' bill that would introduce interventionist
powers and replace the discredited statutory incomes policy; a more considered piece of legislation including measures to strengthen the unions could
follow in the next session. Barbara resisted. She wanted her White Paper to
be seen as a whole; removing the penal sanctions for separate legislation
would reduce her to a quasi-Tory union-basher and give the unions an
entirely genuine reason to unite against her.

Barbara's greatest asset against her critics was the continuing industrial
chaos. The public – including union members – wanted the unions to be
made to behave. What was much harder – as a seminal dispute in February
and March 1969 illustrated – was to find out how to do this. Early in 1969,
the Ford Motor Company had struck a pioneering no-strike deal: any breach
would be penalized by the withdrawal of the enhanced benefits – a whacking
7–10 per cent pay increase, an increased holiday bonus and a guaranteed
week whatever the supply difficulties caused by disputes elsewhere – which
were the sweetener for the deal. The negotiators from the fifteen unions
recognized by Ford accepted the terms. But the shop stewards in the vast
majority of the company's plants promptly rejected them; the shop stewards
were not going to give up their most powerful weapon, the unofficial strike.
The two unions who between them represented nearly three-quarters of
Ford's workforce were the Transport Workers and the Amalgamated Engineering Union. Both formally recognized their members' initially unofficial
strikes. The Ford management took the unions to court, arguing that a

legally enforceable agreement had been breached. The judge decided that the parties had not intended to make a legally enforceable agreement, and threw the action out.

However, the unions, the eventual victors, had refused to recognize the court's initial award of an interim injunction to Ford. Not only had the strike continued, it had spread, the workers entirely ignoring the court's ruling. The judge himself, Mr Justice Geoffrey Lane, said he thought the negotiating table rather than a court room was the place to resolve such matters. The TUC's evidence to the Donovan Commission – that there was no room for a third party in pay negotiations – seemed proven. At the same time, the shop stewards insisted that their real complaint was against the idea of applying sanctions to everyone even if the agreement was breached only by a few. Yet, when Barbara herself did intervene – successfully – to spur the two sides towards an agreement, she came away with the impression that both Hugh Scanlon and Jack Jones were prepared to accept the principle of 'collective sanctions'.

Meanwhile, at Vauxhall's Ellesmere Port factory a strike by just ten platers had led to eleven thousand workers being laid off at Luton. The situation deteriorated quickly and affected the mood in the Commons. While on 3 March a devastating ninety-three Labour backbenchers voted against or abstained at the end of the debate on 'In Place of Strife' – the biggest revolt since Chamberlain was destroyed in 1940 – less than ten days later, after a statement on the continuing Ford dispute with the unions involved publicly at odds with each other, Roy Hattersley turned to Barbara and said, 'We could get the penal clauses through the House today.' It was a fleeting moment.

On 26 March, at the monthly meeting of the Labour Party National Executive, Joe Gormley of the National Union of Mineworkers tabled a resolution rejecting 'any legislation' based on the proposals in the White Paper. Callaghan moved an amendment which merely proposed dropping the word 'any', thereby destroying all chance of support for Barbara's own anodyne alternative calling for continuing consultations. Callaghan's amendment was duly carried and the next morning's papers reported a serious snub to Barbara's plans. It was the first time since 1964 that the NEC had rejected government policy. She was furious. Wilson, just off to Nigeria on an abortive mission to try to end the Biafran war, promised her he would deal with Callaghan on his return. But in his absence, the story of what was instantly interpreted as a leadership bid by Callaghan leapt into the headlines. Increasingly anxious telegrams criss-crossed between Wilson, in Lagos and then Addis Ababa, and No. 10. First, Wilson to his office at home: 'It's being reported here that Callaghan has done a Ray and George [i.e. leaked a self-justifying account of the incident to the press] . . . please give us facts.' In response, No. 10 sent long quotes from that week's *Economist*: 'Mr Callaghan is now very plainly the leader of the internal opposition in the government . . . he is back at the centre of the party stage from which devaluation had removed him . . . if Mr Wilson and Mrs Castle falter now, they will be inviting Mr Callaghan's friends to take over the government.' Wilson responded from Addis Ababa to the Lord President, Fred Peart: 'Am watching Callaghan situation carefully. As you know I will take firm action on my return . . . essential that you watch what [Douglas] Houghton does. Essential that no party meeting on party situation takes place in my absence.' This provoked a response from Marcia Williams, his closest Downing Street aide: 'This is a challenge . . . my strong view is that you should return overnight so that you can spend Wednesday at Westminster and be seen to be back in charge again . . . Your enemies are, as you know, easy to handle, but God save you from the rest.' To Barbara's frustration, though, when Wilson returned he entirely failed to reprimand Callaghan in Cabinet; and although lobby journalists were briefed that a severe dressing-down had been delivered, which achieved something of the same effect, it was at the expense of reinforcing Wilson's reputation for pusillanimity among his cabinet colleagues. In fact it was Crossman who had attacked, to which Callaghan retorted that he had done nothing wrong since no legislation had been agreed; he was within his rights when he had voted against it at the NEC. Wilson, rather feebly in the view of Barbara's supporters Crossman and Jenkins, merely reminded Callaghan that the Cabinet was collectively committed to the White Paper.

The episode, however, had finally convinced Barbara that she must accept Jenkins's proposal for an interim bill, to be announced in the budget at the same time as the abandonment of further prices and incomes legislation. Callaghan must not be given any more scope to establish himself as the next leader of the Labour Party, touting his conscience round the union conferences all summer long while industrial anarchy spread. Barbara concluded that a showdown with the Home Secretary was inevitable, 'Otherwise, Jim will de facto have become the government.' If it forced Callaghan's resignation, she and Wilson decided, it was a risk they would have to take.

The plan for early legislation had the additional merit of bringing Crossman back into close alliance, especially after Barbara appeared to concede that she should forgo the power to order a strike ballot in certain circumstances. Crossman had always argued that if there was to be a bill at all, it must be soon. During the Commons Easter recess in early April, he, Jenkins and Barbara had dinner together to discuss tactics at the Chancellor's house at East Hendred in Oxfordshire. The evening gave Barbara a particularly satisfying opportunity to pronounce on the domestic arrangements of a man she always suspected of patronizing her. Having commented unfavourably on the aspect of the garden (overlooked by other houses), she continued in her diary: 'Supper was a very domesticated affair ... I wasn't surprised that Roy has a taste for expensive meals out in restaurants.'[23] (The criticism rankled enough for Jenkins to repeat it in his own memoirs.)

The TUC now locked eyeballs with the government. On 10 April, four days before the budget and the announcement of an interim industrial relations bill, Vic Feather tried to head it off by suggesting a tripartite agreement between the TUC, the CBI and the government to deal with unofficial strikes (of which there were five reported in that morning's papers). The following day, Barbara and Wilson met the TUC in Downing Street. To Barbara's annoyance, Wilson offered an apparently relaxed timetable for consultation on an alternative to a bill, as the unions declared their total opposition to all the government proposals and muttered barely veiled threats about the future of their financial relationship with the Labour Party. She sent Wilson a note warning: 'I'm afraid you've left [the TUC] with the impression there is a lot of time for consulting them on an "alternative". Are you going to reply to Vic's point that they are opposed to acceleration of legislation?' Wilson responded evasively: 'I was holding that back.'[24] His failure to warn them of the interim legislation would be the cause of much anger.

The weakness in the TUC's position was already evident. In order to substitute for some external force – the CIR – as an industrial relations policeman, it would have to enhance its own powers. But those powers came from its constituent trade unions and there was no evidence that the biggest and strongest – once again, the engineers and the transport workers – would view demands for restraint coming from the TUC any more kindly than from some government agency. In the weeks of painful negotiation that followed and as Wilson staked more and more of his government's credibility on the issue, Vic Feather had to balance trying to head off legislation, as his members insisted he did, with the need to offer enough to the government to cover its embarrassment and keep it in power.

On 14 April, the eve of the budget and of the Chancellor's announcement of an interim bill, Barbara joined Wilson and Feather for a dinner of sandwiches at No. 10. Barbara (like others of Wilson's Cabinet) never enjoyed these prolonged evening sessions where, over brandy and cigars, the

Prime Minister would expand into broad conversational generalities. That night Wilson warned Feather that the bill was coming. 'He didn't bridle or declaim,' Barbara noted in her diary, 'How far [Feather] is genuinely unalarmed . . . I cannot tell. I only know that in public he will trounce them [her proposals] vigorously.'[25]

Two days later, she had to spell out the details of her bill in the biggest parliamentary occasion of her career to date. Barbara hated speaking in the Commons as a minister. She disliked writing out speeches, which she thought should be more spontaneous and responsive to the mood of her audience than her officials were prepared to tolerate. But she took the task with deadly seriousness – too seriously, in the eyes of observers like her PPS John Fraser, who felt that she overprepared, even recording sections of the speech and then listening back to them.

That day, she struggled. The speech was even more honed than usual. (Wilson had insisted he have a look at it and had made a few suggestions. It was, he said, 'the most important speech ever made in parliament by a woman'.) And Barbara was also having to respond to the Tories' new golden boy Iain MacLeod.[26] Against the jeers of the opposition and the sullen, silent Labour members behind her she tried to convince her audience that the state wasn't interested in sending trade unionists to prison but in alerting the conscience of every trade unionist to the damage his actions might do to his fellow trade unionists elsewhere. 'Our major proposals,' she pleaded, 'are conceived in no vindictive spirit, but in a spirit of faith.' Those proposals had now been reduced to two. Strike ballots – which Barbara had believed would reconnect rank and file with the leadership – had at the last minute been abandoned to give unions a chance to put them into their own rules, but the Employment Secretary would have power to enforce a CIR finding in inter-union disputes and would be able to order a twenty-eight-day conciliation pause in unconstitutional stoppages and a return to the status quo while negotiations continued. But her attempt to sound conciliatory about sanctions merely made her sound confused. Confrontation, however she phrased her proposals, was unavoidable.

The following night, 17 April, the Prime Minister, who had been cautious about the idea of a 'short' bill, suddenly decided to stake his now almost non-existent credibility on it. He told the weekly party meeting: 'The bill we are discussing is an essential bill, essential to our economic recovery. Essential to the balance of payments. Essential to full employment . . . I have to tell you that the passage of this bill is essential to [this government's] continuance in office.' Later, he was to claim that he also said the alternative was for the TUC to make its own urgent and effective proposals. But no one reported that at the time. Instead, two signals were sent out: first, that the government would go to the country if it did not get its legislation through the House, and second, that the trade unions were the cause of Britain's economic crisis. When she heard this, Barbara was appalled. She felt the PLP was being bludgeoned into support when 'they had a perfect right to reject my bill'. It was a hostage to fortune that came back with a vengeance; a serious misjudgement, and an ill omen for the conduct of the negotiations to come.

In that week's *Tribune* Michael Foot wrote one of his most celebrated invectives. Under the headline 'The Maddest Scene in Modern History' he wrote: 'An hysterical press campaign, whipped up by ministerial and prime ministerial leakages, clamours for a Labour government to drink the poison that could kill it.' He ended on a biblical note resonant with his Methodist background. 'A Labour government . . . must show that it looks to the rock whence it was hewn and the pit whence it was dug.' The article consummated the alliance between the left and the trade union centre of the party, and to all but the most optimistic suggested the virtual impossibility of getting any industrial relations legislation through the Commons and on to the statute book.

Barbara at once set out to test her belief that she could sell her reforms over the heads of the trade union leaders to ordinary members. Her first stop, on 17 April (the night Wilson addressed his MPs), was the Scottish TUC conference in Dunoon. For all her bravado, she was not at all confident of success. The Scots had the reputation of being the toughest audience in Britain; two days earlier, John Newton, the STUC president, had accused the Prime Minister of being untrustworthy, 'more concerned with provocative political propaganda than sober consultation'. Newspapers warned Barbara of personal hostility and possibly even a walk-out by the crew of the ferry carrying her over to Dunoon. Instead, wearing her 'true colours', a favourite red dress, she scored a resounding personal success, finding herself affectionately mobbed by the ferry's crew and cheered warmly by at least half of the audience at the conference. The *Sun* described her 'employing her full armoury', sometimes 'wheedling and girlish' but with moments when 'she turned sideways on to the audience and stuck out a straight left in the manner of a prize fighter . . . people listened attentively and she will be remembered afterwards with affection.' But, it added, 'There is no evidence that anyone was persuaded to change sides.'

The following day she visited the Rootes car plant at Linwood and was cheered again, especially after she staged another of her publicity coups, departing from the official walkabout to talk to the crowds of shop-floor workers looking on. She gave one a kiss. It was a photographer's dream and they all had the shot; it – and she – got the kind of coverage no politician had ever enjoyed before, and rarely since. The press might think the substance of the bill was thin, but they decided Barbara was brilliant.

The *Financial Times* declared her star of the week. Their political correspondent David Watt, who had written harshly of her in the recent past, now declared his conversion. 'She has the kind of star quality given only to a tiny handful of entertainers in any generation – and to almost no politicians – that of making the crowd lean forward in their seats when she steps onto the stage.' He could not quite allow himself unrestrained enthusiasm: 'We can see that she is courageous, opportunistic, intelligent, self-deceiving, emotional, calculating, principled and ambitious. But we never know . . . which quality is going to win.'

At Westminster, however, the political barometer was dropping fast. Another back-bench survey by the *Sunday Times* revealed that a majority of the MPs questioned opposed the legislation, while a significant minority were prepared to tell pollsters they wanted Wilson himself to go. Once again the party seemed poised on the brink of self-destruction: Callaghan was in alliance with the Tribunite left (an alliance that was to prove enduring), while Roy Jenkins's supporters, the young Turks who later formed the nucleus of the Social Democratic Party, plotted to decouple their leader from the bill. There was nothing, it seemed, to keep Wilson in power except a desire among MPs for self-preservation. Crossman, whose own bill to reform parliament had been withdrawn after meeting insurmountable opposition, dictated a jaundiced but fundamentally accurate account of the state of play to his diary on Sunday 20 April. Barbara's speech in the Commons had been disastrous; abandoning the strike ballot had made her look weak, he claimed (unkindly, since it was a concession for which he had argued), and confused. 'She had apparently produced an appallingly governessy speech . . . when she got to her own proposals on the Industrial Relations Bill she was flaccid and uncertain of what she meant.'[27] Reflecting with the irritated impatience of a man for once not on the inside track, he condemned the way Barbara and Wilson appeared to be sending out inaccurate reports of what had actually been decided at the negotiating sessions.

> There is no inner coherence and we are blundering ahead with Barbara and the Prime Minister just as much a two-man show as ever they were. They launched this thing in December, pushed it through Cabinet by extremely unscrupulous means in January . . . decided to go ahead on the long term plan and then, when it failed, as we predicted it would because they

couldn't sustain consultations, we put on a short term plan. Now we have
agreed on this, we haven't any inner body to plan exactly how to put it
through and what will be the form of our discussions with the trade unions,
the NEC and the Parliamentary Party. It now sticks out a mile that we are
having a quarrel on a phoney issue. If only we were tackling the real
problem of how to bring the trade unions within the law. Instead, as I
predicted last January, we are having a gratuitous head-on collision with
them.[28]

Wilson, watching Callaghan's manoeuvres anxiously out of the corner of
his eye, resolved, once again, to offer the party the smack of firm government. Without consulting Barbara, even though they had only that morning
discussed the matter, on 29 April he replaced her friend, the relaxed
disciplinarian John Silkin, as Chief Whip with the hammer of the left, the
Transport and General Workers-sponsored Bob Mellish.[29] Barbara was devastated. Already shaken by the opposition of her friends, she saw Mellish as
one of her old enemies and his appointment as a move to revive the bullying
tactics used against the Bevanites in the 1950s, in order to get her legislation
through. She dashed off a letter, steaming with rage, although not without
keeping a hand-copied version of it for her own reference. As in all the best
rows, she ranged beyond the immediate cause of dispute.

> Dear Harold, Nothing that has happened in 4½ years has made me as angry
> as this. To me it is inconceivable that a Prime Minister should call on a
> colleague to pilot the most controversial Bill of our whole Parliament
> through the House and then switch Parliamentary pilots in the middle of it
> without even telling her. I still simply cannot believe that you knew what
> you knew this morning and had not the courtesy to take me into your
> confidence. This is indeed the 'manner of government' of which others[30]
> have complained. I must warn you that faith can never be the same again
> and that if the strategy is to railroad my Bill through Parliament on a
> Healey-type regime of reactionary discipline, I will have no part of it.
> Yours, Barbara.

To Crossman, and later in her diary, she was even more vituperative. 'I
am through with Harold now,' she raged, like a betrayed mistress, as if the
experience of his duplicity at first hand had at last caused the scales to fall
from her eyes. Despite her genuine fury, events now became farcical, with
Barbara storming home and retiring to bed, leaving Ted to tell Downing
Street − frantically searching for her by now − that he didn't know where
she was. It must have looked like resignation; but the following morning

they made up. Wilson tried to persuade her that he had moved Silkin only because the 'middle-of-the-road' backbenchers had lost faith in him, and without their support, there was no chance at all of getting the bill through. Barbara, slightly appeased, went out and bought 'three new frocks' to steady her morale before triumphantly taking on the PLP. Harold Wilson's later account of her contribution suggests an enduring gratitude for her capitulation. 'The day was Barbara Castle's. In her most impassioned manner she replied to the debate, almost every sentence being cheered . . . in all my years of party meetings I have never seen an ovation such as she received; the applause went on and on and she had to rise to her feet to acknowledge it.'[31] Barbara doubted the extent of her triumph. 'I have developed an odd capacity for making a lot of my failures (they seem natural) while I suspect the validity of my successes.'

She was right. The ovation for her performance made no difference to the backbenchers' hostility to her proposals. However powerful the arguments on an emotional level, they thought the bill was not worth the risk to the traditional link with the unions; and on a practical level, they knew the likely cost in seats of fighting an election without union money and union organization. Barbara – like many backbenchers – was also picking up danger signals from her normally quiescent constituency. Some Blackburn trade unions and party activists were furious with her plans and it was only loyal constituency officers who held off critical motions. Once, she only escaped censure by eight votes. However, a flying trip to address a thousand party members and trade unionists at a meeting in the town hall soothed local anger. 'She was such a commanding personality, they did not really want to be cross with her,' one local journalist, Eric Lever of the *Lancashire Evening Telegraph*, thought. But she was determined to believe that her strategy was working and that, as long as she carried on the argument, she would make converts.

With each day, the stakes mounted. The new Chief Whip repeated that if the Industrial Relations Bill fell there would be a general election. The message was clear. The polls, showing Wilson the most unpopular Prime Minister since Chamberlain, left none in doubt that an election would mean the dole for dozens – perhaps a hundred – Labour MPs. As a hundred thousand trade unionists marched through central London on May Day in protest, the newspapers were full of reports of revolt on the back benches and of a 'Wilson Must Go' campaign approaching a climax. Barbara joined the backlash in defence of her patron. In a speech in Newcastle on 5 May, she warned that no current member of the Cabinet could serve under any other Prime Minister. The whole government was committed to the Industrial Relations Bill. But she reiterated her determination to win the argument rather than resort to force. 'I personally would reject any attempt to railroad the IR Bill through Parliament by threats of expulsion or "clobbering the left". This is an immensely important issue to our Movement – rightly or wrongly a matter of conscience to many people. I think wrongly: my conscience is clear.'[32] Her friend Joan Lestor, a newly elected MP, wrote an anguished letter to her: 'However down you may feel on the reaction to the white paper, it is not a personal opposition and your personal standing is still high. But the sheer misery and dismay with the rank and file here and in the country cannot be overestimated.'[33]

The appointment of Mellish as Chief Whip, instead of appeasing Wilson's critics, succeeded only in providing them with another target. At the start of the second week of May, PLP chairman Douglas Houghton told a meeting of backbenchers that it was 'neither necessary nor desirable' to force the bill through and that nothing it might do for industrial relations would 'redeem the harm we can do to our movement and to the nation by the disintegration or defeat of the Labour Party'. Wilson was furious. He believed Houghton's objective was to prepare the ground for Callaghan to emerge as the leader of the middle ground, the sensible centre, of the PLP, and he declared the remarks 'unconstitutional' at the following day's Cabinet. Crossman again rounded on Callaghan directly, accusing him of spreading defeatism, and bluntly telling him to get out. Wilson had to intervene to get Callaghan to stay.

At a meeting of the National Executive the next day, Barbara herself launched an attack on the Home Secretary, scorning his view that it was a Labour government's job to 'make trade unions popular'. 'I told him he ought to be ashamed of himself. Our job was to build up the strength, authority and status of the trade union movement so that it could make itself popular.' Briefly, she was able to bask in the approbation of her friends. And though the next day, in this extraordinary semi-public battle for authority within the party, the press came out in favour of cool, calm 'Uncle Jim' Callaghan, who had triggered Barbara's attack by dissociating himself from her policy, Barbara somehow reassured herself that her bill had in fact become the focus of a wider discontent, against the government and its economic policies as a whole. Angrily, she rounded on one of the rebel leaders, her oldest political friend, Michael Foot. 'I told [him] flatly that he had grown fat on a diet of soft options because he had never had to choose.' Callaghan was sacked from the newly established inner cabinet; there was now no union voice in it. Jenkins, Healey, Castle, Crossman and Wilson, who had all progressed smoothly from Oxford to Westminster, together with

Fred Peart (Durham University), took on the trade union movement. Callaghan became the movement's representative in the government; to oppose the plans for legislation was to support Callaghan.

For all her bravado, Barbara had allowed herself to become hopelessly trapped between the commitment to the legislation given by the Prime Minister, backed by the threats of the new Chief Whip, and the trade union movement, who had captured the determined support of the PLP. The unions had two options, and they ran them both. They egged on the rebels in the parliamentary party, and they prepared to make concessions just large enough to make it hard for the government to reject them.

The TUC had called a special congress for 5 June to consider its own alternative to legislation, its 'Programme for Action'. Publication of the bill, being drafted and redrafted, was put off and the 'Programme for Action' became the focus for negotiation, with Vic Feather playing the mediator between his diehards – Jack Jones and Hugh Scanlon – and Wilson, usually late at night over brandy in Downing Street. There was no doubt in anyone's mind that once the TUC had agreed the proposals to be put to the special congress, it would be all but impossible to get further concessions. There was also an open channel between the TUC and senior officials at the Department of Employment. It was by this route that, on 9 May, Vic Feather quietly slipped the government an advance copy of the 'Programme'. It offered two areas of movement, both of which addressed the current concerns caused by the British Steel and Ford disputes. On one, inter-union disputes – both those of recognition and the notorious 'who-does-what' disputes – the TUC was prepared to intervene more aggressively. Officials were dismissive. To make this stick with the wider public who had been promised the strong arm of the law, there had to be sanctions to make sure that unions would toe the TUC line. The TUC's sanctions processes 'are almost too cumbersome to be credible', one official noted in his advice on the draft.[34] But this was a significant move, and although it was still the subject of some manoeuvring, it effectively removed that area of dispute from negotiations.

The TUC was also prepared to condemn strikes which began before the disputes procedure had been exhausted, or which the union leadership would not endorse – unconstitutional or unofficial strikes – and to insist that unions affiliated to the TUC should 'take action to ensure that the workpeople return to work while discussions take place'. For a body like the TUC, whose existence depended on the consent of the great union barons who jealously protected their autonomy, this was another significant move. But it, too, would be hard to sell to the public when some unions did not even have the powers to make their members return to work, let alone the will to use those powers. At dinner on the 9th Barbara and Feather fought bitterly over the TUC's willingness to make members obey its edicts.

On 12 May, the draft of the TUC's 'Programme for Action' was formally discussed. Before the meeting with Wilson and the TUC, Barbara flew up to Southport to evangelize at the National Union of Public Employees' conference. The *Guardian* described her, wearing a barrister's black dress with white lace at the collar, as making 'the most emotional speech of her political career' as she told delegates that trade unionism was about to take 'one of the biggest leaps forward in its whole history'. She was back in time to make an entrance at the Downing Street talks, but if she was hoping for the leap to happen that day, she was disappointed. As the talks – which had to include the entire thirty-strong General Council in order to involve Jack Jones and Hugh Scanlon,[35] the only two who mattered – ground on, Wilson passed Barbara a note: 'I do not think they're going to give us a viable alternative . . . But every hour that goes past strengthens our hands versus the PLP. We shall be able to show how we tried & how at the end of the day they couldn't deliver. Also, what the point was where they failed. This shd shift enough of our people, I hope. [signed] HW'.

It was another misjudgement.

14. The Battle of Downing Street

Barbara Castle was surely correct in believing that a more con‐
structive relationship between unions and a Labour government, a
changed balance of rights and responsibilities, was necessary for the
successful achievement of Social Democracy.

Peter Jenkins, *The Battle of Downing Street*[1]

At the start of what came to be called 'the Battle of Downing Street',
Barbara's officials had warned her that legislation would be impossible
without two key elements: the backing of the Prime Minister and the
acquiescence of the General Secretary of the TUC. Although he frequently
hijacked negotiations, Wilson remained loyal to the cause to the bitter end.
The TUC General Secretary George Woodcock had also accepted that some
kind of legislation was inevitable. But his successor, Vic Feather, made no
such commitment. Even if he had wanted to, he could not have delivered
on it without the agreement of Jack Jones and Hugh Scanlon. Agreement
was not available.

Between them, Jones and Scanlon had nearly three million members and
were expanding aggressively. Altogether, as a recent vote on Woodcock's
ideas for a voluntary incomes policy had shown,[2] the TUC was now almost
evenly divided between radical and conservative tendencies. Jones and
Scanlon, rivals in many a pay negotiation, shared a disenchantment with the
cosy relationship between the TUC and government and between some
union leaders and government, which had slowly developed since the war.
They were both men from the shop-floor who had done time as shop
stewards, and who brought to the challenge of derailing Barbara's plans for
industrial relations legislation the shop steward's negotiating techniques of
exploiting weakness and ratcheting up the pressure. For them, the unofficial

strike might be undesirable (because it challenged the authority of the leadership), but it was effective in the perpetual battle with employers. This was a view indirectly confirmed by the CBI, who told Barbara that the real problem with unofficial strikes was not the number of days lost but the 'wrong decisions forced on management'.[3] The unions' strongest weapon was the ability of their shop stewards to call out a group of workers or a whole plant in the heat of the moment on account of, say, a dismissal, or an unpopular change in working practices. Cooling-off periods and pre-strike ballots were anathema to union leaders, whose success depended on mobilizing their members at the moment of maximum commitment. Any constraint on union power weakened them in their fundamental purpose, the improvement of their members' pay and conditions. However, in the campaign against Barbara's legislation it was not so much their own members (despite their frequent obeisances to 'democracy') that were their troops as the trade union-sponsored MPs at Westminster. And their officers on this battlefield were Jim Callaghan and Douglas Houghton.

Jack Jones distrusted not only Wilson and Barbara (whom he dismissed as academics); he also distrusted Vic Feather, whom he regarded as a product of the Co-operative movement and the TUC, not a real worker. The long evenings of brandy and cigars at No. 10 were exposing the soft underbelly of trade unionism, in Jones's view, and Wilson was prepared to take advantage by pushing ahead with his ignorant determination to curtail the rights on which trade unionists depended for the advancement of their cause. Nor, Jones thought, did any in the government know how to negotiate. Despite his own reputation for aggressive incorruptibility, he condemned the way 'once [Barbara] took a stand, she would argue like hell for it'.[4]

Jones went further. He thought the whole basis of the post-war consensus was mistaken. There was no common ground between unions and government, nor was there any obligation on unions to support Labour in office. He later claimed that Heath was a far easier man to negotiate with than Wilson, although he was happy to work with Michael Foot in the 1974–9 Labour government, for voluntary pay restraint. 'The common good isn't recognized in a capitalist society, is it?' he would demand rhetorically. At the height of the negotiations over 'In Place of Strife', Barbara, who had worked with him when she was Transport Minister and who shared much of his political outlook, took him out to dinner to try to find out what if anything would appease him. She confided in her diary: 'At times like these I feel confident that Jack is a genuine responsible social democrat.' It wasn't a view shared by officials of her such as Conrad Heron, who was in charge of conciliation in the department, or the security services who, during the Ford dispute, sent Barbara a report warning that he was 'more militant than Scanlon'; nor even the then right-wing Labour man Bernard Ingham, who cited Jones as the reason for his own total disenchantment with the union movement.

Despite Jack Jones's low opinion of Vic Feather's talents as a negotiator, by the middle of May 1969 its acting General Secretary had manoeuvred the TUC into a position of strength against the government. Barbara's bill had still not been published (although it was ready in draft), which meant that there was still scope, as far as the unions were concerned, for her to be pushed back further. Meanwhile, the TUC had persuaded its members that there would indeed be legislation unless they accepted some significant concessions – to be put to the entire membership at the special congress. It was clear that once congress had approved the TUC programme, the TUC would find it very hard indeed to move any further. The chances of the government getting legislation through the House in the face of opposition from the TUC were negligible.

To make sure of that, once the interim bill was announced Feather had consolidated a working alliance with Jim Callaghan and Douglas Houghton. The Home Secretary and the chairman of the Labour Party conspired to derail agreed cabinet policy with the acting General Secretary of the TUC in Houghton's Marsham Street flat, a short walk from the Commons. At the very least, no tears would have been shed if the by-product had been the derailing of the Prime Minister himself. To many – not only a paranoid Prime Minister – it looked like a deliberate attempt to put Callaghan into No. 10. From Marsham Street emerged a steady flow of leaks and briefings about the ebb in support for legislation among the PLP. As another part of this strategy, Feather repeatedly overpromoted the chances of a deal and presented Barbara as the hawk and Wilson the dove – a portrayal Wilson later denied, although his well-known dislike of falling out with colleagues may have genuinely persuaded Feather that he wanted to conciliate. Under-lying this presentation, though, must have been Feather's calculation that it gave Wilson the option of cutting loose from Barbara and the industrial relations legislation, and saving himself and his government.

Back-bench MPs, especially those who felt they should have been promoted, were eager to help the man they saw as the future king. Even though Barbara was deeply suspicious of, and hostile to, Callaghan and his cronies, she was still repeatedly caught out by leaks and misrepresentations of meetings she had addressed. '"The PLP is so neurotic," she moaned to Ted after one such betrayal, "that one can only govern in spite of it – not with

it." I went to bed so angry I could hardly sleep. How can a Labour government win with troops like these?'[5]

Callaghan, however, was not the only pretender to the throne. Roy
Jenkins's friends on the back benches, young intellectuals like David Marquand, the Edinburgh academic doing work experience as a Westminster
MP, were anxious that their man was going to be overtaken by events. So
was Barbara's own deputy, Roy Hattersley. On 11 May Hattersley made the
supreme sacrifice: he abandoned tickets for the Rugby League cup final at
Wembley to drive out to East Hendred to tell Jenkins he must distance
himself from the bill. (Jenkins recalled in his autobiography only that his PPS
Tom Bradley 'told me several times that the bill was the only thing standing
between me and the premiership'.[6]) Jenkins knew it was politically impossible
to distance himself from it. On the 16th, Hattersley, whom Barbara never
accused of disloyalty, showed her a letter he was going to send to Wilson. It
was a startling missive from a junior minister actively involved in trying to
unseat the Prime Minister. The letter, he wrote to Wilson, came with
Barbara's knowledge: 'I have not however asked her to comment on it as I
wanted to be able to say that although I believe I am expressing the views of
many members of the Parliamentary Labour Party I do so entirely on my
own initiative.' He then launched into a bitter attack on the whole conduct
of government policy – the tendency to oversell policies as 'vital' shortly
before abandoning them, to try to 'buy off' opposition rather than pursuing
a course on its merits – warning that there was mounting gloom about the
party's electoral prospects. On the same day, Barbara was warned by Jim
Mason, her constituency chairman, that the mood against legislation in
Blackburn – egged on, he believed, by Jones and Scanlon from London –
was becoming increasingly hostile.

Against this background, Barbara and Wilson continued to negotiate to
try to toughen up aspects of the TUC's 'Programme for Action' before its
publication on 19 May. When they didn't meet, they spoke on the phone,
often several times a day. Wilson was acutely aware of the danger of the
union side capturing public opinion and reinforcing party hostility, by
presenting changes as dramatic concessions. After another secret late night
with Vic Feather, there was a new offer of a slight strengthening of the
TUC's powers over individual unions to enforce their undertakings on their
members. Early the next morning Wilson told Barbara by phone that 'he
feared that the disadvantage of the new proposals was that although they
were still not fully effective, they would *look* so good that the government
might be criticised by many of its supporters for turning them down.'[7] He

felt the government might have to feel its way to a 'double-barrelled' system, some way of testing the TUC's promises.

On the 19th the TUC finally published its 'Programme for Action'. It proposed strengthening its existing powers to sort out inter-union disputes, making it possible for the TUC to require a union to order its members back to work. It defined and condemned strikes that were unofficial (not approved by the union leadership) or unconstitutional (embarked upon before the disputes procedure had been exhausted), and it called on unions to strengthen their own procedures so that they had effective sanctions against their members. The ancient cart-horse, as the cartoonist Low saw it, moved. The London evening papers – possibly briefed by Feather – anticipated a government climb-down and in viscerally critical leaders accused the government of handing over the country to the unions – a foretaste of the press reception of any retreat. Neither Wilson nor Barbara Castle now had any alternative but to fight on. They declared the 'Programme' an inadequate substitute for legislation.

The next day, 20 May, the inner cabinet contemplated fall-back positions. Barbara had been secretly warned that the TUC would abandon its own proposals for reform if she pressed on with penal sanctions in her bill, opening up the alarming possibility of ending up with absolutely no advance at all. With the news from her remaining friends in the PLP getting grimmer by the day, she was beginning to think in terms of giving the TUC's ideas time to fail. That could be done either by threatening legislation at a later date, or (as Wilson and Roy Jenkins preferred) by introducing legislation now but not bringing it into force. It was a desperate measure and would produce the merest fig leaf of decency to place over what would amount to capitulation, but the inner cabinet clung to it as a possibility. All too aware that they were not up to the task, Barbara tried to rouse them. 'We mustn't forget we have some powerful cards to play too. [The unions] certainly don't want an election and a Tory government. But we may take us all over the brink . . . it is a risk we must run if we are not to destroy the total credibility of the Government.'

The following day there was yet another fruitless meeting with the TUC, whose position had been strengthened by the timely revelation that their 'Programme for Action' had been unanimously accepted by all the hundred trade-union-sponsored MPs. The threat to withdraw its own reforms if the government pressed on with legislation was made explicit. Wilson retaliated by playing what he thought would be his trump card. He warned the union leaders, as Barbara herself had warned the inner cabinet, that they were about to bring the government down and split the Labour movement. But it made no impression (although Barbara would always argue that this was what 'won the day' for the agreement that ultimately followed). Later, following secret contacts with the TUC, Barbara's officials warned her that there would be no further movement on the part of the unions; their recommendation was to keep up the appearance of negotiation to avoid 'the need for a definitive assessment at this stage of the TUC's Programme [for Action] and a definite statement of the implications for the government's proposals for legislation'.[8]

Later, Wilson revealed to Barbara his personal fall-back position. At his most relaxed, the 'cheeky chappie' declared that he would make the legislation an issue of confidence not in the government (triggering an unwinnable election) but in himself, personally. If the legislation was defeated, he would resign, allowing the government to carry on. 'The Government would drag on for a time and he could use this issue devastatingly against Heath. He clearly visualised that it wouldn't be long before he staged a comeback ... I'm sure, if a crisis *does* come, this is the only way to handle it,' Barbara wrote in her diary.[9] It was a bizarre strategy. How did Wilson believe he could attack the Tories when he would be in opposition to his own party? He appeared to be proposing a course of action that would have split the party more surely than anything the TUC could do, a point Crossman was shortly to drive home to Barbara.

At the end of an exhausting day, Roy Jenkins gave her a drink and (unnecessarily) a little spine-stiffening homily. 'You have become a kind of folk heroine,' he told her, promising (somewhere, surely, a cock crowed) to stick by her. 'But you do realise, don't you, that it has its dangers? It could be very bad for you if you back down now.'

In the midst of the crisis, Barbara made one of the strangest decisions of her political career. Encouraged by Wilson, she set off on a two-week Mediterranean cruise on a rich capitalist's yacht. Two months earlier the founder of the Forte hotel and motorway service station empire, Sir Charles (later Lord) Forte, another notorious opponent of trade unionism, had offered her his yacht to sail around the bays and islands of southern Italy. The Castles and the Fortes had first met during an Italian holiday the previous August, which had been followed up by dinner in London in January. In March, she recorded in her diary that she had a drink with Crossman to invite him and his family to join them 'for a few days'. So, on 23 May, with the TUC about to declare open war on her and the government, she, Ted and the entire Crossman family – Dick, Anne and their two children – set off for Naples escorted by Gino, the head waiter from the Café Royal. 'Barbara is tremendously keen to keep it secret,' 'Double' Crossman wrote, as he recorded the restoration of their previous personal intimacy – and ignoring the fact that he had already told several of his friends about the trip. (The news would leak soon after their return.)

Her officials were astounded. 'The cruise was absolutely inexplicable,' John Burgh, one of those most closely involved in the legislation, recalled. 'How could she go for a cruise in the Mediterranean, bad enough in itself, but on a capitalist's yacht? She must have known how it looked.' Bernard Ingham, despite being number two in the press office, only found out through private office gossip. 'They tried to keep it from me,' he believes. In the increasingly febrile and mistrustful atmosphere, at least one of her officials thought it was all a conspiracy by Wilson: at the very least a plot to discredit Barbara, possibly even a bid to remove her from the scene, thus also removing the main obstacle to setting up a deal with the TUC. Others, like Roy Jenkins (often needled by Barbara for his own relaxed approach to work), defended Wilson and Castle, arguing that she desperately needed a break. It is an episode that both Barbara, and according to his friends, Ted, later found embarrassing to recall.

Conspiracy or not, certainly Feather spotted the opportunity to get Wilson and the two key players from the union side, Jones and Scanlon, alone together, in the hope of convincing the Prime Minister that no more movement on the 'Programme for Action' was possible. A dinner and overnight stay at Chequers was arranged. Feather assured Jones that Barbara, 'the queer one' as he unattractively called her, would not be there. Whatever his view of her at the time, Jones certainly believed that without her a deal was much more likely. But at the last minute, Barbara – who knew all about the meeting, apparently from Wilson himself – decided to break her holiday and fly back.

Roy Hattersley had been asked to devise code names for the parties involved. His first idea, that Barbara should be Gloriana, was – unsurprisingly – rejected. Wilson, apparently oblivious to the risks – or perhaps anticipating the benefits – of her departure, then personally prepared code names for all possible participants in any ship-to-shore radio communication he and Barbara might have. In a bizarre excursion into zoological metaphor he was to become 'Eagle', she 'Peacock', and Crossman 'Owl'. The pecking order continued pointedly: the Chancellor was merely 'Starling', and the Home Secretary – Jim Callaghan – a paltry 'Sparrow'. Vic Feather was 'Rhino', and Jack Jones 'Horse', while the TUC General Council was to be known collectively as 'the Zoo'. The government's penal clauses were to be referred to as 'teeth', and the TUC's sanctions as 'false teeth'. Finally, in the event of some major drama which would demand Barbara's instant recall, the signal 'Aunty has mumps' would be transmitted.

It was a better parlour game than message system. In the event, communications proved almost impossible (it is suggested, perhaps apocryphally, that Crossman sabotaged the radio), and when Conrad Heron went out to collect Barbara and brief her for the Chequers dinner, it was only his wartime experiences in Italy that led him to the harbour master who in turn knew where to find the Forte yacht.[10]

Despite the odd relaxing shopping trip with Anne Crossman (Barbara spending freely) and the presence of the children, which she always enjoyed, Barbara's holiday was not likely to put her in a quiescent frame of mind. Crossman's was not a restful personality. In the unseasonably hot sirocco wind, with the yacht too precious to be risked in any but the safest harbour, it sometimes seemed that only the presence of Ted stopped them coming to blows. One sticky day, the three of them scrambled competitively up a rough, steep path to a restaurant at the top of Mount Epomeo on the island of Ischia, where they drank too much and argued aggressively. Crossman was as bitterly opposed as ever to the whole idea of legislation. In the hot Italian afternoon, with the Forte yacht, the *Maria Luigi II*, lying elegantly in the blue Mediterranean three thousand feet below, he told Barbara she was on the verge of splitting the Labour movement even more damagingly than Ramsay MacDonald had done.

According to Barbara, Crossman said that if she and Harold resigned there would be an election with two sorts of candidates – those backed by the unions, and the rest. She accused him of trying to bludgeon her into admitting that none of this would have happened had they consulted Cabinet first. She blamed his own plan for pension reform for the low morale in the PLP. Crossman told her that if she and Wilson offered the PLP, not to mention Harold's potential usurpers like Callaghan, the choice between the industrial relations legislation plus a likely election, or a new Prime Minister with the hundred-seat majority intact, it was obvious which they would choose. By the time Barbara set off on 1 June for what was to become one of the most infamous political dinner parties in history, she was more fired up than relaxed by her week in the sun.

Briefed by Conrad Heron on the negligible progress of talks between the TUC and officials during the slow journey from Naples to Northolt by military transport aircraft (mainly concerning the substitution of 'must' for 'may' in a paragraph of the TUC document), as soon as Barbara arrived at Chequers, she discussed tactics with Harold in the intimacy of his bedroom, where the Prime Minister was changing his shirt after a round of golf. They agreed that the key vote in the Commons should be not on the substance of the bill, but on the technical question of whether debate on the bill should be 'guillotined' or left open-ended. If there was no cut-off point, they knew the bill would never get through – Crossman's recent parliamentary reform bill had been slowly strangled by an alliance between Foot and the Tory Enoch Powell, masters of procedure, on the floor of the Commons. The vote would be presented as a vote of confidence in Wilson personally. If they were defeated, 'those involved' – Wilson himself, Barbara and maybe Jenkins – would resign 'quietly'. Barbara, not directly commenting on the probable death of her own political career, noted that Wilson 'is resigned to our election defeat and is preoccupied with how he can outmanoeuvre Jim and thwart his ambitions'.

Downstairs Jack Jones, who, no doubt in another of Wilson's private jokes, had been allocated the Prison Room (where the sister of Lady Jane Grey had been locked up by the real Gloriana for two years – faint traces of the Latin inscriptions she had written on the wall are still visible), was reacting with horror to the news that Barbara was, after all, there. 'Don't be difficult,' hissed Vic Feather, who must have been equally disappointed, plying them all with drink.[11]

Barbara was apparently unaware of the personal hostility of Wilson's guests. Trying to establish common interest with Jones, she discussed Feather's likely contribution as TUC General Secretary. But it soon became clear that the game had gone way beyond the possibility of being influenced by cosy personal relations, even if it would ever have been possible to conjure them up given Jones's instinctive suspicion of all official authority, his holier-than-thou incorruptibility and his determination not to be patronized by his hosts or impressed by the grandeur of his surroundings.

The following day, Wilson wrote down a detailed account of the whole affair. Only nine copies of the document were ever made, but it was also selectively shown to cabinet ministers (and later almost certainly to Peter Jenkins when he wrote his account of the drama) in order to strengthen the case for fighting on. Wilson interpreted the entire evening as an attempt by Feather to show him that further movement on the 'Programme for Action' was impossible. According to Wilson, Scanlon and Jones 'did most of the talking'. Their message was simple. First, they would concede no more power to the TUC to intervene in the affairs of individual unions, and were unlikely even to observe the new rules – to which they had already agreed – giving the TUC a say in solving inter-union disputes, let alone sanction the power to interfere in relations between unions and their own members, a precondition of stopping unofficial strikes. All concessions made so far were really just an attempt to head off the government's plans for legislation. Challenged by Barbara to say whether it was just the penal clauses they opposed, or the whole principle of legislation, 'they said firmly, legislation'. They would make it unworkable. Backed by Feather, they declared the end of the 'Woodcock era', in which legislation had been opposed while it went through the House but then accepted once it was in force. Wilson, who quite reasonably regarded this as the pivotal moment of the evening, warned that this would make *them* the government, and he, the Prime Minister, would resign. If he resigned (Barbara noted in her diary, but Wilson did not in his account of the evening) the government would fall because no one else could lead a Labour government. Barbara recorded wryly, '"None of us has ever suggested anyone else", they chorused.' The Prime Minister's minute was less colourful but perfectly explicit: 'I said that in particular if the TUC hoped to crack their whip over Trade Union Group members [of the PLP] to vote against the government it would clearly mean that the TUC, a state within a state, was putting itself above the Government in deciding what a Government could and could not do. They made no attempt to deny this because, as they said, a fundamental principle was at stake.'

It was when Scanlon took up the point Crossman had made a few days earlier as he and Barbara had sat and argued on Ischia, that the most celebrated moment of this evening occurred. 'Get your tanks off my lawn,' Wilson is supposed to have said when the Amalgamated Engineering Union's leader warned of another 1931. 'I reminded [Scanlon] sharply that in that context I was not a Ramsay MacDonald, but in the context of his previous comment, I wasn't a Dubček,' Wilson noted. In other words, he would not split the Labour movement, but nor would he, like the Czech leader who had capitulated to the Soviet tanks the previous summer, roll over before union power. But even as he said it, he and Barbara knew that the moment was rapidly approaching when it would have to be one or the other.

The debate had taken them through roast duck in the Chequers dining room to brandy and cigars upstairs in the gallery. At about midnight, Barbara went to bed, convinced they had to fight on. As if to confirm the trade unionists' suspicions, Vic Feather and Wilson had a final, amicable discussion in Wilson's bedroom, which left Wilson convinced that relations with the union movement could still be rebuilt after legislation. The last thing Wilson did before he went to bed was scribble a note to Barbara, asking her to come and see him first thing in the morning.

As usual, by the time she visited him in his bedroom (where he was having a Churchillian breakfast in bed) she had a plan. She wanted to send a stiff letter to the TUC outlining exactly what needed to be done to toughen up the 'Programme for Action' in a way that would make the penal clauses unnecessary. The TUC had to be able to make sure that the unions obeyed its recommendations and got their members back to work in unofficial strikes by being able to discipline the the unions if necessary. In a proposal which she knew would be entirely unacceptable to the whole union movement, Barbara suggested legislating in a second bill for model union rules, whose adoption would be a condition for registration. The penalty for being an unregistered union would be the loss of immunity from damages. In other words, a Labour government was proposing to take the union movement back to the bad old Taff Vale days when strike action was effectively impossible. On a perfect June morning in the Chequers rose garden, Wilson – to Barbara's astonishment – accepted the idea with enthusiasm. Even Ramsay MacDonald would have turned in his grave at the idea, but she had rashly handed Wilson, the great gambler, one last chip to throw after all the others.

Barbara, compounding her misjudgement of going on holiday in the first place, now returned to Naples, leaving her officials to draft the letter and Wilson to deal with the fallout from it and from the special congress. The following day, after a damp tour of Herculaneum, she and Ted met her chief negotiator Conrad Heron in a restaurant in Risena, where what Ted called the 'Treaty of Herculaneum', the letter to the TUC, was duly signed. Back in London it was delivered to the TUC barely twenty-four hours before the special congress. Barbara's plan was to have it put to, and then rejected by, the unions, putting them (she hoped) on the defensive. Feather thwarted her entirely by simply pretending that he had never received the letter at all.

But he left her officials and Downing Street in no doubt at all that it had arrived. First he contacted Barbara's Permanent Secretary, Denis Barnes, who solemnly noted that Feather refused to believe the letter had been sanctioned by Wilson and blamed Barbara entirely. When Feather finally got through to the Prime Minister himself, he told him the letter was 'a catastrophe'.[12] As ever, Wilson soothed him. The rest of the world remained in ignorance of the government's continuing concerns as it was treated to the spectacle from the special congress held in Croydon of a united trade union movement approving what were generally seen as sound and genuinely well meant, if rather feeble, proposals from the eminently reasonable Vic Feather.

Feather, in carefully moderate language, explained the grounds for opposition to the government's plans. He told delegates, 'We have been puzzled by the government's attitude, puzzled but not angered.' He was puzzled by the assertion that there should be a pay-off for the right to join a trade union, in the form of acceptance of government intervention in trade unions' internal affairs, where surely the right to join a trade union was universally recognized as a basic principle of democracy. He was puzzled by the rush for legislation: could the workers really be to blame for all the country's ills? The government's proposals would not even work, he said: men won't go back to work just because they're faced with a writ; and fines, recoverable after a dispute was ended, would just perpetuate bad relations. Above all, he said, 'Legislation of this kind cannot be effective, but the danger is that when this becomes apparent the government will be forced into a choice – either to abandon it, or to try and stop the gaps by taking even more stringent powers.'

Meanwhile, the unions' own proposals *would* work, he argued. Instead of the government's cooling-off period which only came into force after a strike had begun, under their plans a dispute would trigger an immediate return to the status quo, preventing a strike from even starting. Where the TUC then found against a union, 'the General Council will require unions to satisfy them that they have done all they reasonably can be expected to do to secure compliance with a recommendation . . . including taking action within their own rules, if necessary'. That could mean, he admitted, that some unions' rule books would need updating. In the notorious who-does-what disputes there should not be strikes at all; there, the TUC had a proven track record in settling them. Now, instead of having to wait to be asked to intervene, it could intervene on its own initiative. But all of this would be abandoned if the government persisted in introducing (not implementing, merely introducing) its penal clauses. The TUC position was endorsed by nearly eight million votes to 846,000.

Faced with such rational argument, and compared with what the government's proposals might achieve, it suddenly seemed to those listening to Feather's argument that the only explanation for the government's fighting on was to save its – and specifically, Barbara's – face. Even if her criticisms of the likely effectiveness of the TUC's role, as set out in the letter Feather had suppressed, had been in the public domain, it is unlikely they would have done much to diminish the sudden surge of enthusiasm for allowing the TUC to continue its traditional role of policing all trade union affairs. But her criticisms were not known, and neither, most damagingly, was Barbara there to argue her case or – as she later claimed she would have done – to accept the TUC's terms for peace.

Instead, her officials helped Wilson to draft what Barbara called a 'sour' comment on the special congress, insisting that the government had to fight on to get a deal on unofficial strikes that would stick. It went out under

Barbara's name: in the aftermath of the later defeat, Wilson (anxious that he was being portrayed as the weaker of the two) confirmed that he had been unable to reach his First Secretary on the ship-to-shore telephone, and that it was his decision; he had been determined to 'check the post-Croydon euphoria'. Not for the first time, Barbara and Wilson were at odds over negotiating tactics. But although she recorded that it reduced their room for manoeuvre, there is no evidence that from now on she was arguing for conciliation, as she later claimed. Certainly her department was as utterly committed to legislation as ever, and in the intimate and fevered atmosphere of a department under siege, their total support for the project would have been an important sustaining influence. (Indeed, so bad did the atmosphere become that Bernard Ingham used to go out and use a public phone when he wanted to talk in any detail with journalists. 'Heads were going to roll,' he said later, 'and no one wanted any evidence around that could be used against them.')

Before Barbara had returned from her cruise – they all spent the final day on Capri – a *Daily Express* journalist, John Grant (who later became a Labour MP), had received a copy of the 'Treaty of Herculaneum' which he used to illustrate the 'unyielding attitude' of both Barbara and Wilson.

Cabinet ministers, watching nervously as their Prime Minister appeared determined to drive the whole government into oblivion, once again became restive. On another glorious June day, exactly a week after the Chequers dinner party, the inner cabinet met. In the wake of the enthusiastic reception of what had transpired at the special congress, they were suffering a collective loss of nerve. Most alarmingly, for the first time even Roy Jenkins (whose acolytes were still pressing hard for him to distance himself from the legislation before Callaghan got an unassailable advantage in the phantom leadership contest) began to sound wobbly. Barbara, who had spent the morning and all the previous day bullying her garden back into shape after a fortnight's neglect, now turned on her wilting colleagues. Her diary entry for the session, borne out by official records, steams off the page: 'The history of the Government in the past few months had been one of capitulation – and much good had it done us. The only way to win victories was to stand up to pressures. We could win here too, if only the PLP didn't lose its nerve.'[13] Wilson joined in, explaining that they wanted to test the TUC by offering them the delayed introduction of the penal powers. If they still refused to negotiate unless all threat of sanctions was withdrawn, the government would think again. The idea of the unions calling the shots roused the inner cabinet (without Callaghan still, suspended for his earlier disloyalty, and also without Bob Mellish, the Chief Whip, 'whose nerve couldn't be trusted')[14] to some show of unity. Jenkins dropped his demand – which can only be seen as a back-covering exercise – that support from the full Cabinet be sought. All the same, Barbara recorded that he looked 'shifty'.

Yet when Barbara and Wilson met the TUC the next day, Monday 9 June, Wilson caved in. He was challenged directly by Richard Briginshaw of the print union SOGAT: 'If we strengthen Pararaph 42 [dealing with TUC sanctions on unofficial strikers] will you drop the penal clauses?' 'With barely a moment's hesitation,' Barbara wrote in her diary, 'Harold answered, "Yes."' Barbara thought it was just another negotiating ploy, a challenge to the TUC to knock heads some more, but her officials knew that from that moment the game was up. All the TUC had to do now was to string the government along while continuing to stir up the PLP, and final victory was theirs.

The trade union faction at Cabinet later that day certainly interpreted events since the special congress as proof that peace was now a real prospect. First Mellish and then Callaghan congratulated Wilson and Barbara for their determination in continuing the negotiations, which had brought such dramatic results. Only Peter Shore, in right at the start of 'In Place of Strife' and determined to do something that would enable government to make a prices and incomes policy stick, niggled away at the supposed effectiveness of the TUC proposals. Otherwise, Barbara's colleagues seemed finally to have grasped that the most likely way to persuade her to lay off was to tell her she had already succeeded beyond their expectations. On that basis, Cabinet agreed to back continued negotiations. Secretly, the Industrial Relations Bill, including penal clauses, was printed.

Perhaps Barbara too knew, without admitting it to herself, that the pass had been sold. For the first time, her diary entries become despairing, particularly when Wilson told her after yet another late night over drinks and sandwiches with Vic Feather in his study at No. 10 that he saw the present talks in the same light as his (futile) attempts to try to end Rhodesia's Unilateral Declaration of Independence aboard HMS *Fearless*. At dinner with her officials one night she threatened to resign if Harold sold out. Her health suddenly gave way. For three days she could barely eat, overwhelmed by a nausea that contributed to her general exhaustion.

Still negotiations continued. Barbara's and Wilson's efforts focused on getting a change to the TUC's Rule 11, to strengthen the TUC's powers over its member unions and require that the unions themselves tighten their own rules so that there would be real penalties if a union connived in prolonging an unofficial strike. But the TUC insisted that nothing agreed at Croydon could be changed and that trying to go further risked jeopardizing everything. All they would offer was to put out a circular, a a kind of statement of intent, condemning unofficial strikes and calling on unions to do all they could to get their members back to work. Barbara, fighting on two fronts, had to insist to the inner cabinet that for her own credibility a rule change was the minimum called for.

Newspapers started to report rumours that the negotiations continued only 'to protect Mrs Castle'. On 12 June, Wilson told the TUC that unless a deal was reached, the government would push ahead with legislation the following Wednesday, 17 June. 'TUC given five days to come to heel,' reported the *Guardian*, adding, 'Mr Wilson seems to be protracting the negotiations to protect Mrs Castle, who is a committed champion of the government's legislation.' Barbara was now working up yet another option, involving legislating on model union rules as she had first discussed a fortnight earlier at Chequers. But even her officials, so committed to legislation, were beginning to lose hope. John Burgh, who had done almost all the work on the succeeding drafts of the White Paper and the legislation, wearily submitted yet another aide-memoire on alternatives to the TUC's sanctions, with the covering note for his colleagues in the Prime Minister's private office: 'Jeremy Bentham would have described it as "nonsense on stilts".'

An ailing Barbara set off for a weekend of speaking engagements in the east Midlands and Lincolnshire. She was reported in the *Morning Star* to be weeping with 'petulant passion' during one speech, and when Dick Crossman saw her on the day before the final crisis (to discuss what to give Charles Forte as a 'tribute' for their holiday, news of which had just leaked out, provoking derisive press comment), he found her 'miserable and unhappy'. She had to be convinced that to resign would merely play into Callaghan's hands.

As Barbara trekked, nauseous, by train from Nottingham to Lincoln and Skegness and back to London, still trying to find some way of putting teeth into the TUC proposals for dealing with unofficial strikes, Douglas Houghton delivered the coup de grâce. He leaked to the *Sunday Telegraph* a letter he was about to send to Wilson in his capacity as chairman of the PLP. In it, he warned that penal clauses would not get through the House, and that there was a 'total collapse of confidence' among backbenchers, and a 'yearning for unity' in the run-up to the election. It was a deadly blow to all further attempts to negotiate, the political equivalent of going nuclear. And that allusion to the next election made it clear it was not so much the closing shot in the campaign against legislation as the opening shot in the next campaign: to unseat Wilson and put Callaghan in No. 10.

'The most traumatic day of my political life,' Barbara recorded with, for once, perhaps more justification than drama. On 17 June, with the deadline Wilson himself had set now at hand, the inner cabinet met in a mood of violent and bitter recrimination to decide whether to risk all and back legislation or allow the TUC victory. Wilson and Barbara openly attacked Houghton and accused Callaghan in all but name of collaborating with him. But the damage was done. The Chief Whip, Bob Mellish, showed exactly how the 'so much has been achieved' argument could be used not to encourage but to strangle any further initiative. Confirming Houghton's view that the penal clauses would not get through parliament, he argued: 'The party was saying that the Prime Minister and First Secretary had achieved so much that it would be a tragedy to throw it away.' Wilson retorted that Mellish himself had threatened an election if the PLP didn't back the government. The gloves were off. Barbara bitterly rounded on her old friend Crossman, who was leading the argument against giving her carte blanche to continue negotiations when nothing could get through the PLP unless the TUC supported it. 'If you'd had your way we'd have achieved nothing,' she said, reminding him that there was now a fundamental constitutional issue at stake. If her latest proposal couldn't even be put forward because the TUC wouldn't support it, 'then the government could not govern'.[15]

When the rest of Cabinet joined them for the first of two marathon sessions that day, the opposition had a more coherent case to present than had Wilson and Barbara and – now almost their only totally loyal supporter – the Foreign Secretary Michael Stewart. Ignoring Wilson's warning that accepting the TUC proposals would cost the government 'all credibility both at home and abroad', his opponents returned to their anxiety about the lack of back-bench support and the risk of a Commons defeat. Jim Callaghan set out the case for accepting the TUC's proposal for a 'letter of guidance'. It could, he argued, be made as binding as a change in their rules and it would achieve as much as the government's proposals. Others supported him, most devastatingly Barbara's friend and protégé Peter Shore, who earned Wilson's bitter resentment for turning both on the proposals and on the Prime Minister – for once not sounding (as Wilson had often dismissively remarked) 'like a civil servant' but speaking with a passionate intensity that impressed Barbara, despite herself. Most damningly, Shore asked if she and Wilson were now obsessed with 'winning a victory over the TUC' or were actually interested in having an impact on the number of unofficial strikes.

At lunch time, Cabinet broke without reaching an agreement. Four hours later, they reconvened. No one knew whether the Prime Minister and First Secretary were about to resign and trigger a leadership contest. The rival camps were already jockeying for position. Roy Jenkins – the man who had been determined to have the interim bill in the first place – saw Barbara just before they all reconvened. He no longer thought the fight was worth it, he told her, but agreed that the cost of capitulation – the resignations of Wilson and Barbara – would also be unsustainable. 'She did not recriminate,' he wrote later of her reaction to his betrayal, 'but accepted the news like St Sebastian receiving another arrow.'

As the curtain rose on the final act of the tragedy, a good half of Cabinet – including Tony Benn, who in April had told her 'Keep at it, you are opening up the most important debate we have had for years' – agreed that the terms should be accepted. Benn defended his change of mind: 'To move from absolute silence about industrial disputes to statutory penalties was too big a jump.' But Wilson remained aggressive. He told the Cabinet they had committed themselves months earlier to the interim bill and he would not go now to the TUC and accept their terms. According to Crossman, he was contemptuous of his Cabinet, calling them 'soft' and 'lily-livered'. Jenkins said he showed 'a Lear-like nobility', adding, 'he sounded fairly unhinged at times'. Benn's diaries said he and Barbara were 'extremely bitter'. 'Harold threatened to resign several times and said he wouldn't do what Cabinet wanted him to do and they would have to look for a new Leader, and so on; people were completely unmoved by it. His bluff was called and he just looked weak and petty . . . Barbara was frantic, in the usual Barbara sort of way.' He too thought that if it came to a choice between a Labour government, and Wilson and Barbara, people would prefer to keep the government. A few minutes after 7 p.m., Cabinet was persuaded to accept a compromise proposed by Barbara, giving her and Wilson a free hand with negotiations the following day, although ministers retained their right to accept or reject whatever was said. Wilson and Barbara went to brief the trade union group of MPs. There, they were given the same message again: settle, on the TUC's terms. Finally, the two beleaguered colleagues, entirely isolated from both Cabinet and party, met Vic Feather one last time. Once again, he and Wilson seemed to be on the brink of an understanding. Barbara allowed herself a sudden surge of optimism. 'Wouldn't it be heaven if we could get an amendment to rule 11 and after all show our colleagues up for the cowards and capitulators they are?'[16]

Barbara assumed that Cabinet's restriction on their freedom of nego-tiation would be leaked straight to journalists. Instead, over their toast and marmalade the next day, TUC leaders opened their newspapers to find the reassuring news that their trade union-sponsored colleagues in the Commons would, to a man and woman, oppose the penal clauses and had told Barbara and Wilson so the previous evening. They had withdrawn their support from the government in favour of their paymasters.

Barbara was aware of all this as she rose early for her final attempt to salvage her political career. It was not a morning for hanging on to sleep. For all her euphoria of the previous night, she knew only too well that by night-time there could be a government crisis. She and the Prime Minister might have resigned; she might yet resign on her own. She worked on one last draft of an amended Rule 11. At 10 a.m. she was at Downing Street, immaculate as ever. Everyone else seemed in a kind of stasis of lost conviction and exhaustion. Even her officials had abandoned drafting amendments and tidying the small print. The only paper on the table was her own. Wilson began the final day's negotiations with the bluntest warning. He could not continue, and neither could his government, in a situation 'in which it was unable to introduce effective legislation to deal with unofficial strikes, even though the TUC was unwilling to operate a satisfactory alternative scheme'.[17] In other words, they reached a deal or there would be an election. Although he also continued to hold out the threat of legislation (refusing even to discuss with Barbara that there was a choice other than legislation or a rule change), everyone knew that whatever happened that day, the bill was a dead duck. (Elsewhere in Whitehall, Crossman and Jenkins were agreeing that they would vote Wilson and Barbara down if they even suggested trying to carry on with it.)

Barbara's final proposals for Rule 11 were presented to the TUC. By 11.30 they had been accepted. But not as a rule change: they would use her words only as part of a letter of intent, an idea Wilson and Barbara had resolved was unacceptable. It was Scanlon (for whom Barbara always retained an affection) who first suggested an alternative. He could not, he said, go back to his own members to approve a further transfer of power to the TUC. Perhaps, then, they could all agree a declaration with the same force as the TUC's Bridlington Agreement, made thirty years earlier but still observed and rarely breached, which gave the TUC the power to intervene in cases of inter-union member-poaching. As the two sides separated for their 'doorslab' sandwiches (Barbara's description) and 'sour' beer (Jack Jones even remembered the brewer – Ind Coope), Barbara's senior negotiator Conrad Heron suggested the Bridlington Agreement idea might just provide the way out of the crisis that now loomed. The idea was greeted with relief. Barbara claimed she managed to persuade Wilson, and that Wilson was hawkish to the end; Joe Haines, Wilson's press secretary, who had been at the meeting, believed that Barbara was the problem. He whispered to Wilson that 'it looked like a way out'; Harold waved him away – 'Not until

Barbara's gone.' It was agreed that a 'solemn and binding' commitment by the TUC would be an acceptable alternative. Heron, together with John Burgh, drafted what they later called the 'instrument of surrender', by which the TUC's affiliates would be obliged to accept TUC advice on unofficial stoppages. 'Solemn and binding,' remarked the Permanent Secretary Denis Barnes when Heron briefed him. 'Sounds like a character out of George Eliot.'[18] 'Solomon Binding' it became from then on, a terrible reminder of the derision with which the deal was regarded, even by its authors.

Downstairs, the entire Cabinet had been assembled, ready to approve the deal. The two rivals for the Wilson succession had spent the morning with their followers discussing likely outcomes and making contingency plans for a leadership election. Crossman and Jenkins had agreed that if Wilson and Barbara insisted on resigning, no one else need go with them. Others must have been considering a snap general election. When Wilson announced the deal, there was a feeble attempt at a cheer. It was the last straw for Barbara, who turned on her colleagues in a bitter attack. 'Considering the background of press reports against which we had to negotiate, it is surprising that we achieved anything at all,' she stormed. But before she could really get into her stride, she had to go with the Prime Minister to try to sell the deal to the press.

It was a futile exercise (not enhanced by Wilson ending it abruptly by announcing that Barbara needed to go and get her hair done).[19] No one thought there was anything to discuss beyond the enormity of the fact that the elected government had been unable to get its legislation past the trade unions and had withdrawn it. The headlines the next day unequivocally condemned both parties. 'Surrender' was in the headline of at least three accounts. The *Mirror*, although its industrial correspondent Geoffrey Goodman had written a sympathetic piece (based on a personal interview he had had with Barbara at the end of the previous day when he had found her shattered and despairing), carried a front-page leader written by its Wilson-hating proprietor Cecil King. 'There Exists in Britain a Power Outside Parliament as Great as that which Exists Within' was the headline – this was in the days when tabloids were serious newspapers – and the piece accused Wilson of 'depositing his conscience at TUC headquarters'. Beyond the front pages the damage went, if anything, deeper. Most papers carried selected quotes from the past weeks of threat and negotiation, ranging from Wilson's assertion when the bill was announced that it was 'essential', to his statement to the TUC in late May in which he said, 'The issue is whether this Labour government can continue.'

But there was no discussion now of Wilson's great plan to resign in the face of union or PLP obduracy. Barbara, in the immediate aftermath of the deal, hinted to her officials that she would like to go. She told her private secretary that she wished she could organize a farewell party instead of a party to celebrate the department's new freedom from the burden of rushed legislation. Her officials half thought she might go, and that she should. They were under no illusions as to how resoundingly they had been defeated. But to resign then would have ruthlessly exposed the futility of the so-called victory of the government over the unions, and left Wilson – her own protector – with no protection himself against his enemies. It would also have left her own political career in shreds, and at fifty-nine even the irrepressible Barbara Castle could have had few illusions about the chances of rebuilding it.

Joe Haines thought the joint resignation threat was seriously meant. 'Yes, I think they meant to resign, but equally I knew Harold very well and he never went into a room without knowing the way out. He was the last man ever to paint himself into a corner. He was determined to get something out of it.' As it was, Barbara personally got a generally good press, as the commentators sat down to write their assessment of the Battle of Downing Street. Like Margaret Thatcher later, she became famous for her willingness to fight her corner. She became 'Battling Barbara', identifiable in the headlines by her first name alone. She was widely projected as indomitable (although also prone to weeping at moments of high emotion), tougher than Wilson, and formidable compared with the rest of the weaklings in Cabinet. But it was a reputation based on the newspapers' thorough dislike of the trade union movement, and their enthusiasm for the cause of taming them.

The left were much less impressed. Although they were by definition interventionists, they unanimously condemned Barbara's choice of areas in which to intervene. Her most persistent critic, Alan Watkins in the *New Statesman*, accused her of 'making action and decision ends in themselves' and, perhaps more tellingly, of a kind of vanity: 'She convinces herself not merely that whatever she happens to be up to is socialist – this goes without saying – but that it is the most important activity currently being undertaken in politics.' With the party (even her own constituency party in Blackburn) and with trade unionists and left-wing commentators, she was discredited. She may have had letters of praise from unexpected quarters (the Duke of Devonshire expressed enthusiastic admiration), but it cost her dearly with the people whose support she both wanted and needed if her career was ever to prosper again. Many of her subsequent political and ministerial decisions were damagingly but probably correctly interpreted as attempts to restore her credentials with those who had not understood that her real intention had been to strenghten trade union rights the better to fulfill their responsibilities.

Her reputation for political judgement was also sullied beyond redemption. Even some of her officials, who had rated her so highly as an intelligent, hard-working and decisive minister, acknowledged that she was slow to make the tactical retreat, too fierce in defence of her position and lacking the lightness of touch that could on occasion have retrieved a difficult negotiation. Vic Feather told Cecil King that she should have been a commissar. To attempt such fundamental and controversial reform as a short-term political fix, a way of scoring off the Tories, without considering how to sell the measure to the party or how to contain the risk of alienating the party's main financial backers, the unions, who were already locked in conflict with the government over incomes policy, cost both Barbara and the government much.

History is a kinder judge. 'She genuinely represents the first attempt to come to terms with an abuse of power, and that is an historic achievement,' Bernard Ingham said later. After twenty years of trade union legislation and periods of mass unemployment, many people believe that if Barbara had been able to get her bill through, the end of the twentieth century might have looked very different. There would have been, it is argued, no winter of discontent at the end of the Callaghan government. Labour then might have been returned again; and there would never have been a Prime Minister Thatcher, no tough anti-union laws, and no derogation by government from the commitment to full employment. Instead, Labour, able by virtue of being in power to avoid its disastrous lurch into anarchy in the 1980s, might have been able to find a less destructive way of using North Sea oil revenues to restructure and modernize the economy.

Wilson was more damaged than Barbara, Jenkins less. Callaghan, apparently finished by the devaluation debacle, was restored to his former position as leading challenger. The government, far from proving it was governing, had proved that it could not. If the unions had not actually brought the government down, they could not have done much more to damage it.

'It was a sad story,' Roy Jenkins observed with that impartial generosity Barbara could never have emulated, 'from which [Wilson] and Barbara Castle emerged with more credit than the rest of us.'[20]

15. One of the Lasses

You haven't got to show when you're hurt, you haven't got to
retire to lick your wounds; if you're wounded, then you've got to
clout back harder . . . there must be no displays of mortification,
of being vanquished.

Vic Feather[1]

Barely a month after her crushing defeat over 'In Place of Strife' in June
1969, the *Guardian* and the *Financial Times* reported that Barbara was already
on the rebound. 'Mrs Castle is preparing to launch another of her ministerial
crusades,' said the *Guardian*, 'this time for the implementation of equal pay
for women. It is a cause which seems likely to attract wide Labour support
and could well restore some of the popularity Mrs Castle lost over anti-strike
legislation.' Barbara was clouting back.

She had emerged drained and exhausted from the final defeat in the
industrial relations battle, but it was Wilson who took the battering in the
press and it was his conduct of government that was subjected to withering
scorn – the *Economist* called it 'In Place of Government'. The trade unions,
it was clear to everyone, had won. Pretending otherwise merely made the
government look shifty. Tony Benn went to see Vic Feather a week after
the defeat, on 25 June. 'Vic kept me waiting for a long time, which was an
indication of how powerful he felt: he didn't have to bother very much
about Cabinet Ministers.'[2] Wilson – who, Benn thought, was going mad in
the aftermath of the defeat – was swearing revenge on the ministers who had
failed to back him. He told Barbara: 'You and I must keep together. I am
the only friend you have and you are the only friend I have. I'm like the
elephant: I may appear to forget but I never do.'[3]

Early in July Barbara had to speak late at night in the debate on their

agreement with the TUC. Crossman hurried back from an official trip to
hear her.

> I arrived just as Barbara was getting up to boos and cheers and for the first
> seven minutes she was on her feet, she only got out half a dozen sentences.
> I was sitting right at the end below the Speaker's chair and I saw her
> trembling as she got up, nervous, tense and tiny and somehow pathetic. If
> you are little and can only just see over the top of the dispatch box, if you
> have a high-pitched woman's voice and if you are trying to still the post-
> prandial, alcoholic clouds of noise you are at a terrible disadvantage,
> especially if you are a bit schoolmistressy and try to hector and lecture them
> at the same time. Barbara did her best and the angrier she got the more
> effective she got.[4]

A fortnight later, Wilson offered Barbara a move, to a new, bigger and
better department that would merge transport, housing and planning and
local government. She turned it down, in a way that suggests she was
determined to deny the extent of her defeat. 'My dominant nagging thought
was that I must avoid the danger of becoming Harold's gimmick-maker.
Unless I stayed at one job long enough to carry a policy right through, I
should cease to be regarded as an efficient trouble-shooter and be seen as a
bit of a show-off.'[5] The technique seemed to work. Crossman thought
Barbara was the embodiment of success-by-survival. 'She is determined to
keep her image and she has. She is still regarded as a fine, determined
woman, remarkable in her own way. I wouldn't say that she's successful but
she has proved that you can retain strength not merely in circumstances of
lack of success but in failure.'[6] Surviving meant moving on, new projects,
diversionary action. In 1959, when Barbara had just humiliatingly lost her
'Cyprus torture' libel action, she had bounced back with her campaign
against turnstiles in women's lavatories. On 28 July, she told the Prime
Minister and a reluctant Chancellor that she wanted to introduce an equal
pay bill.

If the timing had been entirely wrong for industrial relations legislation,
it was almost perfect for equal pay. Equal pay had been a TUC objective
since the theosophist Annie Besant led the matchgirls' strike in 1888, but
natural justice had always conflicted with assumptions about the needs of
society. Men needed to work to support a family. Married women did not
need to work, and unmarried women had no family to support and could
not expect to be paid the same as men with obligations. By the 1960s the
balance was changing. New attitudes to women's rights, encouraged by the

new feminism, were one element. New jobs for women in the expanding light engineering and technological sectors of industry meant new recruitment opportunities for trade unions, which almost for the first time started to pay serious attention to the demand for equal pay. Finally, and conclusively, the Employment Secretary was a woman with a record of support for equal pay and an unexpected hole in her legislative programme.

'Equal pay is the oldest wage claim in the history of the British trade union movement,' John Newton, the TUC President, unblushingly told its first ever equal pay conference at the end of 1968. It had been adopted as an objective in 1888, in response to fears that cheaper women's labour would take men's jobs in the new, more mechanized factories. Nearly sixty years later, many industries and professions still operated a marriage bar. In 1944, Churchill had forced a vote of confidence in order to reverse an amendment to the Education Bill giving women teachers the same pay as men won by one of his own MPs, Thelma Cazalet-Kier. Amidst cries of 'Dictator!' a Royal Commission into the question of equal pay was conceded. Cazalet-Kier lost her seat in the 1945 Labour landslide and, despite valiant efforts, was never selected for another.

The Royal Commission report, published in 1948, offered women only partial encouragement. Despite warnings about the 'psychological impact' on men and women alike, it was cautiously in favour of equal pay for the professional Civil Service. However, in all other areas it dismissed equal pay as a mere 'battle cry'. Dwelling on the difficulties of definition, it concluded that it was impossible to deliver 'exact justice between individuals' while 'oiling the wheels of economic progress'. The case in favour of equal pay was left to a strongly worded minority report by three of the four women members of the committee (who included the trade unionist Dame Anne Loughlin and the Principal of Somerville College Oxford, Dr Janet Vaughan). 'The claims of justice between individuals and the development of national productivity point in the same direction,' they declared. Where the majority report claimed that women could only expect lower pay because they were less efficient, the minority report pointed to weak unionization and artificial restrictions on women's employment which undermined their bargaining position.

In 1954, Barbara had been a co-sponsor of a cross-party equal pay bill. In 1955 a Conservative government conceded that equal pay should be phased in over six years in the administrative Civil Service. In the interlude, twenty-seven thousand typists were excluded from comparability on the grounds that they were all women; their work could not be compared with men's, and so they had no claim.

It was the shopworkers' union USDAW that launched what would be the ultimately victorious campaign, in which they played a leading role, with a resolution at the 1963 TUC conference calling for the next Labour government to legislate. Between 1964 and 1970 women accounted for 70 per cent of the growth in trade union membership.[7] Other unions launched their own campaigns, especially in engineering where new jobs were increasingly being taken by women.

Labour included a commitment to legislate in its 1964 manifesto. A tripartite working party with members drawn from the CBI – which also accepted the principle of equal pay – and the TUC, as well as government, was set up by Barbara's predecessor at the Ministry of Labour, Ray Gunter. In July 1966, Barbara recorded in her diary that her suggestion that equal pay should be introduced for government employees in areas such as the naval dockyards and the Royal Mint so as to set an example to the private sector was ignored at an economic policy cabinet committee. In 1967 the Gunter inquiry finally concluded, with all parties accepting the principle of equal pay but declaring against legislation to achieve it. They would rely instead on a voluntary approach. Its cost – which one report had now reckoned at £600 million, or a 3.5 per cent increase in the country's pay bill – was deemed incompatible with the prices and incomes policy.

So Barbara's inheritance when she arrived at the Department of Employment was a certain amount of research and a comfortable arrangement between the main negotiating parties to do nothing. But in June 1968, when she had been at the DEP for just ten weeks, women machinists at Ford's Dagenham plant came out on strike to protest that a new job evaluation scheme had wrongly graded them, undervaluing their skills. Their strike was disrupting production through the plant. The management were desperate, but not so desperate that they would concede regrading the work, which would mean reviewing the grades of thousands of male workers too. Rather than deal with the cumbersome multi-union team of negotiators who were refusing to use Ford's new procedural agreement intended to avoid disputes coming to strike action, and who anyway couldn't agree what kind of a dispute it was (this was the dispute that marked the start of her disenchantment with trade unions),[8] Barbara decided to call in the women themselves. The furniture was rearranged in her office so they could all sit informally together, and she herself sat in the middle of the sofa and gathered them around a large, mumsy teapot. The photographers came in early, in case the talks went too badly for pictures to be taken later.

The ensuing image ensured that Barbara was forever seen as the godmother of equal pay. She wrote later, 'I think I managed to make the

Government look again as if it consisted of human beings and not just cold-blooded economists.' As soon as the pictures were taken and the photographers dismissed, according to Violet Dawson, who was there, Barbara had the teacups removed and got out a 'real drink'. Whether it was the impact of the tea or the alcohol, or merely the chance to meet the management face to face, the meeting led to a settlement. Ironically, it was the settlement more than the original grievance that transformed the strike into an equal pay dispute: the management refused to meet the demand for regrading the machinists' jobs, but they were prepared to reduce their differentials to 92 per cent of a comparable man's wage.

Other women were impressed by what had been achieved by a small, determined group. Out of this dispute came the laboriously named National Joint Action Campaign Committee for Women's Equal Rights, which briefly but effectively became the militant wing of the equal pay campaign. It supported a growing number of stoppages all around the country, organized by women who were determined to copy the Dagenham machinists' victory.

Meanwhile, Barbara was fighting the 1968 round of the statutory prices and incomes policy through the Commons, a matter of huge importance to both foreign perceptions of the British economy and domestic perceptions of the government's ability to exert authority over its own supporters. On 26 June she was ambushed by one of the leading women's rights activists in the Commons, Lena Jeger, with an amendment demanding equal pay, which the whips told Barbara was likely to be carried. Roy Jenkins, the Chancellor, was sitting beside her on the government front bench. They had a whispered conference, Barbara stressing the importance of avoiding defeat, Jenkins anxiously reiterating the fragility of the economy. Barbara won; at the end of the debate, she promised immediate talks on a timetable for phasing in equal pay. She gave seven years as a possible introductory period. Campaigners feared it would just be a prolonged opportunity for employers to wriggle out of their obligations. But the 'talks about talks' strategy succeeded, and rebellion was narrowly averted. Her diary betrays relief at survival rather than celebration of a triumph. 'The only way we can survive these tricky issues is to play them positively and play them long,' she wrote that night.

Perhaps the equal pay issue might have been played even longer had Barbara not hit political catastrophe with 'In Place of Strife'. Certainly when she met the TUC soon after her dramatic Commons pledge, she warned that even the seven years was not a firm commitment. Her caution provoked another back-bench bill. Inside Whitehall, there was little visible progress for most of the next year as yet another round of inquiries was instigated. Barbara was committed to keeping all pay increases inside the pay policy and paid for through productivity deals. She was, as one campaigner[9] remarked later, first and foremost the Secretary of State and a politician. Campaigning for women came much further down her list of priorities.

Nonetheless, she took the opportunities as they came. In October 1968, after months of negotiation, the engineers' national pay negotiations looked close to total breakdown. Barbara and her chief negotiator, Conrad Heron, were called in. Their role was to get a deal that didn't breach pay policy but that didn't provoke a national strike either. Barbara was determined it should also reflect some improvement in the status of women workers. The union side, whose pay rates were still determined in the categories of (in descending order) 'skilled, semi-skilled, labourer, female', wanted women's rates raised to match labourers'. The employers, some of whom now had workforces at least a third female, said it was too expensive. In a traditional negotiating ploy, unions and employers agreed to talk about skilled rates first. But, having done an acceptable deal there, the unions repeated their demand for parity of women and labourers within three years, and the employers flatly refused on the grounds that it exceeded the overall cash available. A national strike suddenly looked dangerously imminent.

Barbara was furious: with the unions, for doing a deal that would exclude women, and with the employers for allowing themselves, in her words, 'to be manoeuvred into this trap'.[10] But if Barbara was furious, her officials were appalled that their minister seemed prepared to intervene in a national negotiation in an area in which she had no official role. They could see a hard-won agreement falling to pieces, a national strike looming. (Even Barbara noted in her diary that her officials were 'reeling under the impact of my ferocity'.) Marion Veitch of the General and Municipal Workers' Union, and the only woman among the negotiators, warned her colleagues that 'the tweezers were replacing the spanner' and that if the two and a half million men covered by the agreement allowed themselves to be bought off at the expense of the five hundred thousand women, they would soon find themselves with no jobs to go to.

Barbara pressed her case at a discreet dinner she organized for engineering magnates, including Arnold Weinstock of GEC and Sir Jack Scamp, the government's favourite industrial relations troubleshooter, at Brown's Hotel in central London. The employers reluctantly admitted that it would be more expensive not to give the women extra than to let the unions' demand go through (although there were dire warnings about the impact on the export drive). Finally, with women at Rolls-Royce and Rootes staging stoppages and walk-outs, both sides accepted a joint working party to look at job evaluation – and the employers kept their word and conceded the extra money for the women. Outside parliament, the National Joint Action Campaign Committee for Women's Equal Rights finally captured the TUC, or at least its public face. It commissioned research among its members which showed that men were earning, on average, 25 per cent more than women, and that despite years of lip-service to the idea of equal pay the gap was actually widening. In November came the one-day conference on equal pay, where the TUC women's officer, Ethel Chipchase, warned the more radical campaigners that they faced an uphill struggle, not only because of employers' opposition but also because of the apathy of many women workers. 'If you want revolution,' she told them, 'you must do it yourselves.' The *Daily Express* nervously reported that it was 'the most militant demonstration of support for equal pay ever sponsored by the TUC'. But it was not yet militant enough for the Campaign Committee, who disregarded TUC advice and marched from Central Hall across Parliament Square to lobby their MPs.

In the aftermath of 'In Place of Strife', Barbara returned to equal pay. In late July 1969, more than a year after her first promise to the Commons to introduce a timetable, Barbara was ready to go to the inner cabinet for approval for a bill. It was, inevitably, a compromise between the two hostile partners in the negotiation. There was to be a five-year phase-in; the TUC wanted two years and thought that any longer would give employers the chance to regrade jobs, segregating women and declaring their work 'unisex' and beyond comparison with men's – a fear borne out by the experience of civil servants ten years earlier. But the CBI's preferred option was no legislation at all, and it had only reluctantly acquiesced in a five-year handover. Barbara had to compromise too over the definition of 'equal work'. The TUC wanted it to cover all work of equal value, the definition proposed by the International Labour Organization. But the CBI wanted the much narrower 'same value'. Barbara's solution, after much work, was 'equal pay for work of the same or broadly similar value'. There was to be a ban on discrimination, which would end the practice of negotiating women's and men's rates separately.

Richard Crossman was an important ally. Now Secretary of State for Health and Social Services, he argued that the new phenomenon of the 'fatherless family' experienced the worst deprivation. Higher wages for women would also ease his problems with the poverty trap, which had led to the erosion of the incentive to work for single mothers (a category of benefit claimant just beginning to register as a problem on DHSS radar). However, Roy Jenkins, although stating that Barbara's proposal was 'inevitable and right', was not at all sure it would be effective. Nor was he reassured as to its economic impact by Barbara's research showing that it would add up to 5 per cent to the pay bill, and perhaps as much as 4 per cent to prices. There was little comfort in the study Barbara had commissioned of the impact on industries like clothing, potteries and electronics, which employed a high proportion of women. Based on the premise of equal pay for the same work, it showed women getting an increase of around 25 per cent. This conclusion (which turned out to be seriously over-optimistic) was embedded in caveats relating to the likely response of other grades of workers who, it was feared, might seek to perpetuate their differentials with women workers.

A month later, in September 1969, as a sweetener in a stern talk about trade union obligations in industrial relations, Wilson made the first oblique announcement to the TUC Conference of the government's intention to legislate. 'It will be clear to every delegate present,' he lectured the increasingly hostile audience as he promised to end injustice in the pay packet, 'that progress on [equal pay] must be based on restraint in incomes policy generally.' Women, in other words, could only get more if the men got less. Barbara, who thought Wilson had accepted that equal pay could not be delivered within a pay policy, was angry. She was suffering pre-conference tension herself, preparing for her first encounter with the Labour rank and file since 'In Place of Strife'. She was, as usual, expecting the worst: she had already had a bet that she would be voted off the NEC. The promise of legislation on equal pay was undoubtedly going to be a much-needed blandishment. But it was not the only announcement she had to make. She was also going to tell delegates that the prices and incomes policy was back, if in weaker form than previously. She knew the news would be badly received. It was imperative to get cabinet approval for equal pay. She recorded that the session went 'much better than I dared hope',[11] but the official cabinet minutes (unusually) paint a different picture. There was little enthusiasm for what was wearily seen as another of Barbara's schemes. Ministers argued that it would mean higher taxes, lower public spending and more unemployment without increasing the national wealth. Roy Jenkins had a new line of reservations – damage to the balance of payments and confidence in the pound. Even her loyal ally Crossman, though admiring her courage in rejecting Wilson's offer of a move after 'In Place of Strife', reflected later that her speech was a disaster, and aimed principally at 'trying to make good her damaged reputation'.[12]

If she felt Cabinet had gone better than she expected, conference went infinitely worse. Although she had the unexpected comfort of being once again elected top of the constituency section of the NEC, her equal pay announcement was immediately overshadowed by union hostility to her confirmation that statutory powers over prices and incomes were to be revived. Barbara was bitterly disappointed and lashed out in her diary against Jack Jones, who resented, she decided, being robbed of the leadership on industrial issues – 'which I am now convinced he wants exclusively concentrated in the hands of the unions'. Part of her disappointment at the hijacking of her conference speech lay in her determination to make equal pay a campaigning issue, proof that the government's concerns were about more than trying to hold down pay and satisfy foreign bankers. When, a fortnight earlier, the inner cabinet had met at Chequers to discuss an election strategy, she had argued passionately for a campaign built around a vision of the kind of society Labour wanted to foster. Equal pay was part of building a more civilized, compassionate and courageous society.

Barbara remained sceptical about the strength of the unions' commitment to equal pay. When she met them to try to guage what they really wanted in terms of a phasing-in period, she could not resist the opportunity to educate them in the realities of equality, starting with the need for women themselves to accept the same conditions of work as men, including night working, and for men to allow women to work alongside them. (Bus drivers in Aldershot were threatening to strike rather than allow women to be trained as drivers.) Her relations with the unions were not improved by her style. Crossman noted (probably exaggerating) in typically feline fashion, that union leaders were said to loathe the sight of her 'because before she sits down she lectures them with one of her emotional tirades'.[13] Nonetheless, equal pay was in the Queen's Speech in the autumn of 1969, and it would be the last piece of legislation on the statute book when parliament was prorogued for the election in May 1970. There was probably no other minister in that Cabinet who could have overcome the combination of inertia and hostility.

The Act showed women that gender should be no bar to justice. Barbara's efforts did not, however, end unequal pay. When she was guest of honour at the thirtieth anniversary of the Equal Pay Act in June 2000, women in all sectors were still earning 18 per cent less than hourly paid men (and part-timers, 41 per cent less). Nor was this triumph one that Barbara might, ideally, have sought. She believed in the rate for the job and, the more socialist option, a minimum wage, which she knew would have been a much more transparent way of raising women's earnings. In 1968, she and Crossman had considered the prospects for introducing a minimum wage for women only, coming in at the very low level of four shillings (20p) an hour and building up from there, but they agreed that the left would 'howl their heads off at any Bill that started as modestly as that'. So nothing was done. In 1969, she told a personnel conference that 90 per cent of those helped by a minimum wage of £13 a week would be women. However, the Ministry of Labour's studies had suggested that a minimum wage fixed at a level to lift people out of pay poverty would add nearly 20 per cent to the national wages bill. It was politically impossible. The introduction of equal pay was partly a response to the Labour government's failure to find a way to lift low-paid workers out of poverty; it was also a ladder out of Barbara's personal political disaster zone.

Barbara found herself a heroine of the new feminist movement despite finding the new feminism as misplaced as the old. Her argument was the one which had divided the suffragette sisters Sylvia and Christabel Pankhurst fifty years earlier. Christabel, Barbara argued later in a short biography of them both,[14] had no interest in how the vote was used, while Sylvia accepted that women's rights could only be secured as part of socialist reforms. Invited in 1968 to celebrate the fiftieth anniversary of women winning the vote, Barbara wrote, 'Preparing my speech was agony because I am too busy exercising my emancipation to have time to think about it . . . Talking to that crowded room full of elderly or ageing earnest women was like trying to talk to a room full of cotton wool.' The feminism of the 1960s and 1970s was 'unhealthy introspection'. Touching on what she called her 'bumpy ride' towards sorting herself out sexually, she wrote, 'I had a mind as well as a vagina and I did not see why the latter should dominate'. Contemporary feminists were 'obsessed with self-discovery in sexual terms,' while 'most women had little interest in political organisation or in the administrative minutiae of equality. Sexual politics took over from social policy . . . a vacuum was left for the counter-revolutionaries who had spent the intervening years preparing every detail of an unequal and repressive society.'[15] The media image was of a woman committed to helping other women, and that equalled feminist. So 'feminist' became part of the vocabulary used to define her, even though it was plain that Barbara's attitudes to other women, at least at the time, were indistinguishable from any moderately progressive male's.

In the early 1970s, she was invited to make a television documentary about the defender of the matchgirls, Annie Besant. Ted wrote the script but Barbara got the credit. When pressed for an opinion, she argued that women wanted to be themselves, not get into parliament. 'Real equality must go down to the mundane things, like how do I get enough to live on, do I or do I not have children, who will help me to bring them up?'[16] What was really happening in the 1960s was that women's attitudes began to catch up with Barbara's own. Some men, like Tony Benn, thought she was motivated by a dislike of men. She attacked male preserves – the trade unions and drink driving – and later she was prepared to insist that men lost a tax advantage so that their wives could be payed child benefit direct. From her attempts, as Stafford Cripps's PPS, to increase the supply of war-rationed nylons in the late 1940s to her support for increased maintenance for separated women, she identified herself with women's interests, but with many other causes as well. Her political motivation was always to improve life for the underdog; gender was relevant only because more underdogs were women than men.

She also brought the perspective of a woman to decision-making at the top. Many would interpret her career as a justification of the campaign to recruit more women MPs. Barbara disagreed. 'I think the only really distinctive contribution women should be expected to make in political life is to get into politics and when in politics behave as naturally and unselfconsciously as possible.'[17] Even though she owed her political career – or at least Blackburn owed their MP – to the determination of the women in the constituency who had demanded a woman on their short list, Barbara was a very late convert to the campaign for all-women short lists. Nor did she seek out women to promote in parliament. She acknowledged the problems women faced in becoming MPs, and once they were there. But she did not believe in changing the system to enable more women to come in until she realized she was arguing the same line as Margaret Thatcher. If she did not quite haul up the ladder behind her, nor did she try to make the climb less steep. However, on a personal level, she helped some aspiring women politicians individually. Betty Boothroyd, Jo Richardson and Janet Anderson all worked for her before being elected and becoming highly successful politicians in their own rights. When a cash shortage forced another friend and later MP, Joan Lestor, to consider giving up a seat she was fighting, Barbara wrote around to friends drumming up support. In the Commons she endured the barracking of the opposition and condescension from her own side as part of the job. Where possible, she exploited it. In Cabinet, the minister who had once complained about the flattery she received did nothing to deter the attentions of her colleagues. In one early Cabinet, a spoof motion was passed to her, signed by Arthur Bottomley, Fred Peart, Ray Gunter and Edward Short: 'That this House, noting the grace, charm, vitality & outstanding good looks of the Minister of Overseas Development, calls upon every hon member to show their appreciation of these unique qualities by all the means in their power.'[18] In the Commons, Tories sent her lubricious notes. One shadow minister, Nigel Fisher, apologized for being rude about a White Paper: 'I had not read [the White Paper] properly before the statement. It is full of good things, and I'm not surprised you were angry – but you did look magnificent.'[19] In the days before token women, Wilson insisted that she stand in the middle for his first cabinet photograph.

Throughout the period of the first two Wilson administrations, there were persistent rumours about Wilson and Barbara having an affair. Twenty years later, the unexpurgated version of the disgruntled spy Peter Wright's *Spycatcher* suggested an explanation.

> Tom Driberg was [an] MP named by Czech defectors. I went to see Driberg myself and he finally admitted that he was providing material to a Czech controller for money. For a while we ran Driberg on, but apart from picking up a mass of salacious detail about Labour Party peccadilloes, he had nothing of interest for us. His only lasting story concerned the time he lent Harold Wilson his flat so that the then Prime Minister could conduct an affair in strict privacy. Driberg was determined to find the identity of the woman who was the recipient of Wilson's favours, and one evening, after Wilson had vacated, he searched the flat and found a letter addressed to the Right Honourable Barbara Castle! Driberg claimed to be horrified by his discovery, and raised it with Wilson, suggesting that he ought to be more careful in case word of his activities ever became public.[20]

Several aspects of the account make it highly improbable. Driberg, who was gay, was the most notorious gossip and philanderer at Westminster, and therefore the most unlikely person for a serving Prime Minister to turn to for help in continuing an illicit affair. Then, in the unusual event of the Prime Minister conducting an affair with a cabinet minister, it seems beyond belief that either he or his mistress should be so careless as to leave an incriminating letter to be found. Driberg was a fantasist with a grudge against Wilson, who had regarded him as far too high a risk to include in government. Nonetheless, in the drinking holes of Westminster and Fleet Street it was a rumour that never quite died and one that Barbara's detractors could use to explain why the woman they found so difficult apparently had such power over the Prime Minister.

Every weekend that she could, Barbara retreated from her exhausting cabinet career to Hell Corner Farm, the small farmhouse with a barn attached built into the side of a hill, that she and Ted had bought in 1964, the year after she and Marjorie had first seen it.

Barbara set about making Hell Corner the centre of the life of her extended family, the permanent home they had never had as children. The barn was converted for Barbara's mother, whose house in London was sold, a move which subsequently caused a predictable dispute with Jimmie about their respective shares of their parent's assets. Moving 'Muvvie' was not a success: she was in her eighties, suddenly cut off from her friends and casual visitors. There was no shop to which she could walk, and only Barbara's housekeeper to keep her company. Her mental health began a sharp decline. But for Barbara, who had no time to visit her mother during the week, it meant she could both be sure of her safety and see her at weekends.

There was still room for Marjorie's three children and later for their families, and several acres of land and an old orchard. The house needed putting in order, and so did the garden, which gave Ted's life a purpose and Barbara a subordinate role. It was somewhere she could go and release the tension and anger of a week in politics, and she found the challenge as absorbing as politics and a good outlet for aggression. Hell Corner was high up in the Chilterns, in steep, beautiful countryside, and it was hard to believe that the M40 was only a couple of miles away and central London less than an hour. Their dog Aldie was taken for long walks along tracks through woods and the high, open fields. The cottage was Barbara's romantic rural idyll where she created a fairy-tale family life. Even the name was a source of endless amusement.

Crossman described one May evening in 1968 when he and his wife Anne went to celebrate Ted's birthday:

We found Barbara sitting on the steep lawn with, behind her, an orchard which must be over 100 years old. There was a nice housekeeper looking after her, with Ted looking like a distinguished old country squire . . . some people call [Barbara] a neurotic and self-centred politican. Sometimes she is, but in the atmosphere of home, she's lovely. She knows how to enjoy home and how to make it enjoyable. She's got very ordinary, middle-class taste in furniture and pictures and books and in none of these ways is she high-falutin'. She and Ted are the nicest kind of people and she is one of the few good things in our Cabinet.[21]

Off duty, digging in the garden or sweating in the kitchen, the tense, driven, passionate cabinet minister became a different person. She was a generous and tolerant great-aunt: Great-aunt Barbara and Great-uncle Ted,

Gabby and Gut to Marjorie's grandchildren, the family whom she had once promised Marjorie she would look after if anything untoward happened. In 1969 her niece Sonya Hinton painted a picture of weekends at Hell Corner, which substantiated Barbara's loving accounts in her diaries: 'She cooks stupendous meals for us, she's a fabulous cook; she doesn't spare her ingredients . . . and she gardens with enormous vigour and she walks and she talks. She enjoys social contacts enormously, I think, but very much at the country pub level, where she meets a cross-section of the local people . . . I would say that she probably hasn't got many intimate friends. And this is why family is so important to her.'[22]

Christmas and Guy Fawkes' were were not informal get-togethers but major family occasions. At Guy Fawkes' there were two parties, one for the children followed by an adult one later. There would be venison, roasted by Barbara. On at least one occasion, the great-nieces and -nephews were dressed as Puritans. Barbara took the instruction of children as seriously as her father did, although, Sonya observed, 'She has little concept of child development and no understanding that you can't reach maturity without being unstable or immature in the process.'[23] At Christmas, as well as entertaining all their friends, family and neighbours on Christmas Eve, she wrote and directed the children in a show and then set fiendish clues for them to follow in order to find their presents.

Barbara and Ted still argued passionately and – to outsiders – frighteningly, but then Barbara always argued with her friends. Both appeared to need the adrenalin rush of a violent, often searing, exchange of views which left the more pacific onlooker appalled. Ted was immensely proud of her and 'spoilt her rotten'. A prototype Denis Thatcher, quick to laugh, the amiable bloke everyone loved, the utterly loyal husband at last, he took Barbara's success for his own. He could claim to be the first man to be married to a cabinet minister. The establishment, to start with, was flummoxed. At their first formal occasion, a City banquet, they were heralded as 'the Minister for Overseas Development and Mrs Castle'. 'We wives,' he would say when they met friends like the Crossmans, 'must look after one another.'

In the *Observer* in 1969, Barbara explained Ted's importance to her:

> Some people ask him what it's like for him having a successful wife, implying that he's not been successful. As a matter of fact, he is a brilliant journalist and one of the best debaters in local government. The only real difference between our successes is that I am bang in the public eye . . . I don't like holding forth about women and men in general, but I'm the

kind of woman who needs, and likes to need, to be the partner of a man. I need Ted, for instance, and I like needing him. If you took away my need for Ted you'd take away part of me . . . I need to have and give affection, just as I need to breathe, and in order to have security and to build my own private cocoon I need this relationship with a particular person.

She told another interviewer: 'If you want to get to the top, first you need the right husband,' adding: 'The price you pay for power – I would rather call it public responsibility – is that it has the first call on your time.' In the *Mirror*, agony aunt Marjorie Proops pondered the impact on Ted's ego. 'Barbara is lucky,' she wrote. 'She and Ted have this kind of tricky marriage problem properly sewn up. She is a domesticated wife.' Barbara, in her role as domesticated wife, described coming back from the country with armfuls of flowers and fresh mushrooms, which she cooked for supper. In the *Daily Mail* she confided: 'Of course, I am very lucky to be married to a very mature man who does not feel he has to dominate a woman. Why, he's simply loving it, having me in the Cabinet. He's coming with me everywhere; he loves meeting people.'

On 17 April 1970 Barbara came home to find the person she so often described to attentive interviewers in such glowing terms was transformed. After six years as an alderman of the Greater London Council – an honorary position arising from his long service as an Islington councillor, which took him to the heart of London politics – Ted had been dropped.

I have never seen him in a more desperate state. He was knocking back whiskies when I arrived and almost shouting aloud with the pain of his humiliation. 'Everywhere and by everybody I am rejected . . . At every stage of my life I have failed. Why? I ask myself. Why? Why?' There were tears of despair in his eyes. 'You can't possibly understand. How could you? You have gone on from success to success. I have gone from rejection to rejection. What am I to do with myself? I go back to London with you. How am I to fill my time? You've no time to spare for me.[24]

Being married to a minister was a lonely and potentially – for a man who had had ambitions himself – an embittering experience. Barbara refused even to gossip with him about life at the top. She was aghast, but not remorseful, at Ted's distress. On the following Monday she bustled off and persuaded Wilson that Ted must have a peerage. As long, of course, as it did not mean she had to be a Lady.

★

There was, in truth, little time for Ted or anyone else in Barbara's working week, especially since Ted took over none of the domestic responsibilities. Barbara thought Roy Jenkins's ten-hour days, interrupted by a good lunch, proof of his dilettante approach to politics. She started early, ate almost nothing, mainly yoghurt and fruit, and often stayed in her office over lunch before finishing late. She found fitting in domestic chores almost impossible. She did her shopping on the run, or more often persuaded her official driver or her secretary to do it for her. Ted, it was accepted, did nothing in or for the house. Barbara had a series of housekeepers, most of whom stayed for years, but she still had to take the decisions and make the plans, and she would not compromise. She maintained her regular monthly visits to Blackburn, travelling on the overnight sleeper, returning the following night, also overnight. One day she recorded how she had managed an NEC meeting, prepared for a session on the Transport Bill, prepared for and answered questions in the Commons, sat in on the Transport Bill committee, done three television interviews and then gone back to the Transport Bill committee for an all-night sitting. 'I am delighted I can do a routine like that without difficulty,' she wrote. The next day she fell asleep in Cabinet and missed the vital debate on immigration. For most of the six years from 1964 to 1970, an economic crisis was either pending or happening. Complex and technical policy papers were debated in Cabinet and in the monetary policy committee that Barbara joined in the last two years of the government. At the same time she was always initiating legislation, drafting it or seeing it through parliament, as well as travelling and negotiating. Her health frequently collapsed under the pressure; at least twice a year she had a bad attack of flu and had to retire to bed.

On top of her other duties, she had her diary to keep up. In early 1968, after a Christmas when first the housekeeper and then Ted had also retired to bed, her own flu turned to pneumonia and Barbara decided she would have to abandon keeping her diary herself and adopt the Crossman technique of dictation. Her press spokesman Chris Hall lived nearby, and his wife Jennie, who already did the job for Crossman, was persuaded to give up part of her weekend to come and take dictation. Barbara would lie on the floor in front of the fire ('Never stand when you can sit, never sit when you can lie,' she would say) and dictate for a couple of hours. Jennie would retire and type up her notes for Barbara to correct later.[25] When Crossman discovered the arrangement he was not amused, but it lasted for more than a year, right through their intense disagreements over 'In Place of Strife'.[26]

Barbara had kept the diary, erratically at first, from the 1950s onwards. In the beginning she wrote up only the events she considered significant –

LEFT: Another one for the photographers. Barbara had a reputation as a good cook, but she rarely had the time and employed a housekeeper once she became an MP.

BELOW: Heading for glory. Barbara at about the time of her appointment as Minister for Overseas Development in 1964.

TOP LEFT: Barbara and her dogs and the hair that needed a wash, on the day of her appointment to the Cabinet. LEFT: Wilson's first Cabinet. In pre-tokenism days, he called Barbara in from the outer edge to stand beside him, a symbol of his power and her obligation. ABOVE: The informal Mrs Castle. She scandalized her more old-fashioned officials by sending out her private secretary to buy her a lipstick, some-times just to get him out of the way.

TOP: Unwanted hug. Hastings Banda of Malawi, a comrade in the fight for freedom who became an oppressor himself. The picture provoked the most offensive correspondence Barbara ever received. ABOVE LEFT: On an early African tour as Overseas Development Minister. Barbara's press officer took the baby away to be washed before presenting it to her for the ultimate photo opportunity. ABOVE RIGHT: At the height of her success as transport minister. Note the open ashtray. She was a heavy smoker, but rarely let herself be caught with a cigarette in her hand.

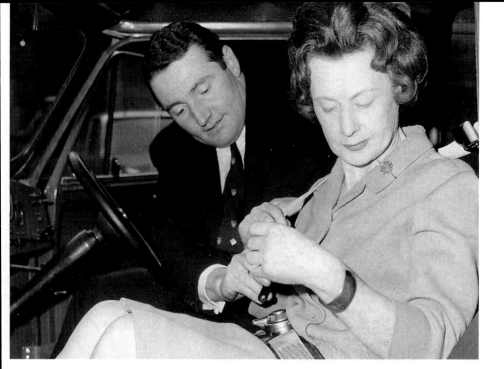

ABOVE: Promoting the seat belts campaign, and Barbara Castle.

OPPOSITE: 'B-day', 9 October 1967. 'I don't want to be remembered as the woman who introduced the breathalyzer' she once complained of her most durable achievement.

LEFT: The most highly rated politician in Britain on holiday in Ireland. Wilson told her he thought she looked so sexy he claimed to have stuck the picture on his shaving mirror.

"Use the whip again, Barbara, I could have sworn I felt it move!"

TOP: 'In Place of Strife.' In the end it was the trade unions who took Wilson and Barbara for a ride. ABOVE: The pay-beds battle. Wrong time, wrong fight. OPPOSITE TOP: Battling Barbara. OPPOSITE MIDDLE: 1970 election. 'I have a haunting feeling there is a silent majority sitting behind its lace curtains waiting to come out & vote Tory,' Barbara wrote in her diary. OPPOSITE BOTTOM: Surrounded by Ted's roses at Hell Corner Farm where she lived from 1965 until her death in 2002.

TOP: Eightieth birthday celebrations in 1991. Barbara's birthday often fell during the Labour conference, a mixed blessing until she became a party icon in the 1990s. ABOVE LEFT: Oldest friends: Barbara and Michael Foot. ABOVE RIGHT: Still as much socialite as socialist. Barbara in 1997, the year she set out to save the party from New Labour.

the Profumo affair, the Khrushchev dinner in 1957, the battle over the bomb in 1960. She did not start her cabinet diaries until three months into the first Wilson government. The diaries are intensely political, never intentionally revealing about herself. The entry about Ted's anguish at losing his place on the GLC is the most personally revelatory passage in the two published volumes. They are a vivid, narrow, sometimes melodramatic journalistic record, unlike Crossman's broad reflective approach. Sometimes they appear strikingly similar in style to the Angela Brazil-type school adventures she used to write for her friend Evelyn in Bradford. In those, there was always a ginger-headed heroine with an impish grin trying hard, sometimes failing, occasionally saving the day. Her diaries reflect the same solipsistic view of the world – 'the naughtiest girl becomes a cabinet minister'. But Barbara, like Crossman, was genuinely interested in exposing the inner workings of government. She believed that an explanation of the daily grind of a cabinet minister, which formed the background to the demand for clear thinking on finely balanced choices, would make people more realistic (and perhaps more forgiving) about politics and politicians.

Hell Corner, Westminster; the third element in Barbara's life was her constituency, Blackburn. Blackburn, she said, was 'the raw stuff of politics'; it was also the epitome of Britain's rust belt, a town in decline. It was a cotton town, and British cotton was finding world competition too tough. It had diversified into making machines for the manufacture of tufted carpets and into breweries. In a BBC series made in the 1960s, Jeremy Seabrook thought Blackburn grim and tyrannical. 'The subculture was a closed system which penetrated every feature of [life], dictated patterns of behaviour, belief and thought.' But it was also on the edge of the wild expanses of the Forest of Bowland. Arthur Wainwright, the great walker and writer, had been its assistant town clerk.

People who saw her in London as well as Blackburn noticed Barbara shift character as she travelled north: the smart, sassy cabinet minister emerged from her sleeper in Blackburn in clothes that were more downbeat, harder-working, less showy. One reporter suggested that, with a cigarette between her lips, she took on an almost masculine air. The town suffered from bad housing, poverty, drunkenness, low pay, and mill owners who pressed Barbara to find a solution to the intractable problems caused by world competition. It also had an energetic local party and a series of strong party agents, who criticized Barbara over Cyprus and even more over 'In Place of Strife'. They did not invariably find her easy to work with. They grumbled about her temper, her time-keeping and her intolerance when arrangements went awry, but they admired her powers of persuasion and they enjoyed basking in her fame. She could not cross from the train station to the White Bull, the modest hotel where she always stayed, without being greeted by someone who recognized her.

Barbara was an assiduous constituency member and described her constituents as her family. She would do street corner meetings,[27] standing on a rickety chair challenging people to come and heckle. She took up individual constituent's cases. No profile is complete without the tale of the Blackburn milkman who was told his eyesight was too bad to have the licence he needed to drive his electric float at two miles an hour round the town: Barbara got the law changed so that he could keep his job. In 1955, when she so nearly lost her seat, she blamed the hostility of the Catholic Church. (Cardinal Basil Hume, later Archbishop of Westminster, was then a local parish priest, and had preached that the Bevanites were crypto-Communists.) She decided to woo it back with a boost for Catholic education, and hunted down the Education Minister to talk to him about a new Catholic school. Tom Taylor, Blackburn Council's Labour leader, was with her:

> Either he didn't want to meet us, or he hadn't got time to meet us, and in the end, knowing the habits of this particular Minister, knowing that he went down to the bar every night round about half past eight, we decided that we would wait for him and lobby him when he arrived . . . after spending three-quarters of an hour with him he promised that the following day he would report back to his officials . . . within two months we were able to announce that we had got a replacement for the school in Blackburn.[28]

One one occasion she infuriated Crossman when as Housing Minister he came to talk to Barbara's local government officials about a new piece of legislation. Unconventionally, Barbara insisted on accompanying him to the meeting. Even more unconventionally, she then argued against the policy. As he recorded in his diaries, Crossman protested: ' "Look Barbara, you put your name to it." She replied, "A Cabinet minister is still allowed personal views as a constituency minister", and continued to denounce it.'[29]

By the late 1960s, Blackburn had a growing immigrant population which Barbara treated with great respect. There is no evidence that her strong opposition to immigration controls cost her votes in the town, where after 1955 her majority rose steadily. Blackburn had long since become her town, and despite the occasional rows with the local party they were proud of their MP, 'the greatest lady in the land'.

1970 had long been earmarked as election year, because in 1971, the government's fifth year, pounds, shillings and pence were to be replaced by decimal currency. Wilson thought decimalization might make the government unpopular and was determined to go to the country ahead of it. In the spring of 1970, the polls began to turn in Labour's favour. Roy Jenkins pulled off the great coup of eliminating the trade deficit. Ironically, Barbara's failure to hold down wage increases had introduced a general feel-good factor. On 14 May, Wilson declared 18 June as election day.

16. Yesterday's Woman

On the morning of Budget day, a series of models were smuggled into Mr Wilson's room in the House of Commons and unveiled before the Campaign Committee with electrifying effect. They showed members of the shadow cabinet in lurid colours and with down-in-the-mouth expressions. 'Yesterday's Men' was to be the theme of a £60,000 publicity campaign.

David Butler and M. Pinto-Duschinsky,
The British General Election of 1970[1]

Election day was to be 18 June, the first anniversary of the humiliation of 'In Place of Strife'. It was not an auspicious day to go to the polls. Labour's majority of ninety-seven was converted into a Tory majority of thirty. Barbara had felt defeat in the air, and privately told intimates that the government did not deserve to win. She blamed complacency at the top for a lacklustre campaign and had been sceptical about Labour's small but steady poll lead. 'I have a haunting feeling there is a silent majority sitting behind its lace curtains waiting to come out & vote Tory,' she wrote in her diary. She was not surprised by her own result: her majority was down to 2,600, and on a much lower turnout. 'As I go round the com. rooms with Ted and George [Eddie, her former agent] I am uneasily aware that there isn't exactly a euphoric rush to the polls.'[2] Barbara had had seven fat years since Wilson had become leader. The next seven were to be very lean indeed.

Inflation and strikes had been two of the dominant issues of the campaign. Five million days had been lost to strikes in the first six months of 1970 – twice as many as in the first half of 1969. One of the unconsidered consequences of her futile attempt to introduce industrial relations legislation had been to remind voters that they had more faith in the Tories' determination to be tough on trade unions than they had in Labour's. Although at first Roy Jenkins's refusal to have a reflationary budget, followed by alarming trade figures just three days before polling day were blamed for the unexpected reverse, on reflection, both left and right were inclined to blame Barbara for their loss of ministerial office.

After her last regretful hint of resignation to her civil servants, Barbara had never betrayed a sense of defeat over 'In Place of Strife'. To her relief, even Vic Feather had temporarily stifled his irritation and campaigned with her in Blackburn. She had made two radio broadcasts on prices and incomes policy. But few other Labour candidates regarded industrial relations as a vote-winning issue – unlike the Tories, who frequently revisited their promise to bring in legislation. Slowly, the backbenchers who had done so much to destroy the bill were forced to accept that their voters did indeed want something done about the perceived strength of the unions.

The day after the election, on 19 June, Harold Wilson took immediate stock of the new political order at a final Downing Street inner cabinet. Barbara was not invited. Desperate for contact, later she hunted him down by phone at Chequers. She got a brisk response and no gossip. Labour was out of power. She was out of favour.

Labour's second six years in office, in stark contrast to its first, had left few memorials. The soaring triumphs of 1945–51, the creation of the NHS and the welfare state, the huge extension of public ownership and the handover of power in India, were replaced in 1970 with little more than a creeping doubt about what Labour governments were for. Any claim the party had to economic competence had been shattered by devaluation; the ambitious proposals for growth and planning had barely left the drawing board. The old boast that Labour knew how to manage the trade unions was palpably untrue, while students demonstrated their anger at the government's support for American policy in Vietnam and its conciliatory approach to Rhodesia. With the exception of Roy Jenkins's iconoclasm at the Home Office – now only a distant memory – nothing radical, it seemed, had been achieved and very little had even been tried. Proposals to reform the House of Lords had been defeated, and a pensions scheme to end poverty in old age had fallen through lack of parliamentary time. The poor, according to a devastating analysis by the newly created Child Poverty Action Group, had actually got poorer. Mr Wilson's second term seemed to have produced little beyond Barbara's popular but undramatic equal pay, seat belts and breathalyser – meagre achievements for a government that had promised to harness the white-hot technological revolution to the cause of socialism.

The Tribunites, led by Michael Foot and Ian Mikardo, thought – and said, often and loudly – that they had been wasted years, when a landslide

majority had been allowed to rot in a feeble subservience to the enemies of
the left within the party and outside it. Out in the country, among the
activists whose disenchantment had contributed to the election defeat, the
sentiment was echoed and magnified. But the discontent was still unfocused
and negative, distinguished mainly by a refusal to support the party. Over
the next ten years that discontent was to become organized, directed and
concentrated on capturing the party's commanding heights. Ostensibly this
new 'outside' left's ambition was to impose the democratic will of the grass
roots on the leadership, a proposal already advanced in the 'Socialist Charter'
launched in *Tribune* in 1969, to keep it responsive to the party activists – a
demand that could be traced back without difficulty to the days of the ILP.
In fact, its objective matured into a sectarian concentration on a redefined
ideological purity which Barbara – old sectarian herself – found absurd and
naive and that Michael Foot was to call 'leftist infantilism'.

For Barbara, life in opposition to the government, rather than to her
own party's leadership, was a new experience. She had to accept that this
opposition was going to be different. Propelled from near-obscurity to the
top table in 1964, she had never even been in the shadow cabinet. For some
of her colleagues – like Denis Healey – it was an entr'acte, a hiatus in an
upward trajectory. Barbara had to face the fact that she was now nearly sixty,
the pensionable age for women; and she also had to acknowledge the
unpopularity of the government in which she had played a leading role.
Typically, for as long as she could, she tried to ignore both. The pressing
question, since she agreed with the general drift of the left's criticisms of the
government, was how to re-establish herself with her traditional constituency
without open disloyalty to the colleagues with whom she had served. 'I
know that the Labour govt failed in major ways,' she acknowledged in her
diary. To intimates she went further. She had told one journalist, towards
the end of the election campaign, that she 'and a number of others' would
not be prepared to take five more years of hard slog just to stand still. 'I
would want to see some radical changes or get the hell out of it.'[3]

She had invited her closest political friends to dinner for the weekend
following the election. Crossman – who had told her only after the election
that, although still an MP, he was going to edit the *New Statesman* – as well
as Tony Benn, Peter Shore, the clever and successful Manchester MP, Harold
Lever and Tommy Balogh, went to her flat in Cholmondley Court to discuss
'new directions'. As usual, they feared that Harold Wilson would be captured
by the right, and the issue was how to prevent it happening. Crossman
eagerly offered the *New Statesman* as platform and champion of the left.

One of Barbara's besetting weaknesses as a politician was an extraordinary capacity for self-deception. She refused to acknowledge that her career was, if not finished, then at the very least grounded. As far as she was concerned, she had opposed much of what had been done in her name as a cabinet minister and was therefore in some obscure way untainted by it. She could not see how damaged she had been not only by 'In Place of Strife', but by mere membership of the Wilson governments. To the horror of her friends, she now proposed to run for the deputy leadership of the party. George Brown, along with Jennie Lee, had been one of the most prominent casualties of the election, and there was no incumbent. Barbara wanted to turn the clock back to the glory days of 1968, when she had looked like Wilson's successor. 'I suddenly said: "Why shouldn't I stand for deputy leader?" which took them all aback,' she wrote in her diary. Crossman, Benn and Shore loyally, and probably dishonestly, promised support. Benn wrote: 'There was a general feeling that Barbara really shouldn't stand and that it was an explosion of feeling rather than a sensible decision, because after her trouble with 'In Place of Strife' her reputation in the Party had dropped very sharply.' Meanwhile, he speculated that he might stand for Chief Whip, an elected position in opposition. For one of the left to stand would at the very least damage the appearance of party cohesion. For two to stand would undoubtedly have been taken as a neo-Bevanite plot and would provoke retaliatory action by the right. A left slate and a right slate would emerge, and the fabric of the party would be shredded once more.

Wilson, dedicated to holding the party together – his main prime-ministerial achievement – was incandescent when Barbara told him her plan. He exploded with pent-up grievance, threatening resignation, attacking her personally. ('What job would *I* have got if Gaitskell had been leader?') Now it was her turn to be taken aback. Blind, as so often, to the wider impact of her plans, she thought his reaction 'very odd'.

> He was in a near neurotic state. He'd been appalled, he said, by what he had learned in the last couple of hours. I said I wanted to run as DL. Denis [Healey] had told him that, if I did, he would too . . . 'Yes, you are free to run but other people are free to make decisions too. I'm free to say that I won't be leader of a divided party. And I won't. The great thing I have done is to unite this party and I don't intend to preside over a party that is splitting again. If you want it that way you must find another leader.'

Barbara, inured by long experience to appeals for unity, was unimpressed. She tried to persuade Wilson that Callaghan and Jenkins, with their estab-lished power bases, were a serious threat to him in a way she would never be. In response, the Wilson entourage set on her. Marcia Williams harangued her about unity and the need to 'keep the right under control'. Barbara retaliated: the only other options were a threat – either Callaghan, with his power base at party headquarters, or Jenkins, who had a growing number of fans in the PLP. But Wilson's team did not see it like that. 'Gerald [Kaufman] followed me out to the car pleading with me not to run "for the sake of the party",' she recorded. Soon it was an eager topic of gossip around Westminster. Cecil King wrote: 'There has been some talk of Barbara Castle standing for the deputy leadership of the PLP. Wilson assured Rupert [Murdoch] that if she did so, she would not get more than twenty votes.'[4]

The leadership elections were still a fortnight away. Barbara was obdurate. 'Harold's behaviour has crystallised for me once again my always latent anxieties about his attitudes. I now believe that he is disastrous as leader. The only thing that keeps him there is the lack of a less disastrous alternative.'

But she knew that the PLP, which had never elected her to anything, was unlikely to start now. Finally Crossman – probably encouraged by Wilson, to whom he had become even closer now he was semi-retired from active politics – passed on to her the unsurprising news that even the Tribune group of MPs wouldn't vote for her, either for the deputy leadership or for the impending shadow cabinet elections (still called the parliamentary committee) because of 'In Place of Strife'. Without further comment in her diary, she pulled back from the contest for deputy leader. Jenkins, 'the man who denied them [the party] growth', romped home to become Wilson's deputy, beating Michael Foot by 133 to 67. Barbara consoled herself as she had before. 'Anyway I don't think I could stomach the intrigues that seem inseparable from leadership.' Entirely unsympathetic to Wilson's position, she was furious with his attitude to her desire to run, and his seeming dismissal of all she had achieved. She clutched at straws. Her candidacy should have shown him that 'I am not to be taken for granted. If that thought doesn't worry him then he is far gone indeed in his subservience to the Right,' she wrote.

The episode was over in the beat of a butterfly's wing. It aroused no publicity, it caused no immediate harm to anyone; but it left a long shadow across Barbara's future. Most immediately, as Ted sadly observed, the peerage that Harold had all but promised Barbara would be arranged for him after his humiliating dismissal as an alderman was now out of the question. But equally, the most important political relationship of her career was evaporating. The mutual support system between Harold and Barbara, forged in the 1950s when Barbara had backed him against the ageing Bevan and at its height in the battle for 'In Place of Strife', now went into slow, painful decline. Wilson never quite deserted her, but moments of intimacy became infrequent, and increasingly he allowed his irritation with her – culminating in a series of humiliations in their final years of government together – to show in public.

It was the last turning point in Barbara's career; even after the debacle of 'In Place of Strife', her sheer determination meant she had continued to be rated as one of the most successful ministers in the government. She had admirers across the old left–right divide, people who respected her political creativity as well as her drive and determination. She had built up credits across politics, she had shown herself capable of modernizing socialism. Then, in 1970, she threw it away. Where she could have tried to become a unifying figure on the centre left, steadying the party in the difficult years of opposition, instead she resumed the old, bitter factionalism; the previous six years, it sometimes seemed, had not happened. Instead of capitalizing on her position as a successful minister and seeking out areas of agreement, she spent the opposition years of the early 1970s fighting for policies that would be unacceptable to a significant part of the PLP and the party rank and file; first she was determined to reverse the party's pro-European position, regardless of the effect it would have on her own government's reputation. She was equally determined to justify her own actions in government by making the party and the unions face up to the need for a pay policy. Although in both cases her arguments were entirely consistent with her own long-held beliefs, they were not without an element of personal calculation. Yet the two battlegrounds she chose cancelled each other out. The pro-pay-policy right would not forgive her inflammatory approach to Europe, while the anti-European left could not accept the need for pay restraint.

At first, it seemed only that loss of ministerial office – an experience in a democracy which is, after all, as inevitable as it is unpredictable – presented new choices. On one level, Barbara was relieved to be out of office, free to enjoy summer days in the garden at Hell Corner. To lose office at a general election carries none of the stigma of being sacked, only the inconvenience of the loss of civil servant expertise and, especially in Barbara's case, the faithful civil service driver. She had no doubt that she wanted to stay at the top. Almost as a matter of course, she stood in the annual elections for the shadow cabinet – an event intended to give democratic legitimacy to the leadership but which serves mainly to exacerbate and illuminate the party's differences. For the first and only time, and without the support of most of the Tribunites (Michael Foot, who had just taken the momentous decision to fight from inside rather than outside the hierarchy, broke ranks and voted for her), she managed to scrape home, last of the successful candidates. But then what?

Her spirits were lifted by the apparent return of her friends on the left; in the autumn, one Frank Allaun, told her she should never have gone to the DEP (something she occasionally admitted to herself): ' "More than one t. unionist used to say to me you ought to be Leader of the party." ' Ted used to tell everyone that she would have been leader but for the mistake of going to the DEP. ' "Of course[Allaun continued], your Bill altered all that. I want you to know that I have a lot of good will towards you; you are so good on so many things. If only you would lie low for a bit on some of the things like prices and incomes policy . . ." I thanked him, but thought to myself that it will be no good anyone trying to lead this party unless we can get the t. unions to face up to political issues *like* prices and incomes policy.'[5] Wilson too pressed her to turn to a new field of endeavour and put the searing defeat of 'In Place of Strife' behind her. She and the party needed to move on. He tried to persuade her to tackle the Social Security brief, as Crossman had suggested she should if they had stayed in office.

Still Barbara, determined to fight the Conservative plans for industrial relations reform, refused to move. If she moved, she would be unable to defend her record. Already travestied, she would be forgotten. Her way back to the party's heart, she believed, lay in persuading her old colleagues that they had misjudged her intentions; she had been right all along. But this was another midjudgement. She had not yet grasped how completely she was on her own, an ex-minister from a government of which no one was proud – indeed, which even its former members were rushing to criticize. Old allies on the left, passed over by Wilson, felt she had betrayed them. She had neither close friends nor disinterested advisers, while in the aftermath of the defeat, the party was sliding down its traditional path into fratricidal chaos.

The Balkanization of the Labour Party, which culminated in the emergence of the Social Democratic Party twelve years later, began on 19 June 1970. Not only the left had found the experience of Labour government a disappointment; so had the right. Wilson, previously the beneficiary of their disquiet and now its author, retreated to lodge in Dick Crossman's house in Vincent Square and simply withdrew from politics at this crucial stage in order to write a book reviewing his six years in power. Others conducted similar reviews more publicly. From left and right, contemplating the wreckage of their hopes, came the raised voices of emerging factions as different emphases evolved into a clash of principle. Planning, the idea around which the party had so optimistically united ten years earlier, had failed. Now, the left sought new ways of controlling the economy, while the right sought new, non-economic, priorities.

Barbara's determination to stay and lead the attack on the Tory industrial relations legislation did not *cause* the divisions that ensued but it embarrassed many in the party, who felt it was simply dishonest; and it was the outrider of a struggle that would only really end with the Blairites' apparent annihilation of the left twenty-five years later.

The Tories' Industrial Relations Bill was rushed into the Commons by Robert Carr, Barbara's successor at the Department of Employment, in the autumn of 1970. It was indeed, as she argued in a welter of newspaper articles, quite different in spirit from hers. The Carr legislation was overtly intended to break the power of trade unionism. It introduced a new Industrial Relations Court with extensive powers to intervene in disputes; it ended the closed shop. But the principle was the same as those underlying Barbara's proposals. It brought the law into collective bargaining and it did so with measures – a cooling-off period and sanctions – which, however much Barbara argued otherwise, were familiar from her own failed attempt to legislate.

The party was divided on how to respond. Election campaign opinion polls showed that significant numbers, even of Labour supporters, thought trade unions were too powerful. A section of opinion in the party argued that outright opposition was unprincipled, and would be seen as surrender to the TUC. Jenkins felt she made 'a most appalling ass of herself, and of the Labour party, by frenziedly opposing the Government's Industrial Relations bill as a monstrous piece of class oppression, despite the fact that it owed about 80 per cent of its inspiration to her own In Place of Strife'.[6] On the other hand, the new left, close to the trade union leadership of Jack Jones and Hugh Scanlon, who claimed Barbara's legislation had unbolted the door for the Tories, were determined that the legislation should be entirely rejected. Barbara was convinced that she should do the rejecting.

In shadow cabinet, Barbara was instructed to pursue a policy of 'moderate opposition'. At a PLP discussion a few days later, her fellow MPs let loose their bile. 'I was taken aback at the bitterness and almost savage hostility to me. Some said they hoped we weren't going to fight the bill by trying to justify my proposals . . . I sat through all the nastiness getting calmer and calmer inside as I always do when I think I am being unfairly attacked. And I was more than ever determined to sweat it out.'[7]

She survived the first debate, admitting, 'I have never been so frightened in all my life.' In her diary she wrote:

The fatal day . . . Ted, who has been wonderfully understanding and not
impatient with my birth pangs for once, ran me down to the House . . .
Poor darling, he'll get the worst of it sitting in the gallery, aching with
anxiety by proxy. I know what hell that can be . . . during the last few days
people have approached me as tho I had been condemned to death,
commiserating with me . . . I knew [Ted] was frightened for me, because
he was so gentle . . . out on to the terrace to gulp some air. (I smoke myself
silly on these occasions.) Suddenly I wondered if a brandy would help. A
nice old Tory insisted on buying me one, and wishing me luck . . . And
then I was on my feet. The words came tumbling out.[8]

To her old private secretary at the DEP Douglas Smith, she said afterwards,
'What a gamble it was for me to insist on leading on the Bill, what a bad
time I had been through and how frightened I'd been.' Soothingly, he
responded that the department had disapproved of her decision but now
thought she had been proved right again.

Few, though, saw the distinction that Barbara spelt out in a Fabian
Society lecture early in 1971 when she presented 'In Place of Strife' as having
been a way of extending democracy and responsibility. Her White Paper's
central idea, she said, had been that 'collective bargaining is essentially a
process by which employees take part in decisions that affect their working
lives . . . it represents the best method so far devised of advancing industrial
democracy'. By contrast, she claimed, Tory industrial relations legislation was
about curbing power. 'It is their alternative to an incomes policy. Create
unemployment and weaken trade unions is the remedy. I prefer: strengthen
the unions and turn their negative power into positive power by bringing
them into decision making.'

For the general public – many of them trade unionists themselves – the
idea of the unions taking responsibility seemed vanishingly remote. The
language of opposition was growing steadily more strident. It was picked up
in parliament. Barbara sounded close to despair. 'This is what frightens me:
the clear tendencies of many trade unionists who think they can settle all
their problems, whether political, social or fiscal, by industrial action. If they
do this they will not undermine the Government but they will undermine
themselves . . . If they do it will probably put paid to there ever being
another Labour government.' Despite the fig-leaf talk of 'principled opposition', Barbara fought the Conservative bill clause by clause, forcing votes,
trying to ambush the government, resorting to every possible tactic in her
determination to prove the difference between her bill and theirs. Her
approach alienated still more of her own backbenchers, many of whom felt

she was being hypocritical in opposing the bill at all, and most of whom resented the repeated late nights and long hours of voting against a bill which they were not going to be able to stop. Warned by the whips of approaching trouble, Barbara dismissed the objectors scornfully as 'dilettantes'.

The more moderate trade unions, especially white-collar ones like the Inland Revenue Staff Federation from which both Jim Callaghan and Douglas Houghton had come and which was now headed by Cyril Plant, were anxious to negotiate with Carr. Feather would have none of it. There were angry rallies and a short, deadly slogan, 'Kill the bill', which only added to the public perception of 'extreme' trade unions. And the tensions simmering unseen below the surface in the union movement were reflected in the Labour Party. Early in 1971 negotiations began, through the newly established liaison committee between the TUC and the NEC, on a new Labour position on industrial relations. The unions wanted a commitment simply to repeal the Tory law. Callaghan – now, mysteriously, a convert to industrial relations legislation in some form – was pushing for an alternative.

The Holy Grail that the majority sought was a way to deliver full employment without also delivering inflation. Public awareness of the link between inflation and unemployment was growing, and there was talk of some kind of informal contract between the unions and the next Labour government. Tommy Balogh had already written about it; by January 1971 Michael Foot was talking about a 'new compact' and suggesting the party present itself 'as the party of consent'. Barbara, familiar with union negotiation in government, was more sceptical. She was particularly anxious about prices and incomes policy, which neither trade unions nor the left in parliament would discuss. Her interventions did nothing to improve her relations with the trade unions. At the party conference in the autumn of 1971, she was not allowed to speak on the Tory bill. It was a disastrous week, made even worse by public celebrations of her birthday. (It was thought to be her sixtieth, although in fact she was sixty-one. 'I don't appreciate obituaries while I'm still alive,' she wrote.) In her diary she confided.

> I wish I could believe in the unions as an instrument for Socialism. And yet the vigour of their fight for their members is an instalment of that socialism in a mixed economy – it is the jump from that short-term assertion of working class rights in a capitalist society to the transformation of that society which, I believe, can and should be achieved by political (parliamentary) means, which is so difficult. Where I quarrel with union leaders like Jack [Jones] – who make so many political demands – is that they won't even recognise the difficulty exists.[9]

The new left regarded Barbara's attitude to the unions as something close to treachery. But she had spent enough time knocking on doors, addressing meetings, to have an instinct for what the voters wanted, and enough time in government to understand both the economic and the symbolic significance of a pay policy. 'It was vital for the air to be cleared with the unions before we got back to power again,' she wrote. After a further year of negotiation on the liaison committee, Barbara noted disparagingly: 'I think that those like Wedgie [Benn][10] who believe we can and must draw up a "joint programme" – a kind of social contract between the TUC and the [next] labour govt – totally fail to appreciate the nature of the TUC beast. It *must* by definition keep some independence of action. What is the crime, then, if the Labour govt demands, by definition, some independence of action too?'

'Barbara can't help annoying people,' Benn wrote at about this time. In December 1971 the extent to which she had annoyed people was brought home: she was knocked off the shadow cabinet. She blamed Roy Jenkins for withdrawing his support. Commentators blamed her attacks on the Tory industrial relations legislation. Harold Wilson leapt to her defence in tacit acknowledgement of the burden she still carried for their joint failure over 'In Place of Strife'. He immediately sent her a note: 'Dearest Barbara, I'm terribly, terribly sorry. I half feared it – and on hearing said it was utterly disgraceful. We know why.[11] There isn't anything I can say, but with all you're going through, this is just too much. And it's a terrible loss to me – after a whole generation of comradeship.'[12]

Later that evening, they met.

> He walked in – white with rage. He had already rushed a charming note to me and told me he had tried to contact me before the party meeting to warn me of what was coming. He swept me off to his room for a drink . . . this is Harold at his most endearing; how can one be anything but loyal to a man who is so loyal to his friends? I have rarely seen him so moved; he talked of me as his old friend for whom he had always had a great affection – and if it had always been merely platonic, he added impishly, that wasn't his fault . . . 'of course' he would keep me on the front bench – in any job I liked . . . what about the social services?

At a dinner that night he declared to the television cameras, 'Barbara will be a member of my next Cabinet.'

It was soothing stuff. But Barbara felt damaged enough to contemplate leaving the front bench. Another old friend rode to the rescue. Crossman, ill and in deep trouble at the *New Statesman* where he too had alienated almost everyone, found time to persuade her to stay in the limelight and take his old brief at Social Security. Otherwise, a fate worse than unpopularity awaited: 'You'll disappear,' he warned her.

Barbara was exhausted. At sixty-one, she had emerged from six hard years in Cabinet to a gruelling eighteen months of opposition. Muvvie was slowly succumbing to dementia. The latest housekeeper had walked out. Worst of all, Ted's heart was giving him serious trouble. It began in the spring of 1971. One night, when the long hours of voting on the Industrial Relations Bill were at their worst, Ted had woken in the early hours to say he couldn't breathe. Barbara was too exhausted even to wake up properly. The following day he had been admitted to hospital. It was the final day's debate on the bill and Barbara had felt unable to leave the front bench. Her secretary Janet Anderson was sent round to Cholmondley Court to let the ambulancemen in. 'They think he has a virus infection and are taking a lot of tests. How serious it is we don't know. I have a chill feeling that all our plans for happy times together are now at risk.'[13] He had spent most of the rest of the year in hospital; finally, in September, he had a major operation. Anxiety about the future recurred. Would she and Ted have a retirement to enjoy? she wondered. Retirement was a mirage that still shimmered far enough ahead to be inviting. More often, what emerges from her diaries is a profound conflict of interest between her political life and her personal responsibilities. Visiting Ted caused her to miss some important meetings, a fact she observed with barely suppressed irritation. The responsibility was delegated largely to friends and family.

Early in 1972, with Ted slowly recovering and staying with her niece, Barbara went on a lecture tour of the States. In Chicago she came face to face with Women's Lib for the first time. 'I was surprised how seriously they took it: they just can't see how funny words like "consciousness raising" are. They loaded me with literature about it which gave me some more fun over breakfast . . . My lecture subject is Women in Politics and I am at a loss to know how to deal with it to an audience which is largely post-graduate.' The *Times*'s New York man Michael Leapman picked up the tale. 'Mrs Barbara Castle berated the American Women's Liberation Movement last night for its obsession with trivialities . . . "If I had bothered about whether I was called Mrs, Miss or Ms," she said, "I would never have worked up to the good neuter title of Minister . . . My consciousness was raised at the age of six . . . women should find a cause bigger than themselves – let us get ourselves obsessed with something bigger than sexual politics. In Britain politics is a crusade. Women, by identifying themselves with the crusade, can break down the conventional barriers more easily."'

Back in Britain, though, she was beginning to recognize that to be a woman is to be different. Each crisis was recorded with a sigh, and the easy confidence of men like Michael Foot in the Commons drove her to despair. Where she would beaver away for hours amassing and digesting facts and statistics, he would breeze into the Chamber, sit and listen, and then intervene – often, she acknowledged, to far greater effect than she did, despite her hours of sedulous application. She frequently lamented the wasted effort in her diary. In the gloom of October 1971, she wrote: 'I really ought to be able to do it on my head, but as always self-doubts are creeping in and I fear I am getting too obscure, just because I can't rattle off effectively disguised platitudes like the chaps can . . . go to bed muttering to myself: "I know I am a second class mind trying to do first class things. It's agony but I believe it is better than to be a first class mind doing second class things."' But to take up the flag of feminism would be an admission of defeat. She flatly rejected an appeal to join an organization a friend was launching called 'Women against the Common Market' with the comment in her diary: 'I really am not prepared to play in the third league.'

If she felt frustrated by her debating performance, she was entirely lost without Ted as her driver. After six years of official chauffeurs and half a lifetime of the faithful Ted, his illness meant she found herself marooned either at Westminster or, more profoundly, at Hell Corner Farm. She resolved, for the first time since Michael Foot had abandoned the attempt to teach her thirty-five years earlier, to learn to drive.

As usual, she took things too seriously. Having taken the decision she plunged in immediately with a retired police officer, who encouragingly told her that her reactions were 'above average despite her age'. On the first day, she spent four hours on hill starts, a prerequisite for driving away from Hell Corner. On the second, after a further four hours wrestling with the polite traffic of Henley-on-Thames, she felt she was on the home straight. But it was not Barbara's year. Writing up the day in her diary, she was still too shocked to find it funny.

> Suddenly I find myself at a sharp left-hand turn, try desperately to remember where I place my hands, negotiate the turn successfully, correct too soon, find myself heading for a wall, panic and put my foot down unconsciously on the accelerator. He grabs the wheel too late, and Bob's my uncle, crash! The wheel catches me painfully in the chest and the front of the car is a

buckled mess. Fortunately I was going pretty slowly in the first place . . .
My chief worry is lest someone recognises me and we have the *Daily
Express* on the doorstep when I get home. For apart from anything else, I
wasn't wearing my seat belt.

Her political career seemed headed just as certainly for the wall. It was a
point at which many would have given up. She had had six years in
government, she had proved herself in Cabinet. If the Heath government
lasted the full five years, she would be sixty-five at the next election. She
could have quietly announced that she was not contesting the next election
and spent her declining years in the garden with Ted. But she did not want
to. She had too much energy to stop; and her life was politics. She did not
like what was happening to the party, and she wanted to go out at the top.
Instead of resignation she set out on another crusade, firing the first shot in
the battle that would define Labour in the last quarter of the twentieth
century.

Europe was the issue that would force the party to define itself with
damaging, provocative, Gaitskellite clarity. There was no room for Wilsonian
fudge here. Either Labour was a party of the market economy, ideologically
flexible, economically pragmatic, at home in Europe. Or it was a British
socialist party, dedicated to achieving a genuine transfer of economic power,
internationalist in its outlook, committed to extending practical friendship to
the new countries of the Commonwealth. George Brown, as Foreign
Secretary in 1967, had persuaded Wilson to join him on a tour of European
capitals which evolved into an application for EEC membership (widely
rumoured to have been the price of keeping Brown in government). General
de Gaulle had blackballed the application magisterially and offensively by
declaring that the British economy wasn't up to it.

A few months after the 1970 election, Barbara noted a change in the
party mood on Europe. She set out to make herself the 'focal point of
opposition to Europe on socialist grounds'.[14] This could, she thought, be a
way out of 'the political doldrums'. For twenty years, she had been arguing
that the Common Market was nothing more than a rich man's club, a
capitalist construct that could only impede the advance of socialism through
its rules restricting state intervention and economic planning. Meanwhile,
the pro-Europeans were the enemy, 'ready to smash the party as long as they
get their beloved Europe'. It was, she concluded triumphantly, 'their socialism'. Jenkins – still Wilson's number two – had made an incendiary speech

in Birmingham appealing to the party to stand for 'honesty and consistency' in Europe. Wilson – and everyone else – read it as an attack on his leadership. To add to the pressure, his even longer-standing rival, James Callaghan, had now indicated his opposition to the Market.

To Barbara, mobilizing anti-Market sentiment in the party seemed an irresistible way of isolating Jenkins and the pro-Marketeers as well as an ideological imperative. When, early in 1971, Prime Minister Heath came back from Europe having succeeded where Wilson had failed, with agreement on entry, Barbara saw it as an opportunity to shift party policy so that it reflected growing hostility to Europe in the wider Labour movement. The Heath deal would require major legislation, and there were splits in the Tory ranks. Heath would need Labour support to get his measures through. The pro-Europeans argued it was an issue above party. For Barbara there was no such thing. She saw it as an opportunity to evict Heath from No. 10, and those who refused to treat it as such were dismissed as crypto-Conservatives. However, the pro-Europeans and uncommitted outnumbered the Labour MPs opposed to Europe, and the annual party conference, where the anti-Market wing's big battalions could be deployed, was still months away.

Barbara dreamt up the idea of demanding a special conference immediately, on the grounds that the PLP might have to vote in principle on the Market before the summer recess. In a paper for the National Executive she suggested – disingenuously – that such a conference should not come to any conclusion on Europe, but merely take note. It would provide an outlet for delegates' feelings without actually committing the party to a course of action. The delegates' feelings were not at issue – the party rank and file was known to be anti-Europe – but her anodyne approach meant unlikely allies such as Callaghan could support her motion. Even the arch-Jenkinsite Shirley Williams backed her (by mistake, she said later, in vain). Barbara won her argument for a conference. Her real intention was to use an amendment to the resolution the conference would debate, to bounce the leadership into demanding a general election on the issue of entry.

Wilson's speech to the conference would be the key. Callaghan, worried about the party's mood, came to see her (Barbara noted on 24 June). 'He had made his own position clear to Harold: he didn't give a damn for the [Common Market] but would do anything to get Heath out. Where did Harold stand? It was imperative that Harold came out openly against the Market at the special conference. [Callaghan] assured me he wasn't trying to stab him in the back; he was convinced Harold was the only one who could lead the party. "Some of us know your capacity to 'drip, drip away' on a subject till you get your own way. You must drip, drip on Harold now."'

But when she carried the message to Wilson, he was deeply suspicious. "Do not trust him, gentle maiden,"' he told her. ' "He only wants to trap me. Do you know that when we were in gov. he came to me and urged that we should switch from an American to a European policy? That man has no steel: used to weep in our b[alance] of p[ayments] crises."' In an impassioned outburst to his old intimate (over several glasses of brandy and water) he went on:

> My job – my one job – is to keep this party united – and I don't mean the PLP, I mean the party in the country. All along I have believed my duty was to be the custodian of party unity . . . I am determined to avoid the splits of 1959. But that means I have got to come out against [Europe] . . . I know I am only a bumbling amateur with no sense of tactics. So you think. But I shall find no difficulty in coming out against the terms. I am about to go through the worst 3 months . . . in my life. The press will crucify me. And the marketeers will never forgive me. But I shall bring the party out of this united and then I am seriously considering giving up the leadership.[15]

Barbara told him reassuringly that he was 'nobly doing the ignoble'. It was not a widely shared sentiment, least of all after he all but completed his shift away from Europe in his speech to the special conference on 17 July. In a lacklustre address designed to appease those opposed without alienating the pro-Marketeers, he claimed he could not accept the terms on which Heath was proposing entry. His assertion was undermined by a declaration from George Thomson,[16] who had led the Labour negotiating team, that the terms would have been perfectly acceptable. The pro-Europe *Mirror* said it was 'Mr Wilson's saddest hour . . . who can explain to [the voters] why the most important issue of a generation has – so far as Labour is concerned – become just a pawn in a game played for party advantage?'

Two days later Barbara herself suffered a wounding reverse and saw what was in her eyes incontrovertible evidence of the perfidy of the pro-Europeans. Scheduled to speak at a PLP meeting against Roy Jenkins – in the awkward position of being deputy leader at odds with party sentiment – she lost an undignified dispute over who should address the meeting last. She was resoundingly defeated by Jenkins, who pulled rank and insisted he had a 'delicate' personal position to explain. She was still fuming when she made her diary entry for 19 July:

> Roy stood up immediately [after Barbara's 'muted' address] to cheers. He launched into a vehement speech (which he had written out and later

circulated to the press) and worked himself up to a great emotional crescendo, not sparing Harold on the way . . . He sat down to tumultuous cheers with people . . . thumping on the desk with both hands. It could have developed into a standing ovation at the drop of a hat. I realised then why he had insisted on speaking last and why the room was so packed; as clearly organised a demo as I have ever seen, and an anti-Wilson demo at that . . . a group of us anti-marketeers adjourned to the smoke room for a Council of War. Mike [Foot] said my speech had been excellent but we all agreed that I had been tricked into muting it. 'This was all planned,' we agreed, 'the knives are out . . .' Roy stopped by our table on the way out . . . I [said] savagely, I had always liked and trusted [him] but never again. Roy was obviously shaken, bridled nervously and moved away.

As far as she was concerned, this was proof that the right was now organizing as the Bevanites had in the 1950s. She went to see Harold. ' "Perhaps now you will listen to some of us," I pleaded with him. "They've always been out to get you and they think this is their chance." He said grimly he had some hard thinking to do.' But Wilson's total conversion to an anti-Market position had yet to be accomplished. After tortuous negotiations over a form of words that would not irrevocably alienate the pro-Europeans, this was finally achieved at the next NEC meeting. At the autumn conference of 1971, the position was confirmed: the party was finally committed to seeking a specific mandate, through a general election, before joining the European Economic Community. And Wilson once again rested on the left for his main support. Barbara felt restored, at least partially, as a figure of influence. In fact, the special conference had exacerbated a rift in the party that took twenty years to heal.

The 1971 Labour Party conference thus committed the party to opposition; from there it was one short step in the mistrustful climate of the early 1970s to insisting that MPs toe the party line – not, the left claimed, as they had been made to toe the line back in the 1950s by the whips, whose authority came ultimately and undemocratically from the right-wing trade union barons, but the constituency party line. The left argued that defeating Heath on the principle of entry to the EEC would force a vote of confidence that Labour could win. Therefore supporting him – bailing him out – over Europe was tantamount to betrayal. All the same, sixty-nine pro-European Labour MPs, led by Roy Jenkins, defied the three-line whip, giving Heath a majority for entry of 112. Had they obeyed the party line, he would have been defeated. The left claimed political treachery; the pro-Europeans, applauded in the press, that the issue was above politics.

It might have ended there had not President Pompidou of France declared there would have to be a French referendum on British entry into Europe. It was the launch pad Tony Benn needed to renew a long campaign he had been fighting for a British referendum specifically on the issue of entry. Barbara supported him enthusiastically, with another bitter attack on the pro-Europeans, as she reported to her diary: 'I pointed out that when conference decided against a referendum in favour of a general election, it also expressed the hope that the PLP would unite behind the conference decision. [Conference] could not have foreseen that so many of our colleagues in the House would make a general election impossible by supporting the gov.' She added in parentheses, 'I thought I did rather well, and later Terry Pitt [a Transport House official] told me it was one of the best speeches he had ever heard at the NEC.'[17] But it did nothing to heal the increasingly unbridgeable division between pro- and anti-Marketeers.

Within a fortnight the referendum policy had been adopted. Roy Jenkins resigned the deputy leadership in protest. 'The schism began at that point,' Roy Hattersley later remarked. Barbara gloated. 'What a mess [Jenkins] has made of things! He ought to have abstained in the first place and not run for the office. Lying low for a bit would have saved both his own position and the party's unity. Now he – and the fanatics who have been egging him on – have the nerve to argue that it is those who are supporting the party line on the CM who are "splitting the party".'[18]

Even Jenkins's friends, like Hattersley, thought he had blundered into a political cul-de-sac. Predictably – and in defiance of Barbara's own advice – the departure of Jenkins to the back benches drove Wilson to build up the right. With his eye once again on the unity of the movement, he used the reshuffle to promote the vanquished Jenkinsites, including Hattersley himself, who became Education spokesman. Denis Healey became shadow chancellor, Callaghan shadow foreign secretary. In the new climate, friends on the left became a little less important; Barbara, seen as the source of schism, was an embarrassment. She did not see it like that. 'It is typical of Harold,' Barbara recorded, plainly through gritted teeth, 'that his reaction to an attack on his leadership should be to strengthen the Right. I fear for the party – terribly. And I know now that if I HAD taken the job Harold offered me – leadership of the House[19] – and used it to establish close personal contact with backbenchers, I might have been in a very strong position now. Perhaps there is some truth in the story that women don't *want* to get to the very top.' She added, returning to her pious self-deception, 'In my case I find intrigue too distasteful.'

The Jenkins resignation, in April 1972, left a gap in the shadow cabinet.

In the by-election against Eric Heffer, who had previously secured the same number of votes as she had for shadow cabinet, Barbara won. It was later claimed by a right-winger, John Golding, that her success was due to his taking a bet on her and rounding up his friends in the Manifesto Group (of right-wing MPs) to support her to make sure that she was elected and he won his bet.[20]

Golding's claim is borne out by the results of the full shadow cabinet election in November when she was voted off again. This time she was shattered. 'I am not only numb – I'm bewildered too. What makes me so personally unpopular? I know I haven't scintillated in the House, but I have been competent. Is it the Left which has written me off? Yet I was on the Tribune list this year. Or have I been the target of the pro-marketeers?'

Overwhelmed by depression as she had never been before, Barbara decided to stand down altogether from the opposition front bench. She would call in the aid of the party en masse to redress the balance inside the PLP. She sketched a letter to Wilson explaining, in an echo of the campaign Benn was already fighting, that she wanted to reconnect with the party in the country: 'I have been alarmed at the growing gap between the party in the House and the party in the country and I cannot think of anything more likely to weaken us as a movement and to rob us of victory at the next election. I want during the coming year to play my part in closing that gap and in preventing the open defiance by some of our colleagues of the wishes of the rank and file.'[21] But still she hesitated: no front-bench job would also mean no reason to speak from the platform at next year's party conference. Ted told her she must come off; Dick said she must stay on. She asked Michael Foot for his opinion. He asked how she felt about it. 'I said I felt pretty exhausted, and the thought of another 12 months' slogging on detailed legislation when I knew the back benchers were not behind me frankly appalled me. "Then don't do it," he said firmly.' Foot, good friend that he had again become, went to see Wilson. The job as shadow social services secretary was hers if she wanted it, he said on his return. But some right-wingers had already been to see Wilson to demand that she wasn't reappointed.[22]

She made her decision public at a meeting in Blackburn. The *Guardian* reported: 'Mrs Castle's statement suggests that she is embarking on a bid to recapture her political youth ... Her bid to reassert her left-wing credentials comes at a moment when there is growing desperation on the Left of the party about its failure to make the party at Westminster do as Conference wishes it to.'

There were kind letters – from Shirley Williams: 'I'm sorry ... you are the ablest woman I have ever met in politics. It is a cruel business, and you have had more than your fair share of its cruelty', and from dozens of Tories, mainly beginning 'I would never vote for you but . . .' Other friends rallied. Hugh Macpherson in *Tribune* wrote:

> Her treatment by the Labour party should be a stern warning to anyone entering politics who harbours any illusion about gratitude in the rough-house of Westminster. There was nothing remotely moderate about the way she has been singled out as the scapegoat for all the troubles with the unions. Of course it was only to be expected that her old adversaries in the party would never vote for her but she was ultimately betrayed by the left and 'moderate' wing of the the party which has such appeal in editorial offices – when Labour is in opposition.

Dick Crossman, newly ousted from the *New Statesman*, who had never been elected even once to the shadow cabinet, wrote angrily in a newspaper column about the curse of moderation in the PLP: 'When she won her seat in 1945, for example, it was already obvious that Barbara Castle had just the combination of radical conviction, political flair and administrative ability to take charge of a big ministry and fight her policies through. Yet never once before she became a real Minister in 1964 was she voted into shadow office by her parliamentary colleagues. And all the political commentators said how wise it was to keep a firebrand like Mrs Castle out in the cold.'

She arranged with Wilson, Foot serving as intermediary, that the social services job would be hers again in a Labour government; meanwhile Douglas Houghton, 'too old to claim a job in the next cabinet' – and, almost as important, not on the NEC and therefore ineligible to be a platform speaker at conference – would take charge. A fortnight later, however, Barbara was still at a loss (and no caretaker spokesman had been appointed). She told her local paper not to write her off, but privately she wondered if she had reached the point of no return. 'My nervous exhaustion continues. It is like the aftermath of a road accident and I find myself waking up in the middle of the night to brood in the darkness about the political dead end I now face.' A week later: 'I crawl home so deeply depressed I don't know how I shall ever pull out of it. Once again I wake up in the night submerged by gloomy thoughts.'

A few days later, the same refrain: 'I wish I knew how to pull out of this terrifying self doubt and gloom. If I hadn't got Ted and [Hell Corner Farm] and the dogs I should go mad. Restored my sanity somewhat by scrubbing the lounge floor.' Unexpectedly, her shadow cabinet defeat ended one source

of misery. She got back on good terms with *Tribune*. Its editor Dick Clements
took her out to lunch. 'I told him I felt at sea these days: "I have no political
base". My loyalties are all with the Left but I could not bring myself just to
try to crawl to cover by applying to join the Tribune group of MPs.' He
told her to make *Tribune* itself her base. 'That would be a different thing. I
really think he may have something there. I know I crave a warm, not arid
Socialism.'

As she acknowledged to Clements, she had nowhere to go in the party.
The Bennite left had written her off ('Barbara really has no future although
she is a very vigorous and active woman,' Benn wrote priggishly when he
decided not to vote for her for the shadow cabinet), and she had little time
for them. There was a series of confrontations with the left on the National
Executive, her last remaining base, over the economy, prices and incomes.
She thought their approach was too often naive and misleading and she did
not disguise it:

> I went on with my usual recklessness to plead eloquently that no gov. could
> manage the economy if the unions insisted on following a policy of laissez
> faire, reminding them that Hughie [Scanlon] had once said to me, I cannot
> accept that any wage claim is ever inflationary. Something like panic set in
> at this. Mik[ardo] said disapprovingly that he was sure the unions would
> play along once they had a gov. that was really trying to do the things they
> wanted. Denis agreed; even Jim and Douglas [Houghton][23] were silent. . . .
> I went away in deep depression, sure that I was a figure of deep suspicion
> once again. Yet all I want is for the trade unions to face up to the
> implications of their own demands and tell us frankly what alternatives they
> want.[24]

A couple of days later, at a joint meeting of the NEC and the PLP, she
barged in again: the next Labour government would face a 'crisis of
impossible expectations'. At party conference, too, when she warned delegates that a rise of £10 a week in pensions would mean finding £1.5 billion:
'We should be committing ourselves to redistribute the national income, not
merely between rich and poor, but between private consumption and public
expenditure. In other words we should need to create an entirely differently
motivated society . . . If conference consciously and courageously made this
choice, no one would be more proud than I.' Later she was told she had
been wrong to put a figure on the £10 promise. 'Is it now anti-Socialist to
face the truth?' she asked her diary angrily. Early in 1973 she criticized a leading Bennite Joan Maynard, who had declared she was in favour of a prices

and incomes policy as long as it was part of a socialist economy. Barbara was dismissive. 'The trouble with that answer, I thought to myself – not for the first time – is that we will never get to a Socialist economy by one leap. The real problem is how to buy the time to build a Socialist economy and how to win people over to Socialism on the way. Sectional selfishness won't do it.'

Barbara was increasingly finding herself on ground where she had never been before: somewhere towards the centre of party thinking. Out on the right wing, now untroubled by the constraints of party office, Roy Jenkins was also trying to swing the party away from the Bennites. In the spring of 1973 he launched a series of speeches setting out an agenda on poverty, inequality and injustice, areas on which he wanted the party's focus to fall. There was little in the speeches with which Barbara could argue and much that she could endorse. She accused him, privately, of plagiarizing ideas from party working groups. Jenkins, as far as she was concerned, was part of a conspiracy against Wilson; his first lieutenant, Dick Taverne, had been deselected by his constituency party in Lincoln for refusing to obey the party line on Europe, then stood as an independent and won.

Jenkins's first speech in the series, delivered in Oxford on 9 March 1973, fed her suspicions. It was widely interpreted as the opening shot in an autumn leadership bid. He attacked the tone of Labour politics and asserted that the election had been lost because the party's policies in government had been too left-wing. Barbara, unsurprisingly, took it personally, although this was almost certainly a reference to Wilson's U-turn on Europe. 'People dislike the conventional slanging matches of politics, and turn away in boredom when they listen to hyperbolic denunciations of the other side for doing what they have a shrewd suspicion the denouncing party would itself be doing if it were in office.' He criticized – in terms Barbara was echoing in her diary – the 'easily-made promises never carried out', and, plainly referring to Europe, dismissed policy made 'to solve internal party problems and pay off old scores'.

Barbara, scheduled to speak in Taunton the following day, hastily redrafted. She was, she declared, 'sick and tired' of Jenkins. She challenged him to tell the country whether he was in favour of the Labour government abandoning its statutory prices and incomes policy, which 'I tried so faithfully – yes, too faithfully – to operate on his behalf. Did he not come to realise, as I realised, that you cannot make a prices and incomes policy work without the consent of the people you represent? Let him tell us whether he was in favour of Mr Harold Wilson's and my agreement with the TUC and of withdrawing "In Place of Strife" . . . I believe it is the voters' memory of those disappointingly over-orthodox and timid years of our government which is preventing them from swinging back to us enthusiastically now.'

The Conservative industrial relations legislation had thrown the unions back into the arms of the Labour Party. Between them, Michael Foot and Jack Jones were devising alternatives to a statutory pay policy. Jones had suggested a conciliation and arbitration service to help resolve disputes, and the party and unions had worked their way towards the idea of a 'social contract' and the creation of a 'climate' by government which, by controlling prices and pumping cash into public services, would make huge pay claims a thing of the past.

By 1973, for the first time, a new generation of trade union leaders were using their block votes to support radical reform. On Europe, economic policy and social policy, the block votes would now swing behind the left instead of the right. But faced with the prospect of power, the left was fragmenting. Foot, increasingly, was the unifier, counselling caution, defending the rights of parliament. It was Tony Benn who led the new left and who increasingly controlled the policy agenda. It was Benn who championed the radical 'Programme for Britain 1973', which promised 'to bring about a fundamental and irreversible shift in the balance of power and wealth in favour of working people and their families'. The government would intervene directly in the economy by taking into public ownership the top twenty-five companies, the 'commanding heights', and setting up a national enterprise board to run them. When Wilson recoiled in alarm at this, ideas for imposing greater control by conference on the party leadership and the PLP were proposed, with MPs mandated to follow the programme agreed at conference and the rank and file given more weight on the NEC.

Barbara could do little more than protest. She found herself urging caution, trying to insist on tempering idealism with realism. She managed to persuade the NEC to initiate an exercise in costing the Programme, but it had little impact. She attacked delegates' refusal to take painful decisions. She was more optimistic about the notion of a social contract and the challenge of costing a new concept: the 'social wage', the amount contributed by government to the pay packet in the form of health and education and other public services. (She calculated it, in early 1974, at £1,000 a year per person.)

Her attendance in the Commons and at NEC meetings had to be balanced with looking after Ted. By slow degrees, the incentive to be at Westminster was waning. She often felt lost and friendless there, and overwhelmed by the weight of her responsibilities at home. The party's anger against her seemed, if anything, to be building rather than retreating. The trade unions were losing their battle against the Tories' industrial relations legislation, and in their frustration blamed Barbara with mounting vehemence for paving the way for it. Jack Jones told anyone who cared to ask that she was completely discredited. She found him icy: 'Talking to him in his evangelical mood I always feel like a modest member from the ranks of the New Model Army getting my moral instructions from the great general,' she wrote in her diary.

She claimed to be suspicious of Foot's conciliatory approach to the party (in 1973, he had only narrowly missed becoming deputy leader), but the fact remained that the unions – and especially Jones, who had become Foot's close ally – were negotiating with him on terms that she had never managed. Although their old affectionate relationship had been restored after the bitterness engendered by 'In Place of Strife', and Foot was a deeply loyal and considerate friend, she did not have the kind of obsessive, terrible-twin conspiratorial friendship with him that she had had with Crossman. Michael and his wife Jill Craigie led a wider, less exclusively political life, diluted by literature and films. The two women had an uneasy relationship. They disagreed about important things, especially the significance of feminism. Jill was a widely read and committed supporter of women's rights, in the vanguard of new-wave feminism. Barbara delighted in regarding feminism as a lesser interest, suitable only for those who could not make it in a man's world. She once sent Jill an original of a Vicky caricature of herself, inscribed 'to my feminist friend'. They went to each other's parties, they ate in each other's houses. But, close as Barbara and Michael were at Westminster, the two couples were never quite intimate.

As for Tony Benn, Barbara, perhaps inspired by rivalry, sometimes admired his courage but more often doubted his judgement. Her own judgement may have been coloured by evidence that Benn was capturing the leadership of the left outside parliament, a constituency Barbara would once have led herself. By 1972, she had dropped to fourth in the NEC elections, which Benn now topped as regularly as she once had. She belonged with the older, more traditional (and ultimately more enduring) soft left, the left that believed in parliament and the strength of institutions, which might be supported but not replaced by the Bennite world of people power and workers' control. They had always had an edgy relationship; Benn, more than ten years younger, more assured, sailing briskly leftwards despite his record in the last Labour government (he had, after all, backed 'In Place of Strife' almost to the end) – and in Barbara's view tending dangerously to the demagogic – was, she thought, too willing to mix with people who did not have Labour's best interests at heart. She noted primly his willingness to accept speaking invitations from groups she considered little better than fellow travellers, and dismissed policy proposals from his supporters in Transport House that refused to take account of the realities an incoming Labour government would face.

Crossman remained her most intimate political friend. In opposition, and especially while he had been editing the *New Statesman*, their old relationship had continued. She told a journalist she had a love–hate relationship with him and, in the more reflective mood that had overtaken her, defined it in her diary: 'I would . . . miss Dick terribly if anything happened to him . . . and [will] miss him when he has completely cut himself off from Parliament-ary politics.'

She did not know it, but he was already terminally ill. Crossman put his problems down to the recurrence of a stomach ulcer, but by the end of 1973 he knew he was dying of cancer. By early 1974, her best and closest political friend, the person who, after Wilson, had done most to promote her career, could barely manage a glass of wine with her at lunch. She harried him about pay relativities, her latest political idea. He told her how tired he was. 'I had a love–hate relationship with him,' she said again, this time to Roy Jenkins. 'More love than hate,' he observed. A few weeks later, Crossman died. 'A great, abrasive, tonic force has gone out of my political life,' she wrote. 'I shall miss him terribly.'

By the time Crossman died, Labour was back in government. Crossman had always intended that his diaries should be his memorial. He had finished preparing the first volume for publication before his final illness, and the *Sunday Times* was due to start serializing them in the autumn of 1974. Crossman, political theorist, knew and intended that publication would provoke a constitutional crisis and was apparently unconcerned whether it happened when his own party was in power. The convention of collective responsibility in Cabinet imposes a thirty-year rule of secrecy (shortened from fifty years by Wilson) to protect the confidence of politicians and officials lest advice and discussion are inhibited by fear of imminent publica-tion. Crossman wanted to expose the workings of government precisely in order to feed the contemporary debate 'while the controversy was still green'.[25] The serialization, delayed and in slightly expurgated and shortened form, happened early in 1975. Only then did the Labour government obtain an injunction in an attempt to prevent the book being published.

Two years earlier, Barbara had discussed publishing her own diaries with Harold Evans and Frank Giles of the *Sunday Times*: 'They insisted that extracts could be made extensively . . . to make a book . . . after all, why not? Dick will be spilling his beans very shortly and I should hate his version of events to go down in history as the only authentic one.'[26] Barbara's plans for her diaries were widely known, and her support for the publication of Crossman's was taken for granted. Yet, in 1975, when she was invited to sign an affidavit on behalf of Crossman's literary executors (who included Michael Foot), saying that the knowledge that someone was keeping a diary would not inhibit her from working with them, she refused (as did all the Cabinet except Patrick Gordon Walker). Furthermore, when Anne Crossman signed an affidavit which said, among other things, that 'my husband knew Barbara Castle was keeping a diary', Barbara said she would publicly deny it. It is hard to explain why[27] – given that she had signed her own contract to publish memoirs based on diaries nearly ten years earlier and that Crossman had so often offered help to her – she would do nothing for him in return. It is possible that she felt she had offended Wilson too much already to risk taking the dead Crossman's side against him, yet by 1975 she certainly intended to publish her own diaries, once Labour was in opposition again, and if the government had won the Crossman case, the work that she had always referred to as her pension plan would have become worthless.

Well before the diaries could be published, in 1969 Barbara – true to her faith in personal publicity – authorized a curious biographical venture in which a journalist, Wilfred De'Ath, was provided with the names of a dozen of Barbara's friends, family and Blackburn party workers. They were all interviewed – including Ted and Barbara – and the results had been published in a slim volume in 1970 entitled *Barbara Castle: A Portrait from Life*; it was an attempt to convey the political flavour of Barbara at home and in her constituency. It is not clear what she was expecting or what she had told the interviewees, but several of them,[28] surprisingly, had not realized their words would appear between hard covers, and Barbara had apparently not considered that some of them would have hard things to say about her. She was furious in particular with her niece Sonya for calling her 'so bloody virtuous that none of the family ever feels completely a person in her presence', and with her former constituency secretary Elaine Strachan, who had reminisced at length about her stinginess and a tendency towards feeling a victim. Barbara moaned about the book, but nonetheless it was serialized in her local paper under the headline, 'Am I Just God's Most Arrogant Bitch?' As part of a campaign of self-promotion, it had limited success.

Money was always an anxious consideration for Barbara. Sometimes she was plain parsimonious, but in in the opposition years, on a back-bench MP's salary – raised in 1972 for the first time in nearly ten years from £3,250 to £3,500 – and with Ted out of work and too ill even to make a contribution to the daily chores, she genuinely struggled. Barbara refused to compromise, entertaining the family (although making them work for it), carrying on with plans to improve the garden, relying on the kindness of friends, especially her secretary Janet Anderson,[29] to drive her back and forth from London. Occasionally, and imbued with a spirit of romance, she did the journey by public transport, but the bus left her ten minutes' walk from the nearest train station in High Wycombe, and dumped her back a dark and lonely half-mile from her Buckinghamshire home. She had a few more driving lessons, but they tailed off without a test ever being attempted.

For much of 1972, Ted needed visiting in hospital. Weekends were spent trying to contain nature at Hell Corner Farm. Muvvie was another anxiety: she was deaf and vague, and prone to damaging falls. Hanging on to Hell Corner against the financial pressures became a constant preoccupation, every family holiday there a reminder of how precious it was. Barbara took on a huge amount of broadcasting and newspaper journalism to keep her income up, but every television appearance provoked a storm of letters. Even when she had a full-time secretary, partly paid for by her publishers who were hoping for a book of memoirs, she could not cope. Only the joys of Hell Corner inspired her.

'What deep satisfaction I get from possessing and running this haven. I like to lie in bed and feel the place full of distant murmurs of happiness. I hope I can make a go of my book [of memoirs] because on its success rest our hopes of being able to retain this unique focus point.'

Time, she knew, was running out. The next chance would be her last.

17. Battling On

Barbara is unchanged from the old days: she wanted her entire legislative programme spelled out in the Queen's Speech. She is just politically greedy, that is the only way of describing her.

Tony Benn, *Against the Tide: Diaries 1973–1977*[1]

The 1970s was the decade of disillusion. Disappointment, such a feeble emotion, shattered British political life. Over the next five years of compromise and defeat, the Labour Party became increasingly unstable, a prelude to becoming, in opposition, unelectable.

The election that Edward Heath called in February 1974 was fought against the background of a miners' strike, in response to which the Conservatives had introduced a three-day working week and issued ministerial advice to save hot water and bath with a friend. Mr Heath boldly asked, 'Who governs Britain?' The answer was obscure. A Conservative majority of thirty had been lost, but Labour did not have enough seats to form a majority government. Heath failed to persuade the Liberals into a coalition. Wilson decided to go it alone and risk a minority administration; he would challenge the opposition to force another election by voting down his government.

The harder the choices, the more intensely the battles were fought. Barbara's greatest political asset remained her special relationship with the party leader, but the old intimacy had gone. Wilson, never as engaged in his third and final administration as he had been in earlier ones, was beginning to find Barbara's unflagging energy overwhelming. As Bernard Donoughue, one of Wilson's kitchen cabinet advisers, noted in his account of working for Harold Wilson, 'She was shrewd, aggressive . . . By 1974 [Wilson] seemed a little frightened of her; even bored by her increasing shrillness.'[2] But Wilson kept his promise and put her in his Cabinet as Secretary of State at the

Department of Health and Social Security. Observers noted that the two most controversial figures on the left and the right of the party – Barbara and Roy Jenkins, who was reluctantly to be Home Secretary again – had both been put in jobs below their obvious abilities. 'A year or two at Social Services,' Barbara wrote with determined optimism, 'and then it will be retirement – or a bigger bid.'[3]

Barbara's miserable four years of eclipse, her hatred of the right and her suspicion of the Bennite left, foreshadowed the turmoil of her next fifteen years in the party. Painfully aware that she no longer had an automatic place in its heart, she struggled for secure political ground. Ten years earlier, she had created that ground for herself, triumphantly forcing personal admiration and the acceptance of her policies. Now, even in a government where all the leading players (except Michael Foot) had been scarred by the rank and file's reaction to their first attempt at office, she stood out as damaged goods. She was sixty-three. She did not feel old, but the appointments at the hairdresser and the ministrations of the TV make-up girls (always the *senior* make-up girl, it was gleefully reported) had become even more essential to her sense of well-being. For bad-hair days she acquired a wig, Lucy. Lucy once got whisked off during a televised walkabout in the ashes of a burnt-out old people's home. It says much for the power of Barbara's personality that the event went entirely unreported.

> Cameras peeped at me through every aperture as I went through the ruined home, watching my feet in case I tripped. Alas I did not watch my head and suddenly, to my horror, I felt 'Lucy' snatched from it by a piece of wire trailing from the roof. The officer said, 'Oh!' I snatched 'Lucy' back and somehow pulled her on my head again, askew – and carried on . . . Some inner grimness of will always comes to my rescue in these crises and I walked on, looking, questioning, and *willing* my entourage to believe they had imagined it . . .[4]

Birthdays were an embarrassment, particularly as they almost always fell during the party conference, and recent years had been so dispiriting and the strain of coping with Ted and her mother so great that she had already warned her constituency that she might not fight another election. However, she agreed to stay on in 1974 because there was plainly a second election coming soon. In truth, she was not ready to go: she wanted to pull it off again. The prospect of getting back into administration and proving once more her creative and managerial capacities restored her self-belief. She had been a great cabinet minister before, and as Secretary of State at the DHSS she could be so again. She was, she wrote, 'supremely confident'. Office would be her route back, the way to remind the party of her commitment and her ability to achieve what they wanted achieved, and to show a wider audience that she had talents too great to be overlooked.

The Department of Health and Social Security was Crossman's final political bequest to Barbara, the politician most likely to use it to push back the frontiers of the welfare state. The department had been created for Crossman in 1968, when Wilson was still thinking of an inner cabinet of departmental overlords. Barbara's capacity for detail and her administrative drive were, Wilson anticipated, ideally suited for the monstrous department. But the merger of Social Security and Health reflected a view of both that was already out of date when it had been proposed. In the immediate post-war era there was a certain synthesis: both dealt with acute poverty – Social Security was mainly about keeping people out of it, and the Department of Health about treating them once they were in it.

By the 1970s, it seemed that many of the assumptions on which the Beveridge Report had been based were out of date. Unexpectedly, as affluence spread, demands on the health service grew. The Department of Health had come to be largely about running a huge nationalized industry while, in an era of full employment, Social Security had become much more about the economics of work and retirement. The departments had their own Permanent Secretaries, and had only recently moved into a shared building; Crossman used to have two offices and would frequently catch his officials out by turning up unexpectedly. The departments would be decoupled again, after twenty years, in 1988.

Barbara's officials at Alexander Fleming House, the 1960s-barbaric headquarters of the DHSS at the Elephant and Castle, a glum district of south London that their presence had failed to revive, viewed her arrival with nervous anticipation. She lived up to her advance billing. She arrived with a clear agenda and, at least one participant at the first large meeting remembered, a handbag. Officials were not yet used to handbags. She also had plans for a political 'cabinet'. Wilson had authorized the idea, and Barbara brought in as a political adviser a young Islington councillor who was a friend of Ted's, Jack Straw, as well as Brian Abel Smith, Professor of Social Administration at the LSE, who had been indispensable to Crossman. 'I appointed Brian for his brain, Jack for guile and low cunning,' she would tell visitors.[5]

Inevitably, the agenda was not entirely of her choosing. At the top was pensions: both occupational pensions and the basic state pension. The latter's immediate uprating had been a key election pledge and had to be negotiated with the new Chancellor, Denis Healey. There was also a pressing need for a decision on the state's role in providing occupational pensions. Barbara wanted to tackle poverty, and there was a demand in the party for action on pay beds.

Pay beds were about politics. Over the previous five years, the issue of allowing NHS doctors to treat private patients in private rooms within NHS hospitals had achieved a political prominence out of all proportion to its actual importance in the efficient functioning of the health service. Barbara saw it as an area where she could once more tackle the producer in the interests of the consumer and impress the party and trade unions, for whom it was an issue of talismanic status. However, as at least one of her special advisers and her officials and her Health Minister were to tell her, private practice would be more effectively tackled simply by improving state provision. The decision to elevate the elimination of pay beds into a ministerial priority was the equivalent of running up the red flag over Alexander Fleming House.

Occupational pensions, by contrast, were a pressing practical matter: there had to be a swift decision on whether to abort the scheme for second pensions introduced by the outgoing Tory minister, Sir Keith Joseph. Joseph had legislated for a funded system of occupational pensions, and it was due to kick in within months. Legislation needed for some aspects of the scheme would have to be started almost immediately. Labour had strongly opposed the Tory bill when it had gone through the House because its provisions were inadequate for the millions of people on low pay or with erratic earnings. It set up only a safety-net 'State Reserve Scheme' for those either with no access to occupational pensions or who could not join or keep up membership of one of the compulsory private schemes. Nor did it do anything to improve women's access to pensions, even though women pensioners constituted one of the most obvious pool of poverty. The State Reserve Scheme would be fully funded – that is, all contributions would go into a fund from which future (rather than current) pensions would be paid. Its size would fluctuate depending on the state of the stock market.

But devising an alternative in a matter of months was a task requiring Herculean feats of labour and determination, and fine political judgement. Retirement pensions, with their awkward combination of public and private provision, were a hard issue for the party. Beveridge had envisaged a basic state pension paid for by flat-rate contributions, on which the elderly could live decently for what were then the relatively few years between retirement and the grave. It was an idea imbued with Labour values of fair shares and equality. Unfortunately, as Labour's research department had observed in work it had carried out in opposition, in practice it failed to produce enough to pay a decent pension to existing pensioners:

> The aims of the Beveridge Report ('to make want under any circumstances unnecessary and to guarantee the minimum income needed for subsistence') looked bold a generation ago, but they are not good enough for the 1970s. It is not enough to raise the threshold of poverty. The wealth of the nation is increasing, standards of living are rising, and those least able to care for themselves – the aged, the sick, the unemployed, the widows, and the low paid with families to care for – have a right to share in the revolution of rising expectations.[6]

The response in the 1940s to the inadequacy of the basic state pension had been the widespread introduction of occupational schemes. By the 1970s, half the workforce were covered by them. But once again, they tended to exclude the lower-paid manual workers and, most especially, women, whose work record was, often unavoidably, patchy. As a result, the inequalities of the workplace were replicated in retirement. For twenty-five years, the party had been considering how to improve pensions so that no pensioner needed to rely on supplementary benefit. As pension provision lacked all political excitement,[7] it was a little-noticed process. Perhaps for that reason, the debate was more pragmatic than ideological, and the right-wing Gaitskellite economist Douglas Jay was able to work in harmony with the Bevanite socialist Dick Crossman. Perhaps they were united by being Wykehamists.

In 1969 Crossman had introduced a scheme largely drawn up by the two of them in the 1950s. First, it was based on the myth of personal insurance, of contributions buying an entitlement when in fact current pensions were paid for out of current contributions. The idea of moving to a more transparent system of paying for pensions out of income tax had been rejected. Future pensioners were investors in their own future, not dependants reliant on the largesse of the nation – a principle Barbara regarded as sacrosanct. Second, given the accomplished fact of occupational pensions, it was accepted that at least an element of the state pension would have to reflect earnings. It was still not a generous scheme, especially not to women because, as Crossman acknowledged to Barbara, he had geared his scheme to the standards of the private sector.

In the more radical mood of the early 1970s, these issues were re-examined. Crossman himself submitted to the atmosphere of ministerial culpability and admitted his scheme was capable of improvement. Barbara, as opposition spokesperson, chaired an NEC subcommittee that devoted long hours to the consideration of the merits of a truly socialist scheme that would pay everyone the same flat-rate pension, thus achieving large-scale redistribution. There had even been some excited discussion about nationalizing insurance companies, which Barbara's instincts had warned her would be rash. 'I see great difficulties . . . particularly if you are going to hand their funds over to a State Holding Co whose duty is to invest those funds on socially desirable rather than purely commercial grounds.'[8]

The Joseph scheme was inadequate, but there was no guarantee that the enormous effort of reversing it would offer an equivalent return. Barbara was undismayed. She had made her first political splash with pensions thirty-one years earlier; now she had the opportunity to update the welfare state, to fit it for the last quarter of the twentieth century. For a politician impatient to get things done, it was a field rich with promise. A proper pension scheme addressing the problems of the low-paid would be one of the keys to the door out of the poverty impasse. (Other aspects of tackling poverty flitted across her horizon; she contemplated alternative ways of delivering benefits in an attempt to find a way out of the newly identified poverty trap.)

Moreover, she disliked being without a piece of legislation; for every single year she had been in office except her first at Overseas Development (when there had been a White Paper) there had been a corresponding bill. She showed no signs of changing now: Tony Benn, with whom Barbara's relations were increasingly frosty as he used his job as Secretary of State for Industry to advance ambitious plans for government intervention, complained bitterly about her selfishness. He and Bob Mellish, once again the government's Chief Whip, exchanged a note in Cabinet as they discussed the legislative programme for the first Queen's Speech: 'TB: Couldn't Barbara deliver the Queen's Speech herself? BM: Yes, but she wouldn't want to refer to any other dept.'[9] Denis Healey told her that her bids for the public spending round were larger than the entire contingency fund.

In the pensions industry and at Westminster, there was something approaching desperation for a settled scheme. There was also a wealth of expertise in the department. Barbara had not only Brian Abel Smith but Crossman's former junior minister Brian O'Malley,[10] who actually understood the subject. Officials were equally well prepared. The Permanent Secretary in charge of Social Security, Sir Lance Errington, observed, as he took up his pen once again: 'We are going to design a new plane from the models that have crashed on the runway.'[11]

O'Malley, the MP for Rotherham, was a skinny, chain-smoking teacher and ex-band leader to whom Barbara became very close. 'Very intelligent,' Crossman thought, 'a strange young man . . . a good mind, quite illiterate.'[12] For Barbara, he was not only a soulmate, but 'a tower of strength. He has absolute mastery in his field and is very good at the dispatch box. Moreover I can trust his judgement and know he will foresee all the snags for me.'[13] Professor Abel Smith was a public-school socialist with 'incomparable knowledge of health and social affairs'. Sharp and clear in his analysis, forthright in his views, he was unafraid of telling Barbara where he thought she was wrong, and was a figure of respect rather than a candidate for cosy, morale-boosting dinners after a long parliamentary day. It was O'Malley who clucked around her and bought her bottles of wine to cheer her after dispiriting hours on committee.

It took O'Malley, Abel Smith and the officials just six months to put together the State Earnings-Related Pension Scheme (SERPS). It was, it was universally agreed, a brilliant piece of work, incorporating the best of Crossman while, by offering considerable help to the private sector, pacifying the industry. It set a standard which raised the game of the private sector. In political terms, it was just what Wilson wanted: popular in the financial press and with the trade unions, while in the medium term – only twenty years – offering dramatic improvements to the living standards of the elderly, with the state buying-in contributions for those approaching retirement. He was so pleased with the reception given to the Green Paper that Barbara felt her early optimism and confidence in her ability to restore her standing were justified. 'Is my eclipse coming to an end?' she asked herself.

A few months later she introduced the bill in hyperbolic terms: 'I believe that the proposals before the House will mark an advance in our provision for old age greater and more enduring even than the breakthrough which Beveridge achieved.' She had worked tirelessly at the bill; but as Secretary of State of a vast empire, she had had other major issues before her too. Most of the work was delegated to O'Malley (who was to die in April 1976, aged only forty-six). Later, she acknowledged to herself that she used to go along to committee sessions of the bill merely to make sure her name, not O'Malley's, was attached to it. Kenneth Clarke, who led opposition to the bill for the Conservatives, soon spotted her vulnerability. He prided himself on annoying her by calling it the O'Malley bill, then would mollify her by calling it after her. After one session of detailed wrangling in standing committee, which she attended largely, it seemed, to prove that she could, her officials were lavish with their praise. 'So my determination to serve on the Committee and hold my corner on it, whatever the additional strain on time and health, has been justified. God knows, I don't want to claim all the credit for the scheme. It has been a joint effort and it ought to be called the Castle/O'Malley Bill.'[14]

The bill succeeded in being generous enough to take all pensioners off means-tested benefit, yet with contributions low enough for the low-paid to be able to afford them. Annual upratings would be linked to either prices or incomes, whichever increase was the greater. To make sure that the eleven million people already in private schemes would not come flooding into the state scheme and overburden it, there were to be state subsidies to private pension companies, to ensure their provision was at the same or at a higher level. The private sector was accommodated, not excluded. It was, she said, 'an unprecedented partnership between the state and occupational schemes'.

When the new earnings-related scheme came on stream, people approaching retirement would be given credits which, for the first time, would allow them to receive an earnings-related pension too. After only twenty years, all employees who had not contracted out of the scheme would be able to claim according to their earnings, including women who had spent some of those years caring for children or elderly relatives. In another revolutionary move, when the scheme was fully mature people would be able to claim their twenty best years' earnings, rather than their final pay – a change which would help both women and manual workers, who often earned most when young and fit.

Women, always the poorest pensioners, were the biggest winners. Barbara, who only two years earlier had stopped parliament introducing a pension scheme which (astoundingly) would have given male MPs better rights than female ones, was triumphant. 'We believe it is no longer tolerable to treat women as second-class citizens entitled to third-class benefits – a by-product of excessive reliance on the concept of dependency,' she told the House of Commons. Overall, women and the low-paid made sweeping gains. Lower-rate 'married women' contributions – which often resulted in elderly widows living on a pittance because they had failed to contribute enough in their working years – were to be phased out, a typical example of Barbara's muscular approach to women's issues. Her insistence that women pay the same contributions as men was balanced by a blatant piece of reverse discrimination, which allowed women the same pension entitlement as men while continuing to retire at sixty. (Twenty years later, an appeal to the European Court would overturn the decision.) Barbara admitted there was no logical justification for it. 'But . . . the lower retirement age for women is some compensation for the lower wages they have been drawing all these years, when, as everyone will agree, many women have been exploited and have been paid merely sweated wages. No one can pretend that they will get real equality in pay and job opportunities for some time ahead.'

The experts were not entirely convinced that the scheme was going to work. From the beginning, one or two commentators questioned its long-term viability. Pay-as-you-go schemes rely on the generosity of generations to come. From the opposition benches, the future Chancellor Nigel Lawson pointed out that the 'either earnings or inflation' uprating link would mean pensioners doing better than the workforce as a whole. Barbara's State Earnings-Related Pension Scheme and the earnings/inflation link for the basic pension were hefty economic burdens to expect the workers to shoulder, and she knew it. Predictions of the ratio of pensioners to workers were vague, but even the published actuarial calculations showed how heavy the cost of supporting pensioners at a decent level of income would become. In less than ten years, her calculations would be undone by new evidence. The 1981 census showed a million more pensioners than she had anticipated at the time the scheme came to maturity. In the mid-1980s, the respected Institute for Fiscal Studies was declaring: 'It is difficult to discuss the future of social security rationally in the shadow of this foolish commitment.' But Barbara's gamble, that the desirability of her scheme would keep it solvent even against the individualistic urges of the generation that grew up under Margaret Thatcher, was at least partly successful. SERPS lives, albeit in truncated form.

SERPS was a pioneering assertion of women's economic independence. Barbara was once again described as an 'ardent feminist'. This misleading impression was enhanced when Wilson asked her to chair his newly established Women's National Commission;[15] 1975 had been declared International Women's Year. Barbara held a reception at Lancaster House to celebrate. 'The irony of it is that I have always found these women's issues a bore, but, having taken on this job . . . at Harold's request, I intend to make a go of it.'[16] Accordingly, a few weeks later she spent a whole morning with the Commission – enough, she felt, to qualify her as a feminist. In May she had a weekend of women's issues in Edinburgh. 'I soon gathered that the Scots are the biggest male chauvinists of the lot and that the women there are resentful at not being treated seriously. It amuses me to see myself cast in the feminist role after a lifetime in which I have hated the whole idea, but, faced with the failure of the Secretary of State for Scotland to turn up to our functions as well as the Lord Provost, I find myself getting pretty militant.'[17]

In September 1974 the pensions White Paper came out, barely six months after the March election and ready to be a central part of the manifesto for the next election, scheduled for 10 October. The government

was once again wrestling with a failing economy, a trade deficit and pressure
to deflate. There was too little room for manoeuvre for economic argument.
Instead, Europe once again became the focus for dissent.

Early in the new Labour government, the Foreign Secretary Jim Callaghan
had begun a tour of European capitals to 'renegotiate' Britain's terms of
entry, in accordance with the manifesto demand for major changes in the
Common Agricultural Policy. Fairer budget finance, a guarantee of no
economic and monetary union and the national retention of power over
regional, fiscal and industrial policies were strong enough commitments for
Enoch Powell to advise anti-Europeans to vote Labour, without being
unacceptable (quite) to Labour's pro-Europeans. The party was committed
to a binding referendum on the new terms within twelve months of the
election. At a time when both the party and – according to the polls – the
electorate were opposed to EEC membership, it was a convenient way of
keeping Europe out of contention. The right, still unhappy with the idea of
a referendum at all, tried to change the manifesto commitment. (What,
Jenkins asked, would be the case if the result was inconclusive, or the turnout embarrassingly low? Surely parliament must then take the decision.) It
was only when Barbara intervened with a Wilson-style appeal to unity that
the row was averted. Wilson was grateful to her, but – later events suggest –
misunderstood the nature of her loyalty.

   A few days after Barbara's sixty-fourth birthday, Labour squeaked home
in the second general election of the year, with a majority of just three. It
was to be Barbara's last; she had taken her two-year-old great-nephew Mark
campaigning with her, as his mother Sonya had campaigned with her nearly
thirty years before. But Barbara played little part in the national campaign;
there was no room in the official party image for an ideological pensioner
with a taste for conflict. The woman on the platform at the daily press
conferences was the charmingly scatty Shirley Williams. It was Williams who
inadvertently triggered the Europe issue. She declared – when pressed – that
she would leave active politics if the referendum went against staying in the
Common Market. It was a question that would return to haunt Barbara.

   Early in 1975, with the economy still floundering, industrial unrest
building and Tony Benn being peculiarly troublesome in his determination
to produce socialism if only in one department, Harold Wilson prepared to
challenge the majority in both the parliamentary and the wider Labour Party,
and call a referendum on the new terms. He would recommend staying in.
It was perhaps the greatest risk of his long career as the finely calibrated

sensor of the party's centre of gravity and was based on the brutally simple calculation that the left had nowhere else to go.

On 21 January, in an unprecedented departure from the constitutional propriety of collective responsibility, he confirmed to Cabinet that ministers who disagreed with the government's position on Europe would not have to resign if they wanted to dissent in the referendum. This was not a random experiment in statecraft so much as a shroud for the party's inescapable divisions over Europe. Wilson, emotionally uncomfortable with conflict, never believed he could afford the luxury of principle if he was to remain leader of a united party. Although his personal politics were as internationalist as Barbara's, if not as anti-Market (although that could only be guessed at), he had early grasped the politics of the matter. For Wilson, Europe was less a matter of principle than a valuable weapon in the constant struggle to stay at the top of the heap of the ambitious, the unscrupulous and the ideological that made up the Labour movement.

Wilson's approach to Europe meant it was widely and almost exclusively analysed in terms of its party-political implications. On several occasions, from a mixture of instinct and self-interest, Barbara pressed him to make a stand on principle, to lead and see who would follow. But Wilson's success was built on his rejection of gesture as much as the shrewd use of symbol. He made his support for Europe conditional on the terms of entry, and thus slipped neatly through the middle of the party. Most, however, saw the renegotiated terms for what they were: window dressing, a fleeting eye-catching distraction from Labour's real concerns. A Yes vote was a vote for the Jenkinsite right's view of the future; a No vote, a vote for socialism in one country, incompatible with capitalist Europe. Like rearmament and the bomb in the 1950s, by the early 1970s, Europe had become the vehicle for an open battle for control of the party. It was not the only parallel. Attitudes to Europe, like attitudes to the bomb, were at least as emotional as rational.

The renegotiations were to be finalized at the Dublin European Community summit early in March 1975. Barbara predicted it would be possible to interpret them as either defeat or triumph, 'a messy muddle in the middle'. But now that the moment had come, Wilson decided he must establish a framework for differing opinions to accommodate the two views of the party, a framework which did not operate as a mechanism for exaggerating and publicizing the differences. At the same time, his survival depended on securing a Yes vote, despite opinion polls which continued to show the general public as well as the great mass of the party were against.

Wilson announced to Cabinet, Barbara wrote, 'a fundamental change in our constitutional convention as casually as if he had been offering us a cup of tea'. He told them: 'As soon as we have made our decision on the terms, I am going to recommend that the minority should be free to campaign in the country on their own point of view.'[18]

Barbara, the veteran Bevanite, could only put down to chagrin the silence of the pro-Marketeers. She gave the plan her immediate and enthusiastic endorsement. She had always been an advocate of the restorative powers of argument. Politics was a crusade, in which one had to fight or die. Her greatest disdain for Jenkins was always reserved for his distaste for a fight. Her own greatest pleasure – as her friends knew to their cost – was an uninhibited exchange of views. The reality that lay ahead – the damage to the party's electoral support caused by open conflict at the top of government, the dire threat of the party campaigning against the Market while Cabinet argued for it – was ignored. Socialism was at stake, the forces of darkness (the City, newspaper magnates and coalitionists) were gathering against it, and the only recourse for the cash-starved anti-Marketeers was organization.

In Cabinet, she declared that every member, from top to bottom of the party, must be free to campaign on his own views. 'Our tolerance as a Cabinet would encourage the whole party to be tolerant,' she claimed optimistically. 'But there was no reason to treat the situation tragically. I was prepared to accept the nation's verdict, whichever way it went. I certainly wasn't going to let such unimportant things as the Common Market wreck my political work or my party's socialist unity.' She added, 'Shirley [Williams] gave me a wry little smile at that.'[19] With her customary energy and focus, Barbara began to plan the chain of events that should follow the anticipated cabinet approval of the renegotiated terms. She found to her surprise that Peter Shore and Michael Foot were cautious about her strategy. Even Jack Jones warned her against being 'too political'. (Benn, meanwhile, was organizing separately and, in his own words, 'pinching' Barbara's work.) Wilson had licensed individual conscience; Barbara planned to organize a mutiny.

Only Judith Hart, a colleague of whom she had often been dismissive, stood shoulder to shoulder with her, drafting minutes and making sure people turned up at meetings. Barbara and friends on the left – the Foots, the Shores, the Benns and the Silkins, with occasional others – had begun to meet regularly at what they called 'husbands and wives' dinners'. They pretended to be social occasions; in fact they were gatherings of a caucus of like-minded ministers who hoped to be able, by united action, to keep the government to the left. Not for the first time, the leading figures of the left found they were too diverse a group to work effectively together; Barbara often complained that lines she thought had been agreed over dinner were disavowed in Cabinet. But Europe was different. Given the black-and-white nature of the referendum, there was no room for disagreement. Early in March a husbands' and wives' dinner hosted by Peter Shore and his wife Liz[20] drew up a carefully orchestrated sequence of press conferences and statements to be launched the moment Cabinet actually approved the new terms. A week later Barbara hosted another planning meeting. She was determined that if the City and the media were to back the Yes campaign, they would call in the party rank and file to back theirs.

On 18 March 1975, Cabinet voted eighteen to six in favour of accepting what were claimed as concessions won by Callaghan and Fred Peart, the Agriculture Minister. The dissenting ministers, as well as Barbara, were Tony Benn, Michael Foot, Peter Shore, John Silkin and Eric Varley. Of these, only Barbara, Benn and Shore played a role in the No campaign.

It has been suggested that Wilson received unreliable intelligence about the state of mind of the dissenters. Barbara, it was put about in the days after Cabinet had approved the terms, might well come back to Wilson out of loyalty and a desire for unity, as she had seemed to do in the NEC debate before the election. But although she undoubtedly recognized the importance of unity (albeit often in an asymmetrical way – on her terms), this was not an issue on which she was prepared to buck her own and the party's instincts. There is no record of her faltering in her determination to campaign to the end, even at the expense of her cabinet job, possibly even of the government itself.

Wilson could not have doubted her convictions, either. At the Cabinet of 18 March, Barbara noted the inadequacies of the renegotiations. But that, she told Wilson as he went round the table taking voices, was not why she could not accept British membership. 'We were asking the British people to remain in an organization in whose principles we said we did not believe,' she declared. Handing power to Brussels, where politics was conducted by negotiation and consensus rather than principle, made socialism in Britain unachievable. It was, declared Benn more pithily, a capitalist club. Barbara continued: 'Harold had said that the theology of the Common Market was dead: long live pragmatic decisions. "But [Wilson added] the pragmatic fact is that, far from rejecting the theology, we have accepted that we cannot challenge it and that the negotiations would have broken down if we had even tried."'

On her way out of Cabinet, under the nose of the cabinet secretary, she pressed Eric Varley to come to that afternoon's campaign launch of the anti-Marketeers. Tipped off, Wilson sent Barbara a message asking her not to attend – an indication of how little he knew of her intentions. At the same time ministers were given strict instructions in a set of guidelines about how to conduct themselves. In an attempt to avoid pitching members of the government against their leadership, and to minimize the damage to the party itself, there were to be no personal attacks or direct personal confrontation. 'No minister should appear on a platform or programme in association with or support of a Member of Parliament of a different political party, or with a representative or any organisation he would not in other circumstances be seen dead with.'

But most controversially – although only the dissenting ministers expressed surprise, it being obvious to most others that licence to disagree could only go a very little way without entirely crippling government – dissenting ministers, and only the dissenting ministers, were not to be allowed to speak in the House on Europe or to conduct any business associated with Europe, including answering questions.

Even if she had been interested in the ground rules, Barbara can barely have had time to think about them during a day that included opening the debate on the second reading of her pensions bill, attending the 'Cabinet against the Market' launch and a meeting of PLP dissenters, as well as soliciting support for a Commons motion echoing the dissenting ministers' statement and underlining how impossible it would be to advance socialism within the EEC:

> In spite of the exertions of our negotiators, the results have fallen far short of our minimum aims [said the statement]. But the gravest disadvantages are political. The rights of our own people and the power of Parliament remain, at the end of the negotiations, subordinate to the non-elected commission and council of ministers in Brussels . . . the strengthening of our industry, the struggle against poverty, the progress towards equality and the mainenance of employment . . . will all be made much more difficult by the Common Market's rules on free movement of capital and of firms.

But that was just the beginning. The most dramatic step was yet to come. Once again the structures of the party, its interlocking circles, were to be wrenched apart. Barbara was engineering a split between Cabinet and party. The final piece of her jigsaw was that the NEC members among the dissenting ministers – Barbara herself, Benn, Foot, Judith Hart (no longer in Cabinet) and the junior minister Joan Lestor – were to sign an incendiary NEC motion in the name of the party chairman Ian Mikardo (but drafted by Barbara and other dissenting ministers at her flat in Cholmondley Court a couple of days earlier) that had the potential to destroy both the government and the Labour movement.

The intention was to capture the party machine for the anti-Marketeers' campaign. So the motion went through the ritual of condemning the Wilson terms of entry. Then the dynamite was planted: the party must oppose the terms that its own government had negotiated and campaign for withdrawal from the Market altogether. The motion would be debated at a special party conference convened to pass judgement on the Wilson terms. 'Mikardo Hurls Down the Party Gauntlet,' yelled the *Guardian*.

Late on the night of 19 March, Barbara was summoned by an explosive Prime Minister.

> Harold [was] . . . angrier than I have ever heard him in my whole life. He was almost beside himself. The venom poured out of him. He had generously allowed us to disagree publicly on the Common Market and what had we done? 'Made a fool of me,' he declared. When he had talked about freedom to dissent he hadn't meant that we should rush out and hold a press conference and organise an anti-Government campaign. No one had done more than he had to keep the party together and he had been pilloried and he had had enough of it . . . 'So this is all the loyalty I get. No one would have brought you back into Government but me'. At that, something snapped in me and I retorted, 'I have never been so insulted in my life. I thought you had chosen me on merit. I am the best Minister you've got and you can have my resignation in ten minutes flat.' He began to climb down. 'You can have mine. Of course I chose you on merit. But this campaign you are organising is intolerable. Some of us are having a meeting in my room in the House. You can come if you like.'

Barbara went. Her diary account – a compelling contemporaneous portrait of a government in crisis – continues:

> A gloomy scene met me as I entered Harold's room. Harold was sitting in his chair, obviously in a shattered state. Mike [Foot] sat at one end of the table opposite him; Jim [Callaghan] at the other, head in hands. 'Have a drink,' said Harold morosely and as I helped myself he added, 'I was very insulting to Barbara just now and I apologize. I withdraw what I said.' I went over and kissed him affectionately on the forehead. 'And I'm sorry if I have upset you, but I am afraid I can't withdraw,' I replied. 'Don't I get a kiss?' said Jim gloomily. 'God knows I need it.' So I kissed him too and sat down next to him. 'I can't understand why Barbara is so chirpy,' he almost groaned. 'Because I don't think the situation is tragic,' I replied. 'Harold,

you must wear with pride this freedom you have given us.' Harold had
obviously calmed down a bit, but he was still in a pretty neurotic state. So
for over an hour we had to listen to him. He wasn't going to accept
Barbara's resignation or anybody else's because he did not intend to preside
over a rump Government. He must represent the whole movement or
nothing at all. But his position was intolerable. Here we had approached
Eric Varley within minutes of Cabinet's decision having been taken,
inviting him to join a press conference that had clearly been pre-arranged
(who the hell did tell tales, I wonder?).

Barbara, unrepentant or possibly simply uninterested in the damage she
risked doing, continued gaily: 'The thing which obviously hit Harold was
the fact that we had got it all worked out beforehand. If he knew I was
responsible for the whole plan, I really would be finished!'

The NEC motion opposing his terms for entry and calling for withdrawal
from Europe was the last straw for Wilson: he warned Barbara and Foot that
he would resign unless it was withdrawn. Callaghan said he would resign
too. A little later the party's general secretary, Ron Hayward, 'drifted in' and
made it plain he would follow the party's instructions to campaign, if that
was what they were. Barbara went on the offensive.

> I made soothing noises from time to time but I couldn't help thinking that
> Harold ought to have foreseen all this. How could the right to dissent have
> any meaning, I asked him, unless it also included the right to make dissent
> effective? Weren't the pro-marketeers going to organise? At this Harold
> said he was as angry at their – particularly Roy's – organising efforts and
> said he was going to try to stop them too, which is absurd. Why shouldn't
> they organise? But Harold went on with his dark hints as to what would
> happen to the party, and not least to the Left, if he resigned. 'Some people
> would go straight into a coalition,' he spat out, adding, 'Roy would, like a
> shot.'

It was Michael Foot, in his new role as conciliator, who set out to try to
ease the pressure on Wilson, promising to look again at the NEC motion.
As the meeting broke up at 1 a.m., Barbara had one last shot, warning
Wilson that the spending cuts the Chancellor was preparing would do more
damage to the party than the battle over Europe. The following day, in a full
cabinet meeting devoted to the issue, Foot conceded the NEC resolution
was a problem. Barbara lamented in her diary later: 'As they grow older,
these Foot brothers all merge into one collective Foot type: rational, radical
and eminently reasonable. They even speak in the same voice and the same

terms: they are natural Liberals.' But Barbara refused to concede. According to Benn, Wilson called the No campaign 'silly and sly' and asked: 'Are the PM and the Treasurer of the Party to have to ask for the right to dissent? Are we to be allowed to attend the conference? . . . I object to Ministers on the NEC campaigning against Government recommendations. People cannot wear two hats, even though we have accepted an agreement to differ. There is a grave economic crisis. Am I in a credible position if hostile NEC action is taken by Ministers?'

Barbara – presumably blocking out any memory of the last time the NEC came out against the government, when it was her legislation they were rejecting – was unrepentant. 'I asked whether, if Cabinet had decided no, anyone believed Roy Jenkins would have meekly stayed silent? Hadn't the European Movement already organised four hundred meetings?' But Foot, backed by Shore, implicitly acknowledged the damaging potential of the NEC motion. Wilson and Callaghan, as well as others who supported the terms, must be able to speak at the special conference, he agreed, and promised to try to deliver a solution. It was Foot again who mollified Ian Mikardo, who claimed to be as unable as Barbara to see the difficulty. Peter Shore argued, 'If the party machine is brought into action a situation would be created from which we could not recover.' Even Benn backed the need for Wilson and Callaghan to be able to speak, and for the NEC to recognize the right to dissent, just as Cabinet had done.

Wilson now sent out another edict about the behaviour of ministers who were also on the NEC.

> It is not a licence to Ministers on the NEC who differ from the government to invoke a coordinated and deliberate programme of activities with the NEC or in other party bodies against the government, or with a view to embarrassing their ministerial colleagues or undermining their position in parliament or on the NEC . . . The last thing I want to see is any weakening of the links between the government and the NEC. But I have a duty to do all I can to ensure that the discussion of this issue does not cause irreparable damage to the Government or to the Party, still less to create a major and harmful split between them.

To underline the parallel Barbara had so conveniently overlooked, Wilson circulated a minute originally sent out on 3 April 1969, when Callaghan had been leading the NEC in revolt over 'In Place of Strife'. It warned that overreaching by the NEC would simply result in NEC members being unable to serve in government. 'The NEC,' he warned, 'would be reduced to a body which was competent merely to discuss and to protest but not to exercise influence or to accept responsibility.'[21] Two days later, on 26 March, the NEC accepted a deal. Barbara, arriving at the meeting 'a little late' was able to put her case to the TV cameras uninterrupted. But once inside Transport House, she had less control.

On paper, the NEC was deciding its position on the Market. But there was no doubt where majority opinion lay: Barbara had already marshalled it behind the Mikardo motion, carefully gathering signatures in advance. When Callaghan was finally allowed to set out his 'achievements' in renegotiation, Barbara recorded, 'some people chatted and others went to the lavatory or the telephone'. But she was forced to accept that the party could not be mobilized behind her anti-Market campaign. Whatever the NEC felt, and regardless of rank-and-file opinion as expressed at the special conference to be held on 26 April, the party had to remain organizationally neutral. It could not be called in as a counterbalance to 'the whole government machine' which Barbara knew would now be brought in to 'bulldoze their views through'.

The No campaign began immediately. It was a resounding failure. Public opinion was as inconstant as the Prime Minister. According to the statistics gathered by David Butler for his *1975 Referendum* analysis, during the previous four years – even while the Conservatives were taking Britain in – there had never been a majority in favour of going in or staying in. Yet as soon as the question asked was changed from 'Should Britain be a member?' to the issue of renegotiated terms and a government endorsement of them, opinion became positive. The referendum question was: 'Do you think that the United Kingdom should stay in the European Community (the Common Market)?' In February 1975, according to Professor Butler,[22] 8 per cent more wanted to accept the terms than to come out. In March it had leapt to 29 per cent and it stayed there, fluctuating a little and ending on 34 per cent on polling day itself. 'It was plain,' Butler and his colleague Uwe Kitzinger concluded, 'that on a subject on which few felt really strongly there was a general willingness to accept opinion leadership, particularly on the Labour side.'

Barbara herself acknowledged the confusion among voters in her constituency. Why was she saying something different from her Prime Minister? To thousands of people it didn't make sense. The commentators saw a way of making it make sense. There was no more appetite in Fleet Street – overwhelmingly in favour of Europe – for detailed textual analysis of the renegotiations than there had been on the NEC. The campaign was about politics, not Europe; it was about left versus right, and in particular it was about whether Labour could be saved from the wild men and women now haranguing the voters about socialism and sovereignty. Tories used routinely to end their speeches with the mantra 'Beware Benn, Foot and Castle.'[23] The Jenkinsites were more circumspect, but the columnists said it for them: 'Whoever loses the Battle for Europe will also lose the war for the heart and mind of the party,' wrote Peter Jenkins, in whose south London house much of the Yes campaign was planned. A victory for the Yes campaign would lead to a major political realignment, he argued, presciently.

Barbara allowed Benn to make the running in the No campaign. With a major department to run and the added burden of complex negotiations with the hospital consultants now in hand, she did little more than the essential in what was clearly a losing campaign. On 20 April, with nearly two months to go, she was telling her fellow dissenting ministers that they were going to lose and that Peter Jenkins was right. Wilson would end up being the prisoner of the right. This fear gave an added desperation to the party battles. Tony Benn prepared a 'strategy for withdrawal', which Barbara approved in principle but whose drafting she deplored. ('Barbara was bossy but brilliant,' Benn noted.) Her copy of the first version of the strategy is scored through with red. 'I cannot get attuned to the over-simplified extremism of the anti-Market case,' she wrote after a revivalist rally with them at the Free Trade Hall in Manchester.

Jim Callaghan would have sympathized. In a renewed bid to capture the party for the No campaign, three days before the special conference Geoff Bish, the party's strongly anti-European research officer, produced a long document attacking the renegotiated terms that he wanted the NEC to approve for distribution to the delegates. Callaghan exploded over what he said were its many inaccuracies, submitted more than two hundred amendments and declared it 'a disgrace to the name of research'. Another fudge resulted in its being distributed 'for information', without formal endorsement.

The special conference itself, it is clear from Barbara's diary, was a flop. Conference voted two to one against the terms, but the majority was small enough to enable the media to describe it as a rebuff for the left. Harold, forced by Labour's strict internal hierarchy to sit next to Barbara, went out of his way to be unpleasant, demonstrating an unexpected line in low point-scoring by carefully positioning a water jug between her and the cameras. The speakers for the No cause were 'unattractive'. 'I got gloomier as the day went on, not about the basic principles, but about our ability to present them,' Barbara commented.

The only relief came when Harold softened to Barbara's praise of his speech. "You lowered the temperature. They are saying Roy made a great mistake in raising it." Harold came to life. "I intend to play it low key throughout. The decision is purely a marginal one. I have always said so. I have never been a fanatic for Europe."' He cheered her some more by promising that Foot would keep his job. 'I felt like telling those right-wing plotters that I had got a message for them: they would never succeed in making a prisoner of Harold.'[24]

The soft talk from Harold, together with her increasing irritation with the 'mish-mash of exaggeration and generalisation' coming from the Benn camp and an overall sense of despair, all contributed to set Barbara against Benn. The latter was determined to make one last pitch to get the party working for their side of the argument and had requisitioned an emergency NEC meeting. 'I am rather surprised and puzzled about what Wedgie is up to,' she wrote. 'I thought all this had been settled at the last NEC.' In the event Benn – now being portrayed in some parts of the press as a Communist fifth-columnist – was up to nothing beyond getting a guarantee that the party would put out some literature reflecting their arguments.

By 1 May, Barbara was as near as she ever came to despair. 'There is no co-ordinated or coherent leadership of the anti case – and such a danger of our being annihilated by the Establishment in the referendum (with disastrous consequences for the Labour Party).' Barbara believed that when she got the chance she could make a good argument in defence of her position. But she rarely got the chance. She had settled her long dispute with the hospital consultants but was now in the midst of highly technical legislation on pensions as well as fighting on the pay beds issue, which was absorbing more and more of her ministerial energy. In the press, she was attacked for conflict and iconoclasm, a woman who was upsetting the nation's heroes and heroines in the medical profession with her prescriptive approach to their livelihood. It was easy to add her to the list of bogeymen the Yes campaign enjoyed wheeling out. A cruel caricature began to take shape: an ideologue sliding down the wrong side of the hill, clinging to the doctrinaire as her hold on the sympathies of her audience fell away. Her profile in the campaign was now so low that she was not included in a rare poll seeking to establish how far individual personalities were influencing people's attitudes to the Market. It made gloomy reading for the anti-Marketeers, all of whose main propo- nents – Foot, Benn, Jack Jones and Clive Jenkins of ASTMS – were disliked more than liked by a wide margin.[25]

The disastrous consequences Barbara feared for the Labour Party were perhaps more personal than she admitted. There was widespread speculation in the press (which everyone assumed was being fed from Jamaica where

Wilson and Callaghan were attending a Commonwealth conference) that all
the dissenting ministers were to be 'slapped down'. Benn reported rumours
that he was to be moved to Barbara's job. 'Harold is evidently implying to
Barbara that I am a competitor for her job, in the hope of neutralising her,'
he concluded.[26]

Barbara tried to take a hand herself in organizing the campaign. In mid-
May one of the few polls the No campaign had been able to afford showed
that Barbara's fears of defeat were all too well founded. If there was the
merest glimmer of hope, it was that the biggest group of potential supporters
were working-class women, and prices were the single most important issue.
Barbara devoted the final days of the campaign to appealing to them. She
took her great-niece Rachel to Brussels on a shopping trip intended to
highlight the cost of baked beans in Belgium and fish fingers in Paris. It got
a lot of coverage, most of it critical (the enthusiastically pro-European
Guardian said it 'disgusted the international press'), while the expense of the
trip was questioned by the cash-strapped National Referendum Campaign.
Barbara's attempt to make people understand in practical terms what was
being debated was dismissed as a failure to appreciate the great sweep of
history.

At the climax of the campaign, on the eve of polling, Barbara joined
Peter Shore to debate the issue at the Oxford Union. They were against
Edward Heath and the Liberal leader Jeremy Thorpe on the motion, 'This
House Says Yes to Europe'. Although she had often debated at the Union
since her Oxford days, she still found it a nerve-racking experience. Her old
sense of intellectual inferiority came flooding back. She prepared exhaustively
– trying to build a case on the real internationalism that would be jeopardized
by membership of an exclusive Europe – and in her view (and that of
sympathizers in the audience) failed catastrophically. Her nadir came when
Thorpe challenged her to resign if the referendum went against her. 'The
audience went wild with delight. Hoots and catcalls drowned any attempt at
reply. I turned and faced them, waiting for the row to die down and then
said emphatically and slowly, "If Britain votes to stay in the Common
Market, my country will need me more than ever." I was rather proud of it
– and I meant it anyway. But the audience shrieked with derision.' She went
home with the 'slow stain of the misery of failure'[27] eating into her soul.

Twenty-four hours later, on 5 June 1975, it emerged that the nation had
voted two to one in favour of staying in. Barbara, buoyed by a flood of
enthusiastic mail after the televised Oxford Union debate, shrugged off
defeat. 'I know I have not much longer to operate in the febrile, exacting
and fulfilling world of power and some instinct makes me want to make the

most of it.'[28] Wilson carefully put his Cabinet back together. Dissent was over, he said firmly at the first post-referendum cabinet meeting, and that night demoted Benn from Industry to Energy and Judith Hart from Overseas Development to Transport – a job she refused to take. It was a sign of his determination to restore what passed for harmony in the party that he entertained Benn, Foot and Barbara Castle in his room late into the night, listening to their demands that Hart should be reinstated. Hart herself ended the mini-crisis by resigning.

Barbara, looking back on the campaign, saw their effort as a bicycle compared with a racing car. The official figures showed the Yes campaign had spent eleven times as much as the No: £1.5 million as against £133,000. It was a sign of the national mood that the No campaign had been able to raise just seven personal donations, of which the largest, from the TGWU, was for a little over £3,000. Barbara was inclined to blame the general lack of professionalism on the umbrella organization, the National Referendum Campaign, through which all other anti-Market organizations had had to work. She had done little for the NRC, and was scathing about an organization that held press conferences miles from Fleet Street, and sent out a message which depended more on the messenger's personal outlook than on any analysis of what might change voters' minds. To add to the NRC's problems, it was only in mid-April that they had got the promised state funding.

The press, almost entirely Euro-enthusiasts, had generally treated the referendum as an internal party row, demonizing Benn and simultaneously building up his standing as a major political player. As Barbara observed with more than a touch of jealousy, 'The press have made Wedgie, not only a hero of the Left, but a major political force. Every day there are articles about him which far from doing him harm, turn him into a political giant, particularly as the criticisms are larded with grudging admissions of his abilities.'

The general conclusion was that Europe was now a closed issue. Twelve years of argument were ended, Wilson said optimistically. The party had survived, intact. There was no coalition between centre-right Labour and the Tories. There were no splits. Yet.

18. Defeat

I stuffed their mouths with gold.

Aneurin Bevan on the doctors, 1948

Barbara's final act on the Westminster stage was her boldest, her most political and her least successful. She set out to improve on Bevan's greatest achievement, the National Health Service. To do so, she had to unpick a delicate settlement and impose in its place an unpopular one. Predictably, the consequences were fury, unpopularity and in the end a compromise that satisfied nobody. It was not, one of her closest advisers admitted later, a proper policy:[1] it was a response to the decline in her own fortunes and the renewal of sectarianism in the Labour movement. Rather than changing her status in the party, her failure confirmed it.

Always, at the back of her mind, was the prospect of winning a triumph that had eluded Bevan. It was a nice political irony that the most frequent obstruction to her ambitions was Michael Foot, her dear friend and Bevan's biographer. In 1974, Foot had become Employment Secretary and guardian of the social contract and the government's pay policy. 'I wonder if Mike will one day write the story of Barbara's battle to bring Nye's reforms up to date with as much approval as he wrote about Nye's compromises,' she wrote. Later, it was: 'I thought ironically that Nye never met the obstruction from the Attlee Cabinet that I was meeting from the Department of Employment under Mike.' Or again: 'So the forces are mobilising against us as they did against Nye – only this time the party would not tolerate the sort of concessions that Nye made. Our job is going to be even harder than his.'

★

Bevan, she might have considered, was remembered for what he succeeded in doing rather than for where he failed. His National Health Service was the jewel in the crown of the post-war settlement: socialism in action, a health service providing the best care available to each, strictly according to need.

Yet because no one had accurately predicted the financial demands it would make, the NHS remained vulnerable even under a Labour government. Within a year of its foundation, Bevan was having to go to the Treasury and ask for more. Nearly thirty years later it still had to be shored up, continually, against a Treasury that gloomily regarded it as a bottomless pit for the taxpayer and against the doctors who, Barbara believed, never quite accepted the principle of a health service paid for by the taxpayer. Every complaint from the British Medical Association about shortage of cash she translated into an attack on the fundamental principle of a freely available tax-funded NHS.[2]

Money was the dominant problem: to run a service in which pressure of demand mounted year on year, to pay for technological innovation and new treatments, but above all to pay the wages of the hundreds of thousands of staff who worked for what had become the biggest employer in Europe. By 1970, when on the eve of the election Wilson and Crossman refused to honour a doctors' pay review recommendation, it was clear the NHS was failing. Thousands of employees – from hospital consultants to hospital porters – felt underpaid and undervalued, as spending on the NHS, shackled to the sickly UK economy, failed to deliver them even standstill pay increases.

Cash crisis brought the language of industrial relations to the NHS. The BMA, representing almost all doctors, abandoned gentlemanly discussion in favour of professional negotiation. Other tiers of staff like the nurses were looking with increasing enthusiasm on trade unions rather than their professional bodies to win them back their standing on the pay ladder. Trade unions, especially the National Union of Public Employees (NUPE) and the Confederation of Health Service Employees (COHSE), were in brisk competition for recruits among the lower-paid.

Partly because of the renewed union activity, the health service had also caught the eye of Labour's policy-makers. The commitment to end prescription charges had been in every manifesto since 1951. But the leftward, egalitarian swing of the party had also led to demands to reopen the Bevanite settlement and exclude private practice from NHS hospitals. Only ten years earlier, the Labour leader Hugh Gaitskell, without attracting any comment at all, had been treated during his final illness in a private hospital. Many of those who could afford it on the left did the same, just as many continued to educate their children privately. When Barbara had needed an operation on her sinuses as a cabinet minister in 1965, she had been given a room to herself. When she faced accusations of being treated privately, ten years later, it had been such an insignificant issue that she had no recollection of whether she had or not. The last Labour government had actually encouraged the combination of private and NHS practice within one hospital in the interests of what was called 'geographical whole-time working', which meant that consultants did not waste time travelling between state and private hospitals.

In the 1970s, for the first time, using private health care became an act of political betrayal. The personal became political and failure to use public services, however inadequate, deprived politicians of the *locus standi* to run them. Many in the party wanted private practice abolished altogether.[3] As a start, pay beds – which allowed doctors to treat their paying patients alongside their NHS patients – must go.

Labour's original, pre-NHS, ambition had been for a full-time salaried medical service – nationalizing the doctors. The doctors had resisted. Aneurin Bevan had conceded the continuance of a fee-based system and private practice within the NHS only at the very last minute and only because he was cornered by the consultants, who, he feared, might smother the infant NHS at birth by refusing to take part in it. He had told a restless party that it was worth sacrificing the ambition for a salaried service to get the consultants on board. 'There is all the difference in the world between plucking fruit when it is ripe and plucking it when it is green.'[4] But from the start there had been suspicions that the arrangement was abused, and that far from strengthening the NHS it was undermining it. Dick Crossman, for example, complained bitterly when his wife Zita was fatally ill in 1953 that her doctor had tried to manoeuvre her into a private bed. By the 1970s, consultants stood accused in some circles of allowing their waiting lists to lengthen in order to recruit patients for their private practices, and of skimping on their NHS patients to see more privately. Some doctors and other hospital staff complained that NHS equipment was being used for private patients without charge. In 1972, the Labour minority on a cross-party Commons committee found enough evidence of abuse to demand the arrangement be abolished.

At the same time, although there was little statistical evidence showing a link between waiting lists and the growth of private practice, NUPE and COHSE had discovered that the most effective weapon in a pay dispute was to hit services to the private beds. Although in the whole health service there were only 4,500 – rarely at more than 50 per cent occupancy – and they accounted for little more than 1 per cent of the patients treated each year, the unions found that angry consultants could make the case for a pay rise with the management on their behalf with satisfying effectiveness.

But pay was only one issue. At the heart of the row that dominated the next two years in the NHS was the battle between unions and consultants for control of the health service. It was an unedifying scrap between the two most powerful groups of producers, conducted with frequent appeals to the interests of, but little genuine regard for, the patients, whose treatment was jeopardized by sporadic industrial action sometimes involving ward orderlies, sometimes doctors and consultants, and occasionally both.

The negotiations for the consultants' new contracts were part of this newly industrialized world of NHS labour relations. Barbara planned to use the opportunity to redefine the way consultants worked. Her widely applauded intention was to make the service less skewed to the teaching hospitals in prosperous south-east England, while at the same time – by weighting pay in favour of those doctors who devoted themselves exclusively to the NHS – signalling the government's disapproval of private practice.

This meant changing the system of bonuses, or what the doctors called 'merit awards', so that they favoured the Cinderella areas of care, the geriatric and mental health consultants who had no prospect of private earnings, rather than the heart specialists in London who could double their NHS pay with just a dozen operations a year. However, it also implied, as one consultant angrily complained, that the consultant who worked forty hours for the NHS and then went sailing was to be regarded more highly than the consultant who, after his forty hours, went off to his private practice. Since Barbara once told consultants to play golf rather than work in private practice, she plainly did think that.

It rapidly became impossible to keep the consultants' contracts and the pay-beds issue apart: taking pay beds away would reduce consultants' earning capacity. It could not be done until their new contracts and the accompanying pay awards had been made. Barbara told the doctors they could not have an inflation-busting pay rise unless they approved her plans to favour whole-time NHS consultants. The consultants had no doubt the contract was the first step to ending all private practice.

Barbara had been committed to abolishing pay beds since at least 1955, when (perhaps because of Dick Crossman's experience) it was a specific pledge in her personal manifesto in the general election that year. It was observed, however, that ending prescription charges, a project she never seriously contemplated, had been a manifesto commitment for even longer. Her critics suspected that because the party and the union movement had elevated pay beds into a touchstone of socialism, she was treating it as a vehicle to revive her flagging standing among the rank and file.

It was a dangerously controversial approach. Her policy adviser, Brian Abel Smith, was blunt. Echoing Bevan's own tactics, he argued that she could achieve the same ends by improving the health service and upping the cost of pay beds, rather than going for a head-on confrontation. 'If we are to get a better health service we must carry the majority of the doctors with us, or at least not turn them hot in fury against us for minimal gain in the short period.'

Within months of the general election in March 1974, the health service unions, led by NUPE, pushed pay beds further up the political agenda. In midsummer, the sparkling new Charing Cross Hospital in West London, swiftly branded the Fulham Hilton, was brought to a standstill after NUPE members started taking action against the private beds on the fifteenth floor. It was a sign of the already tense atmosphere that the BMA's response was to demand government intervention, or, it threatened, it would start its own industrial action. 'We had to shake the thinking of the government,' admitted the doctors' leader Anthony Grabham. 'We had to show them something was going on if the doctors were prepared to work to rule. It was a bucket of cold water.'

It did not have the desired effect. If Barbara had ever been prepared to back off, a medical secretary ('battling grannie' in the *Daily Mail*) called Esther Brookstone now made it impossible to do so. Mrs Brookstone, an old Communist who had once worked for Harry Pollit, the CPGB general secretary, wanted the private wing – which had been built with NHS money – opened to ordinary NHS patients, or, she threatened, all medical support services would be withdrawn. 'Give in . . . or we will starve the patients out,' she was reported as saying. The doctors demanded that Barbara step in. Questions were asked in the House. There was sympathetic disruption in other hospitals. Barbara called in the BMA and the leaders of NUPE and COHSE; the unions were determined to get a commitment on the phasing-out of pay beds, the doctors equally adamant that they would oppose such a move to the last scalpel.

It took all-night negotiations to settle the row, against screaming head-lines that Barbara herself had once had private treatment. The allegations were made by a Dr Leonard Kingdom who treated her for her sinus problems in the 1960s, but neither side could ever produce conclusive evidence. The leaders of the two unions involved, Alan Fisher and Albert Spanswick, used their moment in the headlines to remind Barbara – and a wider audience – that ending pay beds was now their top objective and that the tactics used at

Charing Cross Hospital could be repeated across the country. Under pressure itself from a more radical breakaway group of doctors, the Hospital Consultants and Specialists Association, claiming to represent around half of the eleven thousand consultants in the NHS, the BMA signalled that, whatever might be in the manifesto on which the government had been elected, it regarded pay beds as a legitimate part of the set-up and that it would fight for them with every means at its disposal.

Nonetheless, in July 1974, Barbara emerged with credit from settling the Charing Cross dispute. It was the BMA that was attacked for challenging the government over its legislative plans before those plans had even been presented to parliament. Many observers drew a parallel with the dockers' challenge to Tory industrial legislation three years earlier. Horror was expressed that senior members of the medical profession could even contemplate industrial action.

Over the summer, however, as the second general election loomed, Barbara's officials joined the campaign to try to deflect her from what many of them regarded as nothing more than a rush of doctrinaire socialism. In part of an operation by civil servants across Whitehall (discreetly encouraged by Downing Street) to 'mellow the manifesto', Barbara's Permanent Secretary Sir Philip Rogers delivered a judiciously phrased memorandum, warning of the 'incalculable harm' that would be done by the policy. 'Emotionally it is most appealing,' wrote Sir Philip in a finely honed rebuke, '[but] the implication of a doctrine that no one would be allowed to pay for *additional* services or supplies in any of these fields beyond those provided on the basis of need would obviously be very far reaching indeed.' There were serious practical problems too, he warned. Private practice would be driven into a separate, competing sector which would attract staff at all levels away from the public health service. 'I believe that sizeable competition from a private practice sector at this stage and in this atmosphere could do grave harm to the NHS itself,' he said.

Finally, he produced the killer fact. The cost, in revenue forgone and in servicing the beds as they reverted to the NHS, could be between £25 million and £50 million, he estimated, 'which could be better spent dealing with the problems which make private practice desirable'.

A second paper from department officials produced more detailed and even more alarming arguments against Barbara's policy; the NHS itself could be threatened, it argued. But it also admitted that pay beds were a problem, in that NHS staff cared for private patients for no extra pay, unlike consultants (although the latter worked in their own time), while the patients themselves did not pay the real economic cost to the NHS. At the same time, there *was* real danger from a private sector working in direct competition with the NHS. The paper went on: 'In time a threshold could be reached beyond which it is not sensible nor justifiable to plan services for the whole population within the NHS . . . Had the occasion offered, the department, while recognising the strength of the manifesto commitment, would have advised Ministers that it would not be in the long-term interests of public health generally or of the National Health Service in particular to seek to exclude private practice from NHS hospitals altogether.' These were the arguments that had persuaded Bevan to admit pay beds.

Barbara was unmoved. She dismissed her officials' opinions. Privately, their opposition reinforced her sense of mission. She retorted: 'Quite apart from my own ideological commitment to this, I am convinced that neither the PLP nor the staff of the NHS would tolerate any attempt to renege.'

It was a disingenuous answer in the first of several confrontations with her most senior officials, which led to repeated rumours of threatened mass resignations. It was true that eliminating pay beds had become a popular cry for both the parliamentary party and the unions. But Barbara made no attempt to head off either PLP or NHS staff from their objective; there was no public discussion of priorities, or even, for some months, a coherent explanation of why the fight was worth having. It was a tempting prospect, the chance of renewing her claim to the leadership of the party's sansculottes, of proving her commitment to the ideals of equality and social justice.

The 1974–9 Labour government was even more beset by economic troubles and, latterly, industrial chaos than Wilson's first administration. There was no room for debate about ideals, as Barbara grimly noted in her diaries. Her campaign was fought in the newspapers, where striking doctors were treated as one more sign of the ungovernability of Britain and the incompetence of the government, and most especially of its Health Secretary. Her press officer, Peter Brown, once bravely told her why the press didn't like her: 'They think that in everything you do you have one single thought: how it will serve your ends.'

The difference of outlook between Barbara Castle and her Health Minister Dr David Owen added to the sense of embattlement. Owen, whose ability Barbara rated highly but whose instincts she mistrusted, had initially appeared committed to the abolition of pay beds and was chairing the working party jointly considering pay beds and the consultants' contracts. In a paper for Barbara he set out his arguments. Unmet demand, he said, meant pressure to ration health care by ability to pay rather than need. That in turn distorted the principles on which the NHS was founded. But, he thought, the problem could only be solved with caution. The logical way of ending the distortion would be to abolish private practice, but he recognized that was unacceptable. However, even phasing out pay beds would possibly require compensation – unless it was done slowly enough for facilities to be provided in the private sector to replace the beds lost in NHS hospitals. He recommended a three-year interval.

Barbara dismissed the idea: the aim was to discourage the expansion of the private sector, she reminded him, not give it time to grow. For the same reason she rejected his proposal to allow consultants to work full time for the NHS and do private practice outside it.

When at the general election in October, on what was then a startlingly low turnout of 72 per cent, Labour managed to secure a majority of just three, the doctors believed it unlikely that Barbara would get her proposals through parliament and swore their undying opposition. In a grave misjudgement of her mindset, they hoped to frighten Barbara off. 'This is war,' she told her officials in a fine piece of flag-waving. 'No Government could accept instructions to ignore its own Manifesto.' From the other side, the unions used their conferences to reinforce their determination to get rid of pay beds.

By now the doctors were almost entirely alienated. Their pay claim – which was being pursued by the independent Doctors' and Dentists' Review Body – seemed likely to be squeezed by government pay policy. They were confronting a revolution, a new world without, perhaps, the financial cushion of pay beds and with a restructured contract that would reward best those who worked exclusively for the NHS. David Owen and the Chief Medical Officer (Sir Henry Yellowlees, who was widely known as 'Yellowknees', and occasionally even less flatteringly as 'Yellowbelly') both warned Barbara that crisis was approaching. Barbara was unreceptive. She always suspected Owen's stamina; he was one of those right-wingers whose courage, she thought, deserted them under pressure. On 1 November 1974, in the post-election debate on the Queen's Speech, she made the announcement to MPs that Wilson had banned from the Queen's Speech itself. She told them that she was preparing legislation on pay beds for the coming session.

Barbara professed astonishment at the uproar that resulted. As usual, she had not been speaking from an official draft. Her officials must have hoped they still had time to divert her on to a less confrontational track. When they realized how totally they had failed, they stormed in to see her – first Sir Henry Yellowlees, 'all steamed up', she recorded. 'I had wrecked his credibility with the doctors and he thought he ought to have been consulted.' Next, her Permanent Secretary Sir Philip Rogers, equally angry: 'I must tell you, Secretary of State, that I believe the health service is in more danger than I have ever known.' She wrote to the BMA, some of whose members were already working to rule: 'We were elected on this policy – are you challenging the electorate?'

Her astonishment at their reaction seems the more studied in the context of a remark she made to Ted and carefully entered in her diary. 'I told Ted things were turning out just as I wanted. First, a fight on this issue would put me back just where I wanted in the NEC stakes. Secondly, whatever the militant unions did now on the pay bed issue it would be the consultants who had started the industrial action.'[5] But she had less room for manoeuvre than she was admitting. Now that the pay-bed issue appeared to be going their way, the party and the unions were sliding the goal posts towards a total ban on private practice. She knew, whatever her own feelings, that they had to be diverted. But the charge that a total ban was at the top of her own secret agenda further poisoned her relations with the doctors.

Feelings were inflamed still more when Barbara intervened in David Owen's negotiations over contracts. Locked in fruitless conflict over ways of making it more profitable to work exclusively for the NHS, Owen had been seriously examining the doctors' preferred solution of an 'item of service' contract – in effect, a kind of piece rate – and they were far enough advanced to be about to discuss dates for a pilot scheme. Barbara was appalled. Whatever its merits, she thought, it would hugely inflate their pay without doing anything to achieve her objectives of rewarding NHS full-timers and those who worked in the geographically and medically less glamorous areas.

Unsurprisingly, her intervention in the negotiations at a point where the two sides thought they were nearing a deal was hugely unpopular. Barbara compounded her unpopularity by letting journalists know that she had had to stiffen Owen's backbone, confirming the consultants' view that she was the obstacle to a settlement. Just before Christmas 1974, Barbara presented them with the government's decisions on the new contract and the crisis erupted into open hostilities. She had in fact gone some way to meeting the consultants' demands. Unfortunately, they had thought they were heading in an entirely different direction with David Owen. The meeting broke up in disarray and bad headlines for Barbara. In the new year, some consultants began operating sanctions, in effect a work-to-rule, which within weeks were closing hospital casualty departments and leading to cancelled operations and lengthening waiting lists. Fractious negotiations continued for another four months. Against this background, Barbara launched her next moves in the pay-beds campaign.

Even if she had wanted to, she argued, she could not afford to wait. The strong, competing private sector of which Sir Philip had warned was taking shape with every passing day. Buoyed up by horror stories from the hospital wards, newspapers carried large advertisements for private health insurance. Some trade unions, like the National Union of Seamen, negotiated private health care for their members. Planning applications to convert hotels into private hospitals mounted.

In the department, Barbara was facing something close to mutiny at the top. On New Year's Day 1975 the *Daily Express* reported the startling and unprecedented story that mass resignations within the department were threatened, a story hastily and vehemently denied to Barbara by her Permanent Secretary and the Chief Medical Officer. But there was no doubt that, in contrast to her tight-knit private office, where her private secretary Norman Warner[6] and her special adviser, the young Jack Straw had forged an alliance that was to last for a generation, the policy-makers outside were finding Barbara an almost impossibly demanding minister.

Partly this was because she was making waves where they did not even want to dip a toe in the water. But more fundamentally, her challenging, try-and-stop-me approach to government was anathema to the negotiate-and-compromise tradition of the Civil Service. Her officials were exhausted, they complained, and worse, her demands were destroying the delicate yet pivotal relationship with the Treasury. Demanding too much might mean she got nothing, they warned, reminding her of her prized objective, the inflation-proofing of the NHS budget.

Just as, at the Department of Employment, her civil servants had quietly undermined her, so now – indirectly of course – did some at the Department of Health and Social Security. It would be all too easy for an off-the-record conversation, for example, between the Chief Medical Officer and the BMA, to end up reflected in a piece by Barbara's particular goad, the *Daily Mail* correspondent John Stevenson. One official directly involved in the consultants' negotiations was so out of sympathy with her approach that he had to be moved to other work. But Barbara was untroubled by the resistance she met even at the top of the department. And she regarded as eyewash the paranoid left's conviction that the establishment was out to undermine all good socialists. Any decent minister could impose their will on their officials. Yet the ruffled feathers at the top of her department undoubtedly contributed to the negative reporting of her policies – and also, to her distress, of herself.

There were other grounds for the sense of disintegration which now settled on the health service. Both GPs and junior doctors were threatening resignations or industrial action in pursuit of pay claims. Although they were bought off – for the time being at least – the threats only added to the impression that Barbara Castle, as the Tory spokesman Tim Raison claimed, was 'going round lighting fires' in the NHS.

For all their reservations, DHSS officials dutifully set to work on the pay-beds project. Sir Philip Rogers's warnings about the expansion of the private sector seemed proven by the reports of proposals for new hospitals. Tighter planning controls were proposed, and an end to tax relief on company health insurance schemes. Other ideas were raised: controls on the burgeoning private sector should be considered, such as insisting on paying staff at the same rates as the NHS, repaying the government for training costs and banning private training. At the same time, because of the lack of progress, the health unions upped the ante with more covert threats to spread industrial action in hospitals, delivered via Jack Straw.

Barbara's image of intransigence was misleading. She was now a good deal more supple than she was prepared to admit. She was sufficiently alarmed by the chaos – and the ensuing bad press – that seemed to be on the brink of engulfing the NHS not to want head-on confrontation with the consultants, but she knew she had to be seen to make progress. She abandoned any idea of a dramatic, once-and-for-all, ban on pay beds and suggested instead taking out of service surplus beds (a common occurrence anyway, but capable of being presented as a significant political development), to be followed by the introduction of legislation to enable all pay beds to be phased out by a fixed – but not yet decided – date. And she began to think of ways of putting a ceiling on private-sector development to prevent it sapping the lifeblood of the NHS.

It was hard to tell who was pushing and who pulling. By early March, NUPE was complaining to the Prime Minister that too little progress had been made. Pay beds were being blacked by staff across the country and NUPE said it was the government's fault for reneging on a manifesto commitment. COHSE, not to be outdone, was equally restive. But Barbara had yet to settle the consultants' contract dispute and – despite evidence that the BMA was on the brink of suing for peace – could not risk antagonizing them. Jack Straw, far too astute to give his minister unpalatable advice, suggested a line to take in Cabinet on pay beds. 'Whatever reservations your colleagues may have,' he wrote, 'they must accept that by their collective inclusion of the commitment in the manifesto they have unleashed this tiger and the only way to take control of it is by the government taking action now.' Her diary entries imply that she was struggling to square a circle linking unions, Cabinet and medics. But there is also evidence that she was stirring up the unions.[7] The occasional unguarded diary entry suggests she certainly saw scope for personal advancement. The truth probably lies somewhere between.

On 18 April, she finally reached a bad-tempered compromise with the BMA over consultants' contracts. Naturally, she claimed victory; and it had taken some nippy footwork on her part to get Cabinet to accept the huge pay increase – 34 per cent – recommended by the Doctors' and Dentists' Review Body. But in truth she had not got much of what she wanted. There was no new, closed contract to make it easier for NHS managers to monitor the consultants' hours spent with their NHS patients, while Brian Abel Smith told her bluntly that the final deal was going neither to encourage a better geographical spread of consultants nor to improve the rewards open to the full-timers.[8] The press, although confused, was generally unflattering: it was the death warrant of the social contract, the deal between government and unions intended to deliver economic growth and public services in return for pay restraint, declared the *Express*. *The Times* preferred to attack Barbara personally, accusing her of being weak with the unions and tough with the doctors. The *British Medical Journal* trumpeted the defeat of the 'state medical service'.

But at least the doctors had been ready to sue for peace. Barbara and Owen concluded it was an opportune moment to press on fast with the pay-beds proposals. But Barbara rapidly found that if she was hungry for the next fight, few of her colleagues were. Although she won the approval of Cabinet's social services committee for phasing pay beds out within two and a half years, her cabinet colleagues recoiled in horror at the action she now thought was a parallel imperative: putting a ceiling on private-sector expansion.

Her first critic was closer to home. David Owen told her to let the market decide. Private medicine, without the cushion of NHS facilities, would be too expensive to pose a serious threat. He did not believe controls could be made to work, and his views were well reported. Then the cracks in Cabinet began to show. The Paymaster General, Edmund Dell, warned her that she would be threatening the right of doctors to practise privately. Wilson, from whom Barbara had never been more distant, instructed her not to set a date for legislation. Nonetheless, on 5 May 1975, with half an hour's notice to the BMA, she announced that she would legislate to take powers to license private-sector developments so she could control the supply of private beds. With her department's reluctant and tense acquiescence, a consultative paper was drawn up. (Sir Philip wrote to her: 'None of us pretend to be really happy about these recommendations . . . these discussions show how complicated and difficult the issues are.')[9] By the end of July her ideas had clarified. She wanted a fixed date for the total separation of private practice from the NHS, including out-patient facilities, coupled with a complex licensing system for private-sector developments.

Bevan himself would have quaked at the forces now arrayed against her: the press, the doctors, her department and soon, it emerged, several of her most important cabinet colleagues. Denis Healey, the Chancellor (who some years later punched a reporter for asking whether his wife Edna had had private treatment), was anxious about the cost in terms of revenue forgone and of adding beds to the NHS. It would have to come from her existing budget, he warned. The City millionaire Harold Lever, Chancellor of the Duchy of Lancaster and very close to Wilson – and a good friend to Barbara – warned of the 'unwarrantable interference' of the limit on private-sector development. 'To propose such a limit is bound to lead to major political difficulties with the medical profession' – he played bridge with consultants, Barbara noted – 'I can see no grounds for courting these risks prematurely.'[10]

The department was desperate to minimize controversy over what officials knew would be a deeply unpopular policy, seemingly committed to introducing to health the kind of planning agreements the left wanted in industry. The consultation document was published in August, and the old subterfuge was employed whereby just six weeks were allowed for comments. Even the *Guardian* accused Barbara of 'lurching leftwards' with her plan for controls. She had given in to the unions, the press said, while the *Telegraph*, apoplectic, called it 'Sovietization'.

Barbara based her defence not on the rational position that a burgeoning private sector might severely damage the health service, but on the emotive shorthand of queue-jumping by those with either the money or the insurance to afford it. Although the elevation of the ability to pay over the criterion of medical need undoubtedly violated the founding principle of the NHS, it also allowed her opponents to insist that she was only interested in pleasing the unions through crude egalitarianism, even at the expense of the NHS itself. She was disregarding the right of the law-abiding taxpayer to spend his money as he saw fit, and setting out on a road that could only end in the abolition of private practice. She further undermined her own case by conceding to universities the right to continue private practice since the fees went into research, and on a tour of the Middle East encouraged fee-paying foreigners to continue to come to Britain because they brought prestige to British medicine as well as oil dollars. Queue-jumping, by implication, was acceptable as long as it was done by foreigners and didn't make doctors themselves richer.

Meanwhile, the doctors, bruised by the widespread disapproval of their decision to take industrial action only months earlier, now reinvented themselves as guardians of the health service. At the end of September they agreed their response to the consultation document. 'The proposals . . . would be profoundly damaging to the community, to the NHS and to the medical and dental professions . . . both the content and the manner in which the issues in the document have been presented by the Government are calculated to lead to a full-scale confrontation.' If there was any doubt about their views, it was banished by their conclusion: the doctrine that those who are trained by the state must work for the state, they said, 'must lead ultimately to the justification for the watch-tower, the search-light and the Berlin Wall'.

David Owen recommended retreat. 'The central mistake so far has been to overestimate the necessity of keeping the trade union leaders with us on all aspects of the policy and to underestimate the strength of the leaders of the medical profession . . . I really believe that we must now accept that there are far larger issues involved than the Manifesto or our loyalty to our supporters. Our fundamental loyalty must be to maintain the NHS as we know it.' Barbara, who had not lost touch with what was practical, conceded a conciliatory statement to the BMA and an invitation to talk without preconditions. She knew how little space she had. She had to treat with the doctors and had no reason to disbelieve Owen when he warned that they could sabotage everything else she wanted to achieve. She also knew she had serious problems in Cabinet.

On the other hand all her instincts were to do what the unions wanted, not only because they wanted it but because she thought it was necessary to prove to them that a Labour government still believed in socialism and that there was no need to look elsewhere, perhaps to the non-democratic left (as she privately accused Benn of doing). For so long frustrated by the party's caution in office, she now believed she had to ride the tiger of dissent in order to keep it in the party, to disprove the belief of radicals like the young Hilary Wainwright, who thought that the old socialists were survivors of a bygone age, 'individuals beached on a party that was not the one they thought they had joined'.[11] And it was her moment to prove that it was possible to be a socialist in Cabinet, to live down for all time the humiliation of 'In Place of Strife', to establish her place in the pantheon of Labour heroes.

In the rare moments of relaxation, she talked about her father with her new Permanent Secretary, Sir Patrick Nairne, a far more congenial colleague than the now retired Sir Philip Rogers. Frank Betts, she told him, would have had no time for the compromisers and conciliators. At home, Ted was unflaggingly supportive, and in the department her private secretary Norman Warner came perilously close to taking a political position.

But none was more powerfully behind Barbara than the young Jack Straw. Nearly two years into the job, the student activist turned local councillor had carved out a vital role for himself as special adviser – linkman with the trade unions, with disaffected doctors, with backbenchers, as well as press and policy adviser. He plied her with lines to take and arguments to use in Cabinet; he had a keen eye for trouble ahead and a quick appreciation of defensive strategies. His instincts were at least as radical as Barbara's own, and, as a councillor and activist, he was more exposed to the disaffection that was already corrupting the relationship between leadership and rank and file.[12] But he could not deliver the party – only warn that she was losing it. That autumn, conference ignored her appeals and voted overwhelmingly for a total ban on private medicine.

By mid-October 1975, Barbara was fighting on all other fronts too. She had settled a junior doctors' pay claim, but now the deal was coming unstitched as they started to realize that sticking to the pay policy meant that in order to give more pay to most, some would get less. The BMA had sworn an absolute refusal to accept her pay-bed plans. The cartoonists portrayed her as an ageing shrew. And Harold Wilson had accepted the doctors' argument for a Royal Commission on the health service. Barbara suspected it in the long term as a device to condemn a tax-funded NHS and in the short term as a way of kicking the pay-beds issue into the long grass. Now she had to allow that, politically, it must be conceded. It was announced on 20 October.

Its remit was to consider 'in the interests both of the patients and of those who work in the National Health Service, the best use and management of the financial and manpower resources of the NHS'.[13] In return, Barbara persuaded Wilson to meet the consultants' chief negotiator, the highly adversarial Anthony Grabham, and she won her argument in Cabinet to get a commitment to pay-beds legislation in the Queen's Speech for the 1975–6 session of parliament. Wilson's interest in her department alerted her to the real danger she now faced: losing the Prime Minister's backing.

She had also to reassure David Owen. She set out her assessment of the situation. She was still uncertain, she revealed, that the commitment to legislate (carried, she admitted, only because Michael Foot and Wilson backed it) meant it would actually happen. It would be too dangerous to leave the issue of controls over private beds until a need for them was proven; at that point it would be too late. And there was no going back on phasing out pay beds. 'You would be unwise,' she told him cheerily, 'to underestimate the fury we shall face when the Queen's Speech is known, even if we put the issue of controls completely in suspension.' But she did agree to extend the phasing-out period on the grounds that the doctors' pay increase had now been frozen by the newly introduced flat-rate £6 a week limit, the government's alternative to a statutory pay policy.

It was not enough. In November, the consultants announced they would join the juniors and provide emergency cover only. Barbara, who could see the entire NHS in chaos as unions joined in, blacking pay beds and disrupting services, accused them of striking against the House of Commons. 'I find it unique in the history of strikes in Britain that we should be threatened with action about a piece of legislation before Parliament has even seen it.'

It was the last straw for Wilson. He telephoned to tell her, 'casually', that Arnold Goodman, lawyer to the famous, the man whose calls the Prime Minister always took, was offering to operate as a secret back channel between her and the doctors. Barbara accepted the offer with alacrity. Like everyone at the top of the Labour movement, she had known Goodman for years. Top-flight legal advice dispensed with much charm and no charge had given him an entrée into the highest Labour circles. He was also clever, funny and extremely diplomatic, with an astute mind only partially concealed by his bonhomie and bushy eyebrows. As chairman of the Newspaper Publishers' Association he was a prince of Fleet Street, capable of putting his client's case direct to every editor. Certainly the doctors' leader Anthony Grabham believed he squared the press for him. He was also retained by Barbara's other opponents, the Independent Hospitals' Group.

As Barbara had anticipated, Goodman suggested using the Royal Commission to defuse the whole pay-bed crisis. Barbara, conciliatory in private, agreed that her proposals for the control of private beds could be considered by the Royal Commission but argued that the unions would not tolerate any delay on phasing out pay beds from NHS hospitals. Goodman appeared to suggest he could ease Grabham out of the picture; Barbara pointed out tartly that unless Grabham recommended a deal, the BMA wouldn't accept it. Still, there were grounds for negotiation. Over the next couple of weeks, in total secrecy – unknown even to her Permanent Secretary, and certainly to the Chief Medical Officer – Barbara and the faithful Norman Warner met Goodman in his flat (Goodman always kept her waiting) and thrashed out the essentials of the future compromise over tea and cucumber sandwiches.

Barbara might have guessed that if Goodman was representing Grabham to her as the problem, he would be making parallel noises on the other side. Early in December she discovered that without consulting her, but having clearly discussed it with Goodman, Wilson was to meet the BMA. 'The insult to me is obvious,' she stormed in her diary. But, although she was prepared to threaten resignation, she could no longer write in the intemperate language she had used when six years earlier she discovered he had brought in the right-wing Bob Mellish to push 'In Place of Strife' through the Commons. She had lost the ear of the Prime Minister; Goodman still had it. She was reduced to exhortation. 'I would urge you should refuse to discuss any proposals for negotiation at all as this would lead to the suggestion that any eventual settlement had only been reached because you had overruled me and this makes my position untenable.'[14]

It was a hollow threat. Wilson would not even take her phone calls. Where she had been cheered on from the sidelines and in almost every newspaper in the battle for union reform, she was now without useful support. Goodman had, Grabham admitted later, discussed the doctors' point of view with several newspaper editors, leading to much-improved coverage for the doctors at Barbara's expense. Her colleagues in Cabinet were embarrassed – yet the unions thought she was doing too little. On 6 December the *Daily Mail* summed up the chaos in the NHS – one health authority had warned that even accident and emergency services were on the point of breakdown – with graveyard humour. 'Stay in bed this weekend,' it advised. 'Getting out of bed is so often the first step to the casualty ward.' A *Sun* cartoon, commenting on her revision of the use of available cash as a way out of the junior doctors' dispute, went:

CASTLE to WILSON: 'Oh silly me! I got my sums wrong about the
    doctors' pay! I shall tell them I can't count.'
WILSON (aside): 'I've already told them *she doesn't count!*'

The cartoonists were right. Wilson's intervention cut the ground from under Barbara's feet. It was a savage blow, a public gesture of no confidence. But, after months of bitter dissent, settlement was reached in little more than a fortnight of intense and niggling negotiations. The bones of the deal emerged from the first secret meetings Barbara and Norman Warner had held with Goodman. The government would recognize the right to private practice, in the NHS and in private facilities, while doctors would accept the phasing-out of redundant beds; the only others to go would be those that could be replaced in the private sector. An independent board would adjudicate.

Once more, Barbara tried to present it as a victory. Privately, she knew it was not – it was merely the best she could do in the circumstances: 'I have saved the maximum from the situation in which I was placed and safeguarded the major principles of our policy,' she noted in her assessment of the deal. In fact she had lost on every count: private practice was to continue within the NHS – she had been forced to accept that in remote areas where there was no market for a private hospital, she could not deny a consultant a pay bed – while the party's agenda on ending private practice altogether was now dead. Her only hope was to draft the legislation so that it milked the settlement for the little scope it had.

Far more seriously, Barbara had come off worst among her supporters too. The ink was hardly dry on the settlement before the National Executive was asked to censure her for a deal 'which is clearly divergent from the policy expressed at this year's Labour party conference'.

She didn't take only a political fall. At a party the day after the deal, forgetting she was wearing her bifocal spectacles, she fell down a flight of stairs and ended up with a suspected cracked shin. First, she had to endure emergency care from a Tory MP, Dr Gerard Vaughan. He was apologetic; she horrified. Then, because of the disputes, hardly any London hospitals were working normally. After two days of agony, she agreed to go for an X-ray at one hospital where the outpatients department was functioning. But to her horror, the loyal Norman Warner had warned the casualty consultant she was coming. He was waiting to meet her. The only way she avoided being branded a queue-jumper by the press – who were besieging her flat and in contact with every hospital in London – was by bursting into tears and insisting on being taken to the outpatients' waiting room. It was an ignominious denouement to a brutal political collision which owed much more to naked politics than to idealism.

Barbara had finally reached her limit. She carried on at the DHSS, promoting ideas each one of which might have satisfied a lesser minister. Early in 1976, in an unusually reflective mood, she listed the achievements of the previous two years. Through Brian O'Malley's efforts, they had together delivered a breathtaking pensions reform. She had won a battle no one else would even have tried to fight, to introduce child benefit, a universal entitlement paid to mothers, regardless of whether they were working, not to fathers as a tax break through their pay packets. She claimed credit for the new prominence of the problem of battered wives, the achievement of the joint financing of Social Services and NHS schemes, and most notably protecting the NHS budget (getting the Treasury to recognize a formula for spending increases which acknowledged the additional burden on the budget of rising demand and improving technology). But of the two issues that had dominated her work and provoked scores of savage headlines, 'action on pay beds, the resistance to the worst features of the consultants' proposed new contract', she could report little success. This was not the stuff of epitaphs. Worse, it overshadowed all the genuine, uncontroversial initiatives she and her ministers had taken. David Owen, despite his tendency to chop and change – 'I believe [Barbara said] he could produce great creative changes if only he was less didactic to begin with and climbed down less dramatically' – also had a long list of credits: democratizing the NHS and initiating reform of its structure, trying to redistribute resources within it more fairly and prioritizing neglected issues like mental health. Owen, who was to become Foreign Secretary and later still to help found the SDP and become the bogey of the left, regarded his stint with Barbara Castle as his happiest ministerial office. 'She has a very ideological strand to her personality but it's balanced by a truly critical intellect,' he told one writer ten years later. 'If you could arouse her critical faculty, make a case and convince her, she would ditch the ideology . . . She was also a brilliant delegator. One realised with her very early on that as long as she knew you weren't trying to compete with her for newspaper and television coverage, she was easy to work with.'[15] Few politicians can have achieved as much as she did at the DHSS, and be remembered for so little.

Cabinet Ministers occasionally go out with a bang, a spectacular resignation. Sometimes they retire peacefully as their party loses power. A few are exposed to a lingering political death, a slow and painful erosion of status, all the slower and more painful when the individual concerned has once been within reach of the top of the greasy pole.

Barbara had gone back into government in 1974 with her ambition to get to the very top still afloat, if not exactly buoyant. There were glimmers of the old intimacy with Wilson; but more often there was evidence of his frustration with her. The man who used the word 'socialism' only twice in the election campaign no longer needed a strident socialist conscience at his elbow in Cabinet. And if he did, there was Michael Foot, now bringing to the left the credentials of a 1960s refusenik, prepared to treat with the right and capable of carrying the trade unions. Wilson, preparing his own departure, wanted to hand the chalice of unity on to the man most likely to carry it safely: that would be Callaghan, the pragmatist, who had become Wilson's confidant, the only minister given advance warning of his last decision in government – to resign.

Barbara still had defenders in Cabinet, and Foot was unfailingly kind and generous with his personal support. But he wouldn't back her if her ideas threatened pay policy or rocked the boat too violently. Her detractors noted that her items came up last on the cabinet agenda at the point when discussion might be curtailed by lunch engagements, just as, physically, she was back at the end of the cabinet table, once again unable to catch the Prime Minister's eye or hear discussion between him and the Chancellor.

The Department of Health and Social Security, despite its size and importance in the government's scheme of things, was an unglamorous brief, known around Whitehall as the Ministry of Stealth and Total Obscurity. Its offices, in the dreary high-rises of the Elephant and Castle, were ten minutes by car and light years in political terms from the mighty offices of state occupied by Healey at the Treasury, Callaghan in the Foreign Office and Jenkins at the Home Office. Barbara's efforts to rebrand the DHSS as the central department in the delivery of the social contract merely irritated her colleagues, especially Benn with whose ambitions for workers' control and industrial democracy Barbara was now frequently at odds. In July 1975, a run on the pound triggered Healey's U-turn on economic strategy and renewed debate about a statutory pay policy: Barbara does not record the incident. According to Benn, they had a blazing row:

> Barbara thinks socialism is about the social wage which of course is based on the expenditure of her own Department. Although she argues against a statutory [incomes] policy, she would accept it if it would prevent cuts in the DHSS. Actually she's not on our side at all, she's on the other side. Boy, was she shrieking, throwing her arms in the air. 'Alright, you say I am not fair, but nobody has ever been fair to me.' That revealed the burning sense of personal injustice which makes Barbara tick. She is a tough woman . . . but she is very cynical and she hates my guts.[16]

There were other, less public but more humiliating signs of loss of status. Wilson, who had decided not to move into the Downing Street flat after his third election victory, changed the phone number of his Lord North Street house and Barbara could never again ring him at home, while others – like Lord Goodman during the pay-beds dispute – could always find him. For Wilson, Benn was a threat and had to be taken seriously. But Barbara, with no following at Westminster and a declining one in the wider Labour Party, was just a nuisance. He honoured the old debt from the torrid last days of 'In Place of Strife', but she no longer mattered enough to need appeasing. For Barbara, the cosy intimacy first established twenty-five years earlier on those long train journeys across Canada had ended; intimate episodes were rare and not always entirely altruistic. Soon after the first 1974 election, over a drink in his room in the House, Harold again told her he wanted to make Ted a life peer. The offer coincided with Wilson coming under attack for alleged involvement in a sleazy land deal; it constituted a blood-mingling ceremony, not a restoration of the old relationship – just as his refusal to give Ted a peerage in 1970 had been retribution for Barbara's threatened challenge for the deputy leadership. Ted, however, finally went to the Lords in one of Wilson's most controversial honour lists, which also honoured Marcia Williams.

Early in 1976, tired and bad-tempered, Wilson said in so many words that he had had enough of her and her apparently endless capacity for causing a row when he longed for peace. The particular excuse for his outburst was her decision, despite being Health Secretary (with, it was felt, a responsibility to remain above the fray), to support the David Steel Abortion Act against an attempt to amend it. It was a highly contentious issue within the party and among the Catholic population in Barbara's constituency. (If she had not been going to retire, she would probably have kept her head down, as she always had on this subject in the past.) Barbara commented in her diary: 'He told me categorically that he wasn't going to have me splitting the party. "I'm sick of pulling this party back from the brink. If this goes on I shall throw in my hand – and then see how some of you will get along." "Like who?" I replied, at which he gave me a hostile look, as if to say, "You'd go, for one."'

The press knew all this and reflected it in the way they reported her. She was interesting in Labour terms, but no longer enough of a player on the national scene to be depicted as a threat to the nation (although if necessary she could be presented as such).

As editors and press barons began to panic about the strength of the left and Barbara's own position weakened, the tone of her press changed. Wilson's irritation with her meant the loss of her only power base at the heart of politics. Soon enough, it was reflected in her public image. What had once been her courage became dogmatism, her speeches, shrill scolds. An Alice in Wonderland caricature of Barbara, called the Red Queen, was introduced into the news coverage, a wild-eyed doctrinaire socialist determined to tip Britain from disaster into catastrophe.

Above all, try though she did to fudge her date of birth (how she regretted putting it in *Who's Who* in 1945) and painstaking as she continued to be with her appearance, she was unmistakably getting old, old enough to claim the pension whose uprating had been her first action when she took office. Officials remember the pension book arriving and being buried in a locked drawer. She was a little older than Wilson and Callaghan and

Foot, significantly older than Healey and Jenkins. She was still slim and attractive, she still enjoyed flirting and flashing a leg. But politically she was beginning to look like a survivor from an earlier generation, a dowager. As the commentators knew Wilson's mannerisms and evasions, so they were becoming too familiar to be impressed any more by Barbara's energy and determination as applied to such apparently misguided causes as the pay-beds issue.

The party conference, where once she had been sure of being everyone's heart-throb, became a painful ritual. 'Back at home [after conference] I suddenly got depressed. With the age thing for everyone to seize on (which they would never have guessed if I hadn't told them), and with the very people in the movement who ought to be backing me conspiring against the Government in general and me in particular instead, I temporarily but utterly lost heart. "I want the hell out of it," I said to Ted as he cuddled me in bed. "My only problem is: when I go and the reason I give." And I added viciously, "Let some of them take this pay beds thing on and let us see what *they* can make of it." Ted just listened, stroking my head as gently and staunchly as he has done over the years.'[17] She nearly funked the NEC elections altogether and was only persuaded by her often bilious critic, Ian Mikardo, to stand again. She scraped in, last of the successful candidates.

Party activists, led by Benn, were determined to head off into a world of fantasy economics, where there were no foreign bankers to trigger a run on the pound and no economic crises provoked by intractable problems of underinvestment in industry. In September 1975 Benn published *The Bristol Letter*, a call to arms that was barely compatible with his continued membership of the government. 'In 6000 words he has skilfully put himself at the head of all the discontents in the movement . . . as usual the media have endorsed his claim to be the keeper of the socialist conscience . . . Wedgie's speech covers familiar ground: the fact that Britain is now in a "deep slump" and that only radical policies will cure it. Once again I find a fatal flaw in his analysis: his refusal to tell the movement that, if it wants more investment, it must give up eating the seed corn.'[18]

Time and again, Barbara argued for economic realism, on the NEC and at conference, where pressure for more control by the party over MPs and the government was mounting. 'How can they call on the Government to obey Conference decisions when they refuse themselves to do any realistic arithmetic?' she wrote in 1975. 'They must learn to choose: either they can continue to pass these resolutions as a relief for their own souls, knowing full well the Government cannot meet them all, or they must impose some revolutionary self-discipline on themselves.'

Often she was supporting Foot, although on occasion she was prepared to go further to meet party demands; and unless it was her workforce in the hospitals and social services whose pay rises were being discussed, she was usually more hawkish than the Employment Secretary on pay policy. She could not resist observing that Foot was now as distant from *Tribune*, the newspaper he had edited for nine years, as she had become when she was Employment Secretary.

Barbara's relations with Benn were cool and cooling further. Benn recorded one epic confrontation, at a 'husbands' and wives' dinner' in 1974.

> Barbara turned on me. 'You with your open government, with your facile speeches, getting all the publicity, pre-empting resources – "I'm the big spender, I can't do it without money" – trying to be holier than thou and more left wing than me.' She was extremely angry with me. 'I know we can *only* get this expenditure if we go for a statutory wages policy,' she said, revealing once again her hatred for the trade unions . . . my God, Barbara's hatred really came out. I think she is feeling guilty.[19]

On occasion, they were prepared to acknowledge each other's exceptional abilities. Yet Barbara, inherently questioning, was becoming almost paranoid about Benn. In January 1975, she noted: 'Wedgie as always was warmly adulatory. I am sorry if I think it is a bit calculated, but he certainly does it very well, making one feel successful and wanted just when one needs it most.' Their appreciation of each other's strengths rose as they worked together on the referendum campaign, but even so Barbara was never comfortable with him. 'I do wish he could manage to sound less like a lay preacher helping everyone else to find the right road,' she wrote in February 1975. In April, Benn was writing: 'Barbara was in the chair, bossy but brilliant.' But this was a brief thaw in a relationship that had become icy in opposition and became icy again after the referendum campaign. Barbara distrusted his demagoguery and suspected his charm. 'I feel these days Wedgie has got himself launched so strongly on a tide of challenging everything and everyone that all he can do is to shoot the rapids.' In June 1975, after an all-day session at Chequers on devolution, she wrote: 'Once again I was divided in my mind over Wedgie: a maddening mixture of the bogus theoretician and the genuine visionary.'

But the relationship that was to be crucial was with Jim Callaghan, a man whom she had disliked and distrusted for most of her political life.

★

Barbara was finally forced to acknowledge there was only one way for her career to go: down. She had always loved politics: it had been her life for fifty years, it had driven out almost every other consideration. She had intended to get to the very top, and she could not give it up lightly. But Ted was not well. There had been more, inconclusive, tests (and unpleasant newspaper coverage suggesting the Health Secretary's husband had been getting special treatment). Retirement with Ted would be difficult; retirement without him, impossible.

She had always believed she could make people love her; and she had often succeeded. But now she felt surrounded by hostility and sneering criticism. Colleagues in Cabinet were uniting against her demands for more money. Colleagues in the party attacked her for failing to spend enough. The newspapers just attacked her. Early in 1976 she told her private secretary Norman Warner, to whom she had become very close, that she would resign from Cabinet when the pay-beds legislation went through. She may not have been serious: she did not go and see Wilson until March, by which time she was in fear of losing her job in the light of their increasingly tense relationship. She asked him to let her go out with dignity, and in her own time. 'I don't want the press to be able to say I've been pushed out.' She wanted one last achievement, her pay-beds bill. He was charming and agreeable, and revealed that he too was planning to take early retirement. He said he had given the date to the Queen when he had returned to power in 1974; he would not, however, divulge it to Barbara, insisting that it might yet change. They discussed the succession: 'There are three groups on the Left. There is what is now called the "soft" left, to which you and I and Michael always belonged. There is a middle group and then there are the really vicious group,' Wilson told her, adding, 'Your timetable ought to fit in with mine alright'.[20]

It was their last intimate conversation as two members of government. Twelve days later, on 16 March, Wilson announced his resignation to Cabinet. Barbara, after the most fleeting of pangs of regret, was immediately suspicious. What, she began to wonder, did he mean by it? 'OK, so a man has the right to decide he will give up office, and whatever date he chooses will have its snags, but for Harold to do this gratuitously . . . almost looks like frivolity. Has one the *right* to throw one's party into turmoil for no apparent cause, to face them with a fait accompli because one knows they would plead with one to stay if they knew in time? What exactly *was* Harold up to?'

It did not take long for her to find an answer: Wilson was aiming to ease Callaghan in. Callaghan was the only cabinet minister to have had significant advance warning, the only one who precisely fitted Wilson's description of what his successor must be: 'loyal to the counter-inflationary policy and to Nato [not Benn, then, and a dig at Foot who had long been a leading CND campaigner] . . . ready to work himself to death [not Jenkins] and make a point of getting out into the country and meeting the people . . . Above all, remember the Party is the Party in the country – not the Palace of Westminster, not Smith Square.'

Barbara was planning a 'Stop Jim' campaign almost before she was out of Downing Street. Michael Foot would be her candidate; but the left would have no chance if it was divided. Benn would have to be persuaded to keep his head down this time. Benn, however, dismissed her appeal. It was 'a typical defeatist view', he snorted into his diary. 'She began by saying "Wedgie, we all agree the future is yours." That's a load of nonsense really, the question is what does the Party do *now* to avoid a collapse?'[21]

Stopping Jim was not only about rescuing the party; Barbara knew that of all the potential leaders he was the one with least time for her. Healey – whom she urged to stand as the candidate most likely to be second choice (a misjudgement) – respected her, and appreciated her determination. Jenkins had always appeared to value her political perspective. Benn now disliked her on a personal level but recognized her worth as an experienced left-winger. Foot, of course, would keep her in Cabinet for as long as she wanted to stay. But Callaghan and Barbara were polar opposites. Trade unionist versus middle-class intellectual, pragmatist against Passionara, perhaps their only point in common was a determination not to let the other win. Callaghan in No. 10 meant Barbara on the back benches.

She had no way of influencing her fate. She kept out of Foot's campaign, which was run by young left-wingers led by Neil Kinnock. After the first round, it was clear Callaghan was going to cruise home. By the time the result was announced, on 5 April 1976, Foot had already conceded defeat, and the business of allocating ministerial jobs was under way. 'Mike won't let Jim be nasty to you,' whispered Jill Craigie, sitting beside Barbara on the sofa in Foot's room. But there were limits even to Foot's influence with the new Prime Minister.

Two days later, Cabinet was cancelled; Barbara was summoned to Downing Street. She was kept waiting for fifteen minutes. Then Callaghan sacked her. 'I still didn't believe that a Prime Minister could cut across a legislative programme in mid-session so crudely, so indifferently,' she wrote later, piously, overlooking her promotion in the midst of the Transport Bill eight years earlier.

Barbara made it as hard for him as she could. She argued. She refused to write the conventional resignation letter. '"I want to stay to finish my legislation,"' she told him defiantly, '"and that is what I shall say in my letter to you. And I shall hold a press conference to spell this out. I shall go on to the Standing Committee on the Bill and shall defend it line by line." "Heaven help your successor," he replied mournfully. "Don't worry, Jim," I said cheerfully. "I shan't attack you personally, I shall just tell the truth." '[22]

Later Callaghan told Benn that he 'had to end her career', as if she were an old family pet. He told Foot, 'It might be my first mistake.' Barbara thought they should have fought for her as once the three of them had fought for Judith Hart. Foot, who had insisted on jobs for his own young supporters, always had a niggling worry that he might have done more.

To be out of office in opposition was one thing. To be excluded from a Labour government Barbara found almost intolerable. To add to her grief, Brian O'Malley had had a stroke. Two days before she was sacked, he had died. Barbara was devastated by his death. She felt acutely mortal herself. But she also felt cruelly unprepared for O'Malley's death, and her own political extinction:

> What interests me is the stubbornness of my sense of power and authority. When we lost the last election, I never had this rooted belief that I was part of the government . . . I find it inconceivable that I shall not be at Tuesday's Cabinet; not fighting for a proper rate of child benefit; not introducing the pay beds bill on Monday; not coping with the new problem of the juniors; not conducting our discussions on the consultative document on health priorities; not fighting for the proper treatment of pensions in the next round of pay policy. Authority is ingrained in me in a new way and I just don't believe anyone can discharge it better in DHSS.

The Castle motto throughout had been: 'When the sirens sound, make sure you look your best.' She got her hair done and went to Blackburn for the weekend. Then she went north again, to Rotherham for O'Malley's funeral. She was put in the second row, behind the cabinet ministers, but she was mobbed when she came out. 'That's star quality,' said David Owen. 'Her successor won't have it.'

19. The End of the Affair

I have had a long love affair with the rank and file and I may be a relatively glamorous great-aunt but I want to stay that way in everyone's memory.

Barbara Castle, unpublished diaries, 30 September 1976

Jim Callaghan had taken his revenge. Unexpectedly, the thought that he had intended to humiliate her, to 'discard me cavalierly, like a piece of old junk',[1] made it easier for Barbara to survive her final dismissal than the rejection by her colleagues in the shadow cabinet elections in 1972. Where that had left her demoralized and self-doubting for months, this time, after Easter in the garden at Hell Corner, Barbara soon found compensation in undisturbed weekends and time spent with Ted and the family. As importantly, she rediscovered friends in the party with whom she could unite in scorn for the new Prime Minister. The corridors of Westminster were suddenly full of people who wanted to give her a consoling kiss, to praise her for the scale of her achievements, and to sympathize over her callous treatment. The exceptions were Michael Foot, whom she found bewilderingly loyal to their old enemy – and Wilson, who also refused to criticize Callaghan and who, she complained after his farewell lunch, had turned into a right-winger, 'out of tune with any flick of rebellious fun'.[2]

Once again retirement beckoned. The government's majority was so fragile that at any time a general election might end her political career altogether. She looked around Westminster and at her rediscovered friends in the party with an unfamiliar sense of warmth and a renewed determination to go out undefeated. On 26 April, just over three weeks after she had been sacked, she spoke in front of her cabinet colleagues for the first time as a backbencher, at the monthly meeting of the NEC–Cabinet liaison committee. 'It was quite an effort as I'm still shell-shocked and ill at ease in my new role. But, like a rider who has been thrown, I made myself remount and I delivered a spirited speech.'[3] On the 27th, she made her first intervention from the back benches in the Commons, on the second reading of the Pay Beds Bill for which she had fought so hard. She had not spoken as a government backbencher – 'the lowest form of parliamentary life'[4] – for twenty-five years; she did not even know where she would sit. 'I felt strangely paralysed by shyness. Here I go again, I thought to myself; I'm going to fail to rise to the occasion . . . Mercifully, as soon as the debate started, I came alive . . . I rose for my speech to full benches on our side; all shyness vanished and I was away to a good speech, helped enormously by the cheers of our own lads . . . I sat down to a great cheer and congratulations.'[5] True to her threat to Callaghan, she made sure she was on the standing committee, which went through the bill clause by clause. She would guard her legacy; for the last time she would deny defeat, just as she had denied that she had been beaten over 'In Place of Strife' (or that her wig had been lifted off by a piece of wire). But what motivated her for the rest of her parliamentary career was a determination to show Callaghan – and the rest of the world – that she had been sacked at the height of her powers. She still had the Commons; more importantly, she also had a say in the party through the National Executive, which was entering its long and ultimately disastrous attempt to control the parliamentary party.

The conflict between, on the one hand, the ambitions of the narrowly focused party organizations with their tendency to be inward-looking, and their leaders in government on the other, is a commonplace of modern politics. Labour, committed philosophically to internal accountability and control, had institutionalized the tension. After 1970, the NEC had responded to criticism of Wilson's first administrations by trying to direct the next Labour government's attention entirely to the fulfilment of the party activists' ambitions; it was pushing at the frontiers of its role as the repository of conference sovereignty by acting as a kind of running tribunal by which the Labour government was continually being called to account. Geoff Bish, the secretary of the research department, encouraged by Bennite supporters on the NEC, drafted extravagant policy papers for a mid-term manifesto which reflected the views of enthusiastic constituency party activists. As the government staggered from crisis to expenditure cuts, the NEC kept up an angry chorus of disapproval which made its meetings a constant source of headlines, while Callaghan, uncertain of his majority in parliament, appeared sometimes to have even less support in his party than Wilson. The bitterness at the top was reflected and magnified in constituency parties around the country. Trade union leaders, in particular Jack Jones and Hugh Scanlon, loyally backed the government; but they could no longer control their rank and file.

Barbara saw herself as a voice of reason in the NEC's increasingly partisan debates. Early in 1974 she had fought off a move to ban ministers who chaired NEC committees from developing policy in their own field. 'This Labour government won't succeed . . . if both NEC and Government insist that they must go their separate ways. We need *more* integration, not less, if the thing is to work. And the NEC must not assume that every modification of party policy by a Labour Government is a sign of betrayal rather than closer knowledge of the facts.'[6] But once again the party's ambitions had been hopelessly compromised by economic reality; the Tories' reflation in the early seventies and, in 1973, a sharp rise in oil prices had produced stagflation – raging inflation and no growth. By the end of 1974, the trade deficit was £2.5 billion above predictions, and had added nearly 10 per cent to inflation while savagely reducing growth. In 1975 Cabinet had mutinied when faced with a demand from Healey for further cuts. No one knew quite what to do as Keynesian remedies failed to work; it was new and uncharted territory.

By 1976, the left – backed by reputable economists including Nicolas Kaldor, Healey's own adviser – was attracted by the idea of adopting variants on a siege economy, with import controls to protect British industry while it geared up for a return to growth. In the Cabinet, Tony Crosland – Jim Callaghan's Foreign Secretary until his sudden and premature death in 1977 – argued strongly in favour of import controls; outside it, Barbara, not for the first time, shared Crosland's analysis.[7] Her enthusiasm for controls, however, was tempered by her memory of the unconvincing experience of them in 1964. But they and other government critics were already talking in obsolete terms. Healey believed a trading nation like Britain could not risk any impediment to exports, and chose monetarism, a decision reinforced by the International Monetary Fund's tightly restrictive terms for the £2.5 billion loan the Treasury believed, on the basis of inaccurate forecasts, to be essential. So Chancellor Healey reversed his early expansionist, easy-money approach and clamped down on public spending and pay rates.

Keynesian economics, the guide for every government since the war, was dead. Jim Callaghan read its funeral rites at the party conference in October 1976: 'The cosy world we were told would go on for ever, where full employment would be guaranteed by a stroke of the Chancellor's pen, cutting taxes, deficit spending – that cosy world is gone . . . we used to think you could spend your way out of a recession and increase employment by cutting taxes and boosting Government spending. I tell you in all candour, that option no longer exists.'[8] Healey agreed. His steep deflation taking £2.5 billion out of the economy in 1976 – which, he believed, was eventually vindicated by the turnaround of the economy by 1978 – was the recruiting sergeant for the Campaign for Labour Party Democracy, a pressure group founded in 1972 by a left-wing activist, Vladimir Derer. The CLPD thought that the way to make a Labour government pursue socialist economics was to put MPs under the control of their constituencies by threatening them with the loss of their seats, thereby disempowering the right-wing PLP. Helped by the greater power of the NEC, there would finally be a radical PLP and a radical Cabinet. The alternative, that there might never be enough Labour MPs, radical or not, to form a government, was not considered.

Barbara – unlike, she thought, Benn – knew that the view from Cabinet was more complex than what she called the *simplistes* on the NEC were prepared to acknowledge. The dilemma was always to balance the inevitable constraints with political courage and knowing when to override them. She refused to go into outright opposition. On the back benches she still found herself out of tune with the government, but she was even more irritated by the Bennite Ian Mikardo–Judith Hart axis on the NEC, which was trying to carry forward the revolution-in-industry strategy that Benn had first drafted in the early 1970s, built on huge state backing for industrial 'winners' as a way of revitalizing employment and export prospects. Benn's sideways move from Industry to Energy after the referendum campaign in 1975 had ended his attempt at radical (and, in the view of Wilson, Callaghan and most others, disastrous) reform. Barbara noted: 'I just don't accept Mik and Judith's facile assumption that no cuts of any kind would be necessary if only we would alter our industrial strategy. On the other hand, I'm blowed if I can see why I should underwrite everything done by a government whose policies I criticised so often and so forcibly when I was in the Cabinet.'[9] A few weeks later, she observed: 'I am always glad when opposition for opposition's sake is given a smack on the NEC. Nonetheless I know the right wing – with their attacks on public expenditure and their political cowardice about values – needs a corrective, however crude, from the rank and file.'[10] As the outside left pulled harder and harder at party unity, Barbara – like thousands on the soft left – often found herself isolated, unwilling to follow the far left but disinclined to back the government. Cautious figures on the right warned that for the NEC to promote policies at conference which were unacceptable to the government risked recreating the conditions for a 1931-type split. The breaches of the 1930s and the 1950s were about to be revisited.

The NEC had embarked on an ambitious project, a new programme for the government, to be called 'The Next Three Years'. Barbara was not impressed. She found herself thinking of alternative ways of organizing the NEC's policy-making processes. 'What a way to evolve a policy . . . what ministers should have done was to take charge of the policy sub-committees in their particular field, attend themselves (preferably in the chair), get their political advisers to play an active part; in other words integrate themselves with the NEC's work as I did in the social policy field. The result was that the social policy chapter is the most precise and realistic – as well as visionary – in the whole document.'[11] Eventually the NEC document, replete with ambitious spending and nationalization plans, was passed. However, on the way, a government disclaimer had been inserted, rendering its influence on a future manifesto negligible. Barbara, vigorously attacking Healey, recommended the programme to conference in 1977.

> Of course, Denis, these policies [of deflation] have worked in a certain sense, they always do; in the sense that they cut demand and so cut imports and spending, so they balance our accounts, build up our reserves and send share prices rocketing. They also help to bring down prices by cutting demand because people have not got the money to buy the things they need. But what these policies cannot do and have not done, is to stimulate economic activity, increase our standard of life or create jobs. It is a financiers' recovery, not an economic one, and the success of solvency is no substitute for growth.

But she also warned that there was a desperate need for realism among the delegates. Callaghan, with what was becoming a kind of trademark astuteness, praised her for telling the conference what it needed, as well as what it wanted, to hear.

When Attlee had promoted Callaghan into government thirty years earlier, the old Prime Minister had given him one piece of advice: 'If you are going to negotiate with someone tomorrow, don't insult them today.' Callaghan applied the principle to the left. Where flattery would not work, he simply ignored the provocation. In April 1976, carefully observing the new Prime Minister's style, Barbara noted, amazed, that a proposal to nationalize four clearing banks and six top insurance companies went through the NEC without comment from either Callaghan or the unions. The approach set the tone for Callaghan's premiership. Frustrated herself by the purism and lack of realism of the left which made it easy for government to ignore its ideas, Barbara found herself admiring Callaghan for the first time in their political careers. She was still horrified that a politician's response to the economic crises of the early 1970s could be, as Callaghan's was, to wonder where he might emigrate to. But she watched with a connoisseur's understanding as he charmed and flattered his critics at every opportunity and then carried on doing what he wanted to. Early in 1977 they were on a delegation together to a socialist conference in Norway:

> I began to realise how he had managed to charm the Left-wingers in the Cabinet . . . Jim suggested we all ate together in his private suite. And so we ended the evening high up on the 20th floor [of the hotel] round a large table in Jim's room eating our reindeer steaks and enjoying a panoramic view of the lights of Oslo glittering on the snow. Jim could not have been more matey, insisting on standing us wine though he only had a modest glass of beer himself. [He] couldn't have been nicer. But as I looked at him I thought once again how *dull* his virtues are. He looked more like a neutered Tom than ever. I longed for the sparkle of wit and the touch of devilment of a Nye Bevan, a Michael Foot – or even a Harold Wilson.[12]

At the end of that year, after the pact with the Liberals which had given Labour a new lease of life nearly broke down, Barbara wrote with unaccustomed enthusiasm:

> Jim has kept his cool brilliantly: it is a strange, late flowering in a man who flopped as Chancellor, made no mark as Foreign Secretary and was a reactionary Home Secretary. But it is not just a case of the office making the man, but of the hour making him. Jim got his chance to give the kind of calm, conservative leadership natural to him at a moment when the unions had been frightened out of their wits by the fear . . . of a Thatcher government and when Labour MPs were ready to follow anyone who would save their seats. The trouble is that Harold Wilson threw away all the opportunities for radical change and at the same time was associated with the period of economic difficulties. So all the Labour party is left with is the need to make a success of non-radical economic policies.[13]

Wilson was now beyond the pale as far as Barbara was concerned. He had betrayed the old relationship by his resignation, and she dismissed him as a Prime Minister. She was inclined, like many others, to blame in part the influence of his personal secretary Marcia Williams (now Lady Falkender).

> My feelings about Marcia are mixed. I know (because they have told me) that some of Harold's secretaries who had to work with her hated her. I know too that she is neurotic, because Harold told me so. I remember

how, way back in 1956 when Harold was not even leader of the party, he told me how he had 'stolen' this young typist from Transport House where she was conspiring against the party machine which was then right-wing dominated and, she said, seeking to neutralise his growing political influence. He told me her marriage had broken up, that she was in a terrible emotional state and that he was having an exhausting time with her. But even then he seemed to have become a prisoner of her fierce loyalty and to be almost enjoying the burdens it placed on him. I believe too that she increasingly exploited her special relationship with him, as though it gave her the right to treat him impertinently . . . even in front of others and even when he was Prime Minister. I've seen her do it! As against that she was very kind to me, always pushed me with Harold, always backed me politically. She *was* a good political influence with him in many ways: her instincts were always earthy and usually healthy ones. He did need someone like her at his elbow to prevent him from becoming too pro-establishment. The real flaw in Harold's entourage was not Marcia: it was Harold's passion for surrounding himself with the second rate.[14]

David Ennals, Barbara's hapless successor at the DHSS, also tried to charm her. He was a considerate successor, inviting her to receptions and dinners whenever contacts she had made were paying return visits, or when projects she had initiated came to fruition. Barbara went to the parties, and she freely criticized his decisions. The Pay Beds Bill he left alone; Goodman had already disembowelled it. But in May 1976 he announced that one of Barbara's cherished schemes, the introduction of child benefit, had been postponed indefinitely. Barbara was furious. ' "You don't think I liked doing this?" he said. "You could have done what I would have done and resigned," I replied coldly, turning on my heel.'[15]

Child benefit was all that remained of a manifesto idea to introduce a system of tax credits to replace means-testing. Means-testing meant the poverty trap, where low earners lost more in benefits – for example, free school meals – than they gained from a pay increase. When Barbara had been sacked, she had just agreed the rate at which it should be introduced in 1977. Now it was to be delayed, and probably abandoned, because trade unionists on whose support over pay policy the government was dependent were thought to oppose what would appear to be a tax increase.

From the back benches, Barbara now launched her last campaign to advance the welfare state. Using her position on the NEC she set out to defuse criticism of the benefit among trade unionists. In this she was aided by the first-ever leak of cabinet minutes to the magazine *New Society*, detailing the debate between Ennals and Healey over the decision to postpone child benefit. The minutes, the leaking of which was blamed on Jack Straw although he no longer worked in the DHSS, showed that the decision was a mix of economic pragmatism – the rate Healey said was affordable (£2.40) would mean actually cutting the amount of aid given to families in real terms – and political finessing. Healey claimed that the unions were against, while the unions were told that the PLP was opposed because of the impact on men's pay packets. Barbara got a TUC–NEC working party to examine ways in which the benefit could be introduced. As it was impossible for the trade unions to oppose the new measure openly, they fell into line. In parliament, eighty-five backbenchers supported a Commons motion demanding its introduction. As a result, Healey gave in. Child benefit was phased in over three years and was fully introduced by the 1979 election. 'The government was glad to claim it as the cornerstone of its policy for the family,' Barbara wrote in the epilogue to her second published volume of diaries.

By the autumn of 1976 she was enjoying politics almost more than ever before. The sense that she had nothing more to strive for liberated her from the agonizing self-doubt that had often blighted her public career. She fought with undiminished energy for her vision of socialism, in speeches and on the NEC. Ted tried to dissuade her from standing for the Executive, fearing that she would be knocked off. But Barbara was not ready to give it up before it gave her up. 'I'd rather risk this public humiliation than meekly submit to Jim's dismissal of me . . . the more I study the turgid mediocrity of the Cabinet, the more arrogant I become. I *know* I was a better Minister than most of them rolled together. I believe, for instance, that the government could get away with a much more vigorous economic strategy if only it had some fight in it.'[16] In the event, she did slightly better in the NEC election than in the previous year, which – since she was no longer part of any slate or group – she happily concluded must have been due to personal affection. However, she resolved not to run the following year (and then changed her mind, staying on the NEC until she left the Westminster parliament at the 1979 election).

The 1976 conference itself confirmed her view of the new left, the new Puritans, she thought, quite unplugged from normal human aspirations, especially after they voted against what was to become Margaret Thatcher's most popular working-class policy, council house sales. 'It is a weird, unrealistic atmosphere as though the nearer delegates feel to political extinction the more vivid become their dreams and the more they cling to them . . . Conference merely devalues itself by this kind of unthinking hysteria; making the nonsensical the enemy of the achievable.'[17] But she enjoyed herself, demanding a role in the *End of the Peers* review, in which a young Neil Kinnock starred. She also provoked a near-riot at the Tribune rally (where Neil Kinnock starred again) by tipping off Jack Jones that Ian Mikardo was going to attack the trade unions for what he called their complicity in the government's pay policy. Jones, who had become the government's most important trade union partner, was so incensed that he stormed on to the platform, where he and Mikardo squared up for fisticuffs and had to be pulled apart. After embarrassing herself and the government (quite unintentionally, she claimed, somewhat implausibly) by giving an unflattering interview about Callaghan to *Woman* magazine, published at the start of conference – 'Barbara's vengeance,' said the *Express* – she imposed a public reconciliation on him by asking him to dance with her at the conference ball. The challenge dance was one of Barbara's favourite tactics. She once tried it on Frank Cousins at a TUC conference. Afterwards, she led him back to Frank's feisty wife, Nance. 'Frank is a wonderful dancer,' Barbara said. Nance, the story goes, looked her straight in the eye: 'And I am a wonderful cook. And I'm good in bed too.'[18]

The awkward dance with Callaghan ended less memorably, but it was the start of a series of small personal triumphs that vindicated, she believed, her bitter and unpopular battles of the past two years. Perhaps most astonishingly, her old enemy the BMA gave her an ovation after an impassioned speech about why the NHS was essential. Callaghan's pact with the Liberals in March 1977 – just the kind of coalition politics she most detested – enabled the government to survive for two more years. Barbara's work on the NEC and its myriad committees still absorbed more than half her week.

There was more interest than ever before in the machinery of power. Barbara, as its most recent escapee, was courted by the Whitehall-watchers. In conversation with Rudolf Klein, the leading observer of the NHS, she developed her theory that every action everyone took was informed by politics. There was no such thing as a neutral expert, she said, and that should be accepted, as she had always accepted that her officials had views which, as long as she knew what they were, she could accommodate. 'What mattered most in government was political will . . . [Klein] said what I was saying meant that a government's social policy would depend on who happened to be minister. "It does now," I replied. "In fact it is dictated by the PM. If he wants the social services to be given higher priority he puts a tough Minister in there." '

In a later interview she dismissed the suggestion, popular among conspiracy theorists on the left, that officials could be blamed for obstructing government proposals. It all came down to the courage of the departmental minister, the Cabinet and ultimately the Prime Minister. On the purposes of parliamentary reform she was unequivocal: it should aim to improve the ability of government to carry out its business. The idea of an elected House of Lords, and the enhanced authority that would accompany it, was so unacceptable that she – like Michael Foot – would rather have no reform at all. A bill of rights would also undermine the Commons, while select committees (not then established on departmental lines) were 'pretty amateur affairs' that 'don't really get to the bottom of issues, yet rush into partisan statements'.

On 4 April 1977, Barbara finally announced to her constituents that she would not stand again for parliament. When she had first taken the decision to go, it had seemed easy, even desirable. When it finally happened, she made the announcement with the greatest regret; only the response cheered her. The BBC sent a camera crew *and* a make-up girl to record an interview, after an emotional session with her constituency party.

> I told them that together we would ensure that Blackburn remained Labour for another 32 years. They must choose a Socialist, not a careerist, to follow me. They were clearly a bit stunned by my news . . . I realised once again why I was a Socialist. It wasn't theory (all theories have been taking a bit of a bashing recently). It was practical experience of the hidden gifts of the most unlikely people who have been the despised and neglected of our snobbish society and who are only just beginning to get their chance.

On 26 June, Jack Straw was selected to replace her, as she wished. 'Now I am really on my way to my self-imposed self-effacement.'

But of course, she knew she was not. 'When will it stop mattering to me whether I am the idol of the party rank and file or not? Will I ever be able to wean myself from my present involvement in party life? At present I am curiously suspended between two lives: between the heaven of feeling I still have a major political role to play and the hell of accepting that I no longer have. How soon should one begin to accept death?'[19]

Like an alcoholic on a cure, Barbara had already started making covert plans to return to politics by the back door. The government was preparing to introduce legislation allowing direct elections to the European Parliament.

Barbara, in a typical example of twin-tracking, intended to oppose the legislation because her hostility to Europe and its institutions was undiminished – not least to the parliament, which she regarded as a fig leaf for the European Commission's autocracy and drive towards federalism – and then to stand as a candidate. She wrote in early March 1977: 'One of the things which reconciles me to my own retirement is the realisation that the House of Commons will never play a major political role again. The battleground is shifting inevitably to Brussels.' Barbara would shift with it. Later that same month she went to the north-west England regional party conference. This would be her selection conference, she thought. 'I shall try to rise like a phoenix from the ashes and carry on my political fight in the new European scenario.' She no longer thought it was feasible to campaign for Britain's withdrawal from Europe, even though the left was now doing just that. She had, as Benn said he had, accepted the referendum decision. She pinned her hopes, as Eurosceptics were to do for the next generation, on enlargement of the Community, a wider and looser Europe, confederalism rather than federalism.

In March 1978, a dishonourable episode from her recent past propelled her, for once unwillingly, back into the political limelight. She was accused of searching DHSS files for political advantage. What was unclear was whether it was to damage or to protect the former Liberal leader, Jeremy Thorpe.

Good-looking, charismatic and lightweight, Thorpe – who had bested her so effectively in the Oxford Union debate on Europe less than a year earlier – was the political antithesis of Barbara. At some point after the 1974 elections, when for the first time since the Second World War the Liberals effectively held the balance of power, Thorpe convinced Wilson that he was being smeared by the South African secret service because of his opposition to apartheid. Wilson was an eager audience. As Thorpe may have known, his assertations tallied closely with Wilson's own conspiracy theories.

Barbara's involvement had begun in her last few months in Cabinet. In January 1976, a good-looking man in early middle age appeared in a South Wales court. His name was Norman Scott and he was accused of dishonestly obtaining £14.60 in supplementary benefit. From the dock, he claimed to have been the homosexual lover of the Liberal leader. Thorpe claimed it was part of a deliberate attempt to undermine him. The allegations started a political scandal both notorious and absurd, a scandal which destroyed Thorpe and threatened to drag Barbara's reputation down and with it the future career of her special adviser, Jack Straw.

According to Barbara's diary – possibly amended in the light of subsequent events – Wlson asked Barbara, informally, to explore how the fraud case against Scott had come up.

> He [HW] has got a new idea for his plot to expose the anti-Jeremy machinations . . . 'in which Lady Falkender is naturally taking a great interest'. He believes that the Tories, or someone even more sinister, put Scott up to announcing his alleged association with Jeremy. 'The Tories had this information as long ago as 1972. Why didn't they use it then? My theory is that they thought it would rebound on Heath. But now they see their opportunity to destroy the Liberal Party. They wouldn't be beyond paying Scott to make his allegations now. And what better way of getting maximum publicity than to do it in a court case? So I want you to make some discreet enquiries about the prosecution your department brought against Scott for fraud. How did it originate? How was he discovered? Did he even volunteer the information on which he was prosecuted?' I said I would put Jack on to it as, apart from anything else, he was a barrister. Harold thought this was a good idea, and wanted the information by Monday. So back at the office, I passed the message on to Jack and Norman[20] in confidence. Norman spoke to the Permanent Secretary and Jack went off to do some feretting.[21]

Barbara passed no judgement on this curious request. Wilson's press secretary Joe Haines recalled that she disliked it. Later, she justified it as a legitimate counter-offensive against South Africa's apartheid regime. There were pressing, if less honourable domestic reasons too. The government's majority was down to two; at the very least, it made political sense to keep the Liberals on side. A few days later, according to her diary, she reported back to Harold: 'I hurried into Cabinet early to give Harold the résumé Jack has done of the Scott file. Harold's face dropped a bit when I told him it seemed to show Jeremy's relationship with Scott had been longer and more domesticated than he had so far admitted. My aim is to warn Harold against going overboard for Jeremy too recklessly. He has already made a rather hysterical attack on the press for "hounding" Jeremy and has exposed himself to an attack in a *Mirror* leader today.'[22] Barbara must have known that she was handing Wilson material which could have been explosive if used against Thorpe.

Unlike Wilson, Barbara disliked Thorpe's style of politics and she despised Liberals in general, mere woolly adherents to middle-of-the-road compromise and consensus. But in the context of minority government, Thorpe and the small party he had led since January 1967 had become major players. Thorpe – as his party was just discovering – was a dangerous political friend. There were extensive allegations of homosexuality and there seems little doubt that he had been Scott's lover in the early 1960s. He had also been, at least nominally, his employer for a brief period and had not kept up Scott's National Insurance. In the late 1960s, his lieutenant, another Devon Liberal MP, Peter Bessell, had tried to get hold of the Scott file. Slowly the DHSS was sucked into a much wider and wilder story, involving the shooting of Scott's Great Dane, Rinka, and a murder attempt on Scott himself in which Thorpe was implicated after it emerged that large sums of Liberal money had changed hands for uncertain purposes including recovering incriminating letters he had written to Scott.

None of this was in the public domain when Barbara told Wilson that Scott's relationship with Thorpe had been more extensive than Thorpe had revealed.

On 16 March 1976, a day which stands out even in a decade notorious for corruption and cynicism, Britain's newsdesks were rocked by two wholy unexpected revelations: Princess Margaret and Lord Snowdon were to separate; at the same time (not, it is said, quite by coincidence) came the announcement of Wilson's resignation. There was a third event that day too, which, unlike the other two, newsdesks had anticipated: the opening of the trial of an airline pilot, Andrew Newton, for the shooting of Rinka the dog and the attempted shooting of Scott. By 19 March, Newton had been convicted on the first count although not the second, and was beginning a two-year jail sentence. Scott, the main prosecution witness, had repeated all his allegations against Thorpe in court but emerged branded as a blackmailer. There everything might have rested, had Wilson not – for unfathomable reasons of his own – reignited the story.

Perhaps already bored with retirement, in May 1976 Wilson approached two junior BBC investigative journalists, Barrie Penrose and Roger Courtiour, and told them he had information to help them nail the South African apartheid regime's propaganda machine. He proceeded to divest himself of his paranoias, including his version of Barbara's involvement in the Thorpe affair. 'Barbara should sing like a bird,' Wilson told the journalists, adding cockily, 'she still regards me as her Prime Minister'.[23] Within a couple of days, the two journalists were interviewing Barbara in her office in the Commons. She sent them on to Jack Straw, a man with his political fortune to make, who was even more alarmed than Barbara had been. It was mainly their unhappy response to the journalists' visits which convinced Penrose and Courtiour that they were onto a story. It was the Watergate era. President Nixon had only recently been forced from office. 'They had gathered only snippets of information,' wrote the journalists – who had adopted the Watergate style of speaking of themselves in the third person, '[yet] two very highly placed persons had now reacted to their questions as if they were being accused of some misdemeanour. What was it that put them so much on the defensive?'[24]

The journalists believed that a key file in the Scott case – showing Scott's National Insurance Contributions had been made up by Thorpe – was missing, and were inclined to assume that Barbara must at least know what had happened to it and might have been complicit in its disappearance. Lady Falkender, who had also been extensively interviewed, had further encouraged them to believe that Barbara had been involved. 'The Political Secretary explained that she had been handling Civil Service files for many years. In general everything was a matter of routine but the Scott files seemed to present problems for the DHSS. She could not accept that a file had gone missing, and Barbara Castle, the Social Security Minister at the time, had been asked to make her own enquiries . . . thus the Prime Minister's request for Scott's file had set two rival enquiries in motion.'[25] She also told them, 'If you had looked at those files you knew someone had been up to no good. For example, you could see that officials had co-operated with outside sources to stop the Scott case coming to court at all.'[26] Falkender appeared to have been making enquiries since the government's return to power in 1974. She told the *Mirror*, which serialized *The Pencourt File* early in 1978, that she believed efforts had been made to hold back the Scott prosecution. The motivation was either to maximize – or to minimize – the damage.

Barbara promptly issued a statement insisting the department had behaved correctly throughout. In a Commons debate, she reiterated that, whatever Lady Falkender said, no official documents of any kind had gone to Downing Street. But a kind of frenzy now consumed Westminster and the impression that there had been an establishment cover-up was fuelled when Barbara's successor at the DHSS, David Ennals, admitted that he had been made aware of the Scott case when he was a junior DHSS minister in 1969, when he had been asked to change Scott's National Insurance status. He confirmed that departmental information on individuals 'is held in strict confidence . . . and is not disclosed to third parties without the consent of the person concerned' unless fraud or serious crime was suspected.[27] Furthermore, when he took over from Barbara in 1976, he had instructed the department to launch a detailed inquiry which established 'all the Department's social security records and files relating to Mr Norman Scott can be accounted for . . . with the exception of a folder used to administer a 1962 claim for sickness benefit. This is presumed lost or accidentally destroyed when the local office retaining it was closed in 1967 ... there is no foundation for the suggestion that a file concerning Mr Scott was stolen from the department's local office in Chelsea.' He had even asked the Director General of the BBC, Sir Charles Curran, to call off Penrose and Courtiour because the allegations they were investigating were, he said, 'without foundation'.[28]

Barbara was plainly worried. She had a long phone conversation with Wilson, in which he told her that, at some unspecified time, Thorpe had given him 'a whole lot of paper, nothing to do with pensions at all, relating to alleged threats etc.'[29] Thorpe had also told Wilson at that point that Scott's National Insurance file was missing. Straw's 1976 report on the affair had contained about twenty photocopied pages from various files, and a note that one file – which Wilson thought was the one Thorpe had said was stolen – had been 'weeded'. Wilson remembered someone saying 'be careful, this could be another Watergate'. In the traditional pattern of their relationship, he seems to have played Barbara off against Falkender, telling Barbara that he had seen the transcript of Falkender's long interview with Penrose and Courtiour, and it was 'evil' and 'garrulous'. Barbara noted him saying, 'Haines [is] behind all this'.

In September 1978, Penrose and Courtiour wrote to Barbara, and to Straw – now safely selected to take over from Barbara in Blackburn and researcher for what was then the leading current affairs television programme, Granada TV's *World in Action*. They announced a new edition of their book *The Pencourt File*. 'We know, from the very best sources, and intend to publish, that you did examine Scott's file and removed documents to your home.' Barbara, and in a separate letter, Straw, replied that it was not true. In October, the journalists wrote again, ignoring the earlier charge but introducing a new one, an assertion made by Wilson that Barbara 'may have committed a statutory offence' when she had carried out her investigation at his behest.

Frantic activity ensued. The DHSS said they would underwrite her and Straw's legal costs, and the original report written by Straw – unusually, no copies appear to have been made – was released by Downing Street to the DHSS where Barbara and Straw inspected it. The DHSS solicitor confirmed in writing that no documents mentioned or photocopied in the report were missing. Wilson told Barbara on the phone that he would deny in a witness box that he had said she had committed a statutory offence. However, when Barbara's lawyer begged Wilson, through Falkender, to say as much in writing – a knockout blow to the Penrose/Courtiour allegations – the only reply was a letter from Wilson's lawyer, Peter Carter-Ruck, saying 'Both Sir

Harold and Lady Falkender are disinclined to become further involved in any correspondence in connection with the Scott affair'. A month or so later Carter-Ruck withdrew from the case, having suddenly recalled that his firm had libel-read *The Pencourt File* and therefore had a conflict of interest.

In February 1979, Thorpe went on trial for conspiracy to murder. Even though most of the allegations had by now become familiar breakfast-table fare, it was followed in salacious detail; Thorpe's lawyers finally acknowledged his homosexuality. But he was acquitted. Penrose and Courtiour, whose second edition was on hold pending a guilty verdict, fell silent.

More than twenty years later, Joe Haines exhumed the tale in a memoir, serialized in the *Mail on Sunday* in October 2002, asserting that the whole affair had indeed – as Falkender had first indicated – been an attempt to build up a case against Thorpe with which he could be threatened if he looked as if he might undermine the minority Labour government. Straw, who already had a reputation for a shrewd grasp of political opportunity, would probably have included in his report some suggestion of how the 'longer and more domesticated' relationship between Thorpe and Scott might, if it became necessary, be handled – either in defence, or attack.

It was a disreputable incident, for Barbara and Jack Straw and for Downing Street. They knew it was constitutionally unacceptable for politicians to poke about in a citizen's files in order to discover evidence for covert political purposes. They were clearly uncomfortable with what they had done, and, in interview, Straw remains so. There are also enough loose ends to explain why two conspiracy-obsessed journalists hoping they were on the brink of another Watergate should believe they had a bigger story than any they finally uncovered.

As a peer, Ted had been sent as one of Labour's delegates to the European Parliament. But he was not well. In 1977 he was in and out of hospital with what turned out to be an ulcer; he seemed to rally, then decline again. On the occasions when they were at home at the same time, Barbara found herself looking after him as well as absorbing herself in housework. The first summer after her sacking, she turned Hell Corner inside out: 'The opportunity to go domestic goes to my head like wine. I wake at 6am every morning; wide awake and longing for a cup of tea while I plan the next round of my assault on the turning out of cupboards, the rehanging of pictures, the conversion of old eiderdowns into duvets; the whole process of taking control of my domestic life once again.'[30] Ted felt old and ill and wanted to settle down quietly at Hell Corner. He did not want Barbara to become an MEP; he wanted them both to cultivate their garden. But Barbara was as full of energy as she had ever been, and only enjoyed gardening if it was heavy digging. It was a heatwave year: in the middle of the night after a party, she swam with her neighbours' teenage children in her underwear; and she sat for a wild and vivid portrait by the fashionable artist John Bratby. 'If I retire and there is no Ted to share it with me, I shall have nothing to live for,' she wrote in her diary. However, in August 1978, she confirmed that she would run for Europe. Ted demurred 'a bit unhappily . . . he wants me at home'.[31]

At Christmas that year Barbara noticed a lump in her breast. Once the family had departed and their new year celebrations were over, she went to get it checked out. Ted was on a European Parliament delegation to Rome, and she was alone. Visits to hospital had become a nightmare, the moment when her politicization of the health service and her passion for publicity collided with sneering porters and snooping journalists. The fear that her condition might be leaked added to the dread that she might have the same cancer which, she now remembered, had killed her maternal grandmother.

The news was bleak, as she wrote late that night in London, with a towel under her typewriter so that the neighbours in the flat below would not complain of the noise. '[The consultant] confirmed the good old lump alright. Encouraged by me he pulled no punches. At my age the probability of its being malignant was very high.' The investigation brought home to her the vulnerability of her situation.

> We sat and discussed the macabre alternatives. Alternative No. 1: his friend in the laboratory would let us have the result tomorrow and she might find nothing. But, he added, that didn't necessarily prove benignancy. He might just have missed the malignant bit . . . that brought us to alternative two: that I ought to come into hospital as soon as possible so as to have the lump removed . . . if the cold section showed malignancy I ought to stay in hospital and have the breast removed. But alternative three was already clearly in his mind. 'This thing' he told me, 'might just have started as a tiny pinhead and could have been growing for a couple of years.' So, he added briskly, the malignancy could have spread through my body and into the bones. If that had happened it would be a futile bit of surgery to remove the breast.

The success rate for mastectomy in the late 1970s was only 20–30 per cent. But she *could* live for another ten years.

Well, I could face that too. I have been facing up to death for a long time: after 65 one does have to take it on board as a reasonably imminent possibility . . . I don't mind dying but until I do I want to feel the full tide of life flowing through my veins. It is the death by a thousand X-rays and little diminishments that I dread. It has always been my dream to go out at the high tide. Vanity, I know. The rich abundance of energy of which I have been so proud. Most other people have never had it. How could I hope to hang on to it? I sat belittled in those tiny cubicles, trying to prepare myself to give up health and life with dignity.

However, she did not allow herself to dwell. In the afternoon, she went back to the Commons and debated the European elections manifesto in an NEC committee, and then carried on to another meeting. 'You find yourself behind a curtain,' she said later, 'a kind of shutter comes down between yourself and the rest of humanity. Suddenly you are no longer one of them.'[32] She finally got back to the flat after 11 p.m. 'I cooked myself some bacon and egg and started typing. But it will be bliss when my Teddy is home.'[33] The next day, she went up to Blackburn in the snow and despite a rail strike. There was a lorry drivers' strike on too, and on 21 January the ambulancemen said they would not even answer emergency calls. It was the winter of discontent, the unions protesting at a 5 per cent pay-increase norm, one more pay squeeze after the years of restraint; the government's life was disintegrating, and it seemed when she was told to come in at once for a lumpectomy that Barbara's might be too.

On the morning that she was due to go into hospital, the NEC–TUC liaison committee met. Barbara sat there 'feeling rather shaky' but apparently with no thought of cancelling, as the unions told Callaghan and Healey that they could not contain the industrial anarchy sweeping Britain.

'I must speak,' I said, forcing myself. 'One never knows: it might be the last time.' I signalled to Alf Allen and he called me next . . . I said the social contract had been destroyed by the IMF, which had forced on us financial policies which were not justified by the economic facts. Even so we had been doing very well until this summer . . . And what had caused it [the industrial unrest]? We had ignored communications and ignored psychology . . . Looking Jim straight in the face I said to him: 'If you had gone for 10 per cent I believe the outcome would have been a level of earnings no greater than you are getting now.'

Then she slipped out, with her overnight bag, to the hospital, where she had to persuade the ward sister not to put her in a private room. 'I said, "I'm sorry sister, if you won't allow me to be in the public ward I won't have the operation." I signed the consent form. And when I woke up she was kneeling next to me, and she whispered "Mrs Castle I'm afraid they had to take off your breast." '[34]

Only her most intimate circle of friends ever knew. Somehow, despite the angry relations between unions and government at the height of the strike-ridden winter of 1978–9, the news never leaked into the public domain. Adept at weaving almost every experience into the public face of Barbara Castle, she never publicly acknowledged her mastectomy. Friends suggested to her that it might give heart to other women going through the same trauma, but not even for altruistic motives would she discuss it publicly. It was the one major event that she was not prepared to add to the legend, which already included the most personal: her sense of failure, her feelings of insecurity, the importance she attached to her appearance, even the wig she acquired to see her through her most hectic ministerial days, as well as Ted's despair when he was knocked off the GLC. All these details figured in the diaries and often featured in newspaper articles and in radio and television interviews. But on this one thing, she cared too much. The loss of a breast is an assault on a woman's femininity; Barbara was an intensely feminine person. Her startling good looks were integral to her persona, like her passion for clothes and making up; the slim and sexy, red-haired, blue-eyed politician was her role, a role she was not ready to relinquish despite the surgeon's knife and her approaching seventieth birthday. Her image was her best weapon in an unjust world, her way of overcoming the drawbacks of being a lone woman among the men, and perhaps she could not bear anyone to know that, in her own eyes, she had been diminished. The diary covering the weeks immediately after the operation has been destroyed. It starts again three weeks later.

But Barbara's *annus horribilis* was only just beginning. On 3 May 1979 Labour lost office, and after thirty-four years as an MP, she left the House of Commons. Barely six months later, early on the morning of Boxing Day 1979, after presiding over a family Christmas lunch Ted died in his sleep. Barbara, her friends said, was devastated as she had never been before. Ted, who had never been quite good enough for her, who had been an accessory to her political career but who was her most loyal friend and admirer, her prop and comforter, had gone. They had been married for thirty-five years, just a year longer than she had been in parliament. No parliament, no Ted, the two most important strands in her life removed within months. Exactly four weeks after Ted, her mother Annie, aged ninety-six, 'endearing, much loved and totally exasperating', also died.

Barbara had just started her new life as an MEP, the career move Ted had not wanted her to make, on the territory that had been his when he had been nominated as a member of the European Parliament. She saw him everywhere. 'How does one come to terms with such a loss? Does one keep him alive by endlessly remembering – and nearly destroy oneself? Or move on briskly to new fields of pragmatic common sense and suppress one of life's most significant experiences? Or just go numb and wait for death?' she wrote in an emotional article in *The Times* in May 1980. 'What should one try to do with life when the steady warmth of integration with another person has gone out of it? How does one find meaning in the mutilation left by death? I struggle with the question in the dark night hours and whenever the busyness I seek comes to a stop.'

There was one distraction. Only a fortnight after Ted's death, the serialization of her diaries began in the *Sunday Times*. The spectacular proceedings five years earlier, in which the government had tried to stop the publication of Crossman's diaries on the grounds of breach of confidence, had paved the way for the smooth publication of Barbara's, despite her refusal to contribute to the case for Crossman's defence. After the judge, Lord Widgery, had thrown out the government's case, Wilson had set up an inquiry under Lord Radcliffe. It had confirmed that as long as memoirs and diaries did not breach national security, jeopardize international relations or compromise colleagues (a clause widely breached) there was no reason to stop publication.

Barbara secured a lucrative deal. She was paid £40,000 by the *Sunday Times* (£4,000 more than Crossman), on top of the advance of £25,000 that she had received from her publishers Weidenfeld & Nicolson for the two volumes of diaries, the first tranche as long ago as 1967. And the serialization gave her a platform from which to berate the pusillanimous governments of Wilson and Callaghan, in keeping with the mood of angry radicalism overtaking the party in the aftermath of election defeat. Barbara defended herself against cries of treachery from Crossman's publishers by insisting that it was only because the publication of the Crossman diaries had caused, in the end, so little damage that she had felt able to publish hers. This does not entirely square with the admission in her diaries that she had signed a contract in 1967 for a book 'based on her diaries', on which she had started work during the opposition years after 1970. But perhaps the publication of the actual diaries was not decided upon until after Crossman's were safely out. If this was the case, it is curious that at the height of one argument with Crossman during their 1969 rows over 'In Place of Strife' she taunted him with 'Thank God I've kept a diary, Dick, so there will be someone to challenge the Crossman version of history.' Moreover, the point at issue was whether keeping and using a detailed record of cabinet discussion and official advice added up to a breach of confidence and of collective responsibility. It is hard to see how a book 'based on her diaries' could have avoided being both. When she told Wilson in April 1967 that she was contracted to write her life story, he took it 'very unperturbably [sic], saying that writing one's life was very different from a political book. Oh, Harold!'[35]

Wobbling over the ethics of publication, Barbara had sent her typescript to her friend and admirer, the poverty expert Peter Townsend. His reply, dated 16 March 1977, was brutal. 'It does rather give the impression that a top politician's life is rather like a one-performance repertory company with the politician having the further task of writing or at least re-writing the script.'[36] He suggested more analysis of decision-making, anathema to Barbara's stream-of-consicousness diary keeping. But his warning that publication would finish her political career, she did take to heart. On 28 March, she told Harold Evans, the *Sunday Times* editor, who wanted to get her version into the public domain before the next great tranche of Crossman diaries, that there could be no serialization until her retirement from politics had been announced.

Townsend's criticisms were echoed in the reviews. 'Barbara frequently appeared as the best Minister at Harold Wilson's disposal,' Foot joked. Barbara was furious, and asked him pointedly not to review the second volume. He did, of course, but without mentioning her perfidy over the publication of Crossman's diaries.

Her election as an MEP had not been as easy as she had at first anticipated. The groupings at Westminster ranged from the Bennites on the left to Callaghan and most of his government on the right, with Foot and Barbara somewhere towards the left of centre. But, in the constituencies, the perception was much starker, a simple left–right split. Barbara was a notorious anti-European, and for many constituency selection committees a schismatic left-winger. The pro-European right thought it was hypocritical of her to want to go to the European Parliament, and many of the left – including those on the National Executive – thought she was simply wrong to take part at all. But on her own patch, Barbara, the queen of the north-west England Labour aristocracy which, through its links with Wilson had had the pick of the jobs for more than ten years, was confident that she could choose which of the vast new of Brussels constituencies she would represent.

In the end, she chose Greater Manchester North, Labour's most winnable seat in the country. There had been an uncomfortable moment when it looked as if the Lancashire seat which included Blackburn might choose its candidate first; Barbara would have had a difficult time explaining why she did not want to be selected when the real reason, as she admitted to friends, was that she was not confident she could win it. But in Manchester Town Hall one night in February 1979, she secured the nomination she wanted. It renewed an old link: some of her new constituents still remembered her as Barbara Betts from Hyde Independent Labour Party. To add to her appeal was the fact that she had been sacked by Jim Callaghan, a man now reviled by most party activists. They liked a woman who had made it to the top but had still retained her socialist principles.

Privately, Barbara put her initial difficulty in finding a seat down to being blackballed by right-wingers as she was trying to blackball them. But the real reason was that she was not on form. People found her shrill and vituperative, with only a confused rationale for her decision to stand: she said the European Parliament had no powers. When asked why, then, she wanted to be elected, she explained it was in order to stop it gaining any. She talked, recorded one observer who interviewed her at length, with 'a remarkable degree of uncompromising venom. It really would be very difficult indeed for many Labour moderates to exist under her leadership at Strasbourg.'

The omens for Labour at these first-ever direct elections to the European Parliament in 1979 could scarcely have been worse. In its fifth, painful year of government, with the strikes of the winter barely behind it and increasingly committed to withdrawal from the whole European project, the Labour Party could not have been optimistic about its prospects. But, in June 1979 Barbara became the new MEP for Greater Manchester North. Even before she was elected she had assured herself of the leadership of the British Labour group. She teamed up with John Prescott – 'a very nice chap with the right instincts, but a bit incoherent',[37] with whom she had agreed to try and set up a European equivalent of the Tribune group. At a meeting in Luxembourg that April, she wrote, the other candidates, including the pro-Europeans, 'soon found that I knew the ropes and they did not'. She fought an exhausting campaign around the eight Westminster constituencies that made up her Euro seat without, to begin with, even a car and driver 'and nowhere to wash my smalls' she complained to one party worker.[38] Barbara found it hard to raise campaign funds for a cause that few knew about and that was unpopular among those who did. In the end, Labour did no better than at the previous month's general election, winning just seventeen seats to the Tories' sixty. However, all of Europe was swinging right; the British Labour group was the largest of all the socialist groups in the Parliament.

Barbara then made an overambitious pitch for the leadership of the European Parliament, but could not persuade even her fellow socialists to choose someone with as strong a record of hostility to Europe as herself, and the members chose instead another woman, Simone Veil, the French centre-right candidate.

Barbara was an MEP for ten years. It was not a happy period, although her energy appeared undiminished and she threw herself into her work with her customary determination. She already spoke good French, and worked hard on her German, often spending part of the summer at language schools. But the Parliament was ill-attended and virtually powerless, confirming all Barbara's prejudices about coalitions and consensus. 'It can never be turned into an effective instrument of democratic control on anything remotely resembling House of Commons lines,' she concluded after she left in 1989.[39] She refused to make concessions to the consensual tradition of European politics, turning every issue into a war of attrition as if she was Prime Minister, organizing her Labour group as if she was Chief Whip. She devoted herself to what most regarded as the dull housekeeping job of trying to get some kind of reform of the Common Agricultural Policy, which she regarded as at the heart of the European Community's problems. She initiated the first academic research into the impact of the policy, joining the parliamentary CAP committee and working long hours to master the subject, but made little headway. She fought hard, but in the end unsuccessfully, for a new deal for farmers. Barbara made few intimate friends, relying for company and political support on a handful of people: in particular, her researcher Anita Pollock, later an MEP herself, and the right-wing MEP Derek Enright, whose family were faithful friends until Barbara's death. The loneliness of widowhood followed her from Hell Corner to Brussels and Strasbourg and back again. Even political friends seemed thin on the ground.

In Britain, the Labour Party, now under the leadership of Michael Foot, had become increasingly hostile to the European Community. In 1980 conference voted by more than two to one to reverse its policy and campaign for withdrawal. Barbara thought the decision just one of many mistakes the party was making. As an MEP, she had had no vote in the leadership election but it would have been only old loyalty that would have persuaded her to cast it for Foot, her 'honourable but miscast' political friend.

The following year, Denis Healey and Tony Benn fought for the deputy leadership. Jack Straw, still some years from his political realignment and founding role in New Labour, wrote to Barbara asking for her views on who should win. Barbara was uncertain. Deeply suspicious of Benn for the past ten years, she thought he suffered from having had an overpowerful father who had groomed him for political stardom and condemned him to a life driven by personal ambition. She also viewed with alarm his way of chairing a committee. In her final days on the NEC she observed him at work: 'I suddenly realised why, if Tony Benn ever got the leadership of the Labour party, it would be a disaster ... Wedgie wouldn't offer us too little democracy, but too much. As Tony fumbled his way through the agenda which suddenly got itself packed with manuscript (or even vocal) resolutions ... I was reminded of the shambles to which he reduced the party conference in 1972 ... that lad is just a political boy scout who ends up by killing off his mates with a piece of amateurish chemistry.'[40] On the other hand, her fervent belief in the importance of political will inclined her to support the most determined candidate. To Straw she responded:

> The position for people like you and me (what Harold, God help us, calls the 'soft left') is very difficult. We are not political Calvinists, but we are not right-wing Jesuits either. We hate the Inquisition from whichever religious faith it may come. I think we are political 'William Morrisites', dreaming of a society in which revolutionary change is achieved by love and tolerance and in which collectivism and the pursuit of aesthetic satisfaction are synonymous ... Tony Benn is a Calvinist and he carries with him the aura of witch burnings. But ... I know which side of the barricades I am on, even if I don't like some of the company. Denis Healey's reaction to the Benn campaign is a revelation of the fact that at bottom he is a ruthless bully.[41]

As she explained to Straw, Barbara was still trying to find some middle-left ground to stand on, some way of withstanding the pull of the polarizing extremes. Jack Straw voted for Benn in the second ballot, unlike Neil Kinnock, shortly to become party leader himself, whose decision, together with those of three other Tribunites, to abstain rather than support Benn, probably cost Benn the election. It led to the hard-left breakaway Campaign Group deserting the Tribunites (as well as near-fisticuffs between angry Bennites and the soft left).

Shortly before the party conference, at which the votes were taken in a more poisoned atmosphere than even the old Bevanites could remember, Barbara had written an article for the *New Statesman* setting out a strategy for remaining in Europe. Socialists believed that European law would prevent socialism, in the form of Benn's 'Alternative Economic Strategy', coming to Britain. Barbara's article was a valiant if not entirely honest attempt to explain her own position. 'After years of haggling about the right conditions for our membership, we have suddenly announced that we *know* membership would be incompatible with what a Labour government would want to do and that we are going to wash our hands of the whole show,' she wrote, ignoring her own outright opposition to membership little more than five years earlier. Leaving Europe, she insisted, would lead to years of institutional wrangling which would distract from the real business of sorting out the economy. It would leave the party fighting on a negative for which it would not even be able to claim European funds – unlike the Tories, who would repeat the referendum Yes campaign's superior presentation and organization at a general election, with disastrous consequences for Labour. She argued that a better tactic would be for an incoming Labour government to go ahead with the industrial restructuring the party wanted and which European law appeared to rule out, and challenge Brussels to expel Britain from the Community if it disapproved. This was broadly the position the party took up for the 1983 election, but it cost Barbara the support of a significant minority of the Labour group and, in 1985, the leadership of the Labour group of MEPs.

The 1980s was the decade when socialism and feminism found a new modus vivendi. Barbara began to regret a little her rude rejection of all its manifestations and wonder if it was too late to scramble into what was plainly an important boat. Before she even left parliament, she had been angry at being all but ignored in an exhibition to mark the fiftieth anniversary of women's suffrage. 'I noticed wryly that people like Shirley Summerskill and Anne Taylor had been included in the big blow-ups of the "women in government" while I had been tucked behind at the back with the pictures of the has-beens. OK, so I didn't want to speak at their meeting or go to their wretched garden party, but it was the principle. Damn it all I have done more than any other Minister to carry forward the work the suffragettes began: equal pay, equal pensions, child benefit . . .'[42] But she had rejected a suggestion that her name go forward to head the Equal Opportunities Commission as too narrow a field for her to play on. Meanwhile, for almost the first time in her life, she was being overtaken by other women. Not only was Simone Veil leading the European Parliament in Strasbourg, but Margaret Thatcher ruled at Westminster.

Thatcher had stolen, in 1975, what, for a time, many had thought would be Barbara's prize by becoming the first woman leader of a major party. Thatcher did not – unlike, for example, Jennie Lee – arouse Barbara's envy so much as a kind of distant curiosity. 'The papers are full of Margaret

Thatcher. She has lent herself with grace and charm to every piece of photographer's gimmickry, but don't we all when the prize is big enough? What interests me now is how blooming she looks – she has never been prettier. I am interested because I understand this phenomenon . . . she looks as I looked when Harold made me minister of Transport.'[43]

Women, she was now prepared to concede, did make a difference.

> The excitement of switching to a woman might stir a lot people out of their lethargy. I think it will be a good thing for the Labour Party too. There's a male-dominated party for you – not least because the trade unions are male-dominated, even the ones that cater for women. I remember just before the February election last year pleading on the NEC for us not to have a completely producer-oriented policy . . . because women lose out in the producer-run society. The battle for cash wage increases is a masculine obsession. Women are not sold on it, particularly when it leads to strikes, because the men often don't pass their cash increases on to their wives. What matters to the women is the social wage. Of course, no one listened to me; even to suggest that the battle for cash wage increases might be a mirage is to show disloyalty to trade unionism! I believe Margaret Thatcher's election will force our party to think again; and a jolly good thing too. To me socialism isn't just militant trade unionism. It is the gentle society, in which every producer remembers he is a consumer too.

Like many others, Barbara overestimated the impact of the first woman Prime Minister on the status of women generally. She herself had a much stronger record on promoting women's interests; indeed, beyond the incidental example of her gender, Mrs Thatcher rejected the idea that the state had any role at all in making men and women more equal, and was notoriously bad even at encouraging other women in her party. Yet she and Barbara shared a perspective: both had always been politicians first and women second. So Barbara Castle watched Margaret Thatcher with something approaching admiration as she wrestled with and sometimes tripped on the perils of being a woman politician. In the early 1970s they had met when Thatcher was Education Secretary. 'I am interested in Margaret's technique. She enters the room radiating charm and embraces everyone in a cocoon of courtesy. But she gives nothing away. I think that is counterproductive and I liked her much more when I forced her to be honest about the possibilities, however unfavourable.'[44] She was also interested in the immaculate Thatcher style, a contrast to herself in the 1970s when she was experimenting unsatisfactorily with a less formal look (there were no more 'best hair-do' awards in her final years in government). She thought Thatcher's hair looked too recently done. That no man trusts a woman who has just had her hair permed was one of Barbara's axioms.

For Barbara, politicians' wives were inferior to women politicians, even when they were considerable figures in their own right like Peter Shore's wife Liz, a former deputy Chief Medical Officer and then a leading figure in medical politics, or Caroline Benn, who worked diligently and creatively to promote comprehensive education. But with Thatcher, there was an identity of interest which, although it never came near transcending the gaping political divide, meant that Barbara was on the watch for her as a fellow toiler at the same lathe. This was reflected in one diary entry in October 1975, which gave a more honest account of her life than most newspaper interviews.

The *Observer* had an interview with Margaret Thatcher yesterday in which she suggested that she managed to cope with all domestic chores herself as well as do her political work. . . Sorry, but I don't believe it. Okay, she's not a minister now, but she is Leader of the Opposition and the amount of reading she must have to do is enormous. Or doesn't she? Because I find that I just can't fit in regular domestic work. Cooking is a special-occasion luxury that I do about six times a year . . . as for housework, it's fun. Nothing more satisfying than a good spring clean. I'm positively longing to resign so that I can turn out Mother's storage shed. But when I have work to do at the level I have – and presumably Margaret has – it is quite impossible to do one's own chores.[45]

When things went badly for the Tory leader, Barbara was sympathetic: in March 1977 Thatcher failed in her first attempt to defeat the government on a confidence motion. 'She had the House openly laughing at her before she had done. "You couldn't make a speech like that if you tried" one of our chaps said to me . . . So for Jim, practised, relaxed and an outstanding Parliamentary performer – a man speaking to a male audience – it was a walk-over.'[46] Both women brought to politics a courage and the strong convictions that many of their male colleagues lacked. 'My definition of a left-winger is someone who, when a storm brews, battens down the hatches and sails through it. It is part of his professional response. A love of popularity is the beginning of defeat,' Barbara wrote in a style that could equally have come from Thatcher.[47] The first women to fight their way to the top were moulded by upbringing and circumstance into unexpectedly similar casts, and they adopted the same tactics of confrontation and focus. Male colleagues in the Labour Party thought Thatcher was 'like Barbara, only worse'.

Barbara could not tear herself away entirely from the Westminster political scene. In the 1983 election she insisted on being on the platform at every press conference, even though she was scathingly dismissive of the manifesto – the 'longest suicide note in history', as Wilson's former press man Gerald Kaufman had called it. Barbara saw it as the apotheosis of Bennery, and cheered when the man she regarded as her protégé, Neil Kinnock, replaced Michael Foot a few months later. At the next election campaign in 1987, she spoke at the hubristic Sheffield rally when everyone, including the pollsters, believed Labour was going to win. ('How much did you go over your time?' she angrily demanded of Roy Hattersley, her old junior and now deputy leader of the party, 'because they're not taking it back out of *my* time.') In 1989, having decided to retire from Europe, she marched into the office of the leader of the opposition at Westminster to tell Neil Kinnock that she was ready to go to the Lords, unreformed as it was.

In 1974, she had fussed that Ted's elevation would mean that she would be addressed as 'Lady Castle' – a point of etiquette swiftly dismissed; Beatrice Webb had refused to share in Sidney's title when he was made Baron Passfield in 1929. Barbara Castle took her seat in 1990, an event of some embarrassment to her, given her long hostility to the peerage – although perhaps no more than becoming a MEP. She found the Lords full of old friends and enemies, among them Tom Taylor, Blackburn's long-serving Labour leader, now Lord Taylor. They shared a desk, but Taylor put his foot down at her suggestion he might make her a cup of tea.

But on May Day 1997, when Tony Blair finally led Labour to its first landslide since 1966 and its greatest landslide ever, she was at home at Hell Corner. She was part of Labour's unruly radical left, and there was no room for her at New Labour's top table, nor among the thousands who gathered at the Festival Hall as the polls closed that night. She had, however, already shown that she had one more fight in her.

20. Epilogue

Barbara Castle was more than the heroine of the Labour Movement of the last century. She was a warrior for the institutions that had to be built for a decent society for us all.

Peter Townsend,[1] *Guardian*, 6 May 2002

While all politicians are egocentric, her ego was, in the end and to the end, what she was all about. She was the Norma Desmond of politics, like the protagonist of *Sunset Boulevard* always ready for her close-up.

Gerald Kaufman, *Sunday Telegraph*, 5 May 2002

Barbara was eighty-three when Tony Blair became leader, incidentally creating for her an entirely new role. Out of a mixture of malice and sentiment, she was elevated into an icon of Old Labour and a goad for the New. The shrewish ideologue of the 1970s morphed in the 1990s into the epitome of the virtues of the conviction politician, in favourable contrast with the easy superficialities of New Labour. It was a trajectory followed almost simultaneously in the Conservative Party by Margaret Thatcher, as Tories and commentators reacted against the grey pragmatism of the new Conservative Prime Minister, John Major. For Barbara, on a personal level, it was the final triumph of her long political career: she had only to appear on a platform or in a television studio to be immersed in the love and admiration which she had always craved. But it is a mistake to confuse her desire for recognition with her motivations as a politician. The performance may not have been entirely about politics; the by now notorious demands for the lavish attentions of the make-up artist and the hairdresser had become almost as much a part of the performance as the performance itself. But ultimately she wanted a platform to continue the argument, and the proof of that is the effort she put into researching and writing for her final campaigns at a time when, almost blind and becoming ever more frail, most people would have found the physical demands unsustainable.

'The redefinition of socialism as being more to do with the moral than the material relationships between people was potentially the most important philosophical change in the Labour Party since it was last in office,'[2] wrote Blair's biographer John Rentoul, reviewing Blair's climb to power. Barbara had never seen a distinction: material relationships *were* a moral issue. But while she had been in Europe her old enemies on the right had defected to the new Social Democratic Party, and Labour had become identified with causes, often gratuitously misrepresented in the newspapers and distorted in the policies of local councils, that many voters found bewilderingly alien. Back on the domestic political scene in the 1990s, Barbara, who had always found action more satisfying than reflection, picked up the threads of controversy as if it was 1950 all over again. In the old Bevanite days, single issues like the bomb and Clause 4 had become the totemic symbols of rival attitudes. After 1994, the need to restore the link between the rise in average earnings and the basic state pension, and the Blairite rejection of that link in favour of targeted benefits, became the policy that represented all that was flawed in New Labour's strategy for capturing power.

For nearly ten years, Barbara, at least in her imagination, exercised motherly rights over Neil Kinnock, who had succeeded Michael Foot as Labour leader in 1983. She exhorted him not to let the image doctors destroy him, argued with the way he shifted party policy to accommodate a consumerist society, travelled the country to speak for him. It allowed her to feel that she still had a role to play in British politics; and her own accommodation of important concessions such as the abandonment of unilateral nuclear disarmament as a party objective, as well as her recognition of the role Europe could play in promoting socialism, showed a willingness to continue to engage with the contemporary mood. When, after the bitter disappointment of the 1992 defeat, Kinnock had stood down, to be replaced by John Smith and then, after his death barely two years later, Smith was replaced by Blair, Barbara's last remaining link with the party leadership had gone. She had never even met the new leader until the party conference after his election. Now her only power base was the platform the media eagerly gave her. Fed up with a discredited Tory Party but unable to shake off generations of hostility to Labour, the newspapers were happy to give space to Barbara's campaign on pensions – definitely her last, she told the admiring profile writers who drove down to Hell Corner every few months.

Their adulation allowed them to jeer at Blair without themselves attacking the most popular figure in British politics. On television and radio her quick wit and uncompromising style were a refreshing change from the inoffensive, conciliating manner of the new generation of politicians. Barbara had been suspicious of the Smith regime's cautious spending plans, but she was genuinely appalled by Blair's reverse takeover of the party and its reconstruction in his own image.

New Labour was a party for that creature Barbara was constitutionally unable to comprehend, the floating voter, a party that claimed it was possible to ameliorate the injustices of society without compromising the material ambitions of the majority. Barbara's long-held belief that the party itself needed a sense of mission was dismissed. Blair had drunk at the well of the Clinton US presidential campaign; its manager James Carville claimed: 'Whenever I hear a campaign talk about a need to energise its base, that's a campaign that is going down the toilet.'[3] In pensions, Barbara found an issue that challenged the Blairites, spoke to a wider audience than the party and allowed her to remind a new generation of her own achievements in power.

The three million elderly people who relied only on the basic state pension, which was so low it automatically entitled the recipient to a top-up from Income Support, made up the biggest, most identifiable and most incontrovertibly needy group in Britain. These were the people who had fought in the war and built the peace and, in many cases, voted Labour all their lives. But Barbara's argument with the Labour leadership was less over their need, which no one disputed, than over her insistence that this need must be met by raising the level of the basic state pension for all, rather than applying some kind of means test – whether disguised as a minimum income guarantee or a pensioner credit or Income Support – which would put extra money only into the pockets and purses of the poorest. Barbara regarded the universality of the welfare state as its most socialist element. It was the barricade at which she would rather fall than surrender. But New Labour's election strategy demanded that there be no internal dissent and only the most modest and costed of spending commitments. Universal benefits amid the affluence of the 1990s, when many pensioners were enjoying serial holidays abroad in between days on the golf links of Britain, were philosphically indefensible and economically unsustainable, although it was not disputed that means-tested benefits were expensive – about ten pence in the pound went in administration – or that they failed to reach many of the people who were most in need.

Barbara did not just want a hike in the basic pension; she wanted the restoration of the earnings link that she had introduced and the abolition of which had been an early act of the thrifty Thatcher Chancellor Sir Geoffrey Howe. She also wanted the revival of her earnings-related pensions scheme, SERPS, now reduced by a Conservative review[4] of social security spending. With Peter Townsend, the academic with whom she had first worked more than twenty-five years earlier, she wrote a pamphlet, *We Can Afford the Welfare State*. SERPS, they pointed out, had taken four decades to introduce fully, was cheap to administer and ended pensioner poverty. 'She sought to warn and persuade before it was too late. In her mid-eighties, she went to work with her customary vigour and uncomfortably penetrating style of cross-examination,'[5] Townsend wrote in an appreciation after her death. *We Can Afford the Welfare State* was published in time for the 1996 party conference, and updated every year thereafter.

The 1997 election was now imminent, and party unity deemed essential. Barbara, the Harold Macmillan of the Labour Party when it came to exploiting the frailties of age, tottered to the podium in the Blackpool Winter Gardens and was given a three-minute standing ovation before she reached the microphone. 'I believe good debate only strengthens democracy, not weakens it,' she announced to more cheers. 'This debate puts this pensions issue back in the centre of our party where it should have been in the first place.'[6] For less than one per cent on National Insurance Contributions, she argued, pensioners could over four years be given back the £23 a week they had lost since pensions and earnings were decoupled. Her assault was all that had been feared – and for which the New Labour machine had prepared. To Barbara's lasting fury, her co-leader of the campaign, her old sparring partner Jack Jones, now president of the National Pensioners' Convention, had done a deal with Gordon Brown. There was to be a review, and an immediate increase for the poorest pensioners. For the last time, the trade union block vote was mobilized to defeat her.

Barbara persisted in her campaign for the rest of her life, harrying Social Security Ministers and the Chancellor, Gordon Brown, whenever she could reach him. Her sight was failing steadily through irreversible macular degeneration and, certainly for the last three or four years, she could no longer read at all. She put an advertisement in her parish magazine and recruited a neighbour to come and read to her. Her speeches had not only to be delivered without notes, but prepared without them too. Her inability to read did not, however, lessen the effort she put into establishing the facts and developing an argument. Instead, it made her theatrical skills, on which she had always been able to call when addressing a crowd, more important than ever. Even close friends did not realize quite how blind she had become. In the Lords, she and the trade unionist Muriel, Lady Turner led a series of determined but unsuccessful attacks on government pensions legislation, drafting and moving a series of complex, if ultimately futile, amendments. Her opponents considered her unscrupulous: she refused, they said, to accept their careful explanations of statistics and constantly misrepresented them. But the media loved her. Forty years earlier, she had been the whistle-blower, the vanguard of campaigners for colonial freedom. In the 1990s, it was a role she tried to fulfil again for everyone alientated by the Blair project.

Barbara was more than the Frank Sinatra of Westminster making one more comeback, and the pensions battle was not just a replay of one of her greatest hits, although it was that too. It was a debt of honour to Crossman and to Brian O'Malley, the real political architect of SERPS; ultimately, perhaps, it was the final acknowledgement of her father Frank, for whom she had written her first election pledge in 1916, 'Vote for me, citizuns and I will give you houses.'

Despite being the centrepiece of her campaign against New Labour, the pensions fight was not the only ground on which she took them on. She was bitterly opposed to the reforms of the party's policy-making machinery, both for the way in which the new structure was organized into a series of regional and policy-based talking shops, and for the concomitant downgrad-ing of conference within it, which meant that there was virtually no way of changing policy from the conference floor.

She had become, too, a stalwart of the Animal Rights Campaign. In 1976, when she had first become involved, she had tried to persuade the League Against Cruel Sports to take up the issue of fox hunting selectively, urging them to concentrate on live animal exports and on the outlawing of the use of animals in experiments. 'I . . . tried to show we really did understand the countryside[7] . . . But the purists were in full cry. They were determined to include beagling and fox-hunting, against which the case is by no means so clearly proved . . . and the inclusion of which will result in an uproar that will merely distract attention from our key proposals.'[8] Later she became convinced that all forms of hunting with dogs should be banned. The idea of a pack of hounds after any single animal offended her sense of justice, and she disliked the way the pro-blood sports lobby had, in her view, appropriated the countryside. However, she never allowed political differ-ences to interfere with friendship. She continued to rely on the kindness of a pro-hunting fellow Labour peer, Ann Mallalieu, the daughter of her old Bevanite colleague William 'Curly' Mallalieu. Lady Mallalieu, who lived near Hell Corner, was Barbara's most regular chauffeur between home and the House of Lords.

She also took a continuing interest in the right to roam, for which she had campaigned with Hugh Dalton as a young MP. 'The point of remembering the past is to grasp the future,' she wrote in a seventieth-anniversary celebration of the Kinder Scout Mass Trespass,[9] which had first triggered the campaign for access to uncultured countryside.

William Mellor, Michael Foot had said, was the 'granite conscience of the left'. Barbara Castle had always seen herself in the same role. She wanted not so much to grasp the future as to claw it back. New Labour, a party without a past, privately dismissed her as the battling granny from prehistory, although Blairites whose careers she had launched like Jack Straw and Janet Anderson believed that if she had been of their generation she would have seen Labour's role as they saw it; and it is easy to find similarities of style. Barbara had always been interested in the language the party used and the way it addressed its supporters. She was as aware as any New Labour minister of the importance of presentation and timing, and as astute as any New Labour spin doctor at finding the image of the moment. In a pre-echo of the New Labour Whitehall spin scandals after the 1997 election victory, she had brought her own people into her press office, and had relied heavily on her young special adviser Jack Straw to keep her in touch with feeling in the wider Labour movement. She had had her own coterie of well-off, and sometimes noble, supporters – Lord Faringdon who lent the Keep Left group his stately home at Buscot Park, Lord Campbell of Booker McConnell, Charles Forte who so famously lent her his yacht; she also understood the importance of wooing business leaders, as she showed in her efforts to find a way of neutralizing opposition to equal pay. She believed in listening to ordinary voters and responding to their anxieties: for example, she was early to sense voter hostility to perceived 'welfare scroungers', and the jibe of 'something for nothing' that it provoked in what Frank Field later dubbed the 'hard-working poor'. She understood that government was the art of choosing priorities, but she thought it was the duty of those outside the leadership to hold it to account. She knew quite as much about positioning herself as did the New Labour press officers. But in refusing Barbara a platform and briefing against her they failed to realize that what they dismissed in her as mere posturing was the result of careful research in support of passionately held views. New Labour, Barbara thought, made the mistake of considering her as trivial as it was itself. Blairism, she would argue, was the triumph of cynicism over ideology, the final betrayal.

The differences between Barbara Castle and New Labour go beyond the generational, or the way each defined the other as its antithesis, although both are important. Barbara's socialism had been imbibed at her father's knee. It was a religion without a God, a system of beliefs that touched most

aspects of her life. Both the party and the voters, according to the traditional
view of the Labour left, needed educating in the message of socialism; it was
not an easy option and it would require courage and leadership to implement.
Inevitably, some middle-class Labour voters would be losers. They had to be
convinced that theirs was a worthwhile sacrifice, not reassured that they
would not need to make one. Rather than find out what the voters wanted
and give it to them, the voters should be given what was good for them and
persuaded that they liked it. In this context it is hardly surprising that in the
abstract – on the back benches, in opposition – Barbara tended to the
doctrinaire. However, in office, especially between 1964 and 1970, her
socialist instincts provided her with what would be called, in the language of
Blairism, a route map, a guide to action in almost any circumstance. From
that came the sense of purpose that helped her to carry it through against the
hesitations of the less committed and her own self-doubts. The highest
compliment Barbara could be paid was to be told that a critic or rival had
conceded that he or she knew where they were with her. It suggested that
her constancy of purpose and political will, which she considered the supreme
political virtues, had been recognized. In fact her rhetoric and her apparently
unbending principles gave her – like Margaret Thatcher – a cloak to throw
over an infinitely more flexible approach in office. Little of what she did
derived exclusively from the socialist doctrinal lexicon. Even her enthusiasm
for controls and licences was as much to do with accruing power to herself
as it was with a belief in the role of state intervention.

However, she had the provocative confidence to argue, like Attlee, that
if she was doing it, it must be socialism. She did not need intellectual
pretensions; she was a politician, not a philosopher, and her interest was in
applying socialist principles rather than speculating about their limits. What
emerged was less socialism than Castle-ism, the moulding of general principle
by the character and circumstances of the individual politician, presented as
socialist fundamentalism.

There was one aspect of Barbara's character that marked her out even
from most of her contemporaries on the middle-class left. She was simultaneously extremely cautious with her money – notoriously tight-fisted, her
close friends would say, recalling her in-flight habit of taking home as many
free quarter-bottles of wine as she could persuade the airline to provide her
with – and very modest in her material ambitions. She had been brought up
to regard any form of conspicuous consumption as vulgar and the pursuit of
material success as downright immoral. The only exception was clothes; she
liked them made for her if possible, off the peg if not. They were, with Hell
Corner, her luxury. She was always the first to propose ministerial salary cuts

at times of national economic crisis – to the irritation of her more high-living, or simply more financially stretched, colleagues, who saw it as just another attempt to take the moral high ground. She also supported moves to make British MEPs take only Westminster MPs' salary. She enjoyed luxury, but always felt mildly uncomfortable with it: a case of what she called the 'sensuous puritanism' she had inherited from her father, or the provincial nonconformism of the Yorkshire lass. To take a taxi was a treat, at least if she was paying for it herself, and she rarely kept her ministerial car hanging around as other ministers did.

'For her – and it is interesting that a woman can admit it more freely than a man – principle and position-seeking were one and the same,'[10] Ben Pimlott once observed. Barbara's political conduct was governed primarily by her beliefs and her self-discipline. Her greatest belief, in the end, was in herself. By the late 1950s she had established her political persona, and she would remain true to her own creation. She had great strengths, her officials testify, as a team leader; leadership, in a kind of gung-ho, over-the-top military style, was her métier. She could never build consensus, nor rally support, nor carry people with her, except by challenging them to follow her; nor did she have the subtlety of approach to enable her to flatter or insinuate, nor the clubbability that might have drawn to her the less politically committed. The skills she knew she lacked, she claimed to disdain; her diaries are littered with attacks on the tactics and schemes of her rivals. In a generation of exceptional intellectual ability she did not shine, while her obsessive personality and searchlight mind – both characteristics later attributed to Margaret Thatcher – alienated the more urbane of the '*New Statesman* left', the Oxford-educated journalists with whom Barbara was most closely associated. Even loyal friends like Michael Foot were critical of her narrowness of focus.

Hers was a lifetime of diligence, the peculiarly feminine aptitude for hard study that she elevated into one of her defence mechanisms against a hostile environment. She worked hard, hated to be caught out, and lacked the confidence to carry off a blunder with a self-deprecatory joke. Neither Thatcher nor Castle could easily hold the Commons, an environment demanding physical authority and a loud voice before any consideration of content or substance. Barbara was often accused of being shrill, sometimes even of screeching. For every young woman who watched her and was inspired, there must have been ten more who watched and knew they lacked the courage to try to emulate her. One such was Anne Cryer, who became the MP for Keighley in 1977. In the 1960s she had been a councillor in Darwen, next to Blackburn, from where she watched Barbara with awe. She 'knew she could never be like her', she once said on a radio programme about women at Westminster.

In her final decade Barbara reversed her opposition to positive discrimination for women and backed the campaign for all-women short lists, 'although after that they are on their own', she would remark, darkly. She had no sympathy for the complaints of the 1997 intake of women MPs against their male colleagues and the arcane procedures that they upheld, although on a personal level she tried to support and encourage the women ministers who came to grief in Blair's first government. She sought out the Social Security Secretary Harriet Harman and the Northern Ireland Secretary Mo Mowlam when they ran into trouble with Downing Street.

If her weaknesses were her political style, her love of battle and loathing of consensus, these went with an independence of approach to each new ministerial portfolio. Her political career's most striking, although not its most consistent, feature was her success in identifying issues on which she could make a difference. Many of her major policy initiatives were attempts to bring about change in order to meet problems whose future impact was not yet widely appreciated. In government, this encompassed her insistence on the practical as well as the moral imperative of a more equal distribution of the world's resources, the introduction of the breathalyser, the seat belt and the 70 mph speed limit, and later her pensions reforms and child benefit proposals. But it also encompassed her disastrous attempt to legislate on industrial relations and her misjudged attack on pay beds.

Four months before she died she launched what was to be her final attack on Tony Blair. 'The thing about Tony,' she said in a radio interview picked up by the newspapers on Christmas Eve 2001, 'is that he is always trying to follow what he thinks public opinion wants. He gets himself landed with the wrong priorities because he's not thinking it out for himself from the basis of principle.'[11] It was a criticism she had hinted at many times before, but this time – provoked by the frustration of watching him triumph against all her prejudices – spelt out with forceful clarity. Earlier that year, Blair had won his second general election landslide. The unpalatable truth was that, however much she despised what he was doing and the way he was doing it, he was managing to give the voters and the party what they wanted. He was the first overtly right-wing leader to win elections for Labour; after the barren years of opposition his victories suggested that voters were no longer interested in ideology – nor even ideals – while the party, her party, wanted victory more than ideological purity. Blair's victory made Barbara's socialism impossible and her own record questionable. For she, after all, had been a leading member of the governments whose conduct of the nation's affairs had left a generation of voters unwilling ever to give Labour another chance.

To the end, for Barbara the personal was political and the political struggle was larger than anything else in her life, even than her great-nieces and -nephews, whose childhoods and subsequent careers provided her with a greater sense of fulfilment than even her political fights gave her. At the height of her success, it had seemed that she might actually be able to make socialism popular with a mass audience; in the late 1970s she became identified with the strident, doctrinaire ambition and failure that made Labour unelectable. She fought hard; she won a misplaced reputation, based on a vituperative personal style, for hating well, although in truth she rarely bore personal grudges. In the shambles of Labour's renewed internal warfare, when all passion was suspect, the pendulum swung further against her than her record justified; for the last ten years of her life, it swung back again further than anyone's qualities might deserve.

Her final ambition was to be able to stay at Hell Corner Farm until she died. In October 2000, she blew her funeral savings on a ninetieth birthday party attended by all her family and Labour luminaries ancient and modern, including the Chancellor Gordon Brown and Jack Straw, then Home Secretary, as well as Michael Foot and Jack Jones, and Jim Callaghan's daughter Margaret Jay, then Leader of the House of Lords (but not Callaghan himself – 'There are some people I can't forgive,' she declared). Harold Wilson's widow, Mary – who had put Callaghan and Barbara into the same car at Wilson's funeral in 1995 and asked afterwards, 'Did you have an interesting journey?' – sat beside her at the top table. Marcia Falkender was another guest. Tony Blair was not invited.

Eighteen months later, early in the new year of 2002, Barbara fell backwards down the steep, narrow stairs of the farmhouse. The fall itself might have killed someone less tough and less determined to stay alive. She lived her last few months in pain, often severe; her doctor suspected she had several hairline fractures. She did not complain. But the energy that had sustained her until she was ninety-one suddenly drained away. She died on 3 May 2002.

Notes

Abbreviations

BAB   Barbara Anne Betts
BAC   Barbara Anne Castle
FATW   Barbara Castle, *Fighting All the Way*, Macmillan, 1993
PRO   Public Record Office

1   Faith and Hope

1. Mary Hepworth letters, BAC papers.
2. Mary Hepworth letters, BAC papers.
3. BAC in Sara Maitland (ed.), *Very Heaven: Looking Back at the 1960s*, Virago, 1988.
4. BAC papers.
5. Interview with Vic Feather in Wilfred De'Ath, *Barbara Castle: A Portrait from Life*, Clifton Books, 1970.
6. *Daily Herald*, 10 Mar. 1961.
7. BAC papers.
8. *Observer*, 28 Sept. 1969.
9. See Maitland, *Very Heaven*.
10. Harry Harmer, *The Labour Party 1900–1998*, Longman, 1999.
11. Interview with Feather in De'Ath, *Barbara Castle*.
12. BAC papers.
13. De'Ath, *Barbara Castle*.
14. De'Ath, *Barbara Castle*.
15. De'Ath, *Barbara Castle*.
16. *FATW*.
17. Mary Clark in De'Ath, *Barbara Castle*.
18. See Eric Silver, *Vic Feather*, Gollancz, 1973.

2 A Woman Wot Speaks

1. Macmillan, 1993 p. 61.
2. In J. Marcus (ed.), *The Young Rebecca: Writings of Rebecca West* 1911–1917, Macmillan/Virago, 1982.
3. Nancy Burton, a sociologist, was a year younger than Barbara and provided this author with a vivid account of life at St Hugh's, to which is owed much of what follows.
4. Olive Shapley, *Broadcasting: A Life: The Autobiography of Olive Shapley*, Scarlet Press, 1996. No other description of Barbara suggests that she was 'sturdy'. Perhaps Ms Shapley was retaliating for being described as 'a tall gangling blond' by Barbara in her autobiography.
5. 'Memorandum on the conduct & discipline of junior members of the university', Michaelmas Term 1927, Oxford University Press, a booklet produced for undergraduates.
6. *FATW*.
7. *FATW*, p. 46.
8. Shapley, *Broadcasting: A Life*.
9. The family were sometimes lent a remote and primitive cottage at Blubber-houses, not far from Leeds, by a Fabian friend of Annie's.
10. Nancy Burton, *On the Margin*, privately printed, 1999.
11. BAC letters.
12. Shapley, *Broadcasting: A Life*.
13. BAC in conversation with the author.
14. And did not for another twenty years, until Shirley Catlin, later Williams, was elected.
15. BAC papers.
16. Much anecdotal evidence suggests his dislike for Barbara stems from their earliest acquaintance and his envy of her university career.
17. *Bradford Pioneer*, 9 Oct. 1931.
18. *FATW*.
19. *FATW*.
20. BAC letters and private papers.
21. Frank Betts to Mary Hepworth, BAB papers, 28 Jan. 1932.
22. Olive Shapley, *Broadcasting a Life*.
23. Glyn Jones 1908–92, Governor-General Malawi 1964–6. He was a friend of Jimmie's and Barbara confesses in her autobiography to a 'romantic poignancy' about their short relationship.
24. Letter to Mary Hepworth, 26 July 1932, 'I managed to carry Hyde against disaffiliation'.
25. A. W. Wright, *G. D. H. Cole and Socialist Democracy*, Clarendon Press, 1979.
26. *FATW*.

27. Quoted in *FATW*.
28. Wilfred De'Ath, *Barbara Castle: A portrait from Life*, Clifton Books, 1970.
29. BAB papers.
30. Susan Lawrence 1871–1947, junior Health Minister 1929–31.
31. *FATW*, p. 68.
32. Keble, according to *FATW*.
33. According to his son, Ronald. It is odd that Barbara makes no mention of it, nor does his entry in *Who's Who*.
34. William Mellor, *Direct Action*, Parsons, 1920, p. 55.
35. Quoted in Patricia Hollis and Jennie Lee, *Jennie Lee: A Life*, Oxford University Press, 1997.
36. All letters between Mellor and Barbara are in her private papers.
37. Ronald Mellor believes that his mother never knew of the affair, which he himself only found out about when Barbara published her autobiography in 1993, fifty years after his father died.
38. *FATW*.
39. See Pamela M. Graves, *Labour Women in British Working-Class Politics 1918–1939*, Cambridge University Press, 1994.

3   Directing the Action

1. Parsons, 1920.
2. *FATW*.
3. Mellor, letter to BAB.
4. Ben Pimlott, *Hugh Dalton*, Cape, 1985, p. 206.
5. Mellor, letter to BAB.
6. Mellor, letter to BAB, Feb. 1934.
7. Mellor, letter to BAB Apr. 1934.
8. A device to ensure further debate at a later date, if carried.
9. H. N. Brailsford, 1873–1958, left-wing journalist and polemicist.
10. Arthur Henderson, Labour leader 1931–2 and Foreign Secretary 1929–31.
11. Quoted in Pimlott, *Labour and the Left*.
12. Margaret Cole, wife of G. D. H. Cole; D. N. Pritt 1887–1972, MP for Hammersmith 1935–50, Socialist Leaguer; Victor Gollancz 1893–1967, founder of the Left Book Club; Madame Maisky, wife of the Russian ambassador Ivan Maisky.
13. *FATW* p. 109.
14. *FATW* p. 75.
15. From around mid-1935 Barbara referred to Mellor as 'my husband'.
16. According to family legend, Marjorie's commitment to politics meant the infant Sonya was brought into the Birmingham Council chamber for her feeds (Marjorie was briefly a councillor).

17. Quoted in Pimlott, *Labour and the Left*.
18. Ronald Mellor, papers.
19. *FATW*.
20. *Tribune*, 15 Oct. 1937.
21. *Tribune*, 26 Nov. 1937.

4   Ends and Beginnings

1. Quoted in Michael Foot, *Aneurin Bevan: A Biography, Vol. 1 1897–1945*, MacGibbon & Kee, 1962.
2. Ibid.
3. Patrick Gordon Walker 1907–80, Foreign Secretary 1964–5, who lost his Smethwick seat in a notoriously racist campaign in 1964 and was then defeated at a by-election at Leyton.
4. Quintin Hogg 1907–99, Lord Chancellor 1970–4, 1979–87.
5. Vernon Bartlett 1894–1983, MP for Bridgwater 1938–50.
6. *FATW*, p. 102.
7. B. Donoghue and G. W. Jones, *Herbert Morrison: Portrait of a Politician*, Weidenfeld and Nicolson, 1973.
8. Conversation with Michael Foot.
9. Simon Hoggart and David Leigh, *Michael Foot: A Portrait*, Hodder & Stoughton 1981.
10. Michael Foot, quoted in Hoggart and Leigh, *Michael Foot*.
11. Michael Foot, *Tribune*, twenty-first anniversary celebrations.
12. *Tribune*, 1 Jan. 1937.
13. R. Postgate, *The Life of George Lansbury*, quoted in Ben Pimlott, *Labour and the Left in the 1930s*, Cambridge University Press, 1977.
14. BAB letter to Ted Castle.
15. Wilfred De'Ath, *Barbara Castle: A portrait from Life*, Clifton Books, 1970.
16. *Tribune*, 2 Feb. 1940.
17. *Tribune*, 21 June 1940.
18. Quoted in Peter Clarke, *The Cripps Version: The Life of Sir Stafford Cripps*, Allen Lane, 2002.
19. *Tribune*, 5 March 1937.
20. Paul Addison, *The Road to 1945: British Politics and the Second World War*, Quartet, 1975.
21. See the excellent *The Five Giants: A Biography of the Welfare State*, Nicholas Timmins, HarperCollins, 1995.
22. Addison, *The Road to 1945*.
23. Quoted in Timmins, *Five Giants*.
24. *FATW*, p. 116.
25. But Ian Mikardo, a 'tough self-confident imperturbable character', said on

making his first speech to conference the following year: 'I didn't have butterflies in my stomach – I had a whole flock of whacking pterodactyls flapping about in there.' See Ian Mikardo, *Back Bencher*, Weidenfeld & Nicolson, 1988, p. 76.

26. *FATW*, p. 117.
27. De'Ath, *Barbara Castle*.
28. See Mikardo, *Back Bencher*.
29. Letter to Ted, July 1943.
30. *FATW*, p. 119.
31. Garry Allighan became an MP and for a long time had the distinction of being the only person to be expelled from the Commons by a vote of his colleagues. He had leaked to a journalist friend the proceedings of a meeting of the Parliamentary Labour Party, and was declared to be in contempt of parliament. Such leaks soon became so commonplace as to be beyond notice.
32. Her first attempts to influence legislation were to improve the treatment of women in the new social insurance legislation.
33. According to Sir George Eddie, Barbara's first agent, who had also been Jimmy Maxton's agent. Quoted in De'ath, *Barbara Castle*.
34. *FATW*, p. 131.
35. Anonymous quote in *Sunday Times* profile, July 1967.
36. *Picture Post*, 23 June 1945.
37. There is a mystery about Barbara's selection: George Thomas, later a Speaker of the House and Lord Tonypandy, recounts in his autobiography how he was also selected for Blackburn in 1944 but resigned only a week later to look for a seat nearer his home in Cardiff. Yet all the surviving records show just Barbara and John Edwards. The only explanation is that Thomas's resignation provoked a second selection meeting. The party's records were lost in a move.
38. BAC papers.
39. William Warbey 1903–80, MP for Luton 1941–5, wrote *Ho Chi Minh: His Life and Achievements*, Merlin Press, 1972.
40. *Tribune*, 29 Apr. 1944.
41. *Tribune*, May 1944.
42. De'Ath, *Barbara Castle*.
43. Ibid.
44. Lancashire *Evening Telegraph*, 26 July 1945.

5   Jerusalem

1. Quoted by Hugh Dalton in *The Political Diary of Hugh Dalton: 1918–1940, 1945–1960*, Ben Pimlott (ed.), Cape, 1986.
2. The Palace of Westminster suffered a direct hit in 1941. The Commons was not completely rebuilt until 1950.
3. Hugh Gaitskell, Harold Wilson, Jim Callaghan and Michael Foot.

4. Eric Estorick, *Stafford Cripps: A Biography*, Heinemann 1949.

5. Estorick, *Stafford Cripps*.

6. Who had thought him 'treacherous', in *FATW*.

7. Quoted in Michael Foot, *Aneurin Bevan: A Biography*, Vol. 1 1897–1945, MacGibbon & Kee, 1962.

8. 'Celticus' (Aneurin Bevan), *Why Not Trust the Tories?* Gollancz, 1944.

9. Nigel Nicolson (ed.), *Harold Nicolson, Diaries and Letters 1930–1964*, Weidenfeld & Nicolson, 1968.

10. BAC papers. It is not clear who published the review.

11. But when Blackburn's boundaries were redrawn for the 1950 election and the old two-member constituency was replaced by Blackburn East and West, Barbara won the nomination for the safer seat. By 1964 it was reduced to a single constituency.

12. *FATW*.

13. P. Williams (ed.), *The Diaries of Hugh Gaitskell 1945–1956*, Cape, 1983.

14. It was said to be on this trip that Wilson realized the pound was overvalued.

15. But she never said so to the author of this book.

16. Sir Richard (Otto) Clarke 'Anglo-American Economic Collaboration' in Sir Alec Cairncross (ed.), *War and Peace 1942–49*, Oxford University Press, 1982.

17. *Hansard*, 16 Nov. 1945.

18. Quoted in Anthony Howard, *Crossman: The Pursuit of Power*, Cape, 1990.

19. Lord Thomas Balogh 1905–85, Fellow of Balliol College, Oxford 1945–73; economic adviser to the Treasury 1964–7.

20. In her autobiography (*Fighting All the Way*, Macmillan, 1993), Barbara confesses that she thinks she – or rather, the party – was wrong and had become overdependent on unpopular and unduly restrictive measures.

21. Douglas Jay 1907–96, President of the Board of Trade 1984–7.

22. *Spectator*, June 1948.

23. Robert Owen 1771–1858, social reformer and industrialist.

24. Leah Manning, *A Life for Education: An Autobiography*, Gollancz, 1970. She dedicated her autobiography to Barbara.

25. Conrad Heron, interview with the author.

26. Dr Edith Summerskill, a right-wing Labour MP 1938–61.

6   Fresh Thinking

1. Macmillan, 1993, p. 205.

2. Janet Morgan (ed.), *The Backbench Diaries of Richard Crossman*, Hamish Hamilton/Cape, 1981, 24 Mar. 1955.

3. Aneurin Bevan, *In Place of Fear*, MacGibbon & Kee, 1952, p. 1.

4. Brian Brivati, *Hugh Gaitskell*, Richard Cohen, 1996, p. 122.

5. Morgan, *Backbench Diaries*, 24 Sept. 1952.

6. Morgan, *Backbench Diaries*, 3 Dec 1953.
7. Quoted in Michael Foot, *Aneurin Bevan: A Biography, Vol. 2 1945–1960*, Davis Poynter, 1973.
8. P. Williams (ed.), *The Diaries of Hugh Gaitskell 1945–1956*, Cape, 1983, 25 Jan. 1951.
9. Morrison papers, quoted in John Campbell, *Nye Bevan and the Mirage of British Socialism*, Weidenfeld & Nicolson, 1987.
10. James Callaghan, *Time and Chance*, Collins, 1987.
11. Brivati, *Hugh Gaitskell*.
12. *FATW*.
13. Tony Benn, *Years of Hope: Diaries 1940–1962*, Hutchinson, 1994, 24 Apr. 1951.
14. *FATW*.
15. Roy Jenkins, *A Life at the Centre*, Macmillan, 1991.
16. *Keeping Left*, New Statesman, 1950.
17. According to Jenkins, *A life at the Centre*.
18. Morgan, *Backbench Diaries*, 17 Dec 1951.
19. Morgan, *Backbench Diaries*, 11 Mar. 1952.
20. Morgan, *Backbench Diaries*, 11 Mar. 1952.
21. Foot, *Bevan: A Biography 1945–1960*, p. 362.
22. Bevan, *In Place of Fear* p. 164.
23. Michael Foot, *Aneurin Bevan: A Biography, Vol. 1 1897–1945*, MacGibbon & Kee, 1962, p. 64.
24. Bevan, *In Place of Fear* p. 169.
25. John Campbell, *Nye Bevan and the Mirage of British Socialism*, Weidenfeld & Nicolson, 1987.
26. Undated newspaper report, BAC papers.
27. Ian Mikardo, *Back Bencher*, Weidenfeld & Nicolson, 1988, p. 124.
28. *Sunday Pictorial*, a leading anti-Bevanite paper which retained Crossman as a columnist.
29. Morgan, *Backbench Diaries*, 29 Sept. 1952.
30. Foot, *Bevan: A Biorgraphy 1945–1960*.
31. Minute of PLP meeting, 11 Oct. 1952. Quoted in Brivati, *Hugh Gaitskell*.
32. Quoted in Morgan, *Backbench Diaries*, p. 162.
33. Morgan, *Backbench Diaries*, 14 Oct. 1952.
34. Morgan, *Backbench Diaries*, 23 Oct. 1952.
35. Foot, *Bevan: A Biography 1945–1960*.
36. Morgan, *Backbench Diaries*, 20 Oct. 1952.
37. Ben Pimlott, *The Political Diary of Hugh Dalton 1918–1940, 1945–1960*, Cape, 1986, 13 Nov. 1952.
38. Ted Castle in Mark Jenkins, *Bevanism: Labour's High-Tide*, Spokesman, 1979.
39. Jenkins, *Bevanism*.
40. BAC papers.
41. Marcia Williams, *Inside Number Ten*, Weidenfeld & Nicolson, 1972.

42. BAC papers.
43. BAC papers.
44. Barbara Castle, *It Need Not Happen: The Alternative to German Rearmament*, a *Tribune* pamphlet, 1954.
45. BAC papers.
46. BAC papers.
47. Letter to a party worker, quoted in Foot, *Bevan: A Biography 1945–1960*, p. 436.
48. Morrison had been given an ex-officio seat on the NEC after his defeat in 1952.
49. BAC papers. Crossman's diary does not mention the fellow-traveller line of attack, nor Bevan's defence. However, he dictated his diary at weekly intervals. Barbara's note appears contemporaneous.
50. Alf, later Lord, Robens, 1910– union official, Coal Board chairman and MP.
51. See also Crossman's plans for the Scarborough conference in Morgan, *Backbench Diaries*, 1 Oct. 1954.
52. BAC papers.
53. BAC papers.
54. Morgan, *Backbench Diaries*, 7 Dec. 1951.
55. BAC papers, letter to Desmond Donnell.
56. Morgan, *Backbench Diaries*, 3 Mar. 1955.
57. Campbell, *Nye Bevan*.
58. But Crossman felt there were only two positions – complete neutrality or a nuclear-armed Britain. He also thought it would never be a big issue.
59. Morgan, *Backbench Diaries*, 24 Mar. 1955.
60. Note, Morgan, *Backbench Diaries*, 31 Mar. 1955.
61. Roy Martin, Blackburn agent 1960–8 in Wilfred De'Ath, *Barbara Castle: A Portrait from Life*, Clifton Books, 1970.

7   Bitter Lemons

1. Faber and Faber, 1957.
2. Philip Williams, *Hugh Gaitskell*, Oxford University Press, 1982, p. 327.
3. Anthony Howard and R. West, *The Making of the British Prime Minister*, Cape, 1965.
4. Quoted in Anthony Verrier, *The Road to Zimbabwe* 1890–1980, Cape, 1986.
5. *FATW*.
6. 'The resignation of Colonel Young', in the Colonial Office files at the PRO, Kew, 1959.
7. BAC papers and PRO, Kew, 1959.
8. *Tribune*, 30 Sept. 1955.
9. *FATW*.
10. *Hansard*, 21 Dec. 1955.

11. *Hansard*, 21 Dec. 1955.

12. Quoted in the *Guardian*, 9 Nov. 2002.

13. Interview with the author.

14. Interview with the author.

15. Mandela, with the other defendants, was acquitted, but convicted in 1964 on a new treason charge. He spent twenty-six years in prison. He regarded Barbara, he told her housekeeper at a Trafalgar Square rally in 1998, as a 'great lady'.

16. BAC papers.

17. Janet Morgan (ed.), *The Backbench Diaries of Richard Crossman*. Hamish Hamilton/ Cape, 1981, 12 Nov. 1953.

18. Tony Benn, *Years of Hope: Diaries 1940–1962*, Hutchinson, 1994, 23 Mar. 1958.

19. BAC unpublished diaries, 25 June 1957.

20. George Brown, gifted working-class Gaitskellite, MP 1945–70, deputy leader of the Labour Party 1960–70.

21. Morgan, *Backbench Diaries*, 22 Feb. 1955.

22. BAC unpublished diaries, 3 Apr. 1957.

23. Morgan, *Backbench Diaries*, 26 Sept. 1957.

24. Anthony Crosland, *The Future of Socialism*, Cape, 1956.

25. BAC unpublished diaries, 20 May 1957.

26. *Daily Mirror*, 6 Aug. 1957.

27. Barbara's approach, as a minister, to nationalized industries suggests she had absorbed more of Crosland's analysis than she was prepared to admit.

28. BAC unpublished diaries, 17 Sept. 1957.

29. BAC unpublished diaries, 27 Sept. 1957.

30. BAC unpublished diaries, 27 Sept. 1957.

31. Morgan, *Backbench Diaries*, 4 Oct. 1957.

32. Morgan, *Backbench Diaries*, 4 Oct. 1957.

33. BAC unpublished diaries, 27 Nov. 1957.

34. BAC unpublished diaries, 27 Nov. 1957.

35. Brother of Michael and another Labour MP, Dingle.

36. BAC unpublished diaries, 9 May 1957.

37. Selwyn-Lloyd, party conference 1958.

38. She called herself chairman – 'I don't mind what I'm called as long as I'm in charge.'

39. According to her recollection in conversation with the author, 2002.

40. Her recollection in conversation, 2002.

41. Crossman had criticized the Highland Light Infantry in 1956 and Driberg reiterated Barbara's criticisms in the week after she left Cyprus.

42. Foreign Office records, PRO.

43. BAC unpublished Cyprus diary, 1958.

44. Conversation with BAC, 2002.

45. BAC unpublished diaries, 27 Oct. 1957.

46. *Daily Telegraph*, 22 Sept. 1958.
47. Benn, *Years of Hope*, 23 Sept. 1958.
48. See Charles Foley, *Memoirs of Colonel Grivas*, Longman, 1964.
49. Foreign Office records, PRO.
50. There was some bitterness in the party that she made no effort to thank those who had helped her.
51. *Hansard*, 27 July 1959.
52. Quoted in the *New Statesman*, 14 Feb. 1959.
53. Jeremy Campbell, *Evening Standard*, 10 Sept. 1959.
54. Roy Jenkins, quoted in Brian Brivati, *Hugh Gaitskell*, Richard Cohen, 1996, p. 332.
55. Morgan, *Backbench Diaries*, 19 Oct. 1959.
56. BAC unpublished diaries, 28 Oct. 1959.
57. Labour Party Annual Conference Report, Nov. 1959.
58. Labour Party Annual Conference Report, Nov. 1959.
59. Not in the official transcript.
60. BAC unpublished diaries, 29 Nov. 1959.
61. *New Statesman*, 9 July 1960.

8   Bombshell

1. Lennox-Boyd retired from parliament in 1959, having tried twice to resign over administrative failures in Kenya and Nyasaland.
2. Transcript in BAC's papers.
3. Lionel Davidson, *John Bull*, 28 Feb. 1959.
4. BAC papers, 1943.
5. When this author asked him more about this in 2001, he said it would be 'ungallant' to say.
6. Davidson, *John Bull*.
7. Janet Morgan (ed.), *The Backbench Diaries of Richard Crossman*, Hamish Hamilton/ Cape, 1981, 4th Feb. 1953.
8. Notes made in 1955 for an unpublished article.
9. *People*, 26 Aug. 1962.
10. *Daily Herald*, 31 Jan. 1959.
11. *Daily Herald*, 10 Mar. 1961.
12. *Evening Standard*, 7 Sept. 1959.
13. *Sunday Graphic*, 6 Dec. 1959.
14. Davidson, *John Bull*.
15. *Daily Herald*, 10 Mar. 1961.
16. Davidson, *John Bull*.
17. His second wife Zita had died in 1952 and in 1954 he had married again.
18. Morgan, *Backbench Diaries*, 8 Oct. 1958.

19. Conversation with the author.
20. BAC unpublished diaries, 27 Jan. 1960.
21. BAC unpublished diaries, 16 Mar. 1960.
22. BAC unpublished diaries, 16 Mar. 1960.
23. Brian Brivati, *Hugh Gaitskell*, Richard Cohen, 1996.
24. The main section of the resolution spoke of 'a complete rejection of any defence policy based on the threat of the use of strategic and nuclear weapons'.
25. BAC unpublished diaries, 21 June 1960.
26. BAC unpublished diaries, 30 June 1960.
27. BAC unpublished diaries, 21 Sept. 1960.
28. *Daily Mirror*, 24 Sept. 1960.
29. BAC unpublished diaries, 12 Oct. 1960.
30. Morgan, *Backbench Diaries*, 13 Oct. 1960.
31. BAC unpublished diaries, 3 Nov. 1960.
32. BAC unpublished diaries, 4 Nov. 1960.
33. BAC unpublished diaries, 18 Feb. 1963.
34. Right-wing Labour MP for West Leeds 1949–74.
35. Gaitskellite loyalist and longstanding critics of Barbara.
36. BAC unpublished diaries, 3 Oct. 1963.
37. BAC unpublished diaries, 10 Mar. 1963.
38. BAC unpublished diaries, 25 Mar. 1963.
39. Parliamentary privilege protects MPs from actions for defamation.
40. *Hansard*, 21 Mar. 1963.
41. BAC unpublished diaries, 22 Mar. 1963.
42. BAC unpublished diaries, 25 Mar. 1963.
43. BAC papers.
44. Conversation with the author.
45. BAC unpublished diaries, 27 Sept. 1957.
46. BAC unpublished diaries, 3 Nov. 1960.
47. BAC papers.
48. BAC papers.

9   A Keen and Dedicated Minister

1. Addressing the Oxford Farming Conference in January 1964.
2. Douglas Home once claimed to use matchsticks to help with his economics.
3. Wilson, conference speech, Oct. 1963.
4. Quoted in Ben Pimlott, *Harold Wilson*, HarperCollins, 1992.
5. Barbara Castle, *The Castle Diaries 1964–1970*, Weidenfeld & Nicholson, 1984, Introduction.
6. From 'My First Hundred Days', prepared for the Introduction to Castle, *Diaries 1964–1970*.

7. Driberg and possibly Mikardo may both have been ruled out on security grounds alone. Driberg was uninhibitedly gay, while Mikardo, a frequent traveller in Eastern Europe, was suspected of Communist sympathies.

8. Wilson, Crossman, Castle, Greenwood and Cousins had all written for *Tribune*.

9. Marica Williams, Wilson's personal secretary since 1956, became the most important member of his entourage and remained a close friend until Wilson's death in 1995.

10. The others were Margaret Bondfield, Ellen Wilkinson (both Labour) and Florence Horsburgh (Conservative).

11. Labour Party Annual Conference Report 1959.

12. *Hansard*, 28 Feb. 1964.

13. *Daily Herald*, 22 Jan. 1964.

14. *Sun*, 3 Jan. 1966, profile of BAC by Susan Barnes.

15. BAC papers.

16. Fabian Society working paper, May 1964.

17. Fabian Society working paper, July 1964.

18. Ibid.

19. Fabian Society working paper, May 1964.

20. 'Mandarin Power', an article by BAC based on a talk she gave to officials at Sunningdale, *Sunday Times*, 10 June 1973.

21. Sir Andrew Cohen's 1963 lecture, 'New Work and Ideas in the Field of Technical Cooperation', BAC papers.

22. *Observer*, 1965.

23. Castle, *Diaries 1964–1970*, Introduction.

24. Anthony Verrier, *The Road to Zimbabwe 1890–1980*, Cape, 1986.

25. 'Mandarin Power', *Sunday Times*.

26. And Crossman, whose *Labour in the Affluent Society*, Fabian Tract 325, June 1960, propounded the same view.

27. *Hansard*, 10 Nov. 1964.

28. *Venture*, pre-election issue, Oct. 1964.

29. *Overseas Development: The Work of the New Ministry*, Cmd. 2736, HMSO, Aug. 1965.

30. Ibid.

31. Castle, *Diaries 1964–1970*, 12 Apr. 1965.

32. Hall later became Secretary of the Ramblers' Association.

33. The admiring sobriquet by which she was known in some parts of the continent after her campaign for colonial freedom.

34. Conversation with the author.

35. Castle, *Diaries 1964–1970*, 4 July 1965.

36. Castle, *Diaries 1964–1970*, 8 July 1965.

37. Castle, *Diaries 1964–1970*, 28 Nov. 1965.

38. W. Beckerman (ed.), *The Labour Government's Economic Record*, Duckworth, 1972.

39. Beckerman, *Economic Record*.

40. 'Mandarin Power', *Sunday Times*.

41. Denis Healey, a Leeds MP 1952–92, a future Chancellor and deputy leader of the Labour Party.

42. Janet Morgan (ed.), *Richard Crossman: The Diaries of a Cabinet Minister*, Hamish Hamilton/Cape, 1981, vol 1. 22 Oct. 1964.

43. *Sunday Times*, 4 Dec. 1966.

44. Castle, *Diaries 1964–1970*, 2 Nov. 1965.

45. Morgan, *Crossman: Diaries of a Cabinet Minister 1964–1966*, 14 Nov. 1965.

46. Morgan, *Crossman: Diaries of a Cabinet Minister 1964–1966*, 4 Nov. 1965.

10   Tiger

1. Conservative Party leader 1965–75.

2. Barbara Castle, *The Castle Diaries 1964–1970*, Weidenfeld & Nicolson, 1984, 21 Dec. 1965.

3. Janet Morgan (ed.), *Richard Crossman: The Diaries of a Cabinet Minister 1964–1966*, Hamish Hamilton/Cape, 1975, 22 Dec. 1965.

4. Castle, *Diaries 1964–1970*, 17 Apr. 1965.

5. Not in her papers, but recorded in *FATW*.

6. Norah Beloff, *Observer*, 7 July 1967.

7. She tried to learn again later.

8. Foot to BAC, 22 Dec. 1965.

9. Castle, *Diaries 1964–1970*, 23 Dec. 1965.

10. *Guardian*, 7 Jan. 1966.

11. *Sun*, 3 Jan. 1966, profile of BAC by Susan Barnes.

12. Castle, *Diaries 1964–1970*, 22 Mar. 1968.

13. Castle, *Diaries 1964–1970*, 8 Sept. 1966.

14. Sir Christopher Foster in conversation with the author.

15. Christoper Foster was later an adviser to Mrs Thatcher on the poll tax.

16. *Socialist Commentary*, a long-running forum for policy debate on the right of the party.

17. Max Nicholson, *The System*, Hodder 1967.

18. Castle, *Diaries 1964–1970*, 5–6 Jan. 1966.

19. Marcia Williams, *Inside Number Ten*, Weidenfeld & Nicolson, 1972.

20. Joe Haines, Wilson's press adviser, claimed in his memoirs that he had gone to Barbara in her room at the ministry and persuaded her that the bridge must get the go-ahead.

21. 'Bridged at Last', Radio Humberside, June–July 1981.

22. In fact, road deaths were down to about 3,600 in 2000.

23. Patrick Gordon Walker, quoted in William Plowden, *The Motor Car and Politics 1896–1970*, Bodley Head, 1971.

24. *The Beeching Report*, published in 1963, proposed cutting Britain's rail network by a third.
25. NEC policy paper RD 444, Apr. 1963.
26. Plowden, *Motor Car*, p. 370.
27. *FATW*.
28. Castle, *Diaries 1964–1970*, 17 May 1965.
29. Adam Raphael, *Guardian*, 3 July 1967.
30. BAC private papers.
31. Christopher Foster, private paper.
32. Castle, *Diaries 1964–1970*, 6 Sept. 1967.
33. Castle, *Diaries 1964–1970*, 18 Sept. 1967.
34. Foster, private papers.
35. Conversation with the author.
36. *Economist*, 11 Nov. 1967.

11   The Politics of Barbara Castle

1. Nora Beloff, *Observer*, July 1967.
2. Profile of BAC by Peter Dunn, *Sunday Times*, July 1967.
3. Paul Foot, *The Politics of Harold Wilson*, Penguin, 1968.
4. Peter Shore, an MP 1964–97 and previously head of the Labour Research Department, was Wilson's Personal Private Secretary 1964–6, Minister of Technology 1966, and joined the Cabinet as Minister for Economic Affairs in 1967.
5. Quoted in 'The trade union "problem" since 1960', in Ben Pimlott and Chris Cook (eds), *Trade Unions in British Politics*, Longman, 1982.
6. For the best discussion of government–trade union relations, see Denis Barnes and Eileen Reid, *Governments and Trade Unions: The British Experience 1945–1979*, Heinemann, 1980.
7. *Productivity, Prices and Incomes: Report of Executive Committees of Affiliated Organisations*, 30 Apr. 1965, TUC, 1965, quoted in Barnes and Reid, *Governments and Trade Unions*.
8. G. Dorfman, *Wage Politics in Britain 1945–67*, Charles Knight, 1974.
9. James Callaghan, *Time and Chance*, Collins, 1987.
10. Lord Morris of Aberavon (John Morris) in conversation with the author.
11. Sir Christopher Foster, conversation with the author.
12. Conversation with the author.
13. Quoted in Barbara Castle, *The Castle Diaries 1964–1970*, Weidenfeld & Nicolson, 1984, 13 Feb. 1967; also, conversation with the author.
14. Conversation with the author.
15. John Morris, conversation with the author.

16. There were memorable lapses, e.g. when she released the ODM White Paper to coincide with the one on immigration.
17. Castle, *Diaries 1964–1970*, 28 Feb. 1967.
18. Castle, *Diaries 1964–1970*, 14 Nov. 1967.

12   The Whirlwind

1. Weidenfeld & Nicolson, 1984, 5 Apr. 1968.
2. It was the year Blackburn, Barbara Castle's constituency, went Conservative for the first time since 1945.
3. Janet Morgan (ed.), *Richard Crossman: The Diaries of a Cabinet Minister 1968–1970*, Hamish Hamilton/Cape, 1975, 29 Mar. 1968.
4. Barbara Castle, *The Castle Diaries 1964–1970*, Weidenfeld & Nicolson, 1984, 29 Mar. 1968.
5. Castle, *Diaries 1964–1970*, 3 Apr. 1968.
6. Ibid.
7. Bernard Ingham, *Kill the Messenger*, HarperCollins, 1991.
8. Quoted in Ben Pimlott, *Harold Wilson*, HarperCollins, 1992.
9. Castle, *Diaries 1964–1970*, 6 Sept. 1968.
10. Castle, *Diaries 1964–1970*, 21 Mar. 1968.
11. So the then Labour Minister Walter Monckton told a young Tony Benn.
12. Ingham, *Kill the Messenger*.
13. In 1969 the total was 6.8 million and in 1970 10.7 million. *Department of Employment Cazette*, July 1972.
14. Tony Benn, *Out of the Wilderness: Diaries 1963–1967*, 21 Jan. 1967.
15. Quoted in Robert Taylor, *The TUC from the General Strike to New Unionism*, Palgrave, 2000.
16. Ian Mikardo, *Back Bencher*, Weidenfeld & Nicolson, 1988.
17. Castle, *Diaries 1964–1970*, 9 Apr. 1968.
18. BAC personal papers.
19. Ingham, *Kill the Messenger*.
20. Conversations with the author; and see Denis Barnes and Eileen Reid, *Governments and Trade Unions: The British Experience 1945–1979*, Heinemann, 1980.
21. Castle, *Diaries 1964–1970*, 5 Apr. 1968.
22. Quoted in Castle, *Diaries 1964–1970*, 28 May 1968.
23. Interview with Conrad Heron, senior DEP official.
24. The Ford and the railmen's settlements were both cited as early breaches.
25. Castle, *Diaries 1964–1970*, 1 May 1968.
26. Prime Minister's minute in BAC papers, 27 May 1968.
27. Castle, *Diaries 1964–1970*, 25 Sept. 1968.
28. BAC private papers.

13   The Eye of the Storm

1. HarperCollins, 2000, p. 386.
2. David Watt, *Financial Times*, 19 Apr. 1969.
3. See Geoffrey Goodman, *The Awkward Warrior*, Davis Poynter, 1979.
4. The Civil Service training college at Sunningdale in Berkshire was often used for ministerial conferences.
5. *Sunday Telegraph*, 5 Jan. 1969.
6. MP for Doncaster 1964–97, Deputy Speaker 1983–92.
7. Sir John Burgh, interview with the author.
8. 'An Alternative Approach', paper prepared for the Sunningdale conference, Nov. 1968, BAC papers.
9. Interview with John Fraser.
10. BAC private papers, (her emphasis).
11. Barbara Castle, *The Castle Diaries 1964–1970*, Weidenfeld & Nicolson, 1984, 28 Nov. 1968.
12. Castle, *Diaries 1964–1970*, 4 Dec. 1968.
13. Castle, *Diaries 1964–1970*, 19 Dec. 1968.
14. Castle, *Diaries 1964–1970*, 15 Jan. 1969.
15. Cabinet Office notes, draft, 16 Dec. 1968, raising the question of defining the appropriate time for ministerial intervention.
16. John Burgh, interview. Although in her diaries Barbara records that she was in the office when Ted's call came from the hospital, in a departure from her diaries, which undermines her claims for their accuracy, in her autobiography (*Fighting All the Way*, Macmillan, 1993) she says she was working in the small hours when Ted, in bed in the next room, awoke inspired.
17. Castle, *Diaries 1964–1970*, 15 Jan. 1969.
18. Interview with Bernard Ingham.
19. Interview with John Burgh; interview with Ian Aitken.
20. *Sunday Telegraph*, 5 Jan. 1969.
21. *New Statesman*, 24 Jan. 1969.
22. *Financial Times*, 24 Jan. 1969.
23. Castle, *Diaries 1964–1970*, 8 Apr. 1969.
24. BAC papers.
25. Castle, *Diaries 1964–1970*, 14 Apr. 1969.
26. Conservative shadow chancellor, then Chancellor of the Exchequer until his premature death in 1970.
27. Janet Morgan (ed.), *Richard Crossman: Diaries of a Cabinet Minister 1968–1970*, Hamish Hamilton/Cape, 1975, 17 Apr. 1969.
28. Morgan, *Crossman: Diaries 1968–1970*, 20 Apr. 1969.
29. John Silkin, MP 1963–83, successful solicitor and later centre-left leadership candidate; Bob Mellish, MP 1952–83.

30. George Brown and Ray Gunter, not people whose opinions Barbara would normally quote.
31. Harold Wilson, *The Labour Government 1964–70: A Personal Record*, Weidenfeld & Nicolson, 1971. He wrongly dates the PLP meeting to 23 April.
32. BAC papers.
33. BAC papers.
34. Conrad Heron, PREM13/2726 (DEP papers), PRO. The PREM code signifies Prime Ministers office; 13 signifies correspondence; 2726 is the series of papers relating to 'In Place of Strife', May–June 1969.
35. Neither was a member of the smaller and more senior finance and general purposes committee.

14   The Battle of Downing Street

1. Charles Knight, 1970.
2. The Croydon conference of trade union executives, 1968.
3. CBI response to the TUC's 'Programme for Action'.
4. Jack Jones, interview with the author.
5. Barbara Castle, *The Castle Diaries 1964–1970*, Weidenfeld & Nicolson, 1984, 19 May 1969.
6. He went on: 'I was not tempted to renege . . . The real count against Wilsonism was that it was opportunistic and provided leadership by manoeuvre and not by direction. To replace him by outdoing his own deficiencies would make a discreditable nonsense out of the whole enterprise.'
7. PREM13/2726, PRO.
8. Ibid.
9. Castle, *Diaries 1964–1970*, 21 May 1969.
10. Interview with Conrad Heron.
11. Jack Jones, *Union Man*, Collins, 1986.
12. PREM13/2727, PRO.
13. Castle, *Diaries 1964–1970*, 8 June 1969.
14. Castle, *Diaries 1964–1970*, 9 June 1969.
15. Wilson later refused even to look at the minutes of this meeting which, unusually, remain on file.
16. Castle, *Diaries 1964–1970*, 17 June 1969.
17. PREM13/2727, PRO, 2–13 June 1969.
18. Conrad Heron, interview with the author. See also Bernard Ingham, *Kill the Messenger*, HarperCollins, 1991.
19. In 1969 she won 'best hair-do' award in the *Hairdressers' Journal*, beating Dusty Springfield, the Duchess of Kent and Elizabeth Taylor.
20. Roy Jenkins, *A Life at the Centre*, Macmillan, 1991.

15 One of the Lasses

1. In Wilfred De'Ath, *Barbara Castle: A Portrait from Life*, Clifton Books, 1970, p. 27.
2. Tony Benn, *Office without Power: Diaries 1968–1972*, Hutchinson, 1988, 25 June 1969.
3. Barbara Castle, *The Castle Diaries 1964–1970*, Weidenfeld & Nicolson, 1984, 24 June 1969.
4. Janet Morgan (ed.), *Richard Crossman: The Diaries of a Cabinet Minister 1968–1970*, Hamish Hamilton/Cape, 1975, 3 July 1969.
5. Castle, *Diaries 1964–1970*, 22 July 1969.
6. Morgan, *Crossman: Diaries 1968–1970*, 31 Dec. 1969.
7. Quoted in Sarah Boston, *Women Workers and Trade Unions*, Lawrence & Wishart, 1987.
8. 'I told Denis Barnes we must discuss and clear up our own ideas about what should be done about Donovan and if necessary propose our own sanctions. His eyebrows shot up at this and he said "Good!"' Castle, *Diaries 1964–1970*, 22 June 1968.
9. Betty Lockwood, then Labour's National Women's Officer, later first chair of the Equal Opportunities Commission and a Labour peer.
10. Castle, *Diaries 1964–1970*, 18 Oct. 1968.
11. Castle, *Diaries 1964–1970*, 4 Sept. 1969.
12. Morgan, *Crossman: Diaries 1968–1970*, 12 Oct. 1969.
13. Ibid.
14. Barbara Castle, *Sylvia and Christabel Pankhurst*, Penguin, 1987.
15. In Sara Maitland (ed.), *Very Heaven: Looking Back at the 1960s*, Virago, 1988.
16. Maitland, *Very Heavan*.
17. *Observer*, Oct. 1969.
18. BAC papers.
19. BAC papers.
20. BAC papers.
21. Morgan, *Crossman: Diaries 1968–1970*, 5 May 1968.
22. De'Ath, *Barbara Castle*.
23. Ibid.
24. Castle, *Diaries 1964–1970*, 17 Apr. 1970.
25. Jennie Hall, interview with the author.
26. Crossman, however, was always in arrears, so Jennie was not typing up rival versions of the same day.
27. Her successor Jack Straw keeps them up.
28. Tom Taylor in De'Ath, *Barbara Castle*.
29. Janet Morgan (ed.), *Richard Crossman: The Diaries of a Cabinet Minister 1964–1966*, Hamish Hamilton/Cape, 1975, 5 Nov. 1965.

16 Yesterday's Woman

1. Macmillan, 1970.
2. BAC unpublished diaries, 18 June 1970.
3. BAC unpublished diaries, 16 June 1970.
4. Cecil King, *The Cecil King Diary 1970–74*, Cape, 1975, 29 June 1970.
5. BAC unpublished diaries, 9 Nov. 1970.
6. Roy Jenkins, *A Life at the Centre*, Macmillan, 1991.
7. BAC unpublished diaries, 10 Nov. 1970.
8. BAC unpublished diaries, 26 Nov. 1970.
9. BAC unpublished diaries, 18 Oct. 1971.
10. Tony Benn was Anthony Wedgwood Benn when he was first elected in 1950. Barbara always referred to him as 'Wedgie'. In 1961 he inherited his father's title (Viscount Stansgate) and had to resign from the Commons. He campaigned to change the law, allowing him to renounce his title, and returned to parliament in 1963. In the sweeping proletarianization of the 1970s, 'Wedgwood' disappeared from his name, a piece of window dressing Barbara refused to acknowledge.
11. A reference to Jenkins.
12. BAC papers.
13. BAC unpublished diaries, 5 Apr. 1971.
14. BAC unpublished diaries, 28 Oct. 1970.
15. BAC unpublished diaries.
16. George Thomson b. 1921, Lord Thomson of Norfolk 1977, Labour MP 1952–72, European Commissioner 1973–7.
17. BAC unpublished diaries, 22 Mar. 1972.
18. BAC unpublished diaries, 24 Mar. 1972.
19. Presumably a reference to the time in 1969 when Wilson tried to persuade Barbara to leave the DEP, as there is no other mention in any other source of her rejecting a more recent job offer.
20. BAC unpublished diaries, 16 Feb. 1978.
21. BAC papers.
22. BAC unpublished diaries.
23. Houghton, like Callaghan, had now done a complete volte-face and they were both now arguing for industrial relations legislation. With justification, Barbara wrote in her diary: 'I can hardly recognise them as the same men who wrecked our IR policy!'
24. BAC unpublished diaries, 17 May 1972.
25. Janet Morgan, (ed.), *Richard Crossman: The Diaries of a Cabinet Minister 1964–1966*, Hamish Hamilton/Cape, 1975, Introduction.
26. BAC unpublished diaries, 25 Sept. 1972.
27. This author's efforts to get an answer from her failed.

28. Their interviews have been an invaluable source for the author.
29. A secretarial allowance had been introduced in 1969. In 1972 it was £1,000.

17   Battling On

1. Hutchinson, 1989, 7 Mar. 1974.
2. Bernard Donoghue, *Prime Minister*, Cape, 1987.
3. Barbara Castle, *The Castle Diaries 1974–1976*, Weidenfeld & Nicholson, 1980, 4 Mar. 74.
4. Castle, *Diaries 1974–1976*, 17 Dec. 1974.
5. Jack Straw, *Tribune*, 10 May 2002.
6. Labour Party Research Department Information Paper No. 9, July 1971.
7. Until the 1980s, when in a rare and short-lived triumph, Labour made the State Earning-Related Pension Scheme (SERPS) a political issue and prevented the Conservatives dismantling it.
8. BAC unpublished diaries.
9. Tony Benn, *Against the Tide, Diaries 1973–1977*, Hutchinson, 1989.
10. His private secretary was Alice Perkins. She and Jack Straw later married.
11. Quoted in Nicolas Timmins, *The Five Giants: A Biography of the Welfare State*, HarperCollins, 1995.
12. Janet Morgan (ed.), *Richard Crossman: The Diaries of a Cabinet Minister 1968–1970*, Hamish Hamilton/Cape, 1975, 12 Oct. 1969. O'Malley also got on well with his Tory opposite number Ken Clarke, with whom he shared a passion for jazz. They used to negotiate aspects of the bill at Ronnie Scott's in Soho.
13. Castle, *Diaries 1974–1976*, 2 July 1974.
14. Castle, *Diaries 1974–1976*, 1 May 1974.
15. An umbrella organization for a wide range of women's organizations which Wilson envisaged using as a sounding board. It is an overlooked source of radical policy ideas.
16. Castle, *Diaries 1974–1976*, 15 Jan. 1975.
17. Castle, *Diaries 1974–1976*, 10 May 1975.
18. Castle, *Diaries 1974–1976*, 21 Jan. 1975.
19. Ibid.
20. Elizabeth Shore was a doctor, Assistant Chief Medical Officer 1977–85 and a senior member of the GMC.
21. A change which has since been made: members of the government no longer sit on the NEC which, as Wilson warned, has been reduced to a body 'competent merely to discuss and to protest'.
22. David Butler and Uwe Kitzinger, *The 1975 Referendum*, Macmillan, 1975.
23. See Butler and Kitzinger, *1975 Referendum*, p. 287.
24. Castle, *Diaries 1974–1976*, 26 Apr. 1975.

25. Butler and Kitzinger, *1975 Referendum*, p. 256.
26. Benn, *Against the Tide*, p. 375.
27. Castle, *Diaries 1974–1976*, 4 June 1975.
28. Castle, *Diaries 1974–1976*, 5 June 1975.

18   Defeat

1. Jack Straw, interview with the author, 2002.
2. She had some justification for her suspicions. Anthony Grabham, the imposing and some felt aptly named doctors' leader, had never believed in a tax-funded NHS.
3. The 1970 party conference passed a resolution to this effect.
4. *Hansard*, 3 May 1946.
5. Barbara Castle, *The Castle Diaries 1974–1976*, Weidenfeld & Nicolson, 1980, 4 Nov. 1974.
6. Norman Warner was given a peerage and a quango to run when Jack Straw became Home Secretary in 1997.
7. In 2002, the view of Jack Straw.
8. BAC papers.
9. BAC papers.
10. Castle, *Diaries 1974–1976*, 27 Nov. 1975.
11. Hilary Wainwright, *Labour: A Tale of Two Parties*, Hogarth Press, 1987.
12. This is why Straw was later such an advocate of the reform of the relationship between party and government.
13. The Royal Commission reported in 1978. Among other things, it found that pay beds were not damaging the NHS significantly.
14. Castle, *Diaries 1974–1976*, 2 Dec. 1975.
15. *David Owen, Personally Speaking*, Kenneth Harris, Weidenfeld & Nicolson, 1987.
16. Tony Benn, *Against the Tide, Diaries 1973–1977*, Hutchinson, 1989.
17. Castle, *Diaries 1974–1976*, 7 Oct. 1975.
18. Castle, *Diaries 1974–1976*, 8 Sept. 1975.
19. Benn, *Diaries 1973–1977*, 11 June 1974.
20. Castle, *Diaries 1974–1976*, 4 Mar. 1976.
21. Benn, *Diaries 1973–1977*, 16 Mar. 1976.
22. Castle, *Diaries 1974–1976*, 8 Apr. 1976.

19   The End of the Affair

1. Jonathan Dimbleby, interview with BAC, Yorkshire Television, 1980.
2. BAC unpublished diaries, 28 Apr. 1976.
3. BAC unpublished diaries, 26 Apr 1976.

4. According to Julian Critchley MP, who spent his whole political career 'looking at the back of my colleagues' heads for signs of intelligence'.

5. BAC unpublished diaries, 27 Apr. 1976.

6. Barbara Castle, *The Castle Diaries 1974–1976*, Weidenfeld & Nicolson, 1980, 8 May 1974.

7. The 'what if' school of contemporary historians likes to ponder a Crosland–Castle 'dream ticket' for the leadership.

8. Callaghan, Labour Party Conference Annual Report, Oct. 1976.

9. BAC unpublished diaries, 28 Apr. 1976.

10. BAC unpublished diaries, 4 May 1976.

11. BAC unpublished diaries, 17 May 1976. However, she regarded the policy committees introduced in the 1990s as completely useless because the NEC no longer had effective power.

12. BAC unpublished diaries, 3 Apr. 1977.

13. BAC unpublished diaries, 15 Dec, 1977.

14. BAC unpublished diaries, 7 Feb. 1977.

15. BAC unpublished diaries, 25 May 1976.

16. BAC unpublished diaries, 22 Sept. 1976.

17. BAC unpublished diaries, 29 Sept. 1976.

18. With thanks to Geoffrey Goodman.

19. BAC unpublished diaries, 17 Nov. 1977.

20. Norman Warner, Barbara's private secretary and close colleague. Unusually, he later became a Labour peer.

21. Castle, *Diaries 1974–1976*, 5 Feb. 1976.

22. Castle, *Diaries 1974–1976*, 12 Feb. 1976.

23. Barrie Penrose and Roger Courtiour, *The Pencourt File*, Secker & Warburg, 1978, p. 32.

24. Penrose and Courtiour, *Pencourt File*, p. 35.

25. Penrose and Courtiour, *Pencourt File*, p. 175.

26. *Daily Mirror* serialization, 31 Jan. 1978.

27. *Hansard*, 27 Feb. 1978.

28. *Hansard*, 6 Mar. 1978.

29. BAC papers.

30. BAC unpublished diaries, 26 Aug. 1976.

31. BAC unpublished diaries, 6 Aug. 1978.

32. Conversation with the author.

33. BAC unpublished diaries, 17 Jan. 1979.

34. Conversation with the author.

35. Castle, *Diaries 1964–1970*, 20 Apr. 1967.

36. BAC papers.

37. BAC unpublished diaries, 20 Mar. 1979.

38. John Evans, interview.

39. *FATW*, p. 523.

40. BAC unpublished diaries, 12 Feb. 1979.
41. BAC papers.
42. BAC unpublished diaries, 3 July 1976.
43. Castle, *Diaries 1974–1976*, 5 Feb. 1975.
44. BAC unpublished diaries, 6 Mar. 1972.
45. Castle, *Diaries 1974–1976*, 13 Oct. 1975.
46. BAC unpublished diaries, 23 Mar. 1977.
47. Castle, *Diaries 1974–1976*, 7 Dec. 1975.

20 Epilogue

1. Professor of International Social Policy at the London School of Economics.
2. John Rentoul, *Tony Blair: Prime Minister*, Little, Brown, 2001.
3. Mary Matalin and James Carville, *All's Fair*, quoted in Rentoul, *Tony Blair*.
4. The Conservative review of SERPS reduced the entitlement of new contributors.
5. Peter Townsend, article in the *Guardian*, 6 May 2002.
6. Labour Party Annual Conference Report, 1996.
7. Although once, when she found a baby rabbit nearly drowned in her lavatory, she did not dare to lift it out as a country woman would have done.
8. BAC unpublished diaries, 28 June 1976.
9. 24 April 24 1932, when about 400 walkers deliberately trespassed in order to highlight their demand to open up the Peak District to the public.
10. *Guardian*, 15 June 1993.
11. Quoted in the *Guardian*, 24 Dec. 2001.

Bibliography

Unpublished Sources

Barbara Castle's papers include Labour Party Annual Conference Reports, 1944–2000; NEC minutes, 1950–79; and minutes of the NEC–TUC liaison committee, 1970–9. They also include much other material available in the public domain – official papers published by HMSO, newspaper cuttings, pamphlets and articles from magazines – as well as cabinet papers that are now available in the Public Record Office.

Published material is clearly identified. Where the source is a cabinet paper smuggled out of her office by Barbara Castle, it falls within the category of 'BAC papers'. Where the source is private correspondence, the information given is as full as possible. The main groups of letters cited are those between Barbara Castle and William Mellor, between Barbara Castle and Mary Hepworth, and between Frank Betts and Mary Hepworth.

General Books

Barnes, D. and Reid E., *Governments and Trade Unions: The British Experience 1945–1979*, Heinemann, 1980
Benn, T., *Parliament, People and Power*, Verso, 1992
Bevan, A., *In Place of Fear*, MacGibbon & Kee, 1952
Brookes, P., *Women at Westminster: An Account of Women in the British Parliament 1918–1966*, Peter Davies, 1967
Buchanan, C., *Traffic in Towns*, Penguin/HMSO, 1964
Butler, D. and Butler, G., *Twentieth-Century British Political Facts*, Macmillan, 2000
– and Kavanagh, D., *The British General Election of February 1974*, Macmillan, 1974
– and Kavanagh, D., *The British Election of October 1974*, Macmillan 1974
– and King, A., *The British General Election of 1964*, Macmillan, 1965
– and King, A., *The British General Election of 1966*, Macmillan, 1966
– and Kitzinger, U., *The 1975 Referendum*, Macmillan, 1976

– and Pinto-Duschinsky, M., *The British General Election of 1970*, Macmillan, 1970

Coote, A. and Campbell, B., *Sweet Freedom: The Struggle for Women's Liberation*, Picador, 1982

Crick, M., *Militant*, Faber and Faber, 1984

Crosland, C. A. R., *The Future of Socialism*, Cape, 1956

Crossman, R., *New Fabian Essays*, Turnstile Press, 1952

Donoghue, B., *Prime Minister*, Cape, 1987

Duff, P., *Left, Left, Left: A Personal Account of Six Protest Campaigns 1945–1965*, Allison & Busby, 1971

Foot, M., *Debts of Honour*, Picador, 1981

Freeman, S. and Penrose, B., *Rinkagate: The Rise and Fall of Jeremy Thorpe*, Bloomsbury, 1996

Gordon Walker, P., *Cabinet*, Cape, 1970

Graves, P., *Labour Women in British Working-Class Politics 1918–1939*, Cambridge University Press, 1994

Harmer, H., *The Labour Party 1900–1998*, Longman, 1999

Harris, R., *The Making of Neil Kinnock*, Faber and Faber, 1984

Haseler, S., *The Gaitskellites: Revisionism in the British Labour Party 1951–1964*, Macmillan, 1969

– *The Tragedy of Labour*, Oxford, Blackwell, 1980

Hatfield, M., *The House the Left Built: Inside Labour Policy-Making 1970–75*

Hennessy, P., *Cabinet*, Blackwell, 1986

– *Whitehall*, Secker & Warburg, 1989

– *Never Again Britain 1945–1951*, Cape, 1992

Hill, D. (ed.), *Tribune 40: The First Forty Years of a Socialist Newspaper*, Quartet Books, 1978

Holmes, M., *The Labour Government 1974–79*, Macmillan, 1985

Howard, A. and West, R., *The Making of the British Prime Minister*, Cape, 1965

Hughes, C. and Wintour, P., *Labour Rebuilt: The New Model Party*, Fourth Estate, 1990

Ingham, B., *Kill the Messenger*, HarperCollins, 1991

Jenkins, M., *Bevanism: Labour's High-Tide*, Spokesman Books, 1979

Jenkins, P., *The Battle of Downing Street*, Charles Knight, 1970

Kavanagh, D. and Seldon, A., *The Powers behind the Prime Minister*, HarperCollins, 1999

Kogan, M. and Kogan, D., *The Battle for the Labour Party*, Kogan Page, 1982

Lapping, B., *The Labour Government 1964–1970*, Penguin, 1978

Maitland, S. (ed.), *Very Heaven: Looking Back at the 1960s*, Virago, 1988

Mann, J., *Woman in Parliament*, Odhams Press, 1962

Marcus, J. (ed.), *The Young Rebecca: Writings of Rebecca West 1911–1917*, Macmillan/ Virago, 1982

Marquand, D., *The Progressive Dilemma: From Lloyd George to Kinnock*, Heinemann, 1991

Mellor, W., *Direct Action*, Leonard Parsons, 1920

Middlemas, K., *Politics in Industrial Society*, André Deutsch, 1979

Middleton, L. (ed.), *Women in the Labour Movement*, Croom Helm, 1977

Miliband, R., *Parliamentary Socialism: A Study in the Politics of Labour*, George Allen & Unwin, 1961

Minkin, L., *The Labour Party Conference: A Study in the Politics of Intra-Party Democracy*, Allen Lane, 1978

Mitchell, A. and Wiener, D., *Last Time: Labour's Lessons from the Sixties*, Bellew, 1997

Morris, W., *The Waters of the Wondrous Isles*, Prior, 1979

Mowat, C., *Britain Between the Wars 1918–1940*, Methuen, 1955

Pelling, H., *A Short History of the Labour Party*, Macmillan, 1982

Phillips, M., *The Divided House: Women at Westminster*, Sidgwick & Jackson, 1980

Pimlott, B., *Labour and the Left in the 1930s*, Cambridge University Press, 1977

Plowden, W., *The Motor Car and Politics 1896–1970*, Bodley Head, 1971

Ponting, C., *Breach of Promise: Labour in Power 1964–1970*, Hamish Hamilton, 1987

Rose, R., and King, A., *The British General Election of 1966*, Macmillan, 1967

Rowbotham, S., *A Century of Women: The History of Women in Britain and the United States*, Viking, 1997

Shaw, E., *Discipline and Discord in the Labour Party*, Manchester University Press, 1987

Skidelsky, R., *Oswald Mosley*, Macmillan, 1975

Taylor, R., *The Fifth Estate: Britain's Unions in the Seventies*, Routledge & Kegan Paul, 1978

Taylor, R., *The TUC from the General Strike to New Unionism*, Palgrave, 2000

Thomas, E. (ed.), *Tribune 21: An Anthology of Literary Contributions to the Tribune during Twenty-One Years*, MacGibbon & Kee, 1958

Timmins, N., *The Five Giants: A Biography of the Welfare State*, HarperCollins, 1995

Verrier, A., *The Road to Zimbabwe 1890–1980*, Cape, 1986

Walter, D., *The Oxford Union: Playground of Power*, Macdonald, 1984

Whitehead, P., *The Writing on the Wall: Britain in the Seventies*, Michael Joseph, 1985

Whiteley, P., *The Labour Party in Crisis*, Methuen, 1983

Young, H., *The Crossman Affair*, Weidenfeld & Nicolson, 1993

Diaries, memoirs, biographies and autobiographies

Benn, T., *Out of the Wilderness: Diaries 1963–1967*, Hutchinson, 1987

– *Office without Power: Diaries 1968–1972*, Hutchinson, 1988

– *Against the Tide: Diaries 1973–1977*, Hutchinson, 1989

– *Years of Hope: Diaries 1940–1962*, Hutchinson, 1994

Brivati, B., *Hugh Gaitskell*, Richard Cohen, 1996

Brown, C., *Fighting Talk: The Biography of John Prescott*, Simon & Schuster, 1997

Brown, G., *In My Way*, Penguin, 1971

Callaghan, J., *Time and Chance*, Collins, 1987

Campbell, J., *Roy Jenkins: A Biography*, Weidenfeld & Nicholson, 1983
– *Nye Bevan and the Mirage of British Socialism*, Weidenfeld & Nicholson, 1987
Castle, B., *The Castle Diaries 1974–1976*, Weidenfeld & Nicholson, 1980
– *The Castle Diaries 1964–1970*, Weidenfeld & Nicolson, 1984
– *Fighting All the Way*, Macmillan, 1993
Charlton, L., *Spark in the Stubble: Colin Morris of Zambia*, Epworth Press, 1969
Chester, L., Linklater, M. and May, D., *Jeremy Thorpe: A Secret Life*, André Deutsch, 1979
Clarke, P., *The Cripps Version: The Life of Sir Stafford Cripps*, Allen Lane, 2002
Cooke, C., *The Life of Richard Stafford Cripps*, Hodder & Stoughton, 1957
Crosland, S., *Tony Crosland*, Cape, 1982
Dalyell, T., *Dick Crossman: A Portrait*, Weidenfeld & Nicholson, 1956
De'Ath, W., *Barbara Castle: A Portrait from Life*, Clifton Books, 1970
Dell, E., *A Strange Eventful History*, HarperCollins, 2000
Foot, M., *Aneurin Bevan: A Biography Vol. 1 1897–1945*, MacGibbon & Kee, 1962
– *Aneurin Bevan: A Biography Vol. 2 1945–1960*, Davis Poynter, 1973
Foot, P., *The Politics of Harold Wilson*, Penguin, 1968
Goodman, A., *Tell Them I'm on My Way*, Chapman & Hall, 1983
Goodman, G., *The Awkward Warrior*, Davis Poynter, 1979
Haines, J., *The Politics of Power*, Cape, 1977
Harris, K., *Attlee*, Weidenfeld & Nicolson, 1982
– *David Owen: Personally Speaking*, Weidenfeld & Nicholson, 1987
Hattersley, R., *Fifty Years On: A Prejudiced History of Britain since the War*, Little, Brown, 1997
Healey, D., *The Time of My Life*, Michael Joseph, 1989
Hoggart, S. and Leigh, D., *Michael Foot: A Portrait*, Hodder & Stoughton, 1981
Hollis, P. and Lee, J., *Jennie Lee: A Life*, Oxford University Press, 1997
Horne, A., *Macmillan, 1957–1986*, Macmillan, 1989
Howard, A., *Crossman: The Pursuit of Power*, Cape, 1990
Jenkins, R., *A Life at the Centre*, Macmillan, 1991
Jones, J., *Union Man*, Collins, 1986
Jones, M., *Michael Foot*, Gollancz, 1994
King, C., *The Cecil King Diary 1965–1970*, Cape, 1975
Mackenzie, N. and Mackenzie, J. (eds), *The Diaries of Beatrice Webb, Vol. 4 1924–1943*, Virago, 1985
Manning, L., *A Life for Education: An Autobiography*, Gollancz, 1970
Marquand, D., *Ramsay MacDonald*, Cape, 1977
Martineau, L., *Barbara Castle: A Biography*, André Deutsch, 2000
Mikardo, I., *Back Bencher*, Weidenfeld & Nicholson, 1988
Morgan, J. (ed.), *Richard Crossman: The Diaries of a Cabinet Minister*, Hamish Hamilson/Cape, 1975: Vol. 1, *Minister of Housing 1964–1966*; Vol. 2, *Lord President of the Council and Leader of the House of Commons 1966–1968*; Vol. 3, *Secretary of State for Social Services 1968–1970*

– *The Backbench Diaries of Richard Crossman*, Hamish Hamilton/Cape, 1981

Morgan, K., *Callaghan: A Life*, Oxford University Press, 1997

Owen, D., *Time to Declare*, Michael Joseph, 1991

Pimlott, B., *Hugh Dalton*, Cape, 1985

– (ed.), *The Political Diary of Hugh Dalton 1918–1940, 1945–1960*, Cape, 1986

– *Harold Wilson*, HarperCollins, 1992

Powell, D., *Tony Benn: A Political Life*, Continuum, 2002

Rentoul, J., *Tony Blair: Prime Minister*, Little, Brown, 2001

Shapley, O., *Broadcasting: A Life: The Autobiography of Olive Shapley*, Scarlet Press, 1996

Wheen, F., *Tom Driberg: His Life and Indiscretions*, Chatto, 1990

Williams, M., *Inside Number Ten*, Weidenfeld & Nicolson, 1972

– *Downing Street in Perspective*, Weidenfeld & Nicolson, 1983

Williams, P., *Hugh Gaitskell*, Oxford University Press, 1982

– (ed.), *The Diaries of Hugh Gaitskell 1945–1956*, Cape, 1983

Wilson, H., *The Labour Government 1964–1970: A Personal Record*, Weidenfeld & Nicolson, 1971

– *Final Term: The Labour Government 1974–76*, Weidenfeld & Nicolson/Michael Joseph, 1979

Ziegler, P., *Wilson: The Authorised Life of Lord Wilson of Rievaulx*, Weidenfeld & Nicolson, 1993

Index

AA 217, 218

Abel Smith, Brian 373, 376, 377, 397, 404

Abyssinia, Italian campaign 50–1

Africa: colonial rule 136–7; Mau Mau 137–40; BC's visits 139, 189, 198; BC's reputation 140–1; East African railway 196; Biafran war 293; *see also* Kenya, South Africa, Southern Rhodesia

aid policies 195, 197, 198–200

Aims of Industry 228

Aitken, Ian 285

Alamein, El (1942), 69, 70

Aldermaston marches 167, 172–3

Allaun, Frank 350

Allen, Alf 436

Allen, Douglas 213

Allen, Sir Roger 154

Allighan, Garry 72, 75

Amalgamated Engineering Union (AEU), 251, 265, 292

Anderson, Janet 335, 355, 370, 452

Animal Rights Campaign 451

Anti-Apartheid Movement 179, 187

Associated Press 95

Atkinson, Norman 234, 254

Attlee, Clement: Labour leadership 62, 104; Cripps relationship 62, 85–6; Deputy Prime Minister 68, 79; Prime Minister 82, 85–6, 88, 104, 106, 216; Bevan relationship 84, 106, 108, 114, 118–19; American loan 89–90; foreign policy 92; advice to Callaghan 423; *Picture Post* interview 98; disbands Bevanites 119; Far East policy 125; attack on Bevanite position 127, 129; defence policy 131–2; resignation 133

Bacon, Alice 76, 120, 171, 178

Balogh, Tommy: Keep Left group 93, 194; on controls 93, 145; *New Statesman* 142; influence on BC 194, 211, 218, 230, 242, 243, 346;

influence on Wilson 194, 230, 242; on Hattersley 268; on prices and incomes policy 278; on trade union relations 353

Banda, Hastings 216

Barnes, Denis: on seamen's strike 246; on pay policy 247, 249, 267; industrial relations policy 271, 289–90; on unemployment 278; Feather contact 314; on TUC agreement 322

Barnes, Susan 209

Bartlett, Vernon 62

Barton, Frank 140

Beaverbrook, Lord 64

Beeching, Dr 217, 220, 221

Beloff, Norah 227, 230, 232

Benn, Caroline 445

Benn, Tony: on Bevan 109; MCF 141; Cyprus issue 157; title 186; transport policy 219; on BC 235, 337, 389; on Wilson government 240; European policy 247, 361, 382, 383, 384, 429; on Woodcock 266; on IR Bill 320; on Wilson and BC 320; relationship with BC 346, 347, 364, 367–8, 376, 406, 412, 415, 417, 441–2; party elections (1970), 347; BC on 354; party strategy 362; supporters 365, 368; leadership of left 366; diaries 371; Industry Secretary 376, 380, 422; European referendum (1975), 382, 383, 387, 389, 390–1, 392, 429; moved to Energy 392, 422; reputation 392; relationship with Wilson 412; *The Bristol Letter* 414; leadership question 417, 442; deputy leadership question 441–2; Alternative Economic Strategy 442

Besant, Annie 326, 334

Bessell, Peter 431

Betts, Annie (Ferrand, mother):, politics 5, 12, 32; appearance 8; marriage 8–9; children 9; relationship with BC 11–12, 15, 16, 21, 40, 60; dressmaking 15, 17, 20, 74; BC's education 20; BC's affair with Mellor 33, 36, 39–40, 49,

Betts, Annie (*cont.*)
  51–2, 60, 66–7; husband's illness 66, 74; in
  Golders Green 181–2; in Ibstone 337; old age
  337, 355, 370, 372; death 437
Betts, Frank (father): politics 5, 6, 31, 32, 105;
  influence on BC 5, 6, 7–8, 17, 21, 40, 406,
  451; career 6–7, 9, 10–11, 12, 30; appearance
  7, 8; mistress 8, 14; marriage 8–9; amateur
  dramatics 10, 17–18; finances 10, 11, 14–15,
  18; editor of *Bradford Pioneer* 12, 14, 16;
  disciples 16–17; BC's education 18, 29–30;
  move to Hyde 30; on BC 29–30, 33–4; BC's
  affair with Mellor 36–7, 39–40, 49, 52; illness
  12, 66, 74, 82; death 82, 181
Betts, Marjorie (sister), *see* McIntosh
Betts, Tristram (Jimmie, brother): birth 9,
  education 9, 15, 16, 23; career 5, 23, 29, 30,
  136, 138, 182; photograph 22; on BC's love
  life 33; on Abyssinia 51; marriages 74, 182;
  drinking 182; financial argument 337
Betts family 5, 10–11
Bevan, Aneurin (Nye): background 45; political
  aims 45, 83, 114–16, 256; trade union policy
  45, 72, 78, 126, 127–8, 162; marriage 50, 74;
  relationship with BC 50, 72–3, 74, 79, 84,
  105, 112, 113, 121–2, 125–6, 131–2, 133, 157,
  164; *Tribune* 54, 68, 71, 72, 83; wartime
  policies 62–3, 68–9, 73, 78, 83; expulsion
  from Labour Party 63; on Soviet non-
  aggression pact 64; Foot's career 64; campaign
  against Churchill 69, 83; on Beveridge report
  70–1; *Why Not Trust the Tories?* 80, 83–4;
  Minister for Health and Housing 84, 88, 106;
  NHS 88, 94, 107, 393–4, 395, 397; Gaitskell
  contest 103–6, 108, 124, 126, 129, 161–2,
  164; Minister of Labour 107–8; resignation
  108–9; NEC election (1951), 110–11;
  Bevanites 111–13, 117–19, 121, 124, 128;
  expulsion issue 114; *In Place of Fear* 114–16,
  148, 289; NEC election (1952), 117–18;
  dissolution of Bevanite group 118–19, 122–3,
  127; in shadow cabinet 119; Yugoslavia policy
  121; Third World policy 124; resignation from
  shadow cabinet 124–5; resignation from NEC
  126–8; party treasurership election 126, 129;
  disarmament policy 130–1, 145–6, 147–8,
  149; leadership election 133–4; in shadow
  cabinet 135; status after 1955 election 133;
  shadow cabinet election (1955), 133; leadership
  election attempt 133–4; shadow colonial
  secretary 135–6; shadow foreign secretary 141,
  150; Yugoslavia policy 144–5; economic
  policy 145; 1957 policy review 149; disavowal
  of unilateralism 150–1; Cyprus policy 152–3;

  157, 158; party reform issues 161–4, 170–1;
  death 164
Beveridge, Sir William 65, 70–1
Beveridge Report 70–3, 80, 373, 374–5
Bevin, Ernest: influence 26, 43, 79, 82, 90;
  taxation policy 27; SSIP 31; Socialist League
  32, 42–3; Mellor's criticisms of 44; Minister of
  Labour 68; on Beveridge report 71; Foreign
  Secretary 85; illness 102, 108
Bing, Geoffrey 117
Birmingham Post 232
Bish, Geoff 389, 420
Blackburn constituency: background and politics
  76–7, 101–2; BC's selection 77–8, 335; 1945
  election 79–81; boundaries 101, 102; 1950
  election 102; IR Bill 300, 307, 341; BC in
  341–2, 418, 436; 1970 election 345; BC's
  retirement 428; Straw selection 428
Blair, Tony: Labour leadership 353, 447, 448–9;
  1997 election 446; Cabinet 256; BC's attack
  on 449, 455
Blue Streak 171
Board of Trade 84–6
Bondfield, Margaret 26, 259
Boothby, Robert 62
Boothroyd, Betty 99, 335
Bottomley, Arthur 201, 335
Boyle, Edward 185
Braddock, Bessie 76, 120, 171
Braddock, Thomas 128
Bradford 12–18, 30
Bradford Girls' Grammar School 14–16, 18
Bradford Pioneer 12, 14, 16, 17, 25, 26, 27
Bradley, Tom 285, 307
Brailsford, H. N., 47
Bratby, John 435
breathalyser 215–16, 345
Bridlington Agreement 272, 321
Briginshaw, Richard 318
British Medical Association (BMA): negotiations
  394; pay beds issue 397, 398, 401, 403–4, 407,
  408; leaked conversations 402; BC's statement
  406; BC ovation 427
British Medical Journal 404
British Railways (BR), 211, 217–18, 221–6
British Steel 272, 302
Brockway, Fenner 46, 141
Brookstone, Esther 397
Brown, George: Khrushchev confrontation 145;
  on defence policy 173; leadership challenge
  177, 178; home affairs 178; Department of
  Economic Affairs 188, 213, 244, 248, 260; aid
  cuts 198; relationship with BC 199; National
  Plan 200; drinking 226, 245; South Africa

Brown, George (*cont.*)
arms policy 238–9, 258; devaluation 247;
Foreign Secretary 248, 357; resignation 251,
253, 257, 269; deputy leadership 254; 1970
election defeat 347
Brown, Gordon 2, 450, 456
Brown, Peter 399
Buchanan, Colin 220
Burgh, John 271, 279–80, 283, 310, 318, 322
Burton, Nancy 20, 21, 23
bus transport nationalization 226
Butler, David 344, 388

Cabinet: MacDonald's 28; war 68–9; Wilson's
187–8, 200–1, 205, 237–9, 258, 260–1;
committees 251, 261; Blair's 256
Cadogan, Sir Alexander 95
Calder, Ritchie 65, 67
Callaghan, James: career 75, 207, 423; social life
96; relationship with BC 102, 198, 236, 286–7,
319, 415, 423–4, 427, 456; Bevan resignation
issue 108; Bevanites 110; support for Ted
Castle 120; Cyprus policy 152–3; leadership
bid (1963), 177; shadow chancellor 178;
Chancellor 188, 198, 199; BR issues 222, 224;
popularity 231; NEC elections 235; South
Africa arms policy 239, 258; Home Secretary
240; Kenyan Asian issue 240; sterling crisis
242, 245, 250; devaluation 247, 250; pay
policy 248, 249, 251, 269; resignation from
Treasury 251; Home Secretary 251; on Wilson
252; deputy leadership question 254; response
to BC's White Paper 285, 287–8, 292;
amendment to White Paper 293–4;
relationship with Wilson 293–4, 299, 301,
319, 411; leadership question 293–4, 306–7,
311, 324, 347–8, 411; response to IR Bill 298,
301, 302, 387; BC's attack on 301; sacked from
inner cabinet 301, 316; campaign against IR
Bill 305, 306, 319; response to Tory IR Bill
353; European policy 358–9, 380, 383, 385,
386, 387, 388; shadow foreign secretary 361;
Foreign Secretary 380, 412; European
referendum (1975), 389, 391; Commonwealth
conference 391; leadership 417; sacks BC
417–18, 440; government 419, 421; leadership
style 423–4; Liberal pact 424; winter of
discontent 324, 436
Campaign for Labour Party Democracy (CLPD),
422
Campaign for Nuclear Disarmament (CND), 147,
172–3, 182, 417
Campaign Group 442

Campbell, Sir Jock (*later* Lord), 193–4, 222–3,
225, 452
Campbell, John 116, 131
car ownership 216–18, 219
Carr, Robert 351, 353
Carter, Evelyn 15, 341
Carter-Ruck, Peter 433–4
Carvel, John 86
Carville, James 449
Castle, Barbara (Betts):
LIFE: family background 5–9; birth 5; schools
9–10, 14–15, 16, 18; amateur dramatics 17;
Oxford 19–25, 29–30; Labour Club 23, 24,
25, 28–9; reports Scarborough conference
(1931), 26–7; unemployment 30; joins
Labour Party 32; affair with Mellor 33,
34–40, 48–9; first job 33, 37, 41–2; Hyde
Labour Party 34; public speaking 34, 37;
move to London 41–2; work for Socialist
League 42–3; journalism 51–2, 56–7, 58,
60, 64, 75, 139–43, 145, 370; parliamentary
hopes 53, 75–6; in Soviet Union 56–7; St
Pancras Borough Council election 59, 60;
war work in Ministry of Food 65; Mellor's
death 66–7; speech on Beveridge report 72;
Ted Castle courtship 73–4; marriage 74–5;
Blackburn selection 77–8; Blackburn
election campaign 79–81; PPS to Cripps
84–5, 98, 234, 335; PPS to Wilson 86–8;
Canadian trip 87–8; maiden speech 89; UN
delegate 94–6; parliamentary style 98–100;
Keeping Left 100; Bevanite position 105,
112, 119, 122–3; election to NEC women's
section (1950), 110; NEC election (1951),
109–11; Tribunite brains trust 116–17; NEC
election (1952), 118; NEC election (1953),
123, 128; on German rearmament 123–4;
Bevan's resignation from shadow cabinet
125–6; attacked on NEC 127; on Bevan's
position 128–9; defence policy 131–2,
145–8, 149–50, 172; shadow cabinet election
attempt (1955), 133; African issues 136–41,
160; travels in 1950s 142–5; unilateralism
149; vice chairman of Labour party 153,
157; Cyprus policies 152–9; party
chairmanship 153, 157, 158, 162, 165; libel
case 159; reform issues 162–4; shadow
minister of works 165; leadership challenge
question 175–6; resignation from shadow
cabinet 177; Profumo affair 180–1; overseas
aid spokesman 184; sister's death 184;
Minister for Overseas Development
187–205, 376; African visits 189, 198; White
Paper (1965), 195, 196, 199, 219, 376;

Castle, Barbara (*cont.*)
Rhodesian issue 202–4, 207; Ministry of
Transport 206–29, 254–6; Transport Bill
217, 226–9, 254, 277, 340; NEC elections
235; prices and incomes policy 246, 251;
sterling policy 249; Cabinet industrial
committee 251; deputy leadership question
254; First Secretary 260, 261; Secretary of
State for Employment and Productivity
229–61, 264–5, 350; prices and incomes
policy 267–70, 273–4, 349; industrial
relations 275–6, 278–9; Sunningdale
conference 277–81, 283–4; White Paper
('In Place of Strife'), 284–94; Commons
speech on White Paper 296, 298; IR Bill
294–324; PLP performance 300;
Mediterranean cruise 309–10, 314, 316;
Chequers dinner (June 1968), 311–14;
resignation question 318, 319–20, 321, 323;
equal pay campaign 326–34, 345; speech on
TUC agreement 326; 1970 election 344–5;
life in opposition 345–7, 349–50, 372;
deputy leadership question 347–8; European
policy 349, 357–61, 380–92, 439; shadow
cabinet election (1970), 349–50; opposition
to Conservative IR Bill 351–3; displaced
from shadow cabinet (1971), 354; elected to
shadow cabinet (1972), 362; voted off
shadow cabinet (1972), 362; stands down
from front bench 362–3; attack on Jenkins
365–6; NEC election (1972), 367; *Barbara
Castle: A Portrait from Life* 369; Secretary of
State at DHSS 371–2, 373–4, 402–3, 410;
SERPS 377–9, 450; Women's National
Commission 379; European referendum
(1975), 388–92; NHS issues 393–411; leg
injury 410; NEC elections 414, 426; sacked
by Callaghan 417–18, 419, 440;
parliamentary reform issue 428;
announcement not to stand again 428;
Thorpe files affair 429–34; mastectomy
435–7; Ted's death 437; mother's death
437; MEP 438, 439–41; on Thatcher
443–5; peerage 446; pensions campaign
448–51; 90th birthday party 450; death 456;
PERSON:
APPEARANCE: arguing 231; in Blackburn 341;
on Canada trip 87; childhood 5, 9; dress
57, 72, 74, 169, 297, 303, 453; electioneering
80; hairdresser 210, 372, 418, 445;
importance of 1–2, 73–4, 418, 437; Labour's
pin-up girl 72; mastectomy 437; New York
trip 95; in old age 1–2, 413–14; at Oxford
22; pony-trekking 231; spectacles 72; star

quality 4, 298, 418; as a teenager 17; trade
union tour 297–8; as Transport Minister
208–10; wig 372;
BELIEFS AND OPINIONS: feminism 38–9, 173,
334–6, 355–6, 367, 379, 443–4, 455;
political views in government 233–5;
socialism 67–8, 249–50, 251, 412, 452–3;
CAREER: Commons performance 98–100, 170,
232, 356, 454; constituency 341–2; isolation
253, 362–3; ministerial character 231,
254–6; speeches 72, 169, 296, 303, 326,
334, 450; status 252–3; strengths 454–5;
turning points 349, 357; voting against party
line 234; working day 340;
CHARACTER: argument 183, 231, 338, 382;
care with money 453–4; courage 169–70;
hard work 356, 454; self-deception 347,
361; talking too much 238; temper 22, 23,
73, 102, 210, 228; toughness 73, 169–70;
vehemence 130, 231, 291, 318;
FINANCES: broadcasting and journalism 96,
370; careful with money 453–4; minister's
salary 241; MP's salary 96, 241, 369;
publication of diaries 438; in wartime 60
HEALTH: appendicitis 77; childlessness 96, 167;
flu 254, 340; leg injury 410; loss of sight
450; mastectomy 435–7; pneumonia 250–1,
340; shingles 77; sinus problems 397;
wisdom tooth problem 124
HOMES: Cadmore End cottage 159, 167, 184;
Cholmondley Court flat 122, 170, 181, 346,
355, 384; flat near British Museum 42; Hell
Corner Farm, Ibstone 184, 241, 267, 336–8,
341, 349, 356, 363, 370, 419, 434, 456
INTERESTS: animal rights 451; camping holidays
97; cooking 338, 339, 445; cycling 96;
dancing 74, 427; dog 167, 172, 337; driving
208, 349, 356–7, 370, 451, 454; gardening
337, 370, 419; walking 96–7, 451–2;
RELATIONSHIPS: affair with Mellor 8, 33,
35–40, 53, 60, 57, 65–8, 115; family 184,
337–8; father's influence 5, 7–8, 15, 17, 21,
40, 406, 451, 454; friendships 183, 252–3,
338, 441; marriage 73–5, 121, 167–9,
338–9, 355; at Oxford 21–2; sexual
independence 166–7; social life 96;
supporters 452; *see also* Bevan, Crossman,
Foot, Wilson;
REPUTATION: 'Battling Barbara' 323; election
campaign (1959), 160–1; housewifely image
80, 99, 119–20, 168–70, 339, 445; IR Bill
323–4; in old age 447–8; popularity 231;
Red Queen caricature 2, 413; rumours 120,

Castle, Barbara (*cont.*)
166–7; star quality 4, 298, 418; status in 1967, 231–2;
WRITINGS: *Are Controls Necessary?* 93; diaries 3, 198, 340–1, 368–9, 419, 438–9; *Fighting All the Way* 103; Pankhurst biography 334; papers 2, 3

Castle, Ted: relationship with BC 4, 73–4, 95–6, 102, 120, 355, 416, 435; career 72, 75, 96, 98, 121, 220, 334, 339, 341, 369, 438; first meeting with BC 72–3; divorce 73; appearance 73; political ambitions 73, 117–18, 120–1, 168, 197, 339; marriage 74–5, 119–20, 124, 166–8, 337–40, 355, 363, 419; BC's career 77, 80, 96–7, 157, 170, 252, 259, 299, 306, 339, 344, 348, 362, 401, 414; social life 91, 96, 182, 184; holidays 97; parents 91, 167; love affairs 120, 166; on Bevan's resignation 125; homes 159, 337; CND marches 172; Profumo affair 180, 181; driving 208; health 289, 355, 366, 369, 370, 372, 434–5; 'In Place of Strife' 289; Mediterranean cruise 309–11, 314; peerage 339, 413, 446; death 437

Cazalet-Kier, Thelma 327
Central African Federation 137, 141, 191, 201
Chamberlain, Neville 58, 62, 63, 68, 69, 293
Charing Cross Hospital 397–8
Charles, Prince 260
Chataway, Christopher 159
child benefit 425, 443
Child Poverty Action Group 345
China, BC's visit (1954), 143, 144
Chipchase, Ethel 331
Churchill, Winston: wartime government 63, 68–9, 83; on Ministry of Labour 265; equal pay issue 327; 1945 election 80; Bevan on 83; BC's attitude to 97, 99; premiership 113; Padmore's career 211; rearmament programme 113–14; on radio 119; resignation 132; reputation 164, 209

Civil Service 107, 211–13, 327
Clarke, Kenneth 377
Clarke, Sir Richard 89
Clements, Dick 364
Cohen, Sir Andrew 137, 191–2, 207
Cohen, Helen, Lady 191
Cole, G. D. H., 29, 31, 32, 43
Cole, Margaret 31, 49
Commission for Industrial Relations (CIR), 281, 283, 285, 290, 295
Common Agricultural Policy 380, 441
Communist Party: at Oxford 28; BC's attitude 28; relationship with Labour Party 43, 54, 127–8; United Front 46, 50, 51, 54

Confederation of British Industry (CBI): on strikes 250, 305; industrial relations policy 272; BC's White Paper 286; equal pay issue 328, 331
Confederation of Health Service Employees (COHSE), 396, 397, 399, 405
Conservative Party: Bevan on 80, 83–4, 106; after Suez 148; Cyprus policy 152; Profumo affair 181; denationalization 216; industrial relations policy 270, 277, 284, 350, 351, 366; equal pay policy 327; Thatcher leadership 443–5

Cook, Tom 87
Co-operative movement 47
cotton industry 77, 101
Courtiour, Roger 431–4
Cousins, Frank: Crossman on 151; unilateralist position 173, 174, 176; Ministry of Technology 188; aid cuts issue 198; resignation 227, 235, 245, 246, 247, 267; relationship with BC 233, 267, 427; on incomes 243; TGWU 243, 265; industrial relations White Paper 285, 286
Cousins, Nance 427
Craigie, Jill 96, 367, 417
Cripps, Isobel, Lady 43, 53, 59
Cripps, Sir Stafford: background 43; Socialist League 43, 47, 54, 55; health 43, 58, 94, 102, 107; political views 43, 83; Mellor relationship 45, 58, 59, 85; United Front campaign 51, 55, 58; relationship with BC 53, 59, 79, 84–5, 234; *Tribune* 54–5, 56, 58; Labour expulsion 62–3; ambassador to Moscow 68; 1945 election 83; Board of Trade 84–6; Chancellor 86, 90, 92, 94; resignation 107
Crosland, Anthony: *The Future of Socialism* 148, 221; on Labour party reform 173; in Wilson's Cabinet 205; marriage 209; on NEC 235; relationship with BC 236; Foreign Secretary 423; death 423
Crossman, Anne 170, 309, 311, 369
Crossman, Richard (Dick): background 90–1; relationship with BC 90–1, 149, 150, 151–2, 165, 167, 170, 179, 184, 235, 259–60, 262–3, 309–11, 347, 354–5, 362, 368; political views 91; foreign policy debate 91–2; social life 96; *Keeping Left* 100; on Gaitskell 104–5; career 109, 114, 116, 260, 301, 363; Bevan relationship 111, 112–14, 115, 123, 125–6; Tribunite brains trust 117; NEC elections 118; support for Ted Castle 120; wife Zita's death 121, 184, 395, 396; on Bevan–BC relations 122; Wilson relationship 122–3, 125, 252, 258–9, 262, 350; defence policy 131–2, 146, 147, 149, 151, 173; shadow cabinet election

Crossman, Richard (*cont.*)
attempt 133; pensions scheme 135, 151, 375, 451; African issues 137, 239; journalism 141–2; on *Industry and Society* 149; on nationalization 151; on 1959 election 161; Gaitskell leadership issue 174, 175, 176–7; Wilson's leadership campaign 175, 177; shadow science minister 178; Profumo affair 180; Minister of Housing 188, 205, 220, 342; on BC and Rhodesian UDI 202, 204; on Transport Ministry 206; Transport Bill 228; on BC 233, 246, 262, 326, 333, 337, 363; stands down from NEC 235; South Africa arms policy 239; Leader of the House 240; European policy 247; response to BC's White Paper 287–9, 290, 292, 294; parliamentary reform bill 298, 312; on IR Bill 298–9; attack on Callaghan 301; Mediterranean cruise 309–11; BC's resignation question 318, 322; on Wilson 320; equal pay issue 331, 332, 333; diaries 340–1, 368–9, 438–9; *New Statesman* 346, 355, 363, 368; pay policy 394; leadership election (1970), 347, 349; DHSS 373; on O'Malley 377; death 368
Crossman, Zita 91, 121, 184, 395
Cryer, Anne 454–5
Cudlipp, Hugh 142
Cudlipp, Percy 66
Cunningham, Sir Charles 212
Curran, Sir Charles 433
Cutliffe, Katie 158, 159
Cyprus 152–9

Daily Express 33, 64, 316, 331, 402, 404, 427
Daily Herald 8, 34, 35, 39, 51, 54, 65, 66, 99, 155–6, 181
Daily Mail 157, 158, 339, 397, 402, 409
Daily Mirror 72, 75, 139, 142, 149, 175, 231, 291, 322, 339, 359, 430, 432
Daily Sketch 157
Daily Telegraph 157, 197, 254, 405
Dalton, Hugh: background 44; influence 44, 82–3, 90, 102, 104, 111; on Socialist League 55; rearmament campaign 63; Chancellor 86, 89, 92; resignation 86; National Land Fund 97; relationship with BC 98, 452; on Wilson 110; off NEC 118; on Castles 120; on Bevan– BC relationship 122; German rearmament issue 123; Bevanite information channel 130
Davies, John 270
Dawson, Violet 329
de Freitas, Geoffrey 96
de Gaulle, Charles 357
Deakin, Arthur 126, 129, 131

De'ath, Wilfred 369
deflation 192, 232, 241–2, 243, 247–8, 422
Dell, Edmund 275, 404
demobilization 89
Derer, Vladimir 422
devaluation: (1948), 94, 192; (1967), 224, 239, 250
Devonshire, Duke of 323
Dickinson, Peter 225
Djilas, Mlovan 145
Dobb, Maurice 23
Doctors' and Dentists' Review Body 400, 404
Donnelly, Desmond 130
Donoughue, Bernard 371
Donovan, Lord 271
Donovan Commission/Report 271–3, 274, 276, 277, 279–81, 287, 293
Douglas Home, Sir Alec 186
Driberg, Tom: journalism 32–3; political career 111, 165, 188, 232; reputation 119; African policies 137; Wright story 336
Dub?ek, Alexander 313
Dulles, John Foster 124
Durham Miners' Gala (1953), 120, 256

Economic Affairs, Department of (DEA), 213, 244, 248, 258–9, 260
Economic Brief 274
Economist 197, 227, 230, 269, 278, 288, 294, 325
Eddie, George 77–8, 101–2, 344
Eden, Anthony 125, 132
Edwards, John 78, 86, 102
elections, general: (1929), 28, 50; (1931), 28; (1935), 50, 52; (1945), 79–81, 82; (1950), 102, 103–4, 106; (1951), 111; (1955), 132–3, 342; (1959), 161; (1964), 186–7; (1966), 214, 230, 232–3; (1970), 343, 344–5; (February 1974), 371; (October 1974), 380, 400; (1979), 437; (1983), 446; (1987), 161, 446; (1997), 446
Elizabeth II, Queen 119, 210, 260, 416
Employment and Productivity, Department of (DEP), 259–61, 328, 350
Ennals, David 204, 425, 426, 432
Eno, J. C., 43
Enright, Derek 441
Eoka 154, 158
Equal Opportunities Commission 443
equal pay 326–34, 345, 443
Equal Pay Act 333
Errington, Sir Lance 376
Europe: EEC application 237; Labour policy 349, 357, 360–1, 380–1, 443; BC's position 349, 357–60, 381–2, 442–3; Wilson's position 358–9, 381–2; referendum 361, 380–92;

Europe (*cont.*)
  renegotiations 380, 381, 383; BC as MEP 438, 439–41, 443
European Commission 429
European Parliament 429–30, 435, 438, 439–43
Evans, Harold 368, 439
Evening Standard 64, 97, 160, 256
Everage, Dame Edna 168
Everyman's 58

Fabian Society: BC's position 60, 75, 190, 352; Wilson's position 75; Jimmie's work 136; African issues 137; overseas development issues 190, 195
Falkender, Lady, *see* Williams, Marcia
Faringdon, Gavin, Lord 112, 117, 452
Fay, Stephen 273
Feather, Vic: on Frank Betts 14, 16; *Bradford Pioneer* 14, 16; appearance 16; relationship with BC 16, 26, 290, 303, 345; TUC leadership 276, 290–1, 304; response to industrial relations legislation 295–6, 304, 353; 'Programme for Action' 302, 308, 310, 312; Jones relationship 305, 306; Callaghan–Houghton relationship 306; Wilson meetings 307, 310, 312–13, 317, 320; Croydon congress 314–15; on BC 324; Benn meeting 325; quoted 325
Ferrand, Annie, *see* Betts
Ferrand, Grandma 8
Field, Frank 452
Financial Times 223, 227, 230, 291, 298, 325
Fisher, Alan 397
Fisher, Nigel 335
Fleming, Ann 167
Foley, Charles 155, 159
Foot, Sir Hugh 152–3, 154, 155, 159
Foot, Michael: career 52, 64, 142, 233–4, 241, 349–50, 367, 390, 411; relationship with BC 52–3, 58, 64, 66, 208, 233–4, 349–50, 360, 362, 363, 367, 393, 411–12, 414–15, 417–18, 454; *Tribune* 54, 56, 58, 84, 117, 415; Bevan relationship 64, 84, 108, 114, 115, 118–19, 121, 126, 132, 150; *Keep Left* 92; social life 96; *Keeping Left* 100; unilateralism issue 150; opposition to Gaitskell 171; Aldermaston marches 172; Gaitskell resignation call 173; biography of Wilson 187; Wilson government 188; on Transport Bill 227; BC on 231; Tribune group 234; on IR Bill 297; BC's attack on 301; trade union relations 305, 353; parliamentary reform issue 312; on Wilson government 345–6; party leadership election (1970), 348; Commons performance 356;

influence 366, 367; Crossman's literary executor 369; Employment Secretary 372, 393, 414–15; European policy 382, 383, 384, 385, 386–7, 390, 392; NHS issues 407; leadership campaign 417; relationship with Callaghan 419; Lords reform issue 428; on BC's diaries 439; party leadership 441, 446; at BC's 90th birthday party 456
Foot, Paul 235–6
Ford Motor Company 292–3, 302, 305–6, 328
Forte, Sir Charles 309, 318, 452
Foster, Christopher: career 211, 268, 270; press leak 211–12; influence 213, 220; on Humber bridge 214; on 'social cost' 218; on BR management 222; Parker issue 223, 225, 228, 268; on Marsh 228; on BC 255
Foyle, Christina 288
Fraser, John 281, 296
Fraser, Tom 205, 207–8, 212, 214, 219
Freeman, John: Bevan's resignation 108; resignation 108, 114, 115, 142; Bevanite strategies 111, 119, 121, 125–6; *New Statesman* 142, 166; relationship with BC 166, 188–9
Fulton Commission 211

Gaitskell, Hugh: career 75, 90, 107; relationship with BC 86, 157, 158, 165, 170–1; on Wilson 86–7; devaluation issue 94; Bevan contest 103–6, 106–9, 118, 132; budget 107–8, 114; support for Ted Castle 120; party treasurership 126, 129; party leadership 133–4, 145–6; leadership style 135; Suez 141; defence policy 146–7, 151, 173–4; policy review 148; Cyprus policy 157, 158; response to 1959 election defeat 161–4; party reform issues 161–4, 170–1, 174; affair with Ann Fleming 167; wins no confidence vote 173; leadership issue 174–7; immigration policy 240; last illness 394; death 177
Galsworthy, John 10, 17
General and Municipal Workers' Union 126, 330
George V, King 44
George VI, King 82
Germany, rearmament issue 123–4, 128, 171
Giles, Frank 368
Girling dispute (1968), 277, 280–1, 284
Golding, John 362
Gollancz, Victor 49, 55, 57, 58, 64
Goodman, Arnold 408–9, 412, 425
Goodman, Geoffrey 150, 322
Gormley, Joe 293
Grabham, Anthony 397, 407, 408, 409
Graham, Andrew 290
Grant, John 316

Greater London Council (GLC) 220, 340, 341, 437

Greater Manchester North constituency 439–40

Greene, Sid 256

Greenwood, Anthony (Tony): bomb issue 131–2, 147; Gaitskell leadership question 174; leadership challenge 175–6; Colonial Office 188

Greenwood, Arthur 126

Griffiths, Jim 111

Griffiths-Jones, Eric 140

Grivas, Colonel George 154, 158

Grocer, the 60, 64

Guardian 208, 211–12, 265, 285, 288, 291, 303, 318, 325, 362, 385, 391, 405

Gunn, John 209

Gunter, Ray: Raymond friendship 222, 264; South African arms policy 239; Minister of Labour 245, 259, 264, 271; incomes policy 245, 248, 249; on BC 261, 264, 335; Minister for Power 264; resignation 264, 269; equal pay issue 328

Haines, Joe 321, 323, 430, 433, 434

Haire, Norman 24

Hall, Chris 197–8, 209, 210, 268, 340

Hall, Jennie 197, 340

Hamilton, Mary Agnes 76

Hardie, Keir 13

Harman, Harriet 455

Hart, Judith: Lanarkshire seat 179; secretary,183; response to BC's White Paper 288, 289, 290; European referendum 382, 384; demotion by Wilson 392, 418; industrial strategy 422

Hatch, John 153

Hattersley, Roy: BC's junior minister 268, 277; at Sunningdale 277, 283; on industrial relations 283–4; 'In Place of Strife' debate 293; IR Bill 307; Jenkins relationship 307, 361; code names 310; Education spokesman 361; deputy leadership 446

Hayward, Ron 386

Hazlitt, William 5

Healey, Denis: on Communists 28; career 75, 301, 346; Rhodesian policy 202; in Wilson Cabinet 205, 206; South Africa arms policy 238–9, 258; ministers 255; relationship with BC 262, 417, 423, 441–2; life in opposition 346; shadow chancellor 361; on trade unions 364; Chancellor 374, 376, 412, 421; NHS issues 405; deflation 422, 423; child benefit issue 425–6; winter of discontent 436; deputy leadership 441–2

Healey, Edna 405

Health and Housing, Ministry of 84, 88, 106–7

Health and Social Security, Department of (DHSS), 372, 402–3, 410, 412, 429, 431–3

Heath, Edward: reputation 206; industrial relations policy 284, 309; trade union relations 308; government 357; European policy 358, 360, 391; 1974 election 371; Thorpe case 430

Heffer, Eric 234, 362

Helsby, Sir Lawrence 212

Henderson, Arthur 27, 48, 76

Hepworth, Mary 17, 21, 22, 29, 30, 33

'Herculaneum, Treaty of' 314, 316

Heron, Conrad 271, 305, 311, 314, 321–2, 330

Hinton, Mark 380

Hinton, Rachel 391

Hinton, Sonya (McIntosh, niece), 80, 182, 338, 369, 380

Hitler, Adolf 45, 51, 61, 63

Ho Chi Minh 124

Hogg, Quintin 62

Hollis, Patricia 2

Hore-Belisha, Leslie 207

Horrabin, Frank 31, 47

Hospital Consultants and Specialists Association 398

Houghton, Douglas: career 287, 353, 363; Callaghan relationship 287, 294; IR Bill 301, 305, 306, 318, 319

Houlston, Freda 22

Houston Post 95

Howard, Anthony 171, 187

Howe, Sir Geoffrey 450

Hughes, William 'Billy' 88

Hull, by-election (1966), 214

Humber Bridge 214

Hume, Basil 342

Hutchison, Lester 128

Hyde 30–1, 41, 53, 440

immigration 199, 240, 342

import controls 192–3, 421

'In Place of Strife': title 115, 289; BC's doubts 289–90; Wilson's position 290, 296–7, 300–1, 304, 325, 349; TUC position 290–1, 295, 302–3, 304, 307–8; publication 291; media response 291; prices and income policy 292; NEC rejection 293, 387; Callaghan's position 293–4, 301–2, 306–7, 387; strike ballot question 294, 298; legislation timetable 294–6, 298–9, 306; BC's Commons speech 296, 298; BC's campaign 297–300; negotiations 298, 304, 305, 317–18; Jones–Scanlon position 304–6; aftermath 324, 325, 331, 332, 344; damage to BC's reputation 325, 347, 348, 350,

'In Place of Strife' (*cont.*)
367, 412; BC's presentation 352; *see also* Industrial Relations Bill (Labour)
Independent Hospitals' Group 408
Independent Labour Party (ILP): Betts membership 6; in Bradford 13, 17–18; membership 13, 46; political stance 13–14, 25, 26, 346; Guild of Youth 16, 17; Labour Party relations 27–8, 31–2; disaffiliation 31–2, 46; United Front issue 53–4
India, BC's visit 198
Industrial Relations Bill (Conservative), 351–3, 366
Industrial Relations Bill (Labour): timetable 294–6, 298–9, 306; BC's Commons speech 296, 298; Wilson's position 296–7, 300–1, 308–9, 316–17, 322–3, 324; TUC position 302–3, 304, 307–8, 310, 314–15, 317, 321–2; Callaghan's position 301–2, 306–7, 319, 324; Jones–Scanlon position 304–6, 310; Chequers meeting 310, 311–14; penal clauses 317, 318–19, 320; printed 317; Cabinet discussions 319–20
Industry and Society 149, 150, 151, 156
inflation 344
Ingham, Bernard 265, 278, 279, 290, 316, 324
Inland Revenue Staff Federation 353
Institute for Fiscal Studies 379
International Labour Organization (ILO), 331
International Monetary Fund (IMF), 292, 421, 436
It Need Not Happen 124–5
Ivanov, Eugene 179

Jameson, Storm 49, 69
Jay, Douglas 94, 161, 375
Jay, Margaret 456
Jay, Peter 250
Jeger, Lena 329
Jenkins, Clive 390
Jenkins, Peter 211, 286, 289, 304, 389
Jenkins, Roy: relationship with BC 3, 236, 259–60, 262, 263, 270, 295, 309, 354, 368, 382, 417; career 75, 301; on Bevan 105; opposition to Bevanites 105, 110; on Wilson 109; *Tribune* 117; on election defeat (1959), 161; in Wilson cabinet 205, 206; Home Secretary (1965), 212, 213, 345; on road safety legislation 215; Chancellor 251, 268, 285; incomes policy 251; first budget 257–8, 263; prices and incomes policy 269, 270, 278; mini-budget (1968), 284; response to BC's White Paper 285, 292, 294; home 295; supporters 298, 307, 316, 348, 361, 389; IR Bill policy

307, 308, 309, 316, 317, 320, 324; on BC's cruise 310; reputation 324; equal pay issue 329, 331, 332; working day 340; trade deficit 343, 345; leadership question 347–8, 358, 365; deputy leadership 348, 359–60, 361; on BC's industrial relations policy 351; European policy 357–8, 359–61; resignation from shadow cabinet 361; relationship with Bennites 365; speeches (1973), 365; Home Secretary (1974), 372, 412; European referendum (1975), 380, 386, 387, 390
John O'London's 99
Johnson, Bill 224
Johnson, Lyndon B., 200
Jones, Aubrey 270, 281
Jones, Glyn 30
Jones, Jack: pay policy 251; TGWU leadership 265, 304, 421; response to White Paper 286, 293, 304–5; TUC 'Programme for Action' 302, 303, 310; response to IR Bill 304–5, 307; opinion of Feather 305, 306; Wilson relationship 305; relationship with BC 305, 333, 353, 367, 427; Wilson meetings 310, 312–13, 321; new left relationship 351; industrial relations policy 366; Foot relationship 366, 367; European policy 382, 390; Mikardo relationship 427; pensions issue 450
Jones, J. D., 213
Joseph, Sir Keith 374, 376
Journal of Transport Economics and Politics 227
Jowett, Fred 14

Kaldor, Nicolas 421
Karamanlis, Konstantinos 154
Kaufman, Gerald 348, 446, 447
Keeler, Christine 179–81
Keep Left 92, 100, 149
Keep Left group 92, 93, 96, 99, 106, 109
Keeping Left 100–1, 110
Kenya: Mau Mau 137–40; BC's visit 139; Hola massacre 160, 165, 170; Kenyan Asians 240
Kenyatta, Jomo 240
Kerby, Henry 180
Keynes, Maynard 75, 89, 257, 421
Khama, Seretse 137
Khrushchev, Nikita 145, 147, 149, 341
Kichina, Kamau 138–9
King, Cecil 257, 264, 322, 324, 348
Kingdom, Leonard 397
Kinnock, Neil 181, 417, 427, 442, 446, 448
Kitzinger, Uwe 388
Klein, Rudolf 427
Korean War 106, 108, 143

Labour, Ministry of: wartime role 264; Bevan's position 107; status 244, 265; prices and incomes policy 245, 264; offered to BC 259, 260; Donovan Commission 280; minimum wage study 334

Labour Monthly 128

Labour Party: ILP relations 13, 27–8, 31–2, 46; collapse of government (1931), 25; conference (1931), 26; trade union block vote 26, 78–9, 110, 366, 450; women's representation 38–9, 76; conference (1932), 44; conference (1933), 44; conference (1934), 47; conference (1938), 61; conferences (1942, 1943), 72; voting system 78–9; membership 79; conference (1944), 83; election victory (1945), 81, 82–3; Attlee government 345; election (1950), 102, 103, 106; Bevan–Gaitskell clash 103–6; conference (1950), 116; conference (1951), 104, 110, 116; conference (1952), 117–18; conference (1953), 122–3, 128; conference (1954), 129; Gaitskell leadership 135; Clause 4, 135, 161, 172, 175, 178, 448; nuclear policy 146; reform issues 161–4; conference (1959), 162–4, 165, 181, 189; constitutional reform question 174; conference (1960), 174–5, 176; conference (1961), 177; conference (1962), 178; conference (1963), 189–90; conference (1967), 232; Wilson governments 235–40, 344–5, 399, 420–1; conference (1968), 274, 278; in opposition (1970), 350–1; European policy 357–61; conference (1971), 360; European referendum (1975), 380–92; Callaghan leadership 417, 423–4; conference (1976), 426; EU relations 440–1; Foot leadership 441; conference (1981), 442; Kinnock leadership 446; New Labour 447, 448–9, 452; conference (1996), 450

Laing, R. D., 236

Lancashire Evening Telegraph 300

Lane, Geoffrey 293

Lansbury, George 31, 68

Laski, Harold 79

Lawrence, Susan 34

Lawson, Nigel 379

Leach, William 13–14

League Against Cruel Sports 451

League of Nations 25, 35, 47–8, 50–1

Leapman, Michael 355

Lee, Jennie: biography 2; Frank Wise relationship 32, 50, 67, 74; Bevan relationship 45, 49–50, 64, 74, 121, 151–2; relationship with BC 50, 67, 74, 84, 123, 164, 172, 183, 443; Bristol by-election 71; *Tribune* 84, 117; Bevan's resignation 108; Yugoslavia policy 144–5; on *Industry and Society* 149; Bevan's death 164,

183; reform issues 172; successor 179; 1970 election defeat 347

Left Book Club 55, 58, 62

Lend-Lease 88–9

Lennox-Boyd, Alan 137–40, 159, 160, 165, 192

Lestor, Joan 301, 335, 384

Lever, Eric 300

Lever, Harold 346, 405

Levy, Benn 163

Liberal Party 13, 424, 429, 430

Lloyd George, David 70

Lloyd George, Megan 98

Loughlin, Dame Anne 327

Low (cartoonist), 133, 308

Luxemburg, Rosa 39

Lyttelton, Oliver 137

MacArthur, Douglas 106

McCarthy, Bill 279, 281–2, 283

Macaulay, Sarah 2

MacDonald, Ramsay: Labour government 25, 266, 314; National Government 25–6, 42; expulsion from Labour Party 27, 311; devaluation 28; deposed from Oxford Labour Club presidency 29; Cripps relationship 42

McIntosh, Alistair (brother-in-law), 182

McIntosh, Hugh (nephew), 172, 182, 338

McIntosh, Marjorie (Betts, sister): birth 9; education 8, 9, 10, 15, 16; career 5, 30, 60, 182, 184–5; photograph 22; children 53, 60, 74, 80, 182, 337; relationship with BC 66, 67, 80, 183–4, 241; death 184–5

McIntosh, Philippa (niece), 182, 338

McIntosh, Sonya, *see* Hinton

MacLeod, Iain 296

Macmillan, Douglas 223

Macmillan, Harold: Cripps relationship 62; 'Wind of Change' speech 136; Gaitskell's opposition 148; Cyprus policy 153, 158; on Hola massacre 160; Cabinet reshuffle 179; Profumo affair 179, 180; retirement 186

Macmillan, Margaret 13

Macpherson, Hugh 363

Mail on Sunday 434

Mair, Janet 65

Maisky, Madame 49

Major, John 447

Makarios, Archbishop 153–9

Mallalieu, Ann, Lady 451

Malta 196

Mandelson, Peter 210

Manifesto Group 362

Manning, Leah 98

Margaret, Princess 431

Marples, Ernest 210
Marsh, Richard 228–9, 254, 286
Marshall Plan 91
Martin, Kingsley 142
Martin, Roy 102
Mason, Jim 77, 307
Matthews, Dennis 143
Matthews, Jim 156
Mau Mau 137–40, 160
Maxton, Jimmy 13, 27, 32, 46, 77
May Day Manifesto 236
Maynard, Joan 364–5
Melchett, Lord 224
Mellish, Bob 299, 301, 316–17, 319, 376, 409
Mellor, Edna: character 34–5; finances 35, 52;
    relationship with husband 34–7, 40, 48–9, 52,
    65–6; son 35, 42, 66; divorce issue 36–7, 42,
    49, 52; wartime home 65; husband's death 66
Mellor, Ronald 35, 42, 66
Mellor, William: career 31, 34, 51–2, 58–9, 66,
    77; SSIP 31, 32; appearance 32, 35;
    relationship with BC 33, 35–40, 53, 57, 60,
    65–6, 115; marriage 33, 34–5, 40, 48–9, 64,
    65–6; *Direct Action* 34, 41; Socialist League
    44–6, 47–8, 51, 54–5, 57; health 45, 66;
    Enfield campaign 47, 50; social life 49; United
    Front issue 46, 51, 55, 63; *Tribune* 54, 58;
    dismissal by Cripps 58; death 66–8; influence
    221, 452
Menon, Krishna 67
Metropolitan Water Board 64, 79
Mikardo, Ian: nationalization resolution 83; *Keep
    Left* 92; NEC election (1951), 111; Tribunite
    brains trust 116–17; Summerskill attack on
    127; Gaitskell on 132; shadow cabinet attempt
    133; CND 147; opposition to Gaitskell 171;
    Gaitskell resignation call 173; Wilson
    government 188; NEC election (1967), 232;
    relationship with BC 234, 266–7, 414; Tribune
    group 234; on Wilson's attack on left 246; on
    incomes policy 266–7, 273; on Wilson
    government 345–6; on trade unions 364;
    European policy 384, 385, 387, 388; industrial
    strategy 422, 427
Mills, John Platts 128
Mintoff, Dom 196
Mitchison, Dick 49, 124, 167
Mitchison, Naomi 49–50, 124, 167
Morley, Agnes Headlam 29
Morning Star 318
Morris, Colin 140, 141, 195
Morris, John 212, 219, 223, 253, 254, 255
Morris, William 7, 12, 115
Morrison, Herbert: Minister of Supply 64;

Beveridge report 71; support for BC 79;
    influence 83, 90, 111, 119; affair with 'Red'
    Ellen 88; on 1950 election 106; Foreign
    Secretary 108; Ted Castle relationship 117; off
    NEC 118; deputy leadership 119; Bevan
    dispute 127; leadership election attempt 134
Moss, Stirling 215
Mountbatten, Lord 257
Movement for Colonial Freedom (MCF), 137,
    141, 152, 157, 179, 187
Mowlam, Mo 455
Mozambique 202
Munby, Denys 224, 227
Munich Agreement 58, 61
Murdoch, Rupert 348
Murray, Gilbert 6–7, 14, 15

Nairn, Tom 246
Nairne, Sir Patrick 406
National Board for Prices and Incomes 244, 245,
    265, 278
National Economic Development Council 266
National Executive: ILP relations 27; women's
    representation issue 39, 76; Communist
    relations 54; Socialist League 54, 55; Cripps'
    memorandum 62; BC's election 109–10;
    election (1952), 117–18; election (1953), 123;
    Gaitskell's position 126; unilateralist issue 150;
    on conference decisions 175; Gaitskell's
    leadership 176; pay policy 248, 278, 364, 366;
    European policy 384–8; government relations
    420–1; PLP relations 422; 'The Next Three
    Years' programme 422–3; BC's last years 426
National Freight Authority 219, 221, 226
National Government (1931), 25, 28, 42
National Health Service (NHS): creation 88, 345;
    Bevan's commitment 94, 107; pay beds 374,
    395–400, 403–8, 416; BC's work 393, 405,
    408–11; budget 394, 402; pay negotiations
    394, 400–1, 403–4, 407; private practice issue
    394–5, 397–8, 403; battle between unions and
    consultants 396, 405–8; BC's speech 427
National Insurance Scheme 100
National Joint Action Campaign Committee for
    Women's Equal Rights 329, 331
National Pensioners' Convention 450
National Referendum Campaign (NRC), 391,
    392
National Service 108, 150
National Union of Mineworkers (NUM), 293
National Union of Public Employees (NUPE),
    303, 394, 395, 397
National Union of Railwaymen(NUR), 249, 263
National Union of Seamen 245, 246, 402

nationalization: BC's beliefs 67; Labour manifesto 83; US attitude 90; Balogh's influence 100; Gaitskell's policy 148; Crossman on 151
Neave, Airey 120–1
Nenni, Pietro 128
'New Economic Strategy' 266
New Left Review 246
New Society 425
New Statesman 90, 105, 108, 127, 142–3, 145, 149, 159, 164, 166, 171, 177, 187, 227, 233, 260, 288, 291, 323, 346, 363, 368, 442
News of the World 188
Newton, Andrew 431
Newton, John 297, 327
Nixon, Richard M., 431
North Atlantic Treaty Organization (NATO), 130, 146, 153, 172, 174, 417
North Sea oil 324
Northern Rhodesia 137
Norway, fall (1940), 34
nuclear weapons 130–1, 145–8, 149–51, 170–4
Nyerere, Julius 196

Observer 227, 230, 338
October Club 28
Olivier, Borg 196
O'Malley, Brian 376–8, 410, 418, 451
OPD (defence and overseas policy committee), 201, 204, 237, 261
Orwell, George 57
Overseas Development, Ministry of 186, 187–92, 207
Owen, David: Health Minister 399; pay beds issue 399–400, 404, 406, 407; contracts negotiations 400, 401; relationship with BC 411, 418
Owen, Robert 97
Oxfam 136, 182, 197
Oxford Union 25, 391, 429

Padley, Walter 161
Padmore, Sir Thomas 211–13, 218, 222, 228, 252, 258
Pakistan, BC's visit 198
Pankhurst, Christabel 334
Pankhurst, Sylvia 334
Pannell, Charles 178, 291
Parker, Peter 222–5, 228, 237, 255, 256, 268
Parmoor, Lord 43
passenger transport authorities 220, 226
pay beds 374, 395–400, 403–8, 416
Pay-beds Bill 420, 425
Peace Pledge Union 35
Pearson, Lord 245

Peart, Fred 294, 302, 335, 383
Penrose, Barrie 431–4
pensions: Beveridge plan 374–5; Crossman's scheme 135, 151, 375, 451; cost of rise 364; Joseph's system 374, 376; BC's work 376–9, 443, 448–51
People, The 168
Philip, Prince 210
Philips, Morgan 159
Picture Post 75, 77, 96, 98, 121, 142
Pimlott, Ben 107, 171, 454
Pinto-Duschinsky, M., 344
Pitt, Terry 361
Plant, Cyril 353
Pollitt, Harry 43, 51, 397
Pollock, Anita 441
Pompidou, Georges 361
Pontefract 9–12
Pontefract and District Girls' High School 9–10
Popular Front 58
Powell, Enoch 312, 380
Prescott, John 246, 440
Prices and Incomes Act (1967), 249
Prices and Incomes Board, *see* National Board for Prices and Incomes
prices and incomes policy 243–6, 251, 267–70
Priestley, J.B., 14
Pritt, D.N., 49
Profumo, John 174–81, 341
Programme for Britain 1973, 366
Proops, Marjorie 339
Punch 225

RAC 217
Radcliffe, Lord 438
Rainsborough, Thomas 100
Raison, Tim 403
Ramblers' Association 96, 268
Raymond, Stanley 221–2, 225, 255, 264
Rentoul, John 448
Rhodesia, *see* Northern Rhodesia, Southern Rhodesia
Richardson, Jo 99, 335
Road Hauliers Association 228
road safety 214–15, 226–7, 345
Road Safety Bill 215
Robens, Alf 128, 223
Robinson, Derek 268
Rogers, Sir Philip 398, 400, 402, 403, 406
Rolls-Royce 330
Rootes 330
Ross, William 204

St Hugh's College, Oxford 18, 20–2, 24
St Pancras Borough Council 59
Samuel Hanson & Sons 33, 41–2
Sandys, Duncan 202
Scamp, Sir Jack 330
Scanlon, Hugh: pay policy 251, 364; AEU leadership 265, 304, 421; response to White Paper 286, 293, 304; TUC 'Programme for Action' 302, 303; Wilson meetings 310, 312–13, 321; new left relationship 351
Scott, Norman 429–34
Seabrook, Jeremy 341
Seers, Dudley 194, 200
SERPS, see State Earnings-Related Pension Scheme
Shapley, Olive 20, 22, 23, 24, 28, 30
Shop Assistants Union 33
Shore, Liz 383, 445
Shore, Peter: in Wilson's Cabinet 238; devaluation issue 247; European policy 247, 382, 383, 387, 391; at DEA 249, 251, 279; on industrial relations 279, 281, 283, 317, 319; relationship with BC 346, 347, 382
Short, Clare 207
Short, Edward 335
Shrimsley, Anthony 231, 233
Silkin, John 299, 300, 382, 383
Silverman, Julius 117
Silverman, Sydney 128
Smith, Douglas 352
Smith, Ian 201, 203–4, 240–1
Smith, John 448–9
Snowden, Philip 26, 28, 77, 266
Snowdon, Lord 431
Social Democratic Party (SDP), 298, 350, 411, 448
social wage 366, 412
Socialist Charter 346
Socialist Commentary 127, 227
Socialist League 32, 42–4, 46–8, 50, 54, 55, 112
Socialist Leaguer 47
Socialist Outlook 128
Society for Socialist Inquiry and Propaganda (SSIP), 31–2
Solley, L. J., 128
Soskice, Frank 188, 205
South Africa: British policy 196; arms issue 200, 238, 239, 258; Southern Rhodesia UDI 202; apartheid 430
South East Asia Treaty Organization (SEATO), 125, 130
Southern Rhodesia: Central African Federation 137, 201; British policy 196, 201–4, 207,

240–1, 345; UDI 202–4, 240, 317; OPD role 237; Tiger talks 241; Fearless talks 317
Soviet Union: BC's visit (1937), 56–7; non-aggression pact with Germany 63; influence on BC 67; BC's visit (1954), 143–4; nuclear policy 147
Spanish Civil War 50, 54, 57, 59
Spanswick, Albert 397
Spectator 228, 278
Spencer, Stanley 143, 144
Stalin, Joseph 63, 143
State Earnings-Related Pension Scheme (SERPS), 377–9, 450, 451
Steel, David 413
Stephenson, Tom 96
sterling crisis 242–3
Stevenson, John 402
Stewart, Michael 248, 319
Stolk, Carlos 95
Strachan, Elaine 183, 369
Strachey, John 57, 86–7
Strauss, George 58
Straw, Jack: political adviser to BC 373, 402, 407, 452; pay beds policy 403; relationship with BC 407, 456; blamed for leak 426; Blackburn selection 428, 433; Thorpe files affair 429, 431, 433–4; vote in deputy leadership election 441–2
strikes: seamen (1966), 245–6, 247; British Steel dispute 272; Girling dispute (1968), 277, 280–1, 284; Ford disputes 292–3, 302, 305–6, 328; Vauxhall 293; unofficial 295, 313, 314, 315, 317, 318; equal pay issue 330; election issue (1970), 344
Styles, Mr 33
Suez crisis 141, 148
Summerskill, Edith 76, 99, 127
Summerskill, Shirley 443
Sun 209, 297, 409
Sunday Mirror 231, 233
Sunday Pictorial 91, 140, 141
Sunday Telegraph 318
Sunday Times 192, 201, 225, 231, 273, 288, 298, 368, 438
Sunningdale conference (1968), 277–9, 280–3, 284
Swingler, Stephen 211, 219, 254

tachograph 227
Tanzania 196
Taverne, Dick 365
taxation: Gaitskell's promise 161; selective employment tax 249
Taylor, Anne 443

Taylor, Tom 101–2, 342, 446
Technical Cooperation, Department of 189, 191
Tennyson, Alfred, Lord 19
Terry, Walter 167
Thatcher, Denis 338
Thatcher, Margaret: character 24, 323, 447, 453, 454; housewife superstar 168, 445; trade union legislation 324; view of women in parliament 335; influence 379; council house sales 426; party leadership 443–4; Prime Minister 444–5; memoirs 4
Thomas, George 252
Thomson, George 359
Thorpe, Jeremy 391, 429–34
Times, The 180, 223, 250, 288, 355, 404, 438
Times of Cyprus 155, 159
Tito 121, 144–5
Town and County Councillor 51–2, 56, 58, 60
Townsend, Peter 439, 447, 450
trade unions: block vote 26, 78–9, 110, 366, 450; Bevan's position 45, 72, 78, 126, 127–8, 129, 162; pay restraint 243–6, 247–8; relationship with Wilson government 245–6; BC's position 258, 264, 273–4; sponsorship of MPs 264, 291, 305; industrial relations 270–1
Trades Union Congress (TUC): Transport House 26; Daily Herald 35; road haulage policy 221; pay policy 243–5, 247–9, 251, 274; Congress (1967), 250; Woodcock's role 265–6, 285, 290; industrial relations 270, 273, 276, 293; BC's White Paper 282–3, 296; Feather's leadership 290–1, 305, 312; 'Programme for Action' 302, 303, 307–9, 312; government relations 304; Scanlon–Jones relations 312–13; Croydon congress 314–15, 317–18; negotiations 317–22, 365; Rule 11, 317, 320–1; equal pay issue 328, 331
Transport, Ministry of: status 206; BC at 206–10, 219–20; civil servants 211–13; Humber bridge 214; road safety 214–16, 226; roads policy 216–19, 227–8; railways 220–6; Transport Bill 226–9
Transport and General Workers' Union (TGWU): leadership 126, 173, 251, 265; sponsorship of MPs 264; Ford dispute 292
Transport Bill 226–9, 253, 254, 277, 340
Transport House 26–7, 72, 122, 368, 388
Trend, Burke 258, 290
Triandefyllides, Michael 155
Tribune 54–6, 58–9, 64, 67, 68–9, 71, 83, 84, 85, 105, 111, 117, 118, 121, 123, 127, 129, 139, 147, 149, 171, 188, 233, 236, 297, 346, 363, 364, 415
Tribune group 234, 266, 345, 348, 349, 442

Truman, Harry S., 82
TUC, see Trades Union Congress
Turner, Muriel, Lady 450

unemployment 28, 30, 42, 100–1
unilateralism 131, 149–51, 173, 174–5
Union of Shop, Distributive and Allied Workers (USDAW), 161, 328
United Front campaign 46, 50, 53–5, 62, 64
United Nations 94–5, 147
United States of America: Lend-Lease 88–9; loan 89–90, 92; Marshall Plan 91, 93; BC's visit (1948), 94–5; McCarthyism 124; Indo–China action 124; nuclear weapons 130, 147; loan negotiations 199; Vietnam 200, 234, 237, 345; BC's lecture tour (1972), 355–6

Varley, Eric 383, 386
Vassall, John 180
Vaughan, Gerard 410
Vaughan, Janet 327
Vauxhall 293
Veil, Simone 441, 443
Veitch, Marion 330
Venture 195
Victory for Socialism 173, 179
Vietnam 200, 234, 237, 258, 345
Voluntary Service Overseas (VSO), 197

Wainwright, Arthur 341
Wainwright, Hilary 406
Walden, Brian 232
Walker, Harold 277
Walker, Patrick Gordon 62, 137, 178, 188, 369
Walker, Peter 227–8
Wallis, Mr 58–9
War on Want 124, 197
Warbey, William 79
Ward, Stephen 180–1
Warner, Norman 402, 407–10, 416, 430
Watkins, Alan 227, 291, 323
Watson, Sam 110, 150, 256
Watt, David 298
Waugh, Auberon 228, 278
Webb, Beatrice 22, 35, 43, 57, 70, 76, 446
Webb, Sidney 22, 57, 76, 446
Weidenfeld & Nicolson 438
Weighell, Sid 243
Weinstock, Arnold 330
Welensky, Roy 137
Wesker, Arnold 236
West, Rebecca 19, 184
Wheen, Francis 165
Whitelaw, William 228

Widgery, Lord 438
Wigg, George 177, 179–81
Wilkinson, 'Red' Ellen 31, 35, 88
Williams, Marcia (*later* Lady Falkender):
  relationship with Walter Terry 167;
  relationship with Wilson 188, 284, 294, 424–5,
  458; on civil servants 213; relationship with BC
  348, 456; Wilson honours list 413; Thorpe files
  affair 430, 432–4
Williams, Raymond 236
Williams, Shirley 224, 252, 358, 362, 380, 382
Wilson, Harold: relationship with BC 3, 86–8,
  122, 129, 178–9, 187–8, 199, 230, 231, 233,
  236, 239, 252, 262–3, 299–300, 311–14, 325,
  336, 345, 348–9, 354, 371, 385–6, 389–90,
  412–13, 416, 424–5; Beveridge assistant 70;
  career 75, 129; junior minister to Cripps 85;
  President of Board of Trade 86, 92; social life
  86–7, 96, 262; 'bonfire of controls' 93;
  devaluation issue (1948), 94; Chancellorship
  question 107; resignation 108, 109, 115, 124;
  Bevanite expulsion issue 114; debating skills
  116; Tribunite brains trust 117; NEC election
  (1952), 118; relationship with Crossman
  122–3, 129–30, 252; NEC election (1953),
  123; *The War on World Poverty* 124; in shadow
  cabinet 125–6, 129; Bevan's position 128–9;
  NEC election (1954), 129; leadership of the left
  129–30, 133; defence policy 131, 173; support
  for Gaitskell 133, 135; shadow chancellor 135,
  177; African issues 137; *New Statesman* 142;
  economic policy 142, 145; policy review 148;
  on Bevan's ambitions 150–1; deputy leadership
  question 171; Gaitskell leadership question
  174, 175; leadership challenge 175–6; shadow
  foreign secretary 177; leadership election
  (1963), 177–8; shadow cabinet 178; leadership
  184, 186, 236; Prime Minister 187; Cabinet
  187–8, 201, 237–9, 258, 260–1, 335; 'White
  Heat' speech 189, 190; economic policy
  192–3, 194, 241–3; aid policy 195, 242;
  Vietnam policy 200, 234; Rhodesian UDI
  202–4, 240–1; Cabinet reshuffle 205; on
  Transport Ministry 206, 207–8; Civil Service
  relations 211, 213; on BR 223; Transport Bill
  228; government 236–40, 257–8, 284, 298;
  South African arms policy 238–9; immigration
  policy 240; prices and incomes policy 243–6,
  249, 267, 269, 271; devaluation 250–1;
  Cabinet restructuring 258–61; response to
  BC's White Paper 284–6, 290; relationship
  with Callaghan 293–4, 299, 301, 306, 311; on
  IR Bill 295–7, 307–9, 317–24; Chief Whip
  replacement 299–300; 'Wilson Must Go'
  campaign 300; codenames for BC's cruise
  310–11; Chequers dinner (June 1968), 311–14;
  TUC relations 314–15; resignation question
  319–20; reputation 324, 325; health 325; offer
  of new department to BC 326, 332; equal pay
  issue 332; doctors' pay issue 394; 1970 election
  343, 345, 346; leadership election (1970),
  347–8; life in opposition 350; European policy
  358–9, 360, 365, 381; offers BC shadow social
  services secretary 362; response to Bennite
  policy agenda 366; pensions policy 377;
  Women's National Commission 379; European
  referendum (1975), 380–2, 383–4, 389–92;
  response to NEC anti–Europe motion 389–92;
  Cabinet after referendum 392; NHS issues
  407, 408, 409; resignation question 411, 413;
  land deal 413; resignation 416–17, 431;
  successor 416–17, 419; Thorpe files affair
  429–33; funeral 456
Wilson, Mary 262, 456
Wilson, Sir Reginald 220
Wise, Frank 32, 43, 50, 67, 74
Woman 427
Women's National Commission 379
Wood, Sir Kingsley 71
Woodcock, George: on DEA 246; TUC
  leadership 265–6, 276, 304, 313; industrial
  relations policy 272–3, 279, 304; response to
  BC's proposals 285–6; retirement 290
Woodcraft Folk 11
Wootton, Barbara 184–5
World in Action 433
World War II 63–79
Wright, Peter 336

Yellowlees, Sir Henry 400
Yorkshire Post 99
Young, Colonel 138, 139
Yugoslavia 121, 144–5

Zambia 196, 202
Zilliacus, Konni 128